Understanding
Moral Philosophy

DICKENSON BOOKS OF RELATED INTEREST

Reason and Responsibility: Readings in Some Basic Problems of Philosophy, Third Edition
   edited by Joel Feinberg

Principles of Ethics: An Introduction
   by Paul W. Taylor

Problems of Moral Philosophy: An Introduction to Ethics, Second Edition
   edited by Paul W. Taylor

Understanding Philosophy
   by Tom Regan

Moral Philosophy: An Introduction
   edited by Paul Fink

Philosophical Problems of Causation
   edited by Tom L. Beauchamp

Individual Conduct and Social Norms: A Utilitarian Account of Social Union and the Rule of Law
   by Rolf Sartorius

Freedom and Authority: An Introduction to Social and Political Philosophy
   edited by Thomas Schwartz

Philosophical and Religious Issues: Classical and Contemporary Statements
   edited by Ed. L. Miller

The Logic of Grammar
   edited by Donald Davidson and Gilbert H. Harman

Philosophy of Law
   edited by Joel Feinberg and Hyman Gross

Understanding Moral Philosophy

edited by

James Rachels

University of Miami

DICKENSON PUBLISHING COMPANY, INC.

Encino, California
Belmont, California

ISBN-0-8221-0172-6
Library of Congress Catalog Card Number: 76-4361

Printed in the United States of America
Printing (last digit): 9 8 7 6 5 4 3 2 1

Production Editor: Linda Malevitz Hashmi   Designer: Jill Casty

CONTENTS

CHAPTER SEVEN

Morality and the Law

INTRODUCTION 359

The Dickenson Series in Philosophy

Philosophy, said Aristotle, begins in wonder—wonder at the phenomenon of self-awareness, wonder at the infinitude of time, wonder that there should be anything at all. Wonder in turn gives rise to a kind of natural puzzlement: How can mind and body interact? How is it possible that there can be free will in a world governed by natural laws? How can moral judgments be shown to be true?

Philosophical perplexity about such things is a familiar and unavoidable phenomenon. College students who have experienced it and taken it seriously are, in a way, philosophers already, well before they come in contact with the theories and arguments of specialists. The good philosophy teacher, therefore, will not present his subject as some esoteric discipline unrelated to ordinary interests. Instead he will appeal directly to the concerns that already agitate the student, the same concerns that agitated Socrates and his companions and serious thinkers ever since.

It is impossible to be a good teacher of philosophy, however, without being a genuine philosopher oneself. Authors of the Dickenson Series in Philosophy are no exceptions to this rule. In many cases their textbooks are original studies of problems and systems of philosophy, with their own views boldly expressed and defended with argument. Their books are at once contributions to philosophy itself and models of original thinking to emulate and criticize.

That equally competent philosophers often disagree with one another is a fact to be exploited, not concealed. Dickenson anthologies bring together essays by authors of widely differing outlook. This diversity is compounded by juxtaposition, wherever possible, of classical essays with leading contemporary materials. The student who is shopping for a world outlook of his own has a large and representative selection to choose among, and the chronological arrangements, as well as the editor's introduction, can often give him a sense of historical development. Some Dickenson anthologies treat a single group of interconnected problems. Others are broader, dealing with a whole branch of philosophy, or representative problems from various branches of philosophy. In both types of collections, essays with opposed views on precisely the same questions are included to illustrate the argumentative give and take which is the lifeblood of philosophy.

Joel Feinberg
Series Editor

Preface

We cannot think seriously or deeply about moral issues without doing philosophy. Consider, for example, the issue of abortion:

Some people say that there should be no laws regulating abortion, and some say that such laws are right and proper. We cannot decide who is right without raising philosophical questions about the purpose and scope of the law, and about the proper relation between a community's moral code and its legal system.

Some say that the unborn baby, as well as the mother, has rights that must be respected. Before we can know whether this is true, we must ask philosophical questions about the nature of rights and about the sorts of beings that have rights.

If abortion is to be judged right or wrong, by what standards should the judgment be made? What general moral principles may be invoked?

And are these principles objectively true, or is the whole business of "morality" nothing more than a matter of personal feeling or social convention? Can each individual (or each society) formulate principles to suit himself, or is there some universally valid system of morality which we must all accept if we are to live as we ought?

It is easy to see that such questions force themselves upon us, not only when we consider the problem of abortion, but when we think seriously about any moral issue. These are some of the questions that moral philosophers try to answer.

This anthology is intended as an introduction to moral philosophy. Each chapter is organized around a single major topic, and contains articles by philosophers which explore its various aspects. Some of the writers discuss and criticize the ideas of the others, giving the reader a sense of the back-and-forth dialectic indispensable to philosophical thinking.

This book is for beginning students, but that can be misleading, for in philosophy we do not have the clear distinction, found in other disciplines, between the elementary and the advanced. Mill's *Utilitarianism*, for example, may be read with profit by freshmen; yet its ideas and arguments provide material for scores of doctoral dissertations. Thus, even at the beginning of our study, we are plunged into the most difficult and important issues.

The first chapter, "Is an Objective Morality Possible?", is concerned with the question of whether there really is any such thing as objective moral truth, or whether our value-judgments do nothing more than express our feelings, or the conventions of our society. The next three chapters deal with three of the most important and interesting general ethical theories: ethical egoism, utilitarianism, and Kantian ethics. Chapters five and six take up specific questions concerning the nature of justice and equality, and human rights. Finally, chapter seven deals with the relation between morality and law.

The selections include some great philosophical classics as well as recent contributions by contemporary thinkers. Where possible, I have chosen readings which connect theoretical issues and concrete moral questions; thus, in addition to the theoretical matters mentioned above, you will find discussions of such subjects as abortion, methods of warfare, "reverse discrimination," the rights of animals, privacy, criminal punishment, and so on.

The annotated "Suggestions for Further Reading" found at the end of each chapter are intended to answer the question: "What else can I read, to learn more about these subjects?" Different teachers would answer this question in different ways; these are simply my suggestions. They are not, of course, exhaustive bibliographies; but I do not think that beginning students—or even moderately advanced students, for that matter—need exhaustive bibliographies. Instead they need specific recommendations, and that is what I have provided.

Peter Singer and Tom Beauchamp made suggestions that were a great help to me in assembling this collection. Richard Trudgen of Dickenson Publishing Company—a practically perfect editor—gave continual help and encouragement. My thanks to all of them.

J.R.

Understanding
Moral Philosophy

CHAPTER ONE

Is an Objective Morality Possible?

INTRODUCTION

Most of us have occasionally felt doubts about whether there really is any such thing as objective moral truth. Usually we do not feel these doubts while in vigorous moral argument, or while campaigning for some cause we think is right. Then, we may be filled with self-righteousness, firmly convinced that our cause is just and that those who oppose us are at best misguided or at worst wicked. However, in calmer moments, we may accept the following:

"Morality, when all is said and done, is only a matter of how we feel about things. We have positive feelings about some things, so we call them good. We have negative feelings about other things, so we call them bad. When people disagree in their evaluations—for example, when one person says that capital punishment is good and someone else says it is bad—no one is really right and no one is really wrong. Each person is simply expressing his own feelings, and no one's feelings are any more 'correct' than anyone else's. As for 'objective moral truth'—well, there simply is no such thing. Each person has his own feelings, and that's the end of it."

These are some of the questions that we will consider in this chapter: Is there any such thing as objective moral truth? Or, are our judgments about right and wrong simply expressions of the way we feel about things, or the conventions of our society, and nothing more? Or is the truth something in between?

Many people are skeptical about "objective moral truth" because different societies have different moral standards. In many Muslim societies, for example, polygamy has been regarded as a perfectly acceptable way of life, while in other societies the same practice is thought to be immoral. Among the Jains it is considered morally wrong to kill a bug, while in America every supermarket sells cans of insect poison. Many more examples could be given. The conclusion that many people draw is that, considering these cultural variations, it is naive to believe in the "truth" or "correctness" of any particular moral code. When we criticize the Muslims or the Jains, we are merely assuming our moral code to be superior to theirs. But they could make exactly the opposite assumption. The truth, according to this view, is that each society has its own norms, and that's the end of it. The first two selections in this chapter, "An Anthropologist's Approach to Ethical Principles" by Ralph Linton, and "Ethical Relativism and the Facts of Cultural Relativity" by Kai Nielsen, critically evaluate this version of ethical relativism—Linton from the anthropologist's point of view, and Nielsen from the philosopher's.

The other selections are concerned with the relation between moral judgment, reason, and emotion. For David Hume, writing in the mideighteenth century, the central philosophical question about morals is "whether they be derived from Reason or from Sentiment." In "Morality Is Founded on Sentiment," Hume argues that we cannot recognize anything as good or bad through the use of "Reason alone." Reason "guides and directs" the sentiments, but it is Sentiment and not Reason that finally determines what is good and what is bad, "so that when you pronounce any action or character to be vicious, you mean nothing, but that from the constitution of your nature you have a feeling or sentiment of blame from the contemplation of it."

In our own century this Humean idea has been the inspiration for a theory of moral language known as *emotivism*. According to this theory, moral "statements" are not really statements at all, for they do not say anything that is true or false. Instead, they simple express our emotions. When we say "abortion is wrong" it is like saying "abortion—bah!" Or when we say "Martin Luther King was a good man," it is like saying "hurrah for Martin Luther King!" We say such things to express our attitudes, and to influence the attitudes of others, but *not* to report any sort of moral "truth." Emotivism has been a very powerful influence in contemporary moral philosophy. In "Moral Judgments as Emotive," A. J. Ayer presents and defends his version of emotivism, and in "The Errors of Emotivism," G. J. Warnock argues that this theory is not a correct account of the nature of moral judgment.

I have already mentioned that one reason why many people doubt there is any such thing as objective moral truth is the variety of moral codes found in different societies. There are, of course, many other reasons. Some argue that our moral beliefs merely express attitudes that we have been conditioned to have from early childhood; others point to the difficulty of proving any moral opinion to be true, or the difficulty of reaching agreement on controversial issues. These considerations, and others like them, lead people to believe that morality is nothing more than a matter of personal feeling. Renford Bambrough's "A Proof of the Objectivity of Morals" offers a lively defense of the objectivity of ethics, and he replies to these and other popular arguments against the notion.

Finally, in "Moral Perplexity," W. D. Falk analyzes this whole controversy and concludes that a complete account of morality must allow a large place for both reason *and* emotion in determining what is right and what is wrong.

1

RALPH LINTON
An Anthropologist's Approach to Ethical Principles

RALPH LINTON (1893–1953), the distinguished American anthropologist, made a lifelong study of the Pawnee. His

many works include *The Cultural Background of Personality* (1945) and *Culture and Mental Disorders* (1956).

The problem of whether there are universally applicable ethical principles has been debated by philosophers for centuries, but recent world developments make it of much more than academic interest. Rapid transportation and the increased economic interdependence of all parts of the world are bringing into close contact groups of diverse cultures. If they are to live together peacefully they must develop a basis for common understanding and for the creation of new patterns controlling the interaction of individuals of different societies. Such common understandings in the field of ethics are the only lasting foundation upon which a world State can be built. If the various societies cannot agree to adhere to certain basic ethical principles in their dealings with each other their strength will be spent in wars and preparation for wars, and civilization as we know it will be wiped out.

Another condition which adds urgency to the quest for universal ethical principles is the necessity for revising many of our familiar culture patterns to meet the new conditions imposed by mechanical civilization. The rapid technological and scientific progress of the current era bids fair to alter our daily lives and even our ways of thinking so profoundly that the new

culture patterns will have to be based on universal human needs and social imperatives. We will have to get down to bedrock to create the new patterns of social interaction which the new situation requires. It is incumbent, therefore, on both the social scientist and the philosopher to seek for this solid foundation, a process which involves first of all ascertaining whether such a foundation really exists.

The most important development in social studies has been the emergence of the concept of culture. Anthropologists in particular have been responsible for a new attitude toward the behavior of societies other than our own. Where the previous attitude could be summed up in the old hymn line, "The heathen in his blindness," the present attitude of social scientists is one of interest and willingness to learn. Since a wide variety of cultures have all been able to provide for the needs of the societies with which they were associated, it seems that each of the problems of human existence can be met in a number of different ways. A study of the various solutions should, therefore, be exceedingly helpful in any attempt to devise new behavior patterns congruous with new conditions.

The first impression which one receives from the study of a series of unrelated cultures is one of almost unlimited variety. Since all the varied patterns function successfully as parts of one culture or another, the stage is set for the development of the concept of cultural relativity. The insistence on scientific objectivity, which means the rigid exclusion of all ethical judgments and the substitution of an attitude of "Well, some do and some don't," contributes toward the same end. Actually, many anthropologists have espoused this position and considerable support can be found for it as long as investigation is limited to the overt behavior patterns of various societies. However, when these patterns are analyzed in terms of their functions and interrelations, certain general principles emerge. Behind the seemingly endless diversity of culture patterns there is a fundamental uniformity. To discover what the common factors are and to plan culture changes in conformity with them is the most important task of the social scientist.

It is easy to see why this uniformity exists. All human societies are composed of members of the same mammalian species. Racial differences exist but none of those which have been demonstrated seem to be culturally significant. Every culture has to provide for the same basic physiological and psychological needs of individuals. Moreover, the organization, operation, and perpetuation of societies involve the same basic problems whether the society is in Australia, Africa, or Arkansas. Children have to be produced, fed, sheltered, and trained. The diversified activities by which the various members of a society contribute to the well-being of the whole have to be assigned to individuals who must, in turn, be reimbursed for their services. Leadership in communal activities has to be provided and disputes have to be settled or at least circumscribed before they can disrupt the community.

Each of these things can be done in any one of several different ways, but all of them have to be done if the society is to survive. Moreover, the actual range of variation seems to be strictly delimited. As the social scientist's acquaintance with a large number of cultures improves, he cannot fail to be more impressed with their similarities than with their differences. This is especially the case where his acquaintance extends to continuous first-hand contact with the societies involved. Any individual who is willing to observe and imitate can soon orient himself in any human society. A Cortez or a Pizarro, confronted by a complex civilization most of whose overt behavior patterns were completely alien to his experience, could still grasp the social and political picture and apply the same principles of statecraft which he would have used in Europe.

The existence and nature of a universal ethical system will have to be established through a comparative study of cultures if it is to be accepted by modern societies. One of the most significant emergent culture patterns of modern times is the demand that all assumptions regarding man and nature should be supported by scientifically acceptable evidence. This pattern always meets with resistance from those individuals and groups who base their assumptions on authority. The long struggle between Fundamentalists and Evolutionists as to the processes involved in creation would be a case in point. In our own society the authoritarian assumption regarding ethics is that it is an expression of the divine will, eternal and immutable. As such it is supported by supernatural sanctions. The good are rewarded and the bad punished, if not now, then in some future existence. A little leeway has to be allowed to man in his implementation of the divinely established principles but each religious sect feels entitled to insist on setting its own limitations.

Scientists have no method by which

they can determine what is or is not divinely established or what may be the fate of good or bad men after death. They can only point out that in most cultures the attitude of the deity or deities toward ethical behavior is much less positive than that of the Christian God. Many of the taboos supported by supernatural sanctions seem to have no social implications and the relation of the individual to the deity is commonly conceived of as something quite apart from his relation to other individuals. In fact, it is common practice for worshippers to ask and presumably receive aid from the deity in unethical activities. Moreover, where deities do show ethical orientations these can be explained as part of the general tendency of societies to project upon their deities the attitudes normal to society members. Since the average society member is annoyed by the unethical behavior of others, it is assumed that the deity will also be annoyed.

Under the circumstances it is best for the scientist to keep to the area in which his techniques are applicable. Without either affirming or denying the relation between ethics and the supernatural, he can try to find out what ethical principles, if any, are reflected in all cultures. In an investigation of this sort, experimental methods are precluded. This is a disadvantage common to most studies of social phenomena. Societies simply cannot be put in laboratories under controlled conditions. As a substitute one can employ comparative studies. The lack of controls is partially compensated for by the possibility of following particular social-cultural continua over long periods. This is especially important since changes in even a small series of culture patterns may result in disharmonies which it will take several generations to adjust. Temporary conditions may also mask the basic ethical assumptions of a society. Thus it is a common observation that attitudes on sex behavior become more permissive in all Western cultures in time of war. This is in marked contrast to some "primitive" societies where sex taboos are much more stringently enforced in wartime.

One of the first requirements of a scientific approach to the problem of universal ethical principles is a clear delimitation of the frame of reference within which the comparative studies are to be made. *It must be stressed that the significant units are societies, not individuals.* There is no ethical principle on which all individuals will be found in agreement. Every society includes a sprinkling of imbeciles, psychotics, and actively antisocial persons. It may be added that the last often recognize and give intellectual allegiance to the ethical systems of the societies to which they belong even though they do not adhere to them in their conduct. When we say that a society has a particular ethical system we mean that a large majority of its members accept this system, consciously or otherwise, and that it is reflected in their normal, culturally-patterned behavior. Whether the ethical system is conscious and verbalized or not is in itself a culture pattern. Some societies are even more culture conscious than Europeans while others take their own habits and attitudes completely for granted. Even in those societies whose members have never felt a need for verbalizing ethical principles there are always easily ascertainable standards of what is good and bad conduct and the ethical system can be deduced from these.

Not only is the society the unit for ethical studies but *ethical systems function only in terms of in-groups.* Since the structure of societies is reminiscent of those Chinese sweetmeat boxes filled with smaller fitted boxes which contain still smaller ones, it is often difficult to determine the limits of the group to which ethical systems apply. Thus every society contains a number of family groups which are organized into communities. The communities are, in turn, organized into larger units, tribes at the "primitive" level, which may form part of still larger groupings such as confederacies or states established by conquest. Lastly, the concept of social membership may be extended to include the whole of mankind, as in some Messianic religions, or even, on the basis of a pantheistic philosophy, to include the whole of nature. Needless to say, at this point the emotional affects on which ethics depends for behavioral expression become so diluted that ethical concepts are rarely applied in practice.

In contrast with these extreme extensions of the ethical frame of reference, most groups at the tribal level limit the application of ethics to dealings with tribe members, with animals or objects which are intimately associated with the tribe, such as totems, and with selected supernaturals such as ancestral spirits or local deities. Ethical behavior is prescribed toward and expected from all members of such an in-group. Toward anything outside it, people included, ethical rules in most cases simply do not apply. Thus the Maori of New Zealand, one of the most ingenious and philosophical of Stone Age peoples, showed all the virtues admired by Europeans in dealings with fellow tribesmen. Their attitude toward outsiders can be judged by the following: "A Maori relating an account of an expedition said incidentally, 'On the way I was speaking to a red-haired girl who had just been caught out in the open. . . . My companions remained with the girl

while I went on. . . . As we came back, I saw the head of the red-haired girl lying in the fern by the side of the track, and further on, we overtook one of the Waihou carrying a back load of flesh, which he was taking to our camp to be cooked for food; the arms of the girl were round his neck whilst the body was on his back.'"[1]

It seems that in spite of the common social phenomenon of groups within groups the same ethical system applies to all forms of social interaction within the society. In general, the smaller and more closely knit the unit within the society, the greater the emphasis on ethical considerations in the dealings of the unit's members with each other. Thus all societies reprehend unethical behavior between the members of nuclear families, that is, parents and children, more severely than any other sort. Next in importance come more distant kindred and members of the same village, the relative emphasis differing with the culture. Ethical rules apply with still less vigor to dealings with members of other communities within the society and with least vigor to interaction with socially marginal individuals such as foreign traders or tolerated refugees. With these last two groups, length of association seems to be the most important factor: the longer the association the stronger the tendency to recognize ethical principles in social interaction.

In more advanced societies the existence of a class structure introduces additional variations. Where social classes are fully developed, not barely emergent as in the United States, each class constitutes a subsociety with its own subculture. Dealings between members

1. E. Tregear, *The Maori Race* (A. D. Willis, New Zealand: 1926), p. 358.

of different classes resemble those between members of different communities in their ethical implications. However, the establishment of close individual relationships across class lines, as between master and old servant, increases ethical responsibility on both sides.

To conclude, it seems probable that the extent to which ethical standards are recognized and adhered to in the social interactions of individuals is primarily a function (in the mathematical sense) of the closeness and continuity of association between the individuals involved. This might be explained in psychological terms of identification, but it can also be explained in terms of practical, informal sanctions. To cheat or abuse a person with whom you have to go on interacting afterward is much more likely to bring reprisals than is the same sort of behavior toward a comparative stranger. An excellent example of this principle is seen in the different patterns of treatment of field slaves and house slaves in all slave-holding societies. House slaves are always dealt with more leniently but a much higher level of honesty is expected from them.

Since the ultimate purpose of comparative studies of ethics is to provide guidance in the reorganization of our own culture which is now under way, it may be asked whether data obtained from a comparison of "primitive" societies are applicable to "civilized" ones. Cultures differ greatly in their patterns of overt behavior even under similar circumstances. Thus in a temple recently dedicated in India, the worshipper is requested to remove either his hat or his shoes on entering, according to which is his accustomed gesture of respect. However, the features common to all social-cultural configurations far outweigh the differences. For a study of ethics, the most significant of these differences seems to stem not from "civilization" or "savagery," a distinction based primarily on complexity of culture content, but from the relative stability of societies in terms of both culture and personnel. Isolated, self-perpetuating communities with slowly changing cultures tend to show the greatest uniformity in their members' ideas of right and wrong and the greatest extension of ethical evaluation. The modern city community, with a rapidly changing culture and personnel of heterogeneous origin presents the greatest range of difference in individual opinions.[2]

To return to the problem of universal ethical principles, ethical relativists seem to be particularly intrigued by the differences in the patterns of sex behavior approved in different societies. In fact, many of them seem to follow our own colloquial practice of making "morals" and "sex behavior" equivalent. Different societies do differ more in their attitudes toward sex than in any other activity within the field of ethics, but all of them have very definite rules governing sex behavior and these rules have much in common. Thus all societies prohibit incest and punish it with great vigor. The same holds for rape, although there may be differences in the exact definition of this offense. The main differences in sexual mores lie in attitudes toward premarital chastity and toward exclusive possession of spouses.

Many societies do not expect premarital chastity from either boys or girls. Their attitude toward adolescent affairs is much like our own amused tolerance of "puppy love." Thanks to the period of adolescent sterility, such

2. See numerous discussions by Dr. Robert Redfield and his students on Folk Society and Civilization.

affairs rarely result in pregnancy, so have little implication for the society as a whole. Nearly all societies frown on promiscuity, in the sense of entertaining a large number of partners. In most "primitive" societies the extension of incest taboos to remote relatives and the comparatively small size of the adolescent group limit the possibilities severely. In all societies which permit premarital affairs, it is taken for granted that they will result in the formation of permanent matings and the establishment of new nuclear families.

With one or two doubtful exceptions, marriage is a universal institution. Moreover, the lifelong union of spouses is everywhere the ideal no matter how easy and frequent separations may be in practice. The rights and duties between parents, between parents and offspring, and between children of the same parents are always culturally defined and enforced by ethical sanctions. Thus each parent must make certain contributions toward the economic life of the family. Loyalty to the spouse is expected in most societies and those which permit exceptions limit these to situations in which there is a conflict between the claims of one spouse and those of the other spouse's kindred.

The marriage relation always limits the sex activities of both parties. Although sex relations with more than one individual may be permitted, the available partners and the conditions under which they may enjoy a spouse's favors are always culturally established and ethically sanctioned. Even in polygynous and polyandrous societies, the rights of plural wives or husbands are clearly defined. Thus in many polygynous societies, each wife is entitled to her husband's company for one day in turn. For a husband to spend another wife's day with a favorite is regarded as adultery and more severely reprehended than ordinary adultery, since it strikes at the very roots of the family system.

Permitted sex relations by married people outside marriage are found in about the same number of societies and frequently in the same societies as those which permit premarital experimentation. However, the possible partners are socially designated and the affairs are arranged in such a way as to avoid either disruption of the family unit or ego injury to the spouse. Thus in wife-lending the borrower is, with few exceptions, either a close relative, such as a younger brother, or a friend who does not live in the same community. In either case the man who receives the favor is expected to reciprocate in kind when he is able to do so. Conversely, the wife may have sexual rights in some of the husband's male relatives, but culture patterns establish which ones and the arrangement is thoroughly understood at the time of the marriage.

Both permitted adolescent lovemaking and permitted nonmonogamous sex behavior in marriage reflect a lowered evaluation of sex per se. Where the sexual act is regarded as a normal, pleasurable exercise, like eating, and where parentage is a matter of social ascription rather than biological relationship, the claims of kinship or even friendship are given precedence over those of exclusive possession. At the same time, practically all societies recognize adultery as unethical and punish the offenders. The same man who will lend his wife to a friend or brother will be roused to fury if she goes to another man without his permission.

Turning to the rights and duties between parents and children, the only point at which sex enters is in the almost universal prohibition of sex relations between parent and offspring. As far as known, no society permits sex relations between mother and son while only two or three permit it between father and daughter, and even in these it is limited to royal or sacerdotal groups. The comparative study of other parent-child relations is complicated by the fact that societies differ greatly in the emphasis they place on the nuclear family. In several matrilineal societies, what are ordinarily the paternal functions are shifted from a woman's husband to her brother. In such cases the ethical obligations between a child and his maternal uncle are practically the same as those between a child and his father in patrilineal societies.

In all societies the parents are expected to care for and train children while the children in turn will care for them in old age. In connection with the training, different societies permit differing disciplinary techniques which vary greatly in severity. However, no society approves sadistic behavior on the part of a parent or any sort of discipline which results in permanent injury. With few exceptions, children are expected to accord both parents respect and obedience. Violence against a parent is a major crime in nearly all societies. Since the care and training of children is the primary function of the family as an institution, failure of either side to live up to its obligations in the parent-child relationship is severely reprehended. Supernatural sanctions are invoked more frequently here than in any other type of social interaction.

The obligations between siblings show more variation than those between parents and offspring. In all cases, some degree of loyalty and mutual assistance is prescribed, but the extent of these claims differs enormously in different societies. The rivalry of half-siblings is recognized and allowed for in the ethical systems of most polygynous societies but violence, treachery, and deceit are disapproved. Even in monogamous societies there is always some conflict between the claims of the sibling group and those of the new nuclear families established by its members' marriages. Various societies lay stress on one or the other of these groups as the focus for individual loyalties. Patterns vary from societies which expect the wife to sever all relations with her siblings at marriage to those which regard spouses as only peripherally attached to the functional family. This is, in such cases, a group of real or classificatory siblings. The most nearly universal regulation governing sibling interaction is the prohibition of sex relations, but even here the exceptions are much more numerous than for the parent-child incest rule.

In addition to its basic function of childrearing, the family is normally an economic unit for both production and consumption. This pattern tends to break down under modern urban conditions, but throughout most of the world ethical sanctions are invoked to ensure that each family member contributes to the family economy and also receives an adequate return for his services. In cases where some member seems to receive a disproportionate share of the family income, investigation usually shows that this share is not used for personal benefit but is disbursed to increase the family prestige.

Lastly, the family everywhere is expected to support its members' interests and to present a united front to outsiders. Particular members may be sacrificed for the good of the whole, but to side with another family against one's own is everywhere regarded as wrong.

The only cases in which it might be adjudged right for a man to ignore the interest of his own family are those in which there is a clash between this and the interest of some larger social unit to which the family belongs. In such cases of conflicting loyalties, some cultures prescribe that the family be favored, some the larger group. The significant point is that loyalty to any social unit to which the individual belongs is always regarded as a virtue, disloyalty as a vice.

So much for the ethical patterns governing sex behavior and family life. It can be seen that the similarities far outweigh the differences. The same seems to hold true for another aspect of culture, that is, property, although here also there is considerable difference in the behavior patterns which implement the common values. To understand the ethical values involved, it is necessary to give a brief description of property concepts in general.

All societies recognize personal property in tools, utensils, ornaments, and so forth. The only exceptions are a few completely communistic societies established by sophisticated individuals as a part of religious movements, and no society of this sort has ever had a long duration. The concept of personal property is easily explained in terms of the individual's identification with objects he has made or habitually uses. Similar identification can often be seen in domestic animals. Products of hunting and food gathering, domestic animals and crops, either garnered or in the field, are universally owned by either individuals or the smallest family groupings operating as organized economic units. The principle involved seems to be that the products of skill or labor belong to the individual or group which has exercised these qualities. Private ownership of means of production is mainly a phe-

nomenon of civilization, but it is not unknown in simpler societies. Individuals, families, or even corporate groups often own such productive appliances as canoes or nets and permit others to use them for a fee.

With respect to land or other irreplaceable natural resources all societies retain the right of eminent domain. The differences lie in the point at which the society recognizes a threat to its well-being and takes over. However, subject to this right, there is a universal tendency toward individual or family ownership of land or resources which possess continuing value. Even at the simplest levels of technological development, family hunting territories are usual in regions where game is nonmigratory. More advanced societies recognize ownership of such resources as winter pasture, fishing places, and improved land. With respect to the last, it is a general rule that crops belong to the individuals or groups who have planted them, but the land itself reverts to the society's common holding when it is no longer in use. Most societies have, in addition to individual holdings, waste land of little value whose products can be exploited by any society member.

There are no economically equalitarian societies. Even among nomadic food gatherers the good hunter with a clever wife has more food, better equipment, and more ornaments. Among food-raising peoples the inequalities in wealth may be striking. It is not uncommon in such societies to have natural resources preempted by wealthy families to such a degree that poor individuals are almost excluded from access to them. However, all societies have culturally recognized patterns for the care of the poor or unfortunate. Extension of family ties and disgrace attaching to failure to care for relatives are usually enough to provide food and shelter at a survival level. Charity, as distinct from the fulfillment of family obligations, is also common. In fact, in most uncivilized societies the main incentive for the accumulation of property seems to be the desire to disburse the surplus at public functions, thus acquiring prestige. The principal alternative to this practice is the destruction or interment of surplus property at funerals but this form of ostentatious waste is highly developed in only a few cultures.

Societies living under conditions that preclude any large accumulation of property nearly all have patterns for sharing food and lending surplus tools and weapons. This is quite different from genuine communal ownership, since the owner of the things shared gains prestige and expects reciprocal favors. Under such conditions theft becomes ridiculous and is so regarded. It is said that the Eskimos do not punish thieves but whenever a thief's name is mentioned everybody laughs. In societies where accumulation is possible, theft is everywhere regarded as a crime and is severely punished. Actually, it is rare in most uncivilized communities. This may be due less to ethical considerations than to the ease with which objects which are not mass-produced can be recognized. Only a kleptomaniac would steal something which he could not use or profitably dispose of without immediate detection. It is worth noting in this connection that with the introduction of money into uncivilized societies both hoarding and theft of money usually appear even though attitudes toward theft of other types of property remain unchanged.

All societies recognize economic obligations of the sort involved in exchange of goods and services and the individual who fails to live up to them is punished simply but effectively by exclusion from future exchanges. Attitudes with respect to sharp practices show more diversity but each society defines the areas in which such practices are permitted and usually has rules as to what techniques are or are not permissible. Thus the Yankee of the horse trading era regarded it as quite legitimate to hide the faults of a horse as long as he could do so without a direct lie. The trading was regarded as a sport, a battle of wits waged according to mutually recognized rules. However, once the parties agreed that it was a trade, neither side could withdraw without complete loss of reputation.

Mention has just been made of the culture pattern prohibiting direct lying in a trade. Attitudes toward lying differ greatly in various societies. The North European is almost unique in regarding verbal truth as an ethical value per se. Most societies regard lying as quite permissible under most circumstances and ability to detect the truth regardless of what is said as a legitimate test of intelligence. The judgments of Solomon brought him great credit but it is not recorded that the litigants were embarrassed at being caught in untruth. However, all societies demand truth in at least certain areas of personal interaction and a great many of them seek to insure it by invoking supernatural sanctions, that is, oaths.

Attitudes on offenses against the person appear highly variable at first sight. It would seem that the only offense which is universally reprehended is killing or maiming without justification. All societies recognize and punish the crime of murder as distinct from justifiable homicide, but their definitions of murder differ considerably. Some of the complications disappear when it is recognized that many societies place ego injury through insult on a par with bodily injury. Such injury justifies physical retaliation, often by culturally delimited techniques, as in the *code duello*. However, it is only with the development of government in the modern sense that the problem of preventing physical aggression can be solved. Where blood revenge is a culture pattern, it may serve as a deterrent to initial acts of violence, but once the act has been committed the consequences are an increasing number of violent acts. The most effective technique for preventing violence in the absence of centralized authority is the institution of *wergild* by which the offender has to pay a fine so heavy that he can rarely meet it without the assistance of his relatives. The knowledge that they will have to part with property if one of the kindred maims or kills a member of another kin group insures that they will do their best to prevent the crime from taking place.

It is interesting to note that no society has successfully solved the problem of preventing psychic aggression. The practice of malevolent magic must not be classed under that head since, to societies which believe in it, it ranks as a form of physical attack. Most societies distinguish between justifiable and unjustifiable use of malevolent magic and punish the latter with great severity, since the insidious nature of the magician's attack makes him a potential threat to the whole community. Psychic aggression either directly through curses or indirectly through slander is actionable in many societies. However, the form which such aggression takes varies greatly from one society to another. Many factors are involved in an individual's insult reaction. Even in Europe where the *code duello* had been elaborated for generations, courts of honor

had to be convened to pass on doubtful cases of insult.

Information is now available on a large number of cultures which are so widely distributed in time and space that they provide an adequate sample for comparative studies. There is no society on record which does not have an ethical system. Apparent exceptions are due to the observer's failure to recognize the social limits within which the system is expected to apply. By an ethical system we mean definite ideas regarding what constitutes right or wrong behavior in most situations involving social interaction with a high degree of consistency in the values which these ideas reflect. Whether the society's members consciously generalize from their specific judgments of right and wrong to an abstract ethical system is a different matter. However, a certain amount of generalization is inevitable. There must be agreement on general principles governing the interaction of individuals since the actual situations which may arise are extremely variable. Even in our own law courts, after thousands of years of accumulated experience, every year produces cases for which there are no precedents.

The values reflected in ethical systems seem to be much the same everywhere. However, the relative importance attached to particular values differs considerably from one society to another and even at different points in the history of the same society. Thus one society may attach great importance to chastity per se and organize wide areas of behavior about it while another regards it as secondary to such a value as hospitality. Contrast the British attitudes toward sex during the Regency and a generation later under Queen Victoria. Again, human life may be held so cheap relative to honor that no man is counted as really adult until he has fought a duel, or so dear that killing under any circumstances is punished by death or exile. The important point is that in spite of such variations in the value hierarchy, there is no society which does not have adverse attitudes toward killing society members or in which sexual selectivity is not approved.

Among the values involved in ethical systems, that of insuring the perpetuation and successful functioning of the society always takes first place. Acts which threaten the group are condemned and punished with greater severity than those which threaten only individuals. Note our own attitude toward treason and toward murder. All societies also recognize that there is a point beyond which the interests of the individual must be made subordinate to those of the state. Note the universality of property regulations comparable to our own right of eminent domain. Within the limits set by the priority given to a society's needs, all ethical systems also seek to provide for the physical and psychological needs of individuals. All societies guard persons in the marriage relationship from both physical deprivation and ego injury by recognizing and enforcing their mutual rights and duties. They also provide a high degree of security in all the other relationships within the family group by approving all forms of cooperation and condemning acts which threaten family solidarity. The recognition of personal property militates against both actual deprivation and ego injury while all societies have developed techniques for the distribution of economic surplus to those who are in want. Violence, allowing for the cultural differences in definition of that term, is everywhere condemned and techniques are present to prevent its outbreak and minimize its consequences. This list could be extended considerably in terms of less fundamental values which are common to a very large proportion of the world's cultures if not to all.

The resemblances in ethical concepts so far outweigh the differences that a sound basis for mutual understanding between groups of different cultures is already in existence. The present difficulties seem to stem from two main sources: the first is that societies which share the same values often differ considerably in the relative importance which they attach to them. To judge from historic evidence on the changes which have taken place in various cultures, such differences are by no means insurmountable. A greater difficulty lies in the age-old tendency of every society's members to assume that ethical systems apply only within their own tribe or nation. This attitude is difficult to overcome but the modern world is witnessing a rapid expansion of social horizons. When people learn to think of themselves as members of a single world society, it will be easy for them to agree on a single ethical system.

KAI NIELSEN
Ethical Relativism and the Facts of Cultural Relativity

KAI NIELSEN, professor of philosophy at the City University of New York, is the author of many works in ethics and the philosophy of religion. His books include *Contemporary Critiques of Religion* (1971), *Ethics Without God* (1973); and *Scepticism* (1973).

I

Anthropologists have discussed in great detail the question of cultural relativism. They have commonly assumed that objective moral judgments are possible only if there is a significant cross-cultural agreement over what is *believed* or *felt* to be good and evil. If we can find such agreement we have *eo ipso* found an adequate basis for an objective morality.[1] I want to argue that no such direct moral conclusion can be drawn from facts concerning the relativity of what people take to be right and wrong. That is to say, discovery of a common acceptance among all peoples that certain things are good or bad would not *of itself* establish that they are good or bad.

The material obtainable in anthropological monographs may be necessary for a well-grounded claim that there are objective moral beliefs but it could not be sufficient, for after we had discovered the procedures used by our tribe and by other tribes in making moral appraisals, the question would still remain as to which if any of these procedures could stand up to rational examination. Whether some could or not would never be simply a matter of anthropological investigation but would also involve conceptual inquiry. If analysis disclosed

that certain criteria of moral appraisal could withstand such a logical examination, we would have good grounds for rejecting ethical relativism. Anthropological material could count against this conclusion only if it were established that our very canons of logical and conceptual appraisal were so relative that no amount of discussion or inquiry could give us any cross-cultural Archimedian point from which to reason about conduct. In such a situation there would be good grounds for claiming that there are no ways to appraise rationally various experiments in living.

Elementary considerations of this sort should instill the suspicion that the situation vis-à-vis anthropological discoveries and ethical relativism is much more complex and indirect than it is usually thought to be. It should be said in the beginning that the very dichotomy between what is called absolutism-relativism is anything but a clear one. Exactly what a relativist or an absolutist is supposed to be committed to is

1. See R. Linton, "Universal Ethical Principles: An Anthropological Approach," in R. N. Anshem, ed., *Moral Principles of Action*, (New York: 1952) and "The Problem of Universal Values," in *Method and Perspective in Anthropology*, R. F. Spence, ed. (Minneapolis: 1952); R. Redfield, "The Universally Human and The Culturally Variable," *The Journal of General Education*, vol. X (July 1967), pp. 150–160; C. Kluckhohn, "Ethical Relativity, Sic et Non," *Journal of Philosophy*, vol. LII (1955), pp. 663–667.

From Kai Nielsen, "Ethical Relativism and the Facts of Cultural Relativity," *Social Research*, vol. 33 (1966), pp. 531–551. Reprinted by permission. This article is reprinted unabridged.

not evident. Furthermore, it is not altogether apparent that the two concepts signify exhaustive categories. I contend, for example, that in an ordinary way we do have objective moral knowledge, but I would not call myself an absolutist, for I do not think any moral knowledge is self-evident and I do not know with sufficient clarity what it is to be an absolutist. "Relativism" itself seems to have several meanings. Different people mean different things by it. When a rosy-cheeked, freshly-scrubbed freshman briskly announces to me that he is a relativist, I do not know, and I suspect he does not know, what he means. Perhaps he means that he has just concluded that premarital intercourse might not be such a bad idea after all.

Still it will not do to say that these terms are so vague that we have no sense at all of what they mean or that there is no conflict between so-called objectivists and relativists. I want here to comment on some anthropological literature on this subject and consider the logical relevance of such literature to any theory of ethical relativism.

II

Among anthropologists, Lévy-Bruhl and Ruth Benedict gave a classical formulation of cultural relativism. In the same year that *Principia Ethica* was published, Lévy-Bruhl argued in his *La Morale et la Science des Moeurs* that moral codes and systems "are merely rationalizations of custom." What *is* done, he argued, is right. Where a given culture has a rule that all twins are to be killed at birth or, as in some places in the Amazon, that all captured children of an enemy tribe are first to be adopted and then, during adolescence, to be eaten by the families that adopted them, such mandatory social practices are right (morally obligatory) for that so-

ciety. Morality is simply the body of rules which actually determines conduct in any society. Social structure and expected behavior vary enormously among different cultures, and thus morality—the normal, sanctioned behavior—takes radically different forms. Thirty years later Ruth Benedict, with a much greater store of anthropological information at hand, made the same type of claim. "Morality," she tells us "differs in every society, and is a convenient term for socially approved habits." In a way that would bring chills to one affected by G. E. Moore, she calmly tells us that "It is morally good" means the same as "It is habitual," and what is habitual for the Tapirape is not habitual for the Papago or the American.[2] In a culture which conditions people to amass property and wealth and directs people to seek success, the attainment of extensive property and power will be good, while in a society in which contemplation and fidelity to one's ancestors are stressed above all, the attainment of wealth and power will not be so highly prized. Confronted with an exuberant variety of cultures, anthropologists, until very recently, have been impressed with the differences in human nature and moral rule rather than the similarities. Lévy-Bruhl, Westermarck, Boas, Benedict and Herskovits are the classical sources here.[3]

More recently, the worm has turned and now we find such eminent anthropological authorities as Kroeber, Linton,

2. Ruth Benedict, "Anthropology and the Abnormal," *Journal of General Psychology*, vol. 10 (1934), pp. 59–80.

3. Lévy-Bruhl, *La Morale et la Science des Moeurs* (Paris: 1903); E. Westermarck, *Ethical Relativity* (London: 1932); F. Boas, *Anthropology and Modern Life* (New York: 1928); R. Benedict, *Patterns of Culture* (New York: 1934); and M. Herskovits, *Man and His Works* (New York: 1950).

Redfield, Mead and Kluckhohn emphasizing that there are common denominators amid the variations.[4] There are what they like to call "universal values." Kroeber and Kluckhohn remark that "to say that certain aspects of Nazism were morally wrong, is not parochial arrogance. It is—or can be—an assertion based upon cross-cultural evidence as to the universalities in human needs, potentialities, and fulfilments and upon natural science knowledge with which the basic assumptions of any philosophy must be congruent."[5] They speak of a "raw human nature" and the "limits and conditions of social life." They urge that it is proper to speak of a "common humanity" and our common humanity can serve as a basis for a morality that is *not* completely culturally relative. Amid incredible variation in human ideals there are some commonly accepted ideals of a very general but still fundamental nature resting on a *consensus gentium*. There are certain very general recipes for moral action that all normal members of all cultures take as authoritative. The incest taboo is universal, all cultures regulate sexual behavior, all cultures have some property rights and no culture tolerates indiscriminate lying or stealing. All cultures believe that it is good as a general rule to preserve human life; they draw a distinction between "murder" and "justifiable homicide," such as execution, killing in war, in religious ceremonials and the like. As Redfield points out, there are no societies where a mother is not obliged to care for her children.[6] Neglect of her own child, or abuse of her own or another's child, is universally taken to be wrong. And in all cultures children also have obligations to their parents, though the exact content of those obligations varies considerably from culture to culture. More generally, there are no cultures without moral codes; and, as Linton points out, these codes always function to insure "the perpetuation and successful functioning of the society," though *sometimes* the relevant social unit may be all of mankind. This function takes pride of place—all societies have something very much like our right of eminent domain—but "within the limits set by the priority given to society's needs, all ethical systems also seek to provide for the physical needs of individuals." Man needs society but he has familial needs as well and he has a need for protection from what Linton calls "ego injury," as well as physical injury. All moral codes serve both to protect society and such individual needs, though where there is a conflict an individual's needs are secondary to those of the society.[7]

In short, there are deep-seated needs, distinctive capacities and characteristic human attitudes that are perfectly universal. Universal values are said to be based on these needs and it is on these values that a cross-culturally valid, objective morality rests.

It is indeed true that just what is to count as "incest," "murder," "neglect," "abuse" and the like is to an astounding degree culturally relative. For the Romans, killing one's parents was the most unspeakable of evils, but for the

4. A. L. Kroeber and C. Kluckhohn, *Culture* (Papers of the Peabody Museum of Harvard University); R. Redfield, *The Primitive World and Its Transformations*; Margaret Mead, "Some Anthropological Considerations Concerning Natural Law," *Natural Law Forum*, vol. VI (1961), pp. 51–64. See also footnote one.

5. Kroeber and Kluckhohn, *op. cit.*, p. 64.

6. Redfield, "The Universally Human and the Culturally Variable," *loc. cit.*, pp. 152–153.

7. Linton, "Universal Ethical Principles: An Anthropological View," *loc. cit.*, pp. 645–660.

Scandinavians and the Eskimos it was a duty in order to establish them in Valhalla or to insure a reasonably new model machine in the life to come. But amid this variety we still find a concern to preserve life and there remains some overlap between cultures concerning what is to count as "murder" and what is to count as "justified killing." Similar things could be said for "incest," "neglect," "abuse" and the like. In short, there are, as Kluckhohn concludes, "pan-human universals as regards needs and capacities that shape . . . at least the broad outlines of a morality that transcends cultural difference."[8]

It is Kluckhohn's and Linton's belief that this convergence is not just a fortunate circumstance. Kluckhohn goes so far as to claim that it is a "presumptive likelihood" that certain very general "moral principles somehow correspond to inevitabilities given the nature of the human organism and of the human situation." We humans have many variable needs but "some needs," Kluckhohn argues, "are so deep and so generic that they are beyond the reach of argument; pan-human morality expresses and supports them."[9] (In the last part of that sentence we have metaphysics parading as science.)

III

There is a plenitude of conceptual confusion here. Linton and Kluckhohn are partially aware that an ability to formulate very general moral principles acceptable to all normal members of all cultures establishes very little, for we can always find some common denominator for such formulations if we delete enough detail. We have not discovered anything very interesting or significant when we find out that all normal people in all cultures regard some patterns of sexual behavior as bad and some ways of eating as desirable and that all cultures have some concept of murder. To say that murder is wrong and eating is good is at best minimally informative. Taylor is perfectly justified in saying that "What an ethical absolutist wants to know is . . . whether it is right to let a person die of neglect when he can no longer contribute to a society's economic production, whether it is right to kill unwanted infants, whether monogamy is the best sexual institution, whether a person ought to tell the truth under specified circumstances and so on."[10] If we are troubled by ethical relativism, we generally want to know things of this order: Are there some nonethnocentric objective reasons for our moral belief that we ought not to kill a child whom we do not want? We want to know whether our very strong convictions here could be established as sound, and conflicting convictions extant in other cultures shown to be wrong.

There is a further difficulty for any view that seeks to base morality on some common human nature. Even if there are universal human needs, why should they be satisfied? We all have needs for companionship and sexual satisfaction. But universal as such needs are, they can be so modified and controlled as to become almost nonexistent.[11] Let us see how this occurs. I can ask myself whether I should shun companionship and become self-absorbed, or whether I should become more outgoing

8. Kluckhohn, "Ethical Relativity: Sic et Non," *loc cit.*, p. 668.

9. *Ibid.*, p. 670.

10. P. Taylor, "Social Science and Ethical Relativism," *The Journal of Philosophy*, vol. LV (1958), p. 38.

11. H. D. Monro, "Anthropology and Ethics," *The Australasian Journal of Philosophy* (December, 1955).

and gregarious. A certain amount of contact with others is almost inevitable, but beyond the bare minimum should I seek a life full of friends and the resources of society or should I live in relative isolation? Would it be better for a reflective young man to try to become another Thomas Merton and seek the "voices of silence" and renounce the joys of the flesh, or should he have a wife, family and the art of conversation? Discoveries about universal human needs are not sufficient to resolve questions like these. The fact that people universally have sexual urges does not tell us whether we should make our present sexual patterns more or less permissive. After we find out what the needs of man are, we still have to find out which needs should be allowed to flourish and in what way, and which needs should be inhibited. In seeking what Weston La Barre has aptly called "a more adequate culture," in attempting to decide whether one way of life is better than another, anthropological discoveries *by themselves* can give us no new directions.[12] That there are certain universal needs does not entail the making of any moral judgment at all.

If we try to build our moral house from cross-culturally validated, distinctively human capacities, we get into similar difficulties. It may be the case that men try to develop certain powers or abilities that are distinctively human. Yet in making moral appraisals we must often choose among them since they are sometimes in conflict. Furthermore, why should we develop only the non-conflicting capacities? Why not make a choice among certain conflicting capacities and then develop the capacity we decided to develop? To say the conflicting ones are "perverse" or "abnormal" in a tone that suggests they should not be sought assumes a moral

criterion *not* based on human capacities. That certain capacities or dispositions are common to all men everywhere is not a sufficient ground for developing them or claiming they *ought* to flourish. To say that people should develop these capacities is to say that "people ought to do what other people can do, given the environmental conditions of their cultures." But whether such conformism is desirable is itself a debatable *moral* belief. That we should conform to this belief is not something we could discover in a biological treatise or in a cross-cultural survey of the mores of diverse cultures.

Cross-cultural agreement in moral belief or attitude does not establish ethical objectivism. Similarly cross-cultural difference does not establish ethical relativism. Ethical relativism is the contention that the moral beliefs of different cultures are frequently incompatible and that there are and can be no sound grounds for accepting the moral beliefs of one or more of the groups as correct and rejecting conflicting moral beliefs as mistaken. But universal agreement in moral belief does not establish the soundness of the belief, for the soundness of a moral belief does not depend simply on the number of people who believe it but on whether adequate justifying reasons can be given for holding it. If reasonable people assent to it, we have some reason for assenting to it, but whether a person is either reasonable or a rational moral agent is not dependent on whether or not his beliefs, attitudes and actions are in accordance with majority rule or some *consensus gentium*. Even if a universal concurrence in moral belief and attitude were discovered, the moral relativist could

12. Weston La Barre, "Wanted: A More Adequate Culture," in *Sociology: A Book of Readings,* Samuel Koenig, ed. (New York: 1953) pp. 52–62.

still claim that this agreement does not rest on rational grounds but merely on a contingent and fortuitous similarity or uniformity in what is approved. The moral relativist could reasonably argue that though the agreement is extensive it is quite arbitrary for it has no rational basis. Since it is reinforced by early and persistent social stimulation, it is very persuasive and often very compelling psychologically; just as many of the literati and quasi-literati started to admire Kipling simply because T. S. Eliot did, so people come to approve what they approve because from a very early age they have been told it is *to be* approved. This generally makes for agreement rather than disagreement. But if some others come to have different and conflicting moral beliefs the fact that most do not have these moral beliefs and attitudes does not constitute a sound basis for asserting that the minority is wrong. That there are what Linton calls "universal values" only proves (if it proves anything) that people tend to agree about some very general moral judgments. It says nothing about who (if anyone) is right or which moral views (if any) are sound.

In sum, I wish to say that anthropological facts about the divergence, convergence or complete coincidence of the moral beliefs of different cultures do not establish or refute ethical relativism or conventionalism. People and whole cultures could be in radical disagreement about what they ought to do, and yet ethical relativism would not be established. But if it were shown that a considerable number of contradictory moral claims were equally *sound* and that whole moral codes were in logical conflict but were still equally *well justified*, then conventionalism or ethical relativism would be established. The rather common assumption that if men share moral beliefs then conventionalism and ethical relativism is false is itself false.

IV

Someone might readily agree that the facts of ethical relativity taken by themselves cannot sanction the conclusion that moral principles can never be sound or the moral conclusion that what a group *says* is right is right. That cultures differ radically in their moral beliefs does not of itself establish that "is right" is simply a convenient way of saying "is right in my group," and that all cultures agree that certain things are right does not establish that they are right. Someone might concur in all this and still contend that there is something frightfully unrealistic about stressing this as a bare logical truth, for it follows from what I have been saying that one lone moral radical might have sound reasons for his moral claims while the rest of us are deluded. As it might be the case that everyone believed the earth to be flat when in reality it was round, so it might be the case that everyone believed killing unwanted infants was wrong when in reality it was right or morally indifferent. But while the factual contention is easy enough to understand, the moral claim is, to say the least, paradoxical. In certain important respects it is like saying "Acorns taste good" even when many people, including the utterer, spit them out and make a face whenever they taste them. In such circumstances we are puzzled about what could be *meant* by saying "Acorns taste good." In saying this, what could a person mean, other than something like, "If you would only repeatedly try them, especially when you want something bitter, you will in time come to like them and no longer spit them out but savor them"? But if people, including the man who said this, continued even after such a trial to spit them out we would indeed be very puzzled as to what could be *meant* by "They taste good."

Similarly, if we say "Life ought to be protected," and repeatedly and for no reason sanction killing and have no attitudes opposed to any form of killing, it would no longer be clear what could be meant by saying "Life ought to be protected." Indeed "Life ought to be protected" is *not* equivalent to "I want life protected" or "People generally wish that life be protected," for it is reasonably clear how we could establish the truth of the last two statements, but what would establish the truth of the first statement is not clear. But it is clear that "Life ought to be protected" would not be asserted if no one had an attitude favoring the protection of life.

Whatever we do mean by "a sound moral standard," a standard or claim that ignores what people actually choose, what they do, and how they feel would hardly be a standard at all, much less a sound moral standard. And in finding out what people do and what attitudes they have we obviously must turn to the information that anthropologists and psychologists give us. Here Linton's remarks about the importance of "a comparative study of cultures" is quite in place. Without such information, we are very likely to have an ethnocentric standard. If an anthropologist supplied us with detailed, well-documented information to the effect that all people of normal intelligence sought or desired certain things when fully acquainted with both the causes of their desires and with the probable consequences of having their desires satisfied, it would be conceptually odd to say that what they strove for or desired in those circumstances was not

good or desirable. Such information—if we had it—would indeed be relevant to our understanding of morality and to the establishment of an objective moral code even though it would not by itself establish such a code.

Yet we must not forget that there is indeed a place for the moral reformer and even for the moral radical and iconoclast—the disciplined man who in Nietzsche's terms would "create values." We cannot find out what is good by simply finding out what people—no matter how wide our sample—call "good." In the end each of us must make up his own mind about what is good; we must make our own moral choices on the basis of a disinterested review of the facts. ("Must" has a logical force in both of its occurrences in the preceding sentence.) Iconoclasts such as Jesus or Nietzsche were not saying something unintelligible when they advocated radically new moral standards. But if intelligent, honest and rational men do not commend and seek what Jesus or Nietzsche sought, even when these men are fully aware of the facts that Jesus and Nietzsche were aware of, and know no new facts that would serve to alter the situation, then it would be paradoxical to say that Jesus and Nietzsche were right, and the others were wrong. To this extent, agreement is important in determining the soundness of moral claims, though this is not to say—what is indeed ludicrous—that we could determine what is right and wrong or good and evil by vote. What others do seek and choose is indeed a relevant consideration for a man faced with a moral choice. But it is also relevant that he know the facts of the case, be rational, impartial and prepared to give reasons for his choices. In neglecting these last considerations, the anthropologists, trying to establish an objective morality on our "common human nature," have been wide of their mark. But it remains true that they have stressed an important point concerning morality when they point out that in deciding what is normally good or worthy of pursuit it is crucial to know not only what good redblooded Americans say and believe is the right thing to do, but what all men say and believe is right and worthy of attainment.

This can be overstressed, for it is perfectly true that in many situations an individual need not consider what other peoples do. When a man is deciding whether or not to be unfaithful to his wife, he need not consider what the Arapesh or even the Samoans do. But in thinking about what attitudes people generally should take toward extramarital relations, what the Arapesh and Samoans think and do is relevant. When we reflect in this way, we are in effect thinking about long-range effects; our thinking is to a degree utopian and visionary. If we ask ourselves what sort of lives we would take to be desirable for our children, we should be able to recognize that such long-range considerations are plainly relevant. When we ask about what is worthy of pursuit and what is the best possible life for the human animal, it would indeed be very, very good to know in depth what men everywhere and at all times have sought and have taken as ideal.

In giving us information about peoples' moral attitudes, anthropologists have brought up some facts that are of obvious importance to any adequate understanding of what would constitute a rational morality. Morality is not the province of social science or psychology; the facts obtainable by these disciplines cannot resolve the issue over whether what is *believed* to be right in

my culture really is right in my culture or whether all talk about what is right *sans phrase* is nonsense; but it does not follow from this that facts about man and his nature are irrelevant to sound moral appraisals. If these facts are not relevant then no facts would be. Let us not forget that while moral statements indeed are not factual statements, factual statements are crucially relevant to the appraisal of moral statements.

V

The problem of ethical relativism is an ancient and very tangled one—a problem that cuts to the very heart of our thinking about morality. I have not thought to unravel the whole snarl here, but only to establish two points which are crucial to any adequate treatment of the problem. The two points are these: (1) cultural agreement or difference over what is said to be good and evil will not establish either ethical relativism or ethical objectivism; (2) nonetheless, any extensive cross-cultural agreement over what is humanly desirable cannot reasonably be ignored in the statement of a rational morality. These two points seem to me to be platitudinous, but the literature on the subject amply attests to the fact that these "platitudinous points" have been denied again and again. Yet whether my points are platitudinous or not, my argument still prompts certain questions that need at least a brief consideration.

Throughout my essay there seems to run an unargued claim that there must be a rational or logical basis for morality. I speak of "a rational morality" but do not specify what I mean; I ask if the procedures used by our tribe and other tribes will stand up to rational examination; I argue that in making moral appraisals one must be rational; I examine the ethical relativist's claim that there are and can be no *sound grounds* for claiming the moral beliefs of one culture to be correct and those of another to be mistaken. But surely my analysis is clouded by these unspecified references to a "rational" or "sound" basis for morality. Must there be a rational basis for morality?

This question cannot have a straightforward answer. There is an important sense in which anything that would count as morality must be rational for, by implicit definition, a "moral claim" is a claim that must be supportable by reasons. (The force of the "must" here is logical.) If someone says to another person "Please do this for me," or "I like this," they need not give reasons for their request or avowal, but if someone claims "You should do this for me," or "This is good," it is always appropriate, from a logical point of view at least, to ask why. For "Please do this for me" I can answer "For no reason, I just wish you would." I cannot do this for "You should do this for me" since I cannot appropriately reply "For no reason, I just wish you would." The logic of "should" requires the relevance of "But why should I?" in the way "having mass" requires "having weight."[13] Moral discourse is *in this way* rational discourse.

It must also in another way be rational discourse. By definition a *justified* moral judgment must be reasonable in that it must—logically must—be a judgment that will stand up to an impartial review of the facts, and it must consider the interests of everyone in an impartial way. This is a part of the very logic of moral discourse.[14]

In another way it is an open question whether moral claims must be supportable by reason. We indeed must support a moral judgment by giving reasons, but have we shown that what will count as "good reasons" or even as

"relevant reasons" is determined or even determinable by cross-culturally agreed-on criteria? Is there something in the very logic of moral discourse that dictates that there must be an agreement about this? Certainly this is an open question. Perhaps people actually differ in their criteria as to what will count as "good reasons" in ethics; it may even be that they can on reflection find no shared grounds for deciding what are to count as "good reasons" in ethics. Perhaps the force of the "must" in "There must be agreed-on criteria," is itself *moral* rather than logical, that is to say, it may very well be more like "We must make this marriage work" than like "Red things must be colored." It may in effect give voice, in a disguised but quite understandable way, to an urgent *plea* for a universal morality. But if this is so, we must not forget that this is a *moral plea* and not something that can be determined by a careful philosophical or logical analysis of the concept of morality.

It is also true that a man may perfectly well know what is right and still not do what is right either through weakness of will or, like the fictional character Hud, through a deliberate rejection of the very canons of morality. The former phenomenon is frequent enough; the latter is far more puzzling, for as a matter of *psychological fact* it may remain the case that no one flaunts the very dictates of morality in a thorough and systematic way. Yet it is logically possible that someone might, and it is very questionable whether there is any morally neutral sense of "reason" in which we can find some reason or set of

13. See W. D. Falk, "Goading and Guiding," *Mind*, vol. LXII (1953), pp. 145–171.

14. See J. N. Findlay, *Language, Mind and Value* (London: 1963), chs. IV and IX.

reasons of an absolutely conclusive sort which will prove to a man that he must be moral. There is no Reason somehow embedded in the nature of things that will show him that he *must* so reason.[15]

We need to twist the tiger's tail a little more. People affected by certain "theories" about "the sociology of knowledge" will argue that men not only reason from an established set of facts, but what *are* the facts depends upon the frame of reference, the mental set, the body of presuppositions that men bring to their observations of the facts. This supposedly undercuts my claim that to talk of what is the case (the facts) is one thing and to talk of what ought to be the case (values) is another. It also presumably undercuts my claims that anthropological facts about the moral beliefs and reasoning of other cultures are relevant and important facts to be utilized in moral appraisal and criticism.

But such a criticism does not undermine my argument. In fact if it is taken *literally*, it is obviously and plainly false that what the facts are depends on our frame of reference or "value orientation." That I am writing this paragraph with a green pencil is a plain fact. That it is a fact does not depend on my or anyone else's attitudes, values or beliefs. That people in another culture do not draw a distinction between green and black or that, being preliterate, they have no conception of a pencil, does not make it any less a fact that I am writing this paragraph with a green pencil. As we can be taught to make other color discriminations than those we do in fact habitually make, so people in other cultures can be and are taught to discriminate between what we call a black and a green object and they can also be taught, though here the teaching is vastly more complicated,

what a pencil is even though their culture does not have an artifact that is even remotely like a pencil. There is no case at all for saying that the fact that I am writing this paragraph with a green pencil depends on any "value orientation" or set of moral beliefs that I or anyone else might hold. As this case and millions like it show, facts, for the most part, are not the creatures of our culture pattern, "value orientation," our "existential interpretation" or anything of that order. By the use of true statements we state facts, but they are not for a whole range of cases at any rate the creatures of our cultural or historical imagination.

Yet, as the old saying goes, where there is smoke there is fire. If the above claim were reduced to the claim that our value judgments shape in a radical way our *selection* of what facts are *relevant* and *important* facts then we would have an important and challenging claim. Such stances concerning what is worthwhile and what is good, may even determine which facts are selected for notice and which are not. If a Marxist were to write about the Peloponesian War he would surely select for attention more facts about the economic life of the different Greek poli than did Thucydides. If a man were a Freudian the fact that Luther had hemorrhoids would be a fact to be noticed, but for most non-Freudians it is without historical significance. But in all sobriety we must realize that to say this is not to imply that the facts are determined by our "value-orientation"; but it does mean that in selecting the

15. I have argued that point at length in my "Why Should I Be Moral?," *Methodos*, vol. XV, no. 59–60 (1963), pp. 275–306, "On Looking Back At the Emotive Theory," *Methodos*, vol. XIV, no. 53 (1962) pp. 1–20 and "On Being Moral?" *Philosophical Studies*, vol. XVI, no. 1–2 (January-February, 1965), pp. 1–4.

facts to be recorded in an anthropological or sociological study, judgments of relevance and importance are crucial. They in large measure determine what facts are to be examined.

We need rather fully and carefully to consider a hypothetical case to see how this is so. Suppose a Puerto Rican is considering what position he should take concerning the political status of his country. Should he be for an expanded commonwealth status, for statehood or for an independent Puerto Rico? There are a host of facts that he could consider. With independence there will initially be the maximum freedom of self-determination, but with independence Puerto Rico may well come to have what is in effect a dictatorship. Furthermore, countries like Puerto Rico when independent tend to get very corrupt governments. The presence of officials from the States keeps health and educational standards at a higher level than they otherwise might be, and the investment of American capital will be greater if Puerto Rico does not become a sovereign state. Yet an independent Puerto Rico would free the United States from charges of colonialism. With independence the island could impose its own tariffs and develop its own foreign policy.

Factual considerations or putative factual considerations of this sort would be selected by any rational human being in making such a deliberation; but many facts are completely irrelevant to such a deliberation. Rational human beings do not select as even relevant to the discussion the fact that low tide was at noon, that Mrs. Ferdandez bought a new blue hat or that Puerto Ricans like music. That such facts are irrelevant and that those previously mentioned are relevant is, in part, determined by the attitudes or "value-orientation" of the people involved; but it is not as simple

as that. There are general conditions which are brought to bear in judgments of relevancy and importance. Not all attitudes are relevant. The factual considerations which are relevant are for the most part those that point to the harmful or beneficial consequences for everyone involved in adopting one status rather than another; furthermore precisely which consequences are harmful or beneficial is not simply a function of the attitudes we happen to have, for consequences that are harmful are, among other things, consequences that cause pain, suffering or anguish to the people involved, and consequences which are beneficial are consequences that give rise to fairly permanent states of enjoyment, ease and "peace of mind" to the people involved.[16] That Puerto Rico could impose its own tariffs, would presumably work to the advantage of at least some people. Thus such a factual consideration is relevant in making a decision about what political status Puerto Rico ought to have. In such a situation a reason is a relevant reason for a moral decision, if what the reason asserts to be the case is the case and if, when that which the reason asserts to be the case is the case, something good or bad results or is likely to result, which would not otherwise come about or be likely to come about. But we could make this claim only if we had some prior conception of good and bad. Decisions about relevance and irrelevance involve the imposition of normative standards. Judgments about the weight or merit of admittedly relevant reasons are still more difficult; and such judgments surely involve the imposition of normative standards. In the case men-

16. See my "Appraising Doing the Thing Done," *The Journal of Philosophy*, vol. LVII (November 24, 1960) and my "Moral Truth," *American Philosophical Quarterly*, Monograph No. 1 (1968).

tioned, we have a decision as to which reasons are relevant, but we must also assess the comparative *merit* of the different relevant reasons, in deciding what we ought to do. How are we to decide which of the relevant reasons are the most important? Here one's values and attitudes, sooner or later, are crucial in any selection or weighting. But how, in turn, do we rationally justify adopting those values?

This is indeed a difficult problem—a problem that takes us to the very heart of thinking about morality. I can not here attack this problem.[17] But I will say this: granting that one's attitudes or one's "value orientation" is of fundamental importance in determining a selection of the facts, this still does not, by itself, establish either ethical relativism or cultural relativism. There may well be cross-cultural agreement about certain very fundamental values used in making such a selection. In the first part of my essay I have shown that agreement about what is taken to be desirable or valuable does not of itself establish that what is taken to be desirable is in fact desirable. Such cultural agreement is not *by itself* enough to establish an objective morality. But if there were such agreement, and furthermore, if this agreement were to persist in cases where people did not have mistaken or superstitious *factual* beliefs and where they carefully thought through the consequences of holding these values and took what these values enjoined to heart, we, in such a situation, would have a very strong case for saying that here we have in part at least a basis for a rational and objective morality.

My reference to "rational morality" and my earlier reference to "a rational human being" might be thought to be question begging. The term "rational," it might be argued, does have approbative force, but it makes no objective

reference. The last part of this statement is false. If a man is a rational man, he must be willing to listen to evidence and he must act in accordance with the evidence. Furthermore, where such considerations are relevant, a rational human being must act according to principle and he must grant that if X is a good reason for B's doing Y in Z, it is also a good reason for anyone else relevantly like B and similarly situated. The force of all the above occurrences of "must" is logical. My above remarks are explicative of what is *meant* by "being a rational human being." The recognition of this involves no value judgment on anyone's part. It would be an abuse of the English language to assert that people can fail to act in this manner and still act rationally. And given the conventions of English, people who habitually fail to act in this manner cannot correctly be said to be rational human beings. Moreover, this does not simply reflect the conventions of English, but holds for the concept expressed by the English term "rational human being." Such a convention would hold for any language in which this concept was expressed. The above claim could be stated in German, for example, though we would speak in German of the conventions governing the German term "vernünftiger Mensch."[18]

Furthermore, that our "value orientation" radically influences or even de-

17. I have tried to do this in the articles mentioned in notes 15 and 16 and in my "Justification and Moral Reasoning," *Methodos*, vol. IX no. 33–4, (1957), pp. 77–113 and my "The Good Reasons Approach Revisited," *Arhiv für Rechts und Sozialphilosophie*, vol. 1964 L/4, pp. 445–484.

18. More needs to be said about this than I can say here. I have said some of it in my "Rational Explanations in History," in *Philosophy and History*, Sidney Hook, ed. (New York University Press: 1963), pp. 311–313, "Appealing to Reason," *Inquiry*, vol. V (1962) and "Wanton Reason," *Philosophical Studies* (Maynooth, Ireland), vol. XII (1963).

termines the selection of facts to be used in moral appraisal, does not make us impervious to the facts selected by others with different "value orientations" for appraising the same actions we are appraising. Certain "unwelcome facts" may be brought to our attention which will lead us, if we are rational human beings, to alter our appraisal of an action.

In short, even if there are no cross-culturally agreed-on criteria of relevancy or criteria for deciding which of the relevant facts are the most *important* facts in making moral assessments, it still does not follow that ethical relativism is true, for some people might be mistaken in their judgments of relevancy and importance. We would need some further theoretical argument to show that no one could be mistaken in this respect and that all such criteria are equally valid. But that no one can be mistaken in this way or that all such criteria are of equal worth cannot be determined from the anthropological facts *alone*.

The main thrust of my essay has been to show that, as important as the facts concerning cultural agreement and disagreement are, they will establish neither ethical relativism nor ethical objectivism. It is important to note that if cultural disagreement about what is *said* to be good or bad cannot by itself establish that what is good or bad is relative to the culture, then, as a strict logical consequence, cultural agreement over what is *said* to be good or bad cannot establish that what is so said to be good or bad is indeed good or bad. If the fact of cultural disagreement cannot establish ethical relativity the fact of cross-cultural agreement cannot establish ethical objectivism. In neither case can we move directly from a factual consideration to a moral one.

In thinking intelligently about morality we need to know about the facts of cultural relativity, we need to develop a sensitivity to the cultural determinants of what it is to be reasonable or what it is to "follow Reason," and we need to see how deeply our very forms of life affect our criteria of relevance and our weighing of the various facts appealed to in moral reasoning; but no matter what discoveries we make here, we have not thereby established ethical relativism or, its shadow, ethical objectivism.

3

DAVID HUME
Morality Is Founded on Sentiment

DAVID HUME (1711–1776), the British philosopher and historian, wrote important works on ethics, religion, metaphysics and theory of knowledge, and history. His *A Treatise of Human Nature*, which is probably the greatest philosophical book in the English language, was written when Hume was in his early twenties.

MORAL DISTINCTIONS NOT DERIVED FROM REASON

. . . Those who affirm that virtue is nothing but a conformity to reason; that there are eternal fitnesses and unfitnesses of things, which are the same to every rational being that considers them; that the immutable measures of right and wrong impose an obligation, not only on human creatures, but also on the Deity himself: All these systems concur in the opinion, that morality, like truth, is discern'd merely by ideas, and by their juxta-position and comparison. In order, therefore, to judge of these systems, we need only consider, whether it be possible, from reason alone, to distinguish betwixt moral good and evil, or whether there must concur some other principles to enable us to make that distinction.

If morality had naturally no influence on human passions and actions, 'twere in vain to take such pains to inculcate it; and nothing wou'd be more fruitless than that multitude of rules and precepts, with which all moralists abound. Philosophy is commonly divided into *speculative* and *practical*; and as morality is always comprehended under the latter division, 'tis supposed to influence our passions and actions, and to go beyond the calm and indolent judgments of the understanding. And this is confirm'd by common experience, which informs us, that men are often govern'd by their duties, and are deter'd from some actions by the opinion of injustice, and impell'd to others by that of obligation.

Since morals, therefore, have an influence on the actions and affections, it follows, that they cannot be deriv'd

Excerpted from David Hume, *A Treatise of Human Nature* (1740), Book III, Part I, Section 1; and *An Inquiry Concerning the Principles of Morals* (1751), Section I, and Appendix 1.

from reason; and that because reason alone, as we have already prov'd, can never have any such influence. Morals excite passions, and produce or prevent actions. Reason of itself is utterly impotent in this particular. The rules of morality, therefore, are not conclusions of our reason.

No one, I believe, will deny the justness of this inference; nor is there any other means of evading it, than by denying that principle, on which it is founded. As long as it is allow'd, that reason has no influence on our passions and actions, 'tis in vain to pretend, that morality is discover'd only by a deduction of reason. An active principle can never be founded on an inactive; and if reason be inactive in itself, it must remain so in all its shapes and appearances, whether it exerts itself in natural or moral subjects, whether it considers the powers of external bodies, or the actions of rational beings.

It would be tedious to repeat all the arguments, by which I have prov'd that reason is perfectly inert, and can never either prevent or produce any action or affection. 'Twill be easy to recollect what has been said upon that subject. I shall only recall on this occasion one of these arguments, which I shall endeavour to render still more conclusive, and more applicable to the present subject.

Reason is the discovery of truth or falsehood. Truth or falsehood consists in an agreement or disagreement either to the *real* relations of ideas, or to *real* existence and matter of fact. Whatever, therefore, is not susceptible of this agreement or disagreement, is incapable of being true or false, and can never be an object of our reason. Now 'tis evident our passions, volitions, and actions, are not susceptible of any such agreement or disagreement; being original facts and realities, compleat in themselves, and implying no reference to other passions, volitions, and actions. 'Tis impossible, therefore, they can be pronounced either true or false, and be either contrary or conformable to reason.

This argument is of double advantage to our present purpose. For it proves *directly*, that actions do not derive their merit from a conformity to reason, nor their blame from a contrariety to it; and it proves the same truth more *indirectly*, by shewing us, that as reason can never immediately prevent or produce any action by contradicting or approving of it, it cannot be the source of moral good and evil, which are found to have that influence. Actions may be laudable or blameable; but they cannot be reasonable or unreasonable: Laudable or blameable, therefore, are not the same with reasonable or unreasonable. The merit and demerit of actions frequently contradict, and sometimes control our natural propensities. But reason has no such influence. Moral distinctions, therefore, are not the offspring of reason. Reason is wholly inactive, and can never be the source of so active a principle as conscience, or a sense of morals.

. . . Take any action allow'd to be vicious: Wilful murder, for instance. Examine it in all lights, and see if you can find that matter of fact, or real existence, which you call *vice*. In whichever way you take it, you find only certain passions, motives, volitions and thoughts. There is no other matter of fact in the case. The vice entirely escapes you, as long as you consider the object. You never can find it, till you turn your reflexion into your own breast, and find a sentiment of disapprobation, which arises in you, towards this action. Here is a matter of fact; but 'tis the ob-

ject of feeling, not of reason. It lies in yourself, not in the object. So that when you pronounce any action or character to be vicious, you mean nothing, but that from the constitution of your nature you have a feeling or sentiment of blame from the contemplation of it. Vice and virtue, therefore, may be compar'd to sounds, colours, heat and cold, which, according to modern philosophy, are not qualities in objects, but perceptions in the mind: And this discovery in morals, like that other in physics, is to be regarded as a considerable advancement of the speculative sciences; tho', like that too, it has little or no influence on practice. Nothing can be more real, or concern us more, than our own sentiments of pleasure and uneasiness; and if these be favourable to virtue, and unfavourable to vice, no more can be requisite to the regulation of our conduct and behaviour.

I cannot forbear adding to these reasonings an observation, which may, perhaps, be found of some importance. In every system of morality, which I have hitherto met with, I have always remark'd, that the author proceeds for some time in the ordinary way of reasoning, and establishes the being of a God, or makes observations concerning human affairs; when of a sudden I am surpriz'd to find, that instead of the usual copulations of propositions, *is*, and *is not*, I meet with no proposition that is not connected with an *ought*, or an *ought not*. This change is imperceptible; but is, however, of the last consequence. For as this *ought*, or *ought not*, expresses some new relation or affirmation, 'tis necessary that it shou'd be observ'd and explain'd; and at the same time that a reason should be given, for what seems altogether inconceivable, how this new relation can be a deduction from others, which are entirely different from it. But as authors do not commonly use this precaution, I shall presume to recommend it to the readers; and am persuaded, that this small attention wou'd subvert all the vulgar systems of morality, and let us see, that the distinction of vice and virtue is not founded merely on the relations of objects, nor is perceiv'd by reason.

OF THE GENERAL PRINICIPLES OF MORALS

There has been a controversy started of late, much better worth examination, concerning the general foundation of Morals; whether they be derived from Reason or from Sentiment; whether we attain the knowledge of them by a chain of argument and induction or by an immediate feeling and finer internal sense; whether, like all sound judgment of truth and falsehood, they should be the same to every rational intelligent being; or whether, like the perception of beauty and deformity, they be founded entirely on the particular fabric and constitution of the human species.

The ancient philosophers, though they often affirm that virtue is nothing but conformity to reason, yet in general seem to consider morals as deriving their existence from taste and sentiment. On the other hand, our modern enquirers, though they also talk much of the beauty of virtue and deformity of vice, yet have commonly endeavoured to account for these distinctions by metaphysical reasonings, and by deductions from the most abstract principles of the understanding. Such confusion reigned in these subjects that an opposition of the greatest consequence could prevail between one system and another, and even in the parts of almost each individual system; and yet nobody, till very lately, was ever sensible of it. The elegant Lord Shaftesbury, who first

gave occasion to remark this distinction, and who in general adhered to the principles of the ancients, is not himself entirely free from the same confusion.

It must be acknowledged that both sides of the question are susceptible of specious arguments. Moral distinctions, it may be said, are discernible by pure *reason*; else, whence the many disputes that reign in common life, as well as in philosophy, with regard to this subject: the long chain of proofs often produced on both sides, the examples cited, the authorities appealed to, the analogies employed, the fallacies detected, the inferences drawn, and the several conclusions adjusted to their proper principles. Truth is disputable, not taste; what exists in the nature of things is the standard of our judgment; what each man feels within himself is the standard of sentiment. Propositions in geometry may be proved, systems in physics may be controverted; but the harmony of verse, the tenderness of passion, the brilliancy of wit, must give immediate pleasure. No man reasons concerning another's beauty, but frequently concerning the justice or injustice of his actions. In every criminal trial the first object of the prisoner is to disprove the facts alleged and deny the actions imputed to him; the second, to prove that, even if these actions were real, they might be justified as innocent and lawful. It is confessedly by deductions of the understanding that the first point is ascertained: how can we suppose that a different faculty of the mind is employed in fixing the other?

On the other hand, those who would resolve all moral determinations into *sentiment* may endeavour to show that it is impossible to reason ever to draw conclusions of this nature. To virtue, say they, it belongs to be *amiable*, and vice *odious*. This forms their very nature or essence. But can reason or argumentation distribute these different epithets to any subjects, and pronounce beforehand that this must produce love, and that hatred? Or what other reason can we ever assign for these affections but the original fabric and formation of the human mind, which is naturally adapted to receive them?

The end of all moral speculations is to teach us our duty; and by proper representations of the deformity of vice and beauty of virtue, beget correspondent habits, and engage us to avoid the one and embrace the other. But is this ever to be expected from inferences and conclusions of the understanding, which of themselves have no hold of the affections or set in motion the active powers of men? They discover truths; but where the truths which they discover are indifferent and beget no desire or aversion, they can have no influence on conduct and behaviour. What is honourable, what is fair, what is becoming, what is noble, what is generous, takes possession of the heart and animates us to embrace and maintain it. What is intelligible, what is evident, what is probable, what is true, procures only the cool assent of the understanding and, gratifying a speculative curiosity, puts an end to our researches.

Extinguish all the warm feelings and prepossessions in favour of virtue, and all disgust or aversion to vice; render men totally indifferent towards these distinctions, and morality is no longer a practical study, nor has any tendency to regulate our lives and actions.

These arguments on each side—and many more might be produced—are so plausible that I am apt to suspect they may, the one as well as the other, be solid and satisfactory, and that *reason* and *sentiment* concur in almost all

moral determinations and conclusions. The final sentence, it is probable, which pronounces characters and actions amiable or odious, praiseworthy or blamable; that which stamps on them the mark of honour or infamy, approbation or censure; that which renders morality an active principle and constitutes virtue our happiness, and vice our misery—it is probable, I say, that this final sentence depends on some internal sense or feeling which nature has made universal in the whole species. For what else can have an influence of this nature? But in order to pave the way for such a sentiment, and give a proper discernment of its object, it is often necessary, we find, that much reasoning should precede, that nice distinctions be made, just conclusions drawn, distant comparisons formed, complicated relations examined, and general facts fixed and ascertained. Some species of beauty, especially the natural kinds, on their first appearance command our affection and approbation; and where they fail of this effect, it is impossible for any reasoning to redress their influence, or adapt them better to our taste and sentiment. But in many orders of beauty, particularly those of the finer arts, it is requisite to employ much reasoning in order to feel the proper sentiment; and a false relish may frequently be corrected by argument and reflection. There are just grounds to conclude that moral beauty partakes much of this latter species, and demands the assistance of our intellectual faculties in order to give it a suitable influence on the human mind.

CONCERNING MORAL SENTIMENT

If the foregoing hypothesis be received, it will now be easy for us to determine the question first started, concerning the general principles of morals; and though we postponed the decision of that question, lest it should then involve us in intricate speculations which are unfit for moral discourses, we may resume it at present and examine how far either *reason* or *sentiment* enters into all decisions of praise or censure.

One principal foundation of moral praise being supposed to lie in the usefulness of any quality or action, it is evident that *reason* must enter for a considerable share in all decisions of this kind, since nothing but that faculty can instruct us in the tendency of qualities and actions, and point out their beneficial consequences to society and to their possessor. In many cases this is an affair liable to great controversy: doubts may arise, opposite interests may occur, and a preference must be given to one side from very nice views and a small overbalance of utility. This is particularly remarkable in questions with regard to justice as is, indeed, natural to suppose, from that species of utility which attends this virtue. Were every single instance of justice, like that of benevolence, useful to society, this would be a more simple state of the case, and seldom liable to great controversy. But as single instances of justice are often pernicious in their first and immediate tendency, and as the advantage to society results only from the observance of the general rule and from the concurrence and combination of several persons in the same equitable conduct, the case here becomes more intricate and involved. The various circumstances of society, the various consequences of any practice, the various interests which may be proposed; these, on many occasions, are doubtful, and subject to great discussion and inquiry. The object of municipal laws is to fix all the questions with regard to justice: the debates of civilians, the re-flections of politicians, the precedents of history and public records, are all directed to the same purpose. And a very accurate *reason* or *judgment* is often requisite to give the true determination amidst such intricate doubts arising from obscure or opposite utilities.

But though reason, when fully assisted and improved, be sufficient to instruct us in the pernicious or useful tendency of qualities and actions, it is not alone sufficient to produce any moral blame or approbation. Utility is only a tendency to a certain end; and were the end totally indifferent to us, we should feel the same indifference towards the means. It is requisite a *sentiment* should here display itself, in order to give a preference to the useful above the pernicious tendencies. This sentiment can be no other than a feeling for the happiness of mankind and a resentment of their misery, since these are the different ends which virtue and vice have a tendency to promote. Here therefore *reason* instructs us in the several tendencies of actions, and *humanity* makes a distinction in favour of those which are useful and beneficial.

This partition between the faculties of understanding and sentiment, in all moral decisions, seems clear from the preceding hypothesis. But I shall suppose that hypothesis false; it will then be requisite to look out for some other theory that may be satisfactory, and I dare venture to affirm that none such will ever be found so long as we suppose reason to be the sole source of morals. To prove this, it will be proper to weigh the five following considerations.

I. It is easy for a false hypothesis to maintain some appearance of truth, while it keeps wholly in generals, makes use of undefined terms, and employs comparisons instead of instances. This is particularly remarkable in that philosophy which ascribes the discernment of all moral distinctions to reason alone, without the concurrence of sentiment. It is impossible that in any particular instance this hypothesis can so much as be rendered intelligible, whatever specious figure it may make in general declamations and discourses. Examine the crime of *ingratitude*, for instance, which has place wherever we observe good-will expressed and known, together with good-offices performed, on the one side, and a return of ill-will or indifference with ill-offices or neglect on the other: anatomize all these circumstances and examine, by your reason alone, in what consists the demerit or blame. You never will come to any issue or conclusion.

Reason judges either of *matter of fact* or of *relations*. Enquire then, *first*, where is that matter of fact which we here call *crime*; point it out, determine the time of its existence, describe its essence or nature, explain the sense or faculty to which it discovers itself. It resides in the mind of the person who is ungrateful. He must, therefore, feel it and be conscious of it. But nothing is there, except the passion of ill-will or absolute indifference. You cannot say that these, of themselves, always and in all circumstances are crimes. No, they are only crimes when directed towards persons who have before expressed and displayed good-will towards us. Consequently, we may infer that the crime of ingratitude is not any particular individual *fact*, but arises from a complication of circumstances which, being presented to the spectator, excites the *sentiment* of blame by the particular structure and fabric of his mind.

This representation, you say, is false. Crime, indeed, consists not in a particular *fact*, of whose reality we are assured by *reason*, but it consists in certain *moral relations*, discovered by reason, in the same manner as we discover by reason the truths of geometry or algebra. But what are the relations, I ask, of which you here talk? In the case stated above, I see first good-will and good-offices in one person, then ill-will and ill-offices in the other. Between these, there is a relation of *contrariety*. Does the crime consist in that relation? But suppose a person bore me ill-will or did me ill-offices, and I, in return, were indifferent towards him, or did him good offices. Here is the same relation of *contrariety*, and yet my conduct is often highly laudable. Twist and turn this matter as much as you will, you can never rest the morality on relation, but must have recourse to the decisions of sentiment.

When it is affirmed that two and three are equal to the half of ten, this relation of equality I understand perfectly. I conceive that, if ten be divided into two parts, of which one has as many units as the other, and if any of these parts be compared to two added to three, it will contain as many units as that compound number. But when you draw thence a comparison to moral relations, I own that I am altogether at a loss to understand you. A moral action, a crime, such as ingratitude, is a complicated object. Does the morality consist in the relation of its parts to each other? How? After what manner? Specify the relation: be more particular and explicit in your propositions, and you will easily see their falsehood.

No, say you, the morality consists in the relation of actions to the rule of right; and they are denominated good or ill, according as they agree or disagree with it. What then is this rule of right? In what does it consist? How is it determined? By reason, you say, which examines the moral relations of actions.

So that moral relations are determined by the comparison of action to a rule. And that rule is determined by considering the moral relations of objects. Is not this fine reasoning?

All this is metaphysics, you cry. That is enough; there needs nothing more to give a strong presumption of falsehood. Yes, reply I, here are metaphysics surely; but they are all on your side, who advance an abstruse hypothesis which can never be made intelligible, nor quadrate with any particular instance or illustration. The hypothesis which we embrace is plain. It maintains that morality is determined by sentiment. It defines virtue to be *whatever mental action or quality gives to a spectator the pleasing sentiment of approbation;* and vice the contrary. We then proceed to examine a plain matter of fact, to wit, what actions have this influence. We consider all the circumstances in which these actions agree, and thence endeavour to extract some general observations with regard to these sentiments. If you call this metaphysics and find anything abstruse here, you need only conclude that your turn of mind is not suited to the moral sciences.

II. When a man, at any time, deliberates concerning his own conduct—as, whether he had better, in a particular emergence, assist a brother or a benefactor—he must consider these separate relations, with all the circumstances and situations of the persons, in order to determine the superior duty and obligation; and in order to determine the proportion of lines in any triangle, it is necessary to examine the nature of that figure, and the relation which its several parts bear to each other. But notwithstanding this appearing similarity in the two cases, there is, at bottom, an extreme difference between them. A speculative reasoner concerning triangles or circles considers the several known and given relations of the parts of these figures, and thence infers some unknown relation which is dependent on the former. But in moral deliberations we must be acquainted beforehand with all the objects and all their relations to each other, and from a comparison of the whole fix our choice or approbation. No new fact to be ascertained; no new relation to be discovered. All the circumstances of the case are supposed to be laid before us, ere we can fix any sentence of blame or approbation. If any material circumstance be yet unknown or doubtful, we must first employ our inquiry or intellectual faculties to assure us of it, and must suspend for a time all moral decision or sentiment. While we are ignorant whether a man were aggressor or not, how can we determine whether the person who killed him be criminal or innocent? But after every circumstance, every relation is known, the understanding has no further room to operate, nor any object on which it could employ itself. The approbation or blame which then ensues cannot be the work of the judgment, but of the heart, and is not a speculative proposition or affirmation, but an active feeling or sentiment. In the disquisitions of the understanding, from known circumstances and relations we infer some new and unknown. In moral decisions, all the circumstances and relations must be previously known; and the mind, from the contemplation of the whole, feels some new impression of affection or disgust, esteem or contempt, approbation or blame.

Hence the great difference between a mistake of *fact* and one of *right;* and hence the reason why the one is commonly criminal and not the other.

When Oedipus killed Laius, he was ignorant of the relation, and from circumstances, innocent and involuntary, formed erroneous opinions concerning the action which he committed. But when Nero killed Agrippina, all the relations between himself and the person, and all the circumstances of the fact, were previously known to him; but the motive of revenge, or fear, or interest, prevailed in his savage heart over the sentiments of duty and humanity. And when we express that detestation against him to which he himself, in a little time, became insensible, it is not that we see any relations of which he was ignorant, but that, for the rectitude of our disposition, we feel sentiments against which he was hardened from flattery and a long perseverance in the most enormous crimes. In these sentiments then, not in a discovery of relations of any kind, do all moral determinations consist. Before we can pretend to form any decision of this kind, everything must be known and ascertained on the side of the object or action. Nothing remains but to feel, on our part, some sentiment of blame or approbation, whence we pronounce the action criminal or virtuous.

III. This doctrine will become still more evident if we compare moral beauty with natural, to which in many particulars it bears so near a resemblance. It is on the proportion, relation, and position of parts, that all natural beauty depends; but it would be absurd thence to infer that the perception of beauty, like that of truth in geometrical problems, consists wholly in the perception of relations, and was performed entirely by the understanding or intellectual faculties. In all the sciences, our mind from the known relations investigates the unknown. But in all decisions of taste or external beauty, all the relations are beforehand obvious to the eye; and we thence proceed to feel a sentiment of complacency or disgust, according to the nature of the object and disposition of our organs.

Euclid has fully explained all the qualities of the circle, but has not in any proposition said a word of its beauty. The reason is evident. The beauty is not a quality of the circle. It lies not in any part of the line, whose parts are equally distant from a common centre. It is only the effect which that figure produces upon the mind, whose peculiar fabric of structure renders it susceptible of such sentiments. In vain would you look for it in the circle, or seek it, either by your senses or by mathematical reasoning, in all the properties of that figure.

Attend to Palladio and Perrault, while they explain all the parts and proportions of a pillar. They talk of the cornice, and frieze, and base, and entablature, and shaft, and architrave, and give the descriptions and position of each of these members. But should you ask the description and position of its beauty, they would readily reply that the beauty is not in any of the parts or members of a pillar, but results from the whole, when that complicated figure is presented to an intelligent mind susceptible to those finer sensations. Till such a spectator appear, there is nothing but a figure of such particular dimensions and proportions: from his sentiments alone arise its elegance and beauty.

Again, attend to Cicero while he paints the crimes of a Verres or a Catiline. You must acknowledge that the moral turpitude results in the same manner from the contemplation of the whole, when presented to a being whose organs have such a particular structure and formation. The orator may paint rage, insolence, barbarity on the one side; meekness, suffering, sorrow, innocence on the other. But if you feel no indignation or compassion arise in you from this complication of circumstances, you would in vain ask him, in what consists the crime or villainy, which he so vehemently exclaims against? At what time or on what subject it first began to exist? And what has a few months afterwards become of it, when every disposition and thought of all the actors is totally altered or annihilated? No satisfactory answer can be given to any of these questions upon the abstract hypothesis of morals; and we must at last acknowledge that the crime or immorality is no particular fact or relation which can be the object of the understanding, but arises entirely from the sentiment of disapprobation which, by the structure of human nature, we unavoidably feel on the apprehension of barbarity or treachery.

IV. Inanimate objects may bear to each other all the same relations which we observe in moral agents, though the former can never be the object of love or hatred, nor are consequently susceptible of merit or iniquity. A young tree, which over-tops and destroys its parent, stands in all the same relations with Nero when he murdered Agrippina and, if morality consisted merely in relations, would no doubt be equally criminal.

V. It appears evident that the ultimate ends of human actions can never, in any case, be accounted for by *reason*, but recommend themselves entirely to the sentiments and affections of mankind, without any dependence on the intellectual faculties. Ask a man *why he uses exercise;* he will answer *because he desires to keep his health.* If you then enquire *why he desires health,* he will readily reply *because sickness is painful.* If you push your enquiries further and desire a reason *why he hates*

pain, it is impossible he can ever give any. This is an ultimate end, and is never referred to any other object.

Perhaps to your second question, *why he desires health,* he may also reply that *it is necessary for the exercise of his calling.* If you ask *why he is anxious on that head,* he will answer *because he desires to get money.* If you demend *why? It is the instrument of pleasure,* says he. And beyond this it is an absurdity to ask for a reason. It is impossible there can be a progress *in infinitum;* and that one thing can always be a reason why another is desired. Something must be desirable on its own account, and because of its immediate accord or agreement with human sentiment and affection.

Now as virtue is an end, and is desirable on its own account without fee and reward, merely for the immediate satisfaction which it conveys, it is requisite that there should be some sentiment which it touches, some internal taste or feeling, or whatever you may please to call it, which distinguishes moral good and evil, and which embraces the one and rejects the other.

Thus the distinct boundaries and offices of *reason* and of *taste* are easily ascertained. The former conveys the knowledge of truth and falsehood; the latter gives the sentiment of beauty and deformity, vice and virtue. The one discovers objects as they really stand in nature, without addition and diminution; the other has a productive faculty and, gilding or staining all natural objects with the colours borrowed from internal sentiment, raises in a manner a new creation. Reason, being cool and disengaged, is no motive to action, and directs only the impulse received from appetite or inclination, by showing us the means of attaining happiness or avoiding misery. Taste, as it gives pleasure or pain, and thereby constitutes happiness or misery, becomes a motive to action, and is the first spring or impulse to desire and volition. From circumstances and relations, known or supposed, the former leads us to the discovery of the concealed and unknown; after all circumstances and relations are laid before us, the latter makes us feel from the whole a new sentiment of blame or approbation. The standard of the one, being founded on the nature of things, is eternal and inflexible, even by the will of the Supreme Being; the standard of the other, arising from the eternal frame and constitution of animals, is ultimately derived from that Supreme Will which bestowed on each being its peculiar nature and arranged the several classes and orders of existence.

4

A.J. AYER
Moral Judgements as Emotive

A. J. AYER, Wykeham Professor of Logic at Oxford, first popularized the philosophy of Logical Positivism for the English-speaking world in his book *Language, Truth and Logic* (1936). His other books include *The Problem of Knowledge* (1956), *The Central Questions of Philosophy* (1974), and several more.

The distinctions that I wish to make can best be brought out by an example. Suppose that someone has committed a murder. Then part of the story consists of what we may call the police court details; where and when and how the killing was effected; the identity of the murderer and of his victim; the relationship in which they stood to one another. Next there are the questions of motive: The murderer may have been suffering from jealousy, or he may have been anxious to obtain money; he may have been avenging a private injury, or pursuing some political end. These

From A. J. Ayer, *Philosophical Essays*, St. Martin's Press, Inc., Macmillan & Co., Ltd. (1954), pp. 233–239, 245–249. Reprinted by permission of St. Martin's Press and Macmillan London and Basingstoke. Abridged.

questions of motive are, on one level, a matter of the agent's reflections before the act; and these may very well take the form of moral judgements. Thus he may tell himself that his victim is a bad man and that the world would be better for his removal, or, in a different case, that it is his duty to rid his country of a tyrant, or, like Raskolnikov in *Crime and Punishment*, that he is a superior being who has in these circumstances the right to kill. A psychoanalyst who examines the case may, however, tell a different story. He may say that the political assassin is really revenging himself upon his father, or that the man who persuades himself that he is a social benefactor is really exhibiting a lust for power, or, in a case like that of Raskolnikov, that the murderer does not really believe that he has the right to kill.

All these are statements of fact; not indeed that the man has, or has not, the right to kill, but that this is what he tells himself. They are verified or confuted, as the case may be, by observation. It is a matter of fact, in my usage of the term, that the victim was killed at such and such a place and at such and such a time and in such and such a manner. It is also a matter of fact that the murderer had certain conscious motives. To himself they are known primarily by introspection; to others by various features of his overt behaviour, including what he says. As regards his unconscious motives the only criterion is his overt behaviour. It can indeed plausibly be argued that to talk about the unconscious is always equivalent to talking about overt behaviour, though often in a very complicated way. Now there seems to me to be a very good sense in which to tell a story of this kind, that this is what the man did and that these were his reasons for doing it, is to give a complete description of the facts. Or rather, since one can never be in a position to say that any such description is complete, what will be missing from it will be further information of the same type; what we obtain when this information is added is a more elaborate account of the circumstances of the action, and of its antecedents and consequences. But now suppose that instead of developing the story in this circumstantial way, one applies an ethical predicate to it. Suppose that instead of asking what it was that really happened, or what the agent's motives really were, we ask whether he was justified in acting as he did. Did he have the right to kill? Is it true that he had the right? Is it a fact that he acted rightly? It does not matter in this connection what answer

we give. The question for moral philosophy is not whether a certain action is right or wrong, but what is implied by saying that it is right, or saying that it is wrong. Suppose then that we say that the man acted rightly. The point that I wish to make is that in saying this we are not elaborating or modifying our description of the situation in the way that we should be elaborating it if we gave further police court details, or in the way that we should be modifying it if we showed that the agent's motives were different from what they had been thought to be. To say that his motives were good, or that they were bad, is not to say what they were. To say that the man acted rightly, or that he acted wrongly, is not to say what he did. And when one has said what he did, when one has described the situation in the way that I have outlined, then to add that he was justified, or alternatively that he was not, is not to say any more about what he did; it does not add a further detail to the story. It is for this reason that these ethical predicates are not factual; they do not describe any features of the situation to which they are applied. But they do, someone may object, they describe its ethical features. But what are these ethical features? And how are they related to the other features of the situation, to what we may provisionally call its 'natural' features? Let us consider this.

To begin with, it is, or should be, clear that the connection is not logical. Let us assume that two observers agree about all the circumstances of the case, including the agent's motives, but that they disagree in their evaluation of it. Then neither of them is contradicting himself. Otherwise the use of the ethical term would add nothing to the circumstantial description; it would serve merely as a repetition, or partial repetition, of it. But neither, as I hope to show, is the connection factual. There is nothing that counts as observing the *designata* of the ethical predicates, apart from observing the natural features of the situation. But what alternative is left? Certainly it can be said that the ethical features in some way depend upon the natural. We can and do give reasons for our moral judgements, just as we do for our aesthetic judgements, where the same argument applies. We fasten on motives, point to consequences, ask what would happen if everyone were to behave in such a way, and so forth. But the question is: In what way do these reasons support the judgements? Not in a logical sense. Ethical argument is not formal demonstration. And not in a scientific sense either. For then the goodness or badness of the situation, the rightness or wrongness of the action, would have to be something apart from the situation, something independently verifiable, for which the facts adduced as the reasons for the moral judgement were evidence. But in these moral cases the two coincide. There is no procedure of examining the value of the facts, as distinct from examining the facts themselves. We may say that we have evidence for our moral judgements, but we cannot distinguish between pointing to the evidence itself and pointing to that for which it is supposed to be evidence. Which means that in the scientific sense it is not evidence at all.

My own answer to this question is that what are accounted reasons for our moral judgements are reasons only in the sense that they determine attitudes. One attempts to influence another person morally by calling his attention to certain natural features of the situation, which are such as will be likely to evoke from him the desired response. Or again one may give reasons to oneself as a means of settling on an attitude or, more importantly, as a means of coming to some practical decision. Of course there are many cases in which one applies an ethical term without there being any question of one's having to act oneself, or even to persuade others to act, in any present situation. Moral judgements passed upon the behaviour of historical or fictitious characters provide obvious examples. But an action or a situation is morally evaluated always as an action or a situation of a certain kind. What is approved or disapproved is something repeatable. In saying that Brutus or Raskolnikov acted rightly, I am giving myself and others leave to imitate them should similar circumstances arise. I show myself to be favourably disposed in either case towards actions of that type. Similarly, in saying that they acted wrongly, I express a resolution not to imitate them, and endeavour also to discourage others. It may be thought that the mere use of the dyslogistic word 'wrongly' is not much of a discouragement, although it does have some emotive force. But that is where the reasons come in. I discourage others, or at any rate hope to discourage them, by telling them why I think the action wrong; and here the argument may take various forms. One method is to appeal to some moral principle, as, for example, that human life is sacred, and show that it applies to the given case. It is assumed that the principle is one that already has some influence upon those to whom the argument is addressed. Alternatively, one may try to establish certain facts, as, for example, that the act in question caused, or was such as would be likely to cause, a great deal of unhappiness;

and here it is assumed that the consideration of these facts will modify the hearer's attitude. It is assumed that he regards the increase of human misery as something undesirable, something if possible to be avoided. As for the moral judgement itself, it may be regarded as expressing the attitude which the reasons given for it are calculated to evoke. To say, as I once did, that these moral judgements are merely expressive of certain feelings, feelings of approval or disapproval, is an oversimplification. The fact is rather that what may be described as moral attitudes consist in certain patterns of behaviour, and that the expression of a moral judgement is an element in the pattern. The moral judgement expresses the attitude in the sense that it contributes to defining it. Why people respond favourably to certain facts and unfavourably to others is a question for the sociologist, into which I do not here propose to enter. I should imagine that the utilitarians had gone some way towards answering this question, although theirs is almost certainly not the whole answer. But my concern at present is only to analyse the use of ethical terms, not scientifically to explain it.

I hope that I have gone some way towards making clear what the theory which I am advocating is. Let me now say what it is not. In the first place, I am not saying that morals are trivial or unimportant, or that people ought not to bother with them. For this would itself be a judgement of value, which I have not made and do not wish to make. And even if I did wish to make it it would have no logical connection with my theory. For the theory is entirely on the level of analysis; it is an attempt to show what people are doing when they make moral judgements; it is not a set

of suggestions as to what moral judgements they are to make. And this is true of all moral philosophy, as I understand it. All moral theories, intuitionist, naturalistic, objectivist, emotive, and the rest, in so far as they are philosophical theories, are neutral as regards actual conduct. To speak technically, they belong to the field of metaethics, not ethics proper. That is why it is silly, as well as presumptuous, for any one type of philosopher to pose as the champion of virtue. And it is also one reason why many people find moral philosophy an unsatisfying subject. For they mistakenly look to the moral philosopher for guidance.

Again, when I say that moral judgements are emotive rather than descriptive, that they are persuasive expressions of attitudes and not statements of fact, and consequently that they cannot be either true or false, or at least that it would make for clarity if the categories of truth and falsehood were not applied to them, I am not saying that nothing is good or bad, right or wrong, or that it does not matter what we do. For once more such a statement would itself be the expression of a moral attitude. This attitude is not entailed by the theory, nor do I in fact adopt it. It would indeed be a difficult position to maintain. It would exclude even egotism as a policy, for the decision to consult nothing but one's own pleasure is itself a value judgement. What it requires is that one should live without any policy at all. This may or may not be feasible. My point is simply that I am not recommending it. Neither, in expounding my metaethical theory, am I recommending the opposite. It is indeed to be expected that a moral philosopher, even in my sense of the term, will have his moral standards and that he will sometimes make moral judgements; but these moral judgements cannot be a logical consequence of his philosophy. To analyse moral judgements is not itself to moralize.

Finally, I am not saying that anything that anybody thinks right is right; that putting people into concentration camps is preferable to allowing them free speech if somebody happens to think so, and that the contrary is also preferable if somebody thinks that it is. If my theory did entail this, it would be contradictory; for two different courses of action cannot each be preferable to the other. But it does not entail anything of the sort. On my analysis, to say that something which somebody thinks right really is right is to range oneself on his side, to adhere to that particular standpoint, and certainly I do not adhere to every standpoint whatsoever. I adhere to some, and not to others, like everybody else who has any moral views at all. It is, indeed, true that in a case where one person A approves of X, and another person B approves of not-X, A may correctly express his attitude towards X by saying that it is good, or right, and that B may correctly use the same term to express his attitude towards not-X. But there is no contradiction here. There would be a contradiction if from the fact that A was using words honestly and correctly when he said that X was good, and that B was using words honestly and correctly when he said that not-X was good, it followed that both X and not-X were good, or that X was both good and bad. But this does not follow, inasmuch as the conclusion that X is good, or that not-X is good, itself expresses the attitude of a third party, the speaker, who is by no means bound to agree with both A and B. In this example, indeed, he cannot consistently agree with both, though he may disagree with both if he regards both X and not-X as ethically neutral, or as contraries rather than contradictories in respect of value. It is easy to miss this point, which is essential for the understanding of our position. To say that anything is right if someone thinks so is unobjectionable if it means no more than that anyone is entitled to use the word 'right' to refer to something of which he morally approves. But this is not the way in which it is ordinarily taken. It is ordinarily taken as the enunciation of a moral principle. As a moral principle it does appear contradictory; it is at least doubtful whether to say of a man that he commits himself morally both to X and not-X is to describe a possible attitude. But it may perhaps be construed as a principle of universal moral tolerance. As such, it may appeal to some; it does not, in fact, to me. But the important point is that it is not entailed by the theory, which is neutral as regards all moral principles. And here I may repeat that in saying that it is neutral as regards all moral principles I am not saying that it recommends them all alike, nor that it condemns them all alike. It is not that sort of theory. No philosophical theory is.

But even if there is no logical connection between this metaethical theory and any particular type of conduct, may there not be a psychological connection? Does not the promulgation of such a theory encourage moral laxity? Has not its effect been to destroy people's confidence in accepted moral standards? And will not the result of this be that something mischievous will take their place? Such charges have, indeed, been made, but I do not know upon what evidence. The question how people's conduct is actually affected by their acceptance of a metaethical theory is one for empirical investigation; and in this case, so far as I know, no serious investigation has yet been carried out. My own observations, for what they are worth, do not suggest that those who accept the 'positivist' analysis of moral judgements conduct themselves very differently as a class from those who reject it; and, indeed, I doubt if the study of moral philosophy does, in general, have any very marked effect upon people's conduct. The way to test the point would be to convert a sufficiently large number of people from one metaethical view to another and make careful observations of their behaviour before and after their conversions. Assuming that their behaviour changed in some significant way, it would then have to be decided by further experiment whether this was due to the change in their philosophical beliefs or to some other factor. If it could be shown, as I believe it could not, that the general acceptance of the sort of analysis of moral judgements that I have been putting forward would have unhappy social consequences, the conclusion drawn by illiberal persons might be that the doctrine ought to be kept secret. For my part I think that I should dispute this conclusion on moral grounds, but this is a question which I am not now concerned to argue. What I have tried to show is not that the theory I am defending is expedient, but that it is true.

5

G. J. WARNOCK
The Errors of Emotivism

G. J. WARNOCK is Fellow of Magdalen College, Oxford. His books include *English Philosophy Since 1900* (1958), *Contemporary Moral Philosophy* (1967), and *The Object of Morality* (1971).

It is the central thesis of emotivism that moral discourse is essentially to be characterised by reference to its purpose: As Stevenson puts it, the 'major use' of ethical judgments is 'not to indicate facts, but to *create an influence*'. In any moral discourse the characteristic purpose of the speaker is to influence, not the beliefs, but the *attitudes* of his audience.

From G. J. Warnock, *Contemporary Moral Philosophy*, St. Martin's Press, Inc., Macmillan & Co., Ltd., pp. 24–29. Reprinted by permission of St. Martin's Press and Macmillan London and Basingstoke.

One point, I take it, will be immediately obvious—namely, that this purpose is in no way distinctive of moral discourse. It may well be the case, as Stevenson says, that ethical statements are 'social instruments' for the control, redirection, and modification of 'attitudes'; but so also are advertising posters, television commercials, political speeches, threats, 'committed' works of literature, bribes, and so on. Suppose, for example, that I wish to 'create an influence' in favour of larger families in England. It is clear that there are *many* ways in which I might try to do this—

many species of 'social instruments' of which I might avail myself for the purpose in hand. I might, indeed, engage in moral exhortation, assuring the populace that they ought, that it is right, that perhaps it is positively their duty, to engage more copiously in procreation. But alternatively, or in addition, I might buy space on billboards or time on television, spreading abroad the image of happy, smiling parents among troops of genial, healthy infants. I might make childless adults liable to national service, and give large tax reliefs to the philoprogenitive. I might seek to make out that large families are a mark of the aristocracy, or write novels about the miseries of neglected and solitary old age. It is obvious that all these are ways of 'creating an influence', that they all have the purpose of modifying 'attitudes' and, in consequence, conduct: so that, even if it is true that moral discourse has this purpose, moral discourse is not thereby distinguished from many other things.

But now, is it true that moral discourse *has* this purpose? It is not difficult to see that the answer is: not necessarily, not always. If I set out to 'create an influence' by issuing a moral utterance, then presumably (i) I suppose that my audience does not already have the 'attitude' which my utterance is calculated to promote; also (ii) I wish my audience to have this attitude; and (iii) I think it at least possible that my issuing the utterance will tend to promote adoption of this attitude. But then I may, of course, quite well issue a moral utterance, then presumably (i) I suppose that my audience does not already have someone whose 'attitude' I know to be the same as mine, whom, so to speak, I cannot *move* because he is there already. I may be concerned merely to make my own 'attitude' known to some person to whose reactions to it I am entirely indifferent or, again, who to my knowledge does not care a straw for my opinion. Moral discourse is not always so 'dynamic' as all that. A good deal of what might be called moral chat goes on in the comfortable belief that all parties to it are firmly, perhaps smugly, at one in the attitudes exposed; and though the expression of moral judgments to persons one does not care, or is not able, to influence may be thought somewhat pointless, it is not impossible, and may have some other than the usual point. Thus the alleged dynamic purpose of moral discourse is not only not distinctive of it; it may be quite absent and the discourse be not the less moral for that.

But emotivism is perhaps most seriously in error in its account of the way in which, in moral discourse, 'influence' is exerted. The aptness of moral language to the supposed dynamic ends of moral discourse is sought to be explained by reference to 'emotive meaning'. It is, it is said, because moral words have emotive (and not merely descriptive) meanings that they can play the double role of *evincing* the attitude of the speaker, and exerting *influence* upon the attitude of the addressee. They express my feelings, and will tend to arouse yours. But it is not, I think, difficult to see that this is all wrong, and importantly so.

What *are* emotive words? Why is it that a speaker or writer may be blamed, or in other cases praised, for his employment of emotive language? Emotive words are words that appeal to the feelings or (as of course the term itself suggests) to the emotions. Now this is sometimes, as for instance in certain kinds of literary work, a good thing; for here it may be the intended and entirely proper purpose to appeal to, to stir, the feelings of a reader or an audience. But of course it may often be highly undesirable. A Treasury official, for instance, summarising or commenting upon some issue of economic policy, would justly be rebuked if his minute or memorandum were couched in highly emotive terms. He will do well to avoid, even if he is tempted by, such epithets as 'scandalous', 'fatuous', 'nauseating', or 'birdbrained'. For such language is inimical to the calm and balance of bureaucratic judgment; whereas it is such as his Minister, for example, might use with propriety and effect in the very different context of his electioneering. Now it is clear enough that some moral terms are, in this sense, somewhat emotive; the feelings are quite liable to stir at such a term as 'heroic', and to stir in an opposite sense at such a term as 'blackguardly' or 'vicious'. But the pulses do not beat faster at encountering the word 'right'; there is nothing particularly stirring about 'good', or 'ought'; and if the Treasury official writes, for instance, that the financier's proposition is entirely honest, and even generous, he could scarcely be criticised for using emotive language. The fact is that expressing and appealing to the feelings is incidental to, and actually quite rare in, moral discourse, much as exerting influence is incidental to, and often quite absent from, making moral judgments. 'It would be monstrous to do that!' expresses my feelings, and may stimulate yours; but 'It would be wrong to do that' is most unlikely to do either. It expresses an opinion, not a state of emotional excitement; it gives you, perhaps, my advice against doing something, not a stimulus towards emotional revulsion from doing it. There is nothing, in short, necessarily *emotive* about

moral criticism or approval; moral advice may be given in entirely dispassionate terms. Equally, of course, a piece of discourse may be highly emotive but unconcerned with morals; and one's feelings may quite well run counter to one's moral views.

It is not difficult, in the light of these criticisms, to appreciate why to many the implications of emotivism seemed peculiarly objectionable. We see that it was the characteristic feature—it was put forward, indeed, as the chief claim to originality—of emotivist doctrine to turn away from the informative content, if any, of moral discourse, and instead to locate the essence of moral discourse in its *effects*. In place of the orthodox intuitionist view that a moral judgment, like other judgments, *stated* something and was typically intended to inform, the view was advanced that a moral judgment essentially *did* something, and was typically intended to produce a certain effect. But much as the intuitionists were prevented, by their apparatus of direct 'intuition' and 'self-evident' facts, from having anything of interest to say about moral argument, so, or even more so, for quite different reasons were the emotivists. Briefly: If it is held that a certain kind of discourse is employed essentially to produce an effect, it must follow that the criterion by which such discourse is to be appraised must essentially be the criterion simply of effectiveness. If the point of some tract of discourse is, say, essentially to influence your attitude, to arouse your feelings, then that tract of discourse is good if it succeeds, or is well calculated to succeed, in doing this; it is bad, vulnerable to criticism, if it proves inefficacious, or might have been expected to do so. In logic, it is possible to make a quite clear distinction between an argument's being valid, and an argument's producing conviction; we can well say that a proof, though it convinced, contained a fallacy, or that it was a valid proof, though it happened that no one was convinced by it. The emotivist view leaves no room for an analogous distinction in ethics. Questions of belief, it is allowed, may be rationally debated; we may distinguish here between truth and falsehood, good evidence or bad, between mere prejudice and well-founded belief, belief for good reasons. But on the characteristically moral (as it was supposed) matter of attitudes, there could be no such distinctions; a moral 'argument' so-called might produce its effect or fail to do so, but there was no room for consideration, as a *further question*, as to whether it was a good argument or a bad one. In this way moral discourse emerged—notwithstanding much strenuous special pleading—as essentially in the same boat with propaganda, or advertising, or even intimidation; it was intended to influence people, to affect their feelings and behavior, and was to be assessed not as rational, in terms of good reasons or bad reasons, but as effective or ineffective, in terms of what did or did not yield the results intended. There were many who were able to swallow this startling conclusion; but it was felt in many quarters that something must have gone very wrong.

What *had* gone wrong? Chiefly, I think, two things. First, the emotivists were understandably over-impressed by their idea of bringing in the *purpose*, or function, of moral discourse. It is true that the intuitionists had been distressingly silent on this point. Their view of moral judgments as straightforward (though in certain respects peculiar) truths and falsehoods had appeared to

make a mystery of the relation of such judgments to conduct; they seemed not to have considered at all what moral discourse is *for*. But the emotivists, one might say, were inclined merely to go to the opposite extreme—to dwell, that is, so exclusively on what moral discourse is for, that they scarcely raised seriously the question what it actually is. It is a good thing, no doubt, to appreciate *that* moral discourse is quite often directed to influencing 'attitudes'; but it should have been considered more carefully *how* it does so. For the general purpose, as we have seen, is not an invariable feature of moral utterances and, more importantly, does not distinguish such utterances from many other kinds of linguistic—and for that matter non-linguistic—proceedings.

Second, so far as emotivists did consider how it is that moral discourse may influence attitudes, their account was inadequate, or indeed seriously mistaken. The trouble here arose, in large part, from a certain crudity in their notion of what 'attitudes' are. There was a constant tendency to identify attitudes with *feelings*—to identify, say, my disapproval of someone's behaviour with the disgust or revulsion which I may feel on witnessing it. But this was not merely wrong: it was disastrously wrong. For as a consequence, expressing my disapproval of someone's behaviour became identified with the widely different phenomenon of 'giving vent' to my feelings about it; and my seeking to change someone else's 'attitude' came to be represented as simply an attempt to work on his emotions. Hence the blunder of supposing that moral words as such have 'emotive meaning'; for if I am 'venting' my feelings and working on yours, must it not be the case that I am using emotive language? Thence, finally, the conclusion that moral discourse is essentially nonrational, a matter not of argument but of psychological pressure, not of reasons but of efficacious manipulation. Intuitionism had left gaps—indeed, scarcely anything except gaps—in moral philosophy; but there was a great quantity of muddle in the filling which emotivism supplied.

6

RENFORD BAMBROUGH
A Proof of the Objectivity of Morals

RENFORD BAMBROUGH, of St. John's College, Cambridge, is well known for his work on Greek philosophy, politics, and religion. He is the author of *Reason, Truth, and God* (1969), and other books.

It is well known that recent British philosophy, under the leadership of G. E. Moore and Ludwig Wittgenstein, has defended common sense and common language against what seem to many contemporary philosophers to be the paradoxes, the obscurities and the mystifications of earlier metaphysical philosophers. The spirit in which this work is carried on is well indicated by the titles of two of the most famous of Moore's own papers: "A Defence of Common Sense" and "Proof of an External World." It can be more fully but still briefly described by saying something about Moore's defence of the common sense belief that there are external material objects. His proof of an external world consists essentially in holding up his hands and saying, "Here are two hands; therefore there are at least two material objects." He argues

Excerpted from Renford Bambrough, "A Proof of the Objectivity of Morals," *The American Journal of Jurisprudence* (1969). Reprinted by permission of the author.

that no proposition that could plausibly be alleged as a reason in favor of doubting the truth of the proposition that I have two hands can possibly be more certainly true than that proposition itself. If a philosopher produces an argument against my claim to *know* that I have two hands, I can therefore be sure in advance that *either* at least one of the premises of his argument is false, *or* there is a mistake in the reasoning by which he purports to derive from his premises the conclusion that I do not know that I have two hands. . . .

My proof that we have moral knowledge consists essentially in saying, "We know that this child, who is about to undergo what would otherwise be painful surgery, should be given an anaesthetic before the operation. Therefore we know at least one moral proposition to be true." I argue that no proposition that could plausibly be alleged as a reason in favour of doubting the truth of the proposition that the child should be given an anaesthetic can possibly be more certainly true than that proposition itself. If a philosopher produces an argument against my claim to *know* that the child should be given an anaesthetic, I can therefore be sure in advance that *either* at least one of the premises of his argument is false, *or* there is a mistake in the reasoning by which he purports to derive from his premises the conclusion that I do not know that the child should be given an anaesthetic.

When Moore proves that there is an external world he is defending a common sense belief. When I prove that we have moral knowledge I am defending a common sense belief. The contemporary philosophers who both accept Moore's proof of an external world and reject the claim that we have moral knowledge defend common sense in one field and attack common sense in another field. They hold fast to common sense when they speak of our knowledge of the external world, and depart from common sense when they speak of morality.

When they speak of our knowledge of the external world they not only do not give reasons for confining their respect for common sense to their treatment of that single topic but assume and imply that their respect for common sense is *in general* justified. When they go on to speak of morality they not only do not give reasons for abandoning the respect for common sense that they showed when they spoke of our knowledge of the external world, but assume and imply that they are still showing the same respect for common sense. But this is just what they are *not* doing.

The common sense view is that we *know* that stealing is wrong, that promise keeping is right, that unselfishness is good, that cruelty is bad. Common language uses in moral contexts the whole range of expressions that it also uses in nonmoral contexts when it is concerned with knowledge and ignorance, truth and falsehood, reason and unreason, questions and answers. We speak as naturally of a child's not knowing the difference between right and wrong as we do of his not knowing the difference between right and left. We say that we do not know what to do as naturally as we say that we do not know what is the case. We say that a man's moral views are unreasonable as naturally as we say that his views on a matter of fact are unreasonable. In moral contexts, just as naturally as in nonmoral contexts, we speak of thinking, wondering, asking; of beliefs, opinions, convictions, arguments, conclusions; of dilemmas, problems, solutions; of perplexity, confusion, consistency and inconsistency, of errors and mistakes, of teaching, learning, training, showing, proving, finding out, understanding, realising, recognising and coming to see.

I am not now saying that we are right to speak of all these things as naturally in one type of context as in another, though that is what I do in fact believe. Still less am I saying that the fact that we speak in a particular way is itself a sufficient justification for speaking in that particular way. What I am saying now is that a philosopher who defends common sense when he is talking about our knowledge of the external world must *either* defend common sense when he talks about morality (that is to say, he must admit that we have moral knowledge) *or* give us reasons why in the one case common sense is to be defended, while in the other case it is *not* to be defended. If he does neither of these things we shall be entitled to accuse him of inconsistency.

I *do* accuse such philosophers of inconsistency.

Moore did not expect the sceptic of the senses to be satisfied with his proof of an external world, and I do not expect the moral sceptic to be satisfied with my proof of the objectivity of morals. Even somebody who is not a sceptic of the senses may be dissatisfied with Moore's proof, and even somebody who is not a moral sceptic may be dissatisfied with my proof. In fact, somebody who regards either proof as a strictly valid and conclusive argument for its conclusion may nevertheless be dissatisfied with the proof. He may reasonably wish to be given not only a conclusive demonstration of the truth of the conclusion, but also a detailed answer to the most popular or plausible arguments against the conclusion.

Those who reject the common sense account of moral knowledge, like those who reject the common sense account of our knowledge of the external world, do of course offer arguments in favour of their rejection. In both cases those who reject the common sense account offer very much the same arguments whether they recognise or fail to recognise that the account they are rejecting is in fact the common sense account. If we now look at the arguments that can be offered against the common sense account of moral knowledge we shall be able to see whether they are sufficiently similar to the arguments that can be offered against the common sense account of our knowledge of the external world to enable us to sustain our charge of inconsistency against a philosopher who attacks common sense in one field and defends it in the other. (We may note in passing that many philosophers in the past have committed the converse form of the same *prima facie* inconsistency: They have rejected the common sense account of our knowledge of the external world but

have accepted the common sense account of moral knowledge.)

It will be impossible in a small space to give a full treatment of any one argument, and it will also be impossible to refer to all the arguments that have been offered by moral philosophers who are consciously or unconsciously in conflict with common sense. I shall refer briefly to the most familiar and most plausible arguments, and I shall give to each of them the outline of what I believe to be an adequate answer in defence of the common sense account.

"Moral disagreement is more widespread, more radical and more persistent than disagreement about matters of fact."

I have two main comments to make on this suggestion: the first is that it is almost certainly untrue, and the second is that it is quite certainly irrelevant.

The objection loses much of its plausibility as soon as we insist on comparing the comparable. We are usually invited to contrast our admirably close agreement that there is a glass of water on the table with the depth, vigour and tenacity of our disagreements about capital punishment, abortion, birth control and nuclear disarmament. But this is a game that may be played by two or more players. A sufficient reply in kind is to contrast our general agreement that this child should have an anaesthetic with the strength and warmth of the disagreements between cosmologists and radio astronomers about the interpretation of certain radio-astronomical observations. If the moral sceptic then reminds us of Christian Science we can offer him in exchange the Flat Earth Society.

But this is a side issue. Even if it is true that moral diagreement is more acute and more persistent than other forms of disagreement, it does not follow that moral knowledge is impossible. However long and violent a dispute may be, and however few or many heads may be counted on this side or on that, it remains possible that one party to the dispute is right and the others wrong. Galileo was right when he contradicted the Cardinals: and so was Wilberforce when he rebuked the slave owners.

There is a more direct and decisive way of showing the irrelevance of the argument from persistent disagreement. The question of whether a given type of enquiry is objective is the question whether it is *logically capable* of reaching knowledge, and is therefore an *a priori*, logical question. The question of how much agreement or disagreement there is between those who actually engage in that enquiry is a question of psychological or sociological fact. It follows that the question about the actual extent of agreement or disagreement has no bearing on the question of the objectivity of the enquiry. If this were not so, the objectivity of every enquiry might wax and wane through the centuries as men became more or less disputatious or more or less proficient in the arts of persuasion.

"Our moral opinions are conditioned by our environment and upbringing."

It is under this heading that we are reminded of the variegated customs and beliefs of Hottentots, Eskimos, Polynesians and American Indians, which do indeed differ widely from each other and from our own. But this objection is really a special case of the general argument from disagreement, and it can be answered on the same lines. The beliefs of the Hottentots and the Polynesians about straightforwardly factual matters differs widely from our own, but that does not tempt us to say that science is subjective.

It is true that most of those who are born and bred in the stately homes of England have a different outlook on life from that of the Welsh miner or the Highland crofter, but it is also true that all these classes of people differ widely in their factual beliefs, and not least in their factual beliefs about themselves and each other.

Let us consider some of the moral sceptic's favourite examples, which are often presented as though they settled the issue beyond further argument.

(1) Herodotus reports that within the Persian Empire there were some tribes who buried their dead and some who burned them. Each group thought that the other's practice was barbarous. But (a) they agreed that respect must be shown to the dead; (b) they lived under very different climatic conditions; (c) we can now see that they were guilty of moral myopia in setting such store by what happened, for good or bad reasons, to be their own particular practise. Moral progress in this field has consisted in coming to recognise that burying-versus-burning is not an issue on which it is necessary for the whole of mankind to have a single, fixed, universal standpoint, regardless of variations of conditions in time and place.

(2) Some societies practise polygamous marriage. Others favour monogamy. Here again there need be no absolute and unvarying rule. In societies where women heavily outnumber men, institutions may be appropriate which would be out of place in societies where the numbers of men and women are roughly equal. The moralist who insists that monogamy is right regardless of circumstances, is like the inhabitant of the northern hemisphere who insists that it is always and everywhere cold at Christmas, or the inhabitant of the southern hemisphere who cannot be-

lieve that it is ever or anywhere cold at Christmas.

(3) Some societies do not disapprove of what we condemn as "stealing." In such societies, anybody may take from anybody else's house anything he may need or want. This case serves further to illustrate that circumstances objectively alter cases, the relative is not only compatible with, but actually required by, the objective and rational determination of questions of right and wrong. I can maintain with all possible force that Bill Sykes is a rogue, and that prudence requires me to lock all my doors and windows against him, without being committed to holding that if an Eskimo takes whalemeat from the unlocked igloo of another Eskimo, then one of them is a knave and the other a fool. It is not that we disapprove of stealing and that the Eskimos do not, but that their circumstances differ so much from ours as to call for new consideration and a different judgment, which may be that in their situation stealing is innocent, or that in their situation there is no private property and therefore no possibility of *stealing* at all.

(4) Some tribes leave their elderly and useless members to die in the forest. Others, including our own, provide old age pensions and geriatric hospitals. But we should have to reconsider our arrangements if we found that the care of the aged involved for us the consequences that it might involve for a nomadic and pastoral people: general starvation because the old could not keep pace with the necessary movement to new pastures, children and domestic animals a prey to wild beasts, a life burdensome to all and destined to end with the extinction of the tribe.

"When I say that something is good or bad or right or wrong I commit my- *self, and reveal something of my attitudes and feelings."*

This is quite true, but it is equally and analogously true that when I say that something is true or false, or even that something is red or round, I also commit myself and reveal something of my *beliefs.* Some emotovist and imperativist philosophers have sometimes failed to draw a clear enough distinction between what is said or meant by a particular form of expression and what is implied or suggested by it, and even those who have distinguished clearly and correctly between meaning and implication in the case of moral propositions have often failed to see that exactly the same distinction can be drawn in the case of nonmoral propositions. If I say "this is good" and then add "but I do not approve of it," I certainly behave oddly enough to owe you an explanation, but I behave equally oddly and owe you a comparable explanation if I say "that is true, but I don't believe it." If it is held that I contradict myself in the first case, it must be allowed that I contradict myself in the second case. If it is claimed that I do not contradict myself in the second case, then it must be allowed that I do not contradict myself in the first case. If this point can be used as an argument against the objectivity of morals, then it can also be used as an argument against the objectivity of science, logic, and of every other branch of enquiry.

The parallel between *approve* and *believe* and between *good* and *true* is so close that it provides a useful test of the paradoxes of subjectivism and emotivism. The emotivist puts the cart before the horse in trying to explain goodness in terms of approval, just as he would if he tried to explain truth in terms of belief. Belief cannot be explained without introducing the notion of truth, and approval cannot be explained without introducing the notion of goodness. To believe is (roughly) to hold to be true, and to approve is (equally roughly) to hold to be good. Hence it is as unsatisfactory to try to reduce goodness to approval, or to approval plus some other component, as it would be to try to reduce truth to belief, or to belief plus some other component.

If we are to give a correct account of the logical character of morality we must preserve the distinction between appearance and reality, between seeming and really being, that we clearly and admittedly have to preserve if we are to give a correct account of truth and belief. Just as we do and must hope that what we believe (what seems to us to be true) is and will be in fact true, so we must hope that what we approve (what seems to us to be good) is and will be in fact good.

I can say of another "He thinks it is raining, but it is not," and of myself, "I thought it was raining but it was not." I can also say of another "He thinks it is good, but it is not," and of myself "I thought it was good, but it was not."

"After every circumstance, every relation is known, the understanding has no further room to operate, nor any object on which it could employ itself."

This sentence from the first Appendix to Hume's *Enquiry Concerning the Principles of Morals* is the moral sceptic's favourite quotation, and he uses it for several purposes, including some that are alien to Hume's intentions. Sometimes it is no more than a flourish added to the argument from disagreement. Sometimes it is used in support of the claim that there comes a point in every moral dispute when further reasoning is not so much ineffective as impossible in principle. In either case the answer is once again a firm *tu*

quoque. In any sense in which it is true that there may or must come to a point in moral enquiry beyond which no further reasoning is possible, it is in that same sense equally true that there may or must be a point in any enquiry at which the reasoning has to stop. Nothing can be proved to a man who will accept nothing that has not been proved. Moore recognized that his proof of an external world uses premises which have not themselves been proved. Not even in pure mathematics, that paradigm of strict security of reasoning, can we *force* a man to accept our premises or our modes of inference; and therefore we cannot force him to accept our conclusions. Once again the moral sceptic counts as a reason for doubting the objectivity of morals a feature of moral enquiry which is exactly paralleled in other departments of enquiry where he does *not* count it as a reason for scepticism. If he is to be consistent, he must either withdraw his argument against the objectivity of morals or subscribe also to an analogous argument against the objectivity of mathematics, physics, history, and every other branch of enquiry.

But of course such an argument gives no support to a sceptical conclusion about any of these enquiries. However conclusive a mode of reasoning may be, and however accurately we may use it, it always remains possible that we shall fail to convince a man who disagrees with us. There may come a point in a moral dispute when it is wiser to agree to differ than to persist with fruitless efforts to convince an opponent. But this by itself is no more a reason for doubting the truth of our premises and the validity of our arguments than the teacher's failure to convince a pupil of the validity of a proof of Pythagoras' theorem is a reason for doubting the validity of the proof and the truth of the theorum. It is notorious that even an expert physicist may fail to convince a member of the Flat Earth Society that the earth is not flat, but we nevertheless *know* that the earth is not flat. Lewis Carroll's tortoise ingeniously resisted the best efforts of Achilles to convince him of the validity of a simple deductive argument, but of course the argument *is* valid.

"A dispute which is purely moral is inconclusive in principle. The specifically moral element in moral disputes is one which cannot be resolved by investigation and reflection."

This objection brings into the open an assumption that is made at least implicitly by most of those who use Hume's remark as a subjective weapon: the assumption that whatever is a logical or factual dispute, or a mixture of logic and factual disputes, is necessarily *not* a moral dispute; that nothing is a moral dispute unless it is *purely* moral in the sense that it is a dispute between parties who agree on *all* the relevant factual and logical questions. But the *purely moral* dispute envisaged by this assumption is a pure fiction. The search for the "specifically moral elements" in moral disputes is a wild goose chase, and is the result of the initial confusion of supposing that no feature of moral reasoning is *really* a feature of moral reasoning, or is *characteristic* of moral reasoning, unless it is peculiar to moral reasoning. It is as if one insisted that a ginger cake could be fully characterized, and could only be characterized, by saying that there is ginger in it. It is true that ginger is the peculiar ingredient of a ginger cake as contrasted with other cakes, but no cake can be made entirely of ginger, and the ingredients that are combined with ginger to make ginger cakes are the same as those that are

combined with chocolate, lemon, orange or vanilla to make other kinds of cakes; and ginger itself, when combined with other ingredients and treated in other ways, goes into the making of ginger puddings, ginger biscuits and ginger beer.

To the question "What is the place of reason in ethics?" why should we not answer: "The place of reason in ethics is exactly what it is in other enquiries, to enable us to find out the relevant facts and to make our judgments mutually consistent, to expose factual errors and detect logical inconsistencies"? This might seem to imply that there are some moral judgments which will serve as starting points for any moral enquiry, and will not themselves be proved, as others may be proved by being derived from them or disproved by being shown to be incompatible with them, and also to imply that we cannot engage in moral argument with a man with whom we agree on *no* moral question. In so far as these implications are correct they apply to all enquiry and not only to moral enquiry, and they do not, when correctly construed, constitute any objection to the rationality and objectivity of morality or of any other mode of enquiry. They seem to make difficulties for moral objectivity only when they are associated with a picture of rationality which, though it has always been powerful in the minds of philosophers, can be shown to be an unacceptable caricature.

I have criticised this picture elsewhere, and I shall be returning later in this article to some of its ill effects. Here it is necessary only to underline once again that the moral sceptic is partial and selective in his use of an argument of indefinitely wide scope: If it were true that a man must accept unprovable moral premises before I could prove to him that there is such a thing as moral knowledge it would equally be true that a man must accept an unprovable material object proposition before Moore could prove to him that there is an external world. Similarly, if a moral conclusion can be proved only to a man who accepts unprovable moral premises then a physical conclusion can be proved only to a man who accepts unprovable physical premises.

"There are recognized methods for settling factual and logical disputes, but there are no recognized methods for settling moral disputes."

This is either false, or true but irrelevant, according to how it is understood. Too often those who make this complaint are arguing in a circle, since they will count nothing as a recognized method of argument unless it is a recognized method of logical or scientific argument. If we adopt this interpretation, then it is true that there is no recognized methods of moral argument, but the lack of such methods does not affect the claim that morality is objective. One department of enquiry has not been shown to be no true department of enquiry when all that has been shown is that it cannot be carried on by exactly the methods that are appropriate to some other department of enquiry. We know without the help of the sceptic that morality is not identical with logic or science.

But in its most straightforward sense the claim is simply false. There *are* recognized methods of moral argument. Whenever we say "How would you like it if somebody did this to you?" or "How would it be if we all acted like this?" we are arguing according to recognized and established methods, and are in fact appealing to the consistency-requirement to which I have already re-

ferred. It is true that such appeals are often ineffective, but it is also true that well-founded logical or scientific arguments often fail to convince those to whom they are addressed. If the present objection is pursued beyond this point it turns into the argument from radical disagreement.

Now the moral sceptic is even more inclined to exaggerate the amount of disagreement that there is about methods of moral argument than he is inclined to exaggerate the amount of disagreement of moral belief as such. One reason for this is that he concentrates his attention on the admittedly striking and important fact that there is an enormous amount of immoral *conduct.* But most of those who *behave* immorally appeal to the very same methods of moral argument as those who condemn their immoral conduct. Hitler broke many promises, but he did not explicitly hold that promisebreaking as such and in general was justified. When others broke their promises to him he complained with the same force and in the same terms as those with whom he himself had failed to keep faith. And whenever he broke a promise he tried to *justify* his breach by claiming that other obligations overrode the duty to keep the promise. He did not simply deny that it was his duty to keep promises. He thus entered into the very process of argument by which it is possible to condemn so many of his own actions. He was *inconsistent* in requiring of other nations and their leaders standards of conduct to which he himself did not conform, and in failing to produce *convincing reasons* for his own departures from the agreed standards.

Here we may remember Bishop Butler's remark that the true system of morality can be found by noticing "what all men pretend," however true it may be that not all men live up to their pretensions.

The same point can be illustrated in national politics. When the Opposition complain against an alleged misdemeanour on the part of the Government, they are often reminded that they themselves, when they were in office, behaved in precisely the same way in closely analogous circumstances. They are then able to reply by pointing out that the *then* Opposition complained violently in the House of Commons. In such cases both sides are proceeding by recognized methods of argument, and each side is convicted of inconsistency by appeal to those methods. . . .

In moral philosophy, as in the philosophy of perception, to demonstrate the falsehood of scepticism and the unsoundness of sceptical arguments is an important beginning, but it is only a beginning. It needs to be followed by a positive exposition and description of the character of the knowledge that the sceptic declares not to deserve the name of knowledge, and an explanation of how its character prompts the sceptic to propound his paradoxes, and hence of how his paradoxes contribute to our understanding of its character. To do this for moral scepticism would be to write the book on moral knowledge for which this article cannot be more than a provisional first chapter.

7

W. D. FALK
Moral Perplexity

W. D. FALK is professor of philosophy at the University of North Carolina at Chapel Hill. He is the author of numerous influential papers on moral philosophy.

Every age has its moral perplexities, but our own seems to us have more than its share. And this is not only so because the old days are always the good old days, though there may be something in this too. But it is fair to say that there is less agreement and more uncertainty about moral matters today than, let us say, in the late nineteenth century.

From W. D. Falk, "Moral Perplexity," *Ethics,* vol. 66 (1956), pp. 123–131. Copyright © 1956 by The University of Chicago Press. Reprinted by permission of The University of Chicago Press. This article is reprinted unabridged.

There is more dispute about the rights and duties of parents and children, of husbands and wives, of individuals and the state. There is a rejection of ready-made rules, and, generally, an air of unsettlement.

And there is something else too, namely, a sense of uneasiness about the fact that we are so divided and unsure. We are used to believing that there is a right and wrong about choices and ways of life, and that right thinking, here as elsewhere, can discern truth and dispel error. But now there are not a few who feel that this view itself is on trial. What is added to our moral perplexities is perplexity about morals. People put this by saying that there is some radical error in the traditional view that "reason" can solve moral issues: according to some that "reason" can solve them at all, according to others that it can solve them unaided by religion. There was a time when Immanuel Kant could speak of the two great certainties, the starry heavens above us and the moral law, known by pure reason, within us. In our time both of these seem to be fading into the nebulae.

Such views are a measure of some people's bewilderment, but they need not be correct as a diagnosis. And one may look at the situation more soberly. Because one may say: There is after all no more to the moral condition of our time than could be expected from its character generally. Ours is a time which requires adaptation to big changes all-round. What were sound practices of public finance yesterday are so no longer today; and why should the same not apply to what used to be sound moral practices? Moral codes are rules of thumb for the advancement of individual and social welfare, and as they have been learned they may have to be unlearned. Consider our views on the relations between men and women. At a time when women have careers, when technology changes the economics of the household, medical science the care of the body, psychology our knowledge of mental hygiene, some traditional rules must lose their point, and new ways have to be evolved. This may not be easy and uncontroversial. But it involves none but practical problems. And there is no need for taking the birth pangs of adaptation for the crack of doom.

So one may have different views on the causes of our perplexities. One may attribute them simply to the complexities of a time of change, or to deeper causes, to errors or confusions about right thinking in moral matters. And what I want to discuss are these different diagnoses of the situation.

I might say straightaway that I think that our troubles are both on the practical and on the deeper philosophical level. And this should not be surprising. One cannot doubt that our time is setting us problems for conduct to which we have no ready answers, or which the answer of the past will no longer fit. And it is quite a usual feature of the growth of thought, whether in science or elsewhere, that with big new questions to solve one also has to query what sort of questions these are, and how to solve them. And this is why philosophical questions come up, because philosophy deals with the logic of questions. I might say here, by the way, that philosophers are much misunderstood people. They are either looked down on or admired more than they should be, much as a foreigner in conservative English society. Philosophers have not got a secret key to solving problems at which others fail. Their job is rather to assist question-solving when it gets bogged down in confusion about the questions and about the answers which they permit. This is why there is not really a separate animal in the academic zoo called "philosophy," over and above such creatures as history or physics or economics. Philosophy sits on all thought rather like the shell on the back of the tortoise; and where the tortoise goes there it goes, and as long as the tortoise keeps going it keeps going.

And now let us get on with the job. And here let me say first that not all moral disagreements lead to philosophical worries. Moral disagreements may have different origins, and this is the first point which we must note.

Many of them are simply about the best means toward achieving good ends. Take two parents who are disagreed on the upbringing of their children. Both will think that they should further their good, but one thinks that disciplinarian methods are right, and the other that they are plain wicked and wrong. This would be simply a disagreement about the means toward an agreed end, and, though there may be snags in practice, it is not in principle hard to solve. The facts about child development should decide who is right. And if there actually is much disagreement and uncertainty about this matter today, we may lay this at the door of a new science of infants still in its infancy. And many moral disputes are like this one. A dispute about the wrongness of gambling could be resolved by studying the effects of gambling on people's daily lives. The social effects of ownership will be relevant to disagreement about the right to property. And one could easily multiply examples, so much so that one may come to think that all moral disputes are of this kind. People have said: There is one ultimate end on which agreement can be presupposed: that, above all, we ought to do most good and least harm all-round; and all moral disputes are simply about the best means toward this end. And without doubt it would be a comfort if this were so. Because then, in the last resort, we could solve all moral problems with the aid of science. Psychology, medicine, sociology, economics tell us the story of what leads to what, of the effects of bashing children, of gambling, of private ownership. These sciences would then be our proper advisers on all matters of right and wrong.

Unfortunately this is too sweeping. And it is too sweeping because not all moral disputes arise from disagreement about the best means toward agreed ends. But before I turn to this, let me say that one may also easily underrate the importance of this view. Moral codes, like institutions in general, tend to settle in fixed grooves. We develop a jealous attachment to them. And when one feels most defensive about them, this is often the very moment for revising, "in a cool hour," as Bishop Butler said, what good or harm they really do. And to consult the findings of science at this point will not come amiss.

But, as I say, science cannot help us all the way, because there is another area of moral dispute which relates not to means but to ends. And let me first introduce this area, and then consider how it raises problems.

It seems so natural to say: There is one ultimate end, "above all, do most good and least harm all-round," and on this we are agreed. But, for several reasons, this is far too simple. For one, the formula is too vague. It says we ought to promote people's welfare. But when does a man really fare well? There are many constituents of a good life: freedom from want or fear, health and leisure, justice, freedom of self-expression. And not all of these can be realized to the same extent at the same time. One may have to choose between the one and the other, as, for instance, between economic security and freedom from restraints. So it follows that "do most good and least harm all-round" does not really relate to one ultimate end but to a family of such ends; and that there is a question for deciding in what order of priorities these ends should be realized.

Moreover, even if we are agreed on how to do most good all-round, can one really assume that everyone must be agreed on this as his first aim? I don't think that we can just presuppose this. Someone might come along and say: "Why this at all? Why concern myself with general good instead of my own?" And this raises the problem of convincing him in some way that the furtherance of general good is an end that he ought to make his own. So *the* ultimate moral premise may be a matter for dispute; and unless there is a way of supporting it, the whole edifice of obligations based on it will fall apart.

And, finally, it is also too simple to say that doing most good all-round is what everyone ought to attempt every time and above all. Because there are at any one moment many claimants for a good turn, and one cannot satisfy them all: There are ourselves and others, our children, parents, our group, the present generation and the next, and there is the good of mankind at large. We think that we have some obligation to further most good all-round, but that we have also got special obligations toward those near us, and that we have some rights ourselves. So, once more, there may be situations for choice: where we have to decide which of two conflicting ultimate claims should come first. Remember our example about the upbringing of children. Few parents will dispute that their children's good is their concern. But *how much so*, this is already another matter. It may be true that infinite patience will rear children free of hate and aggression. But to do so to perfection may also consume the time and energy of their parents. How much of their own lives then should parents make over to their children? This is no longer a question of means to ends. It is quite a different sort of question, one of deciding between legitimate and conflicting ends, of how to distribute one's good turns.

And now let us look at the moral perplexities of our time again. It is pretty plain that our major worries are in this area of ultimate ends, and of decisions between them. There have been times when these issues were more concealed by a general consensus of opinion. But in our own time, all the devils of dissent and disorientation seem to be let loose. A Nazi will allow that the good of his children is his responsibility. He will allow high priority to the good of his group, far above that of his parents or friends or of any single individual. But he will deny that the good of other groups is his business; and nothing will persuade him of a right for everyone to be treated humanely. A pacifist will put the preservation of human life before everything else. A Communist will put social justice and economic security before freedom of decision or thought. And he will be far more ready than a liberal individualist would think right to sacrifice the good of the present generation to that of the next. These are all differences about moral premises. And when people apply these premises to daily life, then quite different choices will become right or wrong for them: with the effect that, as we are all in this, we become targets to one another of disapproval and dismay. Everyone feels that the other is wrong-headed beyond comprehension; and opportunities abound for feeling this way.

I said before that perplexity about morals is one of the signs of our time. It is the area of dissent which I have just indicated which is mainly responsible for this. Because dissent about first things raises the question of how to settle it. And on this question we find ourselves in a dilemma. As I said, everyone feels that the other is wrong-headed in placing his priorities where he does. And if the other really is wrong-headed, then there must be a right and a wrong in these matters, and a way of showing what it is. But, in practice, is there such a way? There are few who have not at some time tried and failed. We all know how disputes about first things begin in argument only to end in recrimination; and it is where words fail one that one resorts to bad language. But surely words should not fail one here. If the other is wrong, then there should be a way of putting him right. We have been taught, and believe, that by using "reason" we can put him right. But, as reason is understood, it does not seem to work.

And this is how the philosophical issue has come to be raised. Persistent failure at solving a problem suggests that one has got the wrong measure of it: that one expects too much or the wrong things. So out of the trials and tribulations of our daily experience we are being made to ask: "How can one decide the rights and wrongs of ultimate choices or ways of life at all?"

I must say a little about contemporary trends in response to this question. The keynote, as one would expect, is skepticism of reason. But different conclusions are drawn from this. A very fashionable view is to say that we only fail to convince each other because there is nothing to convince each other of: There just is no arguable right or wrong of ultimate choices. To some people independence ultimately matters more than security and to others not; to some the good of their children is far more important than personal achievement and to others less so. And this is all there is to it. There is no saying that one choice is more "proper" or "rational" than the other. There is no disputing of ultimate tastes. And the reason given is that if there were it should be possible to prove to people that they ought to choose one ultimate course rather than another: One should be able to offer a reason for this. And in the nature of the case, this is impossible. First things, like liberty or doing good to others, one values for them-

selves. And one cannot give people a reason for valuing things for themselves or for valuing one of them more than the other. Because the only reason for valuing things in themselves is in what they are, and if people don't want them knowing what they are, there is nothing to tell them that could convert them. Hume once said that "it was not against reason to prefer the scratching of my little finger to the destruction of the whole world." For if you asked "and why not?" there is nothing one could say. So in the matter of ultimate choices we must tolerate, or may bash each other, but we must not be perplexed at making no headway with arguing.

One may find this "solution" a little hard to take, if not its tolerance too complaisant to tolerate. And let me say that its logic is not as strong as it sounds. It is possible that one ultimate choice should be more right than another even if there is no argument from which to prove this, because not all truths are known by a formal proof. One does not prove by argument that it is raining outside, one just goes and looks. And, maybe, that some ultimate choices are more proper for a human being than others is also something which everyone just has to see for himself. Supposing that one said: "You may not feel this now, but if you thought, you would not have it in your heart to stand by while others suffer." I cannot prove this to you, but it may be true of you, and you would be the one to check on it for yourself. And by saying that one ultimate choice may be more "proper" or "rational" than another, one may just mean this: that it would recommend itself more than the other to a human being who was thoughtful and sincere.

In fact, the main European tradition in ethics is built on a conception like this, and great hopes for a universal and objective ethics used to be pinned on it. Man, it was said, has the moral order in his own nature because he has both a social nature and can reflect. By reflection he can put it to himself what it is to do good or harm; his social nature enables him to respond to these ideas. So when guided by reflection any human being will find the obligation to doing good and not doing harm in his own heart. The right order of choices is laid down for all in their own natures, plain for everyone to see who will trouble to look into himself.

I am referring to this root conception of our ethical tradition because, as we are looking at contemporary trends, it is also under fire today. Its most challenging critic is Jean-Paul Sartre, the French existentialist. Sartre's ideas developed during the war, when Frenchmen were up against having to choose between collaboration and resistance, and where anyone might be in the sort of conflict which Sartre reports of one of his students: Should he stay with his widowed mother whose life depended on him, or join the Free French in an uncertain gamble on doing some good for an anonymous cause? Here was the typical challenge to moral thinking: to solve conflict about ultimate ends and ways of life. And, according to Sartre, none of the traditional formulae will stand the test. Should the student do what will cause most good all-round? The calculus is impossible. And even if possible there would still be the choice between causing most good all-round and protecting his mother. Would it help him to consider which choice would be more right by being more properly human? Again, the formula is too wide and vague to meet the concrete case. Human nature is not uniform and fixed enough to allow expression only in one choice and not in any other. The

conception of the human heart as a book of rules prescribing the same for all, if only consulted properly, is a metaphysical fiction. Should he then seek guidance from his personal feelings, scrutinize his motives, and decide on that which in truth matters to him most? Sartre will not let him have this way out either. One cannot ask: "Is it more proper for *me* to protect my mother or my country?" any more than one can ask: "Is it more proper for a human being to protect his mother or his country?" And one cannot ask this because it is an illusion that by reflection a man could find out about his true feelings so as to guide his choice by them. The only proof of one's true feelings is in the acting. One only knows one's self by what one has decided. And, therefore, in the situation of conflict *there is no known guide to turn to.* Man, Sartre concludes, is "deserted," he must choose in darkness, he must opt for his ultimate goals in default of any knowledge of a better or worse. All the consolation he has is that in freely committing himself one way or another he is not drifting but exercising his human power of cutting the Gordian knot.

This doctrine destroys the illusion that in every complex situation there is one choice which, for everyone alike and quite unmistakably, is more properly human than any other. But, if it has a point here, it does not stop at this. For it goes on to deny that not even in any more personal and more fallible sense could our ultimate choices be guided by any conception of a better or worse. We cannot wait to see on which side our Gordian knot is buttered. Moral thinking in the past was naïve and hopeful enough to think that we could. But the conflicts of modern man have found this out.

One need not follow Sartre all the way, as we shall see in a moment. But even so it becomes clear that right choices of ultimate ends may often have no sure guide in reason. And not everyone will, like Sartre, accept this with stoic pride as the cross of human freedom. So it is not surprising that the present should show one more trend. The trust in reason as a guide to conduct has historically succeeded the view that reason in morals requires the backing of religion. The emancipation of morality from religion on the contemporary scale is a product of recent history. And now that the limits of reason have become more apparent, there are also voices which cry "we told you so." That reason fails us does not mean that there is no right or wrong for human choices; but it shows that we have forgotten to look for instruction in the right place. The true lesson of the present is that we must go back on the divorce of morals from religion.

And with this, the picture of the philosophical situation is complete. Skepticism of reason is its keynote. And if it leaves us with a problem, it is the problem of reassessing what part reason can play.

I should like to say some more about this. And I shall begin with a word about the last view, that return to religious authority is the key to the situation. This is a wide topic, and I cannot do it justice here. All I want to say is that in my opinion this solution would be no cure-all. Because morality, as we understand it, is logically independent of religious authority. And if the skeptics were right, and there were no better or worse in ultimate choices discernible by "reason," then religious authority could not mend things either.

Because how could any authority settle that well-doing is the right, and harm-doing the wrong, choice for a human being? One may say: "But if God says so, surely this should settle it." And, in a way, this is fair enough, for believers at any rate. But we must be clear about the sense in which this is to be taken. For some people will mean by this: "God settles the matter by *saying so*, by *commanding* us to choose in these ways." But this would not be to settle the matter in the required way. It might make people do good or avoid harm in obedience to an order. But it could not produce the conviction that this choice was a morally right one or produce actions which could be called "moral" because they flowed from this conviction. Because one understands by a morally right choice one which is justified purely on the merits of the case and one which one makes independently of anyone's "say-so." And one understands by moral conduct, conduct which is quite unforced from without, coming purely from the inner conviction that the action is right for one in itself. God's command as such, therefore, could not do in place of a rational conviction of right or wrong. Morality, as we understand it, still stands or falls on the possibility of arriving at such a conviction independently of any authority.

But if it is said that "if God says so, this should settle it," one may also mean something else: that what should settle it is that it is *God* who says so, rather than God *saying* so. For one will then be saying: "If God has given the command, then one must take it that he is commanding the right thing; and it is reasonable to take one's instructions from a superior being." And this would be fair enough. But, again, this is not a view which could do in place of an ability on our part to arrive at rational convictions. For, in the first place, it would presuppose that we can form these convictions. We could not even conceive of God as telling what ultimate choices are right for us unless we knew what it was like to distinguish by ourselves between a right or wrong choice. So if skepticism of reason were correct, this view of how God could support us in our ultimate choices would fall to the ground too. And, in the second place, God's support here could not replace independent thinking as much as one may hope. Because the divine rulings tend to be general, as general, in fact, as the general enjoinders to doing well or dealing justly, which one thinks have a plain support in reason too. And, like them, they still leave us without a sure guide when it comes to complex cases: to a choice like that of Sartre's student or to a problem like deciding on the right measure of liberty or social justice in the institution of a given society. Moreover, as the philosophers and divines of the eighteenth century used to stress, without the recourse to "right reason" and independent moral thinking, there would be no check on the interpretations of the divine will by fallible human minds.

I do not therefore think that, if skepticism were right, the return to religion, even if possible on a wide-enough scale, could provide enough of a remedy; nor that our present bewilderment is, in the first place, due to confusions about the right place of religion in morals. The crucial question remains that of skepticism of reason. We must ask: How far is it really justified?

Skepticism often comes from the disappointment of misplaced expectations. There is no comfort in anything, because nothing is good enough to replace the lost hope. And Sartre's views illustrate this. He finds that there is no *sure* way of choosing between one's mother and one's country. So he concludes that there can be *no* way of choosing anything rather than anything else. But this is precisely what does not follow; and the truth, as I see it, is rather that the power of thought to guide ultimate choices is a matter of degree. Some of them are plainly right or wrong—for anyone who deserves the name of a human being. One would have to be a fiend not to have it in one to see that some thought must be given to the good or harm of others. But when it comes to concrete cases, and to matters of conflict, then the big certainties begin to evaporate. How *much* of one's own life is one to give to others? How *much* is one to prefer independence to security? How *much* the good of human kind to that of one's group? These are issues of a different kind, and this must be acknowledged. One has not got enough ground here for saying that only one choice and no other could be right for everyone who is properly human. But nor could one say that every natural basis for a better or worse choice has gone, but rather that the basis for choice has become more personal. One may still make these choices judiciously or not, be guided in them by impartial reflection and honest self-scrutiny, or follow one's blind leanings. For there are qualities of mind on which judiciousness in choice depend at all times. In hard cases they cannot be exercised easily; but this is not enough for saying with Sartre that there is no guide in them at all. If there is not always a choice which is the *one* that is properly human, there is always a properly human way of making one's choices.

We keep confusing ourselves when we call this the way of "reason," and this confusion accounts for much of our disorientation. The point is not that the right choice may not be called the one "guided by reason" but that "reason" may mean so many things. "Reason" makes one think of calculation, of deduction, of learning from experience. But the reason which can guide ultimate choices is none of these; and one draws attention to this when one says that "the good" need not be "the clever." The "reason" of the clever finds out about things unknown. But everyone knows what it is to do good or harm; and if people fail to take notice, then this is not for lack of knowledge. And yet one may say, if loosely, that it is for lack of "using reason." Because "using reason" may also mean: "reminding one's self of what one knows already," "putting it to one's self clearly, vividly, and without reserve." And the properly human choice is the one which is directed by such reminders. In a thoughtless frame of mind one may not mind hurting others; if roused, one may even enjoy it. But if one reminds one's self, sympathetically and plainly, of what doing harm does, one will find that one's own nature will not let one. One finds that harm-doing could not be one's choice as a reflective and normal human being.

And the same principle applies to the more tricky choices between ultimate alternatives. I should say that even with as trivial a choice as that between lambs fry and Wiener schnitzel, one is not condemned, as Sartre will have it, to choose in darkness. Even here one may choose rashly or considerately, with one's eyes open or not, in order to elicit which alternative would truly deserve priority for one. And to choose considerately would here mean: making quite clear to one's self the nature of the alternatives before one; presenting it to one's self that having the one would be forsaking the other; and eliciting one's response to the thought of still opting

for the one even in full view of thereby sacrificing the other. A choice so determined will be the one more truly proper for one than any other; one which I can defend to myself and others; one to the thought of which I can hope to return ever afterward without regret. And to choose between one's mother and one's country, between independence and security, between one's own good and that of others, is only harder and beset more by inner conflict, but in principle no different. Here, too, it is a matter of distinguishing between one's immediate leanings and the well-considered order of one's priorities: the one which sincere reflection on the competing alternatives would show one to express one's true evaluation, the one again with which one could afterward hope to live in peace.

But I want to emphasize that these cases also show more clearly what diverse qualities of mind right choice requires. Philosophers' talk about a simple and unique faculty of moral intuition has here done much to befog the truth. There is not one faculty, there are many qualities of mind which must cooperate. One must have experience of what one is choosing between. One cannot choose well between independence and security any more than between lambs fry and Wiener schnitzel if all one knows is the basic meaning of the words. One must know the savor of living the one as one must know the savor of eating the other. Experience of life and the chance of living it as well as the enterprise to seek it are conditions for making right choices. The real worth of things must be explored; it cannot be deduced. And with big issues like freedom or security this is just the difficulty. We cannot vary the balance of a social order just for the sake of deepening our experience, and if we put our money on trying the one, we easily destroy our chance of trying the other, perhaps even our fitness to try it. This is why it has been said that freedom is more easily lost than gained. Moreover, our own experience is not always enough. To be clear about the good or harm of others, one requires imagination as well, the ability to put one's self into the other fellow's shoes, to extend one's sympathies from the familiar to the unfamiliar by noticing a human being behind the curtain of color, age, class, and distance. This ability, as everyone knows, is not easily exercised; and failure to exercise it lies behind many of our disagreements about the ethics of group relations in the international field. (Though, I should hasten to add, not of all.) And then again right choice requires still another quality of mind. For in order to present the issues to ourselves effectively, we must also be able to relive in the imagination what we know already. One may know of 3,000 flood victims and feel no compunction to help because, as Arthur Koestler once said, "statistics don't bleed"; and, one might add, not *unless one makes them bleed.* And, finally, merely to put the alternatives before one, as when one is choosing between one's self and another, may still not be enough—because one may also do this either halfheartedly or without reserve, with or without self-deceit. And only if done without reserve, will one's proper choice come before one. Now one may follow custom and call this "the choice of reason." But, then, let us be quite clear that moral reason is not that of the scientist or mathematician, whose "reason" has in our time become the paradigm of all reason. One's proper choice is not found under the microscope or by calculation, but it can be found; and not by the exercise of one special faculty but, rather, by the whole man testing *himself* out against an *objective* view of the issues for choice.

I shall only say a little more by way of a summing up. I hope that I have shown why contemporary skepticism goes too far. It is not true that Sartre's student had nothing to guide him. It was up to him to be judicious about his choice or not. True enough, no one else could have *handed* him the answer: Your conscience cannot tell me what I ought to do. But it is also needlessly tough to pretend that in matters like these there could be no answer, no helpful or critical exchange. One cannot prove how anyone ought to choose, but one need not therefore take everyone else's views on ultimate ends, or ways of life, in silence or leave each other confined to the ivory towers of our private consciences. The outsider may help from his experience to make the issues stand out more clearly; he may work on the other's imagination; he may prompt him to reflect in the right way; he may deflate his self-deceits by a calm "if you seriously feel that way, then go right ahead." One should not think that where there is no argument there can be no conversation.

This applies to small things and large, and our big contemporary disagreements about ways of life are not therefore beyond treatment. We do in fact fail in treating them. But then, rather than blame the instrument, we might blame our tardiness in using it in matters in which our interests, or our conceits, are involved.

But I said before that skepticism comes from the disappointment of misplaced expectations. And skeptical disorientation will remain a sign of our time until we have learned to accept moral thinking for what it is and with its limits. What everyone hopes for as a guide are rules by which to settle all cases, applicable with ease, and in the same way to everyone alike. Instead, what we have available is a procedure, calling on many and fallible qualities of mind; a procedure which yields some broad and fairly obvious answers, but which for the rest leaves us to puzzle things out for ourselves, with a margin for error and disagreement too wide for comfort. It may be that we still have to grow up to learn to accept this for a fact: There is no moral Santa Claus in pure reason.

And let me conclude with one gentle reminder. It would not be fair to blame philosophers or "sophists" for forcing this recognition on to us. For what is doing it are once more the circumstances of our time, and philosophers are at best their mouthpiece. Our circumstances are complicating the issues beyond the powers of any book of rules. Not every society has to choose between freedom and social welfare as hard as ours. In the days when economic laissez faire was a working proposition, one could have freedom along with economic welfare without much of a need for choice, or so one could think. But today, with the new means for procuring economic welfare, we must choose. To choose one must think. And even if thinking came to no more than to having a heart and keeping one's head, it would not come to nothing.

Suggestions for Further Reading

The following articles in *The Encyclopedia of Philosophy,* edited by Paul Edwards (New York: Macmillan and The Free Press, 1967), are all helpful. This *Encyclopedia* is a valuable source of information on virtually every philosophical topic.

· Richard B. Brandt, "Ethical Relativism," vol. 3, pp. 75–78.

Jonathan Harrison, "Ethical Subjectivism," vol. 3, pp. 78–81.

Richard B. Brandt, "Emotive Theory of Ethics," vol. 2, pp. 493–496.

Jonathan Harrison, "Ethical Objectivism," vol. 3, pp. 71–75.

A. Phillips Griffiths, "Ultimate Moral Principles: Their Justification," vol. 8, pp. 177–182.

W. T. Stace, *The Concept of Morals* (New York: Macmillan, 1937), chs. 1 & 2. Stace argues against ethical relativism, and in particular against cultural relativism.

John Ladd, ed., *Ethical Relativism* (Belmont, Cal.: Wadsworth, 1973). A good collection of articles arguing the pros and cons of relativism.

Charles L. Stevenson, *Facts and Values* (New Haven: Yale University Press, 1963). Stevenson is the leading proponent of emotivism. This book is a collection of his essays.

Brand Blanshard, "The New Subjectivism in Ethics," *Philosophy and Phenomenological Research,* vol. 9 (1949), pp. 504–511. [Reprinted in P. Edwards and A. Pap (eds.), *A Modern Introduction to Philosophy,* third edition (New York: Free Press, 1973).] Lively criticism of the emotive theory, and a defense of ethical objectivism.

Judith Jarvis [Thomson], "In Defense of Moral Absolutes," *The Journal of Philosophy,* vol. 55 (1958), pp. 1043–1053.

Kai Nielsen, "On Moral Truth," *Studies in Moral Philosophy: American Philosophical Quarterly Monograph No. 1* (1968), pp. 9–25. Nielsen argues that moral judgments are true if they are justified from the moral point of view.

John Searle, "How to Derive 'Ought' from 'Is'," *The Philosophical Review*, vol. 73 (1964), pp. 43–58. [Reprinted in W. D. Hudson (ed.), *The Is-Ought Question* (London: Macmillan, 1969).] Using promise-keeping as his example, Searle argues against Hume that we can derive evaluative conclusions from factual premises—thus "proving" at least some value-judgments to be true.

A. C. Ewing, *The Definition of Good* (London: Routledge & Kegan Paul, 1948). A vigorous defense of ethical objectivism.

CHAPTER TWO

Ethical Egoism

INTRODUCTION

Suppose you find a wallet containing $100; no one saw you find it, and no one knows you have it. But you know that the wallet belongs to a poor man who cannot afford to lose that much money. Should you keep the money, or should you return it?

Again, suppose you have saved enough of your own money to buy some new stereo equipment, but now someone suggests that you give the money for famine relief instead. They may ask: Which is more important, having new stereo equipment or feeding starving children?

Most of us would agree that we ought to return the lost wallet to its rightful owner, and we might also agree that we ought to give at least some of our own money for famine relief. (We might agree that we *ought* to do these things, regardless of what in fact we would do.) But why should we do such things? Why should we look out for *other* people's interests? Why not just look out for our own interests, and let others take care of themselves?

Ethical egoism is an ethical theory that says, in fact, you have no moral obligation to help others. According to this theory, you ought always to do what is in your *own* interests. So, if it is to your own advantage to keep the lost wallet, keep it. And if it is not to your own advantage to give to famine relief, you need not give. More precisely, ethical egoism may be defined as the view that *the right thing for anyone to do, in any circumstances, is whatever would best promote his own interests—* regardless of how other people's interests would be affected. (This theory is sometimes called "universal" or "impersonal" ethical egoism, for reasons explained in this chapter.) Two points should be kept in mind to avoid misunderstanding this theory:

a. Ethical egoism does *not* say that a person should do everything that is to his immediate, short-term advantage. It may be to someone's short-term advantage to smoke cigarettes, for example, because it gives him pleasure; however, this may be to his disadvantage in the long run because it increases his chances of getting lung cancer. Ethical egoism says that a person should do whatever will best promote *all* his interests, taking all factors—long run as well as short term—into account.

b. Ethical egoism does not forbid helping others. In fact, in many circumstances it may be to your own advantage to help others, for you may be paid to do so, or you may expect others eventually to return the favor. In these cases, you ought to do the acts in question because doing them is to your own advantage. Moreover, it is all right for you to help others even when you get nothing out of it, if you want to do so, provided that it does not *harm* your interests in any way. Ethical egoism does not forbid helping others; it simply insists that you never have any *obligation* to give help, unless it is to your own advantage to do so.

Many people have suspected that all human beings are really selfish at heart, that "altruism" is only an illusion, and that all human actions are really motivated by self-interest. So, even when we give to charity, or "sacrifice" our own interests to help others, there is always a selfish motive at work although we may not be at all conscious of it. If we take this view of human nature, then ethical egoism may seem to be a realistic, tough-minded philosophy that pictures people as they really are.

Here confusion has begun to set in. In order to keep things straight, we need to distinguish between *ethical* egoism and *psychological* egoism. Ethical egoism is a theory about how people *ought* to behave. It says that they ought to pursue their own interests. Psychological egoism, on the other hand, is a theory about how in fact people *do* behave. It says that they *are* always motivated by self-interest, in whatever they do. The two theories are, therefore, very different, and we must be careful not to confuse them. Most philosophers today believe that psychological egoism is simply false. In the first selection in this chapter, "Are All Human Actions Motivated by Self-Interest?", Joel Feinberg examines the arguments for and against this hypothesis, and concludes that it cannot be correct.

A first reaction to *ethical* egoism might be that it is an immoral theory; indeed, this can be argued strongly.[1] However, some philosophers have also argued that ethical egoism is a *logically inconsistent* doctrine. According to this view, ethical egoism is indefensible because it is self-contradictory. This is a very surprising claim—the theory certainly does not at first seem self-contradictory—but these philosophers have arguments to back up their claim. These arguments are presented by Brian Medlin in "Ethical Egoism Is Inconsistent," and Kurt Baier in "Self-Interest Is Not the Moral Point of View." Then, in his "Reply to Medlin and Baier," John Hospers tries to demonstrate that their arguments are mistaken, and that ethical egoism is a logically consistent theory.

The exchange between Medlin, Baier, and Hospers illustrates an important aspect of philosophical thinking. Many students, approaching the subject for the first time, have the vague idea that in philosophy the choice among competing views is mainly a matter of personal taste: You survey the available options, pick out the one you like best, and that's your philosophy. Or, if none of the prepackaged models strikes your fancy, you can always make up your own. On this way of thinking, no philosophical view is better or worse than any other; it's just a matter of choosing the one that suits your taste.

But things don't work that way. A philosophical position is no better than the arguments that support it. If there are no good arguments in favor of a certain view, and strong arguments against it, then that view must be rejected, no matter how it appeals to one's emotions. And a "philosopher" who merely gives opinions, with no arguments or solid reasoning to back them up, has little to offer. As you read the selections in this book, you should always ask yourself not only "what view is this writer expounding?" but also *"what arguments* does he give to show that what he says is true?"* Medlin and Baier do not merely state that ethical egoism is false, they try to prove it by rational argument. You should examine their arguments critically. Hospers provides a good lesson in how to do this.

---

1. For a full presentation of this argument, see James Rachels, "Two Arguments Against Ethical Egoism," *Philosophia*, vol. 4 (1974), pp. 297–314.

8

JOEL FEINBERG
Are All Human Actions Motivated by Self-Interest?

JOEL FEINBERG, professor of philosophy at Rockefeller University, is best known for his work in the philosophy of law. He is the author of *Doing and Deserving* (1970) and *Social Philosophy* (1973).

THE THEORY

1. "Psychological egoism" is the name given to a theory widely held by ordinary men, and at one time almost universally accepted by political economists, philosophers, and psychologists, according to which all human actions when properly understood can be seen to be motivated by selfish desires. More precisely, psychological egoism is the doctrine that the only thing anyone is capable of desiring or pursuing ultimately (as an end in itself) is his *own* self-interest. No psychological egoist denies that men sometimes do desire things other than their own welfare—the happiness of other people, for example; but all psychological egoists insist that men are capable of desiring the happiness of others only when they take it to be a *means* to their own happiness. In short, purely altruistic and benevolent actions and desires do not exist; but people sometimes appear to be acting unselfishly and disinterestedly when they take the interests of others to be means to the promotion of their own self-interest.

2. This theory is called *psychological* egoism to indicate that it is not a theory about what *ought* to be the case, but rather about what, as a matter of fact, *is* the case. That is, the theory claims to be a description of psychological facts, not a prescription of ethical ideals. It asserts, however, not merely that all men do as a contingent matter of fact "put their own interests first," but also that they are capable of nothing else, human nature being what it is. Universal selfishness is not just an accident or a coincidence on this view; rather, it is an unavoidable consequence of psychological laws.

The theory is to be distinguished from another doctrine, so-called "ethical egoism," according to which all men *ought* to pursue their own well-being and only their own well-being as an end in itself. This doctrine, being a prescription of what *ought* to be the case, makes no claim to be a psychological theory of human motives; hence the word "ethical" appears in its name to distinguish it from *psychological* egoism.

3. There are a number of types of motives and desires which might reasonably be called "egoistic" or "selfish," and corresponding to each of them is a possible version of psychological egoism. Perhaps the most common version of the theory is that apparently held by Jeremy Bentham.[1] According to this version, all persons have only one

1. See his *Introduction to the Principles of Morals and Legislation* (1789), Chap. I, first paragraph: "Nature has placed mankind under the governance of two sovereign masters, *pain* and *pleasure*. It is for them alone to point out what we ought to do, as well as to determine what we shall do. . . . They govern us in all we do, in all we say, in all we think: every effort we can make to throw off our subjection will serve but to demonstrate and confirm it."

ultimate motive in all their voluntary behavior and that motive is a selfish one; more specifically, it is one particular kind of selfish motive—namely, a desire for one's own *pleasure*. According to this version of the theory, "the only kind of ultimate desire is the desire to get or to prolong pleasant experiences, and to avoid or to cut short unpleasant experiences for oneself."[2] This form of psychological egoism is often given the cumbersome name—*psychological egoistic hedonism.*

PRIMA FACIE REASONS IN SUPPORT OF THE THEORY

4. Psychological egoism has seemed plausible to many people for a variety of reasons, of which the following are typical:

a. "Every action of mine is prompted by motives or desires or impulses which are *my* motives and not somebody else's. This fact might be expressed by saying that whenever I act I am always pursuing my own ends or trying to satisfy my own desires. And from this we might pass on to—'I am always pursuing something for myself or seeking my own satisfaction.' Here is what seems like a proper description of a man acting selfishly, and if the description applies to all men, then it follows that all men in all their actions are selfish."[3]

b. It is a truism that when a person gets what he wants he characteristically feels pleasure. This has suggested to many people that what we really want in every case is our own pleasure, and that we pursue other things only as a means.

c. *Self-Deception.* Often we deceive ourselves into thinking that we desire something fine or noble when what we really want is to be thought

well of by others or to be able to congratulate ourselves, or to be able to enjoy the pleasures of a good conscience. It is a well-known fact that people tend to conceal their true motives from themselves by camouflaging them with words like "virtue," "duty," etc. Since we are so often mislead concerning both our own real motives and the real motives of others, is it not reasonable to suspect that we might *always* be deceived when we think motives disinterested and altruistic? Indeed, it is a simple matter to explain away all allegedly unselfish motives: "Once the conviction that selfishness is universal finds root in a person's mind, it is very likely to burgeon out in a thousand corroborating generalizations. It will be discovered that a friendly smile is really only an attempt to win an approving nod from a more or less gullible recording angel; that a charitable deed is, for its performer, only an opportunity to congratulate himself on the good fortune or the cleverness that enables him to be charitable; that a public benefaction is just plain good business advertising. It will emerge that gods are worshipped only because they indulge men's selfish fears, or tastes, or hopes; that the 'golden rule' is no more than an eminently sound success formula; that social and political codes are created and subscribed to only because they serve to restrain other men's egoism as much as one's own, morality being only a special sort of 'racket' or intrigue using weapons of persuasion in place of

2. C. D. Broad, *Ethics and the History of Philosophy* (New York: The Humanities Press, 1952), Essay 10—"Egoism as a Theory of Human Motives," p. 218. This essay is highly recommended.

3. Austin Duncan-Jones, *Butler's Moral Philosophy* (London: Penguin Books, 1952), p. 96. Duncan-Jones goes on to reject this argument.

bombs and machine guns. Under this interpretation of human nature, the categories of commercialism replace those of disinterested service and the spirit of the horse trader broods over the face of the earth."[4]

d. *Moral Education.* Morality, good manners, decency, and other virtues must be teachable. Psychological egoists often notice that moral education and the inculcation of manners usually utilize what Bentham calls the "sanctions of pleasure and pain".[5] Children are made to acquire the civilizing virtues only by the method of enticing rewards and painful punishments. Much the same is true of the history of the race. People in general have been inclined to behave well only when it is made plain to them that there is "something in it for them." Is it not then highly probable that just such a mechanism of human motivation as Bentham describes must be presupposed by our methods of moral education?

CRITIQUE OF PSYCHOLOGICAL EGOISM: CONFUSIONS IN THE ARGUMENTS

5. *Nonempirical Character of the Arguments.* If the arguments of the psychological egoist consisted for the most part of carefully acquired empirical evidence (well-documented reports of controlled experiments, surveys, interviews, laboratory data, and so on), then the critical philosopher would have no business carping at them. After all, since psychological egoism purports to be a scientific theory of human motives, it is the concern of the experimental psychologist, not the philosopher, to accept or reject it. But as a matter of fact, empirical evidence of the required sort is seldom presented in support of psychological egoism. Psychologists, on the whole, shy away from generaliza-

tions about human motives which are so sweeping and so vaguely formulated that they are virtually incapable of scientific testing. It is usually the "armchair scientist" who holds the theory of universal selfishness, and his usual arguments are either based simply on his "impressions" or else are largely of a nonempirical sort. The latter are often shot full of a very subtle kind of logical confusion, and this makes their criticism a matter of special interest to the analytic philosopher.

6. The psychological egoist's first argument (4a, above) is a good example of logical confusion. It begins with a truism—namely, that all of my motives and desires are *my* motives and desires and not someone else's. (Who would deny this?) But from this simple tautology nothing whatever concerning the nature of my motives or the objective of my desires can possibly follow. The fallacy of this argument consists in its violation of the general logical rule that analytic statements (tautologies) cannot entail synthetic (factual) ones.[6] That every voluntary act is prompted by the agent's own motives is a tautology; hence, it cannot be equivalent to "A person is always seeking something for himself" or "All of a person's motives are selfish," which are synthetic. What the egoist must prove is not merely:

(i) Every voluntary action is prompted by a motive of the agent's own.

but rather:

(ii) Every voluntary action is prompted by a motive of a quite particular kind, namely a selfish one.

4. Lucius Garvin, *A Modern Introduction to Ethics* (Boston: Houghton Mifflin, 1953), p. 37. Quoted here by permission of the author and publisher.
5. *Op. cit.,* Chap. III.
6. See Part D, 15 and 16, below.

Statement (i) is obviously true, but it cannot all by itself give any logical support to statement (ii).

The source of the confusion in this argument is readily apparent. It is not the genesis of an action or the *origin* or its motives which makes it a "selfish" one, but rather the "purpose" of the act or the *objective* of its motives; *not where the motive comes from* (in voluntary actions it always comes from the agent) but *what it aims at* determines whether or not it is selfish. There is surely a valid distinction between *voluntary* behavior, in which the agent's action is motivated by purposes of his own, and *selfish* behavior in which the agent's motives are of one exclusive sort. The egoist's argument assimilates all voluntary action into the class of selfish action, by requiring, in effect, that an unselfish action be one which is not really motivated at all. In the words of Lucius Garvin, "to say that an act proceeds from our own. . .desire is only to say that the act is our own. To demand that we should act on motives that are not our own is to ask us to make ourselves living contradictions in terms."[7]

7. But if argument 4a fails to prove its point, argument 4b does no better. From the fact that all our successful actions (those in which we get what we were after) are accompanied or followed by pleasure it does not follow, as the egoist claims, that the *objective* of every action is to get pleasure for oneself. To begin with, the premise of the argument is not, strictly speaking, even true. Fulfillment of desire (simply getting what one was after) is no guarantee of satisfaction (pleasant feelings of gratification in the mind of the agent). Sometimes when we get what we want we *also* get, as a kind of extra dividend, a warm, glowing feeling of content-

ment; but often, far too often, we get no dividend at all, or, even worse, the bitter taste of ashes. Indeed, it has been said that the characteristic psychological problem of our time is the *dissatisfaction* that attends the fulfillment of our very most powerful desires.

Even if we grant, however, for the sake of argument, that getting what one wants *usually* yields satisfaction, the egoist's conclusion does not follow. We can concede that we normally get pleasure (in the sense of satisfaction) when our desires are satisfied, *no matter what our desires are for*; but it does not follow from this roughly accurate generalization that the only thing we ever desire is our own satisfaction. Pleasure may well be the usual accompaniment of all actions in which the agent gets what he wants; but to infer from this that what the agent always wants is his own pleasure is like arguing, in William James's example,[8] that because an ocean liner constantly consumes coal on its trans-Atlantic passage that therefore the *purpose* of its voyage is to consume coal. The immediate inference from even constant accompaniment to purpose (or motive) is always a *non sequitur*.

Perhaps there is a sense of "satisfaction" (desire fulfillment) such that it is certainly and universally true that we get satisfaction whenever we get what we want. But satisfaction in this sense is simply the "coming into existence of that which is desired." Hence, to say that desire fulfillment always yields "satisfaction" in this sense is to say no more than that we always get what we want when we get what we want, which is to utter a tautology like "a rose is a

7. *Op. cit.*, p. 39.

8. *The Principles of Psychology*, (New York: Henry Holt, 1890), Vol. II, p. 558.

rose." It can no more entail a synthetic truth in psychology (like the egoistic thesis) than "a rose is a rose" can entail significant information in botany.

8. *Disinterested Benevolence.* The fallacy in argument 4b then consists, as Garvin puts it, "in the supposition that the apparently unselfish desire to benefit others is transformed into a selfish one by the fact that we derive pleasure from carrying it out."[9] Not only is this argument fallacious; it also provides us with a suggestion of a counter-argument to show that its conclusion (psychological egoistic hedonism) is false. Not only is the presence of pleasure (satisfaction) as a by-product of an action no proof that the action was selfish; in some special cases it provides rather conclusive proof that the action was *unselfish*. For in those special cases the fact that we get pleasure from a particular action *presupposes that we desired something else*—something other than our own pleasure—as an end in itself and not merely as a means to our own pleasant state of mind.

This way of turning the egoistic hedonist's argument back on him can be illustrated by taking a typical egoist argument, one attributed (perhaps apocryphally) to Abraham Lincoln, and then examining it closely:

Mr. Lincoln once remarked to a fellow-passenger on an old-time mud-coach that all men were prompted by selfishness in doing good. His fellow-passenger was antagonizing this position when they were passing over a corduroy bridge that spanned a slough. As they crossed this bridge they espied an old razor-backed sow on the bank making a terrible noise because her pigs had got into the slough and were in danger of drowning. As the old coach began to climb the hill, Mr. Lincoln called out, "Driver, can't you stop just a moment?" Then Mr. Lincoln jumped out, ran back and lifted the little pigs out of the mud and water and placed them on the bank. When he returned, his companion remarked: "Now Abe, where does selfishness come in on this little episode?" "Why, bless your soul Ed, that was the very essence of selfishness. I should have had no peace of mind all day had I gone on and left that suffering old sow worrying over those pigs. I did it to get peace of mind, don't you see?"[10]

If Lincoln had cared not a whit for the welfare of the little pigs and their "suffering" mother, but only for his own "peace of mind," it would be difficult to explain how he could have derived pleasure from helping them. The very fact that he did feel satisfaction as a result of helping the pigs presupposes that he had a preexisting desire for something other than his own happiness. Then when *that* desire was satisfied, Lincoln of course derived pleasure. The *object* of Lincoln's desire was not pleasure; rather pleasure was the *consequence* of his preexisting desire for something else. If Lincoln had been wholly indifferent to the plight of the little pigs as he claimed, how could he possibly have derived any pleasure from helping them? He could not have achieved peace of mind from rescuing the pigs, had he not a prior concern—on which his peace of mind depended—for the welfare of the pigs for its own sake.

In general, the psychological hedonist analyzes apparent benevolence into a desire for "benevolent pleasure." No doubt the benevolent man does get pleasure from his benevolence, but in most cases, this is only because he has previously desired the good of some person, or animal, or mankind at large. Where there is no such desire, benevolent conduct is not generally found to give pleasure to the agent.

9. *Op. cit.,* p. 39.

10. Quoted from the *Springfield* (Illinois) *Monitor,* by F. C. Sharp in his *Ethics* (New York: Appleton-Century, 1928), p. 75.

9. *Malevolence.* Difficult cases for the psychological egoist include not only instances of disinterested benevolence, but also cases of "disinterested malevolence." Indeed, malice and hatred are generally no more "selfish" than benevolence. Both are motives likely to cause an agent to sacrifice his own interests—in the case of benevolence, in order to help someone else, in the case of malevolence in order to harm someone else. The selfish man is concerned ultimately only with his own pleasure, happiness, or power; the benevolent man is often equally concerned with the happiness of others; to the malevolent man, the *injury* of another is often an end in itself—an end to be pursued sometimes with no thought for his own interests. There is reason to think that men have as often sacrificed themselves to injure or kill others as to help or to save others, and with as much "heroism" in the one case as in the other. The unselfish nature of malevolence was first noticed by the Anglican Bishop and moral philosopher Joseph Butler (1692–1752), who regretted that men are no more selfish than they are.[11]

10. *Lack of Evidence for Universal Self-Deception.* The more cynical sort of psychological egoist who is impressed by the widespread phenomenon of self-deception (see 4c above) cannot be so quickly disposed of, for he has committed no *logical* mistakes. We can only argue that the acknowledged frequency of self-deception is insufficient evidence for his universal generalization. His argument is not fallacious, but inconclusive.

No one but the agent himself can ever be certain what conscious motives really prompted his action, and where motives are disreputable, even the agent may not admit to himself the true nature of his desires. Thus, for every apparent case of altruistic behavior, the psychological egoist can argue, with some plausibility, that the true motivation *might* be selfish, appearance to the contrary. Philanthropic acts are really motivated by the desire to receive gratitude; acts of self-sacrifice, when truly understood, are seen to be motivated by the desire to feel self-esteem; and so on. We must concede to the egoist that all apparent altruism might be deceptive in this way; but such a sweeping generalization requires considerable empirical evidence, and such evidence is not presently available.

11. *The "Paradox of Hedonism" and Its Consequences for Education.* The psychological egoistic Hedonist (e.g., Jeremy Bentham) has the simplest possible theory of human motivation. According to this variety of egoistic theory, all human motives without exception can be reduced to one—namely, the desire for one's own pleasure. But this theory, despite its attractive simplicity, or perhaps because of it, involves one immediately in a paradox. Astute observers of human affairs from the time of the ancient Greeks have often noticed that pleasure, happiness, and satisfaction are states of mind which stand in a very peculiar relation to desire. An exclusive desire for happiness is the surest way to prevent happiness from coming into being. Happiness has a way of "sneaking up" on persons when they are preoccupied with other things; but when persons deliberately and single-mindedly set off in pursuit of happiness, it vanishes utterly from sight and cannot be captured. This is the famous "paradox of hedonism": The single-minded pursuit of happiness is

11. See his *Fifteen Sermons on Human Nature Preached at the Rolls Chapel* (1726), especially the first and eleventh.

necessarily self-defeating, for *the way to get happiness is to forget it;* then perhaps it will come to you. If you aim exclusively at pleasure itself, with no concern for the things that bring pleasure, then pleasure will never come. To derive satisfaction, one must ordinarily first desire something other than satisfaction, and then find the means to get what one desires.

To feel the full force of the paradox of hedonism the reader should conduct an experiment in his imagination. Imagine a person (let's call him "Jones") who is, first of all, devoid of intellectual curiosity. He has no desire to acquire any kind of knowledge for its own sake, and thus is utterly indifferent to questions of science, mathematics, and philosophy. Imagine further that the beauties of nature leave Jones cold: He is unimpressed by the autumn foliage, the snow-capped mountains, and the rolling oceans. Long walks in the country on spring mornings and skiing forages in the winter are to him equally a bore. Moreover, let us suppose that Jones can find no appeal in art. Novels are dull, poetry a pain, paintings nonsense, and music just noise. Suppose further that Jones has neither the participant's nor the spectator's passion for baseball, football, tennis or any other sport. Swimming to him is a cruel aquatic form of calisthenics, the sun only a cause of sunburn. Dancing is coeducational idiocy, conversation a waste of time, the other sex an unappealing mystery. Politics is a fraud, religion mere superstition; and the misery of millions of underprivileged human beings is nothing to be concerned with or excited about. Suppose finally that Jones has no talent for any kind of handicraft, industry, or commerce, and that he does not regret that fact.

What then is Jones interested in? He must desire something. To be sure, he does. Jones has an overwhelming passion for, a complete preoccupation with, his own happiness. The one exclusive desire of his life is *to be happy.* It takes little imagination at this point to see that Jones's one desire is bound to be frustrated. People who—like Jones—most hotly pursue their own happiness are the least likely to find it. Happy people are those who successfully pursue such things as aesthetic or religious experience, self-expression, service to others, victory in competitions, knowledge, power, and so on. If none of these things in themselves and for their own sakes mean anything to a person, if they are valued at all then only as a means to one's own pleasant states of mind—then that pleasure can never come. The way to achieve happiness is to pursue something else.

Almost all people at one time or another in their lives feel pleasure. Some people (though perhaps not many) really do live lives which are on the whole happy. But if pleasure and happiness presuppose desires for something other than pleasure and happiness, then the existence of pleasure and happiness in the experience of some people proves that those people have strong desires for something other than their own happiness—egoistic hedonism to the contrary.

The implications of the "paradox of hedonism" for educational theory should be obvious. The parents least likely to raise a happy child are those who, even with the best intentions, train their child to seek happiness directly. How often have we heard parents say:

I don't care if my child does not become an intellectual, or a football star, or a great artist. I just want him to be a plain average sort of person. Happiness does not require great ambitions and great frustrations; it's not worth it to suffer and become neurotic for the sake of science, art, or do-goodism. I just want my child to be happy.

This can be a dangerous mistake, for it is the child (and the adult for that matter) without "outerdirected" interests who is the most likely to be unhappy. The pure egoist would be the most wretched of persons.

The educator might well beware of "life adjustment" as the conscious goal of the educational process for similar reasons. "Life adjustment" can be achieved only as a by-product of other pursuits. A whole curriculum of "life adjustment courses" unsupplemented by courses designed to incite an interest in things other than life adjustment would be tragically self-defeating.

As for moral education, it is probably true that punishment and reward are indispensable means of inculcation. But if the child comes to believe that the *sole* reasons for being moral are that he will escape the pain of punishment thereby and/or that he will gain the pleasure of a good reputation, then what is to prevent him from doing the immoral thing whenever he is sure that he will not be found out? While punishment and reward then are important tools for the moral educator, they obviously have their limitations. Beware of the man who does the moral thing only out of fear of pain or love of pleasure. He is not likely to be wholly trustworthy. Moral education is truly successful when it produces persons who are willing to do the right thing *simply because it is right,* and not merely because it is popular or safe.

12. *Pleasure as Sensation.* One final argument against psychological hedonism should suffice to put that

form of the egoistic psychology to rest once and for all. The egoistic hedonist claims that all desires can be reduced to the single desire for one's own *pleasure.* Now the word "pleasure" is ambiguous. On the one hand, it can stand for a certain indefinable, but very familiar and specific kind of sensation, or more accurately, a property of sensations; and it is generally, if not exclusively, associated with the senses. For example, certain taste sensations such as sweetness, thermal sensations of the sort derived from a hot bath or the feel of the August sun while one lies on a sandy beach, erotic sensations, olfactory sensations (say) of the fragrance of flowers or perfume, and tactual and kinesthetic sensations from a good massage, are all pleasant in this sense. Let us call this sense of "pleasure," which is the converse of "physical pain," pleasure$_1$.

On the other hand, the word "pleasure" is often used simply as a synonym for "satisfaction" (in the sense of gratification, not mere desire fulfillment.) In this sense, the existence of pleasure presupposes the prior existence of desire. Knowledge, religious experience, aesthetic expression, and other so-called "spiritual activities" often give pleasure in this sense. In fact, as we have seen, we tend to get pleasure in this sense whenever we get what we desire, no matter what we desire. The masochist even derives pleasure (in the sense of "satisfaction") from his own physically painful sensations. Let us call the sense of "pleasure" which means "satisfaction"—pleasure$_2$.

Now we can evaluate the psychological hedonist's claim that the sole human motive is a desire for one's own pleasure, bearing in mind (as he often does not) the ambiguity of the word "pleasure." First, let us take the hedonist to be saying that it is the desire for pleasure₁ (pleasant sensation) which is the sole ultimate desire of all people and the sole desire capable of providing a motive for action. Now I have little doubt that all (or most) people desire their own pleasure, *sometimes*. But even this familiar kind of desire occurs, I think, rather rarely. When I am very hungry, I often desire to eat, or, more specifically, to eat this piece of steak and these potatoes. Much less often do I desire to eat certain morsels simply for the sake of the pleasant gustatory sensations they might cause. I have, on the other hand, been motivated in the latter way when I have gone to especially exotic (and expensive) French or Chinese restaurants; but normally, pleasant gastronomic sensations are simply a happy consequence or by-product of my eating, not the antecedently desired objective of my eating. There are, of course, others who take gustatory sensations far more seriously: the *gourmet* who eats only to savor the textures and flavors of fine foods, and the wine fancier who "collects" the exquisitely subtle and very pleasant tastes of rare old wines. Such men are truly absorbed in their taste sensations when they eat and drink, and there may even be some (rich) persons whose desire for such sensations is the sole motive for eating and drinking. It should take little argument, however, to convince the reader that such persons are extremely rare.

Similarly, I usually derive pleasure from taking a hot bath, and on occasion (though not very often) I even decide to bathe simply for the sake of such sensations. Even if this is equally true of everyone, however, it hardly provides grounds for inferring that *no one ever* bathes from *any* other motive. It should be empirically obvious that we sometimes bathe simply in order to get clean, or to please others, or simply from habit.

The view then that we are never after anything in our actions but our own pleasure—that all men are complete "gourmets" of one sort or another—is not only morally cynical; it is also contrary to common sense and everyday experience. In fact, the view that pleasant sensations play such an enormous role in human affairs is so patently false, on the available evidence, that we must conclude that the psychological hedonist has the other sense of "pleasure"—satisfaction—in mind when he states his thesis. If, on the other hand, he really does try to reduce the apparent multitude of human motives to the one desire for pleasant sensations, then the abundance of historical counter-examples justifies our rejection out of hand of his thesis. It surely seems incredible that the Christian martyrs were ardently pursuing their own pleasure when they marched off to face the lions, or that what the Russian soldiers at Stalingrad "really" wanted when they doused themselves with gasoline, ignited themselves, and then threw the flaming torches of their own bodies on German tanks, was simply the experience of pleasant physical sensations.

13. *Pleasure as Satisfaction.* Let us consider now the other interpretation of the hedonist's thesis, that according to which it is one's own pleasure₂ (satisfaction) and not merely pleasure₁ (pleasant sensation) which is the sole ultimate objective of all voluntary behavior. In one respect, the "satisfaction thesis" is even less plausible than the "physical sensation thesis"; for the latter at least is a genuine empirical hypothesis, test-

able in experience, though contrary to the facts which experience discloses. The former, however, is so confused that it cannot even be completely stated without paradox. It is, so to speak, defeated in its own formulation. Any attempted explication of the theory that all men at all times desire only their own satisfaction leads to an *infinite regress* in the following way:

"All men desire only satisfaction."
"Satisfaction of what?"
"Satisfaction of their desires."
"Their desires for what?"
"Their desires for satisfaction."
"Satisfaction of what?"
"Their desires."
"For what?"
"For satisfaction"—etc., *ad infinitum.*

In short, psychological hedonism interpreted in this way attributes to all people as their sole motive a wholly vacuous and infinitely self-defeating desire. The source of this absurdity is in the notion that satisfaction can, so to speak, feed on itself, and perform the miracle of perpetual self-regeneration in the absence of desires for anything other than itself.

To summarize the argument of sections 11 and 12: The word "pleasure" is ambiguous. Pleasure$_1$ means a certain indefinable characteristic of physical sensation. Pleasure$_2$ refers to the feeling of satisfaction that often comes when one gets what one desires whatever be the nature of that which one desires. Now, if the hedonist means pleasure$_1$ when he says that one's own pleasure is the ultimate objective of all of one's behavior, then his view is not supported by the facts. On the other hand, if he means pleasure$_2$, then his theory cannot even be clearly formulated, since it leads to the following infinite regress: "I desire only satisfaction of my desire for satisfaction of my desire for satisfac-

tion. . .etc., *ad infinitum.*" I conclude then that psychological hedonism (the most common form of psychological egoism), however interpreted, is untenable.

CRITIQUE OF PSYCHOLOGICAL EGOISM: UNCLEAR LOGICAL STATUS OF THE THEORY

14. There remain, however, other possible forms of the egoistic psychology. The egoist might admit that not all human motives can be reduced to the one ultimate desire for one's own pleasure, or happiness, and yet still maintain that our ultimate motives, whether they be desire for happiness (J. S. Mill), self-fulfillment (Aristotle), power (Hobbes) or whatever, are always *self-regarding* motives. He might still maintain that, given our common human nature, wholly disinterested action impelled by exclusively other-regarding motives is psychologically impossible, and that therefore there is a profoundly important sense in which it is true that, whether they be hedonists or not, *all men are selfish.*

Now it seems to me that this highly paradoxical claim cannot be finally evaluated until it is properly understood, and that it cannot be properly understood until one knows what the psychological egoist is willing to accept as evidence either for or against it. In short, there are two things that must be decided: (a) whether the theory is true or false and (b) whether its truth or falsity (its truth value) depends entirely on the *meanings* of the words in which it is expressed or whether it is made true or false by certain *facts,* in this case the facts of psychology.

15. *Analytic Statements.* Statements whose truth is determined solely by the meanings of the words in which they are expressed, and thus can be held

immune from empirical evidence, are often called analytic statements or tautologies. The following are examples of tautologies:

(1) All spinsters are unmarried.
(2) All effects have causes.
(3) Either Providence is the capital of Rhode Island or it is not.

The truth of (1) is derived solely from the meaning of the word "spinster," which is defined (in part) as "unmarried woman." To find out whether (1) is true or false we need not conduct interviews, compile statistics, or perform experiments. All empirical evidence is superflous and irrelevant; for if we know the meanings of "spinster" and "unmarried," then we know not only that (1) is true, but that it is *necessarily* true —that is, that it cannot possibly be false, that no future experiences or observations could possibly upset it, that to deny it would be to assert a logical contradiction. But notice that what a tautology gains in certainty ("necessary truth") it loses in descriptive content. Statement (1) imparts no information whatever about any matter of fact; it simply records our determination to use certain words in a certain way. As we say, "It is true by definition."

Similarly, (2) is (necessarily) true solely in virtue of the meanings of the words "cause" and "effect" and thus requires no further observations to confirm it. And of course, no possible observations could falsify it, since it asserts no matter of fact. And finally, statement (3) is (necessarily) true solely in virtue of the meaning of the English expression "either. . .or". Such terms as "either. . .or," "If. . .then," "and," and "not" are called by logicians "logical constants." The *definitions* of logical constants are made explicit in the so-called "laws of thought"—the law of contradiction, the law of the excluded middle, and the law of identity. These "laws" are not laws in the same sense as are (say) the laws of physics. Rather, they are merely consequences of the *definitions* of logical constants, and as such, though they are necessarily true, they impart no information about the world. "Either Providence is the capital of Rhode Island or it is not" tells us nothing about geography; and "Either it is now raining or else it is not" tells us nothing about the weather. You don't have to look at a map or look out the window to know that they are true. Rather, they are known to be true *a priori* (independently of experience); and, like all (or many)[12] *a priori* statements, they are *vacuous*, that is, devoid of informative content.

The denial of an analytic statement is called a contradiction. The following are typical examples of contradictions: "Some spinsters are married," "Some causes have no effects," "Providence both is and is not the capital of Rhode Island." As in the case of tautologies, the truth value of contradictions (their falsehood) is logically necessary, not contingent on any facts of experience, and uninformative. Their falsity is derived from the meanings (definitions) of the words in which they are expressed.

16. *Synthetic Statements.* On the other hand, statements whose truth or falsity is derived not from the meanings of words but rather from the facts of experience (observations) are called *synthetic.*[13] Prior to experience, there can

12. Whether or not there are some *a priori* statements that are not merely analytic, and hence *not* vacuous, is still a highly controversial question among philosophers.

13. Some philosophers (those called "rationalists") believe that there are some synthetic statements whose truth can be known *a priori* (see footnote 12). If they are right, then the statement above is not entirely accurate.

be no good reason to think either that they are true or that they are false. That is to say, their truth value is *contingent*; and they can be confirmed or disconfirmed only by *empirical* evidence,[14] that is, controlled observations of the world. Unlike analytic statements, they do impart information about matters of fact. Obviously, "It is raining in Newport now," if true, is more informative than "Either it is raining in Newport now or it is not," even though the former *could* be false, while the latter is necessarily true. I take the following to be examples of synthetic (contingent) statements:

(1′) All spinsters are frustrated.
(2′) All events have causes.
(3′) Providence is the capital of Rhode Island.
(3″) Newport is the capital of Rhode Island.

Statement (3′) is true; (3″) is false; and (1′) is a matter for a psychologist (not for a philosopher) to decide; and the psychologist himself can only decide *empirically*, that is, by making many observations. The status of (2′) is very difficult and its truth value is a matter of great controversy. That is because its truth or falsity depends on *all* the facts ("all events"); and, needless to say, not all of the evidence is in.

17. *Empirical Hypotheses.* Perhaps the most interesting subclass of synthetic statements are those generalizations of experience of the sort characteristically made by scientists; for example, "All released objects heavier than air fall," "All swans are white," "All men have Oedipus complexes." I shall call such statements "empirical hypotheses" to indicate that their function is to sum up past experience and enable us successfully to predict or anticipate future experience.[15] They are never logically certain, since it is always

at least conceivable that future experience will disconfirm them. For example, zoologists once believed that all swans are white, until black swans were discovered in Australia. The most important characteristic of empirical hypotheses for our present purposes is their relation to evidence. A person can be said to understand an empirical hypothesis only if he knows how to recognize evidence against it. *If a person asserts or believes a general statement in such a way that he cannot conceive of any possible experience which he would count as evidence against it, then he cannot be said to be asserting or believing an empirical hypothesis.* We can refer to this important characteristic of empirical hypotheses as *falsifiability in principle.*

Some statements only appear to be empirical hypotheses but are in fact disguised tautologies reflecting the speaker's determination to use words in certain (often eccentric) ways. For example, a zoologist might refuse to allow the existence of "Australian swans" to count as evidence against the generalization that all swans are white, on the grounds that the black Australian swans are not "really" swans at all. This would indicate that he is holding *whiteness* to be part of the definition of "swan," and that therefore, the statement "All swans are white" is, for him, "true by definition"—and thus just as

14. Again, subject to the qualification in footnotes 12 and 13.

15. The three examples given above all have the generic character there indicated, but they also differ from one another in various other ways, some of which are quite important. For our present purposes however, we can ignore the ways in which they differ from one another and concentrate on their common character as generalizations of experience ("inductive generalizations"). As such they are sharply contrasted with such a generalization as "All puppies are young dogs," which is analytic.

immune from counterevidence as the statement "All spinsters are unmarried." Similarly, most of us would refuse to allow any possible experience to count as evidence against "2 + 2 = 4" or "Either unicorns exist or they do not," indicating that the propositions of arithmetic and logic are not empirical hypotheses.

18. *Ordinary Language and Equivocation.* Philosophers, even more than ordinary men, are prone to make startling and paradoxical claims that take the form of universal generalizations and hence resemble empirical hypotheses. For example, "All things are mental (there are no physical objects)," "All things are good (there is no evil)," "All voluntary behavior is selfish," and so forth. Let us confine our attention for the moment to the latter which is a rough statement of psychological egoism. At first sight, the statement "All voluntary behavior is selfish" seems obviously false. One might reply to the psychological egoist in some such manner as this:

I *know* some behavior, at least, is unselfish, because I saw my Aunt Emma yesterday give her last cent to a beggar. Now she will have to go a whole week with nothing to eat. Surely, *that* was not selfish of her.

Nevertheless, the psychological egoist is likely not to be convinced, and insist that, in this case, if we knew enough about Aunt Emma, we would learn that her primary motive in helping the beggar was to promote her own happiness or assuage her own conscience, or increase her own self-esteem, and so forth. We might then present the egoist with even more difficult cases for his theory—saints, martyrs, military heroes, patriots, and others who have sacrificed themselves for a cause. If the psychological egoist nevertheless refuses to accept any of these as examples of unselfish behavior, then we have a right to be puzzled about what he is saying. Until we know what he would count as *unselfish* behavior, we can't very well know what he means when he says that all voluntary behavior is *selfish*. And at this point we may suspect that he is holding his theory in a "privileged position"—that of immunity to evidence, that he would allow no *conceivable* behavior to count as evidence against it. What he says then, if true, must be true in virtue of the way he defines—or redefines—the word "selfish." And in that case, it cannot be an empirical hypothesis.

If what the psychological egoist says is "true by redefinition," then I can "agree" with him and say "It is true that in *your* sense of the word 'selfish' my Aunt Emma's behavior was selfish; but in the ordinary sense of 'selfish,' which implies blameworthiness, she surely was not selfish." There is no point of course in arguing about a mere word. The important thing is not what particular words a man uses, but rather whether what he wishes to say in those words is true. Departures from ordinary language can often be justified by their utility for certain purposes; but they are dangerous when they invite equivocation. The psychological egoist may be saying something which is true when he says that Emma is selfish in *his* sense, but if he doesn't realize that his sense of "selfish" differs from the ordinary one, he may be tempted to infer that Emma is selfish in the ordinary sense which implies blameworthiness; and this of course would be unfair and illegitimate. It is indeed an extraordinary extension of the meaning of the word "self-indulgent" (as G. K. Chesterton remarks somewhere) which allows a philosopher to say that a man is self-indulgent when he wants to be burned at the stake.

19. *The Fallacy of the Suppressed Correlative.* Certain words in the English language operate in pairs—for example, "selfish-unselfish," "good-bad," "large-small," "mental-physical." To assert that a thing has one of the above characteristics is to *contrast* it with the opposite in the pair. To know the meaning of one term in the pair, we must know the meaning of the correlative term with which it is contrasted. If we could not conceive of what it would be like for a thing to be bad, for example, then we could not possibly understand what is being said of a thing when it is called "good." Similarly, unless we had a notion of what it would be like for an action to be *unselfish,* we could hardly understand the sentence "So-and-so acted selfishly"; for we would have nothing to contrast "selfishly" with. The so-called "fallacy of the suppressed correlative"[16] is committed by a person who consciously or unconsciously redefines one of the terms in a contrasting pair in such a way that its new meaning incorporates the sense of its correlative.

Webster's Collegiate Dictionary defines "selfish" (in part) as "regarding one's own comfort, advantage, etc. in disregard of, or at the expense of that of others." In this ordinary and proper sense of "selfish," Aunt Emma's action in giving her last cent to the beggar certainly was *not* selfish. Emma *disregarded* her *own* comfort (it is not "comfortable" to go a week without eating) and advantage (there is no "advantage" in malnutrition) *for the sake of* (not "at the expense of") another. Similarly, the martyr marching off to the stake is foregoing (not indulging) his "comfort" and indeed his very life for the sake of (not at the expense of) a cause. If Emma and the martyr then are "selfish," they must be so in a strange new sense of the word.

A careful examination of the egoist's arguments (see especially 4b above) reveals what new sense he gives to the word "selfish." He redefines the word so that it means (roughly) "motivated," or perhaps "intentional." "After all," says the egoist, "Aunt Emma had some *purpose* in giving the beggar all her money, and this purpose (desire, intention, motive, aim) was *her* purpose and no one else's. She was out to further some aim of her own, wasn't she? Therefore, she was pursuing her own ends (acting from her own motives); she was after something *for herself* in so acting, and that's what I mean by calling her action selfish. Moreover, all intentional action —action done 'on purpose,' deliberately from the agent's own motives— is selfish in the same sense." We can see now, from this reply, that since the egoist apparently means by "selfish" simply "motivated," when he says that all motivated action is selfish *he is not asserting a synthetic empirical hypothesis about human motives; rather, his statement is a tautology roughly equivalent to "all motivated actions are motivated."* And if that is the case, then what he says is true enough; but, like all tautologies, it is empty, uninteresting, and trivial.

Moreover, in redefining "selfish" in this way, the psychological egoist has committed the fallacy of the suppressed correlative. For what can we now contrast "selfish voluntary action" with? Not only are there no *actual* cases of unselfish voluntary actions on the new definition; there are not even any *theoretically possible* or *conceivable* cases of unselfish voluntary actions. And if we cannot even conceive of what an unselfish voluntary action would be like, how can we give any sense to the

16. The phrase was coined by J. Lowenberg. See his article "What Is Empirical?" in the *Journal of Philosophy,* May 1940.

expression "selfish voluntary action"? The egoist, so to speak, has so blown up the sense of "selfish" that, like inflated currency, it will no longer buy anything.

20. *Psychological Egoism as a Linguistic Proposal.* There is still one way out for the egoist. He might admit that his theory is not really a psychological hypothesis about human nature designed to account for the facts and enable us to predict or anticipate future events. He may even willingly concede that his theory is really a disguised redefinition of a word. Still, he might argue, he has made no claim to be giving an accurate description of actual linguistic usage. Rather, he is making a proposal to *revise* our usage in the interest of economy and convenience, just as the biologists once proposed that we change the ordinary meaning of "insect" in such a way that spiders are no longer called insects, and the ordinary meaning of "fish" so that whales and seals are no longer called fish.

What are we to say to this suggestion? First of all, stipulative definitions (proposals to revise usage) are never true or false. They are simply useful or not useful. Would it be useful to redefine "selfish" in the way the egoist recommends? It is difficult to see what would be gained thereby. The egoist has noticed some respects in which actions normally called "selfish" and actions normally called "unselfish" are alike, namely they are both motivated and they both can give satisfaction—either in prospect or in retrospect—to the agent. Because of these likenesses, the egoist feels justified in attaching the label "selfish" to *all* actions. Thus one

word—"selfish"—must for him do the work of two words ("selfish" and "unselfish" in their old meanings); and, as a result, a very real distinction, that between actions for the sake of others and actions at the expense of others, can no longer be expressed in the language. Because the egoist has noticed some respects in which two types of actions are alike, he wishes to make it impossible to describe the respects in which they differ. It is difficult to see any utility in this state of affairs.

But suppose we adopt the egoist's "proposal" nevertheless. Now we would have to say that all actions are selfish; but, in addition, we would want to say that there are two different kinds of selfish actions, those which regard the interests of others and those which disregard the interests of others, and, furthermore, that only the latter are blameworthy. After a time our ear would adjust to the new uses of the word "selfish," and we would find nothing at all strange in such statements as "Some selfish actions are morally praiseworthy." After a while, we might even invent two new words, perhaps "selfitic" and "unselfitic," to distinguish the two important classes of "selfish" actions. Then we would be right back where we started, with new linguistic tools ("selfish" for "motivated," "selfitic" for "selfish," and "unselfitic" for "unselfish") to do the same old necessary jobs. That is, until some new egoistic philosopher arose to announce with an air of discovery that "All selfish behavior is really selfitic—there are no truly unselfitic selfish actions." Then, God help us!

9

JOHN HOSPERS
Arguments for Ethical Egoism

JOHN HOSPERS is professor of philosophy at the University of Southern California. He is the author of *Meaning and Truth in the Arts* (1946), *An Introduction to Philosophical Analysis* (1953), *Human Conduct* (1961), and *Libertarianism* (1971). In 1972 Professor Hospers was a candidate for President of the United States on the Libertarian Party ticket.

One word of caution at the outset. Do not confuse "actions conducive to your interest" with "actions which help you but not others"—roughly, selfish actions. There are many *un*selfish actions which surely *are* to your interest to perform. If you do something for someone, he may do something for you some day when you need it badly. If you control your impulses, obey the law, and treat your colleagues nicely even when you don't feel like it, you will earn the respect and esteem of your community, possessions which may stand you in good stead. In short, it is often to your own interest—long-term if not short—to behave in an unselfish manner. Ethical egoism does not deny that you should help others when doing so helps *you.* Perhaps this overlapping of interests occurs most of the time. Ethical egoism only denies that you should help others when *you* will get nothing out of it—neither fame, fortune, nor even personal satisfaction or happiness. Since you should always do what promotes your own interests, and since the unselfish act in these cases does not promote your own interest, there is no reason why you should do it, according to ethical egoism.

Let us first see whether any arguments can be used to *defend* ethical egoism. Most ethical egoists, to be sure,

From *Human Conduct* by John Hospers, © 1961, 1972, by Harcourt Brace Jovanovich, Inc., and reprinted with their permission.

behave egoistically without trying to state any propositions in favor of their doctrine—they do not care about defenses or refutations. If they did want to defend their view, however, what might they say?

We must first distinguish the *personal* ethical egoist from the *impersonal* ethical egoist. The personal ethical egoist is someone who says that *he* should follow his own interests exclusively; he does not say what other people should do. The impersonal ethical egoist, on the other hand, says that *all men* should pursue their own interests exclusively.

1. Let us consider the *personal ethical egoist* first. If he says, "I *shall* follow my own interests," he is only stating what he is going to do and is not giving voice to an ethical theory at all; hence there is as yet no ethical theory to be defended. He is merely making a prediction about how he is going to behave, and a prediction is best defended by its coming true.

But if he says, "I *ought* to pursue my own interests," what reason can he give for making this statement? Suppose that to the question "Why is this wrong?" he answers, "Because it involves the infliction of unnecessary suffering." The reason he gives is a general answer; it covers not only *this* particular act but all other acts which are like it in the specified respect. If this act is wrong, then all acts like it in the specified respect are wrong, regardless of whether they are yours or mine or someone else's. But to give a general reason already goes contrary to the personal ethical egoist's contention. He cannot make any statement about all acts of a certain kind, for he is concerned only with *his own* acts; he says nothing about anyone else's acts. Because he is a personal ethical egoist, he is cut off from being able to state any general reasons or to voice any general ethical principles to uphold his position. Even if he says, "Because *all* persons should pursue their own interest," he is no longer a personal but an impersonal ethical egoist.

He may, however, try to derive his statement "I should pursue only my own interest" from some other statement about what is intrinsically worthwhile or desirable. He may say, "*My* happiness (or whatever else you want to call intrinsically good) is the only intrinsic good there is, and since I should promote the good, I should promote my own happiness." We might then point out to him that if he considers happiness (or anything else) intrinsically good or worth attaining, why is it not worth attaining for everyone else as well as for himself? Why is *he* an exception? The personal ethical egoist is declaring that only *his* happiness, out of that of all the people in the world, is worth striving for; but he gives no reason why he should be thus privileged. In fact, if what he says is true, then not only he but Smith and Jones and you and I and everyone else in the world should do all we can to promote this egoist's happiness; we should promote what is intrinsically good, and his happiness is the only intrinsic good in the world, so we should all neglect our own interests and promote his.

What reasons could he possibly give to back up such a bizarre claim?

a. He may say, "I alone count because there is some characteristic or property which I alone of all men possess and which gives me exclusive title to happiness." Perhaps he is the most talented or brilliant person in the world, or the most powerful, or the most dedicated. But, in the first place, one could question why the possession of these characteristics should entitle him to exclusive attention. And, in the second place, one could point out that even if he possesses the characteristic now, someone else may possess it later (someone else might arise who is more talented than he) and then by his criterion *that* person would be entitled to exclusive attention. (In other words, he would be assenting to the general principle "*Anyone* possessing more of property A than anyone else does should receive exclusive attention.") His view would thus boomerang against him.

b. "But," the personal ethical egoist may say, "there is a way out of this dilemma. I can make sure that it is only to the promotion of my interests to which exclusive attention should be paid. I shall not claim some special property, for someone else might come to possess that property also; I shall say only that I deserve exclusive attention because *I am I*." But this reasoning, of course, will not do either. It is true that being John Jones is something that is true only of John Jones. Even if John Jones is no longer the most talented person in the world, he is still John Jones. But exactly the same thing could be said for everyone else. Being Sam Smith is something that holds true only of Sam Smith. The plea "I deserve X because I am I" is something that everyone could present; if it is a valid plea for Jones it is equally so for Smith.

If something is intrinsically good, then, it is not intrinsically good only when Jones has it. Why, indeed, should it not be intrinsically good wherever it occurs? Hence Jones cannot use his premise about intrinsic good to support the conclusion that he should consider his own interests exclusively.

The personal ethical egoist, however, may say, "I didn't mean that only my own happiness, of all the happiness actual and possible in the world, is intrinsically good. I meant that only my happiness is intrinsically good *for me,* yours is *for you,* and so on for everyone else." Once he has said this, of course, he is no longer a personal but an impersonal ethical egoist, since he has generalized his view to cover other people as well as himself. Let us see, then, what the *impersonal* ethical egoist might say in defense of this view.

2. Certainly the *impersonal ethical egoist* sounds more plausible than the personal ethical egoist. But let us examine exactly what the impersonal ethical egoist could mean by what he says. If he believes that happiness (or anything else) is intrinsically good, then what is being added by the phrases "for you" and "for me"? If happiness is good, isn't it good no matter who has it? The phrases "for you" and "for me" *are* meaningfully used in the context of *instrumental* value: for example, "Insulin is good for you, since you are a diabetic, but not for me since I am not." This statement merely means that the use of insulin is a means toward a certain end in your case but not in mine. "Good for" ordinarily means "good as a means toward." But what is the phrase to mean when what is discussed is not a means toward anything? It would appear that either happiness is intrinsically desirable or it is not; what sense would it make to say that it is good for one person and not for another, or that one happiness is good for one person and not for another, unless we are talking

about it as a means toward something beyond itself—and, consequently, *not* talking about it as an intrinsic good?

"But," the impersonal ethical egoist may object, "this is still not what I mean. What I mean is that the *statement* 'My happiness is good' is true for me but false for you."

What does the impersonal ethical egoist mean this time? How can one and the same statement be both true and false? If it is true that there is a table in this room, then it cannot (at the same time) be false that there is a table in this room; it is nonsense to say that the statement is true for me but false for you. (Something quite different may be meant by it, namely that I see a table in the room and you don't. This statement may be true, of course; but then if it is *true* that I see it and you don't, then it is not also *false* that I see it and you don't.) The same applies to statements about you and me: If it is true that milk is good for you (that is, conducive to your health), then it is not also false that milk is good for you. The statement that milk is good for you is either true or false, but it is not true for you and false for me. Or to put it in still another way, we have two statements:

Milk is conducive to your health.
Milk is not conducive to my health.

If both statements are true (as they might be, for example, if I am allergic to milk), then they are true, not *for* you or me or anyone else but simply true, period. And the same holds if one or both of them is false. When you feel inclined to say that a statement is true for you but false for me, what you have on your hands is *two* statements which you have not distinguished from each other. Thus, you may be inclined to say that the statement "Oysters taste good" is a true statement for you (since you like oysters) and false for me (since I don't like oysters). The truth is that there are *two* statements, one that you like oysters (which is true) and the other that I like oysters (which is false). But the true one is not true just for you, or the false one false for me; the first statement is simply true, and the second one simply false. One is true and the other false even when (as in this example) the statements are *about* you or me. Statements *about* you are not true just *for* you (indeed, what would it mean to say this?). If a statement about you is true (such as that you like oysters), then it is not true for you or for me or for anyone else, but true, period.[1]

Nevertheless, our impersonal ethical egoist may once again absolve himself from our charges against him. He may say, "I didn't really mean to talk about 'good for you' and 'good for me' as if I were talking about intrinsic goods, where that language has no place. Nor did I mean that one and the same statement can be both true and false at the same time, true for one person but false for another. What I really meant was something different. What I should have said is that I should pursue *my* happiness exclusively, and that you should pursue *your* happiness exclusively, and so on for every one else in the world. Putting it that way, I do not have to say anything like 'to you' or 'to me.'"

Very well; at last we have the impersonal ethical egoist's claim without the confusing language. What can we say about this claim? How could the impersonal ethical egoist defend it? He can give the obvious defense at once: "For each person to pursue his own interest exclusively is the best policy because everyone will be happier that way. The world would be a better place to live in if people interfered less with

one another. True, to follow this principle would mean sacrificing some desired things which we get through cooperation, but the sacrifice would be more than made up for by the fact that our lives would not be interfered with by others except when we wanted them to be. Because you would not help me when I was in trouble, I might be inconvenienced, but then neither would I have to help you when you were in a jam. In short, considering it from all angles, the world would be a happier place if each person were left free to pursue his own interest and ignored those of everyone else. Accordingly, that state of affairs is what I am recommending in my egoistic theory."

Here at last we have a possible, and a seemingly quite plausible, position. It does, however, present us with an *empirical claim*—the claim that there would be more happiness in the world if people all pursued their own interests and ignored those of others; and this claim would have to be defended. It is a claim in favor of a completely laissez-faire policy, a universal "rugged individualism." But is it true that if each of us pursued a policy of "splendid isolation" with regard to the interests of other people, we would all be happier? We would gain certain advantages (freedom from interference), but would these advantages be worth the cost? In the hunting-and-fishing stage of man's development, such a view might have been plausible enough; when the land was sparsely settled and I had my hunting domain and you had yours and there was plenty of room and plenty of game for both of us, a policy of mutual noninterference may have been the most

1. For further discussion of this point, see John Hospers, *Introduction to Philosophical Analysis* (Englewood Cliffs, N.J.: Prentice-Hall, 1953), pp. 125–26.

conducive to happiness—at least it would have avoided friction, though it would certainly have caused loneliness. But even if we ignore the need for human companionship and family life, such a policy would produce the maximum happiness only in circumstances where each person could afford to be relatively *independent* of all the others. Such a policy would be disastrous in a complex society such as ours in which each unit is *interdependent* with all the rest. Today people's fates are so tied up with one another—because we are crowded together, because we want things achievable only by cooperation such as industry, medicine, quick transportation, food supply,—that a policy of complete independence (each person making and supplying the foods and clothes he needs for himself) would result in total anarchy. The number of people that exists on this planet today could not possibly continue to exist if everyone were completely independent. John Donne's statement "no man is an island" is far more true today than when he wrote it. More idiomatically, we might say of today's world, "if we don't hang together, we'll all hang separately.". . .

Whatever might be said about the intrinsic value of complete independence, the important fact here is that the person who argues the position just outlined is no egoist at all. Consider: What reason does the impersonal ethical egoist give for his position? Is it an egoistic reason? Not at all: "The world would contain more happiness if people did so and so," he says. But then he is saying that happiness is a good thing, not just his own but the world's. His reasoning is not egoistic but . . . utilitarian; he is, however, a utilitarian with a peculiar twist, for though he shares the utilitarian view that universal happiness is good, he holds (unlike most utilitarians) that the *means* toward universal happiness is the pursuit of one's own interests exclusively. He is egoistic only about the means; about the end toward which exclusive self-interest is a means he is not egoistic but universalistic. Our impersonal ethical egoist, in trying to defend his position plausibly, has deserted his egoism in the process.

10

BRIAN MEDLIN
Ethical Egoism Is Inconsistent

BRIAN MEDLIN is professor of philosophy at Flinders University in Australia.

I believe that it is now pretty generally accepted by professional philosophers

From Brian Medlin, "Ultimate Principles and Ethical Egoism," *Australasian Journal of Philosophy*, vol. 35 (1957), pp. 111–118. Reprinted by permission. This article is reprinted unabridged.

that ultimate ethical principles must be arbitrary. One cannot derive conclusions about what should be merely from accounts of what is the case; one cannot decide how people ought to behave merely from one's knowledge of how they do behave. To arrive at a conclusion in ethics one must have at least one ethical premiss. This premiss, if it be in turn a conclusion, must be the conclusion of an argument containing at least one ethical premiss. And so we can go back, indefinitely but not for ever. Sooner or later, we must come to at least one ethical premiss which is not deduced but baldly asserted. Here we must be a-rational; neither rational nor irrational, for here there is no room for reason even to go wrong.

But the triumph of Hume in ethics has been a limited one. What appears quite neutral to a handful of specialists appears quite monstrous to the majority of decent intelligent men. At any rate, it has been my experience that people who are normally rational resist the above account of the logic of moral language, not by argument—for that can't be done—but by tooth and nail. And they resist from the best motives. They see the philosopher wantonly unravelling the whole fabric of morality. If our ultimate principles are arbitrary, they say, if those principles came out of thin air, then anyone can hold any principle he pleases. Unless moral assertions are statements of fact about the world and either true or false, we can't claim that any man is wrong, whatever his principles may be, whatever his behaviour. We have to surrender the luxury of calling one another scoundrels. That this anxiety flourishes because its roots are in confusion is evident when we consider that we don't call people scoundrels, anyhow, for being mistaken about their facts. Fools, perhaps, but that's another matter. Nevertheless, it doesn't become us to be high-up. The layman's uneasiness, however irrational it may be, is very natural and he must be reassured.

People cling to objectivist theories of morality from moral motives. It's a very queer thing that by doing so they often thwart their own purposes. There are evil opinions abroad, as anyone who walks abroad knows. The one we meet with most often, whether in pub or parlour, is the doctrine that everyone should look after himself. However refreshing he may find it after the high-minded pomposities of this morning's editorial, the good fellow knows this doctrine is wrong and he wants to knock it down. But while he believes that moral language is used to make statements either true or false, the best he can do is to claim that what the egoist says is false. Unfortunately, the egoist can claim that it's true. And since the supposed fact in question between them is not a publicly ascertainable one, their disagreement can never be resolved. And it is here that even good fellows waver, when they find they have no refutation available. The egoist's word seems as reliable as their own. Some begin half to believe that perhaps it is possible to supply an egoistic basis for conventional morality, some that it may be impossible to supply any other basis. I'm not going to try to prop up our conventional morality, which I fear to be a task beyond my strength, but in what follows I do want to refute the doctrine of ethical egoism. I want to resolve this disagreement by showing that what the egoist says is inconsistent. It is true that there are moral disagreements which can never be resolved, but this isn't one of them. The proper objection to the man who says 'Everyone should look after his own interests regardless of the interests of others' is not that he isn't speaking the truth, but simply that he isn't speaking.

We should first make two distinctions. This done, ethical egoism will lose much of its plausibility.

1. UNIVERSAL AND INDIVIDUAL EGOISM

Universal egoism maintains that everyone (including the speaker) ought to look after his own interests and to disregard those of other people except in so far as their interests contribute towards his own.

Individual egoism is the attitude that the egoist is going to look after himself and no one else. The egoist cannot promulgate that he is going to look after himself. He can't even preach that he *should* look after himself and preach this alone. When he tries to convince me that he should look after himself, he is attempting so to dispose me that I shall approve when he drinks my beer and steals Tom's wife. I cannot approve of his looking after himself and himself alone without so far approving of his achieving his happiness, regardless of the happiness of myself and others. So that when he sets out to persuade me that he should look after himself regardless of others, he must also set out to persuade me that I should look after him regardless of myself and others. Very small chance he has! And if the individual egoist cannot promulgate his doctrine without enlarging it, what he has is no doctrine at all.

A person enjoying such an attitude may believe that other people are fools not to look after themselves. Yet he himself would be a fool to tell them so. If he did tell them, though, he wouldn't consider that he was giving them *moral* advice. Persuasion to the effect that one should ignore the claims of morality because morality doesn't pay, to the effect that one has insufficient selfish motive and, therefore, insufficient motive for moral behaviour is not moral persuasion. For this reason I doubt that we should call the individual egoist's attitude an ethical one. And I don't doubt this in the way someone may doubt whether to call the ethical standards of Satan "ethical" standards. A malign morality is none the less a morality for being malign. But the attitude we're considering is one of mere contempt for all moral considerations whatsoever. An indifference to morals may be wicked, but it is not a perverse morality. So far as I am aware, most egoists imagine that they are putting forward a doctrine in ethics, though there may be a few who are prepared to proclaim themselves individual egoists. If the good fellow wants to know how he should justify conventional morality to an individual egoist, the answer is that he shouldn't and can't. Buy your car elsewhere, blackguard him whenever you meet, and let it go at that.

2. CATEGORICAL AND HYPO-THETICAL EGOISM

Categorical egoism is the doctrine that we all ought to observe our own interests, *because that is what we ought to do.* For the categorical egoist the egoistic dogma is the ultimate principle in ethics.

The hypothetical egoist, on the other hand, maintains that we all ought to observe our own interests, because . . . . . If we want such and such an end, we must do so and so (look after ourselves). The hypothetical egoist is not a real egoist at all. He is very likely an unwitting utilitarian who believes mistakenly that the general happiness will be increased if each man looks wisely to his own. Of course, a man may believe that egoism is enjoined on us by God and he may therefore promulgate the doctrine and observe it in his conduct, not in the hope of achieving thereby a remote end, but simply in order to obey God. But neither is *he* a real egoist. He believes, ultimately, that we should obey God, even should God command us to altruism.

An ethical egoist will have to maintain the doctrine in both its universal and categorical forms. Should he retreat to hypothetical egoism he is no longer an egoist. Should he retreat to individual egoism his doctrine, while logically impregnable, is no longer ethical, no longer even a doctrine. He may wish to quarrel with this and if so, I submit peacefully. Let him call himself what he will, it makes no difference. I'm a philosopher, not a rat-catcher, and I don't see it as my job to dig vermin out of such burrows as individual egoism.

Obviously something strange goes on as soon as the ethical egoist tries to promulgate his doctrine. What is he doing when he urges upon his audience that they should each observe his own interests and those interests alone? Is he not acting contrary to the egoistic principle? It cannot be to his advantage to convince them, for seizing always their own advantage they will impair his. Surely if he does believe what he says, he should try to persuade them otherwise. Not perhaps that they should devote themselves to his interests, for they'd hardly swallow that; but that everyone should devote himself to the service of others. But is not to believe that someone should act in a certain way to try to persuade him to do so? Of course, we don't always try to persuade people to act as we think they should act. We may be lazy, for instance. But in so far as we believe that Tom should do so and so, we have a tendency to induce him to do so and so. Does it make sense to say: "Of course you should do this, but for goodness' sake don't"? Only where we mean: "You should do this for

certain reasons, but here are even more persuasive reasons for not doing it." If the egoist believes ultimately that others should mind themselves alone, then, he must persuade them accordingly. If he doesn't persuade them, he is no universal egoist. It certainly makes sense to say: "I know very well that Tom should act in such and such a way. But I know also that it's not to my advantage that he should so act. So I'd better dissuade him from it." And this is just what the egoist must say, if he is to consider his own advantage and disregard everyone else's. That is, he must behave as an individual egoist, if he is to be an egoist at all.

He may want to make two kinds of objection here:

1. That it will not be to his disadvantage to promulgate the doctrine, provided that his audience fully understand what is to their ultimate advantage. This objection can be developed in a number of ways, but I think that it will always be possible to push the egoist into either individual or hypothetical egoism.

2. That it is to the egoist's advantage to preach the doctrine if the pleasure he gets out of doing this more than pays for the injuries he must endure at the hands of his converts. It is hard to believe that many people would be satisfied with a doctrine which they could only consistently promulgate in very special circumstances. Besides, this looks suspiciously like individual egoism in disguise.

I shall say no more on these two points because I want to advance a further criticism which seems to me at once fatal and irrefutable.

Now it is time to show the anxious

layman that we have means of dealing with ethical egoism which are denied him; and denied him by just that objectivism which he thinks essential to morality. For the very fact that our ultimate principles must be arbitrary means they can't be anything we please. Just because they come out of thin air they can't come out of hot air. Because these principles are not propositions about matters of fact and cannot be deduced from propositions about matters of fact, they must be the fruit of our own attitudes. We assert them largely to modify the attitudes of our fellows but by asserting them we express our own desires and purposes. This means that we cannot use moral language cavalierly. Evidently, we cannot say something like 'All human desires and purposes are bad.' This would be to express our own desires and purposes, thereby committing a kind of absurdity. Nor, I shall argue, can we say 'Everyone should observe his own interests regardless of the interests of others.'

Remembering that the principle is meant to be both universal and categorical, let us ask what kind of attitude the egoist is expressing. Wouldn't that attitude be equally well expressed by the conjunction of an infinite number of avowals thus?—

I want myself to come out on top	and	I don't care about Tom, Dick, Harry . . .
and		and
I want Tom to come out on top	and	I don't care about myself, Dick, Harry . . .
and		and
I want Dick to come out on top	and	I don't care about myself, Tom, Harry . . .
and		and
I want Harry to come out on top	and	I don't care about myself, Dick, Tom . . .
etc.		etc.

From this analysis it is obvious that the principle expressing such an attitude must be inconsistent.

But now the egoist may claim that he hasn't been properly understood. When he says 'Everyone should look after himself and himself alone' he means 'Let each man do what he wants regardless of what anyone else wants.' The egoist may claim that what he values is merely that he and Tom and Dick and Harry should each do what he wants and not care about what anyone else may want and that this doesn't involve his principle in any inconsistency. Nor need it. But even if it doesn't, he's no better off. Just what does he value? Is it the well-being of himself, Tom, Dick and Harry or merely their going on in a certain way regardless of whether or not this is going to promote their well-being? When he urges Tom, say, to do what he wants, is he appealing to Tom's self-interest? If so, his attitude can be expressed thus:

I want myself to be happy	and	I want myself not to care about Tom, Dick, Harry . . .
and		
I want Tom to be happy		

We need go no further to see that the principle expressing such an attitude must be inconsistent. I have made this kind of move already. What concerns me now is the alternative position the egoist must take up to be safe from it. If the egoist values merely that people should go on in a certain way, regardless of whether or not this is going to promote their well-being, then he is not appealing to the self-interest of his audience when he urges them to regard their own interests. If Tom has any regard for himself at all, the egoist's blandishments will leave him cold. Further, the egoist doesn't even have his own interest in mind when he says that, like everyone else, he should look after himself. A funny kind of egoism this turns out to be.

Perhaps now, claiming that he is indeed appealing to the self-interest of his audience, the egoist may attempt to counter the objection of the previous paragraph. He may move into "Let each man do what he wants and let each man disregard what others want when their desires clash with his own." Now his attitude may be expressed thus:

I want everyone to be happy   and   I want everyone to disregard the happiness of others when their happiness clashes with his own.

The egoist may claim justly that a man can have such an attitude and also that in a certain kind of world such a man could get what he wanted. Our objection to the egoist has been that his desires are incompatible. And this is still so. If he and Tom and Dick and Harry did go on as he recommends by saying 'Let each man disregard the happiness of others, when their happiness conflicts with his own,' then assuredly they'd all be completely miserable. Yet he wants them to be happy. He is attempting to counter this by saying that it is merely a fact about the world that they'd make one another miserable by going on as he

recommends. The world could conceivably have been different. For this reason, he says, this principle is not inconsistent. This argument may not seem very compelling, but I advance it on the egoist's behalf because I'm interested in the reply to it. For now we don't even need to tell him that the world isn't in fact like that. (What it's like makes no difference.) Now we can point out to him that he is arguing not as an egoist but as a utilitarian. He has slipped into hypothetical egoism to save his principle from inconsistency. If the world were such that we always made ourselves and others happy by doing one another down, then we could find good utilitarian reasons for urging that we should do one another down.

If, then, he is to save his principle, the egoist must do one of two things. He must give up the claim that he is appealing to the self-interest of his audience, that he has even his own interest in mind. Or he must admit that, although 'I want everyone to be happy' refers to ends, nevertheless 'I want everyone to disregard the happiness of others when their happiness conflicts with his own' can refer only to means. That is, his so-called ultimate principle is really compounded of a principle and a moral rule subordinate to that principle. That is, he is really a utilitarian who is urging everyone to go on in a certain way so that everyone may be happy. A utilitarian, what's more, who is ludicrously mistaken about the nature of the world. Things being as they are, his moral rule is a very bad one. Things being as they are, it can only be deduced from his principle by means of an empirical premiss which is manifestly false. Good fellows don't need to fear him. They may rest easy that the world is and must be on their side and the best thing they can do is be good.

It may be worth pointing out that

objections similar to those I have brought against the egoist can be made to the altruist. The man who holds that the principle 'Let everyone observe the interests of others' is both universal and categorical can be compelled to choose between two alternatives, equally repugnant. He must give up the claim that he is concerned for the well-being of himself and others. Or he must admit that, though 'I want everyone to be happy' refers to ends, nevertheless 'I want everyone to disregard his own happiness when it conflicts with the happiness of others' can refer only to means.

I have said from time to time that the egoistic principle is inconsistent. I have not said it is contradictory. This for the reason that we can, without contradiction, express inconsistent desires and purposes. To do so is not to say anything like 'Goliath was ten feet tall and not ten feet tall'. Don't we all want to eat our cake and have it too? And when we say we do we aren't asserting a contradiction. We are not asserting a contradiction whether we be making an avowal of our attitudes or stating a fact about them. We all have conflicting motives. As a utilitarian exuding benevolence I want the man who mows my landlord's grass to be happy, but as a slug-a-bed I should like to see him scourged. None of this, however, can do the egoist any good. For we assert our ultimate principles not only to express our own attitudes but also to induce similar attitudes in others, to dispose them to conduct themselves as we wish. In so far as their desires conflict, people don't know what to do. And, therefore, no expression of incompatible desires can ever serve for an ultimate principle of human conduct.

11

KURT BAIER
Self-Interest Is Not the Moral Point of View

KURT BAIER is professor of philosophy at the University of Pittsburgh. He is the author of *The Moral Point of View* (1958).

Throughout the history of philosophy, by far the most popular candidate for the position of the moral point of view has been self-interest. There are obvious parallels between these two standpoints. Both aim at the good. Both are rational. Both involve deliberation,

Reprinted from Kurt Baier: *The Moral Point of View.* © 1958 by Cornell University. Used by permission of Cornell University Press.

the surveying and weighing of reasons. The adoption of either yields statements containing the word 'ought.' Both involve the notion of self-mastery and control over the desires. It is, moreover, plausible to hold that a person could not have a reason for doing anything whatsoever unless his behavior was designed to promote his own good. Hence, if morality is to have the support of reason, moral reasons must be self-interested, hence the point of view of morality and self-interest must be the same. On the other hand, it seems equally obvious that morality and self-interest are very frequently opposed. Morality often requires us to refrain from doing what self-interest recommends or to do what self-interest forbids. Hence morality and self-interest cannot be the same points of view.

Can we save the doctrine that the moral point of view is that of self-interest? One way of circumventing the difficulty just mentioned is to draw a distinction between two senses of 'self-interest,' shortsighted and enlightened. The shortsighted egoist always follows his short-range interest without taking into consideration how this will affect others and how their reactions will affect him. The enlightened egoist, on the other hand, knows that he cannot get the most out of life unless he pays attention to the needs of others on whose good will he depends. On this view, the standpoint of (immoral) egoism differs from that of morality in that it fails to consider the interests of others even when this costs little or nothing or when the long-range benefits to oneself are likely to be greater than the short-range sacrifices.

This view can be made more plausible still if we distinguish between those egoists who consider each course of action on its own merits and those who, for convenience, adopt certain rules of thumb which they have found will promote their long-range interest. Slogans such as 'Honesty is the best policy,' 'Give to charity rather than to the Department of Internal Revenue,' 'Always give a penny to a beggar when you are likely to be watched by your acquaintances,' 'Treat your servants

kindly and they will work for you like slaves,' 'Never be arrogant to anyone—you may need his services one day,' are maxims of this sort. They embody the "wisdom" of a given society. The enlightened long-range egoist may adopt these as rules of thumb, that is, as *prima-facie* maxims, as rules which he will observe unless he has good evidence that departing from them will pay him better than abiding by them. It is obvious that the rules of behavior adopted by the enlightened egoist will be very similar to those of a man who rigidly follows our own moral code.

Sidgwick appears to believe that egoism is one of the legitimate "methods of ethics," although he himself rejects it on the basis of an "intuition" that it is false. He supports the legitimacy of egoism by the argument that everyone could consistently adopt the egoistic point of view. "I quite admit that when the painful necessity comes for another man to choose between his own happiness and the general happiness, he must as a reasonable being prefer his own, i.e. it is right for him to do this on my principle."[1] The consistent enlightened egoist satisfies the categorical imperative, or at least one version of it, 'Act only on that maxim whereby thou canst at the same time will that it should become a universal law.'

However, no "intuition" is required to see that this is not the point of view of morality, even though it can be universally adopted without self-contradiction. In the first place, a consistent egoist adopts for all occasions the principle 'everyone for himself' which we allow (at most) only in conditions of chaos, when the normal moral order

1. Henry Sidgwick, *The Methods of Ethics*, 7th ed. (London: Macmillan and Co., 1907), pref. to the 6th ed., p. xvii.

breaks down. Its adoption marks the return to the law of the jungle, the state of nature, in which the "softer," "more chivalrous" ways of morality have no place.

This point can be made more strictly. It can be shown that those who adopt consistent egoism cannot make moral judgments. Moral talk is impossible for consistent egoists. But this amounts to a *reductio ad absurdum* of consistent egoism.

Let B and K be candidates for the presidency of a certain country and let it be granted that it is in the interest of either to be elected, but that only one can succeed. It would then be in the interest of B but against the interest of K if B were elected, and vice versa, and therefore in the interest of B but against the interest of K if K were liquidated, and vice versa. But from this it would follow that B ought to liquidate K, that it is wrong for B not to do so, that B has not "done his duty" until he has liquidated K; and vice versa. Similarly K, knowing that his own liquidation is in the interest of B and therefore anticipating B's attempts to secure it, ought to take steps to foil B's endeavors. It would be wrong for him not to do so. He would "not have done his duty" until he had made sure of stopping B. It follows that if K prevents B from liquidating him, his act must be said to be both wrong and not wrong—wrong because it is the prevention of what B ought to do, his duty, and wrong for B not to do it; not wrong because it is what K ought to do, his duty, and wrong for K not to do it. But one and the same act (logically) cannot be both morally wrong and not morally wrong. Hence in cases like these morality does not apply.

This is obviously absurd. For morality is designed to apply in just such cases, namely, those where interests conflict. But if the point of view of morality were that of self-interest, then there could *never* be moral solutions of conflicts of interest. However, when there are conflicts of interest, we always look for a "higher" point of view, one from which such conflicts can be settled. Consistent egoism makes everyone's private interest the "highest court of appeal." But by 'the moral point of view' we *mean* a point of view which is a court of appeal for conflicts of interest. Hence it cannot (logically) be identical with the point of view of self-interest. Sidgwick is, therefore, wrong in thinking that consistent egoism is one of the "legitimate methods of ethics." He is wrong in thinking that an "intuition" is required to see that it is not the correct moral point of view. That it is not can be seen in the same way in which we can "see" that the Court of Petty Sessions is not the Supreme Court.

12

JOHN HOSPERS
Reply to Medlin and Baier

From John Hospers, "Baier and Medlin on Ethical Egoism," *Philosophical Studies*, vol. 12 (1961), pp. 10–16. Reprinted by permission of the author. This article is reprinted unabridged.

In his excellent book *The Moral Point of View*, Professor Kurt Baier attempts to refute ethical egoism—the doctrine that my sole duty is to promote my own interests exclusively—in the following way:

Let B and K be candidates for the presidency of a certain country and let it be granted that it is in the interest of either to be elected, but that only one can succeed. It would then be in the interest of B but against the interest of K if B were elected, and vice versa, and therefore in the interest of B but against the interest of K if K were liquidated, and vice versa. But from this it would follow that B ought to liquidate K, that it is wrong for B not to do so, that B has not 'done his duty' until he has liquidated K; and vice versa. Similarly K, knowing that his own liquidation is in the interest of B and therefore anticipating B's attempts to secure it, ought to take steps to foil B's endeavors. It would be wrong for him not to do so. He would 'not have done his duty' until he had made sure of stopping B. It follows that if K prevents B from liquidating him, his act must be said to be both wrong and not wrong—wrong because it is the prevention of what B ought to do, his duty, and wrong for B not to do it; not wrong because it is what K ought to do, his duty, and wrong for K not to do it. But one and the same act (logically) cannot be both morally wrong and not morally wrong. . . .
This is obviously absurd. For morality is designed to apply in just such cases, namely, those where interests conflict. But if the point of view of morality were that of self-interest, then there could never be moral solutions of conflicts of interest.[1]

We are to assume at the outset that killing K not only seems to be, but really *is* to B's interest and that killing B really *is* to K's interest. (If it were to the interest of each to work out a compromise, then no problem would arise.) Operating on this assumption, what can be said of Professor Baier's one-shot refutation of egoism? His argument can be schematized in the following way:

1. Every adequate ethical theory must be able to provide solutions for conflicts of interest.

2. Ethical egoism is unable to provide solutions for conflicts of interest.

3. Therefore, ethical egoism is not an adequate ethical theory.

So much for the argument for the inadequacy of ethical egoism. But his criticism goes even further:

4. Any view which is guilty of self-contradiction is thereby refuted.

5. Ethical egoism is guilty of self-contradiction.

6. Therefore, ethical egoism is refuted.

We may examine the second argument first, since if a theory is guilty of self-contradiction no further refutation of it is necessary.
Let it be admitted that to say that one and the same act is both right and wrong is to be guilty of a self-contradiction, since the proposition that it is wrong entails that it is not right, and an act cannot be both right and not right. (I shall waive any discussion of a point whose truth is presupposed in Baier's argument, namely that rightness and wrongness are properties. I shall also waive discussion of the possibility that even if they are properties they are to-you and to-me properties, for example, something can be interesting to you and not interesting to me, and rightness might be like interestingness.)
We may admit, then, at least for purposes of the argument, that to say that Brutus killing Caesar was both right and wrong involves a contradiction. But the case presented by Professor Baier is not that of one and the same act being both right and wrong. It is a case of *two* acts, one by B and the other by K. They are two acts of the

1. *The Moral Point of View* (Ithaca, N.Y.: Cornell University Press, 1958), pp. 189–90.

same *kind*, namely attempted murder (or the attempt to foil the murder-attempt of the other), but there is no contradiction in two such acts being attempted or in both being right. It might well be B's duty to try to dispose of K, and K's duty to try to dispose of B. Since there are two acts here, one by B and one by K, the situation of one and the same act being both right and wrong does not arise, and no contradiction arises either.

So much for the argument concerning contradiction. But the inadequacy argument remains, and it seems much more plausible. It is true that we usually expect an ethical theory to be able to settle conflicts of interest; for example, if husband and wife both want custody of the children, we expect the ethical theory to tell us (in conjunction, of course, with empirical premises) which one's wish should be granted; every judge in a courtroom must make such decisions. The judge in arbitrating such a case could not use ethical egoism as a way of settling it, for if it is in the interest of both husband and wife to have the same thing and they can't both have it, he will *have* to decide against the interest of one of them; and egoism, which tells each person to follow his own interest exclusively, can provide no basis for settling the dispute. This does seem to be a very serious criticism.

What would the egoist reply to such a charge? I must first distinguish the *personal* egoist from the *impersonal* egoist. The personal egoist is one who says that *his* sole duty is to promote his own interest exclusively, but makes no pronouncement about what other people should do. (Some would not consider this an ethical theory at all, since it does not fulfill the criterion of generality. And if the theory is restated so as not to talk about duties at all—not "It is my duty to promote my own interest exclusively" but "*I'm going* to promote my

own interest exclusively," which is the kind of thing that most practicing egoists say—then of course there is no ethical theory at all, but only a prediction or expression of determination with regard to one's future behavior.) The impersonal egoist is one who says that the duty of *each and every person* (including himself) is to pursue his own interest exclusively.

How will the egoist react to Baier's inadequacy argument? The personal egoist will not be disturbed at all. According to him, his one duty is to pursue exclusively his own interest; so if he happens to be B he will try to kill K, and if he is K he will try to kill B (and foil K's attempts to kill him); and if he is neither B nor K he will not concern himself with the conflict of interest one way or the other. Of course if there is something in it for him, he will: if he stands to gain a fortune if K wins, then he will do what he can to assist K's victory in order to gain the fortune. But otherwise he will ignore the matter. "But doesn't an ethical theory have to have a means of deciding what to do or say in cases of conflict of interest? If you had to advise B or K, what would you say?" The answer is, of course, that if there is nothing in it for him the personal egoist will not bother to advise either party or to aid either cause. If asked for advice on the matter, he would probably say, "Get lost, you bother me." (Nor would the personal egoist be likely to engage in philosophical discussion. It would hardly be to his interest to allow other people to plant in his minds the seeds of skepticism concerning his egoistic doctrine.)

So far, then, egoism has not been refuted. It has been shown to be inadequate *only if* you expect an ethical theory to arbitrate conflicts of interest. Thus, it *would* be insufficient for the judge in a divorce court. The judge has nothing to gain either way, but he has to decide on a matter of conflict of interest between husband and wife. If the judge were a personal egoist, his principle would simply be to follow *his own* interest; but this principle wouldn't help him at all in dealing with the case at hand. Here he needs instructions, not for promoting his own interest, but for settling cases of conflict of interest between *other* people.

And this, of course, the theory cannot provide; but the personal egoist doesn't mind this at all. He has no wish to arbitrate other people's conflicts of interest. He will gladly leave such activities to the "suckers."

What of the *impersonal* egoist? His view is that he should pursue his own interest exclusively, that B should pursue B's, that K should pursue K's, and so on for everyone else. What will he say in the case of B and K? He will advise K to try to win out over B by whatever means he can, and will advise B to try to win out over K by whatever means he can: in other words, to settle the thing by force or craft, and may the strongest or cleverest man win. Does his advice to B contradict his advice to K? Not at all; he is urging each one to try to gain victory over the other; this is not very different from telling each of the two competing teams to try and win the game. His view does not, of course, provide a *rational* means of settling the conflict of interest, but it does provide a means: it tells each party to try to emerge victorious, though of course only one of them *can* emerge victorious.

So far, there seems to be no difficulty for the impersonal egoist. But, as an impersonal egoist, he does have a stake in the general acceptance of his doctrine; for he does say of other people, not just himself, that each should pursue his own interest exclusively. If he sees B, he will urge B to try to win over K (even if he has nothing to gain personally by B's victory), and if he sees K, he will urge K to try to win over B. But there is, while no outright contradiction, a curious *tactical incongruity* in his view. For if the impersonal egoist advises others to pursue their own interest, might not this interfere with the promotion of *his own* interest, and yet is he not committed by his own doctrine to pursuing his own interest exclusively? If he advises B and K, but neither B nor K is a threat to him, there is no problem; but if I advise my business competitor to pursue his own interest with a vengeance, may he not follow my advice and pursue his own interest so whole-heartedly that he forces me out of business? For the sake of *my own* interest, then, I may be well advised to keep my egoistic doctrine to myself, lest others use it against me.

An impersonal egoist, therefore, may simply prefer to keep his own counsel and not advise others at all. In this case, he escapes the difficulty just as the personal egoist did. He will pursue his own interest regardless of who else opposes it; and while he does, as an impersonal egoist, advise others to pursue *their* own interests, he will do this only when doing it does not imperil *his* interest.

Thus, *if* you are an impersonal egoist, and *if* as an impersonal egoist you have a stake in advising others—and only then—you will feel a conflict between the promotion of your egoistic doctrine and the promotion of your own interests, which will be damaged if others pursue their interests at the expense of yours. But this hardly *refutes* the impersonal egoist's doctrine; it concerns only a tactical matter of when to publicize it.

But now another objection to ethical egoism presents itself. Suppose you are an impersonal egoist, and are suggesting courses of action to your acquaintances. Acquaintance A asks you what to do, and you say to him, "Pursue your own interest exclusively, and if B tries to get the better of you, cut him down. Even if you could save B's life by lifting a finger, there is no reason for you to do so as long as it doesn't promote your interest." Later on, B asks you what you think *he* should do. So you say to him, "Pursue your own interest exclusively, and if A tries to get the better of you, cut him down. Even if you could save A's life by lifting a finger, there is no reason for you to do so as long as it doesn't promote your interest." And you say similar things to your other acquaintances.

Suppose now, that an onlooker heard you say all these things. He might wonder (with good reason) exactly what you were advising—what the general drift of your advice was. You tell A to do what is to his interest and ignore B, so our onlooker thinks you are a friend of A's and an enemy of B's. But then you tell B to do what is to his interest and ignore A, and our onlooker now concludes that you are a friend of B and an enemy of A. And in fact what are you anyway? It sounds to the onlooker as if you are pathologically addicted to changing your mind. Perhaps, like some people, you are so impressed by whoever you are with at the moment that you forget all about the interests of those who aren't right there before you. This might explain the sudden shift in attitude.

But the curious thing is that the egoist doesn't consider this a shift in attitude at all, but a consistent expression of one attitude, the "impersonal egoistic" attitude. But that is just the point of the objection. *Is* it a single consistent attitude? When you are in the presence of A, it is only A's interest that counts; but a moment later, when you are in the presence of B, it is only B's interest that counts. Isn't this very strange? Can the question of whose interests count really depend on whom you happen to be addressing or confronting at the moment?

The charge, in short, is that the impersonal egoist is guilty of issuing *inconsistent directives*. This charge is made, for example, by Dr. Brian Medlin.[2] According to Medlin, when the (impersonal) egoist is talking to himself he says "I want myself to come out on top, and I don't care about Tom, Dick, Harry . . ."; when he is talking to Tom he says (in effect), "I want Tom to come out on top and I don't care about myself, Dick, Harry . . ."; when he is talking to Dick he says, "I want Dick to come out on top, and I don't care about myself, Tom, Harry . . ."; and so on in a conjunction of an infinite number of avowals. "From this analysis," he concludes, "it is obvious that the principle expressing such an attitude must be inconsistent."[3] (The same conclusion follows if the egoist says to Tom, "You alone count," and to Dick, "You alone count," and so on.)

Now, if this is what the impersonal egoist really means to say, then of course what he says *is* inconsistent. But perhaps that is not what he means to say; at any rate, it is not what he *needs* to say. What else might he mean?

It might be suggested, first, that all the egoist wants to say is that if you tend to your interests (happiness, or welfare, or whatever) and I to my interests and Tom to Tom's interests, and so on, everyone will be happier (or have

2. "Ultimate Principles and Ethical Egoism," *Australasian Journal of Philosophy*, 35 (No. 2):111–18 (August 1957).

3. *Ibid.*, p. 115.

more welfare, etc.) than they would if they did not adopt such a completely laissez-faire policy with regard to one another's interests. But two things should be noted about this: (1) If the egoist says this, he is making an *empirical* claim—a claim that human beings will be happier pursuing a policy of splendid isolation with regard to each other than by behaving cooperatively, helping one another in time of need, and so on—and this empirical claim is very dubious indeed; it seems rather to be the case that the welfare of human beings is not independent but *inter*-dependent, and that "no man is an island." If each person pursued his own interest to the exclusion of others, there would be less happiness in the world, not more. But whatever may be said of this empirical claim, (2) when the egoist makes this claim he is no longer an egoist but a utilitarian; he is arguing that the general welfare (or the maximum total fulfillment of human interests) is what should be striven for, and that the best means of achieving it is by a policy of isolation. But in admitting that the general welfare is the end to be aimed at he is already forsaking his egoism.

Is there anything else, then, that the impersonal egoist can be alleged to mean? The charge against him is that his directives to different people are inconsistent with one another. He, Tom, Dick, and Harry cannot each be the *only* person who counts, or the only person he hopes will come out on top. Is not the egoist, if he abandons the utilitarian argument (above) and retreats back to his egoism, caught in the web of inconsistency? Is he not saying to Tom that he hopes Tom will come out on top (and by implication that Dick won't), and then the next moment saying to Dick that he hopes Dick will come out

on top (and by implication that Tom won't), and so on, thereby patting each one on the back before his face and poking him in the nose behind his back?

The egoist *need* not, I think, be guilty of such duplicity. What if he assembled Tom, Dick, Harry, and everyone else into his presence at the same moment? What would he say to them all together? He might say, "I *hope* that each of you comes out on top." But in that case, he *is* saying something self-contradictory, since of course each of them cannot come out on top—only one of them can. But he need not say this; suppose that instead he says, "I hope each of you *tries* to come out on top," or "Each of you should *try* to come out the victor." There is surely no inconsistency here. The hope he is expressing here is the kind of hope that the interested but impartial spectator expresses at a game. Perhaps the egoist likes to live life in a dangerous cutthroat manner, unwilling to help others in need but not desiring others to help him either. He wants life to be spicy and dangerous; to him the whole world is one vast egoistic game, and living life accordingly is the way to make it interesting and exciting. It may be that, if our egoist says this, his egoism is somewhat diluted from the stronger and earlier form of "I hope that you all win" or "Each of you alone counts"—but at least, in this latest formulation, he is not caught in an inconsistency.

Whether or not the egoist, then, is caught in an inconsistency depends on what, exactly, we take him to be saying. It should not be assumed that because the egoist in some formulations of his doctrine is guilty of inconsistency, he is therefore inconsistent in all of them.

Suggestions for Further Reading

Alasdair MacIntyre, "Egoism and Altruism," *The Encyclopedia of Philosophy*, ed. Paul Edwards (New York: Macmillan and The Free Press, 1967), vol. 2, pp. 462–466.

Michael Slote, "An Empirical Basis for Psychological Egoism," *The Journal of Philosophy*, vol. 61 (1964), pp. 530–537. [Reprinted in Joel Feinberg (ed.), *Reason and Responsibility*, third edition (Encino, Cal.: Dickenson, 1975).] Slote argues that if the psychological theories of Hull and Skinner turn out to be correct, then psychological egoism might be established as empirically true.

W. H. Baumer, "Indefensible Impersonal Egoism," *Philosophical Studies*, vol. 18 (1967), pp. 72–75. [Reprinted in Paul Taylor (ed.), *Problems of Moral Philosophy*, second edition (Encino, Cal.: Dickenson, 1972).] Baumer argues, against John Hospers, that ethical egoism *is* a logically inconsistent view.

Jesse Kalin, "On Ethical Egoism," *American Philosophical Quarterly Monograph Series, No. 1: Studies in Moral Philosophy* (1968), pp. 26–41. Kalin defends ethical egoism from some of the charges that have been brought against it.

Richmond Campbell, "A Short Refutation of Ethical Egoism," *Canadian Journal of Philosophy*, vol. 2 (1972), pp. 249–254. Campbell argues that ethical egoism must be rejected because it is incompatible with the principle that "ought" implies "can"—that is, that it can't be true that we *ought* to do something unless we *can* do it.

James Rachels, "Two Arguments Against Ethical Egoism," *Philosophia*, vol. 4 (1974), pp. 297–314. The two arguments are, first, that ethical egoism should be rejected because it is incompatible with the social-political ideal of human freedom; and second, that ethical egoism is simply a wicked view.

Robert G. Olson, *The Morality of Self-Interest* (New York: Harcourt, 1965). Olson defends the view that "the individual is most likely to contribute to social betterment by rationally pursuing his own best long-range interests."

Ayn Rand, "The Objectivist Ethics," *The Virtue of Selfishness* (New York: Signet Books, 1964), pp. 13–35. Ayn Rand is the best-known contemporary advocate of egoism in ethics. This article is a brief presentation of some of her leading ideas. More ambitious readers may want to tackle her very long and sometimes tedious—but often very stimulating—novel, *Atlas Shrugged*. For another presentation and defense of her view (or at least, a view very much like hers), see Nathaniel Branden, "Rational Egoism," *The Personalist*, vol. 51 (1970), pp. 196–211, 305–313. Most people who discuss Miss Rand's views are either so uncritically adulatory, or so blindly hostile, as to make the discussion unprofitable. But for a critical discussion which has neither of these faults, see Robert Nozick, "On the Randian Argument," *The Personalist*, vol. 52 (1971), pp. 282–304.

CHAPTER THREE

Utilitarianism

INTRODUCTION

When we begin to think in a general way about the nature of morality, it is natural to wonder whether there might be one great moral principle that sums up all our duties and obligations. Is there a single "supreme principle of morality" which we should always follow? We have already considered one principle that some people take to be such an ultimate moral rule, the principle of ethical egoism.

Jeremy Bentham proposed another principle which he called "the principle of utility." It says that, whenever we have a choice between alternative actions or social policies, we ought to choose that one that has the best overall consequences for everyone concerned. Or, as Bentham put it, the principle of utility "approves or disapproves of every action whatsoever, according to the tendency which it appears to have to augment or diminish the happiness of the party whose interest is in question: or, what is the same thing in other words, to promote or to oppose that happiness."

Bentham was trained in the law, and he thought of the principle of utility as a guide for legislators. The purpose of the law should be simply to promote the general welfare of all citizens, and *not* to enforce "divine commandments" or "natural moral law" or anything of that sort. Therefore, no type of activity should be prohibited by law unless it is harmful to people: Bentham objected to laws regulating the sexual behavior of "consenting adults," for example, on the grounds that such conduct is not harmful, and because such laws diminish rather than increase human happiness.[1]

Bentham was the leader of a group of philosophical radicals whose aim was to reform the laws and institutions of England along utilitarian lines. One of Bentham's followers was James Mill, the distinguished Scottish philosopher, historian, and economist. James Mill's son, John Stuart Mill, would become the leading advocate of utilitarian moral theory for the next generation, and so the Benthamite movement would continue unabated even after Bentham's death.

Classical utilitarianism—the sort advocated by Bentham and Mill—is characterized by three main features:

a. According to this theory, no action is right or wrong in itself. Actions are right or wrong only on account of their *consequences*. This means that actions such as lying, breaking your promises, and so forth, are only wrong because they have bad consequences, and not because there is anything intrinsically bad about lying or breaking promises. Therefore, right actions will always be actions that have the *best overall consequences*.

b. The goodness or badness of consequences is to be measured by the *happiness* or *unhappiness* that the action causes. Therefore, right actions will always be actions that bring about the *most happiness* or the *least unhappiness*.

1. For more on this point, see Mill, "The Limits to the Authority of the State Over the Individual," Devlin, "Mill on Liberty in Morals," and Dworkin, "Homosexuality, Pornography, and the Law," in chapter seven.

c. Unlike ethical egoism, which says that we need only be concerned about ourselves, utilitarianism says that *each individual's interests are equally as important as any other individual's interests.* Therefore, right actions will always be actions that produce the most happiness or the least unhappiness *for the largest number of people* (or, perhaps, for the largest number of sentient beings—Bentham urges us not to forget the interests of nonhuman animals).

At first glance utilitarianism seems obviously true. It is hard to think of any reason to object to it: How can we possibly quarrel with a theory which enjoins us to increase happiness and reduce suffering? Indeed, the main thrust of the theory seems almost platitudinous.

Yet utilitarianism is one of the most controversial ethical theories. Upon closer inspection it seems to have many faults. For example: Suppose we could increase the general happiness of a society, by a small but definite amount, if we enslave a small segment of the population. The slaves might be less happy than when they were free, but this would be more than compensated for by the increased happiness of the rest of the population. Most of us would consider such an arrangement grotesquely unjust, because we believe that a majority has no right to exploit a minority in this way. Yet, in these circumstances a utilitarian would find it difficult to avoid endorsing such an arrangement. This example shows how considerations of social utility apparently come into conflict with considerations of justice.

(It should be made clear that neither Bentham nor Mill, nor any other utilitarian with whom I am familiar, endorsed slavery. The argument that I have just outlined attempts to bring out an objectionable implication of their *theory*, not an implication of their personal moral views. It should always be kept in mind, when studying the writings of moral philosophers, that a person's moral theory can have implications of which he is not aware and which may conflict with his particular moral beliefs.)

There is another type of objection to utilitarianism: Suppose you have promised to do a certain act *A*. Now you notice that the results of doing *A* would be exactly the same as the results of doing a different act *B*—that is, each act would produce an equal amount of happiness. If so, then according to utilitarianism it doesn't matter which action you perform: There is no good reason why you should do *A* rather than *B*, since in each case the consequences are equally good. But in fact there *does* seem to be one good reason why you should do *A* and not *B*. That reason has nothing to do with the consequences of either act: It is, simply, that *you promised* to do *A*, and so you have an obligation to do it. Utilitarianism, with its emphasis exclusively on consequences, seems unable to account for such obligations.

W. D. Ross outlines several different objections to utilitarian moral theory, including the one connected with promising, in "Difficulties for Utilitarianism." Then in "A Non-Utilitarian Approach to Punishment," H. J. McCloskey focuses attention on the subject of criminal punishment and argues that utilitarianism leads to unacceptable results when applied in that area.

Some philosophers have tried to defend utilitarianism from these criticisms by suggesting that, rather than applying the principle of utility to individual actions, we should apply it to rules or principles of conduct. That is, we should adopt rules of conduct that tend to maximize happiness, and then follow those rules without trying to determine in every case whether each particular action will maximize happiness.

This approach is called *rule-utilitarianism*; it is in contrast with *act-utilitarianism* which says that the rightness or wrongness of each particular action is determined by its own individual set of consequences. In "Promising and Punishment," John Rawls considers whether rule-utilitarianism is any better than act-utilitarianism in accounting for the cases of promise-keeping and punishment.

The remaining selections in this chapter take up a variety of aspects of utilitarian moral theory. "Utilitarianism and the Wrongness of Killing" by Richard Henson considers whether classical utilitarianism can provide a satisfactory account of the ethics of killing; and in "War and Massacre," Thomas Nagel contrasts absolutist and utilitarian arguments concerning methods of warfare. The final reading in this chapter, "Famine, Affluence and Morality" by Peter Singer, argues on utilitarian grounds that citizens of affluent countries have a strict moral duty to contribute large portions of their incomes for famine relief. Here the vast difference between a utilitarian outlook and the type of egoistic ethics considered in chapter two is strikingly clear.

13

JEREMY BENTHAM
The Principle of Utility

JEREMY BENTHAM (1748–1832) was one of the most important British moral and legal philosophers of the modern period. *The Principles of Morals and Legisla-* *tion* (1789), from which the following selection is taken, is his best-known work.

OF THE PRINCIPLE OF UTILITY

I. Nature has placed mankind under the governance of two sovereign masters, *pain* and *pleasure*. It is for them alone to point out what we ought to do, as well as to determine what we shall do. On the one hand the standard of right and wrong, on the other the chain of causes and effects, are fastened to their throne. They govern us in all we do, in all we say, in all we think; every effort we can make to throw off our subjection, will serve but to demonstrate and confirm it. In words a man may pretend to abjure their empire: but in reality he will re-

Excerpted from Jeremy Bentham, *The Principles of Morals and Legislation* (1789).

main subject to it all the while. The *principle of utility*[1] recognizes the subjection, and assumes it for the foundation of that system, the object of which

1. To this denomination has of late been added, or substituted, the *greatest happiness* or *greatest felicity* principle: this for shortness, instead of saying at length *that principle* which states the greatest happiness of all those whose interest is in question, as being the right and proper, and only right and proper and universally desirable, end of human action: of human action in every situation, and in particular in that of a functionary or set of functionaries exercising the powers of government. The word *utility* does not so clearly point to the ideas of *pleasure* and *pain* as the words *happiness* and *felicity* do: nor does it lead us to the consideration of the *number*, of the interests affected; to the *number*, as being the circumstance, which contributes, in the largest

is to rear the fabric of felicity by the hands of reason and of law. Systems which attempt to question it, deal in sounds instead of sense, in caprice instead of reason, in darkness instead of light.

But enough of metaphor and declamation: it is not by such means that moral science is to be improved.

II. The principle of utility is the foundation of the present work; it will be proper therefore at the outset to give an explicit and determinate account of what is meant by it. By the principle of utility is meant that principle which approves or disapproves of every action whatsoever, according to the tendency which it appears to have to augment or diminish the happiness of the party whose interest is in question; or, what is the same thing in other words, to promote or to oppose that happiness. I say of every action whatsoever; and therefore not only of every action of a private individual, but of every measure of government.

III. By utility is meant that property in any object, whereby it tends to produce benefit, advantage, pleasure, good, or happiness, (all this in the present case comes to the same thing) or (what comes again to the same thing) to prevent the happening of mischief, pain, evil, or unhappiness to the party whose interest is considered: if that party be the community in general, then the happiness of the community: if a particular individual, then the happiness of that individual.

IV. The interest of the community is one of the most general expressions that can occur in the phraseology of morals: no wonder that the meaning of it is often lost. When it has a meaning, it is this. The community is a fictitious *body*, composed of the individual persons who are considered as constituting as it were its *members*. The interest of the community then is, what?—the sum of the interests of the several members who compose it.

V. It is in vain to talk of the interest of the community, without understanding what is the interest of the individual. A thing is said to promote the interest, or to be *for* the interest, of an individual, when it tends to add to the sum total of his pleasures: or, what comes to the same thing, to diminish the sum total of his pains.

VI. An action then may be said to be conformable to the principle of utility, or, for shortness' sake, to utility (meaning with respect to the community at large) when the tendency it has to augment the happiness of the community is greater than any it has to diminish it.

VII. A measure of government (which is but a particular kind of action, performed by a particular person or persons) may be said to be conformable to or dictated by the principle of utility, when in like manner the tendency which it has to augment the happiness of the community is greater than any which it has to diminish it.

VIII. When an action, or in particular a measure of government, is supposed by a man to be conformable to the principle of utility, it may be convenient, for the purposes of discourse, to imagine a kind of law or dictate, called a law or dictate of utility: and to speak of the action in question, as being conformable to such law or dictate.

IX. A man may be said to be a

---

proportion, to the formation of the standard here in question; the *standard of right and wrong*, by which alone the propriety of human conduct, in every situation, can with propriety be tried. This want of a sufficiently manifest connexion between the ideas of *happiness* and *pleasure* on the one hand, and the idea of *utility* on the other, I have every now and then found operating, and with but too much efficiency, as a bar to the acceptance, that might otherwise have been given, to this principle.

partizan of the principle of utility, when the approbation or disapprobation he annexes to any action, or to any measure, is determined by and proportioned to the tendency which he conceives it to have to augment or to diminish the happiness of the community: or in other words, to its conformity or unconformity to the laws or dictates of utility.

X. Of an action that is conformable to the principle of utility, one may always say either that it is one that ought to be done, or at least that it is not one that ought not to be done. One may say also, that it is right it should be done; at least that it is not wrong it should be done: that it is a right action; at least that it is not a wrong action. When thus interpreted, the words *ought*, and *right* and *wrong*, and others of that stamp, have a meaning: when otherwise, they have none.

XI. Has the rectitude of this principle been ever formally contested? It should seem that it had, by those who have not known what they have been meaning. Is it susceptible of any direct proof? It should seem not, for that which is used to prove everything else, cannot itself be proved; a chain of proofs must have their commencement somewhere. To give such proof is as impossible as it is needless.

XII. Not that there is or ever has been that human creature breathing, however stupid or perverse, who has not on many, perhaps on most occasions of his life, deferred to it. By the natural constitution of the human frame, on most occasions of their lives men in general embrace this principle, without thinking of it; if not for the ordering of their own actions, yet for the trying of their own actions, as well as of those of other men. There have been, at the same time, not many, perhaps, even of the most intelligent, who have been disposed to embrace it purely and without reserve. There are even few who have not taken some occasion or other to quarrel with it, either on account of their not understanding always how to apply it, or on account of some prejudice or other which they were afraid to examine into, or could not bear to part with. For such is the stuff that man is made of: in principle and in practice, in a right track and in a wrong one, the rarest of all human qualities is consistency.

XIII. When a man attempts to combat the principle of utility, it is with reason drawn, without his being aware of it, from that very principle itself.[2] His arguments, if they prove anything, prove not that the principle is *wrong*, but that, according to the applications he supposes to be made of it, it is *misapplied*. Is it possible for a man to move the earth? Yes; but he must first find out another earth to stand upon.

XIV. To disapprove the propriety of it by arguments is impossible; but, from the causes that have been mentioned, or from some confused or partial view of it, a man may happen to be disposed not to relish it. Where this is the case, if he thinks the settling of his opinions on such a subject worth the trouble, let him take the following steps, and at length, perhaps, he may come to reconcile himself to it.

1. Let him settle with himself, whether he would wish to discard this principle altogether; if so, let him consider what it is that all his reasonings (in matters of politics especially) can amount to?

2. If he would, let him settle with himself, whether he would judge and

2. "The principle of utility (I have heard it said) is a dangerous principle: it is dangerous on certain occasions to consult it." This is as much to say, what? that it is not consonant to utility, to consult utility: in short, that is is *not* consulting it, to consult it.

act without any principle, or whether there is any other he would judge and act by?

3. If there be, let him examine and satisfy himself whether the principle he thinks he has found is really any separate intelligible principle; or whether it be not a mere principle in words, a kind of phrase, which at bottom expresses neither more nor less than the mere averment of his own unfounded sentiments; that is, what in another person he might be apt to call caprice?

4. If he is inclined to think that his own approbation or disapprobation, annexed to the idea of an act, without any regard to its consequences, is a sufficient foundation for him to judge and act upon, let him ask himself whether his sentiment is to be a standard of right and wrong, with respect to every other man, or whether every man's sentiment has the same privilege of being a standard to itself?

5. In the first case, let him ask himself whether his principle is not despotical, and hostile to all the rest of the human race?

6. In the second case, whether it is not anarchical, and whether at this rate there are not as many different standards of right and wrong as there are men? and whether even to the same man, the same thing, which is right today, may not (without the least change in its nature) be wrong tomorrow? and whether the same thing is not right and wrong in the same place at the same time? and in either case, whether all argument is not at an end? and whether, when two men have said, "I like this," and "I don't like it," they can (upon such principle) have anything more to say?

7. If he should have said to himself, No: for that the sentiment which he proposes as a standard must be grounded on reflection, let him say on what particulars the reflection is to turn? if on particulars having relation to the utility of the act, then let him say whether this is not deserting his own principle, and borrowing assistance from that very one in opposition to which he sets it up: or if not on those particulars, on what other particulars?

8. If he should be for compounding the matter, and adopting his own principle in part, and the principle of utility in part, let him say how far he will adopt it?

9. When he has settled with himself where he will stop, then let him ask himself how he justifies to himself the adopting it so far? and why he will not adopt it any farther?

10. Admitting any other principle than the principle of utility to be a right principle, a principle that it is right for a man to pursue; admitting (what is not true) that the word *right* can have a meaning without reference to utility, let him say whether there is any such thing as a *motive* that a man can have to pursue the dictates of it: if there is, let him say what that motive is, and how it is to be distinguished from those which enforce the dictates of utility: if not, then lastly let him say what it is this other principle can be good for?

VALUE OF A LOT OF PLEASURE OR PAIN, HOW TO BE MEASURED

I. Pleasures then, and the avoidance of pains, are the *ends* which the legislator has in view: it behooves him therefore to understand their *value*. Pleasures and pains are the *instruments* he has to work with: it behooves him therefore to understand their force, which is again, in other words, their value.

II. To a person considered *by himself*, the value of a pleasure or pain considered *by itself*, will be greater or less, according to the four following circumstances.[3]

1. Its *intensity.*

2. Its *duration.*

3. Its *certainty* or *uncertainty.*

4. Its *propinquity* or *remoteness.*

III. These are the circumstances which are to be considered in estimating a pleasure or a pain considered each of them by itself. But when the value of any pleasure or pain is considered for the purpose of estimating the tendency of any *act* by which it is produced, there are two other circumstances to be taken into the account; these are,

5. Its *fecundity,* or the chance it has of being followed by sensations of the *same* kind: that is, pleasures, if it be a pleasure: pains, if it be a pain.

6. Its *purity,* or the chance it has of *not* being followed by sensations of the *opposite* kind: that is, pains, if it be a pleasure: pleasures, if it be a pain.

These two last, however, are in strictness scarcely to be deemed properties of the pleasures or the pain itself; they are not, therefore, in strictness to be taken into the account of the value of that pleasure or that pain. They are in strictness to be deemed properties only of the act, or other event, by which such pleasure or pain has been produced; and accordingly are only to be taken into the account of the tendency of such act or such event.

IV. To a *number* of persons, with reference to each of whom the value of a pleasure or a pain is considered, it will be greater or less, according to seven circumstances: to wit, the six preceding ones; *viz.*

1. Its *intensity.*

2. Its *duration.*

3. Its *certainty* or *uncertainty.*

4. Its *propinquity* or *remoteness.*

5. Its *fecundity.*

6. Its *purity.*

And one other; to wit:

7. Its *extent;* that is, the number of persons to whom it *extends;* or, (in other words) who are affected by it.

V. To take an exact account then of the general tendency of any act, by which the interests of a community are affected, proceed as follows. Begin with any one person of those whose interests seem most immediately to be affected by it: and take an account.

1. Of the value of each distinguishable *pleasure* which appears to be produced by it in the *first* instance.

2. Of the value of each *pain* which appears to be produced by it in the *first* instance.

3. Of the value of each pleasure which appears to be produced by it *after* the first. This constitutes the *fecundity* of the first *pleasure* and the *impurity* of the first *pain.*

4. Of the value of each *pain* which appears to be produced by it after the first. This constitutes the *fecundity* of the first *pain,* and the *impurity* of the first pleasure.

5. Sum up all the valued of all the *pleasures* on the one side, and those of

---

3. These circumstances have since been denominated *elements* or *dimensions* of *value* in a pleasure or a pain.

Not long after the publication of the first edition, the following memoriter verses were framed, in the view of lodging more effectually, in the memory, these points, on which the whole fabric of morals and legislation may be seen to rest:

Intense, long, certain, speedy, fruitful, pure
Such marks in *pleasures* and in *pains* endure.
Such pleasures seek, if *private* be thy end:
If it be *public,* wide let them *extend.*
Such *pains* avoid, whichever be thy view:
If pains *must* come, let them *extend* to few.

all the pains on the other. The balance, if it be on the side of pleasure, will give the *good* tendency of the act upon the whole, with respect to the interests of that *individual* person; if on the side of pain, the *bad* tendency of it upon the whole.

6. Take an account of the *number* of persons whose interests appear to be concerned; and repeat the above process with respect to each. *Sum up* the numbers expressive of the degrees of *good* tendency, which the act has, with respect to each individual, in regard to whom the tendency of it is *good* upon the whole: do this again with respect to each individual, in regard to whom the tendency of it is *bad* upon the whole. Take the *balance*; which, if on the side of *pleasure*, will give the general *good tendency* of the act, with respect to the total number of community of individuals concerned; if on the side of pain the general *evil tendency*, with respect to the same community.

VI. It is not to be expected that this process should be strictly pursued previously to every moral judgment, or to every legislative or judicial operation. It may, however, be always kept in view: and as near as the process actually pursued on these occasions approaches to it, so near will such process approach to the character of an exact one.

VII. The same process is alike applicable to pleasure and pain in whatever shape they appear: and by whatever denomination they are distinguished: to pleasure, whether it be called *good* (which is properly the cause or instrument of pleasure), or *profit* (which is dis-

tant pleasure, or the cause or instrument of distant pleasure), or *convenience*, or *advantage*, *benefit*, *emolument*, *happiness*, and so forth: to pain, whether it be called *evil* (which corresponds to *good*), or *mischief*, or *inconvenience*, or *disadvantage*, or *loss*, or *unhappiness*, and so forth.

VIII. Nor is this a novel and unwarranted, any more than it is a useless theory. In all this there is nothing but what the practice of mankind, wheresoever they have a clear view of their own interest, is perfectly conformable to. An article of property, an estate in land, for instance, is valuable, on what account? On account of the pleasures of all kinds which it enables a man to produce, and what comes to the same thing, the pains of all kinds which it enables him to avert. But the value of such an article of property is universally understood to rise or fall according to the length or shortness of the time which a man has in it: the certainty or uncertainty of its coming into possession: and the nearness or remoteness of the time at which, if at all, it is to come into possession. As to the *intensity* of the pleasures which a man may derive from it, this is never thought of, because it depends upon the use which each particular person may come to make of it; which cannot be estimated till the particular pleasures he may come to derive from it, or the particular pains he may come to exclude by means of it, are brought to view. For the same reason, neither does he think of the *fecundity* or *purity* of those pleasures.

14

JOHN STUART MILL
Utilitarianism

JOHN STUART MILL (1806–1873) was the most important nineteenth-century philosopher in the tradition of British empiricism. Mill wrote on a great variety of philosophical issues and, among other things, was an advocate of women's rights (see selection 29 in this book).

CHAPTER II. WHAT UTILITARIANISM IS

. . . The creed which accepts as the foundation of morals, Utility, or the Greatest Happiness Principle, holds that actions are right in proportion as they tend to promote happiness, wrong as they tend to produce the reverse of happiness. By happiness is intended pleasure, and the absence of pain; by unhappiness, pain, and the privation of pleasure. To give a clear view of the moral standard set up by the theory, much more requires to be said; in particular, what things it includes in the ideas of pain and pleasure; and to what extent this is left an open question. But these supplementary explanations do not affect the theory of life on which this theory of morality is grounded—namely, that pleasure, and freedom from pain, are the only things desirable as ends; and that all desirable things (which are as numerous in the utilitarian as in any other scheme) are desirable either for the pleasure inherent in themselves, or as means to the promotion of pleasure and the prevention of pain.

Now, such a theory of life excites in many minds, and among them in some of the most estimable in feeling and purpose, inveterate dislike. To suppose that life has (as they express it) no higher end than pleasure—no better and nobler object of desire and pursuit—they designate as utterly mean and grovelling; as a doctrine worthy only of swine, to whom the followers of Epicurus were, at a very early period, contemptuously likened; and modern holders of the doctrine are occasionally made the subject of equally polite comparisons by its German, French, and English assailants.

When thus attacked, the Epicureans have always answered, that it is not they, but their accusers, who represent human nature in a degrading light; since the accusation supposes human beings to be capable of no pleasures except those of which swine are capable. If this supposition were true, the charge could not be gainsaid, but would then be no longer an imputation; for if the sources of pleasure were precisely the same to human beings and to swine, the rule of life which is good enough for the one would be good enough for the other. The comparison of the Epicurean life to that of beasts is felt as degrading, precisely because a beast's pleasures do not satisfy a human being's conceptions of happiness. Human beings have faculties more elevated than the animal appetites, and when once made conscious of them, do not regard anything as happiness which does not include their gratification. I do not, indeed, consider the Epicureans to have been by any means faultless in drawing out their scheme of

Excerpted from John Stuart Mill, *Utilitarianism* (1861), chs. 2, 3, and 4.

consequences from the utilitarian principle. To do this in any sufficient manner, many Stoic, as well as Christian elements require to be included. But there is no known Epicurean theory of life which does not assign to the pleasures of the intellect, of the feelings and imagination, and of the moral sentiments, a much higher value as pleasures than to those of mere sensation. It must be admitted, however, that utilitarian writers in general have placed the superiority of mental over bodily pleasures chiefly in the greater permanency, safety, uncostliness, &c., of the former—that is, in their circumstantial advantages rather than in their intrinsic nature. And on all these points utilitarians have fully proved their case; but they might have taken the other, and, as it may be called, higher ground, with entire consistency. It is quite compatible with the principle of utility to recognise the fact, that some *kinds* of pleasure are more desirable and more valuable than others. It would be absurd that while, in estimating all other things, quality is considered as well as quantity, the estimation of pleasures should be supposed to depend on quantity alone.

If I am asked, what I mean by difference of quality in pleasures, or what makes one pleasure more valuable than another, merely as a pleasure, except its being greater in amount, there is but one possible answer. Of two pleasures, if there be one to which all or almost all who have experience of both give a decided preference, irrespective of any feeling of moral obligation to prefer it, that is the more desirable pleasure. If one of the two is, by those who are competently acquainted with both, placed so far above the other that they prefer it, even though knowing it to be attended with a greater amount of dis-

content, and would not resign it for any quantity of the other pleasure which their nature is capable of, we are justified in ascribing to the preferred enjoyment a superiority in quality, so far outweighing quantity as to render it, in comparison, of small account.

Now it is an unquestionable fact that those who are equally acquainted with, and equally capable of appreciating and enjoying, both, do give a most marked preference to the manner of existence which employs their higher faculties. Few human creatures would consent to be changed into any of the lower animals, for a promise of the fullest allowance of a beast's pleasures; no intelligent human being would consent to be a fool, no instructed person would be an ignoramus, no person of feeling and conscience would be selfish and base, even though they should be persuaded that the fool, the dunce, or the rascal is better satisfied with his lot than they are with theirs. They would not resign what they possess more than he, for the most complete satisfaction of all the desires which they have in common with him. If they ever fancy they would, it is only in cases of unhappiness so extreme, that to escape from it they would exchange their lot for almost any other, however undesirable in their own eyes. A being of higher faculties requires more to make him happy, is capable probably of more acute suffering, and is certainly accessible to it at more points, than one of an inferior type; but in spite of these liabilities, he can never really wish to sink into what he feels to be a lower grade of existence. We may give what explanation we please of this unwillingness; we may attribute it to pride, a name which is given indiscriminately to some of the most and to some of the least estimable feelings of which mankind are capable; we may refer it to the love of liberty and personal independence, an appeal to which was with the Stoics one of the most effective means for the inculcation of it; to the love of power, or to the love of excitement, both of which do really enter into and contribute to it: but its most appropriate appellation is a sense of dignity, which all human beings possess in one form or other, and in some, though by no means in exact, proportion to their higher faculties, and which is so essential a part of the happiness of those in whom it is strong, that nothing which conflicts with it could be, otherwise than momentarily, an object of desire to them. Whoever supposes that this preference takes place at a sacrifice of happiness—that the superior being, in anything like the equal circumstances, is not happier than the inferior—confounds the two very different ideas, of happiness, and content. It is indisputable that the being whose capacities of enjoyment are low, has the greatest chance of having them fully satisfied; and a highly-endowed being will always feel that any happiness which he can look for, as the world is constituted, is imperfect. But he can learn to bear its imperfections, if they are at all bearable; and they will not make him envy the being who is indeed unconscious of the imperfections, but only because he feels not at all the good which those imperfections qualify. It is better to be a human being dissatisfied than a pig satisfied; better to be Socrates dissatisfied than a fool satisfied. And if the fool, or the pig, is of a different opinion, it is because they only know their own side of the question. The other party to the comparison knows both sides.

It may be objected, that many who are capable of the higher pleasures, occasionally, under the influence of temptation, postpone them to the lower. But this is quite compatible with a full appreciation of the intrinsic superiority of the higher. Men often, from infirmity of character, make their election for the nearer good, though they know it to be the less valuable; and this no less when the choice is between two bodily pleasures, than when it is between bodily and mental. They pursue sensual indulgences to the injury of health, though perfectly aware that health is the greater good. It may be further objected, that many who begin with youthful enthusiasm for everything noble, as they advance in years sink into indolence and selfishness. But I do not believe that those who undergo this very common change, voluntarily choose the lower description of pleasures in preference to the higher. I believe that before they devote themselves exclusively to the one, they have already become incapable of the other. Capacity for the nobler feelings is in most natures a very tender plant, easily killed, not only by hostile influences, but by mere want of sustenance; and in the majority of young persons it speedily dies away if the occupations to which their position in life has devoted them, and the society into which it has thrown them, are not favourable to keeping that higher capacity in exercise. Men lose their high aspirations as they lose their intellectual tastes, because they have not time or opportunity for indulging them; and they addict themselves to inferior pleasures, not because they deliberately prefer them, but because they are either the only ones to which they have access, or the only ones which they are any longer capable of enjoying. It may be questioned whether any one who has remained equally susceptible to both classes of pleasures, ever knowingly and calmly preferred the lower, though many, in all ages, have broken down in an ineffectual attempt to combine both.

From this verdict of the only competent judges, I apprehend there can be no appeal. On a question which is the best worth having of two pleasures, or which of two modes of existence is the most grateful to the feelings, apart from its moral attributes and from its consequences, the judgment of those who are qualified by knowledge of both, or, if they differ, that of the majority among them, must be admitted as final. And there needs be the less hesitation to accept this judgment respecting the quality of pleasures, since there is no other tribunal to be referred to even on the question of quantity. What means are there of determining which is the acutest of two pains, or the intensest of two pleasurable sensations, except the general suffrage of those who are familar with both? Neither pains nor pleasures are homogeneous, and pain is always heterogeneous with pleasure. What is there to decide whether a particular pleasure is worth purchasing at the cost of a particular pain, except the feelings and judgment of the experienced? When, therefore, those feelings and judgment declare the pleasures derived from the higher faculties to be preferable *in kind*, apart from the question of intensity, to those of which the animal nature, disjoined from the higher faculties, is susceptible, they are entitled on this subject to the same regard.

I have dwelt on this point, as being a necessary part of a perfectly just conception of Utility or Happiness, considered as the directive rule of human conduct. But it is by no means an indispensable condition to the acceptance of the utilitarian standard; for that standard is not the agent's own greatest happiness, but the greatest amount of happiness altogether; and if it may possibly be doubted whether a noble character is always the happier for its nobleness, there can be no doubt that it makes other people happier, and that the world in general is immensely a gainer by it. Utilitarianism, therefore, could only attain its end by the general cultivation of nobleness of character, even if each individual were only benefitted by the nobleness of others, and his own, so far as happiness is concerned, were a sheer deduction from the benefit. But the bare enunciation of such an absurdity as this last, renders refutation superfluous.

According to the Greatest Happiness Principle, as above explained, the ultimate end, with reference to and for the sake of which all other things are desirable (whether we are considering our own good or that of other people), is an existence exempt as far as possible from pain, and as rich as possible in enjoyments, both in point of quantity and quality; the test of quality, and the rule for measuring it against quantity, being the preference felt by those who, in their opportunities of experience, to which must be added their habits of self-consciousness and self-observation, are best furnished with the means of comparison. This, being, according to the utilitarian opinion, the end of human action, is necessarily also the standard of morality; which may accordingly be defined, the rules and precepts for human conduct, by the observance of which an existence such as has been described might be, to the greatest extent possible, secured to all mankind; and not to them only, but, so far as the nature of things admits, to the whole sentient creation.

Against this doctrine, however, arises another class of objectors, who say that happiness, in any form, cannot be the rational purpose of human life and action; because, in the first place, it is unattainable: and they contemptuously ask, What right hast thou to be happy? a question which Mr. Carlyle clenches by the addition, What right, a short time ago, hadst thou even *to be?* Next, they say, that men can do *without* happiness; that all noble human beings have felt this, and could not have become noble but by learning the lesson of Entsagen, or renunciation; which lesson, thoroughly learnt and submitted to, they affirm to be the beginning and necessary condition of all virtue.

The first of these objections would go to the root of the matter were it well founded; for if no happiness is to be had at all by human beings, the attainment of it cannot be the end of morality, or of any rational conduct. Though, even in that case, something might still be said for the utilitarian theory; since utility includes not solely the pursuit of happiness, but the prevention or mitigation of unhappiness; and if the former aim be chimerical, there will be all the greater scope and more imperative need for the latter, so long at least as mankind think fit to live, and do not take refuge in the simultaneous act of suicide recommended under certain conditions by Novalis. When, however, it is thus positively asserted to be impossible that human life should be happy, the assertion, if not something like a verbal quibble, is at least an exaggeration. If by happiness be meant a continuity of highly pleasurable excitement, it is evident enough that this is impossible. A state of exalted pleasure lasts only moments, or in some cases, and with some intermissions, hours or days, and is the occasional brilliant flash of enjoyment, not its permanent and steady flame. Of this the philosophers who have taught that happiness is the end of life were as fully aware as those who taunt them.

The happiness which they meant was not a life of rapture; but moments of such, in an existence made up of few and transitory pains, many and various pleasures, with a decided predominance of the active over the passive, and having as the foundation of the whole, not to expect more from life than it is capable of bestowing. A life thus composed, to those who have been fortunate enough to obtain it, has always appeared worthy of the name of happiness. And such an existence is even now the lot of many, during some considerable portion of their lives. The present wretched education, and wretched social arrangements, are the only real hindrance to its being attainable by almost all. . . .

I must again repeat, what the assailants of utilitarianism seldom have the justice to acknowledge, that the happiness which forms the utilitarian standard of what is right in conduct, is not the agent's own happiness, but that of all concerned. As between his own happiness and that of others, utilitarianism requires him to be as strictly impartial as a disinterested and benevolent spectator. In the golden rule of Jesus of Nazareth, we read the complete spirit of the ethics of utility. To do as one would be done by, and to love one's neighbour as oneself, constitute the ideal perfection of utilitarian morality. As the means of making the nearest approach to this ideal, utility would enjoin, first, that laws and social arrangements should place the happiness, or (as speaking practically it may be called) the interest, of every individual, as nearly as possible in harmony with the interest of the whole; and secondly, that education and opinion, which have so vast a power over human character, should so use that power as to establish in the mind of every individual an indissoluble association between his own happiness and the good of the whole; especially between his own happiness and the practice of such modes of conduct, negative and positive, as regard for the universal happiness prescribes: so that not only he may be unable to conceive the possibility of happiness to himself, consistently with conduct opposed to the general good, but also that a direct impulse to promote the general good may be in every individual one of the habitual motives of action, and the sentiments connected therewith may fill a large and prominent place in every human being's sentient existence. If the impugners of the utilitarian morality represented it to their own minds in this its true character, I know not what recommendation possessed by any other morality they could possibly affirm to be wanting to it: what more beautiful or more exalted developments of human nature any other ethical system can be supposed to foster, or what springs of action, not accessible to the utilitarian, such systems rely on for giving effect to their mandates.

The objectors to utilitarianism cannot always be charged with representing it in a discreditable light. On the contrary, those among them who entertain anything like a just idea of its disinterested character, sometimes find fault with its standard as being too high for humanity. They say it is exacting too much to require that people shall always act from the inducement of promoting the general interests of society. But this is to mistake the very meaning of a standard of morals, and to confound the rule of action with the motive of it. It is the business of ethics to tell us what are our duties, or by what test we may know them; but no system of ethics requires that the sole motive of all we do shall be a feeling of duty; on the contrary, ninety-nine hundredths of all our actions are done from other motives, and rightly so done, if the rule of duty does not condemn them. It is the more unjust to utilitarianism that this particular misapprehension should be made a ground of objection to it, inasmuch as utilitarian moralists have gone beyond almost all others in affirming that the motive has nothing to do with the morality of the action, though much with the worth of the agent. He who saves a fellow creature from drowning does what is morally right, whether his motive be duty, or the hope of being paid for his trouble: he who betrays the friend that trusts him, is guilty of a crime, even if his object be to serve another friend to whom he is under greater obligations. But to speak only of actions done from the motive of duty, and in direct obedience to principle: it is a misapprehension of the utilitarian mode of thought, to conceive it as implying that people should fix their minds upon so wide a generality as the world, or society at large. The great majority of good actions are intended, not for the benefit of the world, but for that of individuals, of which the good of the world is made up; and the thoughts of the most virtuous man need not on these occasions travel beyond the particular persons concerned, except so far as is necessary to assure himself that in benefiting them he is not violating the rights—that is, the legitimate and authorized expectations—of any one else. The multiplication of happiness is, according to the utilitarian ethics, the object of virtue: the occasions on which any person (except one in a thousand) has it in his power to do this on an extended scale, in other words, to be a public benefactor, are but exceptional; and on these occasions alone is he called on to consider public utility; in every other case, private utility, the interest or happiness of some few persons, is all he has to attend to. Those alone the influence of whose actions extends to society in general, need concern themselves habitually about so large an object. In the case of abstinences indeed —of things which people forbear to do, from moral considerations, though the consequences in the particular case might be beneficial—it would be unworthy of an intelligent agent not to be consciously aware that the action is of a class which, if practised generally, would be generally injurious, and that this is the ground of the obligation to abstain from it. The amount of regard for the public interest implied in this recognition, is no greater than is demanded by every system of morals; for they all enjoin to abstain from whatever is manifestly pernicious to society. . . .

CHAPTER III. OF THE ULTIMATE SANCTION OF THE PRINCIPLE OF UTILITY

The question is often asked, and properly so, in regard to any supposed moral standard—What is its sanction? what are the motives to obey it? or more specifically, what is the source of its obligation? whence does it derive its binding force? It is a necessary part of moral philosophy to provide the answer to this question; which, though frequently assuming the shape of an objection to the utilitarian morality, as if it had some special applicability to that above others, really arises in regard to all standards. It arises, in fact, whenever a person is called on to *adopt* a standard or refer morality to any basis on which he has not been accustomed to rest it. For the customary morality, that which education and opinion have consecrated, is the only one which presents itself

to the mind with the feeling of being *in itself* obligatory; and when a person is asked to believe that this morality *derives* its obligation from some general principle round which custom has not thrown the same halo, the assertion is to him a paradox; the supposed corollaries seem to have a more binding force than the original theorem; the superstructure seems to stand better without, than with, what is represented as its foundation. He says to himself, I feel that I am bound not to rob or murder, betray or deceive; but why am I bound to promote the general happiness? If my own happiness lies in something else, why may I not give that the preference?

If the view adopted by the utilitarian philosophy of the nature of the moral sense be correct, this difficulty will always present itself, until the influences which form moral character have taken the same hold of the principle which they have taken of some of the consequences—until, by the improvement of education, the feeling of unity with our fellow creatures shall be (what it cannot be doubted that Christ intended it to be) as deeply rooted in our character, and to our own consciousness as completely a part of our nature, as the horror of crime is in an ordinarily well-brought up young person. In the mean time, however, the difficulty has no peculiar application to the doctrine of utility, but is inherent in every attempt to analyse morality and reduce it to principles; which, unless the principle is already in men's minds invested with as much sacredness as any of its applications, always seems to divest them of a part of their sanctity.

The principle of utility either has, or there is no reason why it might not have, all the sanctions which belong to any other system of morals. Those sanctions are either external or internal. Of the external sanctions it is not necessary to speak at any length. They are, the hope of favour and the fear of displeasure from our fellow creatures or from the Ruler of the Universe, along with whatever we may have of sympathy or affection for them or of love and awe of Him, inclining us to do his will independently of selfish consequences. There is evidently no reason why all these motives for observance should not attach themselves to the utilitarian morality, as completely and as powerfully as to any other. Indeed, those of them which refer to our fellow creatures are sure to do so, in proportion to the amount of general intelligence; for whether there be any other ground of moral obligation than the general happiness or not, men do desire happiness; and however imperfect may be their own practice, they desire and commend all conduct in others towards themselves, by which they think their happiness is promoted. With regard to the religious motive, if men believe, as most profess to do, in the goodness of God, those who think that conduciveness to the general happiness is the essence, or even only the criterion, of good, must necessarily believe that it is also that which God approves. The whole force therefore of external reward and punishment, whether physical or moral, and whether proceeding from God or from our fellow men, together with all that the capacities of human nature admit, of disinterested devotion to either, become available to enforce the utilitarian morality, in proportion as that morality is recognised; and the more powerfully, the more the appliances of education and general cultivation are bent to the purpose.

So far as to external sanctions. The internal sanction of duty, whatever our standard of duty may be, is one and the same—a feeling in our own mind; a pain, more or less intense, attendant on violation of duty, which in properly-cultivated moral natures rises, in the more serious cases, into shrinking from it as an impossibility. This feeling, when disinterested, and connecting itself with the pure idea of duty, and not with some particular form of it, or with any of the merely accessory circumstances, is the essence of Conscience; though in that complex phenomenon as it actually exists, the simple fact is in general all encrusted over with collateral associations, derived from sympathy, from love, and still more from fear; from all the forms of religious feeling; from the recollections of childhood and of all our past life; from self-esteem, desire of the esteem of others, and occasionally even self-abasement. This extreme complication is, I apprehend, the origin of the sort of mystical character which, by a tendency of the human mind of which there are many other examples, is apt to be attributed to the idea of moral obligation, and which leads people to believe that the idea cannot possibly attach itself to any other objects than those which, by a supposed mysterious law, are found in our present experience to excite it. Its binding force, however, consists in the existence of a mass of feeling which must be broken through in order to do what violates our standard of right, and which, if we do nevertheless violate that standard, will probably have to be encountered afterwards in the form of remorse. Whatever theory we have of the nature or origin of conscience, this is what essentially constitutes it.

The ultimate sanction, therefore, of all morality (external motives apart) being a subjective feeling in our own minds, I see nothing embarrassing to those whose standard is utility, in the question, what is the sanction of that particular standard? We may answer, the same as of all other moral standards—the conscientious feelings of mankind. Undoubtedly this sanction has no binding efficacy on those who do not possess the feelings it appeals to; but neither will these persons be more obedient to any other moral principle than to the utilitarian one. On them morality of any kind has no hold but through the external sanctions. Meanwhile the feelings exist, a fact in human nature, the reality of which, and the great power with which they are capable of acting on those in whom they have been duly cultivated, are proved by experience. No reason has ever been shown why they may not be cultivated to as great intensity in connexion with the utilitarian, as with any other rule of morals.

There is, I am aware, a disposition to believe that a person who sees in moral obligation a transcendental fact, an objective reality belonging to the province of 'Things in themselves,' is likely to be more obedient to it than one who believes it to be entirely subjective, having its seat in human consciousness only. But whatever a person's opinion may be on this point of Ontology, the force he is really urged by is his own subjective feeling, and is exactly measured by its strength. No one's belief that Duty is an objective reality is stronger than the belief that God is so; yet the belief in God, apart from the expectation of actual reward and punishment, only operates on conduct through, and in proportion to, the subjective religious feeling. The sanction, so far as it is disinterested, is always in the mind itself; and the notion therefore of the transcendental moralists must be, that this sanction will not exist *in* the

mind unless it is believed to have its root out of the mind; and that if a person is able to say to himself, That which is restraining me, and which is called my conscience, is only a feeling in my own mind, he may possibly draw the conclusion that when the feeling ceases the obligation ceases, and that if he find the feeling inconvenient, he may disregard it, and endeavour to get rid of it. But is this danger confined to the utilitarian morality? Does the belief that moral obligation has its seat outside the mind make the feeling of it too strong to be got rid of? The fact is so far otherwise, that all moralists admit and lament the ease with which, in the generality of minds, conscience can be silenced or stifled. The question, Need I obey my conscience? is quite as often put to themselves by persons who never heard of the principle of utility, as by its adherents. Those whose conscientious feelings are so weak as to allow of their asking this question, if they answer it affirmatively, will not do so because they believe in the transcendental theory, but because of the external sanctions. . . .

CHAPTER IV.
OF WHAT SORT OF PROOF THE PRINCIPLE OF UTILITY IS SUSCEPTIBLE

It has already been remarked, that questions of ultimate ends do not admit of proof, in the ordinary acceptation of the term. To be incapable of proof by reasoning is common to all first principles; to the first premises of our knowledge, as well as to those of our conduct. But the former, being matters of fact, may be the subject of a direct appeal to the faculties which judge of fact—namely, our senses, and our internal consciousness. Can an appeal be made to the same faculties on questions of practical ends? Or by what other faculty is cognizance taken of them?

Questions about ends are, in other words, questions about what things are desirable. The utilitarian doctrine is, that happiness is desirable, and the only thing desirable, as an end; all other things being only desirable as means to that end. What ought to be required of this doctrine—what conditions is it requisite that the doctrine should fulfil—to make good its claim to be believed?

The only proof capable of being given that an object is visible, is that people actually see it. The only proof that a sound is audible, is that people hear it: and so of the other sources of our experience. In like manner, I apprehend, the sole evidence it is possible to produce that anything is desirable, is that people do actually desire it. If the end which the utilitarian doctrine proposes to itself were not, in theory and in practice, acknowledged to be an end, nothing could ever convince any person that it was so. No reason can be given why the general happiness is desirable, except that each person, so far as he believes it to be attainable, desires his own happiness. This, however, being a fact, we have not only all the proof which the case admits of, but all which it is possible to require, that happiness is a good: that each person's happiness is a good to that person, and the general happiness, therefore, a good to the aggregate of all persons. Happiness has made out its title as *one* of the ends of conduct, and consequently one of the criteria of morality.

But it has not, by this alone, proved itself to be the sole criterion. To do that, it would seem, by the same rule, necessary to show, not only that people desire happiness, but that they never desire anything else. Now it is palpable that they do desire things which, in common language, are decidedly distinguished from happiness. They desire, for example, virtue, and the absence of vice, no less really than pleasure and the absence of pain. The desire of virtue is not as universal, but it is as authentic a fact, as the desire of happiness. And hence the opponents of the utilitarian standard deem that they have a right to infer that there are other ends of human action besides happiness, and that happiness is not the standard of approbation and disapprobation.

But does the utilitarian doctrine deny that people desire virtue, or maintain that virtue is not a thing to be desired? The very reverse. It maintains not only that virtue is to be desired, but that it is to be desired disinterestedly, for itself. Whatever may be the opinion of utilitarian moralists as to the original conditions by which virtue is made virtue; however they may believe (as they do) that actions and dispositions are only virtuous because they promote another end than virtue; yet this being granted, and it having been decided, from considerations of this description, what *is* virtuous, they not only place virtue at the very head of the things which are good as means to the ultimate end, but they also recognise as a psychological fact the possibility of its being, to the individual, a good in itself, without looking to any end beyond it; and hold, that the mind is not in a right state, not in a state comfortable to Utility, not in the state most conducive to the general happiness, unless it does love virtue in this manner—as a thing desirable in itself, even although, in the individual instance, it should not produce those other desirable consequences which it tends to produce, and on account of which it is held to be virtue. This opinion is not, in the smallest degree, a departure from the Happiness principle. The ingredients of happiness are very various, and each of them is desirable in itself, and not merely when considered as swelling an aggregate. The principle of utility does not mean that any given pleasure, as music, for instance, or any given exemption from pain, as for example health, are to be looked upon as a means to a collective something termed happiness, and to be desired on that account. They are desired and desirable in and for themselves; besides being means, they are a part of the end. Virtue, according to the utilitarian doctrine, is not naturally and originally part of the end, but it is capable of becoming so; and in those who love it disinterestedly it has become so, and is desired and cherished, not as a means to happiness, but as a part of their happiness.

To illustrate this farther, we may remember that virtue is not the only thing, originally a means, and which if it were not a means to anything else, would be and remain indifferent, but which by association with what it is a means to, comes to be desired for itself, and that too with the utmost intensity. What, for example, shall we say of the love of money? There is nothing originally more desirable about money than about any heap of glittering pebbles. Its worth is solely that of the things which it will buy; the desires for other things than itself, which it is a means of gratifying. Yet the love of money is not only one of the strongest moving forces of human life, but money is, in many cases, desired in and for itself; the desire to possess it is often stronger than the desire to use it, and goes on increasing when all the desires which point to ends beyond it, to be encompassed by it, are falling off. It may be then said truly, that money is desired not for the sake of an end, but as part of the end. From being a means to happiness, it has come to be itself a principal ingredient of the individual's conception of happiness. The same may be said of the majority of the great objects of human life—power, for example, or fame; except that to each of these there is a certain amount of immediate pleasure annexed, which has at least the semblance of being naturally inherent in them; a thing which cannot be said of money. Still, however, the strongest natural attraction, both of power and of fame, is the immense aid they give to the attainment of our other wishes; and it is the strong association thus generated between them and all our objects of desire, which gives to the direct desire of them the intensity it often assumes, so as in some characters to surpass in strength all other desires. In these cases the means have become a part of the end, and a more important part of it than any of the things which they are means to. What was once desired as an instrument for the attainment of happiness, has come to be desired for its own sake. In being desired for its own sake it is, however, desired as *part* of happiness. The person is made, or thinks he would be made, happy by its mere possession; and is made unhappy by failure to obtain it. The desire of it is not a different thing from the desire of happiness, any more than the love of music, or the desire of health. They are included in happiness. They are some of the elements of which the desire of happiness is made up. Happiness is not an abstract idea, but a concrete whole; and these are some of its parts. And the utilitarian standard sanctions and approves their being so. Life would be a poor thing, very ill provided with sources of happiness, if there were not this provision of nature, by which things originally indifferent, but conducive to, or otherwise associated with, the satisfaction of our primitive desires, become in themselves sources of pleasure more valuable than the primitive pleasures, both in permanency, in the space of human existence that they are capable of covering, and even in intensity.

Virtue, according to the utilitarian conception, is a good of this description. There was no original desire of it, or motive to it, save its conduciveness to pleasure, and especially to protection from pain. But through the association thus formed, it may be felt a good in itself, and desired as such with as great intensity as any other good; and with this difference between it and the love of money, of power, or of fame, that all of these may, and often do, render the individual noxious to the other members of the society to which he belongs, whereas there is nothing which makes him so much a blessing to them as the cultivation of the disinterested love of virtue. And consequently, the utilitarian standard, while it tolerates and approves those other acquired desires, up to the point beyond which they would be more injurious to the general happiness than promotive of it, enjoins and requires the cultivation of the love of virtue up to the greatest strength possible, as being above all things important to the general happiness.

It results from the preceding considerations, that there is in reality nothing desired except happiness. Whatever is desired otherwise than as a means to some end beyond itself, and ultimately to happiness, is desired as itself a part of happiness, and is not desired for itself until it has become so. Those who desire virtue for its own sake, desire it either because the consciousness of it is a pleasure, or because the consciousness of being without it is a pain, or for both reasons united; as in truth the pleasure and pain seldom exist separately, but almost always together, the same person feeling pleasure in the degree of virtue attained, and pain in not having attained more. If one of these

gave him no pleasure, and the other no pain, he would not love or desire virtue, or would desire it only for the other benefits which it might produce to himself or to persons whom he cared for.

We have now, then, an answer to the question, of what sort of proof the principle of utility is susceptible. If the opinion which I have now stated is psychologically true—if human nature is so constituted as to desire nothing which is not either a part of happiness or a means of happiness, we can have no other proof, and we require no other, that these are the only things desirable. If so, happiness is the sole end of human action, and the promotion of it the test by which to judge of all human conduct; from whence it necessarily follows that it must be the criterion of morality, since a part is included in the whole.

And now to decide whether this is really so; whether mankind do desire nothing for itself but that which is a pleasure to them, or of which the absence is a pain; we have evidently arrived at a question of fact and experience, dependent, like all similar questions, upon evidence. It can only be determined by practised self-consciousness and self-observation, assisted by observation of others. I believe that these sources of evidence, impartially consulted, will declare that desiring a thing and finding it pleasant, aversion to it and thinking of it as painful, are phenomena entirely inseparable, or rather two parts of the same phenomenon; in strictness of language, two different modes of naming the same psychological fact: that to think of an object as desirable (unless for the sake of its consequences), and to think of it as pleasant, are one and the same thing; and that to desire anything, except in proportion as the idea of it is pleasant, is a physical and metaphysical impossibility. . . .

15

W. D. ROSS
Difficulties for Utilitarianism

w. d. ross (1877–1971), the well-known British moral philosopher and Aristotelian scholar, was the author of *Aristotle* (1923), *The Right and the Good* (1930), *Foundations of Ethics* (1939), and other books. He was knighted in 1938 and held important government posts during and after World War II.

It is Utilitarianism in its general form, the view that our sole duty is to produce as much good as possible, that we have now to discuss. If we could persuade ourselves that right just *means* 'calculated to produce the greatest good', the matter would be simple. But we have seen, I hope, that that contention is not at all plausible. If productivity of good is different from rightness but is the universal ground of rightness, how do we know this? There are, I think, only three possibilities. Either it is known by an immediate intuition, or it is established deductively, or it is established inductively. I do not know of any attempt to establish it deductively, and I cannot think of any middle term which could with any plausibility be used to connect the two terms in question. The effective alternatives appear to be intuition and induction. I will first ask whether the proposition has been established inductively. I take leave to quote some sentences from *The Right and the Good.*

Such an enquiry, to be conclusive, would have to be very thorough and extensive. We should have to take a large variety of the acts which we, to the best of our ability, judge to be right. We should have to trace as far as possible their consequences, not only for the persons directly affected but also for those indirectly affected; and to these no limit can be set. To make our inquiry thoroughly conclusive, we should have to do what we cannot do, viz. trace these consequences into an unending future. And even to make it reasonably conclusive, we should have to trace them far into the future. It is clear that the most we could possibly say is that a large variety of typical acts that are judged right appear, so far as we can trace their consequences, to produce more good than any other acts possible to the agents in the circumstances. And such a result is far short of proving the constant connexion of the two attributes. But it is surely clear that no inductive inquiry justifying even this result has ever been carried through. The advocates of utilitarian systems have been so much persuaded either of the identity or of the self-evident connexion of the attributes "right" and "optimific" (or "felicific") that they have not attempted even such an inductive inquiry as is possible.[1]

It is clear, too, that even if we could establish inductively that all optimific acts are right and all right acts optimific, that would not establish that their being optimific is the *ground* of their rightness, which is the proposition we are inquiring into. If we have only proved that the two attributes always go together, that is not enough. We should have to show that all right acts not only are optimific but are right *because* they are optimific. I do not mean to insist that it should be shown that unreflective people always reach their judgement that an act is right because they first judge it to be optimific. To this demand the utilitarian would have

From W. D. Ross, *Foundations of Ethics*, Oxford University Press, 1939. By permission of The Clarendon Press, Oxford. Footnotes edited.

1. *The Right and the Good* (Oxford, 1930), 36.

a perfectly proper answer. He would say, 'Certain types of act have been in practice found to be optimific, and have in consequence been judged to be right; and so, for plain men, the character of rightness has come to seem to belong to such acts directly, in virtue of their being, e.g. fulfilments of promise, and the middle term which established their rightness has come to be forgotten. *Media axiomata* such as "men should keep their promises" have come to be accepted as if they were self-evidently true, and people habitually judge acts to be right on the strength of the *media axiomata*, forgetting the method by which the *media axiomata* have themselves been established'. That is a fair answer. The test I would prefer to impose is a different one, viz. this: when we reflect, do we really come to the conclusion that such an act as promise-keeping owes its rightness to its tendency to produce maximum good, *or* to its being an act of promise-keeping?

It seems clear that Utilitarianism has not established inductively that being optimific is always the ground of rightness, and as a rule utilitarians have not attempted to do so. The reason is simple: it is because it has seemed to them self-evident that this is the only possible ground of rightness. Professor Moore definitely says that for him the principle is self-evident.[2] For my part, I can find no self-evidence about it. And I think I can point to several facts which tell against its truth, and to some which tell against there being even a constant correspondence between the two attributes, optimificness and rightness.

(1) Professor Broad has pointed out one such difficulty. Utilitarians hold that pleasure is either the only good, or is at least a good; and in the latter assertion most people would be, with certain qualifications, in agreement with them.

Then, if any other consequences that an act may have be abstracted from, utilitarians are bound to say that an act which produces the greatest possible amount of pleasure is the right or obligatory act. Now, Professor Broad points out,

among the things which we can to some extent influence by our actions is the number of minds which shall exist, or, to be more cautious, which shall be embodied at a given time. It would be possible to increase the total amount of happiness in a community by increasing the numbers of that community even though one thereby reduced the total happiness of each member of it. If Utilitarianism be true it would be one's duty to try to increase the numbers of a community, even though one reduced the average total happiness of the members, so long as the total happiness in the community would be in the least increased. It seems perfectly plain to me that this kind of action, so far from being a duty, would quite certainly be wrong.[3]

His criticism appears to be clearly justified. We should not merely judge that such action was right because it was optimific; we should judge that it was wrong although it was optimific. It already begins to become clear that it is not our duty to increase to the utmost the total happiness, irrespective of how the happiness is distributed.

Professor Broad does not apply his argument to any other good than pleasure; for it is hedonistic Utilitarianism that he is criticizing.[4] But the same argument will apply to any other form of good, say virtuous action or intelligent

2. *Ethics* (Oxford, 1912), 168–9.

3. *Five Types of Ethical Theory* (London, 1930), 249–50.

4. [*Hedonistic* utilitarians hold that only pleasure is good-in-itself, whereas *ideal* utilitarians hold that there are many different things that are good-in-themselves. Bentham was a hedonistic utilitarian, and Moore was an ideal utilitarian—Ed.]

thought. The utilitarian doctrine involves that all goods are commensurable—that, for instance, in any two virtuous acts there must be different quantities of good which are in a certain ratio to each other, even if we cannot detect the ratio. And a utilitarian should maintain that it is self-evident that if we had to choose between promoting the existence of a certain amount of virtue and intelligence spread out very thin among a certain population, and a slightly smaller amount concentrated in a much smaller population (whose average virtue and intelligence would therefore be greater), we ought to choose the former. But it is clear to me that this is far from self-evident.

Thus we have already a principle which theoretically at any rate is capable of coming into conflict with the principle of producing the greatest total amount of good, viz. the principle which bids us concentrate good in a population of high average virtue and intelligence, rather than spread it out over a population of low average virtue and intelligence, if the choice ever lay between these alternatives.

(2) Consider now a case in which the size of the population is not assumed to be alterable by anything we can do. If the essential utilitarian principle is true, that productivity of maximum good is the sole ground of rightness, it ought to be quite indifferent how an 'extra dose'[5] of happiness should be distributed among the population, provided the total amount of the dose is unaltered. It would be morally just the same whether *A* is made very happy and *B* only very slightly happy, or whether *A* and *B* are both made rather happy, provided that the net gain in happiness for *A* and *B* taken together were equal in both cases. Now if *A* and *B* are people of equal moral worth, we do not really

think that it would be right to distribute happiness unequally between them. Sidgwick, while criticizing some of our supposed intuitions of justice, has the candour to admit that there is one principle of justice that is axiomatic, viz. that of impartiality in the application of general rules.[6] This, in its application to the case we are considering, can only mean that it is *not* morally indifferent how we divide an extra dose of happiness between two individuals, but that in the absence of some relevant difference between them it should be equally divided between them. But though Sidgwick recognizes the 'principle of justice' alongside of the 'principle of rational benevolence' (that which commands us to produce the maximum of good), he seems to assign to it a subordinate position. He would still, I think, say that if we can produce a greater total extra dose of happiness by giving much to *A* and little to *B*, than by giving the same amount to both, we ought to do so. This, however, is a half-way house at which we cannot stop. The principle of justice in the distribution of happiness can in no way be derived from the principle bidding us produce the greatest *total* of happiness. If it is true, as Sidgwick holds, then it is independent of the greatest happiness principle; and if it is independent of it, it is capable of coming into conflict with it. And where it does, I believe we should all judge that it would be rather our duty to produce a smaller increase of total happiness, fairly divided between individuals, than a slightly larger increase, very unfairly divided. Furthermore, I think we should judge not only that there is an independent moral

5. Ibid. 251.

6. *Methods of Ethics* (London, 1907), ed. 7, 380.

principle bidding us divide happiness equally between people of equal moral worth, but also that the same principle bids us divide it, so far as we can, unequally between people of unequal moral worth. This appears to me just as axiomatic as the principle which bids us promote the general happiness, or (more widely) the general good.

(3) A further difficulty for utilitarians arises when we consider the distribution of pleasure between the agent and any one else. For utilitarians, it is always a duty for me to produce a greater pleasure for myself rather than a smaller pleasure for another (except of course where the ulterior consequences of the two acts would weigh the balance in favour of the latter act—but we can ignore this complication). Now the plain truth seems to be that we never judge so in fact. It seems to me that if we are honest with ourselves, which in a matter affecting us so closely it is hard to be, we shall find that we never really think ourselves morally bound to do an act which will increase our own pleasure, except for some ulterior reason, for example where we think that the pleasurable experience will fit us to do our work better, or that the relinquishing it to another person will tend to have a bad effect on his character.

Of these three difficulties for utilitarianism, arising out of the distribution of good, the first two may be dealt with in either of two ways. We may say (a) that quite apart from the duty to produce as much good as possible, there is an independent duty to produce a concentration of good in a smaller number of persons rather than a distribution of an equal amount of it among a larger number, and another independent duty to distribute happiness in proportion to merit. Or we may say (b) that the concentration of good in

a smaller number of persons is itself a good, a good of higher order,[7] as it were, than the good (consisting, say, of virtuous action, intelligent thought, and pleasure) which is thus concentrated; and similarly that the enjoyment of happiness in proportion to merit is itself a good of higher order than the happiness and the merit themselves. In this case the duty to produce such concentrations or such distributions will fall under the general duty of producing good; and our criticism of Utilitarianism will be, so far, less radical than in the other case. We shall not have established a duty other than the duty of producing good. We shall simply have shown that Utilitarianism in naming virtuous action, intelligent thought, and pleasure as the things that are good has overlooked two important goods of higher order.

It is difficult to choose between these two views. On the whole I incline towards the latter. It seems to me that the existence of a greater concentration of good is not only something in which we should in fact take greater satisfaction than in the wider and thinner distribution of the same total amount of good, but something in which it is *reasonable* to take satisfaction, i.e. is a greater good. And similarly I think it is reasonable to take satisfaction in a distribution of happiness in proportion to merit rather than in a distribution not in proportion to merit. If we had before us in imagination two communities in which the total amounts of virtue and of happiness were equal, but in one the good were happy and the bad wretched, and in the other the bad were happy and the good were wretched, I think it would be reasonable to say that the state of the first community is a bet-

7. In a mathematical, not in a moral sense.

ter state than that of the second, and one which on that ground we ought to do our best to bring about rather than the other.

In answer to the third objection also, a utilitarian might be tempted to say that a good of higher order is involved. He might say that the enjoyment of pleasure by a man as a result of another man's action is a good of higher order, while the enjoyment of pleasure by a man as a result of his own action is not such a good. It is clear, however, that this is not true. Suppose that A, desiring to produce pleasure for B, produces it for himself, and that B, desiring to produce pleasure for himself, produces it for A. No one thinks A's enjoyment in the first case less of a good than his enjoyment in the second, though in the first it has been produced by himself and in the second by B.

The utilitarian might then seek to amend his suggestion by saying 'the enjoyment of pleasure by a man as a result of another man's action *directed to that end* is a good of higher order, while the enjoyment of pleasure by a man as a result of his own action directed to that end is not such a good, and that is why it is a duty to produce pleasure for others and not a duty to produce it for oneself'. But he is not entitled to make this amendment. For on his own showing the duty of doing an act depends on the results produced, or (according to a different form of the theory) on the results intended; and he is not entitled to reckon a difference between the two *motives* as a difference in the results produced or intended.

Yet here also our argument does not necessarily point to a duty quite distinct from that of producing a maximum of good. For, while for a third person the enjoyment of pleasure by A is the same kind of thing as its enjoyment by B, A's own pleasure stands in quite a different relation to A from that in which B's pleasure stands to A. There is at least some ground for thinking that for A they may be good only in quite different senses of 'good', B's pleasure being for A a morally suitable object of satisfaction, and A's pleasure being for A only an *inevitable* object of satisfaction, having nothing morally suitable or unsuitable about it. If this be the true account, the hard fact (one of the most certain facts in morals) that we have a duty to produce pleasure for others, and have not a duty to produce it for ourselves, will involve us in admitting that it is only things that are good in the sense of being morally suitable objects of satisfaction, and not those that are good in the sense of being inevitable but morally neutral objects of satisfaction, that we have a duty to produce.

I pass now to an objection connected not with the distribution of pleasure but with the fact that we may by our action produce pleasure for some people and pain for others. On the utilitarian view, to each dose of pleasure there is some dose of pain that is exactly equal. The one may be represented by $+x$, the other by $-x$. Now for a utilitarian it is morally indifferent whether by your act you produce x units of pleasure for A and inflict y units of pain on B, or confer $x-y$ units of pleasure on one of them, since in each case you produce a net increment of $x-y$ units of pleasure. But we should in fact, I think, always judge that the infliction of pain on any person is justified only by the conferment not of an equal but of a substantially greater amount of pleasure on some one else (assuming the persons to be of equal worth). We do not, in fact, think that persons other than ourselves are simply so many pawns in the game of producing the maximum of pleasure, or good. We think they have definite rights, or at least claims, not to be made means to the giving of pleasure to others; and claims that ought to be respected unless the net pleasure, or good, to be gained for the community by other action is very considerable. We think the principle 'do evil to no one' more pressing than the principle 'do good to every one', except when the evil is very substantially outweighed by the good. This consideration seems to be perfectly clear, and it is strange that it has been overlooked by the utilitarians.

I pass next to a group of difficulties for Utilitarianism arising from our sense of special duties towards individuals, based on special relations between them and the agent. These seem to fall under three general heads. There is first the sense which we all possess that we have a special duty to make compensation to any one for any wrong we have done him. When I have wronged some one, he has ceased to be merely what Utilitarianism regards him as being, one out of many possible recipients or receptacles of good, between whom the choice is to be made simply on the basis of the question how the maximum good is to be achieved. He has become some one with a *special* claim on my effort, over and above the claim which all men have to my beneficence.

There is similarly the claim which those have from whom we have accepted benefits in the past. This again is a claim which, in fact, I believe every one recognizes, and it is evident that it is on it that our special duty to parents and friends in the main depends.

These two responsibilities—the responsibility for compensation and for rendering good for good—arise incidentally from past actions having another purpose. But, thirdly, there are obligations arising from acts whose ex-press object was to create them. Our name for these acts is 'promises'; a promise is just the voluntary making of something obligatory on us which would not, or need not, have been obligatory before. To make this clear, we must in the first place distinguish (as we do, more or less clearly, in ordinary life) between the making of a promise and the announcement of an intention. There are cases in which it is difficult to know whether some one is making a promise or is merely announcing an intention; but that does not affect the fact that the two things are in principle quite different. As Sidgwick remarks, 'If I merely assert my intention of abstaining from alcohol for a year, and then after a week take some, I am (at worst) ridiculed as inconsistent; but if I have pledged myself to abstain, I am blamed as untrustworthy.'[8] The announcement of an intention is merely a statement about one's present state of mind; a promise is a statement about the future. But, secondly, not every statement about one's own behaviour in the future is a promise. If I merely say incidentally in conversation with some one that I shall be at a certain place at a certain time, that does not constitute a promise to be there. To make a promise, there must be a more or less clear intimation to another person that he can *rely* upon me to do something which he, at least, regards as a service to him. The difference between this and a mere statement about the future can be seen from the fact that when I have merely made a statement about the future, what he relies upon, if he expects me to fulfil it, is my unchangeability, while, when I make a promise, what he relies upon is my sense of duty.

A promise being this, an intentional

8. *Methods of Ethics*, 304.

intimation to some one else that he can rely upon me to behave in a certain way, it appears to me perfectly clear, that, quite apart from any question of the greatness of the benefits to be produced for him or for society by the fulfilment of the promise, a promise gives rise to a moral claim on his part that the promise be fulfilled. This claim will be enhanced if there are great benefits that will arise from the fulfilment of the promise in contrast to its violation; or it may be overridden if the fulfilment of the promise is likely to do much more harm than good. But through all such variations it remains as a solid fact in the moral situation; and it arises solely from the fact that a promise has been made, and not from the consequences of its fulfilment. I would go so far as to say that the existence of an obligation arising from the making of a promise is so axiomatic that no moral universe can be imagined in which it would not exist.

These seem to me to be the main difficulties in the way of accepting Utilitarianism as a complete ethical creed; these are the principles of duty which seem to emerge as distinct from the principle 'promote the maximum good'.

16

H. J. MCCLOSKEY
A Non-Utilitarian Approach to Punishment

H. J. MCCLOSKEY is professor of philosophy at La Trobe University in Australia. He is the author of *Meta-* *Ethics and Normative Ethics* (1969) and *John Stuart Mill: A Critical Study* (1971).

Although the view that punishment is to be justified on utilitarian grounds has obvious appeal, an examination of utilitarianism reveals that, consistently and accurately interpreted, it dictates unjust punishments which are unacceptable to the common moral consciousness. In this rule-utilitarianism is no more satisfactory than in act-utilitarianism. Although the production of the greatest good, or the greatest happiness, of the greatest number is obviously a relevant consideration when determining which punishments may properly be inflicted, the question as to which punishment is just is a distinct and more basic question and one which must be answered before we can determine which punishments are morally permissible. That a retributivist theory, which is a particular application of a general principle of justice, can account more satisfactorily for our notion of justice in punishment is a positive reason in its support.

From H. J. McCloskey, "A Non-Utilitarian Approach to Punishment," *Inquiry*, vol. 8 (1965), pp. 249–263. Reprinted by permission. This article is reprinted unabridged.

I. INTRODUCTION
At first glance there are many obvious considerations which seem to suggest a

utilitarian approach to punishment. Crime is an evil and what we want to do is not so much to cancel it out after it occurs as to prevent it. To punish crime when it occurs is, at best, an imperfect state of affairs. Further, punishment, invoking as it does evils such as floggings, imprisonment, and death, is something which does not commend itself to us without argument. An obvious way of attempting to justify such deliberately created evils would be in terms of their utility.

This is how crime and punishment impress on first sight. A society in which there was no crime and no punishment would be a much better society than one with crime and resulting punishments. And punishment, involving evils such as deliberately inflicted suffering and even death, and consequential evils such as the driving of some of its victims into despair and even insanity, and so forth, harming and even wrecking their subsequent lives, and often also the lives of their relatives and dependents, obviously needs justification. To argue that it is useful, that good results come from such punishment, is to offer a more plausible justification than many so-called retributive justifications. It is obviously more plausible to argue that punishment is justified because society has a right to express its indignation at the actions of the offender, or because punishment annuls and cancels out the crime, or because the criminal, being a human being, merits respect and hence has a right to his punishment. Such retributive type justifications have some point, but they are nonetheless implausible in a way that the utilitarian justification is not. Yet I shall be concerned to argue that the key to the morality of punishment is to be found in terms of a retributive theory, namely, the theory that evils should be distributed according to desert and that the vicious deserve to suffer. In so arguing, I shall be bringing together and adding to a number of arguments I have set out elsewhere.[1]

II. HOW OUR COMMON MORAL CONSCIOUSNESS VIEWS PUNISHMENT

Is the punishment which commends itself to the moral consciousness always useful punishment? And is all punishment that is useful such that we should consider it to be morally just and permissible? Punishment which we commonly consider to be just is punishment which is deserved. To be deserved, punishment must be of an offender who is guilty of an offence in the morally relevant sense of 'offence.' For instance, the punishing of a man known to be innocent of any crime shocks our moral consciousness and is seen as a grave injustice. Similarly, punishment of a person not responsible for his behaviour, for example, a lunatic, is evidently unjust and shocking. Punishment for what is not an offence in the morally significant sense of 'offence' is equally unjust. To punish a man who has tried his hardest to secure a job during a period of acute and extensive unemployment for 'having insufficient means of support,' or to punish a person under a retroactive law is simply unjust. So too, if the offence for which the person punished is one against a secret law which it was impossible for him to know of, the punishment is gravely unjust. Similarly, punishment of other innocent people—for example, as scapegoats—to deter others, is unjust

1. "An Examination of Restricted Utilitarianism," *Philosophical Review*, Vol. LXVI, 4 (Oct., 1957); 'The Complexity of the Concepts of Punishment,' *Philosophy*, Vol. XXXVII, pp. 307–325 (Oct., 1962).

and morally wrong. So too is collective punishment—killing all the members of a village or family for the offences of one member. Whether such punishments successfully deter seems irrelevant to the question of their justice. Similarly, certain punishments of persons who are offenders in the morally relevant sense of 'offenders' also impress us as gravely unjust. We now consider to have been gravely unjust the very severe punishments meted out to those punished by hanging or transportation and penal servitude for petty thefts in the 18th century. Comparable punishments, for example, hanging for shoplifting from a food market, would be condemned today as equally unjust. It is conceivable that such unjust punishments may, in extreme circumstances, become permissible, but this would only be so if a grave evil has to be perpetrated to achieve a very considerable good.

In brief, our moral consciousness suggests that punishment, to be just, must be merited by the committing of an offence. It follows from this that punishment, to be justly administered, must involve care in determining whether the offending person is really a responsible agent. And it implies that the punishment must not be excessive. It must not exceed what is appropriate to the crime. We must always be able to say of the person punished that he deserved to be punished as he was punished. It is not enough to say that good results were achieved by punishing him. It is logically possible to say that the punishment was useful but undeserved, and deserved but not useful. It is not possible to say that the punishment was just although undeserved.

These features of ordinary moral thinking about just punishment appear to be features of which any defensible theory of punishment needs to take note. Punishment of innocent people—through collective punishments, scapegoat punishment, as a result of inefficient trial procedures, corrupt police methods, mistaken tests of responsibility, etc., or by using criteria of what constitute offences which allow to be offences, offences under secret and retroactive laws—is unjust punishment, as is punishment which is disproportionate with the crime. Thus the punishment which we consider, after critical reflection, to be just punishment, is punishment which fits a retributive theory. It is to be noted that it is just punishment, not morally permissible punishment, of which this is being claimed. Sometimes it is morally permissible and obligatory to override the dictates of justice. The retributive theory is a theory about justice in punishment and tells only part of the whole story about the morality of punishment. It points to a very important consideration in determining the morality of punishment—namely, its justice—and explains what punishments are just and why they are just.

Before proceeding further, some comment should be made concerning these allusions to 'what our common moral consciousness regards as just or unjust.' Utilitarians frequently wish to dismiss such appeals to our moral consciousness as amounting to an uncritical acceptance of our emotional responses. Obviously they are not that. Our uncritical moral consciousness gives answers which we do not accept as defensible after critical reflection, and it is the judgements which we accept after critical reflection which are being appealed to here. In any case, before the utilitarian starts questioning this approach, he would do well to make sure that he himself is secure from similar criticism. It might well be argued that his appeal to the principle of utility itself rests upon an uncritical emotional acceptance of what prima facie appears to be a high-minded moral principle but which, on critical examination, seems to involve grave moral evils. Thus the problem of method, and of justifying the use of this method, is one which the utilitarian shares with the nonutilitarian. It is not possible here to argue for the soundness of this mode of argument beyond noting that whether an intuitionist or noncognitivist meta-ethic be true, this sort of appeal is what such meta-ethical theories suggest to be appropriate.

III. WHAT UTILITARIANISM APPEARS TO ENTAIL IN RESPECT OF PUNISHMENT

Is all useful punishment just punishment, and is all just punishment useful? Here it is necessary first to dispose of what might not unfairly be described as 'red herring.' A lot of recent utilitarian writing is to the effect that punishment of the innocent is logically impossible, and hence that utilitarianism cannot be committed to punishment of the innocent. Their point is that the concept of punishment entails that the person being punished be an actual or supposed offender, for otherwise we do not call it punishment but injury, harm-infliction, social quarantining, and so forth. There are two good reasons for rejecting this argument as nothing but a red herring. Not all unjust punishment is punishment of the innocent. Much is punishment which is excessive. Thus even if punishment of the innocent were not logically possible, the problem of justice in punishment would remain in the form of showing that only punishments commensurate with the offence were useful. Secondly, the verbal point leaves

the issue of substance untouched. The real quarrel between the retributionist and the utilitarian is whether a system of inflictions of suffering on people without reference to the gravity of their offences or even to whether they have committed offences, is just and morally permissible. It is immaterial whether we call such deliberate inflictions of sufferings punishment, social surgery, social quarantining, and so forth. In any case, as I have elsewhere tried to show, the claim is evidently false. We the observers and the innocent victims of such punishment call it punishment, unjust punishment. In so referring to it there is no straining of language.

To consider now whether all useful punishment is just punishment. When the problem of utilitarianism in punishment is put in this way, the appeal of the utilitarian approach somewhat diminishes. It appears to be useful to do lots of things which are unjust and undesirable. Whilst it is no doubt true that harsh punishment isn't necessarily the most useful punishment, and that punishment of the guilty person is usually the most useful punishment, it is nonetheless easy to call to mind cases of punishment of innocent people, of mentally deranged people, of excessive punishment, and so forth, inflicted because it was believed to be useful. Furthermore, the person imposing such punishment seems not always to be mistaken. Similarly, punishment which is just may be less useful than rewards. With some criminals, it may be more useful to reward them. As Ross observes:

A utilitarian theory, whether of the hedonistic or of the 'ideal' kind, if it justifies punishment at all, is bound to justify it solely on the ground of the effects it produces. . . . In principle, then, the punishment of a guilty person is treated by utilitarians as not different in kind from the imposition of inconvenience, say by quarantine regulations, on innocent individuals for the good of the community.[2]

What is shocking about this, and what most utilitarians now seek to avoid admitting to be an implication of utilitarianism, is the implication that grave injustices in the form of punishment of the innocent, of those not responsible for their acts, or harsh punishments of those guilty of trivial offences, are dictated by their theory. We may sometimes best deter others by punishing, by framing, an innocent man who is generally believed to be guilty, or by adopting rough and ready trial procedures, as is done by army courts martial in the heat of battle in respect of deserters, and so forth; or we may severely punish a person not responsible for his actions, as so often happens with military punishments for cowardice, and in civil cases involving sex crimes where the legal definition of insanity may fail to cover the relevant cases of insanity. Sometimes we may deter others by imposing ruthless sentences for crimes which are widespread, as with car stealing and shoplifting in food markets. We may make people very thoughtful about their political commitments by having retroactive laws about their political affiliations, and we may, by secret laws, such as make to be major crimes what are believed simply to be antisocial practices and not crimes at all, usefully encourage a watchful, public-spirited behaviour. If the greatest good or the greatest happiness of the greatest number is the foundation of the morality and justice of punishment, there can be no guarantee that some such injustices may not be dictated by it. Indeed, one would expect that it would depend on the details of the situation and on the general features of the society, which punishments and institutions of pun-

ishment were most useful. In most practical affairs affecting human welfare, for example, forms of government, laws, social institutions, and so forth, what is useful is relative to the society and situation. It would therefore be surprising if this were not also the case with punishment. We should reasonably expect to find that different punishments and systems of punishment were useful for different occasions, times, communities, peoples, and be such that some useful punishments involved grave and shocking injustices. Whether this is in fact the case is an empirical matter which is best settled by social and historical research, for there is evidence available which bears on which of the various types of punishments and institutions work best in the sense of promoting the greatest good. Although this is not a question for which the philosopher *qua* philosopher is well equipped to deal, I shall nonetheless later briefly look at a number of considerations which are relevant to it, but only because the utilitarian usually bases his defence of utilitarianism on his alleged knowledge of empirical matters of fact, upon his claim to know that the particular punishments and that system of punishment which we regard as most just, are most conducive to the general good. J. Bentham, and in our own day, J. J. C. Smart, are among the relatively few utilitarians who are prepared—in the case of Smart, albeit reluctantly—to accept that utilitarian punishment may be unjust by conventional standards, but morally right nonetheless.

Against the utilitarian who seeks to argue that utilitarianism does not involve unjust punishment, there is a very simple argument, namely, that whether

2. W. D. Ross, *The Right and the Good*, Oxford University Press, Oxford 1930, p. 56.

or not unjust punishments are in fact useful, it is logically possible that they will at some time become useful, in which case utilitarians are committed to them. Utilitarianism involves the conclusion that if it is useful to punish lunatics, mentally deranged people, innocent people framed as being guilty, and so forth, it is obligatory to do so. It would be merely a contingent fact, if it were a fact at all, that the punishment which works is that which we consider to be morally just. In principle, the utilitarian is committed to saying that we should not ask "Is the punishment deserved?" The notion of desert does not arise for him. The only relevant issue is whether the punishment produces greater good.

IV. WHAT UTILITARIANISM IN FACT ENTAILS IN THE LIGHT OF EMPIRICAL CONSIDERATIONS

What is the truth about the utility of the various types of punishments? As I have already suggested, it would be astonishing if, in the sphere of punishment, only those punishments and that institution of punishment we consider to be just, worked best. To look at particular examples.

In an article cited above, I argued that a utilitarian would be committed to unjust punishment, and used the example of a sheriff framing an innocent Negro in order to stop a series of lynchings which he knew would occur if the guilty person were not immediately found, or believed to have been found.[3] I suggested that if the sheriff were a utilitarian he would frame an innocent man to save the lives of others. Against this example, it is suggested that we cannot know with certainty what the consequences of framing the Negro would be, and that there may be other important consequences besides the prevention of

lynchings. Utilitarians point to the importance of people having confidence in the impartiality and fairness of the legal system, a belief that lawful behavior pays, and so forth. However, as the example is set up, only the sheriff, the innocent victim and the guilty man and not the general public, would know there had been a frameup. Further, even if a few others knew, this would not mean that everyone knew; and even if everyone came to know, surely, if utilitarianism is thought to be the true moral theory, the general body of citizens ought to be happier believing that their sheriff is promoting what is right rather than promoting nonutilitarian standards of justice. Since complex factors are involved, this example is not as decisive as is desirable. It can readily be modified so as to avoid many of these complications and hence become more decisive. Suppose a utilitarian were visiting an area in which there was racial strife, and that, during his visit, a Négro rapes a white woman, and that race riots occur as a result of the crime, white mobs, with the connivance of the police, bashing and killing Negroes, and so forth. Suppose too that our utilitarian is in the area of the crime when it is committed such that his testimony would bring about the conviction of a particular Negro. If he knows that a quick arrest will stop the riots and lynchings, surely, as a utilitarian, he must conclude that he has a duty to bear false witness in order to bring about the punishment of an innocent person. In such a situation, he has, on utilitarian theory, an evident duty to bring about the punishment of an innocent man. What unpredictable consequences, and so forth, are present here other than of a kind that are present in every moral

3. "An Examination of Restricted Utilitarianism," op. cit., pp. 468–469.

situation? Clearly, the utilitarian will not be corrupted by bearing false witness, for he will be doing what he believes to be his duty. It is relevant that it is rare for any of us to be in a situation in which we can usefully and tellingly bear false witness against others.

We may similarly give possible examples of useful punishments of other unjust kinds. Scapegoat punishment need not be and typically is not of a framed person. It may be useful. An occupying power which is experiencing trouble with the local population may find it useful to punish, by killing, some of the best loved citizen leaders, each time an act of rebellion occurs; but such punishments do not commend themselves to us as just and right. Similarly, collective punishment is often useful—consider its use in schools. There we consider it unjust but morally permissible because of its great utility. Collective punishments of the kind employed by the Nazis in Czechoslovakia—destroying a village and punishing its inhabitants for the acts of a few—are notorious as war crimes. Yet they appear to have been useful in the sense of achieving Nazi objectives. It may be objected that the Nazi sense of values was mistaken, that such punishment would not contribute towards realizing higher values and goods. But it is partly an accident of history that it was the Nazis who, in recent times, resorted to this method. If we had had to occupy a Nazi territory with inadequate troops, this might have been the only effective way of maintaining order. As with human affairs generally, it would depend on many factors, including the strength of our troops, the degree of hostility of the occupied people, their temper and likely reaction to this sort of collective punishment, and so forth. Punishment of relatives could also be useful. It would be an interesting social experiment in those modern democracies which are plagued by juvenile delinquency, for parents as well as the teenage delinquents to be punished. Such punishment would be unjust but it might well be useful. It would need a number of social experiments to see whether it is or is not useful. It is not a matter we can settle by intuitive insight. If it did prove useful, it is probable people would come to think of such punishment of parents as punishment for the offence of being a parent of a delinquent! This would obscure the awareness of the injustice of such punishment, but it would nonetheless be unjust punishment.

Similarly with punishment for offences under secret and retroactive laws. Such laws, it is true, would be useful only if used sparingly and for very good reasons but it is not hard to imagine cases where the use of a retroactive law might be useful in the long as well as in the short run. That a plausible case could have been made out for introducing retroactive laws in postwar Germany on utilitarian grounds as well as on the other sorts of grounds indicated by legal theorists, suggests that such cases do occur. They may be the most useful means, they may, in the German case, even have been morally permissible means and the means of achieving greater total justice; but they are nonetheless means which in themselves are unjust. Retroactive laws are really a kind of secret law. Their injustice consists in this; and secret laws, like them, seem useful if used sparingly and with discretion. The Nazis certainly believed them to be very useful but again it will no doubt be said that this was because their system of values was mistaken. However, unless the system of values includes respect for considerations of justice, such secret laws are possibly useful instruments for promoting good.

In our own community we define 'offence' in such a way, with various laws, that we condone unjust punishment because of its utility. The vagrancy law is a very useful law but what it declares to be an offence is hardly an offence in the morally relevant sense. And it is not difficult to imagine countries in which it would be useful to have a law making it an offence to arouse the suspicions of the government. Suppose there were a democratic revolution in Spain, or in Russia, which led to the perilous existence of a democratic government. Such a government might find that the only way in which it could safely continue in existence was by having such a law and similar laws involving unjust punishments. It would then have to consider which was morally more important—to avoid the unjust punishments which such a law involves, or to secure and make permanent a democratic form of government which achieved greater over-all injustice. That is, it would face conflicting claims of justice.

In an ignorant community it might well be useful to punish as responsible moral agents 'criminals' who in fact were not responsible for their actions but who were generally believed to be responsible agents. The experts suggest that many sex offenders and others who commit the more shocking crimes, are of this type, but even in reasonably enlightened communities the general body of citizens do not always accept the judgments of the experts. Thus, in communities in which enlightened opinion generally prevails (and these are few) punishment of mentally deranged 'criminals' would have little if any deterrent value, whereas in most communities some mentally deranged people may usefully be punished, and in ignorant, backward communities very

useful results may come from punishing those not responsible for their actions. Similarly, very undesirable results may come from not punishing individuals generally believed to be fully responsible moral agents. Yet, clearly, the morality of punishing such people does not depend on the degree of the enlightenment of the community. Utilitarian theory suggests that it does, that such punishment is right and just in ignorant, prejudiced communities, unjust in enlightened communities. The utility of such punishment varies in this way, but not its justice. The tests of responsible action are very difficult to determine, although this need not worry the utilitarian who should use the test of utility in this area as elsewhere. However, to make my point, we need not consider borderline cases. The more atrocious and abominable the crime, the more pointless its brutality is, the more likely it is that the criminal was not responsible and the more likely that the general public will believe him to be fully responsible and deserving of the severest punishment.

Utilitarians often admit that particular punishments may be useful but unjust and argue that utilitarianism becomes more plausible and indeed, acceptable, if it is advanced as a theory about the test of rules and institutions. These utilitarians argue that we should not test particular punishments by reference to their consequences; rather, we should test the whole institution of punishment in this way, by reference to the consequences of the whole institution.

This seems an incredible concession; yet rule-utilitarianism enjoys widespread support and is perhaps the dominant version of utilitarianism. It is argued that particular utilitarian punishments may be unjust but that useful systems of punishment are those which are just systems in the judgment of our reflective moral consciousness. This modification of utilitarianism involves a strange concession. After all, if the test of right and wrong rules and institutions lies in their utility, it is surely fantastic to suggest that this test should be confined to rules and institutions, unless it is useful so to confine its application. Clearly, when we judge the utility of particular actions, we should take note of the effects on the institution or rule, but surely, it is individual acts and their consequences which ultimately matter for the utilitarian. There are therefore good reasons for believing that the half-hearted utilitarianism of rule-utilitarianism involves an indefensible compromise between act-utilitarianism and Ross's theory of a plurality of irreducible prima facie duties.

To consider now the implications of rule-utilitarianism. As with act-utilitarianism, it would be surprising if what was useful was also at all times just, and that what was the most useful institution of punishment was the same under all conditions and for all times. For example, what we in Australia regard as useful and just, fair trial procedures—and these are an important part of justice in punishment—for example, rules about the burden of proof, strict limitation of newspaper comment before and during the trial, selection of the jury, provision of legal aid for the needy, and so forth, differ from those found useful in dictatorships. Also, obviously a country emerging from the instability of a great revolution cannot afford to take risks with criminals and counter-revolutionaries which a stable, secure, well established community can afford to take. In Australia we can take the risk of allowing a few traitors to escape deserved punishment as a result of our careful procedures directed at ensuring that the innocent be not punished in error. During a war we may take fewer risks but at the expense of injustices. In an unstable community, immediately after a revolution, a more cavalier approach to justice is usually found to be the most useful approach. And there are differences within any one community. What is useful for civil courts is not necessarily what is most useful for military courts, and the most useful 'institution' for the whole community may be a mixture of different systems of justice and punishment. Thus not only particular punishments but also whole institutions of punishment may be useful but of a kind we consider to be gravely unjust. It is these difficulties of utilitarianism—of act- and rule-utilitarianism—and the facts which give rise to these difficulties which give to the retributive theory, that the vicious deserve to suffer, its initial plausibility.

V. POSITIVE CONSIDERATIONS FOR A RETRIBUTIVE THEORY OF PUNISHMENT

There are many positive considerations in support of the retributive theory of punishment, if it is constructed as the theory that the vicious deserve to suffer. Firstly, it is a particular application of a general principle of justice, namely, that equals should be treated equally and unequals unequally. This is a principle which has won very general acceptance as a self-evident principle of justice. It is the principle from which the more celebrated, yet opposed accounts of justice, are derived. It is a principle which has wide application and which underlies our judgments of justice in the various areas. We think of it as applying—other things being equal—to fair prices, wages and treatment generally. It is in terms of such a principle that we think that political discrimination against women and peoples of special races is unjust, and that against children, just. Justice in these areas involves treating equals equally, unequals unequally— where the equals are equal in the relevant respect, and the unequals unequal in the relevant respect. Hence it is that we think it just to deny women some jobs because of their weaker physique, but unjust to exclude a woman from a post such as librarian or violinist if she is more proficient as such than other candidates for the post. So too with justice and punishment. The criminal is one who has made himself unequal in the relevant sense. Hence he merits unequal treatment. In this case, unequal treatment amounts to deliberate infliction of evils—suffering or death.

We now need to consider whether our retributive theory implies that there is a duty to punish with full, deserved punishment. Look at the other areas of justice, for example, wage justice. If it is just, say, to pay a labourer £20 a week, there is no breach of justice if the employer shows benevolence and pays £25, whereas there is a grave breach if he pays only £15. Similarly with retributive justice, but in a reverse way. We do not act unjustly if, moved by benevolence, we impose less than is demanded by justice, but there is a grave injustice if the deserved punishment is exceeded. If the deserved punishment is inflicted, all we need to do to justify it is to point out that the crime committed deserved and merited such punishment. Suppose that the just punishment for murder is imprisonment for 15 years. Suppose also that the judge knows that the murderer he is about to sentence will never be tempted to commit another murder, that he is deeply and genuinely remorseful, and that others will not be encouraged to commit murders if he is treated

leniently. If the judge imposed a mild penalty we should probably applaud his humanity, but if he imposed the maximum penalty we should not be entitled to condemn him as unjust. What we say in cases like this is that the judge is a hard, even harsh, man, not that he is an unjust man.

Is only deserved punishment morally permissible? Obviously not. Here we might take an analogy with other parts of morality. It is wrong to lie, to break promises, or to steal. This is not to say that we are never obliged to lie, break promises, steal, and so forth. What it means is that we need to have another, conflicting, more stringent duty which overrides the duty to tell the truth, keep our promise, or not steal, if we are to be justified in lying, breaking our promise, or stealing. Similarly with justice in punishment. The fact that a punishment is just entitles the appropriate authority to inflict it, but that is not to say that it must be inflicted nor that more cannot properly be inflicted. Many considerations may weigh with the relevant authority and make it morally right to inflict more or less than is strictly just; and not all such considerations will be utilitarian considerations—some may be other considerations of justice. We determine what punishment ought to be inflicted by taking into account firstly what punishment is deserved, and then other considerations. Relevant here are considerations such as that the criminal's wife and children may be the real victims of the punishment, that the criminal would be unable to make restitution to the person whose property he has stolen; of benevolence, for example, in not imposing the punishment because the criminal has already suffered greatly in blinding himself in attempting to blow a safe; of the general good, as in making an example of the criminal and inflicting more than the deserved punishment because of the grave consequences that will come about if this type of crime is not immediately checked, and so forth. Production of the greatest good is obviously a relevant consideration when determining which punishment may properly be inflicted, but the question as to which punishment is just is a much more basic and important consideration. When considering that question we need to determine whether the person to be punished committed an offence in the morally relevant sense of 'offence' and what punishment is commensurate with the offence.

It is important here to note and dismiss a commonly made criticism of this retributive theory, namely, that there is no objective test of the gravity of a crime except in terms of the penalty attached to the crime. If the penalty is hanging, then, it is argued, the crime is a serious one; if the penalty is a £2 fine, it is a trivial offence. This criticism is often reinforced by the contention that if all the people in any given group were to make out lists of crimes in order of their gravity, they would give significantly different lists such that what appear as grave crimes on one list are minor crimes on other lists. Obviously, if this criticism were sound, it would mean that one very important element of the retributive theory would be nullified, for punishment could not be other than commensurate with the offence. However, this criticism is unsound and rests on a number of confusions.

It is true that we speak of a crime as serious if the penalty is hanging, but this is not to say that it is therefore a grave crime in the morally significant sense of 'grave crime.' The fact that hanging was the penalty for stealing a loaf of bread made that a serious offence in one sense but not in another, for we speak of the punishment as gravely disproportionate and as treating the offence as much more serious than it really is. It is on this basis that we can and do speak of penalties as being too light or too heavy, even where similar offences have similar penalties. It is unjust that the theft of a loaf of bread should meet with the same punishment as murder. Further, the fact that we reach different conclusions about the relative gravity of different crimes constitutes no difficulty for the retributive theory. Most of us would agree that murder is a very serious crime and that shoplifting a cake of soap is a considerably lesser offence. We should perhaps differ about such questions as to whether kidnapping is more or less serious than blackmail, whether embezzlement should be treated as a lesser crime than housebreaking, whether stealing a car worth £2,000 is less serious than stealing £2,000 worth of jewelry. We do disagree, and most of us would have doubts about the right order of the gravity of crimes. This shows very little. We have the same doubts—and disagreements—in other areas of morality where we are uncertain about which duties are more stringent, and where we differ from others in our ordering of duties. Similarly, utilitarians differ among themselves about goods such that if a group of utilitarians were asked to list goods in their order of goodness we could confidently expect different lists of different goods and of goods listed in different orders. But this would not show that utilitarianism is therefore a theory to be discounted. It shows simply that whatever theory of punishment is adopted, there will be disagreements and uncertainties as to precisely what it dictates. With the utilitarian theory, the uncertainty and doubts arise concerning the assessments of the value of the goods and the determination of which goods should be promoted by punishment. With the retributive theory the difficulties arise in determining the relative gravity of offences; and there,

clearly, the appropriate method of seeking to resolve our doubts is neither to look at what punishments are in fact imposed, nor at what punishments will produce the greatest good, but rather to look at the nature of the offence itself.

17

JOHN RAWLS
Promising and Punishment

JOHN RAWLS is professor of philosophy at Harvard University. His book *A Theory of Justice* (1971) was hailed by

reviewers as the most important work of moral philosophy to appear in many years.

In this paper I want to show the importance of the distinction between justifying a practice and justifying a particular action falling under it, and I want to explain the logical basis of this distinction and how it is possible to miss its significance. While the distinction has frequently been made, and is now becoming commonplace, there remains the task of explaining the tendency either to overlook it altogether, or to fail to appreciate its importance.

To show the importance of the distinction I am going to defend utilitarianism against those objections which have traditionally been made against it in connection with punishment and the obligation to keep promises. I hope to show that if one uses the distinction in question then one can state utilitar-

ianism in a way which makes it a much better explication of our considered moral judgments than these traditional objections would seem to admit. Thus the importance of the distinction is shown by the way it strengthens the utilitarian view regardless of whether that view is completely defensible or not.

To explain how the significance of the distinction may be overlooked, I am going to discuss two conceptions of rules. One of these conceptions conceals the importance of distinguishing between the justification of a rule or practice and the justification of a particular action falling under it. The other conception makes it clear why this distinction must be made and what is its logical basis.

From John Rawls, "Two Concepts of Rules," *The Philosophical Review*, vol. 64 (1955), pp. 3–18. Reprinted by permission of the author and the editors of *The Philosophical Review*. The latter parts of this article, and footnotes, are omitted.

I

The subject of punishment, in the sense of attaching legal penalties to the violation of legal rules, has always been a troubling moral question. The trouble about it has not been that people disagree as to whether or not punishment is justifiable. Most people have held that, freed from certain abuses, it is an acceptable institution. Only a few have rejected punishment entirely, which is rather surprising when one considers all that can be said against it. The difficulty is with the justification of punishment: Various arguments for it have been given by moral philosophers, but so far none of them has won any sort of general acceptance; no justification is without those who detest it. I hope to show that the use of the aforementioned distinction enables one to state the utilitarian view in a way which allows for the sound points of its critics.

For our purposes we may say that there are two justifications of punishment. What we may call the retributive view is that punishment is justified on the grounds that wrongdoing merits punishment. It is morally fitting that a person who does wrong should suffer in proportion to his wrongdoing. That a criminal should be punished follows from his guilt, and the severity of the appropriate punishment depends on the depravity of his act. The state of affairs where a wrongdoer suffers punishment is morally better than the state of affairs where he does not; and it is better irrespective of any of the consequences of punishing him.

What we may call the utilitarian view holds that on the principle that bygones are bygones and that only future consequences are material to present decisions, punishment is justifiable only by reference to the probable consequences of maintaining it as one of the devices of the social order. Wrongs committed in the past are, as such, not relevant considerations for deciding what to do. If punishment can

be shown to promote effectively the interest of society it is justifiable, otherwise it is not.

I have stated these two competing views very roughly to make one feel the conflict between them: One feels the force of *both* arguments and one wonders how they can be reconciled. From my introductory remarks it is obvious that the resolution which I am going to propose is that in this case one must distinguish between justifying a practice as a system of rules to be applied and enforced, and justifying a particular action which falls under these rules; utilitarian arguments are appropriate with regard to questions about practices, while retributive arguments fit the application of particular rules to particular cases.

We might try to get clear about this distinction by imagining how a father might answer the question of his son. Suppose the son asks, "Why was *J* put in jail yesterday?" The father answers, "Because he robbed the bank at *B*. He was duly tried and found guilty. That's why he was put in jail yesterday." But suppose the son had asked a different question, namely, "Why do people put other people in jail?" Then the father might answer, "To protect good people from bad people" or "To stop people from doing things that would make it uneasy for all of us; for otherwise we wouldn't be able to go to bed at night and sleep in peace." There are two very different questions here. One question emphasizes the proper name: It asks why *J* was punished rather than someone else, or it asks what he was punished for. The other question asks why we have the institution of punishment: Why do people punish one another rather than, say, always forgiving one another?

Thus the father says in effect that a

particular man is punished, rather than some other man, because he is guilty, and he is guilty because he broke the law (past tense). In his case the law looks back, the judge looks back, the jury looks back, and a penalty is visited upon him for something he did. That a man is to be punished, and what his punishment is to be, is settled by its being shown that he broke the law and that the law assigns that penalty for the violation of it.

On the other hand we have the institution of punishment itself, and recommend and accept various changes in it, because it is thought by the (ideal) legislator and by those to whom the law applies that, as a part of a system of law impartially applied from case to case arising under it, it will have the consequence, in the long run, of furthering the interests of society.

One can say, then, that the judge and the legislator stand in different positions and look in different directions: one to the past, the other to the future. The justification of what the judge does, *qua* judge, sounds like the retributive view; the justification of what the (ideal) legislator does, *qua* legislator, sounds like the utilitarian view. Thus both views have a point (this is as it should be since intelligent and sensitive persons have been on both sides of the argument); and one's initial confusion disappears once one sees that these views apply to persons holding different offices with different duties, and situated differently with respect to the system of rules that make up the criminal law.

One might say, however, that the utilitarian view is more fundamental since it applies to a more fundamental office, for the judge carries out the legislator's will so far as he can determine it. Once the legislator decides to

have laws and to assign penalties for their violation (as things are there must be both the law and the penalty) an institution is set up which involves a retributive conception of particular cases. It is part of the concept of the criminal law as a system of rules that the application and enforcement of these rules in particular cases should be justifiable by arguments of a retributive character. The decision whether or not to use law rather than some other mechanism of social control, and the decision as to what laws to have and what penalties to assign, may be settled by utilitarian arguments; but if one decides to have laws then one has decided on something whose working in particular cases is retributive in form.

The answer, then, to the confusion engendered by the two views of punishment is quite simple: One distinguishes two offices, that of the judge and that of the legislator, and one distinguishes their different stations with respect to the system of rules which make up the law; and then one notes that the different sorts of considerations which would usually be offered as reasons for what is done under the cover of these offices can be paired off with the competing justifications of punishment. One reconciles the two views by the time-honored device of making them apply to different situations.

But can it really be this simple? Well, this answer allows for the apparent intent of each side. Does a person who advocates the retributive view necessarily advocate, as an *institution*, legal machinery whose essential purpose is to set up and preserve a correspondence between moral turpitude and suffering? Surely not. What retributionists have rightly insisted upon is that no man can be punished unless he is guilty, that is, unless he has broken the law. Their fundamental criticism of the utilitarian account is that, as they interpret it, it sanctions an innocent person's being punished (if one may call it that) for the benefit of society.

On the other hand, utilitarians agree that punishment is to be inflicted only for the violation of law. They regard this much as understood from the concept of punishment itself. The point of the utilitarian account concerns the institution as a system of rules: Utilitarianism seeks to limit its use by declaring it justifiable only if it can be shown to foster effectively the good of society. Historically it is a protest against the indiscriminate and ineffective use of the criminal law. It seeks to dissuade us from assigning to penal institutions the improper, if not sacrilegious, task of matching suffering with mortal turpitude. Like others, utilitarians want penal institutions designed so that, as far as humanly possible, only those who break the law run afoul of it. They hold that no official should have discretionary power to inflict penalties whenever he thinks it for the benefit of society; for on utilitarian grounds an institution granting such power could not be justified.

The suggested way of reconciling the retributive and the utilitarian justifications of punishment seems to account for what both sides have wanted to say. There are, however, two further questions which arise, and I shall devote the remainder of this section to them.

First, will not a difference of opinion as to the proper criterion of just law make the proposed reconciliation unacceptable to retributionists? Will they not question whether, if the utilitarian principle is used as the criterion, it fol-lows that those who have broken the law are guilty in a way which satisfies their demand that those punished deserve to be punished? To answer this difficulty, suppose that the rules of the criminal law are justified on utilitarian grounds (it is only for laws that meet his criterion that the utilitarian can be held responsible). Then it follows that the actions which the criminal law specifies as offenses are such that, if they were tolerated, terror and alarm would spread in society. Consequently, retributionists can only deny that those who are punished deserve to be punished if they deny that such actions are wrong. This they will not want to do.

The second question is whether utilitarianism doesn't justify too much. One pictures it as an engine of justification which, if consistently adopted, could be used to justify cruel and arbitrary institutions. Retributionists may be supposed to concede that utilitarians *intend* to reform the law and to make it more humane; that utilitarians do not *wish* to justify any such thing as punishment of the innocent; and that utilitarians may appeal to the fact that punishment presupposes guilt in the sense that by punishment one understands an institution attaching penalties to the infraction of legal rules, and therefore that it is logically absurd to suppose that utilitarians in justifying *punishment* might also have justified punishment (if we may call it that) of the innocent. The real question, however, is whether the utilitarian, in justifying punishment, hasn't used arguments which commit him to accepting the infliction of suffering on innocent persons if it is for the good of society (whether or not one calls this punishment). More generally, isn't the utilitarian committed in principle to accepting many practices which he, as a morally sensitive person, wouldn't want to accept? Retributionists are inclined to hold that there is no way to stop the utilitarian principle from justifying too much except by adding to it a principle which distributes certain rights to individuals. Then the amended criterion is not the greatest benefit of society *simpliciter*, but the greatest benefit of society subject to the constraint that no one's rights may be violated. Now while I think that the classical utilitarians proposed a criterion of this more complicated sort, I do not want to argue that point here. What I want to show is that there is *another* way of preventing the utilitarian principle from justifying too much, or at least of making it much less likely to do so: namely, by stating utilitarianism in a way which accounts for the distinction between the justification of an institution and the justification of a particular action falling under it.

I begin by defining the institution of punishment as follows: A person is said to suffer punishment whenever he is legally deprived of some of the normal rights of a citizen on the ground that he has violated a rule of law, the violation having been established by trial according to the due process of law, provided that the deprivation is carried out by the recognized legal authorities of the state, that the rule of law clearly specifies both the offense and the attached penalty, that the courts construe statutes strictly, and that the statute was on the books prior to the time of the offense. This definition specifies what I shall understand by punishment. The question is whether utilitarian arguments may be found to justify institutions widely different from this and such as one would find cruel and arbitrary.

This question is best answered, I think, by taking up a particular accusation. Consider the following from Carritt:

. . .the utilitarian must hold that we are justified in inflicting pain always and only to prevent worse pain or bring about greater happiness. This, then, is all we need to consider in so-called punishment, which must be purely preventive. But if some kind of very cruel crime becomes common, and none of the criminals can be caught, it might be highly expedient, as an example, to hang an innocent man, if a charge against him could be so framed that he were universally thought guilty; indeed this would only fail to be an ideal instance of utilitarian 'punishment' because the victim himself would not have been so likely as a real felon to commit such a crime in the future; in all other respects it would be perfectly deterrent and therefore felicific.

Carritt is trying to show that there are occasions when a utilitarian argument would justify taking an action which would be generally condemned; and thus that utilitarianism justifies too much. But the failure of Carritt's argument lies in the fact that he makes no distinction between the justification of the general system of rules which constitutes penal institutions and the justification of particular applications of these rules to particular cases by the various officials whose job it is to administer them. This becomes perfectly clear when one asks who the "we" are of whom Carritt speaks. Who is this who has a sort of absolute authority on particular occasions to decide that an innocent man shall be "punished" if everyone can be convinced that he is guilty? Is this person the legislator, or the judge, or the body of private citizens, or what? It is utterly crucial to know who is to decide such matters, and by what authority, for all of this must be written into the rules of the institution. Until one knows these things one doesn't know what the institution is whose justification is being challenged; and as the utilitarian principle applies to the institution one doesn't know whether it is justifiable on utilitarian grounds or not.

Once this is understood it is clear what the countermove to Carritt's argument is. One must describe more carefully what the *institution* is which his example suggests, and then ask oneself whether or not it is likely that having this institution would be for the benefit of society in the long run. One must not content oneself with the vague thought that, when it's a question of *this* case, it would be a good thing if *somebody* did something even if an innocent person were to suffer.

Try to imagine, then, an institution (which we may call "telishment") which is such that the officials set up by it have authority to arrange a trial for the condemnation of an innocent man whenever they are of the opinion that doing so would be in the best interests of society. The discretion of officials is limited, however, by the rule that they may not condemn an innocent man to undergo such an ordeal unless there is, at the time, a wave of offenses similar to that with which they charge him and telish him for. We may imagine that the officials having the discretionary authority are the judges of the higher courts in consultation with the chief of police, the minister of justice, and a committee of the legislature.

Once one realizes that one is involved in setting up an *institution*, one sees that the hazards are very great. For example, what check is there on the officials? How is one to tell whether or not their actions are authorized? How is one to limit the risks involved in allowing such systematic deception? How is one to avoid giving anything short of

complete discretion to the authorities to telish anyone they like? In addition to these considerations, it is obvious that people will come to have a very different attitude towards their penal system when telishment is adjoined to it. They will be uncertain as to whether a convicted man has been punished or telished. They will wonder whether or not they should feel sorry for him. They will wonder whether the same fate won't at any time fall on them. If one pictures how such an institution would actually work, and the enormous risks involved in it, it seems clear that it would serve no useful purpose. A utilitarian justification for this institution is most unlikely.

It happens in general that as one drops off the defining features of punishment one ends up with an institution whose utilitarian justification is highly doubtful. One reason for this is that punishment works like a kind of price system: By altering the prices one has to pay for the performance of actions it supplies a motive for avoiding some actions and doing others. The defining features are essential if punishment is to work in this way; so that an institution which lacks these features, for example, an institution which is set up to "punish" the innocent, is likely to have about as much point as a price system (if one may call it that) where the prices of things change at random from day to day and one learns the price of something after one has agreed to buy it.

If one is careful to apply the utilitarian principle to the institution which is to authorize particular actions, then there is *less* danger of its justifying too much. Carritt's example gains plausibility by its indefiniteness and by its concentration on the particular case. His argument will only hold if it can be shown that there are utilitarian arguments which justify an institution whose publicly ascertainable offices and powers are such as to permit officials to exercise that kind of discretion in particular cases. But the requirement of having to build the arbitrary features of the particular decision into the institutional practice makes the justification much less likely to go through.

II

I shall now consider the question of promises. The objection to utilitarianism in connection with promises seems to be this: It is believed that on the utilitarian view when a person makes a promise the only ground upon which he should keep it, if he should keep it, is that by keeping it he will realize the most good on the whole. So that if one asks the question "Why should I keep *my* promise?" the utilitarian answer is understood to be that doing so in *this* case will have the best consequences. And this answer is said, quite rightly, to conflict with the way in which the obligation to keep promises is regarded.

Now of course critics of utilitarianism are not unaware that one defense sometimes attributed to utilitarians is the consideration involving the practice of promise-keeping. In this connection they are supposed to argue something like this: It must be admitted that we feel strictly about keeping promises, more strictly than it might seem our view can account for. But when we consider the matter carefully it is always necessary to take into account the effect which our action will have on the practice of making promises. The promisor must weigh, not only the effects of breaking his promise on the particular case, but also the effect which his breaking his promise will have on the practice itself. Since the practice is of great

utilitarian value, and since breaking one's promise always seriously damages it, one will seldom be justified in breaking one's promise. If we view our individual promises in the wider context of the practice of promising itself we can account for the strictness of the obligation to keep promises. There is always one very strong utilitarian consideration in favor of keeping them, and this will insure that when the question arises as to whether or not to keep a promise it will usually turn out that one should, even where the facts of the particular case taken by itself would seem to justify one's breaking it. In this way the strictness with which we view the obligation to keep promises is accounted for.

Ross has criticized this defense as follows: However great the value of the practice of promising, on utilitarian grounds, there must be some value which is greater, and one can imagine it to be obtainable by breaking a promise. Therefore there might be a case where the promisor could argue that breaking his promise was justified as leading to a better state of affairs on the whole. And the promisor could argue in this way no matter how slight the advantage won by breaking the promise. If one were to challenge the promisor his defense would be that what he did was best on the whole in view of all the utilitarian considerations, which in this case *include* the importance of the practice. Ross feels that such a defense would be unacceptable. I think he is right insofar as he is protesting against the appeal to consequences in general and without further explanation. Yet it is extremely difficult to weigh the force of Ross's argument. The kind of case imagined seems unrealistic and one feels that it needs to be described. One is inclined to think that it would either turn out that such a case came under an exception defined by the practice itself, in which case there would not be an appeal to consequences in general on the particular case, or it would happen that the circumstances were so peculiar that the conditions which the practice presupposes no longer obtained. But certainly Ross is right in thinking that it strikes us as wrong for a person to defend breaking a promise by a general appeal to consequences. For a general utilitarian defense is not open to the promisor: It is not one of the defenses allowed by the practice of making promises.

Ross gives two further counterarguments: First, he holds that it overestimates the damage done to the practice of promising by a failure to keep a promise. One who breaks a promise harms his own name certainly, but it isn't clear that a broken promise always damages the practice itself sufficiently to account for the strictness of the obligation. Second, and more important, I think, he raises the question of what one is to say of a promise which isn't known to have been made except to the promisor and the promisee, as in the case of a promise a son makes to his dying father concerning the handling of the estate. In this sort of case the consideration relating to the practice doesn't weigh on the promisor at all, and yet one feels that this sort of promise is as binding as other promises. The question of the effect which breaking it has on the practice seems irrelevant. The only consequence seems to be that one can break the promise without running any risk of being censured; but the obligation itself seems not the least weakened. Hence it is doubtful whether the effect on the practice ever weighs in the particular case; certainly it cannot account for the strictness of the obligation where it fails to obtain. It seems to follow that a utilitarian account of the obligation to keep promises cannot be successfully carried out.

From what I have said in connection with punishment, one can foresee what I am going to say about these arguments and counterarguments. They fail to make the distinction between the justification of a practice and the justification of a particular action falling under it, and therefore they fall into the mistake of taking it for granted that the promisor, like Carritt's official, is entitled without restriction to bring utilitarian considerations to bear in deciding whether to keep *his* promise. But if one considers what the practice of promising is one will see, I think, that it is such as not to allow this sort of general discretion to the promisor. Indeed, the point of the practice is to abdicate one's title to act in accordance with utilitarian and prudential considerations in order that the future may be tied down and plans coordinated in advance. There are obvious utilitarian advantages in having a practice which denies to the promisor, as a defense, any general appeal to the utilitarian principle in accordance with which the practice itself may be justified. There is nothing contradictory, or surprising, in this: Utilitarian (or aesthetic) reasons might properly be given in arguing that the game of chess, or baseball, is satisfactory just as it is, or in arguing that it should be changed in various respects, but a player in a game cannot properly appeal to such considerations as reasons for his making one move rather than another. It is a mistake to think that if the practice is justified on utilitarian grounds then the promisor must have complete liberty to use utilitarian arguments to decide whether or not to keep his promise. The practice forbids this general defense; and it is a purpose of the practice to do this. Therefore what the above arguments presuppose—the idea that if the utilitarian view is accepted then the promisor is bound if, and only if, the application of the utilitarian principle to his own case shows that keeping it is best on the whole—is false. The promisor is bound because he promised: Weighing the case on its merits is not open to him.

Is this to say that in particular cases one cannot deliberate whether or not to keep one's promise? Of course not. But to do so is to deliberate whether the various excuses, exceptions and defenses, which are understood by, and which constitute an important part of, the practice, apply to one's own case. Various defenses for not keeping one's promise are allowed, but among them there isn't the one that, on general utilitarian grounds, the promisor (truly) thought his action best on the whole, even though there may be the defense that the consequences of keeping one's promise would have been *extremely* severe. While there are too many complexities here to consider all the necessary details, one can see that the general defense isn't allowed if one asks the following question: What would one say of someone who, when asked why he broke his promise, replied simply that breaking it was best on the whole? Assuming that his reply is sincere, and that his belief was reasonable (that is, one need not consider the possibility that he was mistaken), I think that one would question whether or not he knows what it means to say "I promise" (in the appropriate circumstances). It would be said of someone who used this excuse without further explanation that he didn't understand what defenses the practice, which defines a promise, allows to him. If a child were to use this excuse one would correct him; for it is part of the way one is taught the concept of a promise to be corrected if one uses this excuse. The point of having the practice would be lost if the practice did allow this excuse.

It is no doubt part of the utilitarian view that every practice should admit the defense that the consequences of abiding by it would have been extremely severe; and utilitarians would be inclined to hold that some reliance on people's good sense and some concession to hard cases is necessary. They would hold that a practice is justified by serving the interests of those who take part in it; and as with any set of rules there is understood a background of circumstances under which it is expected to be applied and which need not—indeed which cannot—be fully stated. Should these circumstances change, then even if there is no rule which provides for the case, it may still be in accordance with the practice that one be released from one's obligation. But this sort of defense allowed by a practice must not be confused with the general option to weigh each particular case on utilitarian grounds which critics of utilitarianism have thought it necessarily to involve.

18

RICHARD G. HENSON
Utilitarianism and the Wrongness of Killing

RICHARD G. HENSON, who is professor of philosophy at Rutgers University, is known to his colleagues not only as a philosopher but as the author of satirical verses and song lyrics.

We know that philosophical theories are often advanced, attacked, and defended without being *stated* in sufficient detail so that anyone is quite clear what they amount to: The history of philosophical theories is a history of programs. Utilitarianism is a confirming instance. Though there have recently been in English several books and innumerable articles on the subject, it is striking how haphazard and sketchy are the applications of the theory to any but the hoary cases on which it has been argued that it founders: The innocent man who is to be "punished" as an example, the imprudent promise made to a dying friend on a desert island, and so on.

I shall discuss the application of utilitarianism to some problems of life and death, and particularly to cases of killing people. My thesis is that hedonistic utilitarianism cannot without substantial revision be brought into consonance with our common views on certain of these matters. My arguments do not turn at all, so far as I can see, on any considerations about justice, some of which have long been recognized as troublesome for utilitarians.

I

There is some variation in terminology among even recent authors, so I must say first what I mean by "utilitarianism." I take it that this is a generic term for any thesis to the effect that the normative moral terms—for example, "right," "wrong," "ought"—are to be applied to human actions solely on the basis of the goodness or badness of the consequences of those actions. This is a rather general formula, which already invites a host of questions, most of which I want now to avoid. So I shall offer a brief characterization of a more specific view, a form of "act-utilitarianism" which is very like that which Moore expounds and criticizes in his *Ethics:*[1] An act *A* is right for a given person to perform in a given situation only if there is no other act *B* open to him which would produce a more favorable balance of good consequences relative to bad ones; if there is such an act *B*, then *A* is wrong. (It is normally assumed that certain other moral predicates, like "ought," "obligation," "duty" can be defined in terms of "right" and "wrong," or at least that their application can be similarly characterized: Thus my version above spoke of the application of "the normative moral terms." I shall not attempt here any definition or full enumeration of those terms.)

As so far adumbrated, the theory assigns such predicates as "right" and "wrong" on the basis of the goodness and badness of consequences, but says nothing about what determines such

From Richard G. Henson, "Utilitarianism and the Wrongness of Killing," *The Philosophical Review*, vol. 80 (1971), pp. 320–337. Reprinted by permission of the author and the editors of *The Philosophical Review*. This article is reprinted unabridged.

1. G. E. Moore, *Ethics*, Ch. 1.

goodness or badness; on this point, utilitarianism is generally divided into two species, hedonistic and "ideal." The former regards pleasure as the only sort of consequence which is good in itself—that is, without regard to yet further consequences—and pain as the only thing which is bad in itself; or else (on this point the classic texts are divided) it regards *happiness* as the only thing which is good in itself and unhappiness as the only thing which is bad in itself. Bentham was pretty strictly a pleasure/pain man; Mill explicitly identified happiness with "pleasure and the absence of pain" and then equivocated. The so-called ideal utilitarians regard pleasure and happiness as *among* the things which are good in themselves, but claim that there are others: knowledge, artistic achievement, beauty, and such emotional states as affection, for instance.

This brief explanation will perhaps raise yet another host of questions which I hope to avoid. I shall say only that I confine myself in this paper to *hedonistic* utilitarianism: Having so announced, I shall feel free to drop the qualifier.

But which kind of hedonistic utilitarianism? The happiness kind or the pleasure kind? Well, for the most part I shall cast my argument in terms of happiness; but I shall sometimes switch to pleasure. I do this not because there is no difference between happiness and pleasure: On the contrary, the differences are many and profound. I do it rather because I think that most of my arguments apply equally well[2] to either version of hedonistic utilitarianism, and it reduces the tedium to mention only happiness in the exposition. I do not often mention pleasure except where the argument or the particular example pertains only to it.

My definition of utilitarianism included reference to a "favorable balance of good consequences relative to bad ones." We need to unpack this a bit. If we are hedonistic utilitarians, we must suppose that something like the following is true. (1) At any given time, any given person is at some "hedonic level" or other, positive or negative or neutral—that is, either happy (in some degree or other) or unhappy (in some degree or other). (2) The range of possible hedonic levels forms (or approximates) a continuum—one's hedonic level can move up or down either continuously or by very small increments. (3) There is in principle some "hedonic metric" such that the hedonic state of a given person at a given time can be compared with any state of himself at another time or with that of another person at any time. (4) This "hedonic metric" is such that cardinal numbers (positive and negative) can be assigned to hedonic levels. (5) A hedonic arithmetic and calculus are thus possible: A person's "hedonic sum" can be (in principle) computed for any given period of time and his "hedonic index" (that is, average hedonic level) for that time computed; and hedonic sums and indexes of *groups* of people can similarly be determined.

These assumptions, give or take a nicety, are what I take it a hedonistic utilitarian is committed to, and I shall sum them up as "the assumption that happiness is cardinal."

Now I do not intend to discuss the plausibility of this assumption nor shall I justify my claim that a hedonistic util-

---

2. Except that the assumption of cardinality, discussed immediately below, is perhaps wilder as applied to happiness than as applied to pleasure. Except for that assumption, the "happiness" form seems more plausible. This is not necessarily to its credit; depending on how the concept of happiness is explicated, it may prove plausible because trivial.

itarian must make it; but unless some such assumption is made, it seems to me rank nonsense to speak of "a balance of happiness over unhappiness" or "the act which produces the greatest net pleasure." I shall pretend here to regard the assumption that happiness is cardinal as true.

I shall employ the term "hedon" to name the unit which measures happiness and unhappiness. The hedon is an instantaneous quantity: That is, it measures the hedonic level at which a person is at an instant, rather than the sum of his happiness through a given period. It quantifies such a notion as "very happy" rather than "a lot of happiness." I shall postulate a measure such that a person at a level of 10 hedons is very happy and at -10 very unhappy. At the moment when you hear that your child is born and he and his mother are doing fine, you might be elevated to (say) 12 hedons; and your average hedonic level over the first three days might be 8.2. If you get a lot of happiness from a gift, say, of a record, this will be measurable in hedon-hours: Perhaps in the first month you will have spent ten hours listening to it, at an average of 1.3 hedons higher than you would have enjoyed had you not had that record; thus you have gotten 13 differential hedon-hours of happiness from it—plus, of course, whatever you may have gotten from thinking about it, bragging about it, and the like.

This is to (pretend to) render more precise the notion that the (or a) *right* act in a given situation is one than which no other open to the agent would produce a more favorable balance of good consequences relative to bad: We can now say that such an act is one whose total consequences will have a net differential value *(n.d.v.)* in *hedon-hours* which is not exceeded by the *n.d.v.* of the total consequences of any other act open to the agent. I speak of hedon-*hours* because obviously a positive hedonic state is better, the longer it lasts; of *differential* value because the preferable act is the one which most *improves* the hedonic states of those whom it affects, the one which makes the most *difference* from what the situation would have been without that act; of the *net d.v.* of the *total* consequences because an act will normally have some positive and some negative hedonic consequences and both are relevant. An act may of course be right without producing a positive *n.d.v.*; if so, it is because no act open to the agent in the situation would have done so, and no *other* act open to him would have produced a smaller negative *n.d.v.* An act may be wrong without producing a negative *n.d.v.*; if so, it is because some other act open to the agent would have produced a greater positive *n.d.v.* One speaks, however, of an act as *"tending to be right"* in virtue of there being some positive *d.v.* which would attach to a given consequence of it—which is to say merely that the consequence counts in favor of its being right, though it may be overweighed by some combination of negative *d.v.*'s of other consequences or of the superior positive *n.d.v.* of some other act. I shall also speak of acts as tending to be right *simpliciter* (rather than of so tending in virtue of some particular consequence) where the *n.d.v.* of the totality of its consequence is positive.

II

I can now approach the problem of this paper by posing one of those bizarre questions from the Philosophers' Wonderland—though it is recognizably related to pressing problems of public policy. If one could choose between creating a population of 1,000 people at an average level of 2 hedons and one of 500 people at an average level of 3 hedons—the distribution of hedons to be equally fair, in the two cases—which ought he, as a utilitarian, to choose?

Talk of maximizing happiness, or gaining the most favorable hedonic balance, might suggest that the former choice would be obligatory: It would produce a total of 2,000 hedons through a unit of time, as contrasted with the 1,500 generated by the second option, and thus seems to have the "more favorable balance" required by utilitarianism as I stated it above. But it seems a much more sympathetic reading to say that that statement was incomplete, and should have read "more favorable balance of good consequences relative to bad ones, *per person*"; that is, that what a proper utilitarian should maximize is the hedonic *average* of persons affected, rather than the number of hedons itself.[3] But this, while it is fine for some kinds of case, has ludicrous consequences. For consider a population which has an average hedonic level of, say, 1.3; and suppose that the hedonic indexes of its members can each be reasonably expected to remain roughly constant for a long time (if they live). Now consider a member whose level is −5.1 or −3.3, or 0, or even +.9: such a person, and indeed *any* person whose level is below 1.3, is *ipso facto* lowering the average. If any such person were to die, the hedonic average of the whole population would rise; this would in itself be a good consequence, the kind which we have just said a utilitarian should seek to bring about; to bring it about would tend to be right; indeed, to fail to bring it about would—unless one were doing something else instead which had better consequences—be wrong. (Given some reasonable assumptions and definitions which I shall not

detail here, it would even be someone's *obligation* to kill him.)

Well, clearly something is wrong somewhere: But let us pursue this line of thought two steps further. Note first that in being below average, hedonically—"hedonically deprived," as we might say—the fellow in question is probably like about half the population: If it is right to kill him, then it is right to kill about half the population. But note second that as you kill those who are in the lower half of the population, hedonically speaking, you are steadily raising the average, so that some who used to be just above average will now be below it. Eventually, the conscientious utilitarian will be playing "Ten Little Indians" with the last ten people alive (if he is happy enough himself to have lasted so long).

One thing wrong with this fantasy, of course, is that we have been assuming that the hedonic level of individual persons in the happier half is not lowered by the deaths of those in the unhappier half, and this is unrealistic. We can put it this way: If several numbers are averaged and then one of them which is not equal to the average is dropped and the average is recomputed without it, one finds (of course) a new average. Thus when a person who is hedonically below par is removed from the population, the average would rise by some differential amount d provided everyone else maintained his previous hedonic index: Let us call d the "recomputation effect" of his death. But when a person dies, people are affected by his death in a variety of hedonically significant ways— that is, some of the survivors, at least,

---

3. I specified above that the two distributions were to be equally fair. It should be clear that I am expressing sympathy for the maximization of hedonic averages not at the cost of fairness, but at the cost of the hedonic *total*, where the latter is maximized merely by multiplying people.

do *not* maintain their previous hedonic levels: Let us call the net hedonic change c which is a *causal* consequence of a given person's death the "contingent effect" of his death.[4] So far, we have been talking as if only the recomputation effect were significant, and that of course is silly. But when we correct that error, the consequences of the theory are still utterly unacceptable: We still have the result that it tends to be right to kill any person, provided *(a)* he is below average, hedonically, and *(b)* the contingent effect c of his death will not be sufficiently negative to outweigh the recomputation effect d. More generally, it tends to be right to kill anyone provided the sum $(d + c)$ is positive. For most people, the condition will not be fulfilled, but for some it presumably will; and a theory which has the consequence that it would tend to be right to kill any such person is clearly false.[5]

Since I shall need to refer to this argument, I hereby christen it: the argument, that is, whose premises are utilitarian theory and whose conclusion is that whenever one can kill someone who satisfies the above condition (that $[d + c]$ be positive) such an act tends to be right. I call it, with some hyperbole, the "paneuthanasia argument."

I have been assuming that once a person is dead, he has no hedonic index at all, and so can simply be omitted from any computation of the hedonic index of the population. It might be suggested that this is a mistake, and that we should include anyone who is dead, counting his hedonic index as zero. This procedure will yield somewhat different results, but not more acceptable ones (see Section III). (Theological views about an afterlife—which is generally thought to be hedonically extravagant, one way or another—will be discussed briefly below.)

My reader will have noticed a certain oddity in the argument so far. It is plausible to say that one should do things which will raise the general hedonic index; but I have been concentrating on a very special way of doing this—namely, eliminating those people whose index is below the general index. This particular way of raising the average has the peculiarity that it does not (unless accidentally) raise the average of any particular person, nor does it raise the hedonic total of the population: It is this, I think, which gives the impression of trickery to the paneuthanasia argument.[6] Recognizing this peculiarity, I confess my inability to say whether it really *constitutes* trickery: I am inclined to think that the difficulty is a deep one in utilitarian theory, not a surface sophistry in my argument. I submit that if someone killed several of the *happiest* people in a population, thus *lowering* the hedonic average, we should not want to say that the lowering was somehow spurious in that it had not resulted from the lowering of the index of any particular person who was affected: *Those who were killed* were affected, and with a mighty affect, and adversely. To be sure, I do not think that this brings out the main reason we should

4. We are considering the suggestion that one should act so as to maximize the general hedonic index of the population—the *living* population, I suppose. In Sec. III, where I try to classify the full hedonic consequences of a death, I take into account the differential hedonic effect also on the deceased.

5. In the last two paragraphs of Sec. III I reply to an objection which might be felt here instead (or also).

6. Note, however, that this source of putative trickery does not occur in the special case (logically, but perhaps not statistically, "special") in which the victim's hedonic average for the remainder of his life would have been (not only below average, but) negative. For in this case, the hedonic total of the group *is* raised, in that a negative quantity is subtracted from it; and the victim's is also raised, if my approach in Sec. III is sound, from a negative quantity to zero.

object to their being killed: But my object in this paper is to show that utilitarianism simply does *not* account for our
objections to killing people. In any case,
I shall now offer another argument to
support this conclusion—one which,
unlike the paneuthanasia argument,
does not depend on the recomputation
effect. The paneuthanasia argument
does suggest, at least, that the "more
sympathetic reading" which I proposed
at the beginning of Section II will not do
as it stands.

III

Even if we do not resort to the recomputation effect—which would generally be
slight, at best, for a single death in a
large population—killing someone will
often have *some* consequences which
are hedonically positive, and which thus
tend to make it right. I think of several
places where the utilitarian might find
negative hedon-hours with which to
weigh the scales against it: *(i)* in the
events which cause or attend dying; *(ii)*
in the state of death; *(iii)* in the hedonic
consequences for the survivors; *(iv)* in
the hedon-hours which the deceased
would have enjoyed if he had lived.[7]

It is important that *none* of these
sources will yield a negative balance in
every case, that each will yield positive
rather than negative balances in some
cases, and that only the third seems
even likely to yield preponderantly
negative values with any regularity.[8] To
discuss them in order: *(i)* This source
cannot—surprisingly, I think—yield
any appreciable quantity of negative
hedon-hours for the utilitarian to use.
For it is only such pain as is necessary to
effect death as can be counted: Any excess will count not for the wrongness of
killing, but for the wrongness of torturing, terrorizing, or even (simply) allowing needless suffering. (I do not question

the adequacy of utilitarianism in accounting for the wrongness of these
things.) And since death can be brought
about quite painlessly, we can say that
the utilitarian is not entitled to count
any pain toward the wrongness of killing per se. At most, we might allow that
which is necessary to effect death in a
certain way, where no other way is open
to the agent.[9] *(ii)* Our ignorance of the
hereafter embarrasses the smooth flow
of the analysis. But I shall not linger
here, beyond remarking that this source
cannot help the utilitarian much. For
one thing, probably few utilitarians
accept a theology which would speak to
the problem; for another, some of those
theologies which do so tell us that killing a saint initiates an eternity of positively infinite hedon-hours and thus has
a tendency to be right than which a
stronger could not be conceived, while
killing an unrepentant sinner initiates a
presumably equal quantity of negative
ones. Surely this is not the sort of help
the utilitarian needs.[10] *(iii)* From this
source there may well issue mostly
negative hedon-hours. But we cannot

7. If we are thinking of a general relaxation
of the prohibition of killing, another important effect would come into play, in that people would
presumably become much more anxious about
being killed: See Sec. V.

8. The preceding generalizations are based
on the assumption that either the state of death
has no hedonic index or some conservative and
familiar Christian beliefs about it are true.

9. A *quick* death, even at a high (negative)
hedon level would make for few hedon-hours: For
example, two minutes at -40 hedons (presumably
an excruciating pain) would yield only -1.33
hedon-hours, which is substantially preferable to
the average P.T.A. meeting.

10. Someone will object that the saint would
have enjoyed that plenitude of hedon-eons even if
he had been permitted to live out his span, so they
should not be credited to the *n.d.v.* of the act of
killing him. This raises several subtle questions: I
reply only that killing him while he is saintly ob-
viates the risk of his becoming unsaintly, and thus
blowing it all.

say that a death always generates a negative balance from this source; and surely we do not feel that such a balance must be verified before we can pronounce a killing wrong. *(iv)* I should not admit, without large qualifications, that one could *ever* be very confident that a given person will enjoy a positive hedonic balance if he is permitted to live for any substantial period of time; one must (as Aristotle says Solon says) see the end. But suppose I grant that one can *sometimes* say that: I take it as an unquestionable truth that one must *usually* be very doubtful whether that condition holds for any given person— and one does *not* feel any similar and consequent doubt that it would be wrong to kill him. Moreover, this fourth source is, more dramatically than the others, a sword-handled sword. For if we are seriously to stress the claim that what is wrong with killing a certain person is that it deprives him of the positive hedonic balance which he would otherwise have enjoyed, we must admit that it is very often wrong *not* to kill another, because *he* will, if he lives, suffer a negative balance. If we make the (optimistic) assumption that one out of two persons will enjoy a favorable hedonic balance for the remainder of his natural life, and if we base our judgment solely on this fourth condition, the odds will be one to two that we ought to kill the next stranger we meet.

One might naturally reply that, since we cannot be *sure* that a given person is destined for a negative balance, we should not risk doing something wrong—namely, killing him; but the utilitarian ought to be equally anxious about *not* killing him: that might well be wrong, instead. But each consideration is fantastic. No one seriously supposes that the reason, or *a* reason, why you should not kill the next stranger

you meet is that perhaps he is destined to be a shade happier than the average stranger.

I should stress that I think it clear that these sources do not just fail, individually, to provide enough negative hedon-hours, in many cases: If *that* were the problem, one might hope to explain the wrongness of killing, case by case, in virtue of a few hedon-hours attributable to this source and a few to that one. Normally—I am not speaking of the harrowing cases where (say) *someone* must die because the rescue plane will carry only part of the party, or the provisions will keep only half of them alive—these conditions do not even come into consideration. No normal person would try to justify a murder by saying "It wasn't really a painful death," or "His soul went to the good place," or "He won't be missed," or "He wouldn't really have been happy if he had lived." Killing a person is too grave an offense for such defenses to matter, or for the denials of such remarks to be *needed* as reasons for its wrongness.

To summarize the argument, then, as it stands without reliance on the recomputation effect: (1) According to utilitarian theory as I have sketched it, an act of killing (like any other act) tends to be right if the net differential value of its consequences is positive. (2) The possible sources of hedon-hours (and thus of *n.d.v.*) which bear on the question are the ones I list in the first paragraph of this section. (3) We can easily imagine a variety of cases in which *(a)* the *n.d.v.* derived from those sources is positive but in which *(b)* no one would suppose that that positive *n.d.v.* had any tendency to legitimize killing. Conversely, one would not feel that he had to establish a negative *n.d.v.* from these (or any) sources, in order to know that a killing was wrong, nor would he feel any need to establish that some other act had a superior positive *n.d.v.*

I anticipate the following objection: "Let *w* be some act which is clearly wrong. Now to show that, on utilitarian theory, *w* would be right would indeed be to refute the theory: But all you (Henson) are doing is showing that some such acts 'tend to be right'—that is, are felicific—and this does not refute anything. To get a refutation, you must show also that no alternative would be *more* felicific."

A weighty objection, I think. But *(i)* I can describe cases—admittedly bizarre—in which there are no more felicific alternatives: and if there are philosophical difficulties about enumerating alternative acts open to the agent, these are difficulties for the utilitarian; his theory presupposes that they are resolvable. *(ii)* To show that *w* is felicific is to show that (according to utilitarianism) if one's alternatives were doing *w* and doing nothing (hedonically speaking,) *w* would be right; and I suppose it follows that doing *w* would be morally preferable to doing nothing—but surely the fact that a killing would be felicific does not in general make performing it morally preferable to doing nothing. *(iii)* I have urged—not argued, because it seems too elementary, once it is noticed, to require argument—that felicificity is, in any normal case, just not the tree to bark up, in connection with killing a human being. As its presence does not justify, so its absence is not needed to condemn, the killing of a person.

IV

It is worth looking briefly at the considerations which we normally bring to bear against euthanasia, to see whether the utilitarian can gain any support from them: because what I have suggested as a consequence of utilitar-

ianism is a sort of cancerous euthanasia, growing wildly out of control. I take it that euthanasia will have no color of acceptability except when there is no reason to hope for cure or remedy for the disability which makes it seem eligible in the first place; and it is hard to be sure what constitutes reason to hope. Tomorrow, one thinks, the miracle drug may be found. I agree that this is often a good reason for not performing a mercy killing; but I do not see how it could be employed by a utilitarian. After all, our decisions must always be based on the hedonic probabilities, if we are utilitarians—and wherever the hope of cure is faint, the *probabilities* are that the victim will live in pain until he dies. If nevertheless we are not to kill him, on the ground that it is not impossible that a cure should be discovered, that must be because we regard even a little life in even moderate comfort as worth a great deal—worth so much that we are almost always willing to countenance a great deal of suffering on the very slim chance that there might be a little more of such life. This is just not a utilitarian attitude.

The importance of this last point can easily be missed. I am not suggesting that euthanasia is always wrong; I am not suggesting that continuation of life itself, in one who is reduced, as we say, to the level of a vegetable, is or should be regarded as desirable. I *am* saying that where there is any faintest hope of significant recovery, we labor and sacrifice to preserve life, even where the odds are enormous that the patient's future hedonic balance will be overwhelmingly negative. "The point of that," it will be urged, "is that without life, he cannot enjoy *any* happiness." Agreed: Nor can he achieve any further wisdom or love any more. But the quoted objection does not meet my point—that he will almost certainly (if he lives) suffer much more misery, and that even if he does eventually recover. If we were really guided by the sense that we should try to maximize the *n.d.v.* of his remaining life, we should kiss him good-by and painlessly cut his losses.

One might still miss the force of my argument because he dwells on the extreme cases, in which—*as I agree*— euthanasia might be warranted. But I am claiming that, for all that utilitarianism can tell us, a person ought to be killed merely to save him from moderate unhappiness hereafter, provided he would not be too much missed.

One opposes euthanasia also on the ground that it is highly undesirable that people should come to take killing lightly: The odds are so heavily against its being right that we regard any breach of the taboo as setting a psychological precedent which is extremely dangerous; and perhaps we oppose it also on the ground that it is a source of intense anguish for a normal person to kill anyone—certainly for him to kill anyone for whom he cares. These too are respectable reasons, but ones whose force in connection with the problem I have been discussing is much attenuated. For first, if the utilitarian rationale I have presented in favor of killing the hedonically deprived were sound, it would be obligatory that a great deal of killing be done, and it would not in that case be undesirable to break down the psychological resistance to killing. And second, as concerns the anguish which killing entails for the killer, much of that presumably accrues from his realization that it is tabooed, and probably wrong. If my line of argument were correct, and much killing were in fact right, we might hope that people would come to recognize the fact; and then the anguish which arises from the conviction that it is wrong would gradually be dis-

sipated. Some would no doubt remain, but surely not at its present level: and in time, people would get into the swing of it. . . .

I conclude that hedonistic utilitarianism cannot account for the gravity with which we view the taking of human life, and indeed that in this area it has consequences which are downright bizarre. And in view of the fact that this is, as I have remarked, the most gross and uncontroversial sort of wrong which one person can inflict on another, I conclude that utilitarianism must be rejected—or sharply modified—whatever decision posterity might make on its well-advertised difficulties with justice.

V

It may be thought that my argument— especially in the first stage, where it depends on the recomputation effect— tells against *act*-utilitarianism, but not against *rule*-utilitarianism.[11] Because, one might think, if it were part of the "public morality," and thus sanctioned

11. The distinction between these two kinds of utilitarianism has not been spelled out to the general satisfaction of the experts. The distinctive claim of rule-utilitarianism, which seems at least to meet some widely felt difficulties in the kind of view I have been discussing, is that *under certain circumstances* it is right to act upon a certain rule the general acceptance of which would have better consequences than the acceptance of any other, and to act upon it even in particular cases in which so acting has *worse* consequences than acting in some other way. For brief exposition and criticism of rule-utilitarianism, see William Frankena, *Ethics* (Englewood Cliffs, 1963), pp. 21–25 and Richard Brandt, *Ethical Theory* (Englewood Cliffs, 1963), Ch. 15. Both Brandt and Alan Donagan mention murder as something which might be "justified" in some cases by act-utilitarianism but not by rule-utilitarianism. See Brandt, "Toward a Credible Form of Utilitarianism," originally published in Castaneda and Nakhnikian (eds.), *Morality and the Language of Conduct* (Detroit, 1963); Donagan, "Is There a Credible Form of Utilitarianism?," in Michael Bayles (ed.), *Contemporary Utilitarianism* (Garden City, 1968). (Brandt's article is reprinted by Bayles.)

in law, that the hedonically deprived could rightfully be killed, anxiety about being thought unhappy (which is already a grave burden for us) would become a terror, vastly decreasing the general hedonic index. Thus if such killing were to be the rule, it would be seriously dyshedonic, and so it could not rightly be accepted as the rule.

The premises seem right enough: But I do not infer that hedonistic rule-utilitarianism might be viable; I infer rather that *no* form of *hedonistic* utilitarianism is defensible. For why should a person be terrified of being thought unhappy, and thus of being killed? Why should he not rather ask himself whether he *is* unhappy—and will remain so—and would just as soon die? Largely, no doubt, because he is afraid of death: and since we (at least I) cannot easily say *what* people fear in death, and since we probably fear rather different things, it is impossible to be sure how the fear of death bears on hedonism. Granting this—granting, therefore, that what I say hereafter will be said with this cloud hanging over it—I shall ignore the expectation of bliss or pain in the beyond in my remaining remarks. I justify that move on three grounds: *(i)* the *ad hominem* ground that utilitarians generally have not relied on such factors and would be embarrassed if they had to resort to them; *(ii)* the ground that consistent resort to such considerations would (as I have suggested but not shown) lead to various counterintuitive consequences; *(iii)* the fact (as I take it to be) that what I have yet to say applies to most people who do not act in fear or hope of postmortem hedon-hours, as well as to those who do.

I suppose, then, that if happiness is the only thing which is good in itself and unhappiness the only thing bad, it is irrational for a person to want to live when the evidence available to him indicates that the probabilities are in favor of his having a negative hedonic balance for the remainder of his (natural) life; but surely a normal person *does* want to go on living, even under those circumstances. Either, then, happiness and unhappiness are not the only things good and bad in themselves, or our normal person is irrational.

Now I shall not insist that a "normal" person *must* be counted as rational: I have not specified the uses of the terms so that such a claim would be plausible. But if normal people do not show by their behavior that they regard life as worth living only when it offers a positive hedonic balance, we can certainly ask the utilitarian what led him to suppose that happiness is the only thing worth having. While we should not want to hold a latter-day utilitarian to the *ipse dixit* of a founding father, it is worth noting that Mill thought his hedonism derived from the facts about what people actually valued:[12] and one does not have to be a "naturalist"[13] to believe that what we actually value must be the ethicist's starting point in determining what is valuable, and that to get beyond that point will require careful and subtle arguments.

My response then to the suggestion that rule-utilitarianism might solve the difficulties I have raised, even if act-utilitarianism cannot, is as follows: The "rule" version certainly looks like an improvement, in this respect; but it relies on the (undisputed) premise that people—even people whose hedonic prospects are dim—are distressed by the threat of death; and I take that fact to

12. See esp. the famous third paragraph of Ch. 4 of *Utilitarianism*.

13. I use the term "naturalist" in the technical sense prevalent in recent Anglo-American ethical theory, for one who holds that ethical (or value) judgments are identical in meaning with empirical statements of some sort.

show that they do not regard a favorable hedonic balance as a necessary condition of life's being worth living; and *that* suggests that the utilitarianism I have criticized fails in its hedonistic aspect rather than in its "act" aspect.

It is probably best to remark explicitly that I have *not* argued that there can be no sound nonhedonistic utilitarianism; that happiness is cardinal; or that life, or human life, is to be venerated just as such.

VI

If I am right, the puzzle remains how it could be so little noticed that such a widely discussed theory fails to account for such a prominent datum. I have a suggestion, if not one which takes us very far. The suggestion is that when we think about cases which involve the death of a person, we treat them (some of us), without quite noticing that we are treating them, as if death were somehow the hedonic equivalent of a marvelously great pain. I do not mean that we *believe* that death is invariably very painful: I mean rather that when we pretend to be using the "hedonic calculus" to show how utilitarianism would cope with some specific case—as we who teach ethics, at any rate, often do—we tacitly count a death, normally, as if it were convertible into some huge number of hedon-hours, and place it in the "con" column. This is, at any rate, what *I* have tended to do, nagged often by a vague sense that something was awry.

If one does this because he thinks that to cause death *is* (normally) to cause great unhappiness or pain, he is (I have argued) mistaken; if he does it because he thinks that to cause death is (normally) the *moral equivalent* of causing much distress, he may be right, but he is no longer a hedonistic utilitarian: He is admitting that an act can be a great

wrong without having the only feature which, on utilitarian theory, would make it (even *tend* to be) so.

I have suggested an explanation[14] of the general failure to notice that utilitarianism is so inept in accounting for our views about death—namely, that we (some of us) have tended tacitly to count death as a great deprivation of hedon-hours. But, as I said, that does not take us very far: for we should ask, why did we do *that*? I have a suggestion here too: Perhaps we did it because we had already pretty well decided that utilitarianism was true, or near enough (needing some patching up, perhaps, to cope with the difficulties about justice); and we knew that killing was (generally) wrong, even apart from any consideration of how the survivors would be affected, whether the victim would have enjoyed a favorable hedonic balance if he had lived, and so on; and the only way to secure that utilitarianism be right and killing wrong was for us to treat death as a very great pain. So we did.[15]

14. Another possible explanation occurs to me, which may apply to more people than the one offered in the text—though not, I think, to me. It is that despite the fact that the theory is explicitly formulated in terms of pleasure and/or happiness, one might tend to think instead of utility *however the recipient conceives it* as the factor which a proper utilitarian ought to maximize. It then is a serious matter to deprive a person of anything which he values highly, whatever its connection with pleasure or happiness; and most people do so value their own lives. This conception of utilitarianism strikes me as a considerable change from that of Bentham and Mill; Jan Narveson, who defends it in *Morality and Utility* (Baltimore, 1967) thinks otherwise. Since his kind of utilitarianism is not hedonistic, it is not touched by my arguments. I think it is open to grave objections, but that is another story.

15. I am indebted to Malcolm Greenaway for counterexamples which stood in a many-one relationship to the things I said about euthanasia in an earlier version of the paper; to Jack W. Meiland and Amelie O. Rorty for various probings; and to Priscilla D. Smith for trenchant objections to Sec. V.

19

THOMAS NAGEL
War and Massacre

THOMAS NAGEL is professor of philosophy at Princeton University. He is the author of *The Possibility of Altruism* (1970), and numerous influential articles on ethics and the philosophy of mind.

From the apathetic reaction to atrocities committed in Vietnam by the United States and its allies, one may conclude that moral restrictions on the conduct of war command almost as little sympathy among the general public as they do among those charged with the formation of U.S. military policy. Even when restrictions on the conduct of warfare are defended, it is usually on legal grounds alone: Their moral basis is often poorly understood. I wish to argue that certain restrictions are neither arbitrary nor merely conventional, and that their validity does not depend simply on their usefulness. There is, in other words, a moral basis for the rules of war, even though the conventions now officially in force are far from giving it perfect expression.

I

No elaborate moral theory is required to account for what is wrong in cases like the Mylai massacre, since it did not serve, and was not intended to serve, any strategic purpose. Moreover, if the participation of the United States in the Indo-Chinese war is entirely wrong to begin with, then that engagement is incapable of providing a justification for *any* measures taken in its pursuit—not only for the measures which are atroci-

From Thomas Nagel, "War and Massacre," *Philosophy and Public Affairs*, vol. 1 (1971–1972), pp. 123–144. Copyright © 1972 by Princeton University Press. Reprinted by permission of Princeton University Press. This article is reprinted unabridged.

ties in every war, however just its aims.

But this war has revealed attitudes of a more general kind, that influenced the conduct of earlier wars as well. After it has ended, we shall still be faced with the problem of how warfare may be conducted, and the attitudes that have resulted in the specific conduct of this war will not have disappeared. Moreover, similar problems can arise in wars or rebellions fought for very different reasons, and against very different opponents. It is not easy to keep a firm grip on the idea of what is not permissible in warfare, because while some military actions are obvious atrocities, other cases are more difficult to assess, and the general principles underlying these judgments remain obscure. Such obscurity can lead to the abandonment of sound intuitions in favor of criteria whose rationale may be more obvious. If such a tendency is to be resisted, it will require a better understanding of the restrictions than we now have.

I propose to discuss the most general moral problem raised by the conduct of warfare: the problem of means and ends. In one view, there are limits on what may be done even in the service of an end worth pursuing—and even when adherence to the restriction may be very costly. A person who acknowledges the force of such restrictions can find himself in acute moral dilemmas.

This paper grew out of discussions at the Society for Ethical and Legal Philosophy, and I am indebted to my fellow members for their help.

He may believe, for example, that by torturing a prisoner he can obtain information necessary to prevent a disaster, or that by obliterating one village with bombs he can halt a campaign of terrorism. If he believes that the gains from a certain measure will clearly outweigh its costs, yet still suspects that he ought not to adopt it, then he is in a dilemma produced by the conflict between two disparate categories of moral reason: categories that may be called *utilitarian* and *absolutist.*

Utilitarianism gives primacy to a concern with what will *happen.* Absolutism gives primacy to a concern with what one is *doing.* The conflict between them arises because the alternatives we face are rarely just choices between *total outcomes:* They are also choices between alternative pathways or measures to be taken. When one of the choices is to do terrible things to another person, the problem is altered fundamentally; it is no longer merely a question of which outcome would be worse.

Few of us are completely immune to either of these types of moral intuition, though in some people, either naturally or for doctrinal reasons, one type will be dominant and the other suppressed or weak. But it is perfectly possible to feel the force of both types of reason very strongly; in that case the moral dilemma in certain situations of crisis will be acute, and it may appear that every possible course of action or inaction is unacceptable for one reason or another.

II

Although it is this dilemma that I propose to explore, most of the discussion will be devoted to its absolutist component. The utilitarian component is straightforward by comparison, and has

a natural appeal to anyone who is not a complete skeptic about ethics. Utilitarianism says that one should try, either individually or through institutions, to maximize good and minimize evil (the definition of these categories need not enter into the schematic formulation of the view), and that if faced with the possibility of preventing a great evil by producing a lesser, one should choose the lesser evil. There are certainly problems about the formulation of utilitarianism, and much has been written about it, but its intent is morally transparent. Nevertheless, despite the addition of various refinements, it continues to leave large portions of ethics unaccounted for. I do not suggest that some form of absolutism can account for them all, only that an examination of absolutism will lead us to see the complexity, and perhaps the incoherence, of our moral ideas.

Utilitarianism certainly justifies *some* restrictions on the conduct of warfare. There are strong utilitarian reasons for adhering to any limitation which seems natural to most people—particularly if the limitation is widely accepted already. An exceptional measure which seems to be justified by its results in a particular conflict may create a precedent with disastrous long-term effects.[1] It may even be argued that war involves violence on such a scale that it is never justified on utilitarian grounds—the consequences of refusing to go to war will never be as bad as the war itself would be, even if atrocities were not committed. Or in a more sophisticated vein it might be claimed that a uniform policy of never resorting to military force would do less harm in the long

1. Straightforward considerations of national interest often tend in the same directions: The inadvisability of using nuclear weapons seems to be overdetermined in this way.

run, if followed consistently, than a policy of deciding each case on utilitarian grounds (even though on occasion particular applications of the pacifist policy might have worse results than a specific utilitarian decision). But I shall not consider these arguments, for my concern is with reasons of a different kind, which may remain when reasons of utility and interest fail.[2]

In the final analysis, I believe that the dilemma cannot always be resolved. While not every conflict between absolutism and utilitarianism creates an insoluble dilemma, and while it is certainly right to adhere to absolutist restrictions unless the utilitarian considerations favoring violation are overpoweringly weighty and extremely certain—nevertheless, when that special condition is met, it may become impossible to adhere to an absolutist position. What I shall offer, therefore, is a somewhat qualified defense of absolutism. I believe it underlies a valid and fundamental type of moral judgment—which cannot be reduced to or overridden by other principles. And while there may be other principles just as fundamental, it is particularly important not to lose confidence in our absolutist intuitions, for they are often the only barrier before the abyss of utilitarian apologetics for large-scale murder.

III

One absolutist position that creates no problems of interpretation is pacifism: the view that one may not kill another person under any circumstances, no matter what good would be achieved or evil averted thereby. The type of absolutist position that I am going to discuss is different. Pacifism draws the conflict with utilitarian considerations very starkly. But there are other views according to which violence may be undertaken, even on a large scale, in a clearly just cause, so long as certain absolute restrictions on the character and direction of that violence are observed. The line is drawn somewhat closer to the bone, but it exists.

The philosopher who has done most to advance contemporary philosophical discussion of such a view, and to explain it to those unfamiliar with its extensive treatment in Roman Catholic moral theology, is G. E. M. Anscombe. In 1958 Miss Anscombe published a pamphlet entitled *Mr. Truman's Degree*,[3] on the occasion of the award by Oxford University of an honorary doctorate to Harry Truman. The pamphlet explained why she had opposed the decision to award that degree, recounted the story of her unsuccessful opposition, and offered some reflections on the history of Truman's decision to drop atom bombs on Hiroshima and Nagasaki, and on the difference between murder and allowable killing in warfare. She pointed out that the policy of deliberately killing large numbers of civilians either as a means or as an end in itself did not originate with Truman, and was com-

2. These reasons, moreover, have special importance in that they are available even to one who denies the appropriateness of utilitarian considerations in international matters. He may acknowledge limitations on what may be done to the soldiers and civilians of other countries in pursuit of his nation's military objectives, while denying that one country should in general consider the interests of nationals of other countries in determining its policies.

3. (Privately printed.) See also her essay "War and Murder," in *Nuclear Weapons and Christian Conscience*, ed. Walter Stein (London,

1963). The present paper is much indebted to these two essays throughout. These and related subjects are extensively treated by Paul Ramsey in *The Just War* (New York, 1968). Among recent writings that bear on the moral problem are Jonathan Bennett, "Whatever the Consequences," *Analysis* 26, no. 3 (1966): 83–102; and Philippa Foot, "The Problem of Abortion and the Doctrine of the Double Effect," *The Oxford Review* 5 (1967): 5–15. Miss Anscombe's replies are "A Note on Mr. Bennett," *Analysis* 26, no. 3 (1966): 208, and "Who Is Wronged?" *The Oxford Review* 5 (1967): 16–17.

mon practice among all parties during World War II for some time before Hiroshima. The Allied area bombings of German cities by conventional explosives included raids which killed more civilians than did the atomic attacks; the same is true of certain fire-bomb raids on Japan.

The policy of attacking the civilian population in order to induce an enemy to surrender, or to damage his morale, seems to have been widely accepted in the civilized world, and seems to be accepted still, at least if the stakes are high enough. It gives evidence of a moral conviction that the deliberate killing of noncombatants—women, children, old people—is permissible if enough can be gained by it. This follows from the more general position that any means can in principle be justified if it leads to a sufficiently worthy end. Such an attitude is evident not only in the more spectacular current weapons systems but also in the day-to-day conduct of the nonglobal war in Indochina: the indiscriminate destructiveness of antipersonnel weapons, napalm, and aerial bombardment; cruelty to prisoners; massive relocation of civilians; destruction of crops; and so forth. An absolutist position opposes to this the view that certain acts cannot be justified no matter what the consequences. Among those acts is murder— the deliberate killing of the harmless: civilians, prisoners of war, and medical personnel.

In the present war such measures are sometimes said to be regrettable, but they are generally defended by reference to military necessity and the importance of the long-term consequences of success or failure in the war. I shall pass over the inadequacy of this consequentialist defense in its own terms. (That is the dominant form of moral criticism of the war, for it is part of what people mean when they ask, "Is it worth it?") I am concerned rather to account

for the inappropriateness of offering any defense of that kind for such actions.

Many people feel, without being able to say much more about it, that something has gone seriously wrong when certain measures are admitted into consideration in the first place. The fundamental mistake is made there, rather than at the point where the overall benefit of some monstrous measure is judged to outweigh its disadvantages, and it is adopted. An account of absolutism might help us to understand this. If it is not allowable to *do* certain things, such as killing unarmed prisoners or civilians, then no argument about what will happen if one doesn't do them can show that doing them would be all right.

Absolutism does not, of course, require one to ignore the consequences of one's acts. It operates as a limitation on utilitarian reasoning, not as a substitute for it. An absolutist can be expected to try to maximize good and minimize evil, so long as this does not require him to transgress an absolute prohibition like that against murder. But when such a conflict occurs, the prohibition takes complete precedence over any consideration of consequences. Some of the results of this view are clear enough. It requires us to forgo certain potentially useful military measures, such as the slaughter of hostages and prisoners or indiscriminate attempts to reduce the enemy civilian population by starvation, epidemic infectious diseases like anthrax and bubonic plague, or mass incineration. It means that we cannot deliberate on whether such measures are justified by the fact that they will avert still greater evils, for as intentional measures they cannot be justified in terms of any consequences whatever.

Someone unfamiliar with the events of this century might imagine that utilitarian arguments, or arguments of national interest, would suffice to deter measures of this sort. But it has become evident that such considerations are insufficient to prevent the adoption and employment of enormous antipopulation weapons once their use is considered a serious moral possibility. The same is true of the piecemeal wiping out of rural civilian populations in airborne antiguerrilla warfare. Once the door is opened to calculations of utility and national interest, the usual speculations about the future of freedom, peace, and economic prosperity can be brought to bear to ease the consciences of those responsible for a certain number of charred babies.

For this reason alone it is important to decide what is wrong with the frame of mind which allows such arguments to begin. But it is also important to understand absolutism in the cases where it genuinely conflicts with utility. Despite its appeal, it is a paradoxical position, for it can require that one refrain from choosing the lesser of two evils when that is the only choice one has. And it is additionally paradoxical because, unlike pacifism, it permits one to do horrible things to people in some circumstances but not in others.

IV

Before going on to say what, if anything, lies behind the position, there remain a few relatively technical matters which are best discussed at this point.

First, it is important to specify as clearly as possible the kind of thing to which absolutist prohibitions can apply. We must take seriously the proviso that they concern what we deliberately do to people. There could not, for example, without incoherence, be an absolute prohibition against *bringing about* the death of an innocent person. For one may find oneself in a situation in which, no matter what one does, some innocent people will die as a result. I do not

mean just that there are cases in which someone will die no matter what one does, because one is not in a position to affect the outcome one way or the other. That, it is to be hoped, is one's relation to the deaths of most innocent people. I have in mind, rather, a case in which someone is bound to die, but who it is will depend on what one does. Sometimes these situations have natural causes, as when too few resources (medicine, lifeboats) are available to rescue everyone threatened with a certain catastrophe. Sometimes the situations are manmade, as when the only way to control a campaign of terrorism is to employ terrorist tactics against the community from which it has arisen. Whatever one does in cases such as these, some innocent people will die as a result. If the absolutist prohibition forbade doing what would result in the deaths of innocent people, it would have the consequence that in such cases nothing one could do would be morally permissible.

This problem is avoided, however, because what absolutism forbids is *doing* certain things to people, rather than bringing about certain *results*. Not everything that happens to others as a result of what one does is something that one has *done* to them. Catholic moral theology seeks to make this distinction precise in a doctrine known as the law of double effect, which asserts that there is a morally relevant distinction between bringing about the death of an innocent person deliberately, either as an end in itself or as a means, and bringing it about as a side effect of something else one does deliberately. In the latter case, even if the outcome is foreseen, it is not murder, and does not fall under the absolute prohibition, though of course it may still be wrong for other reasons (reasons of utility, for example). Briefly, the principle states that one is sometimes permitted knowingly to bring about as a side effect of one's actions something which it would be absolutely impermissible to bring about deliberately as an end or as a means. In application to war or revolution, the law of double effect permits a certain amount of civilian carnage as a side effect of bombing munitions plants or attacking enemy soldiers. And even this is permissible only if the cost is not too great to be justified by one's objectives.

However, despite its importance and its usefulness in accounting for certain plausible moral judgments, I do not believe that the law of double effect is a generally applicable test for the consequences of an absolutist position. Its own application is not always clear, so that it introduces uncertainty where there need not be uncertainty.

In Indochina, for example, there is a great deal of aerial bombardment, strafing, spraying of napalm, and employment of pellet- or needle-spraying antipersonnel weapons against rural villages in which guerrillas are suspected to be hiding, or from which small-arms fire has been received. The majority of those killed and wounded in these aerial attacks are reported to be women and children, even when some combatants are caught as well. However, the government regards these civilian casualties as a regrettable side effect of what is a legitimate attack against an armed enemy.

It might be thought easy to dismiss this as sophistry: If one bombs, burns, or strafes a village containing a hundred people, twenty of whom one believes to be guerrillas, so that by killing most of them one will be statistically likely to kill most of the guerrillas, then isn't one's attack on the group of one hundred a *means* of destroying the guerrillas and civilians, as is impossible in an

aerial attack on a small village, then one cannot regard as a mere side effect the deaths of those in the group that one would not have bothered to kill if more selective means had been available.

The difficulty is that this argument depends on one particular description of the act, and the reply might be that the means used against the guerrillas is not: killing everybody in the village—but rather: obliteration bombing of the *area* in which the twenty guerrillas are known to be located. If there are civilians in the area as well, they will be killed as a side effect of such action.[4]

Because of casuistical problems like this, I prefer to stay with the original, unanalyzed distinction between what one does to people and what merely happens to them as a result of what one does. The law of double effect provides an approximation to that distinction in many cases, and perhaps it can be sharpened to the point where it does better than that. Certainly the original distinction itself needs clarification, particularly since some of the things we do to people involve things happening to them as a result of other things we do. In a case like the one discussed, however, it is clear that by bombing the village one slaughters and maims the civilians in it. Whereas by giving the only available medicine to one of two sufferers from a disease, one does not kill the other, even if he dies as a result.

The second technical point to take up concerns a possible misinterpretation of this feature of the position. The absolutist focus on actions rather than outcomes does not merely introduce a new, outstanding item into the catalogue of evils. That is, it does not say that the worst thing in the world is the deliberate murder of an innocent per

---

4. This counterargument was suggested by Rogers Albritton.

son. For if that were all, then one could presumably justify one such murder on the ground that it would prevent several others, or ten thousand on the ground that they would prevent a hundred thousand more. That is a familiar argument. But if this is allowable, then there is no absolute prohibition against murder after all. Absolutism requires that we *avoid* murder at all costs, not that we *prevent* it at all costs.[5]

Finally, let me remark on a frequent criticism of absolutism that depends on a misunderstanding. It is sometimes suggested that such prohibitions depend on a kind of moral self-interest, a primary obligation to preserve one's own moral purity, to keep one's hands clean no matter what happens to the rest of the world. If this were the position, it might be exposed to the charge of self-indulgence. After all, what gives one man a right to put the purity of his soul or the cleanness of his hands above the lives or welfare of large numbers of other people? It might be argued that a public servant like Truman has no right to put himself first in that way; therefore if he is convinced that the alternatives would be worse, he must give the order to drop the bombs, and take the burden of those deaths on himself, as he must do other distasteful things for the general good.

But there are two confusions behind the view that moral self-interest underlies moral absolutism. First, it is a confusion to suggest that the need to preserve one's moral purity might be the *source* of an obligation. For if by committing murder one sacrifices one's moral purity or integrity, that can only be because there is *already* something wrong with murder. The general reason against committing murder cannot therefore be merely that it makes one an immoral person. Secondly, the notion

that one might sacrifice one's moral integrity justifiably, in the service of a sufficiently worthy end, is an incoherent notion. For if one were justified in making such a sacrifice (or even morally required to make it), then one would not be sacrificing one's moral integrity by adopting that course: One would be preserving it.

Moral absolutism is not unique among moral theories in requiring each person to do what will preserve his own moral purity in all circumstances. This is equally true of utilitarianism, or of any other theory which distinguishes between right and wrong. Any theory which defines the right course of action in various circumstances and asserts that one should adopt that course, ipso facto asserts that one should do what will preserve one's moral purity, simply because the right course of action *is* what will preserve one's moral purity in those circumstances. Of course utilitarianism does not assert that this is *why* one should adopt that course, but we have seen that the same is true of absolutism.

V

It is easier to dispose of false explanations of absolutism than to produce a true one. A positive account of the matter must begin with the observation that war, conflict, and aggression are relations between persons. The view that it can be wrong to consider merely the overall effect of one's actions on the general welfare comes into prominence when those actions involve relations

5. Someone might of course acknowledge the *moral relevance* of the distinction between deliberate and nondeliberate killing, without being an absolutist. That is, he might believe simply that it was *worse* to bring about a death deliberately than as a secondary effect. But that would be merely a special assignment of value, and not an absolute prohibition.

with others. A man's acts usually affect more people than he deals with directly, and those effects must naturally be considered in his decisions. But if there are special principles governing the manner in which he should *treat* people, that will require special attention to the particular persons toward whom the act is directed, rather than just to its total effect.

Absolutist restrictions in warfare appear to be of two types: restrictions on the class of persons at whom aggression or violence may be directed and restrictions on the manner of attack, given that the object falls within that class. These can be combined, however, under the principle that hostile treatment of any person must be justified in terms of something *about that person* which makes the treatment appropriate. Hostility is a personal relation, and it must be suited to its target. One consequence of this condition will be that certain persons may not be subjected to hostile treatment in war at all, since nothing about them justifies such treatment. Others will be proper objects of hostility only in certain circumstances, or when they are engaged in certain pursuits. And the appropriate manner and extent of hostile treatment will depend on what is justified by the particular case.

A coherent view of this type will hold that extremely hostile behavior toward another is compatible with treating him as a person—even perhaps as an end in himself. This is possible only if one has not automatically stopped treating him as a person as soon as one starts to fight with him. If hostile, aggressive, or combative treatment of others always violated the condition that they be treated as human beings, it would be difficult to make further distinctions on that score *within* the class of hostile actions. That point of view, on

the level of international relations, leads to the position that if complete pacifism is not accepted, no holds need be barred at all, and we may slaughter and massacre to our hearts' content, if it seems advisable. Such a position is often expressed in discussions of war crimes.

But the fact is that ordinary people do not believe this about conflicts, physical or otherwise, between individuals, and there is no more reason why it should be true of conflicts between nations. There seems to be a perfectly natural conception of the distinction between fighting clean and fighting dirty. To fight dirty is to direct one's hostility or aggression not at its proper object, but at a peripheral target which may be more vulnerable, and through which the proper object can be attacked indirectly. This applies in a fist fight, an election campaign, a duel, or a philosophical argument. If the concept is general enough to apply to all these matters, it should apply to war—both to the conduct of individual soldiers and to the conduct of nations.

Suppose that you are a candidate for public office, convinced that the election of your opponent would be a disaster, that he is an unscrupulous demagogue who will serve a narrow range of interests and seriously infringe the rights of those who disagree with him; and suppose you are convinced that you cannot defeat him by conventional means. Now imagine that various unconventional means present themselves as possibilities: You possess information about his sex life which would scandalize the electorate if made public; or you learn that his wife is an alcoholic or that in his youth he was associated for a brief period with a proscribed political party, and you believe that this information could be used to blackmail him into withdrawing his candidacy; or you can have a team of your supporters flatten the tires of a crucial subset of his supporters on election day; or you are in a position to stuff the ballot boxes; or, more simply, you can have him assassinated. What is wrong with these methods, given that they will achieve an overwhelmingly desirable result?

There are, of course, many things wrong with them: Some are against the law; some infringe the procedures of an electoral process to which you are presumably committed by taking part in it; very importantly, some may backfire, and it is in the interest of all political candidates to adhere to an unspoken agreement not to allow certain personal matters to intrude into a campaign. But that is not all. We have in addition the feeling that these measures, these methods of attack are *irrelevant* to the issue between you and your opponent, that in taking them up you would not be directing yourself to that which makes him an object of your opposition. You would be directing your attack not at the true target of your hostility, but at peripheral targets that happen to be vulnerable.

The same is true of a fight or argument outside the framework of any system of regulations or law. In an altercation with a taxi driver over an excessive fare, it is inappropriate to taunt him about his accent, flatten one of his tires, or smear chewing gum on his windshield; and it remains inappropriate even if he casts aspersions on your race, politics, or religion, or dumps the contents of your suitcase into the street.[6]

The importance of such restrictions may vary with the seriousness of the case; and what is unjustifiable in one case may be justified in a more extreme one. But they all derive from a single principle: that hostility or aggression should be directed at its true object. This means both that it should be directed at the person or persons who provoke it and that it should aim more specifically at what is provocative about them. The second condition will determine what form the hostility may appropriately take.

It is evident that some idea of the relation in which one should stand to other people underlies this principle, but the idea is difficult to state. I believe it is roughly this: Whatever one does to another person intentionally must be aimed at him as a subject, with the intention that he receive it as a subject. It should manifest an attitude to *him* rather than just to the situation, and he should be able to recognize it and identify himself as its object. The procedures by which such an attitude is manifested need not be addressed to the person directly. Surgery, for example, is not a form of personal confrontation but part of a medical treatment that can be offered to a patient face to face and received by him as a response to his needs and the natural outcome of an attitude toward *him*.

Hostile treatment, unlike surgery, is already addressed *to* a person, and does not take its interpersonal meaning from a wider context. But hostile acts can serve as the expression or implementation of only a limited range of attitudes to the person who is attacked. Those attitudes in turn have as objects

6. Why, on the other hand, does it seem appropriate, rather than irrelevant, to punch someone in the mouth if he insults you? The answer is that in our culture it is an insult to punch someone in the mouth, and not just an injury. This reveals, by the way, a perfectly unobjectionable sense in which convention may play a part in determining exactly what falls under an absolutist restriction and what does not. I am indebted to Robert Fogelin for this point.

certain real or presumed characteristics or activities of the person which are thought to justify them. When this background is absent, hostile or aggressive behavior can no longer be intended for the reception of the victim as a subject. Instead it takes on the character of a purely bureaucratic operation. This occurs when one attacks someone who is not the true object of one's hostility—the true object may be someone else, who can be attacked through the victim; or one may not be manifesting a hostile attitude toward anyone, but merely using the easiest available path to some desired goal. One finds oneself not facing or addressing the victim at all, but operating on him—without the larger context of personal interaction that surrounds a surgical operation.

If absolutism is to defend its claim to priority over considerations of utility, it must hold that the maintenance of a direct interpersonal response to the people one deals with is a requirement which no advantages can justify one in abandoning. The requirement is absolute only if it rules out any calculation of what would justify its violation. I have said earlier that there may be circumstances so extreme that they render an absolutist position untenable. One may find then that one has no choice but to do something terrible. Nevertheless, even in such cases absolutism retains its force in that one cannot claim *justification* for the violation. It does not become *all right*.

As a tentative effort to explain this, let me try to connect absolutist limitations with the possibility of justifying *to the victim* what is being done to him. If one abandons a person in the course of rescuing several others from a fire or a sinking ship, one *could* say to him, "You understand, I have to leave you to save the others." Similarly, if one subjects an unwilling child to a painful surgical procedure, one can say to him, "If you could understand, you would realize that I am doing this to help you." One could *even* say, as one bayonets an enemy soldier, "It's either you or me." But one cannot really say while torturing a prisoner, "You understand, I have to pull out your fingernails because it is absolutely essential that we have the names of your confederates"; nor can one say to the victims of Hiroshima, "You understand, we have to incinerate you to provide the Japanese government with an incentive to surrender."

This does not take us very far, of course, since a utilitarian would presumably be willing to offer justifications of the latter sort to his victims, in cases where he thought they were sufficient. They are really justifications to the world at large, which the victim, as a reasonable man, would be expected to appreciate. However, there seems to me something wrong with this view, for it ignores the possibility that to treat someone else horribly puts you in a special relation to him, which may have to be defended in terms of other features of your relation to him. The suggestion needs much more development; but it may help us to understand how there may be requirements which are absolute in the sense that there can be no justification for violating them. If the justification for what one did to another person had to be such that it could be offered to him specifically, rather than just to the world at large, that would be a significant source of restraint.

If the account is to be deepened, I would hope for some results along the following lines. Absolutism is associated with a view of oneself as a small being interacting with others in a large world. The justifications it requires are primarily interpersonal. Utilitarianism is associated with a view of oneself as a benevolent bureaucrat distributing such benefits as one can control to countless other beings, with whom one may have various relations or none. The justifications it requires are primarily administrative. The argument between the two moral attitudes may depend on the relative priority of these two conceptions.[7]

VI

Some of the restrictions on methods of warfare which have been adhered to from time to time are to be explained by the mutual interests of the involved parties: restrictions on weaponry, treatment of prisoners, and so forth. But that is not all there is to it. The conditions of directness and relevance which I have argued apply to relations of conflict and aggression apply to war as well. I have said that there are two types of absolutist restrictions on the conduct of war: those that limit the legitimate targets of hostility and those that limit its character, even when the target is acceptable. I shall say something about each of these. As will become clear, the principle I have sketched does not yield an unambiguous answer in every case.

First let us see how it implies that attacks on some people are allowed, but not attacks on others. It may seem paradoxical to assert that to fire a machine gun at someone who is throwing hand grenades at your emplacement is to treat him as a human being. Yet the relation with him is direct and straightforward.[8] The attack is aimed specifically against the threat presented by a dangerous adversary, and not against a peripheral target through which he happens to be vulnerable but which has nothing to do with that threat. For

example, you might stop him by machine-gunning his wife and children, who are standing nearby, thus distracting him from his aim of blowing you up and enabling you to capture him. But if his wife and children are not threatening your life, that would be treat them as means with a vengeance.

This, however, is just Hiroshima on a smaller scale. One objection to weapons of mass annihilation—nuclear, thermonuclear, biological, or chemical—is that their indiscriminateness disqualifies them as direct instruments for the expression of hostile relations. In attacking the civilian population, one treats neither the military enemy nor the civilians with that minimal respect which is owed to them as human beings. This is clearly true of the direct attack on people who present no threat at all. But it is also true of the character of the attack on those who *are* threatening you, viz., the government and military forces of the enemy. Your aggression is directed against an area of vulnerability quite distinct from any threat presented by them which you may be justified in meeting. You are taking aim at them through the mundane life and survival of their countrymen, instead of aiming at the destruction of their military capacity. And of course it does not require hydrogen bombs to commit such crimes.

This way of looking at the matter also helps us to understand the importance of the distinction between com-

7. Finally, I should mention a different possibility, suggested by Robert Nozick: that there is a strong general presumption against benefiting from the calamity of another, whether or not it has been deliberately inflicted for that or any other reason. This broader principle may well lend its force to the absolutist position.

8. It has been remarked that according to my view, shooting at someone establishes an I-thou relationship.

batants and noncombatants, and the irrelevance of much of the criticism offered against its intelligibility and moral significance. According to an absolutist position, deliberate killing of the innocent is murder, and in warfare the role of the innocent is filled by noncombatants. This has been thought to raise two sorts of problems: first, the widely imagined difficulty of making a division, in modern warfare, between combatants and noncombatants; second, problems deriving from the connotation of the word "innocence."

Let me take up the latter question first.[9] In the absolutist position, the operative notion of innocence is not moral innocence, and it is not opposed to moral guilt. If it were, then we would be justified in killing a wicked but noncombatant hairdresser in an enemy city who supported the evil policies of his government, and unjustified in killing a morally pure conscript who was driving a tank toward us with the profoundest regrets and nothing but love in his heart. But moral innocence has very little to do with it, for in the definition of murder "innocent" means "currently harmless," and it is opposed not to "guilty" but to "doing harm." It should be noted that such an analysis has the consequence that in war we may often be justified in killing people who do not deserve to die, and unjustified in killing people who do deserve to die, if anyone does.

So we must distinguish combatants from noncombatants on the basis of their immediate threat or harmfulness. I do not claim that the line is a sharp one, but it is not so difficult as is often supposed to place individuals on one side of it or the other. Children are not combatants even though they may join the armed forces if they are allowed to grow up. Women are not combatants just be-

cause they bear children or offer comfort to the soldiers. More problematic are the supporting personnel, whether in or out of uniform, from drivers of munitions trucks and army cooks to civilian munitions workers and farmers. I believe they can be plausibly classified by applying the condition that the prosecution of conflict must direct itself to the cause of danger, and not to what is peripheral. The threat presented by an army and its members does not consist merely in the fact that they are men, but in the fact that they are armed and are using their arms in the pursuit of certain objectives. Contributions to their arms and logistics are contributions to this threat; contributions to their mere existence as men are not. It is therefore wrong to direct an attack against those who merely serve the combatants' needs as human beings, such as farmers and food suppliers, even though survival as a human being is a necessary condition of efficient functioning as a soldier.

This brings us to the second group of restrictions: those that limit what may be done even to combatants. These limits are harder to explain clearly. Some of them may be arbitrary or conventional, and some may have to be derived from other sources; but I believe that the condition of directness and relevance in hostile relations accounts for them to a considerable extent.

Consider first a case which involves both a protected class of noncombatants and a restriction on the measures that may be used against combatants. One provision of the rules of war which is universally recognized, though it seems to be turning into a dead letter in Vietnam, is the special status of medical personnel and the wounded in warfare.

9. What I say on this subject derives from Anscombe.

It might be more efficient to shoot medical officers on sight and to let the enemy wounded die rather than be patched up to fight another day. But someone with medical insignia is supposed to be left alone and permitted to tend and retrieve the wounded. I believe this is because medical attention is a species of attention to completely general human needs, not specifically the needs of a combat soldier, and our conflict with the soldier is not with his existence as a human being.

By extending the application of this idea, one can justify prohibitions against certain particularly cruel weapons: starvation, poisoning, infectious diseases (supposing they could be inflicted on combatants only), weapons designed to maim or disfigure or torture the opponent rather than merely to stop him. It is not, I think, mere casuistry to claim that such weapons attack the men, not the soldiers. The effect of dum-dum bullets, for example, is much more extended than necessary to cope with the combat situation in which they are used. They abandon any attempt to discriminate in their effects between the combatant and the human being. For this reason the use of flame-throwers and napalm is an atrocity in all circumstances that I can imagine, who-

ever the target may be. Burns are both extremely painful and extremely disfiguring—far more than any other category of wound. That this well-known fact plays no (inhibiting) part in the determination of U.S. weapons policy suggests that moral sensitivity among public officials has not increased markedly since the Spanish Inquisition.[10]

Finally, the same condition of appropriateness to the true object of hostility should limit the scope of attacks on an enemy country: its economy, agriculture, transportation system, and so forth. Even if the parties to a military conflict are considered to be not armies or governments but entire nations (which is usually a grave error), that does not justify one nation in warring against every aspect or element of another nation. That is not justified in a conflict between individuals, and nations are even more complex than individuals, so the same reasons apply. Like a human being, a nation is engaged in countless other pursuits while waging war, and it is not in those respects that it is an enemy.

The burden of the argument has been that absolutism about murder has a foundation in principles governing all one's relations to other persons, whether aggressive or amiable, and that

---

10. Beyond this I feel uncertain. Ordinary bullets, after all, can cause death, and nothing is more permanent than that. I am not at all sure why we are justified in trying to kill those who are trying to kill us (rather than merely in trying to stop them with force which may also result in their deaths). It is often argued that incapacitating gases are a relatively humane weapon (when not used, as in Vietnam, merely to make people easier to shoot). Perhaps the legitimacy of restrictions against them must depend on the dangers of escalation, and the great utility of maintaining *any* conventional category of restriction so long as nations are willing to adhere to it.

Let me make clear that I do not regard my argument as a defense of the moral immutability of the Hague and Geneva Conventions. Rather, I believe that they rest partly on a moral foundation,

and that modifications of them should also be assessed on moral grounds.

But even this connection with the actual laws of war is not essential to my claims about what is permissible and what is not. Since completing this paper I have read an essay by Richard Wasserstrom entitled "The Laws of War" (forthcoming in *The Monist*), which argues that the existing laws and conventions do not even attempt to embody a decent moral position: that their provisions have been determined by other interests, that they are in fact immoral in substance, and that it is a grave mistake to refer to them as standards in forming moral judgments about warfare. This possibility deserves serious consideration, and I am not sure what to say about it, but it does not affect my view of the moral issues.

these principles, and that absolutism, apply to warfare as well, with the result that certain measures are impermissible no matter what the consequences.[11] I do not mean to romanticize war. It is sufficiently utopian to suggest that when nations conflict they might rise to the level of limited barbarity that typically characterizes violent conflict between individuals, rather than wallowing in the moral pit where they appear to have settled, surrounded by enormous arsenals.

VII

Having described the elements of the absolutist position, we must now return to the conflict between it and utilitarianism. Even if certain types of dirty tactics become acceptable when the stakes are high enough, the most serious of the prohibited acts, like murder and torture, are not just supposed to require unusually strong justification. They are supposed *never* to be done, because no quantity of resulting benefit is thought capable of *justifying* such treatment of a person.

The fact remains that when an absolutist knows or believes that the utilitarian cost of refusing to adopt a prohibited course will be very high, he may hold to his refusal to adopt it, but he will find it difficult to feel that a moral dilemma has been satisfactorily resolved. The same may be true of someone who rejects an absolutist requirement and adopts instead the course yielding the most acceptable consequences. In either case, it is possible to feel that one has acted for reasons insufficient to justify violation of the opposing principle. In situations of deadly conflict, particularly where a weaker party is threatened with annihilation or enslavement by a stronger one, the argument for resorting to atroc-

ities can be powerful, and the dilemma acute.

There may exist principles, not yet codified, which would enable us to resolve such dilemmas. But then again there may not. We must face the pessimistic alternative that these two forms of moral intuition are not capable of being brought together into a single, coherent moral system, and that the world can present us with situations in which there is no honorable or moral course for a man to take, no course free of guilt and responsibility for evil.

The idea of a moral blind alley is a perfectly intelligible one. It is possible to get into such a situation by one's own fault, and people do it all the time. If, for example, one makes two incompatible promises or commitments—becomes engaged to two people, for example—then there is no course one can take which is not wrong, for one must break one's promise to at least one of them. Making a clean breast of the whole thing will not be enough to remove one's reprehensibility. The existence of such cases is not morally disturbing, however, because we feel that the situation was not unavoidable: One had to do something wrong in the first place to get into it. But what if the world itself, or someone else's actions, could face a previously innocent person with a choice between morally abominable courses of action, and leave him no way to escape with his honor? Our intuitions rebel at the idea, for we feel that the construct-

11. It is possible to draw a more radical conclusion, which I shall not pursue here. Perhaps the technology and organization of modern war are such as to make it impossible to wage as an acceptable form of interpersonal or even international hostility. Perhaps it is too impersonal and large-scale for that. If so, then absolutism would in practice imply pacifism, given the present state of things. On the other hand, I am skeptical about the unstated assumption that a technology dictates its own use.

ibility of such a case must show a contradiction in our moral views. But it is not in itself a contradiction to say that someone can do X or not do X, and that for him to take either course would be wrong. It merely contradicts the supposition that *ought* implies *can*— since presumably one ought to refrain from what is wrong, and in such a case it is impossible to do so.[12] Given the limitations on human action, it is naïve to suppose that there is a solution to every moral problem with which the world can face us. We have always known that the world is a bad place. It appears that it may be an evil place as well.

12. This was first pointed out to me by Christopher Boorse.

20

PETER SINGER
Famine, Affluence, and Morality

PETER SINGER is senior lecturer in philosophy at La Trobe University in Australia. He is the author of *Democracy and Disobedience* (1973) and *Animal Liberation* (1975).

As I write this, in November 1971, people are dying in East Bengal from lack of food, shelter, and medical care. The suffering and death that are occurring there now are not inevitable, not unavoidable in any fatalistic sense of the term. Constant poverty, a cyclone, and a civil war have turned at least nine million people into destitute refugees; nevertheless, it is not beyond the capacity of the richer nations to give enough assistance to reduce any further suffering to very small proportions. The decisions and actions of human beings can prevent this kind of suffering. Unfortunately, human beings have not made the necessary decisions. At the individual level, people have, with very few exceptions, not responded to the situation in any significant way. Generally speaking, people have not given large sums to relief funds; they have not written to their parliamentary representatives demanding increased government assistance; they have not demonstrated in the streets, held symbolic fasts, or done anything else directed toward providing the refugees with the means to satisfy their essential needs. At the government level, no government has given the sort of massive aid that would enable the refugees to survive for more than a few days. Britain, for instance, has given rather more than most countries. It has, to date, given £14,750,000. For comparative purposes, Britain's share of the nonrecoverable development costs of the Anglo-French Concorde project is already in excess of £275,000,000 and on present estimates will reach £440,000,000. The implication is that the British government values a super-

From Peter Singer, "Famine, Affluence, and Morality," *Philosophy and Public Affairs*, vol. 1 (1971–1972), pp. 229–241. Copyright © 1972 by Princeton University Press. Reprinted by permission of Princeton University Press. This article is reprinted unabridged.

sonic transport more than thirty times as highly as it values the lives of the nine million refugees. Australia is another country which, on a per capita basis, is well up in the "aid to Bengal" table. Australia's aid, however, amounts to less than one-twelfth of the cost of Sydney's new opera house. The total amount given, from all sources, now stands at about £65,000,000. The estimated cost of keeping the refugees alive for one year is £464,000,000. Most of the refugees have now been in the camps for more than six months. The World Bank has said that India needs a minimum of £300,000,000 in assistance from other countries before the end of the year. It seems obvious that assistance on this scale will not be forthcoming. India will be forced to choose between letting the refugees starve or diverting funds from her own development program, which will mean that more of her own people will starve in the future.[1]

These are the essential facts about the present situation in Bengal. So far as it concerns us here, there is nothing unique about this situation except its magnitude. The Bengal emergency is just the latest and most acute of a series of major emergencies in various parts of the world, arising both from natural and from man-made causes. There are also many parts of the world in which people die from malnutrition and lack of food independent of any special emergency. I take Bengal as my example only because it is the present concern, and because the size of the problem has ensured that it has been given adequate publicity. Neither individuals nor governments can claim to be unaware of what is happening there.

What are the moral implications of a situation like this? In what follows, I shall argue that the way people in relatively affluent countries react to a situation like that in Bengal cannot be justified; indeed, the whole way we look at moral issues—our moral conceptual scheme—needs to be altered, and with it, the way of life that has come to be taken for granted in our society.

In arguing for this conclusion I will not, of course, claim to be morally neutral. I shall, however, try to argue for the moral position that I take, so that anyone who accepts certain assumptions, to be made explicit, will, I hope, accept my conclusion.

I begin with the assumption that suffering and death from lack of food, shelter, and medical care are bad. I think most people will agree about this, although one may reach the same view by different routes. I shall not argue for this view. People can hold all sorts of eccentric positions, and perhaps from some of them it would not follow that death by starvation is in itself bad. It is difficult, perhaps impossible, to refute such positions, and so for brevity I will henceforth take this assumption as accepted. Those who disagree need read no further.

My next point is this: If it is in our power to prevent something bad from happening, without thereby sacrificing anything of comparable moral importance, we ought, morally, to do it. By "without sacrificing anything of comparable moral importance" I mean without causing anything else comparably bad to happen, or doing something that is wrong in itself, or failing to promote some moral good, comparable in significance to the bad thing that we can prevent. This principle seems almost as

1. There was also a third possibility: that India would go to war to enable the refugees to return to the lands. Since I wrote this paper, India has taken this way out. The situation is no longer that described above, but this does not affect my argument, as the next paragraph indicates.

uncontroversial as the last one. It requires us only to prevent what is bad, and not to promote what is good, and it requires this of us only when we can do it without sacrificing anything that is, from the moral point of view, comparably important. I could even, as far as the application of my argument to the Bengal emergency is concerned, qualify the point so as to make it: If it is in our power to prevent something very bad from happening, without thereby sacrificing anything morally significant, we ought, morally, to do it. An application of this principle would be as follows: If I am walking past a shallow pond and see a child drowning in it, I ought to wade in and pull the child out. This will mean getting my clothes muddy, but this is insignificant, while the death of the child would presumably be a very bad thing.

The uncontroversial appearance of the principle just stated is deceptive. If it were acted upon, even in its qualified form, our lives, our society, and our world would be fundamentally changed. For the principle takes, firstly, no account of proximity or distance. It makes no moral difference whether the person I can help is a neighbor's child ten yards from me or a Bengali whose name I shall never know, ten thousand miles away. Secondly, the principle makes no distinction between cases in which I am the only person who could possibly do anything and cases in which I am just one among millions in the same position.

I do not think I need to say much in defense of the refusal to take proximity and distance into account. The fact that a person is physically near to us, so that we have personal contact with him, may make it more likely that we *shall* assist him, but this does not show that we *ought* to help him rather than another who happens to be further away. If we accept any principle of impartiality, universalizability, equality, or whatever, we cannot discriminate against someone merely because he is far away from us (or we are far away from him). Admittedly, it is possible that we are in a better position to judge what needs to be done to help a person near to us than one far away, and perhaps also to provide the assistance we judge to be necessary. If this were the case, it would be a reason for helping those near to us first. This may once have been a justification for being more concerned with the poor in one's own town than with famine victims in India. Unfortunately for those who like to keep their moral responsibilities limited, instant communication and swift transportation have changed the situation. From the moral point of view, the development of the world into a "global village" has made an important, though still unrecognized, difference to our moral situation. Expert observers and supervisors, sent out by famine relief organizations or permanently stationed in famine-prone areas, can direct our aid to a refugee in Bengal almost as effectively as we could get it to someone in our own block. There would seem, therefore, to be no possible justification for discriminating on geographical grounds.

There may be a greater need to defend the second implication of my principle—that the fact that there are millions of other people in the same position, in respect to the Bengali refugees, as I am, does not make the situation significantly different from a situation in which I am the only person who can prevent something very bad from occurring. Again, of course, I admit that there is a psychological difference between the cases; one feels less guilty about doing nothing if one can point to others, similarly placed, who have also done nothing. Yet this can make no real difference to our moral obligations.[2] Should I consider that I am less obliged to pull the drowning child out of the pond if on looking around I see other people, no further away than I am, who have also noticed the child but are doing nothing? One has only to ask this question to see the absurdity of the view that numbers lessen obligation. It is a view that is an ideal excuse for inactivity; unfortunately most of the major evils— poverty, overpopulation, pollution—are problems in which everyone is almost equally involved.

The view that numbers do make a difference can be made plausible if stated in this way: If everyone in circumstances like mine gave £5 to the Bengal Relief Fund, there would be enough to provide food, shelter, and medical care for the refugees; there is no reason why I should give more than anyone else in the same circumstances as I am; therefore I have no obligation to give more than £5. Each premise in this argument is true, and the argument looks sound. It may convince us, unless we notice that it is based on a hypothetical premise, although the conclusion is not stated hypothetically. The argument would be sound if the conclusion were: If everyone in circumstances like mine were to give £5, I would have no obligation to give more than £5. If the conclusion were so stated, however, it would be obvious that the argument has no bearing on a situation in which it is not the case that everyone else gives £5. This, of course, is the actual situation. It is more or less certain that not everyone in circumstances like mine will give £5. So there will not be enough to provide the needed food, shelter, and medical care. Therefore by giving more than £5 I will prevent more suffering than I would if I gave just £5.

It might be thought that this argument has an absurd consequence. Since

the situation appears to be that very few people are likely to give substantial amounts, it follows that I and everyone else in similar circumstances ought to give as much as possible, that is, at least up to the point at which by giving more one would begin to cause serious suffering for oneself and one's dependents— perhaps even beyond this point to the point of marginal utility, at which by giving more one would cause oneself and one's dependents as much suffering as one would prevent in Bengal. If everyone does this, however, there will be more than can be used for the benefit of the refugees, and some of the sacrifice will have been unnecessary. Thus, if everyone does what he ought to do, the result will not be as good as it would be if everyone did a little less than he ought to do, or if only some do all that they ought to do.

The paradox here arises only if we assume that the actions in question— sending money to the relief funds—are performed more or less simultaneously, and are also unexpected. For if it is to be expected that everyone is going to contribute something, then clearly each is not obliged to give as much as he would have been obliged to had others not been giving too. And if everyone is not acting more or less simultaneously, then those giving later will know how much more is needed, and will have no obligation to give more than is necessary to reach this

2. In view of the special sense philosophers often give to the term, I should say that I use "obligation" simply as the abstract noun derived from "ought," so that "I have an obligation to" means no more, and no less, than "I ought to." This usage is in accordance with the definition of "ought" given by the *Shorter Oxford English Dictionary:* "the general verb to express duty or obligation." I do not think any issue of substance hangs on the way the term is used; sentences in which I use "obligation" could all be rewritten, although somewhat clumsily, as sentences in which a clause containing "ought" replaces the term "obligation."

amount. To say this is not to deny the principle that people in the same circumstances have the same obligations, but to point out that the fact that others have given, or maybe expected to give, is a relevant circumstance: Those giving after it has become known that many others are giving and those giving before are not in the same circumstances. So the seemingly absurd consequence of the principle I have put forward can occur only if people are in error about the actual circumstances—that is, if they think they are giving when others are not, but in fact they are giving when others are. The result of everyone doing what he really ought to do cannot be worse than the result of everyone doing less than he ought to do, although the result of everyone doing what he reasonably believes he ought to do could be.

If my argument so far has been sound, neither our distance from a preventable evil nor the number of other people who, in respect to that evil, are in the same situation as we are, lessens our obligation to mitigate or prevent that evil. I shall therefore take as established the principle I asserted earlier. As I have already said, I need to assert it only in its qualified form: If it is in our power to prevent something very bad from happening, without thereby sacrificing anything else morally significant, we ought, morally, to do it.

The outcome of this argument is that our traditional moral categories are upset. The traditional distinction between duty and charity cannot be drawn, or at least, not in the place we normally draw it. Giving money to the Bengal Relief Fund is regarded as an act of charity in our society. The bodies which collect money are known as "charities." These organizations see themselves in this way—if you send them a check, you will be thanked for your "generos-

ity." Because giving money is regarded as an act of charity, it is not thought that there is anything wrong with not giving. The charitable man may be praised, but the man who is not charitable is not condemned. People do not feel in any way ashamed or guilty about spending money on new clothes or a new car instead of giving it to famine relief. (Indeed, the alternative does not occur to them.) This way of looking at the matter cannot be justified. When we buy new clothes not to keep ourselves warm but to look "well-dressed" we are not providing for any important need. We would not be sacrificing anything significant if we were to continue to wear our old clothes, and give the money to famine relief. By doing so, we would be preventing another person from starving. It follows from what I have said earlier that we ought to give money away, rather than spend it on clothes which we do not need to keep us warm. To do so is not charitable, or generous. Nor is it the kind of act which philosophers and theologians have called "supererogatory"—an act which it would be good to do, but not wrong not to do. On the contrary, we ought to give the money away, and it is wrong not to do so.

I am not maintaining that there are no acts which are charitable, or that there are no acts which it would be good to do but not wrong not to do. It may be possible to redraw the distinction between duty and charity in some other place. All I am arguing here is that the present way of drawing the distinction, which makes it an act of charity for a man living at the level of affluence which most people in the "developed nations" enjoy to give money to save someone else from starvation, cannot be supported. It is beyond the scope of my argument to consider whether the distinction should be redrawn or abolished altogether. There would be many other possible ways of drawing the distinction—for instance, one might decide that it is good to make other people as happy as possible, but not wrong not to do so.

Despite the limited nature of the revision in our moral conceptual scheme which I am proposing, the revision would, given the extent of both affluence and famine in the world today, have radical implications. These implications may lead to further objections, distinct from those I have already considered. I shall discuss two of these.

One objection to the position I have taken might be simply that it is too drastic a revision of our moral scheme. People do not ordinarily judge in the way I have suggested they should. Most people reserve their moral condemnation for those who violate some moral norm, such as the norm against taking another person's property. They do not condemn those who indulge in luxury instead of giving to famine relief. But given that I did not set out to present a morally neutral description of the way people make moral judgments, the way people do in fact judge has nothing to do with the validity of my conclusion. My conclusion follows from the principle which I advanced earlier, and unless that principle is rejected, or the arguments shown to be unsound, I think the conclusion must stand, however strange it appears.

It might, nevertheless, be interesting to consider why our society, and most other societies, do judge differently from the way I have suggested they should. In a well-known article, J. O. Urmson suggests that the imperatives of duty, which tell us what we must do, as distinct from what it would be good to do but not wrong not to do, function so as to prohibit behavior that is intolerable if men are to live together in society.[3] This may explain the origin and

continued existence of the present division between acts of duty and acts of charity. Moral attitudes are shaped by the needs of society, and no doubt society needs people who will observe the rules that make social existence tolerable. From the point of view of a particular society, it is essential to prevent violations of norms against killing, stealing, and so on. It is quite inessential, however, to help people outside one's own society.

If this is an explanation of our common distinction between duty and supererogation, however, it is not a justification of it. The moral point of view requires us to look beyond the interests of our own society. Previously, as I have already mentioned, this may hardly have been feasible, but it is quite feasible now. From the moral point of view, the prevention of the starvation of millions of people outside our society must be considered at least as pressing as the upholding of property norms within our society.

It has been argued by some writers, among them Sidgwick and Urmson, that we need to have a basic moral code which is not too far beyond the capacities of the ordinary man, for otherwise there will be a general breakdown of compliance with the moral code. Crudely stated, this argument suggests that if we tell people that they ought to refrain from murder and giving everything they do not really need to famine relief, they will do neither, whereas if we tell them that they ought to refrain from murder and that it is good to give to famine relief but not wrong not to do so, they will at least re-

3. J. O. Urmson, "Saints and Heroes," in *Essays in Moral Philosophy*, ed. Abraham I. Melden (Seattle and London, 1958), p. 214. For a related but significantly different view see also Henry Sidgwick, *The Methods of Ethics*, 7th edn. (London, 1907), pp. 220–221, 492–493.

frain from murder. The issue here is: Where should we draw the line between conduct that is required and conduct that is good although not required, so as to get the best possible result? This would seem to be an empirical question, although a very difficult one. One objection to the Sidgwick-Urmson line of argument is that it takes insufficient account of the effect that moral standards can have on the decisions we make. Given a society in which a wealthy man who gives five percent of his income to famine relief is regarded as most generous, it is not surprising that a proposal that we all ought to give away half our incomes will be thought to be absurdly unrealistic. In a society which held that no man should have more than enough while others have less than they need, such a proposal might seem narrow-minded. What it is possible for a man to do and what he is likely to do are both, I think, very greatly influenced by what people around him are doing and expecting him to do. In any case, the possibility that by spreading the idea that we ought to be doing very much more than we are to relieve famine we shall bring about a general breakdown of moral behavior seems remote. If the stakes are an end to widespread starvation, it is worth the risk. Finally, it should be emphasized that these considerations are relevant only to the issue of what we should require from others, and not to what we ourselves ought to do.

The second objection to my attack on the present distinction between duty and charity is one which has from time to time been made against utilitarianism. It follows from some forms of utilitarian theory that we all ought, morally, to be working full time to increase the balance of happiness over misery. The position I have taken here would not lead to this conclusion in all circumstances, for if there were no bad occurrences that we could prevent without sacrificing something of comparable moral importance, my argument would have no application. Given the present conditions in many parts of the world, however, it does follow from my argument that we ought, morally, to be working full time to relieve great suffering of the sort that occurs as a result of famine or other disasters. Of course, mitigating circumstances can be adduced—for instance, that if we wear ourselves out through overwork, we shall be less effective than we would otherwise have been. Nevertheless, when all considerations of this sort have been taken into account, the conclusion remains: We ought to be preventing as much suffering as we can without sacrificing something else of comparable moral importance. This conclusion is one which we may be reluctant to face. I cannot see, though, why it should be regarded as a criticism of the position for which I have argued, rather than a criticism of our ordinary standards of behavior. Since most people are self-interested to some degree, very few of us are likely to do everything that we ought to do. It would, however, hardly be honest to take this as evidence that it is not the case that we ought to do it.

It may still be thought that my conclusions are so wildly out of line with what everyone else thinks and has always thought that there must be something wrong with the argument somewhere. In order to show that my conclusions, while certainly contrary to contemporary Western moral standards, would not have seemed so extraordinary at other times and in other places, I would like to quote a passage from a writer not normally thought of as a way-out radical, Thomas Aquinas.

Now, according to the natural order instituted by divine providence, material goods are provided for the satisfaction of human needs. Therefore the division and appropriation of property, which proceeds from human law, must not hinder the satisfaction of man's necessity from such goods. Equally, whatever a man has in superabundance is owed, of natural right, to the poor for their sustenance. So Ambrosius says, and it is also to be found in the *Decretum Gratiani:* "The bread which you withhold belongs to the hungry; the clothing you shut away, to the naked; and the money you bury in the earth is the redemption and freedom of the penniless."[4]

I now want to consider a number of points, more practical than philosophical, which are relevant to the application of the moral conclusion we have reached. These points challenge not the idea that we ought to be doing all we can to prevent starvation, but the idea that giving away a great deal of money is the best means to this end.

It is sometimes said that overseas aid should be a government responsibility, and that therefore one ought not to give to privately run charities. Giving privately, it is said, allows the government and the noncontributing members of society to escape their responsibilities.

This argument seems to assume that the more people there are who give to privately organized famine relief funds, the less likely it is that the government will take over full responsibility for such aid. This assumption is unsupported, and does not strike me as at all plausible. The opposite view—that if no one gives voluntarily, a government will assume that its citizens are uninterested in famine relief and would not wish to be forced into giving aid—seems more plausible. In any case, unless there were a definite probability that by refusing to give one would be helping to bring about massive government assistance, people who do refuse to make voluntary contributions are refusing to prevent a certain amount of suffering without being able to point to any tangible beneficial consequence of their refusal. So the onus of showing how their refusal will bring about government action is on those who refuse to give.

I do not, of course, want to dispute the contention that governments of affluent nations should be giving many times the amount of genuine, no-strings-attached aid that they are giving now. I agree, too, that giving privately is not enough, and that we ought to be campaigning actively for entirely new standards for both public and private contributions to famine relief. Indeed, I would sympathize with someone who thought that campaigning was more important than giving oneself, although I doubt whether preaching what one does not practice would be very effective. Unfortunately, for many people the idea that "it's the government's responsibility" is a reason for not giving which does not appear to entail any political action either.

Another, more serious reason for not giving to famine relief funds is that until there is effective population control, relieving famine merely postpones starvation. If we save the Bengal refugees now, others, perhaps the children of these refugees, will face starvation in a few years' time. In support of this, one may cite the now well-known facts about the population explosion and the relatively limited scope for expanded production.

This point, like the previous one, is an argument against relieving suffering that is happening now, because of a belief about what might happen in the future; it is unlike the previous point in

4. *Summa Theologica*, II-II, Question 66, Article 7, in *Aquinas, Selected Political Writings*, ed. A. P. d'Entreves, trans. J. G. Dawson (Oxford, 1948), p. 171.

that very good evidence can be adduced in support of this belief about the future. I will not go into the evidence here. I accept that the earth cannot support indefinitely a population rising at the present rate. This certainly poses a problem for anyone who thinks it important to prevent famine. Again, however, one could accept the argument without drawing the conclusion that it absolves one from any obligation to do anything to prevent famine. The conclusion that should be drawn is that the best means of preventing famine, in the long run, is population control. It would then follow from the position reached earlier that one ought to be doing all one can to promote population control (unless one held that all forms of population control were wrong in themselves, or would have significantly bad consequences). Since there are organizations working specifically for population control, one would then support them rather than more orthodox methods of preventing famine.

A third point raised by the conclusion reached earlier relates to the question of just how much we all ought to be giving away. One possibility, which has already been mentioned, is that we ought to give until we reach the level of marginal utility—that is, the level at which, by giving more, I would cause as much suffering to myself or my dependents as I would relieve by my gift. This would mean, of course, that one would reduce oneself to very near the material circumstances of a Bengali refugee. It will be recalled that earlier I put forward both a strong and a moderate version of the principle of preventing bad occurrences. The strong version, which required us to prevent bad things from happening unless in doing so we would be sacrificing something of comparable moral significance, does seem to require reducing ourselves to the level of mar-

ginal utility. I should also say that the strong version seems to me to be the correct one. I proposed the more moderate version—that we should prevent bad occurrences unless, to do so, we had to sacrifice something morally significant—only in order to show that even on this surely undeniable principle a great change in our way of life is required. On the more moderate principle, it may not follow that we ought to reduce ourselves to the level of marginal utility, for one might hold that to reduce oneself and one's family to this level is to cause something significantly bad to happen. Whether this is so I shall not discuss, since, as I have said, I can see no good reason for holding the moderate version of the principle rather than the strong version. Even if we accepted the principle only in its moderate form, however, it should be clear that we would have to give away enough to ensure that the consumer society, dependent as it is on people spending on trivia rather than giving to famine relief, would slow down and perhaps disappear entirely. There are several reasons why this would be desirable in itself. The value and necessity of economic growth are now being questioned not only by conservationists, but by economists as well.[5] There is no doubt, too, that the consumer society has had a distorting effect on the goals and purposes of its members. Yet looking at the matter purely from the point of view of overseas aid, there must be a limit to the extent to which we should deliberately slow down our economy: for it might be the case that if we gave away, say, forty percent of our Gross National Product, we would slow down the economy so much that in absolute terms we would

5. See, for instance, John Kenneth Galbraith, *The New Industrial State* (Boston, 1967); and E. J. Mishan, *The Costs of Economic Growth* (London, 1967).

be giving less than if we gave twenty-five percent of the much larger GNP that we would have if we limited our contribution to this smaller percentage.

I mention this only as an indication of the sort of factor that one would have to take into account in working out an ideal. Since Western societies generally consider one percent of the GNP an acceptable level for overseas aid, the matter is entirely academic. Nor does it affect the question of how much an individual should give in a society in which very few are giving substantial amounts.

It is sometimes said, though less often now than it used to be, that philosophers have no special role to play in public affairs, since most public issues depend primarily on an assessment of facts. On questions of fact, it is said, philosophers as such have no special expertise, and so it has been possible to engage in philosophy without committing oneself to any position on major public issues. No doubt there are some issues of social policy and foreign policy about which it can truly be said that a really expert assessment of the facts is required before taking sides or acting, but the issue of famine is surely not one of these. The facts about the existence of suffering are beyond dispute. Nor, I think, is it disputed that we can do something about it, either through orthodox methods of famine re-

lief or through population control or both. This is therefore an issue on which philosophers are competent to take a position. The issue is one which faces everyone who has more money than he needs to support himself and his dependents, or who is in a position to take some sort of political action. These categories must include practically every teacher and student of philosophy in the universities of the Western world. If philosophy is to deal with matters that are relevant to both teachers and students, this is an issue that philosophers should discuss.

Discussion, though, is not enough. What is the point of relating philosophy to public (and personal) affairs if we do not take our conclusions seriously? In this instance, taking our conclusion seriously means acting upon it. The philosopher will not find it any easier than anyone else to alter his attitudes and way of life to the extent that, if I am right, is involved in doing everything that we ought to be doing. At the very least, though, one can make a start. The philospher who does so will have to sacrifice some of the benefits of the consumer society, but he can find compensation in the satisfaction of a way of life in which theory and practice, if not yet in harmony, are at least coming together.

Suggestions for Further Reading

J. J. C. Smart, "Utilitarianism," *The Encyclopedia of Philosophy*, ed. Paul Edwards (New York: Macmillan and The Free Press, 1967), vol. 8, pp. 206–212.

J. J. C. Smart and Bernard Williams, *Utilitarianism: For and Against* (Cambridge: Cambridge University Press, 1973). This short book consists of two essays. The first is a revised version of Smart's monograph *An Outline of a System of Utilitarian Ethics* (Melbourne: Melbourne University Press, 1961), in which he defends act-utilitarianism; and the second is Williams's "A Critique of Utilitarianism." This book also contains a very good annotated bibliography.

T. L. S. Sprigge, "A Utilitarian Reply to Dr. McCloskey," *Inquiry*, vol. 8 (1965), pp. 264–291. This is a reply to McCloskey's "A Non-Utilitarian Approach to Punishment."

Jan Narveson, "Utilitarianism and New Generations," *Mind*, vol. 76 (1967), pp. 62–72. Narveson defends utilitarianism from the charge that, "If utilitarianism is correct, then we must be obliged to produce as many children as possible, so long as their happiness would exceed their misery"—because doing so would increase the total amount of happiness in the world.

James Cargile, "Utilitarianism and the Desert-Island Problem," *Analysis*, vol. 25 (1964), pp. 23–24. Cargile believes that utilitarianism gives a true account of what makes actions right, but that we need a different sort of account of what makes human beings good—for, there may be some right actions that only bad people would do! For more on this, see Cargile's "On Consequentialism," *Analysis*, vol. 29 (1969), pp. 78–88.

The following are two very useful paperback collections of essays on utilitarianism:

Michael D. Bayles, ed., *Contemporary Utilitarianism* (Garden City, New York: Doubleday Anchor Books, 1968). This book contains the article by Sprigge listed above.

Samuel Gorovitz, ed., *Mill: Utilitarianism. Text and Critical Essays* (Indianapolis: Bobbs-Merrill, 1971). This book contains the articles by Narveson and Cargile listed above.

CHAPTER FOUR

Kantian Ethics

INTRODUCTION

The system of ethical ideas developed by the great German philosopher Immanuel Kant is an alternative to both egoism and utilitarianism. Unlike the egoists, Kant did not believe that we ought to seek only our own good; and unlike the utilitarians, Kant did not think that the rightness or wrongness of actions should be judged solely by their tendency to promote happiness or misery.

Instead, Kant believed that the good person must obey certain moral *rules*, simply because he sees that it is right to do so. Kant gives these instructions for determining which rules ought to be obeyed: First, when you are contemplating a certain action, ask yourself what rule you would be following if you did that action. Then ask whether you would be willing for everyone to follow that rule, in any similar situation. If so, then the rule may be obeyed and the action is permissible; if not, then the rule must not be followed and the action is wrong. Kant sums up this advice in a principle which he calls The Categorical Imperative. This, he says, is the supreme principle of morality:

Act only on that maxim whereby thou canst at the same time will that it should become a universal law.

Kant gives several examples of such "maxims": Don't make promises you don't intend to keep; don't commit suicide; develop your talents; assist others in distress.

The Categorical Imperative is an *imperative* because it gives directions as to how we ought to behave; it is *categorical* because it has no exceptions and it is absolutely binding on us regardless of our desires or inclinations. Such maxims are contrasted with what Kant called "hypothetical" imperatives. Hypothetical imperatives tell us what to do *provided that* we have certain desires. They have the form *"If* you want to achieve such-and-such an end, then you ought to do so-and-so." For example: "If you want to become a doctor, then you ought to take premedical courses in college." This is something that you ought to do *provided that* you have the relevant desire; for someone who does *not* want to become a doctor there may be no reason at all to take premedical courses. Maxims coming under The Categorical Imperative are not like this: They tell us what we ought to do regardless of our desires. We ought to assist others in distress, and we ought not to make false promises, regardless of whether we want to or not.

We should follow such rules, Kant says, not merely because we have desires that would otherwise be frustrated, but because it would not be rational to reject them. Compliance with The Categorical Imperative is required by reason itself; it is the supreme principle of rationality in conduct. We can begin to see why Kant says this if we consider that it would be *inconsistent* of us not to act on principles that we would want others to accept, or to act on principles that we would want others to reject. For example, suppose I refuse to help others in distress, but when I am in distress I want

184 · Kantian Ethics

others to help me. The "maxim" in question is "assist others in distress," and consistency requires that, if I think that others ought to follow this rule, then I ought to follow it myself.

The basic idea here is that moral principles must be universal in scope, and that they must apply to everyone alike. This idea has been adopted by many contemporary writers. The distinguished Oxford philosopher R. M. Hare has made it a central element of his moral philosophy; Hare's development of the idea is presented in "The Case of the Debtors."[1] Then in "What if Everyone Did That?" Colin Strang approaches the same idea from a somewhat different direction, by analyzing the familiar moral argument.

Another central idea of Kant's is that we should treat persons—"rational beings"—not merely as means to our ends, but as ends in themselves. In fact, he says that an alternative formulation of The Categorical Imperative is:

So act as to treat humanity, whether in thine own person or in that of any other, in every case as an end withal, never as a means only.

R. S. Peters explores this Kantian idea in "Respect for Persons," and in "Persons and Punishment," Herbert Morris considers the implications of this idea for the theory of criminal punishment.

Kant placed great importance on doing one's duty *for its own sake,* and not for any further end. The only thing that is perfectly good in itself, Kant said, is a "good will"—that is, the will of a person who does what the moral law (The Categorical Imperative) requires, simply because he sees that the moral law requires it. This is the person who acts, not from desire or inclination, but from "respect for (the moral) law." Richard Taylor criticizes this doctrine, along with some of Kant's other leading ideas, in "Critique of Kantian Morality."

1. Professor Hare's views are more complex than these remarks indicate. In fact, he endorses utilitarianism and rejects many of Kant's ideas. The selection included in this chapter only takes up the issue of universalizability, which is a Kantian idea that Hare *does* accept.

21

IMMANUEL KANT
Foundations of the Metaphysics of Morals

IMMANUEL KANT (1724–1804) was one of the most profoundly influential figures in the history of modern philosophy. His writings on metaphysics and the limits of human knowledge are equally as important as his ethical works. Kant lived all his life in Königsburg, East Prussia, where he was professor of philosophy. He was known as a witty conversationalist and as a man of extremely regular habits; it was said that the housewives of Königsburg set their clocks by his daily walk.

Nothing can possibly be conceived in the world, or even out of it, which can be called good without qualification, except a *good will*. Intelligence, wit, judgment, and the other *talents* of the mind, however they may be named, or courage, resolution, perseverance, as qualities of temperament, are undoubtedly good and desirable in many respects; but these gifts of nature may also become extremely bad and mischievous if the will which is to make use of them, and which, therefore, constitutes what is called *character*, is not good. It is the same with the *gifts of fortune*. Power, riches, honor, even health, and the general well-being and contentment with one's condition which is called *happiness*, inspire pride, and often presumption, if there is not a good will to correct the influence of these on the mind, and with this also to rectify the whole principle of acting, and adapt it to its end. The sight of a being who is not adorned with a single feature of a pure and good will, enjoying unbroken prosperity, can never give pleasure to an impartial rational spectator. Thus a good will appears to constitute the indispensable condition even of being worthy of happiness.

. . .

The second[1] proposition is: That an action done from duty derives its moral worth, *not from the purpose* which is to be attained by it, but from the maxim by which it is determined, and therefore does not depend on the realization of the object of the action, but merely on the *principle of volition* by which the action has taken place, without regard to any object of desire. It is clear from what precedes that the purposes which we may have in view in our actions, or their effects regarded as ends and springs of the will, cannot give to actions any unconditional or moral worth. In what, then, can their worth lie if it is not to consist in the will and in reference to its expected effect? It cannot lie anywhere but in the *principle of the will* without regard to the ends which can be attained by the action. For the will stands between its *a priori* principle, which is formal, and its *a posteriori* spring, which is material, as between two roads, and as it must be determined by something, it follows that it must be determined by the formal principle of volition when an action is done from duty, in which case every material principle has been withdrawn from it.

The third proposition, which is a consequence of the two preceding, I

Excerpted from T. K. Abbott's translation (1898) of Kant's *Grundlegung zur Metaphysik der Sitten* (1785).

1. [The first proposition was that to have moral worth an action must be done from a sense of duty.]

would express thus: *Duty is the necessity of acting from respect for the law*. I may have *inclination* for an object as the effect of my proposed action, but I cannot have *respect* for it just for this reason that it is an effect and not an energy of will. Similarly, I cannot have respect for inclination, whether my own or another's; I can at most, if my own, approve it; if another's, sometimes even love it, that is, look on it as favorable to my own interest. It is only what is connected with my will as a principle, by no means as an effect—what does not subserve my inclination, but overpowers it, or at least in case of choice excludes it from its calculation—in other words, simply the law of itself, which can be an object of respect, and hence a command. Now an action done from duty must wholly exclude the influence of inclination, and with it every object of the will, so that nothing remains which can determine the will except objectively the *law*, and subjectively *pure respect* for this practical law, and consequently the maxim[2] that I should follow this law even to the thwarting of all of my inclinations.

Thus the moral worth of an action does not lie in the effect expected from it, nor in any principle of action which requires to borrow its motive from this expected effect. For all these effects—agreeableness of one's condition, and even the promotion of the happiness of others—could have been also brought about by other causes, so that for this there would have been no need of the will of a rational being; whereas it is in this alone that the supreme and unconditional good can be found. The pre-eminent good which we call moral can therefore consist in nothing else than *the conception of law* in itself, *which certainly is only possible in a rational being*, in so far as this conception, and not the expected effect, determines the will. This is a good which is already present in the person who acts accordingly, and we have not to wait for it to appear first in the result.[3]

. . .

The conception of an objective principle, in so far as it is obligatory for a will, is called a command (of reason), and the formula of the command is called an Imperative.

All imperatives are expressed by the word *ought* [or *shall*], and thereby indicate the relation of an objective law of

2. A *maxim* is the subjective principle of volition. The objective principle *(i.e.,* that which would also serve subjectively as a practical principle to all rational beings if reason had full power over the faculty of desire) is the practical *law*.

3. It might be here objected to me that I take refuge behind the word *respect* in an obscure feeling instead of giving a distinct solution of the question by a concept of the reason. But although respect is a feeling, it is not a feeling *received* through influence, but is *self-wrought* by a rational concept, and therefore, is specifically distinct from all feelings of the former kind, which may be referred either to inclination or fear. What I recognize immediately as a law for me, I recognize with respect. This merely signifies the consciousness that my will is *subordinate* to a law, without the intervention of other influences on my sense. The immediate determination of the will by the law, and the consciousness of this, is called *respect,* so that this is regarded as an *effect* of the law on the subject, and not as the *cause* of it. Respect is properly the conception of a worth which thwarts my self-love. Accordingly it is something which is considered neither as an object of inclination nor of fear, although it has something analogous to both. The *object* of respect is the *law* only, that is, the law which we impose on *ourselves,* and yet recognize as necessary in itself. As a law, we are subjected to it without consulting self-love; as imposed by us on ourselves, it is a result of our will. In the former aspect it has an analogy to fear, in the latter to inclination. Respect for a person is properly only respect for the law (of honesty, etc.) of which he gives us an example. Since we also look on the improvement of our talents as a duty, we consider that we see in a person of talents, as it were, the *example of a law* (viz. to become like him in this by exercise), and this constitutes our respect. All so-called moral *interest* consists simply in *respect* for the law.

reason to a will which from its subjective constitution is not necessarily determined by it (an obligation). They say that something would be good to do or to forbear, but they say it to a will which does not always do a thing because it is conceived to be good to do it. That is practically *good*, however, which determines the will by means of the conceptions of reason, and consequently not from subjective causes, but objectively, that is, on principles which are valid for every rational being as such. It is distinguished from the *pleasant* as that which influences the will only by means of sensation from merely subjective causes, valid only for the sense of this or that one, and not as a principle of reason which holds for every one.

A perfectly good will would therefore be equally subject to objective laws (viz., laws of good), but could not be conceived as *obliged* thereby to act lawfully, because of itself from its subjective constitution it can only be determined by the conception of good. Therefore no imperatives hold for the Divine will, or in general for a *holy* will; *ought* is here out of place because the volition is already of itself necessarily in unison with the law. Therefore imperatives are only formulae to express the relation of objective laws of all volition to the subjective imperfection of the will of this or that rational being, for example, the human will.

. . .

Finally, there is an imperative which commands a certain conduct immediately, without having as its condition any other purpose to be attained by it. This imperative is *categorical*. It concerns not the matter of the action, or its intended result, but its form and the principle of which it is itself a result; and what is essentially good in it consists in the mental disposition, let

the consequence be what it may. This imperative may be called that of *morality*.

. . .

There is therefore but one categorical imperative, namely, this: *Act only on that maxim whereby thou canst at the same time will that it should become a universal law.*

Now if all imperatives of duty can be deduced from this one imperative as from their principle, then, although it should remain undecided whether what is called duty is not merely a vain notion, yet at least we shall be able to show what we understand by it and what this notion means.

Since the universality of the law according to which effects are produced constitutes what is properly called *nature* in the most general sense (as to form)—that is, the existence of things so far as it is determined by general laws—the imperative of duty may be expressed thus: *Act as if the maxim of thy action were to become by thy will a universal law of nature.*

We will now enumerate a few duties, adopting the usual division of them into duties to ourselves and to others, and into perfect and imperfect duties.[4]

1. A man reduced to despair by a series of misfortunes feels wearied of

4. It must be noted here that I reserve the division of duties for a future *metaphysics of morals;* so that I give it here only as an arbitrary one (in order to arrange my examples). For the rest, I understand by a perfect duty one that admits no exception in favor of inclination, and then I have not merely external but also internal perfect duties. This is contrary to the use of the word adopted in the schools; but I do not intend to justify it here, as it is all one for my purpose whether it is admitted or not. [*Perfect* duties are usually understood to be those which can be enforced by external law; *imperfect,* those which cannot be enforced. They are also called respectively *determinate* and *indeterminate, officia juris* and *officia virtutis.*]

life, but is still so far in possession of his reason that he can ask himself whether it would not be contrary to his duty to himself to take his own life. Now he inquires whether the maxim of his action could become a universal law of nature. His maxim is: From self-love I adopt it as a principle to shorten my life when its longer duration is likely to bring more evil than satisfaction. It is asked then simply whether this principle founded on self-love can become a universal law of nature. Now we see at once that a system of nature of which it should be a law to destroy life by means of the very feeling whose special nature it is to impel to the improvement of life would contradict itself, and therefore could not exist as a system of nature; hence that maxim cannot possibly exist as a universal law of nature, and consequently would be wholly inconsistent with the supreme principle of all duty.[5]

2. Another finds himself forced by necessity to borrow money. He knows that he will not be able to repay it, but sees also that nothing will be lent to him unless he promises stoutly to repay it in a definite time. He desires to make this promise, but he has still so much conscience as to ask himself: Is it not unlawful and inconsistent with duty to get out of a difficulty in this way? Suppose, however, that he resolves to do so, then the maxim of his action would be expressed thus: When I think myself in want of money, I will borrow money and promise to repay it, although I know that I never can do so. Now this principle of self-love or of one's own advantage may perhaps be consistent with my whole future welfare; but the question now is, Is it right? I change then the suggestion of self-love into a universal law, and state the question thus: How would it be if my maxim were a universal law? Then I see at once that it could never hold as a universal law of

nature, but would necessarily contradict itself. For supposing it to be a universal law that everyone when he thinks himself in a difficulty should be able to promise whatever he pleases, with the purpose of not keeping his promise, the promise itself would become impossible, as well as the end that one might have in view in it, since no one would consider that anything was promised to him, but would ridicule all such statements as vain pretenses.

3. A third finds in himself a talent which with the help of some culture might make him a useful man in many respects. But he finds himself in comfortable circumstances and prefers to indulge in pleasure rather than to take pains in enlarging and improving his happy natural capacities. He asks, however, whether his maxim of neglect of his natural gifts, besides agreeing with his inclination to indulgence, agrees also with what is called duty. He sees then that a system of nature could indeed subsist with such a universal law, although men (like the South Sea islanders) should let their talents rest and resolve to devote their lives merely to idleness, amusement, and propagation of their species—in a word, to enjoyment; but he cannot possibly *will* that this should be a universal law of nature, or be implanted in us as such by a natural instinct. For, as a rational being, he necessarily wills that his faculties be developed, since they serve him, and have been given him, for all sorts of possible purposes.

4. A fourth, who is in prosperity, while he sees that others have to contend with great wretchedness and that he could help them, thinks: What concern is it of mine? Let everyone be as happy as Heaven pleases, or as he can

5. [On suicide cf. further *Metaphysik der Sitten*, p. 274.]

make himself; I will take nothing from him nor even envy him, only I do not wish to contribute anything to his welfare or to his assistance in distress! Now no doubt, if such a mode of thinking were a universal law, the human race might very well subsist, and doubtless even better than in a state in which everyone talks of sympathy and goodwill, or even takes care occasionally to put it into practice, but, on the other side, also cheats when he can, betrays the rights of men, or otherwise violates them. But although it is possible that a universal law of nature might exist in accordance with that maxim, it is impossible to *will* that such a principle should have the universal validity of a law of nature. For a will which resolved this would contradict itself, inasmuch as many cases might occur in which one would have need of the love and sympathy of others, and in which, by such a law of nature, sprung from his own will, he would deprive himself of all hope of the aid he desires.

These are a few of the many actual duties, or at least what we regard as such, which obviously fall into two classes on the one principle that we have laid down. We must be *able to will* that a maxim of our action should be a universal law. This is the ·canon of the moral appreciation of the action generally. Some actions are of such a character that their maxim cannot without contradiction be even *conceived* as a universal law of nature, far from it being possible that we should *will* that it *should* be so. In others, this intrinsic impossibility is not found, but still it is impossible to *will* that their maxim should be raised to the universality of a law of nature, since such a will would contradict itself. It is easily seen that the former violate strict or rigorous (inflexible) duty; the latter only laxer (meritorious) duty. Thus it has been

completely shown by these examples how all duties depend as regards the nature of the obligation (not the object of the action) on the same principle.

If now we attend to ourselves on occasion of any transgression of duty, we shall find that we in fact do not will that our maxim should be a universal law, for that is impossible for us; on the contrary, we will that the opposite should remain a universal law, only we assume the liberty of making an *exception* in our own favor or (just for this time only) in favor of our inclination. Consequently, if we considered all cases from one and the same point of view, namely, that of reason, we should find a contradiction in our own will, namely, that a certain principle should be objectively necessary as a universal law, and yet subjectively should not be universal, but admit of exceptions. As, however, we at one moment regard our action from the point of view of a will wholly conformed to reason, and then again look at the same action from the point of view of a will affected by inclination, there is not really any contradiction, but an antagonism of inclination to the precept of reason, whereby the universality of the principle is changed into a mere generality, so that the practical principle of reason shall meet the maxim half way. Now, although this cannot be justified in our own impartial judgment, yet it proves that we do really recognize the validity of the categorical imperative and (with all respect for it) only allow ourselves a few exceptions which we think unimportant and forced from us.

. . .

Supposing, however, that there were something *whose existence* has *in itself* an absolute worth, something which, being *an end in itself*, could be a source of definite laws, then in this and this alone would lie the source of a possible categorical imperative, that is, a practical law.

Now I say: Man and generally any rational being *exists* as an end in himself, *not merely as a means* to be arbitrarily used by this or that will, but in all his actions, whether they concern himself or other rational beings, must be always regarded at the same time as an end. All objects of the inclinations have only a conditional worth; for if the inclinations and the wants founded on them did not exist, then their object would be without value. But the inclinations themselves, being sources of want, are so far from having an absolute worth for which they should be desired that, on the contrary, it must be the universal wish of every rational being to be wholly free from them. Thus the worth of any object which is *to be acquired* by our action is always conditional. Beings whose existence depends not on our will but on nature's, have nevertheless, if they are rational beings, only a relative value as means, and are therefore called *things*; rational beings, on the contrary, are called *persons*, because their very nature points them out as ends in themselves, that is, as something which must not be used merely as means, and so far therefore restricts freedom of action (and is an object of respect). These, therefore, are not merely subjective ends whose existence has a worth *for us* as an effect of our action, but *objective ends*, that is, things whose existence is an end in itself—an end, moreover, for which no other can be substituted, which they should subserve *merely* as means, for otherwise nothing whatever would possess *absolute worth*; but if all worth were conditioned and therefore contingent, then there would be no supreme practical principle of reason whatever.

If then there is a supreme practical principle or, in respect of the human will, a categorical imperative, it must be one which, being drawn from the conception of that which is necessarily an end for everyone because it is *an end in itself*, constitutes an *objective* principle of will, and can therefore serve as a universal practical law. The foundation of this principle is: *rational nature exists as an end in itself.* Man necessarily conceives his own existence as being so; so far then this is a *subjective* principle of human actions. But every other rational being regards its existence similarly, just on the same rational principle that holds for me, so that it is at the same time an objective principle from which as a supreme practical law all laws of the will must be capable of being deduced. Accordingly the practical imperative will be as follows: *So act as to treat humanity, whether in thine own person or in that of any other, in every case as an end withal, never as means only.* We will now inquire whether this can be practically carried out.

To abide by the previous examples:

First, under the head of necessary duty to oneself: He who contemplates suicide should ask himself whether his action can be consistent with the idea of humanity *as an end in itself.* If he destroys himself in order to escape from painful circumstances, he uses a person merely as a *mean* to maintain a tolerable condition up to the end of life. But a man is not a thing, that is to say, something which can be used merely as means, but must in all his actions be always considered as an end in himself. I cannot, therefore, dispose in any way of a man in my own person so as to mutilate him, to damage or kill him. (It belongs to ethics proper to define this principle more precisely, so as to avoid all misunderstanding, for example, as to the amputation of the limbs in order to preserve myself; as to exposing my life to danger with a view to preserve it, etc. This question is therefore omitted here.)

Secondly, as regards necessary duties, or those of strict obligation, towards others: He who is thinking of making a lying promise to others will see at once that he would be using another man *merely as a means,* without the latter containing at the same time the end in himself. For he whom I propose by such a promise to use for my own purposes cannot possibly assent to my mode of acting towards him, and therefore cannot himself contain the end of this action. This violation of the principle of humanity in other men is more obvious if we take in examples of attacks on the freedom and property of others. For then it is clear that he who transgresses the rights of men intends to use the person of others merely as means, without considering that as rational beings they ought always to be esteemed also as ends, that is, as beings who must be capable of containing in themselves the end of the very same action.[6]

·*Thirdly,* as regards contingent (meritorious) duties to oneself: It is not enough that the action does not violate humanity in our own person as an end in itself, it must also *harmonize with* it. Now there are in humanity capacities of greater perfection which belong to the end that nature has in view in regard to humanity in ourselves as the subject; to neglect these might perhaps be consistent with the *maintenance* of humanity as an end in itself, but not with the *advancement* of this end.

Fourthly, as regards meritorious duties towards others: The natural end which all men have is their own happiness. Now humanity might indeed subsist although no one should contribute anything to the happiness of others, provided he did not intentionally withdraw anything from it; but after all, this would only harmonize negatively, not positively, with *humanity as an end in itself,* if everyone does not also endeavor, as far as in him lies, to forward the ends of others. For the ends of any subject which is an end in himself ought as far as possible to be *my* ends also, if that conception is to have its *full* effect with me.

This principle that humanity and generally every rational nature is *an end in itself* (which is the supreme limiting condition of every man's freedom of action), is not borrowed from experience, *first,* because it is universal, applying as it does to all rational beings whatever, and experience is not capable of determining anything about them; *secondly* because it does not present humanity as an end to men (subjectively), that is, as an object which men do of themselves actually adopt as an end; but as an objective end which must as a law constitute the supreme limiting condition of all our subjective ends, let them be what we will; it must therefore spring from pure reason. In fact the objective principle of all practical legislation lies (according to the first principle) in *the rule* and its form of universality which makes it capable of being a law (say, for example, a law of nature); but the *subjective* principle is in the *end;*

6. Let it not be thought that the common: *quod tibi non vis fieri,* etc., could serve here as the rule or principle. For it is only a deduction from the former, though with several limitations, it cannot be a universal law, for it does not contain the principle of duties to oneself, nor of the duties of benevolence to others (for many a one would gladly consent that others should not benefit him, provided only that he might be excused from showing benevolence to them), nor finally that of duties of strict obligation to one another, for on this principle the criminal might argue against the judge who punishes him, and so on.

now by the second principle, the subject of all ends is each rational being inasmuch as it is an end in itself. Hence follows the third practical principle of the will, which is the ultimate condition of its harmony with the universal practical reason, viz., the idea of *the will of every rational being as a universally legislative will.*

On this principle all maxims are rejected which are inconsistent with the will being itself universal legislator. Thus the will is not subject to the law, but so subject that it must be regarded *as itself giving the law,* and on this ground only subject to the law (of which it can regard itself as the author).

22

R. M. HARE
The Case of the Debtors

R. M. HARE is White's Professor of Moral Philosophy in the University of Oxford. He is the author of *The Language of* *Morals* (1952), *Freedom and Reason* (1963), and other works.

Ethical theory, which determines the meanings and functions of the moral words, and thus the 'rules' of the moral 'game', provides only a clarification of the conceptual framework within which moral reasoning takes place; it is therefore, in the required sense, neutral as between different moral opinions. But it is highly relevant to moral reasoning because, as with the rules of a game, there could be no such thing as moral reasoning without this framework, and the framework dictates the form of the reasoning. It follows that naturalism is not the only way of providing for the

From R. M. Hare, *Freedom and Reason* (Oxford: Oxford University Press, 1963), pp. 89–98. © 1963 Oxford University Press. By permission of The Clarendon Press, Oxford. The portion of Professor Hare's book reprinted here is an extract from a longer argument, and the interested reader should consult the rest of chapter six, and the following chapters of *Freedom and Reason,* for an understanding of how this portion fits into his complete argument.

possibility of moral reasoning; and this may, perhaps, induce those who have espoused naturalism as a way of making moral thought a rational activity to consider other possibilities.

The rules of moral reasoning are, basically, two, corresponding to the two features of moral judgements which I argued for in the first half of this book, prescriptivity and universalizability. When we are trying, in a concrete case, to decide what we ought to do, what we are looking for (as I have already said) is an action to which we can commit ourselves (prescriptivity) but which we are at the same time prepared to accept as exemplifying a principle of action to be prescribed for others in like circumstances (universalizability). If, when we consider some proposed action, we find that, when universalized, it yields prescriptions which we cannot accept, we reject this action as a solution to our moral problem—if we cannot universalize the prescription, it cannot become an 'ought'.

It is to be noticed that, troublesome as was the problem of moral weakness when we were dealing theoretically with the logical character of the moral concepts, it cannot trouble us here. For if a person is going to reason seriously at all about a moral question, he has to presuppose that the moral concepts are going, in his reasoning, to be used prescriptively. One cannot start a moral argument about a certain proposal on the basis that, whatever the conclusion of it, it makes no difference to what anybody is to do. When one has arrived at a conclusion, one may then be too weak to put it into practice. But *in arguing* one has to discount this possibility; for, as we shall see, to abandon the prescriptivity of one's moral judgements is to unscrew an essential part of the logical mechanism on which such arguments rely. This is why, if a person were to say 'Let's have an argument about this grave moral question which faces us, but let's not think of any conclusion we may come to as requiring anybody to *do* one thing rather than another', we should be likely to accuse him of flippancy, or worse.

I will now try to exhibit the bare bones of the theory of moral reasoning that I wish to advocate by considering a very simple (indeed oversimplified) example. As we shall see, even this very simple case generates the most baffling complexities; and so we may be pardoned for not attempting anything more difficult to start with.

The example is adapted from a well-known parable.[1] *A* owes money to *B*, and *B* owes money to *C*, and it is the law that creditors may exact their debts by putting their debtors into prison. *B* asks himself, 'Can I say that I ought to take this measure against *A* in order to make him pay? 'He is no doubt *inclined* to do this, or *wants* to do it. Therefore, if there were no question of universalizing his prescriptions, he would assent readily to the *singular* prescription 'Let me put *A* into prison'. But when he seeks to turn this prescription into a moral judgement, and say, 'I *ought* to put *A* into prison because he will not pay me what he owes', he reflects that this would involve accepting the principle 'Anyone who is in my position ought to put his debtor into prison if he does not pay'. But then he reflects that *C* is in the same position of unpaid creditor with regard to himself (*B*), and that the cases are otherwise identical; and that if anyone in this position ought to put his debtors into prison, then so ought *C* to put him (*B*) into prison. And to accept the moral prescription '*C* ought to put me into prison' would commit him (since, as we have seen, he must be using the word 'ought' prescriptively) to accepting the singular prescription 'Let *C* put me into prison'; and this he is not ready to accept. But if he is not, then neither can he accept the original judgement that he (*B*) ought to put *A* into prison for debt. Notice that the whole of this argument would break down if 'ought' were not being used prescriptively, the step from '*C* ought to put me into prison' to 'Let *C* put me into prison' would not be valid.

The structure and ingredients of this argument must now be examined. We must first notice an analogy between it and the Popperian theory of scientific method. What has happened is that a provisional or suggested moral principle has been rejected because one of its particular consequences proved unacceptable. But an important difference between the two kinds of reasoning must also be noted; it is what we should expect, given that the data of sci-

1. Matthew xviii. 23.

entific observation are recorded in descriptive statements, whereas we are here dealing with prescriptions. What knocks out a suggested hypothesis, on Popper's theory, is a singular statement of fact: the hypothesis has the consequence that p; but not-p. Here the logic is just the same, except that in place of the observation-statements 'p' and 'not-p' we have the singular *prescriptions* 'Let C put B into prison for debt' and its contradictory. Nevertheless, given that B is disposed to reject the first of these prescriptions, the argument against him is just as cogent as in the scientific case.

We may carry the parallel further. Just as science, seriously pursued, is the search for hypotheses and the testing of them by the attempt to falsify their particular consequences, so morals, as a serious endeavor, consists in the search for principles and the testing of them against particular cases. Any rational activity has its discipline, and this is the discipline of moral thought: to test the moral principles that suggest themselves to us by following out their consequences and seeing whether we can accept *them*.

No argument, however, starts from nothing. We must therefore ask what we have to have before moral arguments of the sort of which I have given a simple example can proceed. The first requisite is that the facts of the case should be given; for all moral discussion is about some particular set of facts, whether actual or supposed. Secondly we have the logical framework provided by the meaning of the word 'ought' (that is, prescriptivity and universalizability, both of which we saw to be necessary). Because moral judgements have to be universalizable, B cannot say that he ought to put A into prison for debt without committing himself to the

view that C, who is *ex hypothesi* in the same position *vis-à-vis* himself, ought to put *him* into prison; and because moral judgements are prescriptive, this would be, in effect, prescribing to C to put him into prison; and this he is unwilling to do, since he has a strong inclination not to go to prison. This inclination gives us the third necessary ingredient in the argument: If B were a completely apathetic person, who literally did not mind what happened to himself or to anybody else, the argument would not touch him. The three necessary ingredients which we have noticed, then, are (1) facts; (2) logic; (3) inclinations. These ingredients enable us, not indeed to arrive at an evaluative conclusion, but to *reject* an evaluative proposition. We shall see later that these are not, in all cases, the only necessary ingredients.

In the example which we have been using, the position was deliberately made simpler by supposing that B actually stood to some other person in exactly the same relation as A does to him. Such cases are unlikely to arise in practice. But it is not necessary for the force of the argument that B should *in fact* stand in this relation to anyone; it is sufficient that he should consider hypothetically such a case, and see what would be the consequences in it of those moral principles between whose acceptance and rejection he has to decide. Here we have an important point of difference from the parallel scientific argument, in that the crucial case which leads to rejection of the principle can itself be a supposed, not an observed, one. That hypothetical cases will do as well as actual ones is important, since it enables us to guard against a possible misinterpretation of the argument which I have outlined. It might be thought that what moves B is the *fear* that C will actually do to him as he does to *A*—as happens in the gospel parable. But this fear is not only irrelevant to the moral argument; it does not even provide a particularly strong nonmoral motive unless the circumstances are somewhat exceptional. *C* may, after all, not find out what *B* has done to *A*; or *C*'s moral principles may be different from *B*'s, and independent of them, so that what moral principle *B* accepts makes no difference to the moral principles on which *C* acts.

Even, therefore, if *C* did not exist, it would be no answer to the argument for *B* to say 'But in my case there is no fear that anybody will ever be in a position to do to me what I am proposing to do to *A*'. For the argument does not rest on any such fear. All that is essential to it is that *B* should disregard the fact that he plays the particular role in the situation which he does, without disregarding the inclinations which people have in situations of this sort. In other words, he must be prepared to give weight to *A*'s inclinations and interests as if they were his own. This is what turns selfish prudential reasoning into moral reasoning. It is much easier, psychologically, for *B* to do this if he is actually placed in a situation like *A*'s *vis-à-vis* somebody else; but this is not necessary, provided that he has sufficient imagination to envisage what it is like to be *A*. For our first example, a case was deliberately chosen in which little imagination was necessary; but in most normal cases a certain power of imagination and readiness to use it is a fourth necessary ingredient in moral arguments, alongside those already mentioned, viz. logic (in the shape of universalizability and prescriptivity), the facts, and the inclinations or interests of the people concerned.

It must be pointed out that the ab-

sence of even one of these ingredients may render the rest ineffective. For example, impartiality by itself is not enough. If, in becoming impartial, *B* became also completely dispassionate and apathetic, and moved as little by other people's interests as by his own, then, as we have seen, there would be nothing to make him accept or reject one moral principle rather than another. That is why those who, like Adam Smith and Professor Kneale, advocate what have been called 'Ideal Observer Theories' of ethics, sometimes postulate as their imaginary ideal observer not merely an impartial spectator, but an impartially *sympathetic* spectator.[2] To take another example, if the person who faces the moral decision has no imagination, then even the fact that someone can do the very same thing to him may pass him by. If again, he lacks the readiness to universalize, then the vivid imagination of the sufferings which he is inflicting on others may only spur him on to intensify them, to increase his own vindictive enjoyment. And if he is ignorant of the material facts (for example about what is likely to happen to a person if one takes out a writ against him), then there is nothing to tie the moral argument to particular choices.

The best way of testing the argument which we have outlined will be to

2. It will be plain that there are affinities, though there are also differences, between this type of theory and my own. For such theories see W. C. Kneale, *Philosophy*, xxv (1950), 162; R. Firth and R. B. Brandt, *Philosophy and Phenomenological Research*, xii (1951/2), 317, and xv (1954/5), 407, 414, 422; and J. Harrison, *Aristotelian Society*, supp. vol. xxviii (1954), 132. Firth, unlike Kneale, says that the observer must be 'dispassionate', but see Brandt, op. cit., p. 411 n. For a shorter discussion see Brandt, *Ethical Theory*, p. 173. Since for many Christians God occupies the role of 'ideal observer', the moral judgements which they make may be expected to coincide with those arrived at by the method of reasoning which I am advocating.

consider various ways in which somebody in B's position might seek to escape from it. There are indeed a number of such ways; and all of them may be successful, at a price. It is important to understand what the price is in each case. We may classify these manœuvres which are open to B into two kinds. There are first of all the moves which depend on his using the moral words in a different way from that on which the argument relied. We saw that for the success of the argument it was necessary that 'ought' should be used universalizably and prescriptively. If B uses it in a way that is either not prescriptive or not universalizable, then he can escape the force of the argument, at the cost of resigning from the kind of discussion that we thought we were having with him. We shall discuss these two possibilities separately. Secondly, there are moves which can still be made by B, even though he is using the moral words in the same way as we are. We shall examine three different sub-classes of these.

Before dealing with what I shall call the *verbal* manœuvres in detail, it may be helpful to make a general remark. Suppose that we are having a simple mathematical argument with somebody, and he admits, for example, that there are five eggs in this basket, and six in the other, but maintains that there are a dozen eggs in the two baskets taken together; and suppose that this is because he is using the expression 'a dozen' to mean 'eleven'. It is obvious that we cannot compel him logically to admit that there are not a dozen eggs, in *his* sense of 'dozen'. But it is equally obvious that this should not disturb us. For such a man only appears to be dissenting from us. His dissent is only apparent, because the proposition which his words express is actually consistent with the conclusion which we wish to draw; he *says* 'There are a dozen eggs'; but he *means* what we should express by saying 'There are eleven eggs'; and this we are not disputing. It is important to remember that in the moral case also the dissent may be only apparent, if the words are being used in different ways, and that it is no defect in a method of argument if it does not make it possible to prove a conclusion to a person when he is using words in such a way that the conclusion does not follow.

It must be pointed out, further (since this is a common source of confusion), that in this argument nothing whatever hangs upon our *actual* use of words in common speech, any more than it does in the arithmetical case. That we use the sound 'dozen' to express the meaning that we customarily do use it to express is of no consequence for the argument about the eggs; and the same may be said of the sound 'ought'. There is, however, something which I, at any rate, customarily express by the sound 'ought', whose character is correctly described by saying that it is a universal or universalizable prescription. I hope that what I customarily express by the sound 'ought' is the same as what most people customarily express by it; but if I am mistaken in this assumption, I shall still have given a correct account, so far as I am able, of that which I express by this sound.[3] Nevertheless, this account will interest other people mainly in so far as my hope that they understand the same thing as I do by 'ought' is fulfilled; and since I am moderately sure that this is indeed the case with many people, I hope that I may be of use to them in elucidating the logical properties of the concept which they thus express.

3. Cf. Moore, *Principia Ethica*, p. 6.

At this point, however, it is of the utmost importance to stress that the fact that two people express the same thing by 'ought' does not entail that they share the moral opinions. For the formal, logical properties of the word 'ought' (those which are determined by its *meaning*) are only one of the four factors (listed earlier) whose combination governs a man's moral opinion on a given matter. Thus ethics, the study of the logical properties of the moral words, remains morally neutral (its conclusions neither are substantial moral judgements, nor entail them, even in conjunction with factual premisses); its bearing upon moral questions lies in this, that it makes logically impossible certain combinations of moral and other prescriptions. Two people who are using the word 'ought' in the same way may yet disagree about what ought to be done in a certain situation, either because they differ about the facts, or because one or other of them lacks imagination, or because their different inclinations make one reject some singular prescription which the other can accept. For all that, ethics (that is, the logic of moral language) is an immensely powerful engine for producing moral agreement; for if two people are willing to use the moral word 'ought', and to use it in the same way (viz. the way that I have been describing), the other possible sources of moral disagreement are all eliminable. People's inclinations about most of the important matters in life tend to be the same (very few people, for example, like being starved or run over by motor cars); and, even when they are not, there is a way of generalizing the argument, to be described in the next chapter, which enables us to make allowances for differences in inclinations. The facts are often, given sufficient patience, ascertainable. Imagination can be cultivated. If these three factors are looked after, as they can be, agreement on the use of 'ought' is the only other necessary condition for producing moral agreement, at any rate in typical cases. And, if I am not mistaken, this agreement in use is already there in the discourse of anybody with whom we are at all likely to find ourselves arguing; all that is needed is to think clearly, and so make it evident.

23

COLIN STRANG
What if Everyone Did That?

COLIN STRANG is reader in philosophy at the University of Newcastle-upon-Tyne. He has also written on the philosophy of Plato and Aristotle.

From Colin Strang, "What if Everyone Did That?" *Durham University Journal,* vol. 53 (1960), pp. 5–10. Reprinted by permission of the *Durham University Journal.* This article is reprinted unabridged.

I want to discuss the force and validity of the familiar type of ethical argument epitomized in my title. A typical example of it would be: 'If everyone refrained from voting the result would be disastrous, therefore *you* ought to vote.' Now since the argument is addressed to the person concerned simply *qua* member of the class of people entitled to vote, it could be addressed with equal force to any member or all members of that class indifferently; so the conclusion might just as validly be: 'Therefore *everyone* ought to vote.'

There is no doubt that this argument has some force. People *are* sometimes impressed by it. But it is not nearly so obvious that it is a valid one, that is, that they *ought* to be impressed by it.

One way of not being impressed by it is to reply: 'Yes, but everyone *won't* refrain from voting, so there will be no disaster, so it's all right for me not to vote.' But this reply is beside the point. The argument never claimed that this one abstention would lead to disaster, nor did it claim that universal abstention (which *would* be disastrous) would occur; indeed it implied, on each point, the very opposite. This brings out the important fact that the argument does not appeal to the consequences of the action it condemns and so is not of a utilitarian type, but that it is applicable, if anywhere, just where utilitarian arguments do *not* apply.

The objector, who remains unimpressed, will continue: 'Granted that my first objection is beside the point, I still can't see how you get from your premiss to your conclusion. Your premiss is, roughly: "Everyone's nonvoting is to be deplored," and your conclusion is: "Everyone's voting is obligatory." Why should it be irrational to accept the premiss but deny the conclusion? In any case the validity of the argument cannot depend on its form alone. Plenty of arguments of the very same form are plainly invalid. For instance, if every-

one switched on their electric fires at 9 a.m. sharp there would be a power breakdown, therefore no one should; furthermore, this argument applies not only to 9 a.m. but to all times, so no one should ever switch on an electric fire. Again, if everyone taught philosophy whole-time we should all starve, so no one should; or if everyone built houses or did anything else whatever (bar farming) whole-time, we should all starve; and if everyone farmed we would be without clothes or shelter and would die of exposure in winter, so no one should farm. It rather looks, on your kind of argument, as if every whole-time activity is forbidden to everyone. Conversely, if no one farmed we would all starve, so everyone should farm; if no one made clothes we would all die of exposure, so everyone ought to make clothes—and so on. So it also looks, on your kind of argument, as if all sorts of part-time activity are obligatory on everybody. You surely do not mean to commit yourself to enjoining self-sufficiency and condemning specialization? What I want to know is why some arguments of this form are valid (as you claim) while others are not (as you admit).'

In face of this kind of objection the obvious move is to place certain restrictions on the use of arguments of this form, and to show that only those satisfying certain conditions are valid while the rest are not. This is in fact the move adopted in two recent treatments of this problem: One is by A. C. Ewing (*Philosophy*, January 1953), and the other by M. G. Singer (*Mind*, July 1955). These two are independent, since Singer makes no mention of Ewing; and Ewing, incidentally, regards himself as doing pioneer work in the subject, being able to quote only one previous treatment of it (C. D. Broad, *International Journal of*

Ethics, 1915–16). But the restrictions these two wish to impose on the argument seem to me *ad hoc*; they fail to explain why the argument is valid in the remaining cases, and it is just this that I aim to discover.

Compare the voting case with this one: 'If everyone here refuses to dig a latrine the camp will be insanitary, therefore everyone ought to dig one.' Surely the conclusion we want is, rather: 'therefore *someone* ought to dig one.' In the voting case, on the other hand, given the premiss 'If everyone refused to vote there would be no government,' the conclusion 'therefore someone ought to vote' clearly will not do; and even the conclusion 'therefore everyone ought to vote' is hardly cogent on the reasonable assumption that a 10% abstention will do no harm. If the argument is to be at all cogent it must make some reference to the percentage vote (say n%) needed, thus: If more than (100−n)% of the electorate abstained there would be no government'; this allows us to draw an acceptable conclusion, that is, 'therefore n% must vote to avert anarchy and one must dig to avert disease.' But our argument has gained in cogency and precision (being now of a simple utilitarian kind) only at the expense of being no longer effective, or even seemingly so, against the defaulter. He will reply: 'All right, so n% ought to vote (someone ought to dig), but why me?' However, there is hope yet for the moralist. To the retort 'Why me?' the argument may not suggest any obvious reply; but the retort itself does suggest the counter-retort 'Why not you?', to which again there is no obvious reply. An impasse is thus reached in which the moralist cannot say why the defaulter should vote or dig, and the defaulter cannot say why he should not. Evidently it was a mistake to amend the original argument, and yet there seemed to be something wrong with it as it stood; and yet, as it stood, it still seemed to be giving an answer, however obscurely, to the baffling question 'Why me?': 'Because if *everyone* did that . . .'

To return to the camp: Certainly it is agreed by all members of the party that some digging ought to be done, and it is also agreed that the duty does not lie on anyone outside the party. But just where it lies within the party is hard to say. It does not lie on everyone, nor on anyone in particular. Where then? Whatever the answer to that apparently pressing question may be, we all know what would in fact happen. Someone would volunteer, or a leader would allot duties, or the whole party would cast lots. Or, if the thing to be done were not a once-and-for-all job like digging latrines but a daily routine like washing up, they might take it in turns.

Although various acceptable answers to the question how the duties are to be allotted are readily listed, they leave us quite in the dark as to just *who* ought to dig, wash up, etc. That question hardly seems to arise. In the absence of an argumentative defaulter there is no call to think up reasons why I or you should do this or that or reasons why I or you should not, and we are left with the defaulter's 'Why me?' and the moralist's 'Why not you?' unanswered.

Our enquiry has made little progress, but the fog is beginning to lift from the territory ahead. We are evidently concerned with communities of people and with things that must be done, or not done, if the community is to be saved from damage or destruction; and we want to know whose duty it is to do, or not to do, these things. The complexity of the problem is no longer in doubt. (1) There are some things that need doing once, some that need doing at regular intervals, and some that need doing all the time. (2) Some things need doing by one person, some by a number of people which can be roughly estimated, and some by as many as possible. (3) In practice, who shall do what (though not who *ought* to do what) is determined by economic factors, or by statutory direction (for example service with the armed forces in war, paying income tax), or merely by people's inclinations generally, that is when enough people are inclined to do the thing anyway.

Somewhere in this territory our quarry has its lair. The following dialogue between defaulter and moralist on the evasion of income tax and military service begins the hunt. Our first steps are taken on already familiar ground:

Defaulter: £100 is a drop in the ocean to the exchequer. No one will suffer from their loss of £100, but it means a good deal to me.
Moralist: But what if everyone did that and offered the same excuse?
D.: But the vast majority won't, so no one will suffer.
M.: Still, would you say it was *in order* for anyone whatever to evade tax and excuse himself on the same grounds as you do?
D.: Certainly.
M.: So it would be quite in order for *everyone* to do the same and offer the same excuse?
D.: Yes.
M.: Even though disaster would ensue for the exchequer and for everyone?
D.: Yes. The exchequer would no more miss my £100 if *everyone* evaded than they would if only I evaded. They wouldn't miss anyone's individual evasion. What they would miss would be the aggregate £1,000,000,000 or so, and

that isn't my default or yours or anyone's. So even if everyone evades it is still all right for me to evade; and if it's all right for me to evade it's all right for everyone to evade.
M.: You seem now to be in the paradoxical position of saying that if everyone evaded it would be disastrous, and yet no one would be to blame.
D.: Paradoxical, perhaps, but instructive. I am not alarmed. Let me recur to one of your previous questions: You asked whether it would be in order for all to evade and give the same excuse. I now want to reply: No, it would not be in order, but only in the sense that it would be disastrous; but it *would* be in order in the sense that each person's grounds for evasion would still be as valid as they would have been if he had been the *only* evader and no disaster had ensued. In other words, none of the defaulters would be to blame for the disaster—and certainly not one of them would blame himself: On the contrary, each one would argue that had he paid he would have been the only one to pay and thus lost his £100 without doing himself or anyone else any good. He would have been a mug to pay.
M.: But surely there can't be a disaster of this kind for which no one is to blame.
D.: If anyone is to blame it is the person whose job it is to circumvent evasion. If too few people vote, then it should be made illegal not to vote. If too few people volunteer, then you must introduce conscription. If too many people evade taxes, then you must tighten up your system of enforcement. My answer to your 'If everyone did that' is 'Then someone had jolly well better see to it that they don't'; it doesn't impress me as a reason why *I* should, however many people do or don't.
M.: But surely you are being inconsis-

tent here. Take the case of evading military service.

D.: You mean not volunteering in time of crisis, there being no conscription? I do that too.

M.: Good. As I was saying, aren't you being inconsistent? You think *both* that it is all right not to volunteer even if too few other people volunteer (because one soldier more or less could make no difference), *and* think that you ought to be conscripted.

D.: But that is not at all inconsistent. Look: The enemy threatens, a mere handful volunteer, and the writing is on the wall; my volunteering will not affect the outcome, but conscript me with the rest to stay the deluge and I will come without a murmur. In short, no good will come of my volunteering, but a great good will come of a general conscription which gathers me in with the rest. There is no inconsistency. I should add that my volunteering would in fact do positive harm: All who resist and survive are to be executed forthwith. There will be one or two heroes, but I did not think you were requiring me to be heroic.

M.: I confirm that I was not, and I concede that your position is not inconsistent, however unedifying. As I see it, the nub of your position is this: Given the premiss 'if everyone did that the result would be disastrous' you cannot conclude 'therefore *you* oughtn't' but only 'therefore someone ought to see to it that they don't.' If you are right, the 'if everyone did' argument, as usually taken, is invalid. But then we are left with the question: Whence does it derive its apparent force?

D.: Whence, indeed?

(interval)

M.: Suppose when you give your justification for evading ('no one will miss *my* contribution') I reply: But don't you think it *unfair* that other people should bear the burden which you shirk and from the bearing of which by others you derive benefit for yourself?

D.: Well, yes, it is rather unfair. Indeed you make me feel a little ashamed; but I wasn't prepared, and I'm still not, to let your pet argument by without a fight. Just where does fairness come into it?

M.: I think I can see. Let me begin by pushing two or three counters from different points on the periphery of the problem with the hope that they will meet at the centre. First, then: If someone is morally obliged (or permitted or forbidden) to do some particular thing, then there is a reason why he is so obliged. Further, if someone is obliged to do something for a particular reason, then anyone else whatever is equally obliged provided the reason applies to him also. The reason why a particular person is obliged to do something will be expressible in general terms, and could be expressed by describing some class to which he belongs. My principle then reads as follows: If someone is obliged to do something *just because* he is a member of a certain class, then any other member of that class will be equally obliged to do that thing. You yourself argued, remember, that any member of the class of people whose contribution would not be missed (here I allude to your reason for evasion) was no less entitled to evade than you.

D.: Agreed.

M.: My second counter now comes into play. 'Fairness,' you will agree, is a moral term like 'rightness.' An act is unfair if it results in someone getting a greater or lesser share of something (whether pleasant or unpleasant) than he ought to get—more or less than his fair share, as we say.

Now there are a number of things, burdensome or otherwise, which need to be done if the community is not to suffer. But who precisely is to do them? Why me? Why not me? You will also agree, I hope, to the wide principle that where the thing to be done is burdensome the burden should be fairly distributed?

D.: Certainly. I seldom dispute a truism. But in what does a fair distribution consist?

M.: In other words: Given two people and a burden, how much of it ought each to bear? I say: *Unless there is some reason why one should bear more or less of it than the other, they should both bear the same amount.* This is my Fairness Principle. It concerns both the fair allocation of the burden to some class of community members and the fair distribution of it within that class (and this may mean dividing the class into subclasses of 'isophoric' members): There must always be a *reason* for treating people differently. For instance, people who are unfit or above or below a certain age are exempted or excluded from military service, and for good reasons; women are exempted or excluded from certain kinds of military service, for what Plato regarded as bad reasons; those with more income pay more tax, while those with more children pay less, and for good reasons—and so on. You will have noticed that the typical complaint about unfair dealings begins with a 'why': 'Why did they charge me more than him?' (unfair distribution), or 'Why should married couples be liable for so much surtax?' (unfair allocation). The maxim governing differential treatment, that is, which is behind the reasons given for it, seems to be: From each according to his resources, to each according to his need. You might argue that my principle about equal burdens is no more than a special case of this maxim. But that

principle is all I need for my argument and all I insist on; I shall not stick my neck out further than necessary.

D.: It is not, thus far, too dangerously exposed, I think.

M.: Good. We are now ready to move a little nearer to the core of the problem. But first compare the two principles I have advanced. The first was: If a thing is obligatory etc. for one person, then it is obligatory etc. for anyone in the same class (that is the class relevant to the reason given). This is a license to argue from one member of a class to all its members; we will call it the Universalization Principle (U-Principle). The second, which is my Fairness Principle, is: A burden laid on a particular class is to be shared equally by all its members, unless there is reason to the contrary. This, in contrast to the first, is a license to argue from the class itself to each of its members. I take it, by the way, that these two principles are independent, that neither follows from the other.

D.: Granted, granted. I am impatient to know what light all this throws on your 'if everyone did' argument.

M.: I am coming to that. You will remember that you used the U-Principle yourself to argue that if it's all right for you to evade it's all right for everyone else. But it was no use to me in pressing my case, and we can now see why: It argues from one to all, and there was no *one* to argue from. Nor, of course, could I argue from the consequences of your act. 'Why me?' you asked, and I had then no reply. But I did at least have a retort: 'Why not you?'. Now it seems to me that it is just my Fairness Principle that lies behind the effectiveness of this retort, for by it you can be shown to have a duty in cases like this unless you can show that you have not. You would have to show, in the military service example, that you were not a member of the class on which the duty of military service is normally (and we will assume, fairly) regarded as lying. But you cannot show this: You cannot claim to be under age or over age or blind or lame. All you claim is that you have a certain property, the property of being one whose contribution won't be missed, which is shared by every other member of the military class; and this claim, so far from being a good reason for not volunteering, now stands revealed as no reason at all.

D.: Still, you didn't dispute my point that the blame for a disaster following upon wholesale evasion lay upon those whose duty it was, or in whose power it lay, to prevent such evasion.

M.: You certainly had a point, but I can see now that you made too much of it. I concede that the authorities failed in their duty, but then the military class as a whole failed in theirs too. The duty of both was ultimately the same, to ensure the safety of the state, just as the duty of wicket-keeper and long-stop is the same, to save byes. To confine the blame to the authorities is like saying that it's all right to burn the house down so long as it's insured or that the mere existence of a police force constitutes a general license to rob banks. As for the individual defaulter, you wanted to absolve him from all blame—a claim which seemed at once plausible and paradoxical: plausible because he was not, as you rightly pointed out, to blame for the disaster (it was not his duty to prevent that, since it was not in his power to do so); paradoxical because he was surely to blame for *something,* and we now know what for: failure to bear his share of the burden allotted to his class.

D.: Maybe, but it still seems to me that if I volunteer and others don't I shall be taking on an unfair share of it, and *that* can't be fair. Then again if I don't volunteer I shall be doing less than my share, and *that* can't be fair either. Whichever I do, there's something wrong. And that can't be right.

M.: There are two mistakes here. Whichever you do there's something wrong, but nothing unfair; the only wrong is people failing in their duty. Fairness is an attribute of distributions, and whether you volunteer or not neither you nor anyone else are distributing anything. Nor, for that matter, are fate or circumstances, for they are not persons. That is your first mistake. Your second is this: You talk as if the lone volunteer will necessarily do more than his fair share. He may, but he needn't. If he does, that is his own look out: *volenti non fit iniuria.*

D.: It's more dangerous to fight alone than as one among many. How can he ration the danger?

M.: He can surrender or run away. Look, he isn't expected to be heroic or to do, or even attempt, the impossible. If two are needed to launch and man the lifeboat, the lone volunteer can only stand and wait: *He also* serves. The least a man can do is offer and hold himself ready, though sometimes it is also the most he can do.

D.: Let it be so. But I am still in trouble about one thing: Suppose I grant all you say about fairness and the defaulter, I'm still not clear why you choose to make your point against him in just the mysterious way you do, that is, by fixing him with your glittering eye and beginning 'If everyone did that.'

M.: It is a little puzzling, isn't it? But not all that puzzling. After all, the premiss states and implies a good deal: (1) It states that wholesale evasion will have such and such results; (2) it states or implies that the results will be bad; (3) it implies strongly that a duty to prevent them must lie *somewhere*; (4) it implies that the duty does not lie solely on the person addressed (otherwise a quite different kind of argument would apply); (5) it implies, rather weakly, that nevertheless the person addressed has no better excuse for doing nothing about it than anyone else has. The conclusion is then stated that he ought to do something about it. A gap remains, to be sure; but it can't be a very big one, or people wouldn't, as they sometimes do, feel the force of the argument, however obscurely. The 'Why me?' retort brings out implication (4), while the 'Why not you?' counter-retort brings out implication (5); and we didn't really have very far to go from there.

The argument is clearly elliptical and needs filling out with some explicit reference to the Fairness Principle. I would formalize it as follows:

Unless such and such is done, undesirable consequences X will ensue;

the burden of preventing X lies upon class Y as a whole;

each member of class Y has a *prima facie* duty to bear an equal share of the burden by doing Z;

you are a member of class Y;

therefore you have a *prima facie* duty to do Z.

I have introduced the notion of a *prima facie* duty at this late stage to cover those cases where only a few members of class Y are required to do Z and it would be silly to put them all to work. In the latrine case only one person needs to dig, and in America only a small proportion of fit persons are required for short-term military service. In such cases it is considered fair to select the requisite number by lot. Until the lot is cast I must hold myself ready; if I am selected my *prima facie* duty becomes an actual duty; if I am spared, it lapses. Why selection by lot should be a fair method I leave you to work out for yourself.

Notice that the argument only holds if the thing to be done is burdensome. Voting isn't really very burdensome; indeed a lot of people seem to enjoy it, and this accounts for the weakness of the argument in this application. If the thing to be done were positively enjoyable one might even have to invoke the Fairness Principle against overindulgence.

Notice, finally, that the argument doesn't apply unless there is a fairly readily isolable class to which a burden can be allotted. This rules out the farming and such like cases. You can't lay it down that the burden of providing food for the nation (if it *is* a burden) lies on the farmers (that is, the class that provides food for the nation), for that is a tautology, or perhaps it implies the curious proposition that everyone *ought* to be doing the job he *is* doing. Might one say instead that *everyone* has a *prima facie* duty to farm, but that the duty lapses when inclination, ability and economic reward conspire to select a sufficient farming force? Farfetched, I think. The matter might be pursued, but only at the risk of tedium. Well, are you satisfied?

D.:   Up to a point. Your hypothesis obviously calls for a lot more testing yet. But I have carried the burden a good deal further than my fair share of the distance; let others take it from here.

24

R. S. PETERS
Respect for Persons

R. S. PETERS, of the University of London Institute of Education, is best known as a philosopher of education. His works in that area include *Authority, Responsibility, and Education* (1959) and *Ethics and Education* (1966). He has written books on other subjects as well, such as *Hobbes* (1956) and *The Concept of Motivation* (1958).

Kant held that respect for persons was derivative from respect for law. He argued that though respect is a feeling, it is not a feeling received through influence, but is

self-wrought by a rational concept, and, therefore, is specifically distinct from all feelings of the former kind, which may be referred either to inclination or fear. What I recognize immediately as a law for me, I recognize with respect. . . . The object of respect is the law only, and that, the law which we impose on ourselves, and yet recognize as necessary in itself. . . . Respect for a person is properly our respect for the law (of honesty, etc.) of which he gives us an example.

The difficulty about this view is that contempt for persons seems, prima facie at any rate, quite compatible with meticulousness in acting on principles. One could take careful account of a person's interests, for instance, as a guardian might that of his ward, and yet have and show contempt for him as a person. It does not look, therefore, as if the appraisal which goes with respect for law or principles necessarily either coincides with or implies that which is necessary for respect for persons.

Kant, however, had a distinctive concept of law, at least in the practical sphere, in that for him the thought of such laws was inseparable from that of the autonomous rational beings who created them. The principles of practical reason were not "out there" to discover; they were not, as in Plato's system, principles permeating the nature of things which a rational being might discern; they were the creation of individuals possessed of reason and desire. Kant's conception of law was therefore inseparable from his belief in the activity, dignity, and worth of rational individuals who created it. For him the existence of individual rational beings was not just a fact about the world; it was a fact of supreme ethical importance. The notion of "persons" picked out not simply the fact; it also bore witness to the ethical importance of the fact. And this fact was intimately connected with the activity of men as rational beings in deliberating about what they ought to do.

THE MEANING OF "RESPECT FOR PERSONS"

There is much to be said for this doctrine of Kant in that the notion of being a person is connected with "being on the inside" of those experiences which are characteristic of practical reason, of acting on principles, and of determining the future in the light of knowledge of the past and awareness of what may be. Choice, which is intimately connected with the exercise of practical reason, is too narrow a concept; for it implies deliberation between alternatives. It does not cover such things as the grasp of rules, the formulation and statement of intentions, and the making of promises by means of which individuals determine the future. Notions like that of "endeavor" used by Spinoza to characterize a general tendency to persist in a form of being are too general; for they apply also to plants and other homeostatic systems which are not conscious of themselves or of the past and future. The notion is much more that of an assertive point of view; of judgments, appraisals, intentions, and decisions that shape events, their characteristic stamp being determined by previous ones that have given rise to permanent or semipermanent dispositions. The shaping of a pattern of life in this way is constitutive of what we call an individual person. When it is said that a man who brainwashes others, or who settles their lives for them without consulting them shows lack of "respect for persons," the implication is that he does not treat others seriously as agents or as determiners of their own destiny, and that he disregards their feelings and view of the world. He either refuses to let them be in a situation where their intentions, decisions, appraisals, and choices can operate effectively, or he purposely interferes with or nullifies their capacity for self-direction. He ensures that for them the question "What ought I do?" either scarcely arises or serves as a cork on a tide of events whose drift derives from elsewhere. He denies them the dignity which is the due of a self-determining agent who is capable of valuation and choice and who has a point of view of his own about his own future and interests.

The notion of a "person," which is picked out by reference to such notions connected with being an assertive point of view, is narrower than the wider notion of being an "individual." For instance, the individual's awareness of pain, or his visual experience, is not necessarily a manifestation of his existence as a person; if it were so dogs and octopuses would be persons. Yet the principle of consideration of interests could be applied to dogs without ever treating them as persons. A policy would have to be pursued which took account of avoiding pain for them and maximizing their opportunities for satisfaction. This would be done without "respect for persons"; for the dog's point of view about his forms of satisfaction would not be taken into account.

It is possible, too, for individual men and women to live together in society without any clear consciousness of themselves as persons. They might be thought of as having claims or interests, as occupying a certain status; but their view of such matters as individuals might be totally disregarded. Societies are really nothing more than groups of individuals who are initiated into and who accept and maintain a public system of rules. Nevertheless it is quite possible for people to live in societies without any awareness of the determining role of individuals. Indeed they may not distinguish clearly between a social order and a natural order and may think that individual men are comparatively impotent in relation to both of them. Though we might say that they were potentially individual persons who had been conditioned to accept a rather womb-like existence, they might nevertheless have no consciousness of themselves as persons. They might be conscious only of their particular social roles and of their general kinship with other members of the society. They might have neither respect for persons nor consciousness of either themselves or others as persons in any important sense.

People only begin to think of themselves as persons, centers of valuation, decision, and choice, in so far as the fact that consciousness is individuated into distinct centers, linked with distinct physical bodies and with distinctive points of view, is taken to be a matter of importance in a society. And they will only really develop as persons in so far as they learn to think of themselves as such. The concept of being a person, in other words, is derivative from the valuation placed in a society upon the determining role of individual points of view. Individuals will only tend to assert their rights as individuals, to take pride in their achievements, to deliberate carefully and choose "for themselves" what they ought to do, and to develop their own individual style of emotional reaction—in other words they will only tend to manifest all the various properties which we associate with being "persons"—if they are encouraged to do so. They would be persons all right in the sense that the moral laws were true in virtue of which they had such rights; but if such rights were not recognized they would not be treated as persons, would not think of themselves as such. Even in a society which, because of the importance which it attaches to individual points of view, is permeated by the concept of a person, an individual who was systematically discouraged and sat on might have such a low opinion of himself that we might be inclined to say of him that he simply had not got the concept of himself "as a person." What we might mean is that he had the concept of a person but that, because of special circumstances, he was incapable of applying it to himself. Presumably, at certain periods, slaves have been in just this predicament.

In our society being a person matters very much. Individuals are encouraged to judge and choose things "for themselves"; they are held responsible for the consequences of their actions as individuals and are praised and blamed accordingly; they feel pride for things well done and guilt and remorse for things badly done. They are encouraged to be the determiners of their own destiny and, to a certain extent, they *are* so because our society encourages this form of individual assertion. This consciousness of being an individual person rather than just a member of a group is therefore both exhilerating and sobering. The sense of mastery and making an impact on the shape of things is mingled with apprehension for the consequences of failure. Men, however, come to value it very much for what there is in it, as distinct from the value attached to it by their society. Indeed were it not the case that there is much in it to prize, it is difficult to see how societies would come to attach such overriding value to the assertion of an individual point of view.

This consciousness of being a person reaches its zenith, perhaps, in the experience of entering into and sustaining a personal relationship which is based on reciprocal agreement, where the bonds that bind people together derive from their own appraisals and choice, not from any status or institutional position. They create their own world by voluntarily sharing together and mingling their own individual perspectives on and developments of the public life of their society. The obligations, mainly of a contractual nature, which sustain their relationship are felt to be more binding than most duties simply because they are explicitly undertaken and because they create pools of predictability in a realm which was previously subject only to the play of natural appetites and aversions within a world marked out by impersonal traditions and institutional pressures.

A person who is conscious of his own agency in shaping events is also aware of the irksomeness of external forces that may prevent or impede him in doing what he wants. He has learned, however, to come to terms with the confines of nature; for his concept of himself as an agent develops *pari passu* with the concept of a nature which is unaffected by human whims and wishes. It is only in the autistic thinking of the infant, or in magic, that the natural world is subject to human whims and wishes. But he is vividly aware of the irksomeness of constraints imposed on him by other men; for he knows that these are alterable and often unnecessary, as well as frustrating to his purposes. But most irksome of all is the refusal by others to let him determine his own destiny and order his own preference in any major respect by conceiving of goals, deliberating about alternatives, and attempting to implement those of his choosing. To be treated as a moron or merely as an instrument of the purposes of other men, and to have his feelings completely disregarded is intolerable for a man who is conscious of his own potentialities as a self-determining agent. It may not be so, of course, for a man who has always been a slave and who has no consciousness of what he might achieve as an agent; there is no reason to suppose that slaves were discontented with their lot as long as they viewed their situation as part of the order of things.

THE QUESTION OF JUSTIFICATION

It has been argued that in so far as a man has the concept of himself and of others as persons, he must have been initiated into a society in which there is a general norm which attaches importance to the assertive points of view emanating from individual centers of consciousness. A man develops as a person as this concept of himself and of others develops. He also comes to value what is involved in being a person for what there is in it, as distinct from the importance attached to it by the social norm. To ask him, therefore, whether persons ought to be respected is rather like asking a man whether he ought to be afraid of a dangerous situation; for the concept of respect is necessary to explicate what is meant by a person. If he has the concept of person and understands it fully from "the inside" (that is, not just as an anthropologist might "understand," or fail to understand, a concept purely on the basis of external observation), then he must also have the notion that it matters that individuals represent distinct assertive points of view.

The explication of a concept, however, never settles a question of policy. The problem is to produce an argument to establish that any rational being must have the concept of a person and therefore respect others and himself as such. The procedure must therefore be to return to the situation of practical reason and to show that respect for persons is a presupposition that any participant in such a situation must accept. An argument must be advanced to show that it would be impossible for a man to take part seriously in the situation of practical reason who lacked this basic attitude to his fellow participants.

Such an argument is not far to seek. Indeed it has been implicit, as would be expected, if the lines of the analysis of "person" are correct, in the various characterizations of what it means to be a person. Central among these are experiences connected with the individual being the determiner of his own destiny, and with representing an assertive point of view. These phrases are attempts to intimate the sort of presuppositions that any man must have about himself and about others if he is to enter into any rational discussion with them about what ought to be done. In the foregoing chapters on Freedom and The Consideration of Interests it was argued that any man entering such a discussion seriously must claim freedom from interference for doing what there are reasons for doing and must assume that consideration must be accorded to him in so far as he has interests whose nature he wants to determine. If he was going to be subject to arbitrary interference, and if no prima facie attention was going to be paid to his assessment of his interests, such a discussion would lack any point. He must presume, too, that what holds for himself holds also for any other man who seriously joins with him in trying to answer such questions. Within such a discussion, too, the principle of impartiality requires that he listen to what people say and assent to or dissent from their contributions according to relevant criteria, for example, the quality of arguments adduced, and ignore irrelevant considerations such as the color of the eyes or hair of the contributors. These general principles governing the situation of practical reason are precisely those which safeguard the experiences which we most intimately associate with being a person, that is, not being arbitrarily interfered with in respect of the execution of our wants and decisions and not having our claims and interests ignored or treated in a partial or prejudiced manner.

It may be found, of course, that particular people are inarticulate or stupid, or that they are dishonest in the manner in which they advance claims. All such factors are relevant to the attention paid to particular people on particular occasions. But the argument is not meant to show that anyone must do anything particular on any particular occasions. Rather it relates to prima facie principles which a man must *in general* accept if he is determined to settle things, in so far as he can, by discussion.

The norm of respect for persons, therefore, picks out as crucial those types of experiences, which are a selection from the more varied range of experiences located at an individual center of consciousness, which are of cardinal importance for those entering seriously into discussion with their fellows about courses of action or ways of living. "Respect for persons" is therefore a principle which summarizes the attitude which we must adopt towards others with whom we are prepared seriously to discuss what ought to be done. Their points of view must be taken into account as sources of claims and interests; they must be regarded as having a prima facie claim for noninterference in doing what is in their interest; and no arbitrariness must be shown towards them as participants in discussion. To have the concept of a person is to see an individual as an object of respect in a form of life which is conducted on the basis of those principles which are presuppositions of the use of practical reason.

25

HERBERT MORRIS
Persons and Punishment

HERBERT MORRIS is professor of philosophy and professor of law at the University of California at Los Angeles. He has written on a variety of topics in the philosophy of law, and edited *Freedom and Responsibility* (1961).

They acted and looked . . . at us, and around in our house, in a way that had about it the feeling—at least for me—that we were not people. In their eyesight we were just things, that was all. Malcolm X

We have no right to treat a man like a dog. Governor Maddox of Georgia

Alfredo Traps in Durrenmatt's tale discovers that he has brought off, all by himself, a murder involving considerable ingenuity. The mock prosecutor in the tale demands the death penalty "as reward for a crime that merits admiration, astonishment, and respect." Traps is deeply moved; indeed, he is exhilerated, and the whole of his life becomes more heroic, and ironically, more precious. His defense attorney proceeds to argue that Traps was not only innocent but incapable of guilt, "a victim of the age." This defense Traps disavows with indignation and anger. He makes claim to the murder as his and demands the prescribed punishment—death.

The themes to be found in this macabre tale do not often find their way into philosophical discussions of punishment. These discussions deal with large and significant questions of whether or not we ever have the right to punish, and if we do, under what conditions, to what degree, and in what manner. There is a tradition, of course, not notable for its

From Herbert Morris, "Persons and Punishment," *The Monist*, vol. 52 (1968), pp. 475–501. Reprinted by permission of the author and The Open Court Publishing Company, LaSalle, Illinois. This article is reprinted unabridged.

present vitality, that is closely linked with motifs in Durrenmatt's tale of crime and punishment. Its adherents have urged that justice requires a person be punished if he is guilty. Sometimes—though rarely—these philosophers have expressed themselves in terms of the criminal's *right to be punished*. Reaction to the claim that there is such a right has been astonishment combined, perhaps, with a touch of contempt for the perversity of the suggestion. A strange right that no one would ever wish to claim! With that flourish the subject is buried and the right disposed of. In this paper the subject is resurrected.

My aim is to argue for four propositions concerning rights that will certainly strike some as not only false but preposterous: first, that we have a right to punishment; second, that this right derives from a fundamental human right to be treated as a person; third, that this fundamental right is a natural, inalienable, and absolute right; and, fourth, that the denial of this right implies the denial of all moral rights and duties. Showing the truth of one, let alone all, of these large and questionable claims, is a tall order. The attempt or, more properly speaking, the first steps in an attempt, follow.

1. When someone claims that there is a right to be free, we can easily imagine situations in which the right is infringed and easily imagine situations in which there is a point to asserting or claiming the right. With the right to be

punished, matters are otherwise. The immediate reaction to the claim that there is such a right is puzzlement. And the reasons for this are apparent. People do not normally value pain and suffering. Punishment is associated with pain and suffering. When we think about punishment we naturally think of the strong desire most persons have to avoid it, to accept, for example, acquittal of a criminal charge with relief and eagerly, if convicted, to hope for a pardon or probation. Adding, of course, to the paradoxical character of the claim of such a right is difficulty in imagining circumstances in which it would be denied one. When would one rightly demand punishment and meet with any threat of the claim being denied?

So our first task is to see when the claim of such a right would have a point. I want to approach this task by setting out two complex types of institutions both of which are designed to maintain some degree of social control. In the one a central concept is punishment for wrongdoing and in the other the central concepts are control of dangerous individuals and treatment of disease.

Let us first turn attention to the institutions in which punishment is involved. The institutions I describe will resemble those we ordinarily think of as institutions of punishment; they will have, however, additional features we associate with a system of just punishment.

Let us suppose that men are constituted roughly as they now are, with a rough equivalence in strength and abilities, a capacity to be injured by each other and to make judgments that such injury is undesirable, a limited strength of will, and a capacity to reason and to conform conduct to rules. Applying to the conduct of these men are a group of rules, ones I shall label 'primary,' which closely resemble the core rules of our

criminal law, rules that prohibit violence and deception and compliance with which provides benefits for all persons. These benefits consist in noninterference by others with what each person values, such matters as continuance of life and bodily security. The rules define a sphere for each person, then, which is immune from interference by others. Making possible this mutual benefit is the assumption by individuals of a burden. The burden consists in the exercise of self-restraint by individuals over inclinations that would, if satisfied, directly interfere or create a substantial risk of interference with others in proscribed ways. If a person fails to exercise self-restraint even though he might have and gives in to such inclinations, he renounces a burden which others have voluntarily assumed and thus gains an advantage which others, who have restrained themselves, do not possess. This system then, is one in which the rules establish a mutuality of benefit and burden and in which the benefits of noninterference are conditional upon the assumption of burdens.

Connecting punishment with the violation of these primary rules, and making public the provision for punishment, is both reasonable and just. First, it is only reasonable that those who voluntarily comply with the rules be provided with some assurance that they will not be assuming burdens which others are unprepared to assume. Their disposition to comply voluntarily will diminish as they learn that others are with impunity renouncing burdens they are assuming. Second, fairness dictates that a system in which benefits and burdens are equally distributed have a mechanism designed to prevent a maldistribution in the benefits and burdens. Thus, sanctions are attached to noncompliance with the primary rules so as to induce compliance with the primary rules among those who may be disinclined to obey. In this way the likelihood of an unfair distribution is diminished.

Third, it is just to punish those who have violated the rules and caused the unfair distribution of benefits and burdens. A person who violates the rules has something others have—the benefits of the system—but by renouncing what others have assumed, the burdens of self-restraint, he has acquired an unfair advantage. Matters are not even until this advantage is in some way erased. Another way of putting it is that he owes something to others, for he has something that does not rightfully belong to him. Justice—that is punishing such individuals—restores the equilibrium of benefits and burdens by taking from the individual what he owes, that is, exacting the debt. It is important to see that the equilibrium may be restored in another way. Forgiveness—with its legal analogue of a pardon—while not the righting of an unfair distribution by making one pay his debt is, nevertheless, a restoring of the equilibrium by forgiving the debt. Forgiveness may be viewed, at least in some types of cases, as a gift after the fact, erasing a debt, which had the gift been given before the fact, would not have created a debt. But the practice of pardoning has to proceed sensitively, for it may endanger in a way the practice of justice does not, the maintenance of an equilibrium of benefits and burdens. If all are indiscriminately pardoned less incentive is provided individuals to restrain their inclinations, thus increasing the incidence of persons taking what they do not deserve.

There are also in this system we are considering a variety of operative principles compliance with which provides some guarantee that the system of punishment does not itself promote an unfair distribution of benefits and burdens. For one thing, provision is made for a variety of defenses, each one of which can be said to have as its object diminishing the chances of forcibly depriving a person of benefits others have if that person has not derived an unfair advantage. A person has not derived an unfair advantage if he could not have restrained himself or if it is unreasonable to expect him to behave otherwise than he did. Sometimes the rules preclude punishment of classes of persons such as children. Sometimes they provide a defense if on a particular occasion a person lacked the capacity to conform his conduct to the rules. Thus, someone who in an epileptic seizure strikes another is excused. Punishment in these cases would be punishment of the innocent, punishment of those who do not voluntarily renounce a burden others have assumed. Punishment in such cases, then, would not equalize but rather cause an unfair distribution in benefits and burdens.

Along with principles providing defenses there are requirements that the rules be prospective and relatively clear so that persons have a fair opportunity to comply with the rules. There are, also, rules governing, among other matters, the burden of proof, who shall bear it and what it shall be, the prohibition on double jeopardy, and the privilege against self-incrimination. Justice requires conviction of the guilty, and requires their punishment, but in setting out to fulfill the demands of justice we may, of course, because we are not omniscient, cause injustice by convicting and punishing the innocent. The resolution arrived at in the system I am describing consists in weighing as the greater evil the punishment of the innocent. The primary function of the system of rules was to provide individuals with a sphere of interest immune from interference. Given this goal, it is determined to be a greater evil for society to interfere unjustifiably with an individual by depriving him of good than for the society to fail to punish those that have unjustifiably interfered.

Finally, because the primary rules are designed to benefit all and because the punishments prescribed for their violation are publicized and the defenses respected, there is some plausibility in the exaggerated claim that in choosing to do an act violative of the rules an individual has chosen to be punished. This way of putting matters brings to our attention the extent to which, when the system is as I have described it, the criminal "has brought the punishment upon himself" in contrast to those cases where it would be misleading to say "he has brought it upon himself," cases, for example, where one does not know the rules or is punished in the absence of fault.

To summarize, then: First, there is a group of rules guiding the behavior of individuals in the community which establish spheres of interest immune from interference by others; second, provision is made for what is generally regarded as a deprivation of some thing of value if the rules are violated; third, the deprivations visited upon any person are justified by that person's having violated the rules; fourth, the deprivation, in this just system of punishment, is linked to rules that fairly distribute benefits and burdens and to procedures that strike some balance between not punishing the guilty and punishing the innocent, a class defined as those who have not voluntarily done acts violative of the law, in which it is evident that the evil of punishing the innocent is re-

garded as greater than the nonpunishment of the guilty.

At the core of many actual legal systems one finds, of course, rules and procedures of the kind I have sketched. It is obvious, though, that any ongoing legal system differs in significant respects from what I have presented here, containing 'pockets of injustice.'

I want now to sketch an extreme version of a set of institutions of a fundamentally different kind, institutions proceeding on a conception of man which appears to be basically at odds with that operative within a system of punishment.

Rules are promulgated in this system that prohibit certain types of injuries and harms.

In this world we are now to imagine when an individual harms another his conduct is to be regarded as a symptom of some pathological condition in the way a running nose is a symptom of a cold. Actions diverging from some conception of the normal are viewed as manifestations of a disease in the way in which we might today regard the arm and leg movements of an epileptic during a seizure. Actions conforming to what is normal are assimilated to the normal and healthy functioning of bodily organs. What a person does, then, is assimilated, on this conception, to what we believe today, or at least most of us believe today, a person undergoes. We draw a distinction between the operation of the kidney and raising an arm on request. This distinction between mere events or happenings and human actions is erased in our imagined system.[1]

1. "When a man is suffering from an infectious disease, he is a danger to the community, and it is necessary to restrict his liberty of movement. But no one associates any idea of guilt with such a situation. On the contrary, he is an object of commiseration to his friends. Such steps as science recommends are taken to cure him of his dis-

214 · Kantian Ethics

There is, however, bound to be something strange in this erasing of a recognized distinction, for, as with metaphysical suggestions generally, and I take this to be one, the distinction may be reintroduced but given a different description, for example, 'happenings with *X* type of causes' and 'happenings with *Y* type of causes.' Responses of different kinds, today legitimated by our distinction between happenings and actions may be legitimated by this new manner of description. And so there may be isomorphism between a system recognizing the distinction and one erasing it. Still, when this distinction is erased certain tendencies of thought and responses might naturally arise that would tend to affect unfavorably values respected by a system of punishment.

Let us elaborate on this assimilation of conduct of a certain kind to symptoms of a disease. First, there is something abnormal in both the case of conduct, such as killing another, and a symptom of a disease such as an irregular heart beat. Second, there are causes for this abnormality in action such that once we know of them we can explain the abnormality as we now can explain the symptoms of many physical diseases. The abnormality is looked upon as a happening with a causal explanation rather than an action for which there were reasons. Third, the causes that account for the abnormality interfere with the normal functioning of the body, or, in the case of killing with what is regarded as a normal functioning of an individual. Fourth, the abnormality is in some way a part of the individual, necessarily involving his body. A well going dry might satisfy our three foregoing conditions of disease symptoms, but it is hardly a disease or the symptom of one. Finally, and most obscure, the abnormality arises in some way from within the individual. If Jones is hit with a mallet by Smith, Jones may reel about and fall on James who may be injured. But this abnormal conduct of Jones is not regarded as a symptom of disease. Smith, not Jones, is suffering from some pathological condition.

With this view of man the institutions of social control respond, not with

ease, and he submits as a rule without reluctance to the curtailment of liberty, involved meanwhile. The same method in spirit ought to be shown in the treatment of what is called 'crime.'"
Bertrand Russell, *Roads to Freedom* (London: George Allen and Unwin Ltd., 1918), p. 135.
"We do not hold people responsible for their reflexes—for example, for coughing in church. We hold them responsible for their operant behavior—for example, for whispering in church or remaining in church while coughing. But there are variables which are responsible for whispering as well as coughing, and these may be just as inexorable. When we recognize this, we are likely to drop the notion of responsibility altogether and with it the doctrine of free will as an inner causal agent."
B. F. Skinner, *Science and Human Behavior* (1953), pp. 115–6.
"Basically, criminality is but a symptom of insanity, using the term in its widest generic sense to express unacceptable social behavior based on unconscious motivation flowing from a disturbed instinctive and emotional life, whether this appears in frank psychoses, or in less obvious form in neuroses and unrecognized psychoses. . . . If criminals are products of early environmental influences in the same sense that psychotics and neurotics are, then it should be possible to reach them psychotherapeutically."
Benjamin Karpman, "Criminal Psychodynamics," *Journal of Criminal Law and Criminology*, 47 (1956), p. 9.
"We, the agents of society, must move to end the game of tit-for-tat and blow-for-blow in which the offender has foolishly and futiley engaged himself and us. We are not driven, as he is, to wild and impulsive actions. With knowledge comes power, and with power there is no need for the frightened vengeance of the old penology. In its place should go a quiet, dignified, therapeutic program for the rehabilitation of the disorganized one, if possible, the protection of society during the treatment period, and his guided return to useful citizenship, as soon as this can be effected."
Karl Menninger, "Therapy, Not Punishment," *Harper's Magazine* (August 1959), pp. 63–64.

punishment, but with either preventive detention, in case of 'carriers,' or therapy in the case of those manifesting pathological symptoms. The logic of sickness implies the logic of therapy. And therapy and punishment differ widely in their implications. In bringing out some of these differences I want again to draw attention to the important fact that while the distinctions we now draw are erased in the therapy world, they may, in fact, be reintroduced but under different descriptions. To the extent they are, we really have a punishment system combined with a therapy system. I am concerned now, however, with what the implications would be were the world indeed one of therapy and not a disguised world of punishment and therapy, for I want to suggest tendencies of thought that arise when one is immersed in the ideology of disease and therapy.

First, punishment is the imposition upon a person who is believed to be at fault of something commonly believed to be a deprivation where that deprivation is justified by the person's guilty behavior. It is associated with resentment, for the guilty are those who have done what they had no right to do by failing to exercise restraint when they might have and where others have. Therapy is not a response to a person who is at fault. We respond to an individual, not because of what he has done, but because of some condition from which he is suffering. If he is no longer suffering from the condition, treatment no longer has a point. Punishment, then, focuses on the past; therapy on the present. Therapy is normally associated with compassion for what one undergoes, not resentment for what one has illegitimately done.

Second, with therapy, unlike punishment, we do not seek to deprive the person of something acknowledged as a good, but seek rather to help and to benefit the individual who is suffering by ministering to his illness in the hope that the person can be cured. The good we attempt to do is not a reward for desert. The individual suffering has not merited by his disease the good we seek to bestow upon him but has, because he is a creature that has the capacity to feel pain, a claim upon our sympathies and help.

Third, we saw with punishment that its justification was related to maintaining and restoring a fair distribution of benefits and burdens. Infliction of the prescribed punishment carries the implication, then, that one has 'paid one's debt' to society, for the punishment is the taking from the person of something commonly recognized as valuable. It is this conception of 'a debt owed' that may permit, as I suggested earlier, under certain conditions, the nonpunishment of the guilty, for operative within a system of punishment may be a concept analogous to forgiveness, namely pardoning. Who it is that we may pardon and under what conditions—contrition with its elements of self-punishment no doubt plays a role—I shall not go into though it is clearly a matter of the greatest practical and theoretical interest. What is clear is that the conceptions of 'paying a debt' or 'having a debt forgiven' or pardoning have no place in a system of therapy.

Fourth, with punishment there is an attempt at some equivalence between the advantage gained by the wrongdoer—partly based upon the seriousness of the interest invaded, partly on the state of mind with which the wrongful act was performed—and the punishment meted out. Thus, we can understand a prohibition on 'cruel and

unusual punishments' so that disproportionate pain and suffering are
avoided. With therapy attempts at pro-
portionality make no sense. It is perfectly plausible giving someone who
kills a pill and treating for a lifetime
within an institution one who has broken a dish and manifested accident
proneness. We have the concept of
'painful treatment.' We do not have the
concept of 'cruel treatment.' Because
treatment is regarded as a benefit,
though it may involve pain, it is natural
that less restraint is exercised in bestowing it, than in inflicting punishment. Further, protests with respect to
treatment are likely to be assimilated to
the complaints of one whose leg must be
amputated in order for him to live, and,
thus, largely disregarded. To be sure,
there is operative in the therapy world
some conception of the "cure being
worse than the disease," but if the disease is manifested in conduct harmful to
others, and if being a normal operating
human being is valued highly, there
will naturally be considerable pressure
to find the cure acceptable.

Fifth, the rules in our system of
punishment governing conduct of individuals were rules violation of which
involved either direct interference with
others or the creation of a substantial
risk of such interference. One could
imagine adding to this system of primary rules other rules proscribing preparation to do acts violative of the primary rules and even rules proscribing
thoughts. Objection to such suggestions
would have many sources but a principal one would consist in its involving
the infliction of punishment on too great
a number of persons who would not, because of a change of mind, have violated
the primary rules. Though we are interested in diminishing violations of the
primary rules, we are not prepared to

punish too many individuals who would
never have violated the rules in order to
achieve this aim. In a system motivated
solely by a preventive and curative
ideology there would be less reason to
wait until symptoms manifest themselves in socially harmful conduct. It is
understandable that we should wish at
the earliest possible stage to arrest the
development of the disease. In the punishment system, because we are dealing
with deprivations, it is understandable
that we should forbear from imposing
them until we are quite sure of guilt. In the
therapy system, dealing as it does with
benefits, there is less reason for forbearance from treatment at an early stage.

Sixth, a variety of procedural safeguards we associate with punishment
have less significance in a therapy system. To the degree objections to double
jeopardy and self-incrimination are
based on a wish to decrease the chances
of the innocent being convicted and
punished, a therapy system, unconcerned with this problem, would disregard such safeguards. When one is out to
help people there is also little sense in
urging that the burden of proof be on
those providing the help. And there is
less point to imposing the burden of
proving that the conduct was pathological beyond a reasonable doubt. Further,
a jury system which, within a system of
justice, serves to make accommodations
to the individual situation and to introduce a human element, would play no
role or a minor one in a world where expertise is required in making determinations of disease and treatment.

In our system of punishment an attempt was made to maximize each individual's freedom of choice by first of all
delimiting by rules certain spheres of
conduct immune from interference by
others. The punishment associated with
these primary rules paid deference to an

individual's free choice by connecting punishment to a freely chosen act violative of the rules, thus giving some plausibility to the claim, as we saw, that what a person received by way of punishment he himself had chosen. With the world of disease and therapy all this changes and the individual's free choice ceases to be a determinative factor in how others respond to him. All those principles of our own legal system that minimize the chances of punishment of those who have not chosen to do acts violative of the rules tend to lose their point in the therapy system, for how we respond in a therapy system to a person is not conditioned upon what he has chosen but rather on what symptoms he has manifested or may manifest and what the best therapy for the disease is that is suggested by the symptoms.

Now, it is clear I think, that were we confronted with the alternatives I have sketched, between a system of just punishment and a thoroughgoing system of treatment, a system, that is, that did not reintroduce concepts appropriate to punishment, we could see the point in claiming that a person has a right to be punished, meaning by this that a person had a right to all those institutions and practices linked to punishment. For these would provide him with, among other things, a far greater ability to predict what would happen to him on the occurrence of certain events than the therapy system. There is the inestimable value to each of us of having the responses of others to us determined over a wide range of our lives by what we choose rather than what they choose. A person has a right to institutions that respect his choices. Our punishment system does; our therapy system does not.

Apart from those aspects of our therapy model which would relate to serious limitations on personal liberty, there are clearly objections of a more profound kind to the mode of thinking I have associated with the therapy model.

First, human beings pride themselves in having capacities that animals do not. A common way, for example, of arousing shame in a child is to compare the child's conduct to that of an animal. In a system where all actions are assimilated to happenings we are assimilated to creatures—indeed, it is more extreme than this—whom we have always thought possessed of less than we. Fundamental to our practice of praise and order of attainment is that one who can do more—one who is capable of more and one who does more is more worthy of respect and admiration. And we have thought of ourselves as capable where animals are not of making, of creating, among other things, ourselves. The conception of man I have outlined would provide us with a status that today, when our conduct is assimilated to it in moral criticism, we consider properly evocative of shame.

Second, if all human conduct is viewed as something men undergo, thrown into question would be the appropriateness of that extensive range of peculiarly human satisfactions that derive from a sense of achievement. For these satisfactions we shall have to substitute those mild satisfactions attendant upon a healthy well-functioning body. Contentment is our lot if we are fortunate; intense satisfaction at achievement is entirely inappropriate.

Third, in the therapy world nothing is earned and what we receive comes to us through compassion, or through a desire to control us. Resentment is out of place. We can take credit for nothing but must always regard ourselves—if there are selves left to regard once actions disappear—as fortunate recipients of benefits or unfortunate carriers of disease who must be controlled. We know that within our own world human beings who have been so regarded and who come to accept this view of themselves come to look upon themselves as worthless. When what we do is met with resentment, we are indirectly paid something of a compliment.

Fourth, attention should also be drawn to a peculiar evil that may be attendant upon regarding a man's actions as symptoms of disease. The logic of cure will push us toward forms of therapy that inevitably involve changes in the person made against his will. The evil in this would be most apparent in those cases where the agent, whose action is determined to be a manifestation of some disease, does not regard his action in this way. He believes that what he has done is, in fact, 'right' but his conception of 'normality' is not the therapeutically accepted one. When we treat an illness we normally treat a condition that the person is not responsible for. He is 'suffering' from some disease and we treat the condition, relieving the person of something preventing his normal functioning. When we begin treating persons for actions that have been chosen, we do not lift from the person something that is interfering with his normal functioning but we change the person so that he functions in a way regarded as normal by the current therapeutic community. We have to change him and his judgments of value. In doing this we display a lack of respect for the moral status of individuals, that is, a lack of respect for the reasoning and choices of individuals. They are but animals who must be conditioned. I think we can understand and, indeed, sympathize with a man's preferring death to being forcibly turned into what he is not.

Finally, perhaps most frightening of all would be the derogation in status of all protests to treatment. If someone believes that he has done something right, and if he protests being treated and changed, the protest will itself be regarded as a sign of some pathological condition, for who would not wish to be cured of an affliction? What this leads to are questions of an important kind about the effect of this conception of man upon what we now understand by reasoning. Here what a person takes to be a reasoned defense of an act is treated, as the action was, on the model of a happening of a pathological kind. Not just a person's acts are taken from him but also his attempt at a reasoned justification for the acts. In a system of punishment a person who has committed a crime may argue that what he did was right. We make him pay the price and we respect his right to retain the judgment he has made. A conception of pathology precludes this form of respect.

It might be objected to the foregoing that all I have shown—if that—is that if the only alternatives open to us are a *just* system of punishment or the mad world of being treated like sick or healthy animals, we do in fact have a right to a system of punishment of this kind. But this hardly shows that we have a right *simpliciter* to punishment as we do, say, to be free. Indeed, it does not even show a right to a just system of punishment, for surely we can, without too much difficulty, imagine situations in which the alternatives to punishment are not this mad world but a world in which we are still treated as persons and there is, for example, not the pain and suffering attendant upon punishment. One such world is one in which there are rules but responses to their violation is not the deprivation of some good but forgiveness. Still another type of world would be one in which violation of the rules were responded to by merely comparing the conduct of the person to something commonly regarded as low or filthy, and thus, producing by this mode of moral criticism, feelings of shame rather than feelings of guilt.

I am prepared to allow that these objections have a point. While granting force to the above objections I want to offer a few additional comments with respect to each of them. First, any existent legal system permits the punishment of individuals under circumstances where the conditions I have set forth for a just system have not been satisfied. A glaring example of this would be criminal strict liability which is to be found in our own legal system. Nevertheless, I think it would be difficult to present any system we should regard as a system of punishment that would not still have a great advantage over our imagined therapy system. The system of punishment we imagine may more and more approximate a system of sheer terror in which human beings are treated as animals to be intimidated and prodded. To the degree that the system is of this character it is, in my judgment, not simply an unjust system but one that diverges from what we normally understand by a system of punishment. At least some deference to the choice of individuals is built into the idea of punishment. So there would be some truth in saying we have a right to any system of punishment if the only alternative to it was therapy.

Second, people may imagine systems in which there are rules and in which the response to their violation is not punishment but pardoning, the legal analogue of forgiveness. Surely this is a system to which we would claim a right as against one in which we are made to suffer for violating the rules. There are several comments that need to be made

about this. It may be, of course, that a high incidence of pardoning would increase the incidence of rule violations. Further, the difficulty with suggesting pardoning as a general response is that pardoning presupposes the very responses that it is suggested it supplant. A system of deprivations, or a practice of deprivations on the happening of certain actions, underlies the practice of pardoning and forgiving, for it is only where we possess the idea of a wrong to be made up or of a debt owed to others, ideas we acquire within a world in which there have been deprivations for wrong acts, that we have the idea of pardoning for the wrong or forgiving the debt.

Finally, if we look at the responses I suggested would give rise to feelings of shame, we may rightly be troubled with the appropriateness of this response in any community in which each person assumes burdens so that each may derive benefits. In such situations might it not be that individuals have a right to a system of punishment so that each person could be assured that inequities in the distribution of benefits and burdens are unlikely to occur and if they do, procedures exist for correcting them? Further, it may well be that, everything considered, we should prefer the pain and suffering of a system of punishment to a world in which we only experience shame on the doing of wrong acts, for with guilt there are relatively simple ways of ridding ourselves of the feeling we have, that is, gaining forgiveness or taking the punishment, but with shame we have to bear it until we no longer are the person who has behaved in the shameful way. Thus, I suggest that we have, wherever there is a distribution of benefits and burdens of the kind I have described, a right to a system of punishment.

I want also to make clear in concluding this section that I have argued, though very indirectly, not just for a right to a system of punished, but for a right to be punished once there is in existence such a system. Thus, a man has the right to be punished rather than treated if he is guilty of some offense. And, indeed, one can imagine a case in which, even in the face of an offer of a pardon, a man claims and ought to have acknowledged his right to be punished.

2. The primary reason for preferring the system of punishment as against the system of therapy might have been expressed in terms of the one system treating one as a person and the other not. In invoking the right to be punished, one justifies one's claim by reference to a more fundamental right. I want now to turn attention to this fundamental right and attempt to shed light—it will have to be little, for the topic is immense—on what is meant by 'treating an individual as a person.'

When we talk of not treating a human being as a person or 'showing no respect for one as a person' what we imply by our words is a contrast between the manner in which one acceptably responds to human beings and the manner in which one acceptably responds to animals and inanimate objects. When we treat a human being merely as an animal or some inanimate object our responses to the human being are determined, not by his choices, but ours in disregard of or with indifference to his. And when we 'look upon' a person as less than a person or not a person, we consider the person as incapable of a rational choice. In cases of not treating a human being as a person we interfere with a person in such a way that what is done, even if the person is involved in the doing, is done not by the person but by the user of the person. In extreme cases there may even be an elision of a causal chain so that we might say that X

killed Z even though Y's hand was the hand that held the weapon, for Y's hand may have been entirely in X's control. The one agent is in some way treating the other as a mere link in a causal chain. There is, of course, a wide range of cases in which a person is used to accomplish the aim of another and in which the person used is less than fully free. A person may be grabbed against his will and used as a shield. A person may be drugged or hypnotized and then employed for certain ends. A person may be deceived into doing other than he intends doing. A person may be ordered to do something and threatened with harm if he does not and coerced into doing what he does not want to. There is still another range of cases in which individuals are not used, but in which decisions by others are made that affect them in circumstances where they have the capacity for choice and where they are not being treated as persons.

But it is particularly important to look at coercion, for I have claimed that a just system of punishment treats human beings as persons; and it is not immediately apparent how ordering someone to do something and threatening harm differs essentially from having rules supported by threats of harm in case of noncompliance.

There are affinities between coercion and other cases of not treating someone as a person, for it is not the coerced person's choices but the coercer's that are responsible for what is done. But unlike other indisputable cases of not treating one as a person, for example using someone as a shield, there is some choice involved in coercion. And if this is so, why does the coercer stand in any different relation to the coerced person than the criminal law stands to individuals in society?

Suppose the person who is threatened disregards the order and gets the threatened harm. Now suppose he is told, "Well, you did after all bring it upon yourself." There is clearly something strange in this. It is the person doing the threatening and not the person threatened who is responsible. But our reaction to punishment, at least in a system that resembles the one I have described, is precisely that the person violating the rules brought it upon himself. What lies behind these different reactions?

There exist situations in the law, of course, which resemble coercion situations. There are occasions when in the law a person might justifiably say "I am not being treated as a person but being used" and where he might properly react to the punishment as something "he was hardly responsible for." But it is possible to have a system in which it would be misleading to say, over a wide range of cases of punishment for noncompliance, that we are using persons. The clearest case in which it would be inappropriate to so regard punishment would be one in which there were explicit agreement in advance that punishment should follow on the voluntary doing of certain acts. Even if one does not have such conditions satisfied, and obviously such explicit agreements are not characteristic, one can see significant differences between our system of just punishment and a coercion situation.

First, unlike the case with one person coercing another 'to do his will,' the rules in our system apply to all, with the benefits and burdens equally distributed. About such a system it cannot be said that some are being subordinated to others or are being used by others or gotten to do things by others. To the extent that the rules are thought to be to the advantage of only some or to the extent there is a maldistribution of benefits

and burdens, the difference between coercion and law disappears.

Second, it might be argued that at least any person inclined to act in a manner violative of the rules stands to all others as the person coerced stands to his coercer, and that he, at least, is a person disadvantaged as others are not. It is important here, I think, that he is part of a system in which it is commonly agreed that forbearance from the acts proscribed by the rules provides advantages for all. This system is the accepted setting; it is the norm. Thus, in any coercive situation, it is the coercer who deviates from the norm, with the responsibility of the person he is attempting to coerce, defeated. In a just punishment situation, it is the person deviating from the norm, indeed he might be a coercer, who is responsible, for it is the norm to restrain oneself from acts of that kind. A voluntary agent diverging in his conduct from what is expected or what the norm is, on general causal principles, is regarded as the cause of what results from his conduct.

There is, then, some plausibility in the claim that, in a system of punishment of the kind I have sketched, a person chooses the punishment that is meted out to him. If, then, we can say in such a system that the rules provide none with advantages that others do not have, and further, that what happens to a person is conditioned by that person's choice and not that of others, then we can say that is a system responding to one as a person.

We treat a human being as a person provided: first, we permit the person to make the choices that will determine what happens to him and second, when our responses to the person are responses respecting the person's choices. When we respond to a person's illness by treating the illness it is neither a case of treating or not treating the individual as a person. When we give a person a gift we are neither treating or not treating him as a person, unless, of course, he does not wish it, chooses not to have it, but we compel him to accept it.

3. This right to be treated as a person is a fundamental human right belonging to all human beings by virtue of their being human. It is also a natural, inalienable, and absolute right. I want now to defend these claims so reminiscent of an era of philosophical thinking about rights that many consider to have been seriously confused.

If the right is one that we possess by virtue of being human beings, we are immediately confronted with an apparent dilemma. If, to treat another as a person requires that we provide him with reasons for acting and avoid force or deception, how can we justify the force and deception we exercise with respect to children and the mentally ill? If they, too, have a right to be treated as persons are we not constantly infringing their rights? One way out of this is simply to restrict the right to those who satisfy the conditions of being a person. Infants and the insane, it might be argued, do not meet these conditions, and they would not then have the right. Another approach would be to describe the right they possess as a prima facie right to be treated as a person. This right might then be outweighed by other considerations. This approach generally seems to me, as I shall later argue, inadequate.

I prefer this tack. Children possess the right to be treated as persons but they possess this right as an individual might be said in the law of property to possess a future interest. There are advantages in talking of individuals as having a right though complete enjoyment of it is postponed. Brought to our attention, if we ascribe to them the

right, is the legitimacy of their complaint if they are not provided with opportunities and conditions assuring their full enjoyment of the right when they acquire the characteristics of persons. More than this, all persons are charged with the sensitive task of not denying them the right to be a person and to be treated as a person by failing to provide the conditions for their becoming individuals who are able freely and in an informed way to choose and who are prepared themselves to assume responsibility for their choices. There is an obligation imposed upon us all, unlike that we have with respect to animals, to respond to children in such a way as to maximize the chances of their becoming persons. This may well impose upon us the obligation to treat them as persons from a very early age, that is, to respect their choices and to place upon them the responsibility for the choices to be made. There is no need to say that there is a close connection between how we respond to them and what they become. It also imposes upon us all the duty to display constantly the qualities of a person, for what they become they will largely become because of what they learn from us is acceptable behavior.

In claiming that the right is a right that human beings have by virtue of being human, there are several other features of the right, that should be noted, perhaps better conveyed by labelling them 'natural.' First, it is a right we have apart from any voluntary agreement into which we have entered. Second, it is not a right that derives from some defined position or status. Third, it is equally apparent that one has the right regardless of the society or community of which one is a member. Finally, it is a right linked to certain features of a class of beings. Were we fundamentally different than we now are, we would not have it. But it is more than that, for the right is linked to a feature of human beings which, were that feature absent—the capacity to reason and to choose on the basis of reasons—, profound conceptual changes would be involved in the thought about human beings. It is a right, then, connected with a feature of men that sets men apart from other natural phenomena.

The right to be treated as a person is inalienable. To say of a right that it is inalienable draws attention not to limitations placed on what others may do with respect to the possessor of the right but rather to limitations placed on the dispositive capacities of the possessor of the right. Something is to be gained in keeping the issues of alienability and absoluteness separate.

There are a variety of locutions qualifying what possessors of rights may and may not do. For example, on this issue of alienability, it would be worthwhile to look at, among other things, what is involved in abandoning, abdicating, conveying, giving up, granting, relinquishing, surrendering, transferring, and waiving one's rights. And with respect to each of these concepts we should also have to be sensitive to the variety of uses of the term 'rights.' What it is, for example, to waive a Hohfeldian 'right' in his strict sense will differ from what it is to waive a right in his 'privilege' sense.

Let us look at only two concepts very briefly, those of transferring and waiving rights. The clearest case of transferring rights is that of transferring rights with respect to specific objects. I own a watch and owning it I have a complicated relationship, captured in this area rather well I think by Hohfeld's four basic legal relationships, to all persons in the world with respect to the watch. We crudely capture these complex relationships by talking of my

'property rights' in or with respect to the watch. If I sell the watch, thus exercising a capacity provided by the rules of property, I have transferred rights in or with respect to the watch to someone else, the buyer, and the buyer now stands, as I formerly did, to all persons in the world in a series of complex relationships with respect to the watch.

While still the owner, I may have given to another permission to use it for several days. Had there not been the permission and had the person taken the watch, we should have spoken of interfering with or violating or, possibly, infringing my property rights. Or, to take a situation in which transferring rights is inappropriate, I may say to another "go ahead and slap me—you have my permission." In these types of situations philosophers and others have spoken of 'surrendering' rights or, alternatively and, I believe, less strangely, of 'waiving one's rights.' And recently, of course, the whole topic of 'waiving one's right to remain silent' in the context of police interrogation of suspects has been a subject of extensive litigation and discussion.

I confess to feeling that matters are not entirely perspicuous with respect to what is involved in 'waiving' or 'surrendering' rights. In conveying to another permission to take a watch or slap one, one makes legally permissible what otherwise would not have been. But in saying those words that constitute permission to take one's watch one is, of course, exercising precisely one of those capacities that leads us to say he has, while others have not, property rights with respect to the watch. Has one then waived his right in Hohfeld's strict sense in which the correlative is a duty to forebear on the part of others?

We may wish to distinguish here waiving the right to have others forbear to which there is a corresponding duty on their part to forbear, from placing oneself in a position where one has no legitimate right to complain. If I say the magic words "take the watch for a couple of days" or "go ahead and slap me," have I waived my right not to have my property taken or a right not to be struck or have I, rather, in saying what I have, simply stepped into a relation in which the rights no longer apply with respect to a specified other person? These observations find support in the following considerations. The right is that which gives rise, when infringed, to a legitimate claim against another person. What this suggests is that the right is that sphere interference with which entitles us to complain or gives us a right to complain. From this it seems to follow that a right to bodily security should be more precisely described as 'a right that others not interfere without permission.' And there is the corresponding duty not to interfere unless provided permission. Thus when we talk of waiving our rights or 'giving up our rights' in such cases we are not waiving or giving up our right to property nor our right to bodily security, for we still, of course, possess the right not to have our watch taken without permission. We have rather placed ourselves in a position where we do not possess the capacity, sometimes called a right, to complain if the person takes the watch or slaps us.

There is another type of situation in which we may speak of waiving our rights. If someone without permission slaps me there is an infringement of my right to bodily security. If I now acquiesce or go further and say "forget it" or "you are forgiven," we might say that I had waived my right to complain. But here, too, I feel uncomfortable about what is involved. For I do have the right to complain (a right without a corre-

sponding duty) in the event I am slapped and I have that right whether I wish it or not. If I say to another after the slap, "you are forgiven" what I do is not waive the right to complain but rather make illegitimate my subsequent exercise of that right.

Now, if we turn to the right to be treated as a person, the claim that I made was that it was inalienable, and what I meant to convey by that word of respectable age is that (a) it is a right that cannot be transferred to another in the way one's right with respect to objects can be transferred and (b) that it cannot be waived in the ways in which people talk of waiving rights to property or waiving, within certain limitations, one's right to bodily security.

While the rules of the law of property are such that persons may, satisfying certain procedures, transfer rights, the right to be treated as a person logically cannot be transferred anymore than one person can transfer to another his right to life or privacy. What, indeed, would it be like for another to have our right to be treated as a person? We can understand transferring a right with respect to certain objects. The new owner stands where the old owner stood. But with a right to be treated as a person what could this mean? My having the right meant that my choices were respected. Now if I transfer it to another this will mean that he will possess the right that my choices be respected? This is nonsense. It is only each person himself that can have his choices respected. It is no more possible to transfer this right than it is to transfer one's right to life.

Nor can the right be waived. It cannot be waived because any agreement to being treated as an animal or an instrument does not provide others with the moral permission to so treat us. One can volunteer to be a shield, but then it is one's choice on a particular occasion to be a shield. If without our permission, without our choosing it, someone used us as a shield, we may, I should suppose, forgive the person for treating us as an object. But we do not thereby waive our right to be treated as a person, for that is a right that has been infringed and what we have at most done is put ourselves in a position where it is inappropriate any longer to exercise the right to complain.

This is the sort of right, then, such that the moral rules defining relationships among persons preclude anyone from morally giving others legitimate permissions or rights with respect to one by doing or saying certain things. One stands, then, with respect to one's person as the nonowner of goods stands to those goods. The nonowner cannot, given the rule-defined relationships, convey to others rights and privileges that only the owner possesses. Just as there are agreements nonenforceable because void is contrary to public policy, so there are permissions our moral outlook regards as without moral force. With respect to being treated as a person, one is 'disabled' from modifying relations of others to one.

The right is absolute. This claim is bound to raise eyebrows. I have an innocuous point in mind in making this claim.

In discussing alienability we focused on incapacities with respect to disposing of rights. Here what I want to bring out is a sense in which a right exists despite considerations for refusing to accord the person his rights. As with the topic of alienability there are a host of concepts that deserve a close look in this area. Among them are according, acknowledging, annulling, asserting, claiming, denying, destroying, exercising, infringing, insisting upon, interfering with, possessing, recognizing and violating.

The claim that rights are absolute has been construed to mean that 'assertions of rights cannot, for any reason under any circumstances be denied.' When there are considerations which warrant refusing to accord persons their rights, there are two prevalent views as to how this should be described: there is, first, the view that the person does not have the right, and second, the view that he has rights but of a prima facie kind and that these have been outweighed or overcome by the other considerations. "We can conceive times when such rights must give way, and, therefore, they are only prima facie and not absolute rights." (Brandt)

Perhaps there are cases in which a person claims a right to do a certain thing, say with his property, and argued that his property rights are absolute, meaning by this he has a right to do whatever he wishes with his property. Here, no doubt, it has to be explained to the person that the right he claims he has, he does not in fact possess. In such a case the person does not have and never did have, given a certain description of the right, a right that was prima facie or otherwise, to do what he claimed he had the right to do. If the assertion that a right is absolute implies that we have a right to do whatever we wish to do, it is an absurd claim and as such should not really ever have been attributed to political theorists arguing for absolute rights. But, of course, the claim that we have a prima facie right to do whatever we wish to do is equally absurd. The right is not prima facie either, for who would claim, thinking of the right to be free, that one has a prima facie right to kill others, if one wishes, unless there are moral considerations weighing against it?

There are, however, other situations in which it is accepted by all that a person possesses rights of a certain kind, and the difficulty we face is that of according the person the right he is claiming when this will promote more evil than good. The just act is to give the man his due and giving a man what it is his right to have is giving him his due. But it is a mistake to suppose that justice is the only dimension of morality. It may be justifiable not to accord to a man his rights. But it is no less a wrong to him, no less an infringement. It is seriously misleading to turn all justifiable infringements into noninfringements by saying that the right is only prima facie, as if we have, in concluding that we should not accord a man his rights, made out a case that he had none. To use the language of 'prima facie rights' misleads, for it suggests that a presumption of the existence of a right has been overcome in these cases where all that can be said is that the presumption in favor of according a man his rights has been overcome. If we being to think the right itself is prima facie, we shall, in cases in which we are justified in not according it, fail sufficiently to bring out that we have interfered where justice says we should not. Our moral framework is unnecessarily and undesirably impoverished by the theory that there are such rights.

When I claim, then, that the right to be treated as a person is absolute what I claim is that given that one is a person, one always has the right so to be treated, and that while there may possibly be occasions morally requiring not according a person this right, this fact makes it no less true that the right exists and would be infringed if the person were not accorded it.

4. Having said something about the nature of this fundamental right I want now, in conclusion, to suggest that the denial of this right entails the denial of all moral rights and duties. This requires bringing out what is surely intuitively clear that any framework of rights and duties presupposes individuals that have the capacity to choose on the basis of reasons presented to them, and that what makes legitimate actions within such a system are the free choices of individuals. There is, in other words, a distribution of benefits and burdens in accord with a respect for the freedom of choice and freedom of action of all. I think that the best way to make this point may be to sketch some of the features of a world in which rights and duties are possessed.

First, rights exist only when there is some conception of some things valued and others not. Secondly, and implied in the first point, is the fact that there are dispositions to defend the valued commodities. Third, the valued commodities may be interfered with by others in this world. A group of animals might be said to satisfy these first three conditions. Fourth, rights exist when there are recognized rules establishing the legitimacy of some acts and ruling out others. Mistakes in the claim of right are possible. Rights imply the concepts of interference and infringement, concepts the elucidation of which requires the concept of a rule applying to the conduct of persons. Fifth, to possess a right is to possess something that constitutes a legitimate restraint on the freedom of action of others. It is clear, for example, that if individuals were incapable of controlling their actions we would have no notion of a legitimate claim that they do so. If, for example, we were all disposed to object or disposed to complain, as the elephant seal is disposed to object when his territory is invaded, then the objection would operate in a causal way, or approximating a causal way, in getting the behavior of noninterference. In a system of rights, on the other hand, there is a point to appealing to the rules in legitimating one's complaint. Implied, then, in any conception of rights are the existence of individuals capable of choosing on the basis of considerations with respect to rules. The distribution of freedom throughout such a system is determined by the free choice of individuals. Thus any denial of the right to be treated as a person would be a denial undercutting the whole system, for the system rests on the assumption that spheres of legitimate and illegitimate conduct are to be delimited with regard to the choices made by persons.

This conclusion stimulates one final reflection on the therapy world we imagined.

The denial of this fundamental right will also carry with it, ironically, the denial of the right to treatment to those who are ill. In the world as we now understand it, there are those who do wrong and who have a right to be responded to as persons who have done wrong. And there are those who have not done wrong but who are suffering from illnesses that in a variety of ways interfere with their capacity to live their lives as complete persons. These persons who are ill have a claim upon our compassion. But more than this they have, as animals do not, a right to be treated as persons. When an individual is ill he is entitled to that assistance which will make it possible for him to resume his functioning as a person. If it is an injustice to punish an innocent person, it is no less an injustice, and a far more significant one in our day, to fail to promote as best we can through adequate facilities and medical care the treatment of those who are ill. Those human beings who fill our mental institutions are entitled to more than they do in fact receive; they should be viewed as possessing the right to be treated as a person so that our responses to them may increase the likelihood that they will enjoy fully the right to be so treated. Like the child the mentally ill person has a future interest we cannot rightly deny him. Society is today sensitive to the infringement of justice in punishing the innocent; elaborate rules exist to avoid this evil. Society should be no less sensitive to the injustice of failing to bring back to the community of persons those whom it is possible to bring back.

26

RICHARD TAYLOR
Critique of Kantian Morality

RICHARD TAYLOR is professor of philosophy at the University of Rochester. He is the author of *Metaphysics* (1963), *Good and Evil* (1970), *Freedom, An-* *archy, and the Law* (1973), and other books. Professor Taylor is also an authority on bees.

It is not my intention to give any detailed exposition of Kant's ethical system. I propose instead to discuss certain of Kant's basic ideas in order to illustrate a certain approach to ethics that I think is essentially wrong. For this I could have chosen the ideas of some other modern moralist, but I prefer to illustrate my points by Kant's thought. I am doing this first because of his great fame and the reverence with which many philosophers still regard him, and secondly because it would be difficult to find any modern thinker who has carried to such an extreme the philosophical presuppositions that I am eager to repudiate. I shall, thus, use some of Kant's ideas to show how the basic ideas of morality, born originally of men's practical needs as social beings and having to do originally with men's practical relations with each other, can, under the influence of philosophy, become so detached from the world that they become pure abstractions, having no longer anything to do with morality insofar as this is a practical concern of men. Philosophical or metaphysical morals thereby ceases to have much connection with the morality that is the abiding practical concern of men and becomes, instead, a purely intellectual thing, something to contemplate and appreciate, much as one would ap- preciate a geometrical demonstration. Its vocabulary, which is the very vocabulary of everyday morals, no longer has the same meaning, but instead represents a realm of pure abstractions. Intellectually satisfying as this might be, it is nevertheless highly dangerous, for it leads men to suppose that the problems of ethics are essentially intellectual problems, that they are simply philosophical questions in need of philosophical answers. The result is that the eyes of the moralist are directed away from the world, in which moral problems are the most important problems there are, and toward a really nonexistent realm, a realm of ideas rather than things. The image of the philosophical and metaphysical moralist, who is quite lacking in any knowledge of the world and whose ideas about it are of the childish sort learned in a Sunday school, is a familiar one. He is a moralist whose dialectic is penetrating and whose reasoning is clear—he grapples with many philosophical problems of morality and has many subtle answers to philosophical difficulties—but who has little appreciation of the pain and sorrow of the world beyond the knowledge that it is there.

DUTY AND LAW

Laws, as practical rules of human invention, find no place in Kant's metaphysical morals. The Moral Law that replaces them is sundered from any practical human concerns, for it seemed to Kant that men's practical ends and their moral obligations were not only quite different things but, more often than not, were actually opposed to each other. Obligations, which were originally only relations between men arising from mutual undertakings for mutual advantage, similarly disappear from the Kantian morality, to be replaced by an abstract sort of *moral* obligation that has no connection whatsoever with any earthly good. Duties—which were originally and are still imposed by rulers on subjects, masters on servants, employers on workmen, and so on, in return for certain compensations, privileges, and rights—are replaced by Kant with Duty in the abstract. This abstract Duty is deemed by him to be the sole proper motive of moral conduct; yet, it is not a duty *to* anyone, or a duty to do any particular thing. Men have always understood the notion of one's duty to sovereign or master, and Christians well understood the idea of duty toward God. In such cases, one's duty consisted simply of compliance with commands. But in Kant's system, duties are sundered from particular commands, and Duty becomes something singular and metaphysical. We are, according to this system, to do always what Duty requires, for no other reason than that Duty does require it. Beyond a few heterogeneous examples for illustration, we never learn from Kant just what this is, save only that it is the obligation to act from respect for the Moral Law. A man must cling to life, for example, and give no thought to suicide—not because any lawgiver or God has commanded it, not because things might work out all right for him if he sticks it out a little longer, but just because Duty requires it. A man must also help others in distress; not, again, because any man or God has admonished him to, not just because they need him, or because he

cares for them, or because he wants to see their baneful condition improved—indeed, it is best that he have no such feelings at all—but just because it is his Duty.

THE GOOD WILL

It is in such terms that Kant defined the *good will*, declaring it to be the only thing in the universe that is unqualifiedly good. Now we normally think of a man of good will as one who loves his fellow men, as one whose happiness is sympathetically bound up with that of others, and as one who has a keen and constant desire to abolish the suffering around him and make the lot of his neighbor more tolerable than it might be without his helping hand. Not so for Kant. Indeed, he dismisses the actions of such persons, "so sympathetically constituted that . . . they find an inner satisfaction in spreading joy, and rejoice in the contentment of others which they have made possible," as devoid of any moral worth. Human conduct, to have any genuine moral worth, must not spring from any such amiable feelings as these; these are, after all, nothing but human feelings; they are not *moral* incentives. To have genuine moral worth, according to this moralist, our actions must spring from the sense of Duty and nothing else. And one acts dutifully if he acts, not from love or concern for his fellows, but from respect for the Moral Law.

THE CATEGORICAL IMPERATIVE

The Moral Law assumed, in Kant's thought, the form of an imperative, or command. But unlike any command that was ever before heard by any man, this one issues from no commander! Like a question that no one ever asks, or an assertion that no one ever affirms, it is a command that no God or man ever promulgates. It is promulgated by Reason. Nor is this the humble rationality of living, mortal men; it is Reason itself, again in the abstract. And unlike what one would ordinarily think of as a command, this one has no definite content. It is simply the form, Kant says, not of any actual laws, but of The Law, which is again, of course, something abstract. It has, unlike any other imperative of which one has ever heard, no purpose or end. It is not the means to the achievement of anything; and it has no relation to what anyone wants. For this reason Kant called it the Categorical Imperative, a command that is supposed to command absolutely and for its own sake. The Categorical Imperative does not bid us to act in a manner calculated to advance human well-being, for the weal and woe of men has for Kant no necessary connection with morality. It does not bid us to act as we would want others to act, for what any men want has no more bearing on morals than what they happen to feel. This Imperative does not, in fact, bid us to do anything at all, nor, indeed, even to have any generous or sympathetic motive, but only to honor some maxim or rational principle of conduct. We are, whatever we do, to act in such a manner that we could, consistently with reason, will this maxim to be a universal Law, even a Law of Nature, binding on all rational beings. Kant does not ask us to consider how other rational beings, thus bound, might feel about our maxims, for again, how anyone happens to feel about anything has no bearing on morality anyway. It is Reason that counts. It is not the living and suffering human beings who manage sometimes to be reasonable but most of the time are not. It is not men's needs and wants, or any human desires, or any practical human goods. To act immorally is to act contrary to Reason; it is to commit a sort of metaphysical blunder in the relationship between one's behavior and his generalized motive. Human needs and feelings have so little to do with this that they are not even allowed into the picture. If a man reaches forth to help the sick, the troubled, or the dying, this must not be done from any motive of compassion or sentiment of love. Such love, as a feeling, is dismissed by Kant as "pathological," because it is not prompted by that rational respect for Duty that filled Kant with such awe. Indeed, Kant thought that such human feelings as love and compassion should not even be allowed to cooperate in the performance of Duty, for we must act solely *from* Duty, and not merely *in accordance* with it. Such feelings as love, sympathy, and friendship are therefore regarded by Kant as positively dangerous. They incline men to do from sheer goodness of heart what should be done only from Reason and respect for the Moral Law. To be genuinely moral, a man must tear himself away from his inclinations as a loving human being, drown the sympathetic promptings of his heart, scorn any fruits of his efforts, think last of all of the feelings, needs, desires, and inclinations either of himself or of his fellows and, perhaps detesting what he has to do, do it anyway—solely from respect for the Law.

RATIONAL NATURE AS AN END

This Moral Law is otherwise represented by Kant as respect for Rational Nature, something that again, of course, exists only in the abstract but is, presumably, somehow exemplified in men and, Kant thought, in God. Indeed, it is the only thing in men that Kant considered worthy of a philosopher's attention. Because men are deemed to embody this Rational Nature, human nature is declared to be an End in Itself, to possess an absolute Worth, or Dignity. This kind of absolute End is not like ordinary ends or goals, something relative to the aims or purposes of any creature. It is not anything anyone wants or would be moved to try to achieve. It is, like so many of Kant's abstractions, an absolute end. And the Worth that he supposes Rational Nature to possess is no worth *for* or *to* anything; it, too, is an abstract or absolute Worth. Kant peoples a veritable utopia, which he of course does not imagine as existing, with these Ends in Themselves, and calls it the Kingdom of Ends. Ends in Themselves are, thus, not to be thought of as those men that live and toil on earth; they are not suffering, rejoicing, fumbling, living, and dying human beings; they are not men that anyone has ever seen, or would be apt to recognize as men if he did see them, or apt to like very much if he did recognize them. They are abstract things, reifications of Rational Nature, fabricated by Kant and now called Rational Beings or Ends in Themselves. Their purpose, unlike that of any creature under the sun, is not to sorrow and rejoice, not to love and hate, not to beget offspring, not to grow old and die, and not to get on as best they can to such destinies as the world has allotted them. Their purpose is just to *legislate*—to legislate morally and rationally for this rational Kingdom of Ends.

THE SIGNIFICANCE OF KANT

Kant's system thus represents the rational, logical conclusion of the natural or true morality that was begotten by the Greeks, of the absolute distinction that they drew, and that men still want to draw. This is the distinction between what *is*, or the realm of observation and science, and what *ought* to be, or the realm of obligation and morals. No one has ever suggested that Kant was irrational, and although it is doubtful that his ideas have ever had much impact on human behavior, they have had a pro-

found impact on philosophy, which has always prized reason and abstraction and tended to scorn fact. Kant's metaphysical system of morals rests on notions that are still a part of the fabric of our intellectual culture and inheritance. His greatest merit is that he was consistent. He showed men what sort of metaphysic of morals they must have—if they suppose that morality has any metaphysic, or any logic and method of its own. He showed what morality must be if we suppose it to be something rational and at the same time nonempirical or divorced from psychology, anthropology, or any science of man. That general conception of morals is, of course, still common in philosophy, and still permeates judicial thought, where it expresses itself in the ideas of guilt and desert. A man is thought to be "deserving" of punishment if he did, and could have avoided doing, something "wrong." Our basic moral presuppositions, in short, are still very much the same as Kant's, and Kant shows where they lead. We still assume, as he did, a basic dichotomy between what in fact *is* and what morally *ought* to be, between what the Greeks called convention and nature. Like the Greeks, and like Kant, we still feel a desperate need to *know* what, by nature or by some natural or rational moral principle, *ought* to be. Kant was entirely right in insisting that no knowledge of what in fact is—no knowledge of human nature, of history, of anthropology, or psychology—can yield this knowledge. But Kant did not consider, and many philosophical minds still think it somehow perverse to consider, that there may be no such knowledge—and not merely because no man has managed to attain it, but because there may really be nothing there to know in the first place. There may be no such thing as a true morality. Perhaps the basic facts of morality are, as Protagoras thought, conventions; that is, the practical formulas, some workable and some not, for enabling men to achieve whatever ideas and aspirations happen to move them. In the Kantian scheme, such considerations have nothing to do with morality, which is concerned, not with what is, but with what morally ought to be, with what is in his strange sense commanded. According to the Protagorean scheme, on the other hand, such considerations exhaust the whole subject of morals. Here we are, human beings, possessed of needs, feelings, capacities, and aims that are for the most part not of our creation but are simply part of our endowment as human beings. These are the grist, the data, and the subject matter of morals. The problem is how we get from where we are to where we want to go. It is on our answer to this question that our whole happiness and our worth as human beings depends. Our problem is not whether our answers accord with nature or even with truth. Our problem is to find those answers that do in fact work, whose fruits are sunlight, warmth, and satisfaction in our lives as we live them.

Suggestions for Further Reading

Kant's ethical writings:

> *Foundations of the Metaphysics of Morals,* translated by Lewis White Beck (Indianapolis: Bobbs-Merrill, 1959).

> *Critique of Practical Reason,* translated by Lewis White Beck (Indianapolis: Bobbs-Merrill, 1956).

> *The Metaphysical Principles of Virtue,* translated by James Ellington (Indianapolis: Bobbs-Merrill, 1964).

> *The Metaphysical Elements of Justice,* translated by John Ladd (Indianapolis: Bobbs-Merrill, 1965).

> *Lectures on Ethics,* translated by Louis Infield (New York: Harper Torchbooks, 1963).

H. B. Acton, *Kant's Moral Philosophy* (London: Macmillan, 1970). A good readable introduction to Kant's ethics. This short book is a volume in the series *New Studies in Ethics.*

W. D. Ross, *Kant's Ethical Theory* (Oxford: Clarendon Press, 1954). A critical commentary on Kant's *Foundations.* This book is more difficult than Acton's.

Marcus G. Singer, "Generalization in Ethics," *Mind,* vol. 64 (1955), pp. 361–375. This article discusses the same issue as Strang's "What if Everyone Did That?" Singer's book *Generalization in Ethics* (New York: Knopf, 1961) gives a longer treatment.

Alasdair MacIntyre, "What Morality Is Not," *Philosophy,* vol. 32 (1957), pp. 325–335. [Reprinted in G. Wallace and A. D. M. Walker (eds.), *The Definition of Morality* (London: Methuen, 1970).] MacIntyre argues that moral judgments are not necessarily universalizable.

Philippa Foot, "Morality as a System of Hypothetical Imperatives," *The Philosophical Review,* vol. 81 (1972), pp. 305–316. Mrs. Foot argues that an adequate morality may be founded entirely on hypothetical imperatives; categorical "oughts" are not necessary at all.

R. S. Downie and Elizabeth Telfer, *Respect for Persons* (London: George Allen & Unwin, 1969). The most complete treatment available of this difficult concept.

Robert Paul Wolff, ed., *Kant: Foundations of the Metaphysics of Morals Text and Critical Essays* (Indianapolis: Bobbs-Merrill, 1969). A good collection of essays on Kant's ethics by a variety of philosophers.

CHAPTER FIVE

Justice and Equality

INTRODUCTION

Suppose two people apply for a certain job: One is a white man, and the other is a black woman. The woman is actually better qualified for the job than the man, yet the man is hired—simply because the employer doesn't like blacks, and moreover, he thinks that "women have no business doing jobs that ought to be done by men." Here most of us would say not only that the employer's action was wrong, but that it was a violation of *justice* as well.

The requirement that we treat people justly is one of the basic rules of morality. The concept of justice plays an especially important part in our assessment of social institutions: Justice is, as John Rawls puts it, "the primary virtue" of social institutions and practices. If we think that a law or social policy is unjust, we may feel that it cannot be tolerated, no matter how "useful" it might be on other grounds.

The first two selections in this chapter deal with the general question of what justice is. Rawls develops a theory in "Justice as Fairness," according to which the rules of justice are those which would be accepted by rational, impartial people. A. D. Woozley approaches the problem somewhat differently in "Injustice" by considering when, and on what grounds, we would consider an act or social policy *un*just.

The next three selections deal with specific moral issues: the liberation of women, "reverse discrimination," and the treatment of nonhuman animals. In one way or another, these issues all involve the question of *equal treatment*. It is a familiar idea that we should treat all human beings as equals; it is often said that this is the fundamental rule of justice. Racism, sexism, and other discriminatory practices are unjust precisely because they do not treat all people as equals. Instead, some are treated as inherently superior to others. However, as Peter Singer points out, all people are *not* equals in intelligence, abilities, physical endowments, and so on. So what sense is there in treating everyone as equals, if they are not? The answer is that the principle of equality only requires that we treat people as equals *unless there is a relevant difference between them*. If one man is sick and another is healthy, then we need not treat them as equals when we dispense medical care, for there is a relevant difference between them. If one student has worked hard and has mastered the subject matter of a course, while another student has not worked at all and has learned nothing, we need not give them the same grade, for there is a relevant difference here also. In these cases the principle of equality is not violated, even though people are treated differently. However, if two people are given different degrees of health care, or different grades, *merely* because one is black and the other is white, this is a violation of the principle of equality, since a person's race is irrelevant to the treatment in question.

Similarly, it is a violation of the principle of equality if a person is discriminated against merely because she is female, in cases where sex is irrelevant to the treatment in question. As a result of the women's liberation movement, many males have recently become conscious of the injustices women suffer; however, the struggle for women's rights has a long history. John Stuart Mill was one of the cause's most effective spokesmen, and his analysis of "The Subjection of Women" is still very much worth considering. It is reprinted here in part.

The question of what we may do to remedy past injustices raises some difficult problems. What if a group of citizens is unfairly discriminated against over a long period of time, until they come to occupy the lowest economic and social positions in the society—is it then permissible to practice "reverse discrimination" in order to correct this situation? For example, suppose blacks have been discriminated against and one result is that there are relatively few black lawyers. Moreover, because of the generally prejudiced situation, it is much harder for a black person to qualify for admission to the law schools. Is it then permissible to establish quotas in the law schools and to guarantee admission for a certain number of black applicants, even if it means turning down some better-qualified whites, as a means to correcting the unjust situation? This, of course, is not merely a theoretical question; it is a practical problem now being faced all over the United States. Some argue that such "reverse discrimination" is necessary to counteract the effects of past racism and sexism; others argue that it is just as unfair to accept an applicant because she is black or female as it is to reject the applicant because she is black or female. Thomas Nagel discusses this issue in "Equal Treatment and Compensatory Discrimination."

Finally, in "All Animals Are Equal," Peter Singer argues that the principle of equal treatment should not be restricted only to human beings. Singer makes a powerful case for reassessing all our attitudes toward nonhuman animals, and in doing so he brings out important aspects of the idea of equality.

27

JOHN RAWLS
Justice as Fairness

1. It might seem at first sight that the concepts of justice and fairness are the same, and that there is no reason to distinguish them, or to say that one is more fundamental than the other.[1] I think that this impression is mistaken. In this paper I wish to show that the fundamental idea in the concept of justice is fairness; and I wish to offer an analysis of the concept of justice from this point of view. To bring out the force of this claim, and the analysis based upon it, I shall then argue that it is this aspect of justice for which utilitarianism, in its classical form, is unable to account, but which is expressed, even if misleadingly, by the idea of the social contract.

From John Rawls, "Justice as Fairness," *The Philosophical Review*, vol. 67 (1958), pp. 164–194. Reprinted by permission of the author and the editors of *The Philosophical Review*. This article is reprinted unabridged.

1. An abbreviated version of this paper (less than one-half the length) was presented in a symposium with the same title at the American Philosophical Association, Eastern Division, December 28, 1957, and appeared in the *Journal of Philosophy*, LIV, 653–662.

To start with I shall develop a particular conception of justice by stating and commenting upon two principles which specify it, and by considering the circumstances and conditions under which they may be thought to arise. The principles defining this conception, and the conception itself, are, of course, familiar. It may be possible, however, by using the notion of fairness as a framework, to assemble and to look at them in a new way. Before stating this conception, however, the following preliminary matters should be kept in mind.

Throughout I consider justice only as a virtue of social institutions, or what I shall call practices.[2] The principles of justice are regarded as formulating restrictions as to how practices may define positions and offices, and assign thereto powers and liabilities, rights and duties. Justice as a virtue of particular actions or of persons I do not take up at all. It is important to distinguish these various subjects of justice, since the meaning of the concept varies according to whether it is applied to practices, particular actions, or persons. These meanings are, indeed, connected, but they are not identical. I shall confine my discussion to the sense of justice as applied to practices, since this sense is the basic one. Once it is understood, the other senses should go quite easily.

Justice is to be understood in its customary sense as representing but *one* of the many virtues of social institutions, for these may be antiquated, inefficient, degrading, or any number of other things, without being unjust. Justice is not to be confused with an all-inclusive vision of a good society; it is only one part of any such conception. It is important, for example, to distinguish that sense of equality which is an aspect of the concept of justice from that sense of equality which belongs to a more comprehensive social ideal. There may well be inequalities which one concedes are just, or at least not unjust, but which, nevertheless, one wishes, on other grounds, to do away with. I shall focus attention, then, on the usual sense of justice in which it is essentially the elimination of arbitrary distinctions and the establishment, within the structure of a practice, of a proper balance between competing claims.

Finally, there is no need to consider the principles discussed below as *the* principles of justice. For the moment it is sufficient that they are typical of a family of principles normally associated with the concept of justice. The way in which the principles of this family resemble one another, as shown by the background against which they may be thought to arise, will be made clear by the whole of the subsequent argument.

2. The conception of justice which I want to develop may be stated in the form of two principles as follows: First, each person participating in a practice, or affected by it, has an equal right to the most extensive liberty compatible with a like liberty for all; and second, inequalities are arbitrary unless it is reasonable to expect that they will work out for everyone's advantage, and provided the positions and offices to which they attach, or from which they may be gained, are open to all. These principles express justice as a complex of three

2. I use the word "practice" throughout as a sort of technical term meaning any form of activity specified by a system of rules which defines offices, roles, moves, penalties, defenses, and so on, and which gives the activity its structure. As examples one may think of games and rituals, trials and parliaments, markets and systems of property. I have attempted a partial analysis of the notion of a practice in a paper "Two Concepts of Rules," *Philosophical Review*, LXIV (1955), 3–32.

ideas: liberty, equality, and reward for services contributing to the common good.[3]

The term "person" is to be construed variously depending on the circumstances. On some occasions it will mean human individuals, but in others it may refer to nations, provinces, business firms, churches, teams, and so on. The principles of justice apply in all these instances, although there is a certain logical priority to the case of human individuals. As I shall use the term "person," it will be ambiguous in the manner indicated.

The first principle holds, of course, only if other things are equal: that is, while there must always be a justification for departing from the initial position of equal liberty (which is defined by the patterns of rights and duties, powers and liabilities, established by a practice), and the burden of proof is placed on him who would depart from it, nevertheless, there can be, and often there is, a justification for doing so. Now, that similar particular cases, as defined by a practice, should be treated similarly as they arise, is part of the very concept of a practice; it is involved in the notion of an activity in accordance with rules.[4] The first principle expresses an analogous conception, but as applied to the structure of practices themselves. It holds, for example, that there is a presumption against the distinctions and classifications made by legal systems and other

practices to the extent that they infringe on the original and equal liberty of the persons participating in them. The second principle defines how this presumption may be rebutted.

It might be argued at this point that justice requires only an equal liberty. If, however, a greater liberty were possible for all without loss or conflict, then it would be irrational to settle on a lesser liberty. There is no reason for circumscribing rights unless their exercise would be incompatible, or would render the practice defining them less effective. Therefore no serious distortion of the concept of justice is likely to follow from including within it the concept of the greatest equal liberty.

The second principle defines what sorts of inequalities are permissible; it specifies how the presumption laid down by the first principle may be put aside. Now by inequalities it is best to understand not *any* differences between offices and positions, but differences in the benefits and burdens attached to them either directly or indirectly, such as prestige and wealth, or liability to taxation and compulsory services. Players in a game do not protest against there being different positions, such as batter, pitcher, catcher, and the like, nor to there being various privileges and powers as specified by the rules; nor do the citizens of a country object to there being the different offices of government such as president, senator, gover-

---

3. These principles are, of course, well-known in one form or another and appear in many analyses of justice even where the writers differ widely on other matters. Thus if the principle of equal liberty is commonly associated with Kant (see *The Philosophy of Law*, tr. by W. Hastie, Edinburgh, 1887, pp. 56 f.), it may be claimed that it can also be found in J. S. Mill's *On Liberty* and elsewhere, and in many other liberal writers. Recently H. L. A. Hart has argued for something like it in his paper "Are There Any Natural Rights?," *Philosophical Review*, LXIV (1955), 175–191. The injustice of inequalities which are not won in return for a contribution to the

common advantage is, of course, widespread in political writings of all sorts. The conception of justice here discussed is distinctive, if at all, only in selecting these two principles in this form; but for another similar analysis, see the discussion by W. D. Lamont, *The Principles of Moral Judgment* (Oxford, 1946), ch. v.

4. This point was made by Sidgwick, *Methods of Ethics*, 6th ed. (London, 1901), Bk. III, ch. v, sec. 1. It has recently been emphasized by Sir Isaiah Berlin in a symposium, "Equality," *Proceedings of the Aristotelian Society*, n.s. LVI (1955–56), 305 f.

nor, judge, and so on, each with their special rights and duties. It is not differences of this kind that are normally thought of as inequalities, but differences in the resulting distribution established by a practice, or made possible by it, of the things men strive to attain or avoid. Thus they may complain about the pattern of honors and rewards set up by a practice (for example, the privileges and salaries of government officials) or they may object to the distribution of power and wealth which results from the various ways in which men avail themselves of the opportunities allowed by it (for example, the concentration of wealth which may develop in a free price system allowing large entrepreneurial or speculative gains).

It should be noted that the second principle holds that an inequality is allowed only if there is reason to believe that the practice with the inequality, or resulting in it, will work for the advantage of *every* party engaging in it. Here it is important to stress that *every* party must gain from the inequality. Since the principle applies to practices, it implies that the representative man in every office or position defined by a practice, when he views it as a going concern, must find it reasonable to prefer his condition and prospects with the inequality to what they would be under the practice without it. The principle excludes, therefore, the justification of inequalities on the grounds that the disadvantages of those in one position are outweighed by the greater advantages of those in another position. This rather simple restriction is the main modification I wish to make in the utilitarian principle as usually understood. When coupled with the notion of a practice, it is a restriction of consequence[5], and one which some utilitarians, for example, Hume and Mill, have used in their discussions of justice without realizing apparently its significance, or at least without calling attention to it.[6] Why it is a significant modification of principle, changing one's conception of justice

5. In the paper referred to above, footnote 2, I have tried to show the importance of taking practices as the proper subject of the utilitarian principle. The criticisms of so-called "restricted utilitarianism" by J. J. C. Smart, "Extreme and Restricted Utilitarianism," *Philosophical Quarterly*, VI (1956), 344–354, and by H. J. McCloskey, "An Examination of Restricted Utilitarianism," *Philosophical Review*, LXVI (1957), 466–485, do not affect my argument. These papers are concerned with the very general proposition, which is attributed (with what justice I shall not consider) to S. E. Toulmin and P. H. Nowell-Smith (and in the case of the latter paper, also, apparently, to me); namely, the proposition that particular moral actions are justified by appealing to moral rules, and moral rules in turn by reference to utility. But clearly I meant to defend no such view. My discussion of the concept of rules as maxims is an explicit rejection of it. What I did argue was that, in the *logically special* case of practices (although actually quite a common case) where the rules have special features and are not moral rules at all but legal rules or rules of games and the like (except, perhaps, in the case of promises), there is a peculiar force to the distinction between justifying particular actions and justifying the system of rules themselves. Even then I claimed only that restricting the utilitarian principle to practices as defined strengthened it. I did not argue for the position that this amendment alone is sufficient for a complete defense of utilitarianism as a general theory of morals. In this paper I take up the question as to how the utilitarian principle itself must be modified, but here, too, the subject of inquiry is not all of morality at once, but a limited topic, the concept of justice.

6. It might seem as if J. S. Mill, in paragraph 36 of Chapter v of *Utilitarianism*, expressed the utilitarian principle in this modified form, but in the remaining two paragraphs of the chapter, and elsewhere, he would appear not to grasp the significance of the change. Hume often emphasizes that *every* man must benefit. For example, in discussing the utility of general rules, he holds that they are requisite to the "well-being of every individual"; from a stable system of property "every individual person must find himself a gainer in balancing the account. . . ." "Every member of society is sensible of this interest; everyone expresses this sense to his fellows along with the resolution he has taken of squaring his actions by it, on the conditions that others will do the same." *A Treatise of Human Nature*, Bk. III, Pt. II, Section II, paragraph 22.

238 · Justice and Equality

entirely, the whole of my argument will show.

Further, it is also necessary that the various offices to which special benefits or burdens attach are open to all. It may be, for example, to the common advantage, as just defined, to attach special benefits to certain offices. Perhaps by doing so the requisite talent can be attracted to them and encouraged to give its best efforts. But any offices having special benefits must be won in a fair competition in which contestants are judged on their merits. If some offices were not open, those excluded would normally be justified in feeling unjustly treated, even if they benefited from the greater efforts of those who were allowed to compete for them. Now if one can assume that offices are open, it is necessary only to consider the design of practices themselves and how they jointly, as a system, work together. It will be a mistake to focus attention on the varying relative positions of particular persons, who may be known to us by their proper names, and to require that each such change, as a once for all transaction viewed in isolation, must be in itself just. It is the system of practices which is to be judged, and judged from a general point of view: Unless one is prepared to criticize it from the standpoint of a representative man holding some particular office, one has no complaint against it.

3. Given these principles one might try to derive them from a priori principles of reason, or claim that they were known by intuition. These are familiar enough steps and, at least in the case of the first principle, might be made with some success. Usually, however, such arguments, made at this point, are unconvincing. They are not likely to lead to an understanding of the basis of the principles of justice, not at least as prin-

ciples of justice. I wish, therefore, to look at the principles in a different way.

Imagine a society of persons amongst whom a certain system of practices is *already* well established. Now suppose that by and large they are mutually self-interested; their allegiance to their established practices is normally founded on the prospect of self-advantage. One need not assume that, in all senses of the term "person," the persons in this society are mutually self-interested. If the characterization as mutually self-interested applies when the line of division is the family, it may still be true that members of families are bound by ties of sentiment and affection and willingly acknowledge duties in contradiction to self-interest. Mutual self-interestedness in the relations between families, nations, churches, and the like, is commonly associated with intense loyalty and devotion on the part of individual members. Therefore, one can form a more realistic conception of this society if one thinks of it as consisting of mutually self-interested families, or some other association. Further, it is not necessary to suppose that these persons are mutually self-interested under all circumstances, but only in the usual situations in which they participate in their common practices.

Now suppose also that these persons are rational: They know their own interests more or less accurately; they are capable of tracing out the likely consequences of adopting one practice rather than another; they are capable of adhering to a course of action once they have decided upon it; they can resist present temptations and the enticements of immediate gain; and the bare knowledge or perception of the difference between their condition and that of others is not, within certain limits and in itself, a source of great dissatisfaction. Only the last point adds anything to the usual definition of rationality. This definition should allow, I think, for the idea that a rational man would not be greatly downcast from knowing, or seeing, that others are in a better position than himself, unless he thought their being so was the result of injustice, or the consequence of letting chance work itself out for no useful common purpose, and so on. So if these persons strike us as unpleasantly egoistic, they are at least free in some degree from the fault of envy.[7]

Finally, assume that these persons have roughly similar needs and interests, or needs and interests in various ways complementary, so that fruitful cooperation amongst them is possible; and suppose that they are sufficiently equal in power and ability to guarantee that in normal circumstances none is able to dominate the others. This condition (as well as the others) may seem excessively vague; but in view of the conception of justice to which the argument leads, there seems no reason for making it more exact here.

Since these persons are conceived as engaging in their common practices, which are already established, there is no question of our supposing them to come together to deliberate as to how they will set these practices up for the first time. Yet we can imagine that from time to time they discuss with one another whether any of them has a legitimate complaint against their established institutions. Such discussions are perfectly natural in any normal society. Now suppose that they have settled on doing this in the following way. They first try to arrive at the principles by which complaints, and so practices themselves, are to be judged. Their procedure for this is to let each person propose the principles upon which he wishes his complaints to be tried with the understanding that, if acknowl-

edged, the complaints of others will be similarly tried, and that no complaints will be heard at all until everyone is roughly of one mind as to how complaints are to be judged. They each understand further that the principles proposed and acknowledged on this occasion are binding on future occasions. Thus each will be wary of proposing a principle which would give him a peculiar advantage, in his present circumstances, supposing it to be accepted. Each person knows that he will be bound by it in future circumstances the peculiarities of which cannot be known, and which might well be such that the principle is then to his disadvantage. The idea is that everyone should be required to make *in advance* a firm commitment, which others also may reasonably be expected to make, and that no one be given the opportunity to tailor the canons of a legitimate complaint to fit his own special condition, and then to discard them when they no longer suit his purpose. Hence each person will propose principles of a general kind which will, to a large degree, gain their sense from the various applications to be made of them, the particular circumstances of which being as yet unknown. These principles will express the conditions in accordance with which each is the least unwilling to have his interests limited in the design of practices, given the competing interests of the others, on the supposition that the interests of others will be limited likewise. The restrictions which

7. It is not possible to discuss here this addition to the usual conception of rationality. If it seems peculiar, it may be worth remarking that it is analogous to the modification of the utilitarian principle which the argument as a whole is designed to explain and justify. In the same way that the satisfaction of interests, the representative claims of which violate the principles of justice, is not a reason for having a practice (see sec. 7), unfounded envy, within limits, need not to be taken into account.

would so arise might be thought of as those a person would keep in mind if he were designing a practice in which his enemy were to assign him his place.

The two main parts of this conjectural account have a definite significance. The character and respective situations of the parties reflect the typical circumstances in which questions of justice arise. The procedure whereby principles are proposed and acknowledged represents constraints, analogous to those of having a morality, whereby rational and mutually self-interested persons are brought to act reasonably. Thus the first part reflects the fact that questions of justice arise when conflicting claims are made upon the design of a practice and where it is taken for granted that each person will insist, as far as possible, on what he considers his rights. It is typical of cases of justice to involve persons who are pressing on one another their claims, between which a fair balance or equilibrium must be found. On the other hand, as expressed by the second part, having a morality must at least imply the acknowledgment of principles as impartially applying to one's own conduct as well as to another's, and moreover principles which may constitute a constraint, or limitation, upon the pursuit of one's own interests. There are, of course, other aspects of having a morality: The acknowledgment of moral principles must show itself in accepting a reference to them as reasons for limiting one's claims, in acknowledging the burden of providing a special explanation, or excuse, when one acts contrary to them, or else in showing shame and remorse and a desire to make amends, and so on. It is sufficient to remark here that having a morality is analogous to having made a firm commitment in advance; for one must acknowledge the princi-

ples of morality even when to one's disadvantage.[8] A man whose moral judgments always coincide with his interests could be suspected of having no morality at all.

Thus the two parts of the foregoing account are intended to mirror the kinds of circumstances in which questions of justice arise and the constraints which having a morality would impose upon persons so situated. In this way one can see how the acceptance of the principles of justice might come about, for given all these conditions as described, it would be natural if the two principles of justice were to be acknowledged. Since there is no way for anyone to win special advantages for himself, each might consider it reasonable to acknowledge equality as an initial principle. There is, however, no reason why they should regard this position as final; for if there are inequalities which satisfy the second principle, the immediate gain which equality would allow can be considered as intelligently invested in view of its future return. If, as is quite likely, these inequalities work as incentives to draw out better efforts, the members of this society may look upon them as concessions to human nature: They, like us, may think that people ideally should want to serve one another. But as they are mutually self-interested, their acceptance of these inequalities is merely the acceptance of the relations in which they actually stand, and a recognition of

8. The idea that accepting a principle as a moral principle implies that one generally acts on it, failing a special explanation, has been stressed by R. M. Hare, *The Language of Morals* (Oxford, 1952). His formulation of it needs to be modified, however, along the lines suggested by P. L. Gardiner, "On Assenting to a Moral Principle," *Proceedings of the Aristotelian Society*, n.s. LV (1955), 23–44. See also C. K. Grant, "Akrasia and the Criteria of Assent to Practical Principles," *Mind*, LXV (1956), 400–407, where the complexity of the criteria for assent is discussed.

the motives which lead them to engage in their common practices. *They* have no title to complain of one another. And so provided that the conditions of the principle are met, there is no reason why they should not allow such inequalities. Indeed, it would be short-sighted of them to do so, and could result, in most cases, only from their being dejected by the bare knowledge, or perception, that others are better situated. Each person will, however, insist on an advantage to himself, and so on a common advantage, for none is willing to sacrifice anything for the others.

These remarks are not offered as a proof that persons so conceived and circumstanced would settle on the two principles, but only to show that these principles could have such a background, and so can be viewed as those principles which mutually self-interested and rational persons, when similarly situated and required to make in advance a firm commitment, could acknowledge as restrictions governing the assignment of rights and duties in their common practices, and thereby accept as limiting their rights against one another. The principles of justice

may, then, be regarded as those principles which arise when the constraints of having a morality are imposed upon parties in the typical circumstances of justice.

4. These ideas are, of course, connected with a familiar way of thinking about justice which goes back at least to the Greek Sophists, and which regards the acceptance of the principles of justice as a compromise between persons of roughly equal power who would enforce their will on each other if they could, but who, in view of the equality of forces amongst them and for the sake of their own peace and security, acknowledge certain forms of conduct insofar as prudence seems to require. Justice is thought of as a pact between rational egoists the stability of which is dependent on a balance of power and a similarity of circumstances.[9] While the previous account is connected with this tradition, and with its most recent variant, the theory of games,[10] it differs from it in several important respects which, to forestall misinterpretations, I will set out here.

First, I wish to use the previous conjectural account of the background of

9. Perhaps the best known statement of this conception is that given by Glaucon at the beginning of Book II of Plato's *Republic.* Presumably it was in various forms, a common view among the Sophists; but that Plato gives a fair representation of it is doubtful. See K. R. Popper, *The Open Society and Its Enemies,* rev. ed. (Princeton, 1950), pp. 112–118. Certainly Plato usually attributes to it a quality of manic egoism which one feels must be an exaggeration; on the other hand, see the Melian Debate in Thucydides, *The Peloponnesian War,* Book V, ch. VII, although it is impossible to say to what extent the views expressed there reveal any current philosophical opinion. Also in this tradition are the remarks of Epicurus on justice in *Principal Doctrines,* XXXI-XXXVIII. In modern times elements of the conception appear in a more sophisticated form in Hobbes *The Leviathan* and in Hume *A Treatise of Human Nature,* Book III, Pt. II, as well as in the

writings of the school of natural law such as Pufendorf's *De jure naturae et gentium.* Hobbes and Hume are especially instructive. For Hobbes's argument see Howard Warrender's *The Political Philosophy of Hobbes* (Oxford, 1957). W. J. Baumol's *Welfare Economics and the Theory of the State* (London, 1952), is valuable in showing the wide applicability of Hobbes's fundamental idea (interpreting his natural law as principles of prudence), although in this book it is traced back only to Hume's *Treatise.*

10. See J. von Neumann and O. Morgenstern, *The Theory of Games and Economic Behavior,* 2nd ed. (Princeton, 1947). For a comprehensive and not too technical discussion of the developments since, see R. Duncan Luce and Howard Raiffa, *Games and Decisions: Introduction and Critical Survey* (New York, 1957). Chs. VI and XIV discuss the developments most obviously related to the analysis of justice.

justice as a way of analyzing the concept. I do not want, therefore, to be interpreted as assuming a general theory of human motivation: When I suppose that the parties are mutually self-interested, and are not willing to have their (substantial) interests sacrificed to others, I am referring to their conduct and motives as they are taken for granted in cases where questions of justice ordinarily arise. Justice is the virtue of practices where there are assumed to be competing interests and conflicting claims, and where it is supposed that persons will press their rights on each other. That persons are mutually self-interested in certain situations and for certain purposes is what gives rise to the question of justice in practices covering those circumstances. Amongst an association of saints, if such a community could really exist, the disputes about justice could hardly occur; for they would all work selflessly together for one end, the glory of God as defined by their common religion, and reference to this end would settle every question of right. The justice of practices does not come up until there are several different parties (whether we think of these as individuals, associations, or nations and so on, is irrelevant) who do press their claims on one another, and who do regard themselves as representatives of interests which deserve to be considered. Thus the previous account involves no general theory of human motivation. Its intent is simply to incorporate into the conception of justice the relations of men to one another which set the stage for questions of justice. It makes no difference how wide or general these relations are, as this matter does not bear on the analysis of the concept.

Again, in contrast to the various conceptions of the social contract, the several parties do not establish any particular society or practice; they do not covenant to obey a particular sovereign body or to accept a given constitution.[11] Nor do they, as in the theory of games (in certain respects a marvelously sophisticated development of this tradition), decide on individual strategies adjusted to their respective circumstances in the game. What the parties do is to *jointly* acknowledge certain *principles* of appraisal relating to their common *practices* either as already established or merely proposed. They accede to standards of judgment, not to a given practice; they do not make any specific agreement, or bargain, or adopt a particular strategy. The subject of their acknowledgment of certain principles of judgment, fulfilling certain general conditions, to be used in criticizing the arrangement of their common affairs. The relations of mutual self-interest between the parties who are similarly circumstanced mirror the conditions under which questions of justice arise, and the procedure by which the principles of judgment are proposed and acknowledged reflects the contraints of having a morality. Each aspect, then, of the preceding hypothetical account serves the purpose of bringing out a feature of the notion of justice. One could, if one liked, view the principles of justice as the "solution" of this highest order "game" of adopting, subject to the procedure described, principles of argument for all coming particular "games" whose peculiarities one can in no way foresee. But this comparison, while no doubt helpful, must not obscure the fact that this highest order "game" is of a special

11. For a general survey see J. W. Gough, *The Social Contract*, 2nd ed. (Oxford, 1957), and Otto von Gierke, *The Development of Political Theory*, tr. by B. Freyd (London, 1939), Pt. II, ch. II.

sort.[12] Its significance is that its various pieces represent aspects of the concept of justice.

Finally, I do not, of course, conceive the several parties as necessarily coming together to establish their common practices for the first time. Some institutions may, indeed, be set up *de novo*; but I have framed the preceding account so that it will apply when the full complement of social institutions already exists and represents the result of a long period of development. Nor is the account in any way fictitious. In any society where people reflect on their institutions they will have an idea of what principles of justice would be acknowledged under the conditions described, and there will be occasions when questions of justice are actually discussed in this way. Therefore if their practices do not accord with these principles, this will affect the quality of their social relations. For in this case there will be some recognized situations wherein the parties are mutually aware

that one of them is being forced to accept what the other would concede is unjust. The foregoing analysis may then be thought of as representing the actual quality of relations between persons as defined by practices accepted as just. In such practices the parties will acknowledge the principles on which it is constructed, and the general recognition of this fact shows itself in the absence of resentment and in the sense of being justly treated. Thus one common objection to the theory of the social contract, its apparently historical and fictitious character, is avoided.

5. That the principles of justice may be regarded as arising in the manner described illustrates an important fact about them. Not only does it bring out the idea that justice is a primitive moral notion in that it arises once the concept of morality is imposed on mutually self-interested agents similarly circumstanced, but it emphasizes that, fundamental to justice, is the concept of fairness which relates to right dealing

12. The difficulty one gets into by a mechanical application of the theory of games to moral philosophy can be brought out by considering among several possible examples, R. B. Braithwaite's study, *Theory of Games as a Tool for the Moral Philosopher* (Cambridge, 1955). On the analysis there given, it turns out that the fair division of playing time between Matthew and Luke depends on their preferences, and these in turn are connected with the instruments they wish to play. Since Matthew has a threat advantage over Luke, arising purely from the fact that Matthew, the trumpeter, prefers both of them playing at once to neither of them playing, whereas Luke, the pianist, prefers silence to cacophony, Matthew is alloted 26 evenings of play to Luke's 17. If the situation were reversed, the threat advantage would be with Luke. See pp. 36 f. But now we have only to suppose that Matthew is a jazz enthusiast who plays the drums, and Luke a violinist who plays sonatas, in which case it will be fair, on this analysis, for Matthew to play whenever and as often as he likes, assuming, of course, as it is plausible to assume, that he does not care whether Luke plays or not. Certainly something has gone wrong. To each according to

his threat advantage is hardly the principle of fairness. What is lacking is the concept of morality, and it must be brought into the conjectural account in some way or other. In the text this is done by the form of the procedure whereby principles are proposed and acknowledged (Section 3). If one starts directly with the particular case as known, and if one accepts as given and definite the preferences and relative positions of the parties, whatever they are, it is impossible to give an analysis of the moral concept of fairness. Braithwaite's use of the theory of games, insofar as it is intended to analyze the concept of fairness, is, I think, mistaken. This is not, of course, to criticize in any way the theory of games as a mathematical theory, to which Braithwaite's book certainly contributes, nor as an analysis of how rational (and amoral) egoists might behave (and so as an analysis of how people sometimes actually do behave). But it is to say that if the theory of games is to be used to analyze moral concepts, its formal structure must be interpreted in a special and general manner as indicated in the text. Once we do this, though, we are in touch again with a much older tradition.

between persons who are cooperating with or competing against one another, as when one speaks of fair games, fair competition, and fair bargains. The question of fairness arises when free persons, who have no authority over one another, are engaging in a joint activity and amongst themselves settling or acknowledging the rules which define it and which determine the respective shares in its benefits and burdens. A practice will strike the parties as fair if none feels that, by participating in it, they or any of the others are taken advantage of, or forced to give in to claims which they do not regard as legitimate. This implies that each has a conception of legitimate claims which he thinks it reasonable for others as well as himself to acknowledge. If one thinks of the principles of justice as arising in the manner described, then they do define this sort of conception. A practice is just or fair, then, when it satisfies the principles which those who participate in it could propose to one another for mutual acceptance under the afore-mentioned circumstances. Persons engaged in a just, or fair, practice can face one another openly and support their respective positions, should they appear questionable, by reference to principles which it is reasonable to expect each to accept.

It is this notion of the possibility of mutual acknowledgment of principles by free persons who have no authority over one another which makes the concept of fairness fundamental to justice. Only if such acknowledgment is possible can there be true community between persons in their common practices; otherwise their relations will appear to them as founded to some extent on force. If, in ordinary speech, fairness applies more particularly to practices in which there is a choice

whether to engage or not (for example, in games, business competition), and justice to practices in which there is no choice (for example, in slavery), the element of necessity does not render the conception of mutual acknowledgment inapplicable, although it may make it much more urgent to change unjust than unfair institutions. For one activity in which one can always engage is that of proposing and acknowledging principles to one another supposing each to be similarly circumstanced; and to judge practices by the principles so arrived at is to apply the standard of fairness to them.

Now if the participants in a practice accept its rules as fair, and so have no complaint to lodge against it, there arises a prima facie duty (and a corresponding prima facie right) of the parties to each other to act in accordance with the practice when it falls upon them to comply. When any number of persons engage in a practice, or conduct a joint undertaking according to rules, and thus restrict their liberty, those who have submitted to these restrictions when required have the right to a similar acquiescence on the part of those who have benefited by their submission. These conditions will obtain if a practice is correctly acknowledged to be fair, for in this case all who participate in it will benefit from it. The rights and duties so arising are special rights and duties in that they depend on previous actions voluntarily undertaken, in this case on the parties having engaged in a common practice and knowingly accepted its benefits.[13] It is not, however, an obligation which

13. For the definition of this prima facie duty, and the idea that it is a special duty, I am indebted to H. L. A. Hart. See his paper "Are There Any Natural Rights?," *Philosophical Review*, LXIV (1955), 185 f.

presupposes a deliberate performative act in the sense of a promise, or contract, and the like.[14] An unfortunate mistake of proponents of the idea of the social contract was to suppose that political obligation does require some such act, or at least to use language which suggests it. It is sufficient that one has knowingly participated in and accepted the benefits of a practice acknowledged to be fair. This prima facie obligation may, of course, be overridden: It may happen, when it comes one's turn to follow a rule, that other considerations will justify not doing so. But one cannot, in general, be released from this obligation by denying the justice of the practice only when it falls on one to obey. If a person rejects a practice, he should, so far as possible, declare his intention in advance, and avoid participating in it or enjoying its benefits.

This duty I have called that of fair play, but it should be admitted that to refer to it in this way is, perhaps, to extend the ordinary notion of fairness. Usually acting unfairly is not so much the breaking of any particular rule, even if the infraction is difficult to detect (cheating), but taking advantage of loop-holes or ambiguities in rules, availing oneself of unexpected or special circumstances which make it impossible to enforce them, insisting that rules be enforced to one's advantage when they should be suspended, and more generally, acting contrary to the intention of a practice. It is for this reason that one speaks of the sense of fair play: Acting fairly requires more than simply being able to follow rules; what is fair must often be felt, or perceived, one wants to say. It is not, however, an unnatural extension of the duty of fair play to have it include the obligation which participants who have knowingly accepted the benefits of their common practice owe to each other to act in accordance with it when their performance falls due; for it is usually considered unfair if someone accepts the benefits of a practice but refuses to do his part in maintaining it. Thus one might say of the tax-dodger that he violates the duty of fair play: He accepts the benefits of government but will not do his part in releasing resources to it; and members of labor unions often say that fellow workers who refuse to join are being unfair: They refer to them as "free riders," as persons who enjoy what are the supposed benefits of unionism, higher wages, shorter hours, job security, and the like, but who refuse to share in its burdens in the form of paying dues, and so on.

The duty of fair play stands beside other prima facie duties such as fidelity and gratitude as a basic moral notion; yet it is not to be confused with them.[15] These duties are all clearly distinct, as would be obvious from their definitions. As with any moral duty, that of fair play implies a constraint on self-interest in particular cases; on occasion it enjoins

---

14. The sense of "performative" here is to be derived from J. L. Austin's paper in the symposium, "Other Minds," *Proceedings of the Aristotelian Society*, Supplementary Volume (1946), pp. 170–174.

15. This, however, commonly happens. Hobbes, for example, when invoking the notion of a "tacit covenant," appeals not to the natural law that promises should be kept but to his fourth law of nature, that of gratitude. On Hobbes's shift from fidelity to gratitude, see Warrender, *op. cit.*, pp. 51–52, 233–237. While it is not a serious criticism of Hobbes, it would have improved his argument had he appealed to the duty of fair play. On his premises he is perfectly entitled to do so. Similarly Sidgwick thought that a principle of justice, such as every man ought to receive adequate requital for his labor, is like gratitude universalized. See *Methods of Ethics*, Bk. III, ch. v, Sec. 5. There is a gap in the stock of moral concepts used by philosophers into which the concept of the duty of fair play fits quite naturally.

conduct which a rational egoist strictly defined would not decide upon. So while justice does not require of anyone that he sacrifice his interests in that *general position* and procedure whereby the principles of justice are proposed and acknowledged, it may happen that in particular situations, arising in the context of engaging in a practice, the duty of fair play will often cross his interests in the sense that he will be required to forego particular advantages which the peculiarities of his circumstances might permit him to take. There is, of course, nothing surprising in this. It is simply the consequence of the firm commitment which the parties may be supposed to have made, or which they would make, in the general position, together with the fact that they have participated in and accepted the benefits of a practice which they regard as fair.

Now the acknowledgment of this constraint in particular cases, which is manifested in acting fairly or wishing to make amends, feeling ashamed, and the like, when one has evaded it, is one of the forms of conduct by which participants in a common practice exhibit their recognition of each other as persons with similar interests and capacities. In the same way that, failing a special explanation, the criterion for the recognition of suffering is helping one who suffers, acknowledging the duty of fair play is a necessary part of the criterion for recognizing another as a person with similar interests and feelings as oneself.[16] A person who never under any circumstances showed a wish to help others in pain would show, at the same time, that he did not recognize that they were in pain; nor could he have any feelings of affection or friendship for anyone; for having these feelings implies, failing special

circumstances, that he comes to their aid when they are suffering. Recognition that another is a person in pain shows itself in sympathetic action; this primitive natural response of compassion is one of those responses upon which the various forms of moral conduct are built.

Similarly, the acceptance of the duty of fair play by participants in a common practice is a reflection in each person of the recognition of the aspirations and interests of the others to be realized by their joint activity. Failing a special explanation, their acceptance of it is a necessary part of the criterion for their recognizing one another as persons with similar interests and capacities, as the conception of their relations in the general position supposes them to be. Otherwise they would show no recognition of one another as persons with similar capacities and interests, and indeed, in some cases perhaps hypothetical, they would not recognize one another as persons at all, but as complicated objects involved in a complicated activity. To recognize another as a person one must respond to him and act towards him in certain ways; and these ways are intimately connected with the various prima facie duties. Acknowledging these duties in *some* degree, and so having the elements of morality, is not a matter of choice, or of intuiting moral qualities,

16. I am using the concept of criterion here in what I take to be Wittgenstein's sense. See *Philosophical Investigations*, (Oxford, 1953); and Norman Malcolm's review, "Wittgenstein's *Philosophical Investigations*," *Philosophical Review*, LXIII (1954), 543–547. That the response of compassion, under appropriate circumstances, is part of the criterion for whether or not a person understands what "pain" means, is, I think, in the *Philosophical Investigations*. The view in the text is simply an extension of this idea. I cannot, however, attempt to justify it here. Similar thoughts are to be found, I think, in Max Scheler, *The Nature of Sympathy*, tr. by Peter Heath (New Haven, 1954). His way of writing is often so obscure that I cannot be certain.

or a matter of the expression of feelings or attitudes (the three interpretations between which philosophical opinion frequently oscillates); it is simply the possession of one of the forms of conduct in which the recognition of others as persons is manifested.

These remarks are unhappily obscure. Their main purpose here, however, is to forestall, together with the remarks in Section 4, the misinterpretation that, on the view presented, the acceptance of justice and the acknowledgment of the duty of fair play depends in every day life solely on there being a *de facto* balance of forces between the parties. It would indeed be foolish to underestimate the importance of such a balance in securing justice; but it is not the only basis thereof. The recognition of one another as persons with similar interests and capacities engaged in a common practice must, failing a special explanation, show itself in the acceptance of the principles of justice and the acknowledgment of the duty of fair play.

The conception at which we have arrived, then, is that the principles of justice may be thought of as arising once the constraints of having a morality are imposed upon rational and mutually self-interested parties who are related and situated in a special way. A practice is just if it is in accordance with the principles which all who participate in it might reasonably be expected to propose or to acknowledge before one another when they are similarly circumstanced and required to make a firm commitment in advance without knowledge of what will be their peculiar condition, and thus when it meets standards which the parties could accept as fair should occasion arise for them to debate its merits. Regarding the participants themselves, once persons knowingly

engage in a practice which they acknowledge to be fair and accept the benefits of doing so, they are bound by the duty of fair play to follow the rules when it comes their turn to do so, and this implies a limitation on their pursuit of self-interest in particular cases.

Now one consequence of this conception is that, where it applies, there is no moral value in the satisfaction of a claim incompatible with it. Such a claim violates the conditions of reciprocity and community amongst persons, and he who presses it, not being willing to acknowledge it when pressed by another, has no grounds for complaint when it is denied; whereas he against whom it is pressed can complain. As it cannot be mutually acknowledged it is a resort to coercion; granting the claim is possible only if one party can compel acceptance of what the other will not admit. But it makes no sense to concede claims the denial of which cannot be complained of in preference to claims the denial of which can be objected to. Thus in deciding on the justice of a practice it is not enough to ascertain that it answers to wants and interests in the fullest and most effective manner. For if any of these conflict with justice, they should not be counted, as their satisfaction is no reason at all for having a practice. It would be irrelevant to say, even if true, that it resulted in the greatest satisfaction of desire. In tallying up the merits of a practice one must toss out the satisfaction of interests the claims of which are incompatible with the principles of justice.

6. The discussion so far has been excessively abstract. While this is perhaps unavoidable, I should now like to bring out some of the features of the conception of justice as fairness by comparing it with the conception of

justice in classical utilitarianism as represented by Bentham and Sidgwick, and its counterpart in welfare economics. This conception assimilates justice to benevolence and the latter in turn to the most efficient design of institutions to promote the general welfare. Justice is a kind of efficiency.[17]

Now it is said occasionally that this form of utilitarianism puts no restrictions on what might be a just assignment of rights and duties in that there might be circumstances which, on utilitarian grounds, would justify institutions highly offensive to our ordinary sense of justice. But the classical utilitarian conception is not totally unprepared for this objection. Beginning with the notion that the general happiness can be represented by a social utility function consisting of a sum of individual utility functions with identical weights (this being the meaning of the maxim that each counts for one and no more than one),[18] it is commonly assumed that the utility functions of individuals are similar in all essential respects. Differences between individuals

are ascribed to accidents of education and upbringing, and they should not be taken into account. This assumption, coupled with that of diminishing marginal utility, results in a prima facie case for equality, for example, of equality in the distribution of income during any given period of time, laying aside indirect effects on the future. But even if utilitarianism is interpreted as having such restrictions built into the utility function, and even if it is supposed that these restrictions have in practice much the same result as the application of the principles of justice (and appear, perhaps, to be ways of expressing these principles in the language of mathematics and psychology), the fundamental idea is very different from the conception of justice as fairness. For one thing, that the principles of justice should be accepted is interpreted as the contingent result of a higher order administrative decision. The form of this decision is regarded as being similar to that of an entrepreneur deciding how much to produce of this or that commodity in view of its marginal revenue,

17. While this assimilation is implicit in Bentham's and Sidgwick's moral theory, explicit statements of it as applied to justice are relatively rare. One clear instance in *The Principles of Morals and Legislation* occurs in ch. x, footnote 2 to section XL: ". . . justice, in the only sense in which it has a meaning, is an imaginary personage, feigned for the convenience of discourse, whose dictates are the dictates of utility, applied to certain particular cases. Justice, then, is nothing more than an imaginary instrument, employed to forward on certain occasions, and by certain means, the purposes of benevolence. The dictates of justice are nothing more than a part of the dictates of benevolence, which, on certain occasions, are applied to certain subjects. . . ." Likewise in *The Limits of Jurisprudence Defined*, ed. by C. W. Everett (New York, 1945), pp. 117 f., Bentham criticizes Grotius for denying that justice derives from utility; and in *The Theory of Legislation*, ed. by C. K. Ogden (London, 1931), p. 3, he says that he uses the words "just" and "unjust" along with other words "simply as collective terms including the ideas of

certain pains or pleasures." That Sidgwick's conception of justice is similar to Bentham's is admittedly not evident from his discussion of justice in Book III, ch. v of *Methods of Ethics*. But it follows, I think, from the moral theory he accepts. Hence C. D. Broad's criticisms of Sidgwick in the matter of distributive justice in *Five Types of Ethical Theory* (London, 1930), pp. 249–253, do not rest on a misinterpretation.

18. This maxim is attributed to Bentham by J. S. Mill in *Utilitarianism*, ch. v, paragraph 36. I have not found it in Bentham's writings, nor seen such a reference. Similarly James Bonar, *Philosophy and Political Economy* (London, 1893), p. 234 n. But it accords perfectly with Bentham's ideas. See the hitherto unpublished manuscript in David Baumgardt, *Bentham and the Ethics of Today* (Princeton, 1952), Appendix IV. For example, "the total value of the stock of pleasure belonging to the whole community is to be obtained by multiplying the number expressing the value of it as respecting any one person, by the number expressing the multitude of such individuals" (p. 556).

or to that of someone distributing goods to needy persons according to the relative urgency of their wants. The choice between practices is thought of as being made on the basis of the allocation of benefits and burdens to individuals (these being measured by the present capitalized value of their utility over the full period of the practice's existence), which results from the distribution of rights and duties established by a practice.

Moreover, the individuals receiving these benefits are not conceived as being related in any way: They represent so many different directions in which limited resources may be allocated. The value of assigning resources to one direction rather than another depends solely on the preferences and interests of individuals as individuals. The satisfaction of desire has its value irrespective of the moral relations between persons, say as members of a joint undertaking, and of the claims which, in the name of these interests, they are prepared to make on one another;[19] and it is this value which is to be taken into account by the (ideal) legislator who is conceived as adjusting the rules of the

system from the center so as to maximize the value of the social utility function.

It is thought that the principles of justice will not be violated by a legal system so conceived provided these executive decisions are correctly made. In this fact the principles of justice are said to have their derivation and explanation; they simply express the most important general features of social institutions in which the administrative problem is solved in the best way. These principles have, indeed, a special urgency because, given the facts of human nature, so much depends on them; and this explains the peculiar quality of the moral feelings associated with justice.[20] This assimilation of justice to a higher order executive decision, certainly a striking conception, is central to classical utilitarianism; and it also brings out its profound individualism, in one sense of this ambiguous word. It regards persons as so many *separate* directions in which benefits and burdens may be assigned; and the value of the satisfaction or dissatisfaction of desire is not thought to depend in any way on the moral relations in which individuals stand, or

---

19. An idea essential to the classical utilitarian conception of justice. Bentham is firm in his statement of it: "It is only upon that principle [the principle of asceticism], and not from the principle of utility, that the most abominable pleasure which the vilest of malefactors ever reaped from his crime would be reprobated, if it stood alone. The case is, that it never does stand alone; but is necessarily followed by such a quantity of pain (or, what comes to the same thing, such a chance for a certain quantity of pain) that the pleasure in comparison of it, is as nothing: and this is the true and sole, but perfectly sufficient, reason for making it a ground for punishment" (*"The Principles of Morals and Legislation*, ch. II, sec. iv. See also ch. X, sec. x, footnote 1). The same point is made in *The Limits of Jurisprudence Defined*, pp. 115 f. Although much recent welfare economics, as found in such important works as I. M. D. Little, *A Critique of Welfare Economics*, 2nd ed. (Oxford, 1957) and K. J. Arrow, *Social Choice and Individual Values* (New York, 1951), dispenses with the idea of

cardinal utility, and use instead the theory of ordinal utility as stated by J. R. Hicks, *Value and Capital*, 2nd ed. (Oxford, 1946), Pt. I, it assumes with utilitarianism that individual preferences have value as such, and so accepts the idea being criticized here. I hasten to add, however, that this is no objection to it as a means of analyzing economic policy, and for that purpose it may, indeed, be a necessary simplifying assumption. Nevertheless it is an assumption which cannot be made in so far as one is trying to analyze moral concepts, especially the concept of justice, as economists would, I think, agree. Justice is usually regarded as a separate and distinct part of any comprehensive criterion of economic policy. See, for example, Tibor Scitovsky, *Welfare and Competition* (London, 1952), pp. 59–69, and Little, *op. cit.*, ch. VII.

20. See J. S. Mill's argument in *Utilitarianism*, ch. v, pars. 16–25.

on the kinds of claims which they are willing, in the pursuit of their interests, to press on each other.

7. Many social decisions are, of course, of an administrative nature. Certainly this is so when it is a matter of social utility in what one may call its ordinary sense: that is, when it is a question of the efficient design of social institutions for the use of common means to achieve common ends. In this case either the benefits and burdens may be assumed to be impartially distributed, or the question of distribution is misplaced, as in the instance of maintaining public order and security or national defense. But as an interpretation of the basis of the principles of justice, classical utilitarianism is mistaken. It *permits* one to argue, for example, that slavery is unjust on the grounds that the advantages to the slaveholder as slaveholder do not counterbalance the disadvantages to the slave and to society at large burdened by a comparatively inefficient system of labor. Now the conception of justice as fairness, when applied to the practice of slavery with its offices of slaveholder and slave, would not allow one to consider the advantages of the slaveholder in the first place. As that office is not in accordance with principles which could be mutually acknowledged, the gains accruing to the slaveholder, assuming them to exist, cannot be counted as in *any* way mitigating the injustice of the practice. The question whether these gains outweigh the disadvantages to the slave and to society cannot arise, since in considering the justice of slavery these gains have no weight at all which requires that they be overridden. Where the conception of justice as fairness applies, slavery is *always* unjust.

I am not, of course, suggesting the absurdity that the classical utilitarians approved of slavery. I am only rejecting a type of argument which their view allows them to use in support of their disapproval of it. The conception of justice as derivative from efficiency implies that judging the justice of a practice is always, in principle at least, a matter of weighing up advantages and disadvantages, each having an intrinsic value or disvalue as the satisfaction of interests, irrespective of whether or not these interests necessarily involve acquiescence in principles which could not be mutually acknowledged. Utilitarianism cannot account for the fact that slavery is always unjust, nor for the fact that it would be recognized as irrelevant in defeating the accusation of injustice for one person to say to another, engaged with him in a common practice and debating its merits, that nevertheless it allowed of the greatest satisfaction of desire. The charge of injustice cannot be rebutted in this way. If justice were derivative from a higher order executive efficiency, this would not be so.

But now, even if it is taken as established that, so far as the ordinary conception of justice goes, slavery is always unjust (that is, slavery by definition violates commonly recognized principles of justice), the classical utilitarian would surely reply that these principles, as other moral principles subordinate to that of utility, are only generally correct. It is simply for the most part true that slavery is less efficient than other institutions; and while common sense may define the concept of justice so that slavery is unjust, nevertheless, where slavery would lead to the greatest satisfaction of desire, it is not wrong. Indeed, it is then right, and for the very same reason that justice, as ordinarily understood, is usually right. If, as ordinarily understood, slavery is always unjust, to this extent the utilitarian conception of justice might be admitted to differ from that of common moral opinion. Still the utilitarian would want to hold that, as a matter of moral principle, his view is correct in giving no special weight to considerations of justice beyond that allowed for by the general presumption of effectiveness. And this, he claims, is as it should be. The every day opinion is morally in error, although, indeed, it is a useful error, since it protects rules of generally high utility.

The question, then, relates not simply to the analysis of the concept of justice as common sense defines it, but the analysis of it in the wider sense as to how much weight considerations of justice, as defined, are to have when laid against other kinds of moral considerations. Here again I wish to argue that reasons of justice have a *special* weight for which only the conception of justice as fairness can account. Moreover, it belongs to the concept of justice that they do have this special weight. While Mill recognized that this was so, he thought that it could be accounted for by the special urgency of the moral feelings which naturally support principles of such high utility. But it is a mistake to resort to the urgency of feeling; as with the appeal to intuition, it manifests a failure to pursue the question far enough. The special weight of considerations of justice can be explained from the conception of justice as fairness. It is only necessary to elaborate a bit what has already been said as follows.

If one examines the circumstances in which a certain tolerance of slavery is justified, or perhaps better, excused, it turns out that these are of a rather special sort. Perhaps slavery exists as an inheritance from the past and it proves necessary to dismantle it piece by piece; at times slavery may conceivably be an advance on previous institutions. Now while there may be some excuse for slavery in special conditions, it is never an excuse for it that it is sufficiently advantageous to the slaveholder to outweigh the disadvantages to the slave and to society. A person who argues in this way is not perhaps making a wildly irrelevant remark; but he is guilty of a moral fallacy. There is disorder in his conception of the ranking of moral principles. For the slaveholder, by his own admission, has no moral title to the advantages which he receives as a slaveholder. He is no more prepared than the slave to acknowledge the principle upon which is founded the respective positions in which they both stand. Since slavery does not accord with principles which they could mutually acknowledge, they each may be supposed to agree that it is unjust: It grants claims which it ought not to grant and in doing so denies claims which it ought not to deny. Amongst persons in a general position who are debating the form of their common practices, it cannot, therefore, be offered as a reason for a practice that, in conceding these very claims that ought to be denied, it nevertheless meets existing interests more effectively. By their very nature the satisfaction of these claims is without weight and cannot enter into any tabulation of advantages and disadvantages.

Furthermore, it follows from the concept of morality that, to the extent that the slaveholder recognizes his position vis-a-vis the slave to be unjust, he would not choose to press his claims. His not wanting to receive his special advantages is one of the ways in which he shows that he thinks slavery is unjust. It would be fallacious for the legislator to suppose, then, that it is a ground for having a practice that it brings advantages greater than disadvantages, if those for whom the practice is designed, and to whom the advantages flow, acknowledge that they have no moral title to them and do not wish to receive them.

For these reasons the principles of justice have a special weight; and with respect to the principle of the greatest satisfaction of desire, as cited in the general position amongst those discussing the merits of their common practices, the principles of justice have an absolute weight. In this sense they are not contingent; and this is why their force is greater than can be accounted for by the general presumption (assuming that there is one) of the effectiveness, in the utilitarian sense, of practices which in fact satisfy them.

If one wants to continue using the concepts of classical utilitarianism, one will have to say, to meet this criticism, that at least the individual or social utility functions must be so defined that no value is given to the satisfaction of interests the representative claims of which violate the principles of justice. In this way it is no doubt possible to include these principles within the form of the utilitarian conception; but to do so is, of course, to change its inspiration altogether as a moral conception. For it is to incorporate within it principles which cannot be understood on the basis of a higher order executive decision aiming at the greatest satisfaction of desire.

It is worth remarking, perhaps, that this criticism of utilitarianism does not depend on whether or not the two assumptions, that of individuals having similar utility functions and that of diminishing marginal utility, are interpreted as psychological propositions to be supported or refuted by experience, or as moral and political principles expressed in a somewhat technical language. There are, certainly, several advantages in taking them in the latter fashion.[21] For one thing, one might say that this is what Bentham and others really meant by them, at least as shown by how they were used in arguments for social reform. More importantly, one could hold that the best way to defend the classical utilitarian view is to interpret these assumptions as moral and political principles. It is doubtful whether, taken as psychological propositions, they are true of men in general as we know them under normal conditions. On the other hand, utilitarians would not have wanted to propose them merely as practical working principles of legislation, or as expedient maxims to guide reform, given the egalitarian sentiments of modern society.[22] When pressed they might well have invoked the idea of a more or less equal capacity of men in relevant respects if given an equal chance in a just society. But if the argument above regarding slavery is correct, then granting these assumptions as moral and political principles makes no difference. To view individuals as equally fruitful lines for the allocation of benefits, even as a matter of moral principle, still leaves the mistaken notion that the satisfaction of desire has value in itself

21. See D. G. Ritchie, *Natural Rights* (London, 1894), pp. 95 ff., 249 ff. Lionel Robbins has insisted on this point on several occasions. See *An Essay on the Nature and Significance of Economic Science*, 2nd ed. (London, 1935), pp. 134–43, "Interpersonal Comparisons of Utility: A Comment," *Economic Journal*, XLVIII (1938), 635–41, and more recently, "Robertson on Utility and Scope," *Economica*, n.s. XX (1953), 108 f.

22. As Sir Henry Maine suggested Bentham may have regarded them. See *The Early History of Institutions* (London, 1875), pp. 398 ff.

irrespective of the relations between persons as members of a common practice, and irrespective of the claims upon one another which the satisfaction of interests represents. To see the error of this idea one must give up the conception of justice as an executive decision altogether and refer to the notion of justice as fairness: that participants in a common practice be regarded as having an original and equal liberty and that their common practices be considered unjust unless they accord with principles which persons so circumstanced and related could freely acknowledge before one another, and so could accept as fair. Once the emphasis is put upon the concept of the mutual recognition of principles by participants in a common practice the rules of which are to define their several relations and give form to their claims on one another, then it is clear that the granting of a claim the principle of which could not be acknowledged by each in the general position (that is, in the position in which the parties propose and acknowledge principles before one another) is not a reason for adopting a practice. Viewed in this way, the background of the claim is seen to exclude it from consideration; that it can represent a value in itself arises from the conception of individuals as separate lines for the assignment of benefits, as isolated persons who stand as claimants on an administrative or benevolent largesse. Occasionally persons do so stand to one another; but this is not the general case, nor, more importantly, is it the case when it is a matter of the justice of practices themselves in which participants stand in various relations to be appraised in accordance with standards which they may be expected to acknowledge before one another. Thus however mistaken

the notion of the social contract may be as history, and however far it may overreach itself as a general theory of social and political obligation, it does express, suitably interpreted, an essential part of the concept of justice.[23]

8. By way of conclusion I should like to make two remarks: First, the original modification of the utilitarian principle (that it require of practices that the offices and positions defined by them be equal unless it is reasonable to suppose that the representative man in *every* office would find the inequality to his advantage), slight as it may appear at first sight, actually has a different conception of justice standing behind it. I have tried to show how this is so by developing the concept of justice as fairness and by indicating how this notion involves the mutual acceptance, from a general position, of the principles on which a practice is founded, and how this in turn requires the exclusion from consideration of claims violating the principles of justice. Thus the slight alteration of principle reveals another family of notions, another way of looking at the concept of justice.

Second, I should like to remark also that I have been dealing with the *concept* of justice. I have tried to set out the kinds of principles upon which judgments concerning the justice of practices may be said to stand. The analysis will be successful to the degree

23. Thus Kant was not far wrong when he interpreted the original contract merely as an "Idea of Reason"; yet he still thought of it as a *general* criterion of right and as providing a general theory of political obligation. See the second part of the essay, "On the Saying 'That may be right in theory but has no value in practice'" (1793), in *Kant's Principles of Politics*, tr. by W. Hastie (Edinburgh, 1891). I have drawn on the contractarian tradition not for a general theory of political obligation but to clarify the concept of justice.

that it expresses the principles involved in these judgments when made by competent persons upon deliberation and reflection.[24] Now every people may be supposed to have the concept of justice, since in the life of every society there must be at least some relations in which the parties consider themselves to be circumstanced and related as the concept of justice as fairness requires. Societies will differ from one another not in having or in failing to have this notion but in the range of cases to which they apply it and in the emphasis which they give to it as compared with other moral concepts.

A firm grasp of the concept of justice itself is necessary if these variations, and the reasons for them, are to be understood. No study of the development of moral ideas and of the differences between them is more sound than the analysis of the fundamental moral concepts upon which it must depend. I have tried, therefore, to give an analysis of the concept of justice which should apply generally, however large a part the concept may have in a given morality, and which can be used in explaining the course of men's thoughts about justice and its relations to other moral concepts. How it is to be used for this purpose is a large topic which I cannot, of course, take up here. I mention it only to emphasize that I have been dealing with the concept of justice itself and to indicate what use I consider such an analysis to have.

24. For a further discussion of the idea expressed here, see my paper, "Outline of a Decision Procedure for Ethics," in the *Philosophical Review*, LX (1951), 177–197. For an analysis, similar in many respects but using the notion of the ideal observer instead of that of the considered judgment of a competent person, see Roderick Firth, "Ethical Absolutism and the Ideal Observer," *Philosophy and Phenomenological Research*, XII (1952), 317–345. While the similarities between these two discussions are more important than the differences, an analysis based on the notion of a considered judgment of a competent person, as it is based on a kind of judgment, may prove more helpful in understanding the features of moral judgment than an analysis based on the notion of an ideal observer, although this remains to be shown. A man who rejects the conditions imposed on a considered judgment of a competent person could no longer profess to *judge* at all. This seems more fundamental than his rejecting the conditions of observation, for these do not seem to apply, in an ordinary sense, to making a moral judgment.

28

A. D. WOOZLEY
Injustice

A. D. WOOZLEY, professor of philosophy at the University of Virginia, has written on Greek philosophy, theory of knowledge, metaphysics, ethics, and the philosophy of law.

From A. D. Woozley, "Injustice," *Studies in Ethics: American Philosophical Quarterly Monograph Series No. 7* (1973), pp. 109–122. Reprinted by permission of the author and the editor of the *American Philosophical Quarterly*. This article is reprinted unabridged.

Although philosophers and nonphilosophers alike have written much about justice, they have not always observed the distinction between questions of analysis and questions of criteria, that is, the distinction between what justice is and how to determine instances or noninstances of it. Thus, claims to characterize justice (a) in terms of fairness, and (b) in terms of equality are not merely different claims but claims of different kinds. That a given distribution is unequal among the recipients may be, and, depending on the context, is a good reason for saying that it is unfair, but it is not identical with its being unfair. We can ask whether a distribution is fair, and whether it is equal. But when we go on to ask why it is fair and why it is equal, we are asking questions that are very different from each other: In the first case we are seeking a justification of the claim that the distribution is fair; in the second case we are accepting that the distribution is equal, and seeking a justification of it being so. In short, even if it were true that the only way to treat men fairly is to treat them equally, treating them fairly, although it would consist in treating them equally, would not be conceptually identical with treating them equally. The core meaning of "fair" is a moral meaning, the core meaning of "equal" is not. "It is unfair to treat men unequally" is a significant assertion, and a moral assertion. "It is unequal to treat men unfairly" is not a moral assertion, and would need some torturing even to make into a significant assertion. And the proposition that all men are created equal is so conspicuously false if regarded as a factual proposition that it has to be interpreted as a moral proposition *about* equality if it is to have the ghost of a chance of being true, let alone be the self-evident truth that Thomas Jefferson proclaimed it to be.

Again philosophers have had comparatively little to say about injustice—which is surely the more interesting of the two. Here, perhaps, we have a case of what J. L. Austin used to call "trouser words," with "injustice" wearing the trousers. Justice is the least and the most anaemic of the virtues, about which it is difficult to get excited except where it is refused or threatened. We are liable to think of "unjust" as the contradictory of "just." Here we are wrong, for it is a contrary, but, as it is the only morally interesting contrary, the error is understandable and has no serious consequences: It is not the absence of justice that we get excited about, but the absence of justice where it should be present. Failure to be just, not merely not being just, is what matters, and failure to be just is injustice.

We might start by saying that injustice is unfair discrimination between persons or classes of persons in the distribution of advantages or disadvantages, and that discrimination is unfair if and only if it is based on factors which are not relevant to the distribution. (This will soon need some qualifying.) The injustice of second-class citizenship consists in discriminating between whites and blacks, Aryans and Jews, in general A's and B's, where the dissimilarities between the A's and the B's, although they may be many, obvious, and considerable, are not relevant to the rights and capacities of citizenship; and it is not merely that there is nothing about white pigmentation or black pigmentation which is relevant, but that there is nothing about being a white or being a black which is relevant.

To justify something, such as a practice or an institution, is to show that it is right, or at least that it is reasonable to suppose it to be right; and one way of being right is to be just. But it is not the only way, for the just is a species of the right. It is further in my view possible (although many would dispute this) for a practice to be right, even although it is unjust. Treating people unjustly can sometimes be right and be shown to be right, to be justified in terms of social utility. Because "justify" has come to bear this wider meaning, of showing to be right (or, from another aspect, making right), we need another word with the more limited scope of showing to be just, or making just; perhaps "justicise" would do.

This first step of analyzing injustice as unfair discrimination, and unfair discrimination as discrimination based on factors not relevant to the distribution of the advantages or disadvantages involved, is only a first step.

Next, can we either list or give any general characterization of the factors which are relevant to questions of discrimination? Clearly they are factors about the patients in the case, those being treated unjustly, not factors about either the agents in the case or others who may be affected. If General Electric is treating its employees in Waynesboro, Virginia unjustly by paying them lower rates than it pays its employees in Schenectady, New York for doing exactly the same work, the injustice derives from facts about those employees, for example, that neither the needs nor the merits of those in Virginia are different from those in New York; it does not derive at all from facts about the agent, for example, that General Electric does not have to keep its wage rates as low as job demand permits in order to stay competitive with rival manufacturers; and it does not derive at all from facts about others affected, such as the selling trade or the consumer. It may be unjust to the latter that G.E. lower cost products from Virginia are sold at the same price as the identical, but higher cost products from New York; but even if it is, then not reflecting lower costs of production in a lower selling price is no part of the injustice to the employees at the Waynesboro plant. This is the important distinction between "justify" and "justice" coming in again. If G.E. can be charged with unjust discrimination against its Waynesboro employees, it is not the beginning of a rebuttal for the company to say that it must keep wage rates down to the lowest level that local conditions will permit—although that might be the beginning of a rebuttal of the charge that is discrimination against Waynesboro employees is not justified. Again, maintaining a uniform selling price to the trade may or may not result in unjust treatment of the consumer, and it may or may not be justified. But whether or not it is unjust to the consumer, and whether or not it is justified, has nothing whatever to do with the question whether paying a lower wage rate to employees in Virginia than to those in New York is or is not unjust to the former.

As a beginning of a list of relevant factors, I have mentioned merits and needs. I am sure they are both relevant, but I am not sure that they are alike in the way that they are relevant. If a number of men have equal needs, if you are in some way such as that of an employer or a welfare agency responsible for meeting those needs, if you have sufficient resources available to meet them, and if you then give some men more than they need and (whether consequentially or not) others less than they need, you are treating the latter unjustly. In that situation you have a double duty and they have a double right: You have the duty to respond to their needs and the duty not to discriminate in meeting their needs; and they have the two correlative rights.

In the case where you do not have the first duty you may still have the second. Even if you do not have the duty to respond to their needs, then, if you do respond to their equal needs but do not respond equally, you are being unjust. Having a duty not to discriminate in responding to equal needs does not imply having first a duty to respond to the needs. A father does not have the duty to meet the needs of his neighbor's children which he has to meet the needs of his own; but if he does respond to the former, discrimination, if it leaves the needs of some but not others inadequately met, is unjust. But the principle of treating like cases alike, if it is not to be vacuous, needs careful handling. If the needs of the recipients are equal, failure to meet them equally is unjust. That is to say, a pattern of distribution which gave some more than they needed, but others less than they needed, would be unjust: The latter could justifiably complain that they had been treated unfairly. It is less obviously true that a pattern of distribution which gave some more than they needed, but none less than they needed, would be unjust. No doubt the latter would often protest that they had been treated unfairly, but it is not clear that they would be right; and, indeed, I do not think they would be. We thus have to distinguish between a weak version and a strong version of the principle of treating like cases alike.

Weak version. It is fair (not unfair) to treat like cases alike. This version does not entail that it is unfair to treat like cases unalike. Fairness permits the treating of like cases alike.

Strong version. It is fair (only fair) to treat like cases alike. This does entail that it is unfair to treat like cases unalike. Fairness demands the treating of like cases alike. The weak version

clearly is true, that is, it is never the case that it would be unfair to treat like cases alike. "Like" has to be understood as "relevantly alike": *A*'s being like *B* in any old respect at all, regardless of the nature of the distribution, will not do. And equally clearly the weak version does not entail that it is unfair to treat like cases unalike. From the proposition that it is not unfair to treat like cases alike, nothing whatever follows about the unfairness (or fairness) of treating like cases unalike.

The strong version on the other hand, that it is only fair to treat like cases alike, clearly does have the entailment which the weak version does not: If it is only fair to treat like cases alike, then it is unfair not to, which is to say that it is unfair to treat like cases unalike. And it is the strong version of the "treat like cases alike" slogan which we are inclined to hold (of course it carries the weak version with it) and which we appeal to in what we think to be cases of injustice, viz., the injustice of treating like cases unalike. But, unless it is modified, the strong version is false: It is *not* always the case that it would be only fair to treat like cases alike—or that it would be unfair not to. If *A*'s and *B*'s needs are equal, then while it would be unfair totally to disregard that fact in making your distribution to them, it would not be unfair, having given equally to each what will satisfy his needs, then to give the whole of the surplus to *A*. *B* might protest that it was unfair that *A* got more than he himself did—many beneficiaries under a will have so protested—but he would be wrong, unless there was some further respect, other than need, in which *B* (possibly *A* also) had a claim on your distribution. If a father in the bequests which he makes to his two sons *A* and *B* has fairly met their needs, he does no injustice to *B* if he leaves the whole of the rest of the estate to *A*—unless there is some further respect, other than need, in which the distinction between like cases is unjust.

What this brings out is that the strong version is more complicated than the weak version. A modified strong version would be true, viz., that, if *A*'s and *B*'s needs are equal, it is only fair not to treat them as if they were unequal before reaching the point of meeting their needs. But the unmodified strong version summarized in the ambiguous slogan "treat like cases alike" is not true.

From Aristotle on it has seemed natural to think of injustice within the context of distribution of advantages or disadvantages (for example, on the one hand emoluments, tax reliefs, exemptions; and on the other fines, taxes, military conscription), and of discrimination in the distribution which was not based solely on relevant factors about those who came out well or badly from the discrimination. This makes us think of injustice as something between the treatment of one individual and that of another, between the treatment of some individuals and that of others, between the treatment of one class and that of other classes, etc. The basic cry of injustice thus seems to be the child's "He has got more than I have" or "He has got one and I have not" or, on the other side of the account, "I was punished and he was not." It looks as if the only question we have is that of determining what are the justicising factors, of only one of which I have so far talked, viz., need. That is one question, but not, I think, the only one. There is also the question whether it is correct at all to define justice and injustice in terms of distribution and discrimination. I doubt whether it is; I do not doubt that the most conspicuous cases of injustice are those involving discrimination, but I am inclined to think that there is something more fundamental, that it is not so much the discrimination itself that is offensive as what is involved in the discrimination.

I find the second question more interesting than the first, the question of justicising factors, but I think the second can usefully be approached through the first. I am not going to attempt to make a complete list of justicising factors, but shall mention some that are commonly propounded and that have been held to be in one way or another relevant to the question whether discrimination is essential to injustice. The three sources that I have had primarily in mind are: Henry Sidgwick, *The Methods of Ethics* (6th Edition, 1901) Book III, Chapter V; A. M. Honoré, "Social Justice," *McGill Law Journal*, vol. 78 (1962) revised and reprinted in Robert S. Summers (ed.) *Essays in Legal Philosophy* (1968); and Nicholas Rescher, *Distributive Justice* (1966) Chapter 4. Not surprisingly, there is a high degree of agreement between these sources (and others, too, which could be added) about the justicising factors. I give what is substantially, although not precisely, Honoré's list (not in his order):

1. Need
2. Desert—Achievement
3. Desert—Ability
4. Transaction
5. Special Relation
6. Conformity to Rule

In every case the person to be treated, justly or unjustly, has a claim on the agent, and the agent in not meeting the claim is guilty of injustice. This accords with the distinction made by Kant and again by Mill between justice and the rest of morals, the duties of justice being those which have correlative rights in the other party, other moral duties being those which do not: We have a duty to keep our bargains, for example, contracts, wage agreements, conditions of service, etc. (= Honoré's *transactions*), and the other party has a right that we should; we may also have a duty of benevolence to others, but they have no right that we should be benevolent towards them. Failure in either would be moral failure, but only failure in the first would be injustice.

From the fact that we have a plurality of justicising factors it does not logically follow that there will be conflicts between them. It could be the case that they fell into an order which could be numbered from 1 to *n*, such that any factor outranked any other factor with a higher numeral; and I am not sure that Honoré, for example, does not believe that *need* outranks all the rest. But it seems to me clear that neither that particular claim, not the more general claim that some hierarchical ordering is possible, can in fact be sustained. And even under a single heading there can be conflicts, for example, conflicting needs. Perhaps it is not necessary to stress that the issue is not always justice versus something else, say utility, but it seems at least worth pointing out, because in practical issues where questions of justice and injustice arise there is a human tendency to oversimplify. For example, in the school issue over busing children to achieve integration it is surely oversimple to suppose that justice points in one direction only. What follows in the remainder of this paper should be understood as being

acknowledged to be subject to possible conflicts, not only between the different factors, but also under the heading of a single factor.

1. NEED

This is the factor which I have so far used in my examples, and I do not think more requires to be said about it now. If you have the duty of meeting needs, and you do not match distribution to needs, you are treating unjustly those to whom you give too little or nothing. We should distinguish between

(a) the criticism we might want to make of a society which, say, prefers to expend its wealth on missionary wars, or space spectaculars, or conspicuous consumption than on welfare and poverty programs,

and

(b) the criticism we might want to make of the inequitable legislation for, and operation of, welfare and poverty programs.

In (a) we are complaining about wrong priorities but not directly about injustice (although wrong priorities may breed injustice); in (b) we are complaining about injustice. Meeting the needs of some families, but failing to meet those of others, because they are hesitant to apply or ignorant how to, is clearly unjust. But even in this category of needs it should be noted that, although discrimination (whether intentional or negligent) nearly always is an element of the injustice, it does not have to be. The injustice of failing to pay a living wage is not conditional on discrimination, that is, on paying some people better; it is possible to treat *everybody* unjustly by paying them less than they need. Fat cats among executives or stockholders are not necessary to the validity of a union's claim of injustice to the workers.

2. DESERT—ACHIEVEMENT

That a man has got less for what he did than he deserved, for example, by way of payment or reward, or more than he deserved, for example, by way of damages awarded against him or punishment, is perhaps the oldest cry of injustice. If not getting what you merited by your performance is not a paradigm case of injustice, what could be? Failure here is failure in Aristotle's distributive justice and the feeling for desert as a justicising factor is what lies at the root of objections to the views of penal and social reformers such as Barbara Wootton, who would have us in the area of crime give up thinking in terms of responsibility and punishment and think instead in terms of social utility. The objection to Barbara Wootton is less that for what he did the convicted man deserves to be punished than that he does *not* deserve to be submitted to therapy however securely beyond the stage of uncertain experiment the therapy may be.

Note that, as in the case of need, injustice in responding to the deserts of achievement does not require unjust discrimination, although very often that is the injustice that will be complained of. A man's getting less than he deserved for what he did is doubly unjust if somebody else got more than he, but it would still be unjust if nobody else got more, even if nobody else was involved at all.

3. DESERT—ABILITY

I have separated ability from achievement as a justicising factor (although neither Honoré nor Rescher does) because it seems to me far less clearly a justicising factor at all. They both find

it unjust to a man to deny him what by ability he is qualified for; and so also does J. Feinberg in his "Justice and Personal Desert" (*Nomos*, vol. VI). Incidentally, being qualified must not be confused with being eligible. One can be well qualified, moderately well qualified, poorly qualified, and so forth; and in considering rival candidates for an appointment, we *weigh* their qualifications. Eligibility, on the other hand, is an either/or, on/off business. I may be excellently qualified to be President of the USA, but I am not, and never can become, eligible; and of the millions of those who are eligible few are qualified. Again, the fact that I am qualified for a job is a good reason for appointing me (provided that, if there are elibigility conditions, I meet them); the fact that I am eligible for the job is, at most, a good reason for considering me. Nepotism in making appointments may be objectionable, but I doubt whether it is objectionable on the ground that it is unjust to the better qualified candidates for the job—unless other factors than simply ability are to be taken into account (as I think they normally are). If an employer in appointing a new secretary cares to disregard the excellent qualifications of Miss *A* in favor of the attractions of Miss *B* whose talents are strictly those of a businessman's playgirl, has he been unjust to Miss *A*? Not, I think, unless other factors are involved such as (1) a statement or an implied statement in the advertisement for the job that the candidate judged to be best qualified in secretarial skills would be appointed or (2) the existence of a convention or a rule that in competitive appointments the candidate judged to be best qualified is the one appointed. But then the injustice is, not failing to treat according to ability, but failing to act according to a specially or generally authorized expectation that you will treat according to ability. It can be imprudent not to appoint according to ability and it can be morally objectionable, but I doubt whether the moral objection can be that it is unjust *simpliciter* to disregard ability.

An objector might cite as counterexamples the injustice of denying civil rights to blacks or to women; that (to state the case at its mildest) plenty of blacks who have been prevented from registering as voters have been as well qualified to vote as plenty of whites who are registered; or that women have had it made difficult or even impossible for them to get into jobs and positions for which their ability is no less than that of male competitors. I do not deny the injustice of these examples, but I question whether they are always and clearly counterexamples. The fight for such rights has, on the whole, been the fight against discrimination, not the fight against nonrecognition of ability by itself. Nonrecognition of ability can be unjust, viz., where on the one hand the ability is claimed or is so conspicuous as to stand in no need of claiming and where on the other hand it is denied through hypocrisy or prejudice. What lies at the base of this is, I think, the injustice of affront or insult to which I shall be coming back shortly. The treatment of suppressed minorities (or majorities) whether they are blacks, women, Catholics in Northern Ireland, Jews in Russia, or whatever, is an affront in a way in which merely not to get a job because the boss has a weakness for dumb blondes is not.

I wonder whether the view that ability carries desert, which is a view that is widely held, with the consequences that it is unjust not to treat according to ability, does not perhaps rest on a confusion between ability and demonstration of ability. In many cases, where a choice has to be made between candidates, it is made on the basis of competition in a test or examination; and the choice is made on the performance or display of ability therein. If the man who has performed best does not get the job, he can protest at the injustice of it, because by his achievement, by his showing his superior ability, he deserved the job. There are, of course, possible complications to this: For example, it might be that, although *A* performed best, *B* showed more promise; in such a case it might be imprudent, or even wrong, not to appoint *B*; and, as showing promise is a way of showing ability, it might even be unjust to *B* not to appoint him. Again, *B* may have performed better than *A* over part of the examination, but not over the whole because he was taken ill during it, or from some other uncontrollable cause; in this case it might be unjust to *B* not to appoint him. And the method of selecting the performances that are to count as demonstrating ability may be open to criticism. This is especially liable to happen in situations where what matters is not just having an ability but also being on form or on a winning streak; for example, the method of selecting professional golfers either in this country or in Great Britain to play against each other in the Ryder Cup is frequently criticized on these grounds. But here it does seem to me more a matter of inefficiency or plain bad luck, rather than injustice. What is unjust is the denial of an asked-for opportunity to display an ability, if there is some evidence of its possession. So, it can be unjust to be refused an opportunity of displaying your ability, and it can be unjust not to be treated in accordance with your achievement in displaying it: But I am still unconvinced that it is unjust simply not to be treated in accordance with your known ability—unless, as I have hinted already, the failure to treat you so can reasonably be described in terms of affront.

4. TRANSACTIONS

The justice of transactions is approximately Aristotle's diorthotic justice: the justice of restoring the *status quo* exemplified by payment for services, compensation for harm done—and on the view generally taken by Anglo-American law that promises require consideration, the keeping of bargains and fulfillment of contracts. The injustice of transactions is simply the injustice of taking something for nothing, of getting something at somebody else's expense when he was not a willing party to your doing so. I have nothing more to say about it until I come back to asking whether there is any common thread running through the list of justicising factors.

5. SPECIAL RELATIONS

This is on Honoré's list but not on Rescher's. I am strongly disinclined to accept it. No doubt special relationships, contractual (for example, husband-wife) familial (for example, father-son), official (for example, ruler, judge, policeman, and so forth, those over whom they have authority) and others produce special duties, but only where they also produce special rights do they make possible justice and injustice. A father who does not provide in his will for his son, where there is no special reason why he should not, may be open to moral criticism for not doing so, but unless the son has a claim under another heading such as need, or transaction, or rule, unfairness does not

seem to enter into it. The special relations such as the contractual and the official that do make possible fair or unfair treatment clearly do fall under other headings, and I see no reason to retain this one. That the world would be a worse place if familial duties were not accepted and discharged is not identical with its being a more unjust place if they were not. Old people may be treated thoughtlessly, carelessly, heartlessly by their self-centered sons and daughters, but not in the absence of other factors unjustly.

6. CONFORMITY TO RULE

This either is itself or comprehends the most important factor of all. It is not merely that each of us has a claim that our society's rules should both be fair and be fairly operated, but also each of us has a claim that they should be observed. If the rule in question, whether being one of law, of positive morality, of custom, or of convention, serves a beneficial social purpose, it does so only provided that it is generally observed. For any individual to gain whatever advantages he does from breaking the rule or from treating himself as being exempt from it, it is in general necessary that others should not be breaking it: The situation has to be seen not just as the simple situation of A gaining an advantage by breaking a rule, but as the complex situation of A gaining an advantage by breaking a rule, which all (or most) others are keeping. Consequently the strongest argument against such a would-be rule breaker is neither that his conduct will, or is liable to, through its consequences undermine society (for in the case of most individuals its chances of doing so are negligible), nor that society would be undermined if everybody did the same (for it well might not), but simply the unfairness of his securing an advantage which depends on his breaking a rule in circumstances in which most others are keeping it. So the claim that we should conform to the rules does not depend on their being either legal or moral rules; it depends on those being the rules by which the game is being played. (It is not easy to be precise about what constitutes something being such a rule. But it can be as little as its being a matter of reasonable expectation, which is enough to create a rule, and to open the way for just and unjust treatment of others.)

What I want to suggest is that the notion (or notions) of reasonable expectations, or of the right to expect, is the basic notion of justice, and that injustice consists in treating people differently—more accurately, worse—than they have a right to expect. What treatment a man can reasonably expect, or has a right to expect, sometimes depends on the existence of rules, sometimes does not. We have thus two different types of case; we also have an ambiguity in "reasonable expectation" which we have to be careful about.

We can expect *that* people will in given circumstances behave in a certain way, and we can expect people in given circumstances *to* behave in a certain way; and expecting that they will . . . and expecting them to . . . are very different things.

(Certainly the range of use of each of these expressions does overlap the range of use of the other, so that within that overlap they are interchangeable; I am in this paper concerned with the non-overlapping portions of their respective ranges, for example, the case where *A* can expect *B* to behave in a certain way at the same time as he cannot expect that he will.)

We expect that people will behave in a certain way because there is a rule prescribing such behavior.

(a) At its weakest this is simply a regularity type expectation. We can and do expect that people will go on obeying this rule just because they always/ usually have; or, as in the case of a new rule, we can expect that they will obey it because they always/usually have obeyed the rules. What makes this expectation reasonable or one which we have a right to or are entitled to hold is its inductive backing. (Note that "can" in "we can expect" does not mean "are able to" or even "are allowed to," but "are entitled to," "have a right to," "would be justified in," and so forth.) A simple illustration of the regularity type expectation (although not one depending on rules) would be that of Kant's neighbors setting their watches by his walking habits. These were so regular day after day that they could expect that they would continue, and they would be entitled to feel that something had gone wrong if he suddenly changed his walking schedule. They might feel, if they had really come to rely on his walking habits to determine the accuracy of their watches, that he had let them down if he suddenly changed, although they would not be *entitled* to feel so if there was nothing more to their relationship with Kant than I have supposed. They would be in the same position as the son who received far less under his father's will than he had counted on getting (provided, that is, that his counting on getting much more had been based just on evidence and not at all on promises or even strong hints by the father).

(b) Then we can introduce the notions of people accepting a rule, of feeling committed to it, or feeling bound by it. These are notions which are perhaps different from, although related to, each other. The differences do not matter to the present topic so I will use "feeling bound by" to stand for them all.

We can expect that people will behave in a certain way as prescribed by a rule, not just because they always/usually have, but because we can expect them to feel bound by it, and consequently because we can expect them to behave as prescribed. We are entitled to expect them to behave that way, or to demand that they should, for various possible reasons such as undertakings given, explicitly or implicitly, or society's dependence on reciprocity of sacrifice. Expectation that they will behave in the prescribed way is vulnerable to counterevidence, but expectation-to is not, or not directly, since it can be vulnerable to counterevidence showing *incapacity* to behave that way. We can have evidence about their past conduct or about their present plans and intentions such that we cannot expect that they will keep to the rule; but consistently and simultaneously with that we can expect them to keep to the rule. And in the absence of such counterevidence we can expect that . . . because we can expect them to. . . .

(c) Thus we can expect a man to behave in a certain way even though we cannot expect that he will because we know too much about him for such an expectation to be reasonable. A demand on a person does not fail to be reasonable just because the expectation that he will meet it fails to be reasonable. Because what we can expect a man to do is what we can rightfully demand of him, not only are there situations in which we can expect him to do what we cannot expect that he will do, but also there are situations in which we can expect that he will do what we cannot expect him to do. Kant's neighbors again illustrate the latter: They could expect that Kant would stick to his walking habits but they could not expect him to stick to them. They would not be entitled to

complain of his letting them down if he suddenly changed his schedule; for them to be entitled to complain, not only would Kant have to know that they were relying on him as their watch-regulator, but they would have to know that he knew, and he would have to know that they knew that he knew.

The claim of justice within the context of rules is the claim that reasonable expectations of conformity to rule should not be disappointed. And the basic claim is that of expectation to, which may range up from expecting a man, or an official, or a government, etc., not to depart from the regularities and customs upon which we are known to be depending, to expecting him or them to behave in the way prescribed·by the rule because he or they can be expected to feel bound by it. Injustice consists in failing to treat the victims of it in the way in which they can expect to be treated, at the same time, perhaps, as treating them in exactly the way in which they can expect that they will be treated.

This can be generalized to any case where one can expect to. . . including, that is, cases where even in the absence of rules one can expect to. . . . And there certainly are such cases. I can expect *A* to keep his promise to do *x* because he authorized me to expect that he would. The fact that by promising he authorized an expectation is the reason why he has the obligation to do what he promised to do. His obligation is not logically dependent on promises being a practice (in J. Rawls's sense), although the fact that they are such a practice may reinforce the obligation. Breaking a promise is unjust because it is somehow an affront or an insult to the promisee as a human being, in this case the insult of first conferring a right on him and then behaving as if you had not, and that I suggest is what injustice fundamentally is—the affront done to a man as a human being by not treating him in the way that he can expect to be treated. It is, I suspect, no accident that it is indignation rather than merely anger that we feel at injustice, whether we or others are its victims, and that indignation is still true enough to the etymology of the word to be dependent on viewing the treatment that arouses our indignation as somehow belittling or affronting the worth of the victim. Even where we are justified in treating people unjustly (and unhappily we sometimes may be) we are not to be admired for growing the calluses which make us insensitive to the affront we are doing them. The injustice which is done by discrimination when it is unjust (and not all discrimination is unjust) is the insult given to those discriminated against, the insult being rubbed in by letting them see others not relevantly different being better treated. The injustice done to women or to blacks does not absolutely consist in, although it is compounded by, their being discriminated against; the injustice is the insult of being held to lack the capacity of the qualifications which they clearly do not lack.

It is an affront to have a crying need denied or ignored, to have shown your worth by achievement and to have it belittled. It is inefficient, and socially wasteful, not to treat people according to their abilities, but it is not obviously unjust, unless on other grounds they could expect to be so treated. What is insulting about discrimination against, for example, women or blacks is not so much the failure to allow them to develop and exercise their abilities as the implied denial that they possess them. The boss who employs dolly girls rather than competent stenographers simply because he finds the former easier to look at is not being unjust to the latter; he would be, if he pretended that they were not as good stenographers as the dollies, and gave that as his reason for not employing them.

In this paper I have said nothing about canons or maxims of justice and injustice. I have been concerned solely with making some suggestions about the notion of justice, or rather the notion of injustice, itself. It seems advisable to be clear about that before going on to discuss the practically more demanding and emotionally more charged questions about canons. It may, for instance, be true that justice demands equality; but that truth, if it is one, should not be confused with the falsehood that justice *is* equality.

29

JOHN STUART MILL
The Subjection of Women

The object of this Essay is to explain as clearly as I am able, the grounds of an

Excerpted from John Stuart Mill, *The Subjection of Women* (1869).

opinion which I have held from the very earliest period when I had formed any opinions at all on social or political matters, and which, instead of being weakened or modified, has been constantly growing stronger by the progress of reflection and the experience of life: That the principle which regulates the existing social relations between the two sexes—the legal subordination of one sex to the other—is wrong in itself, and now one of the chief hindrances to human improvement; and that it ought to be replaced by a principle of perfect equality, admitting no power or privilege on the one side, nor disability on the other.

In the first place, the opinion in favour of the present system, which entirely subordinates the weaker sex to the stronger, rests upon theory only; for there never has been trial made of any other: so that experience, in the sense in which it is vulgarly opposed to theory, cannot be pretended to have pronounced any verdict. And in the second place, the adoption of this system of inequality never was the result of deliberation, or forethought, or any social ideas, or any notion whatever of what conduced to the benefit of humanity or the good order of society. It arose simply from the fact that from the very earliest twilight of human society, every woman (owing to the value attached to her by men, combined with her inferiority in muscular strength) was found in a state of bondage to some man. Laws and systems of polity always begin by recognising the relations they find already existing between individuals. They convert what was a mere physical fact into a legal right, give it the sanction of society, and principally aim at the substitution of public and organized means of asserting and protecting these rights, instead of the irregular and lawless conflict of physical strength. Those who had already been compelled to obedience became in this manner legally bound to it. Slavery, from being a mere affair of force between the master and the slave, became regularized and a matter of compact among the masters, who, binding themselves to one another for common protection, guaranteed by their collective strength the private possessions of each, including his slaves. In early times, the great majority of the male sex were slaves, as well as the whole of the female. And many ages elapsed, some of them ages of high cultivation, before any thinker was bold enough to question the rightfulness, and the absolute social necessity, either of the one slavery or of the other. By degrees such thinkers did arise: and (the general progress of society assisting) the slavery of the male sex has, in all the countries of Christian Europe at least (though, in one of them, only within the last few years) been at length abolished, and that of the female sex has been gradually changed into a milder form of dependence. But this dependence, as it exists at present, is not an original institution, taking a fresh start from considerations of justice and social expediency—it is the primitive state of slavery lasting on, through successive mitigations and modifications occasioned by the same causes which have softened the general manners, and brought all human relations more under the control of justice and the influence of humanity. It has not lost the taint of its brutal origin.[1] No presumption in its favour, therefore, can be drawn from the fact of its existence. The only such pre-

1. I am far from pretending that wives are in general no better treated than slaves; but no slave is a slave to the same lengths, and in so full a sense of the word, as a wife is. Hardly any slave, except one immediately attached to the master's person, is a slave at all hours and all minutes; in general he has, like a soldier, his fixed task, and when it is done, or when he is off duty, he disposes, within certain limits, of his own time, and has a family life into which the master rarely intrudes. "Uncle Tom" under his first master had his own life in his "cabin," almost as much as any man whose work

sumption which it could be supposed to have, must be grounded on its having lasted till now, when so many other things which came down from the same odious source have been done away with. And this, indeed, is what makes it strange to ordinary ears, to hear it asserted that the inequality of rights between men and women has no other source than the law of the strongest. . .

The subjection of women to men being a universal custom, any departure from it quite naturally appears unnatural. But how entirely, even in this case, the feeling is dependent on custom, appears by ample experience. Nothing so much astonishes the people of distant parts of the world, when they first learn anything about England, as to be told that it is under a queen: the thing seems to them so unnatural as to be almost incredible. To Englishmen this does not seem in the least degree unnatural, because they are used to it; but they do feel it unnatural that women should be soldiers or members of parliament. In the feudal ages, on the contrary, war and politics were not thought unnatural to women, because not unusual; it seemed natural that women of the privileged classes should be of manly character, inferior in nothing but bodily strength to their husbands and fathers. The independence of women seemed rather less unnatural to the Greeks than to other

ancients, on account of the fabulous Amazons (whom they believed to be historical), and the partial example afforded by the Spartan women; who, though no less subordinate by law than in other Greek states, were more free in fact, and being trained to bodily exercises in the same manner with men, gave ample proof that they were not naturally disqualified for them. There can be little doubt that Spartan experience suggested to Plato, among many other of his doctrines, that of the social and political equality of the two sexes. . . . .

All causes, social and natural, combine to make it unlikely that women should be collectively rebellious to the power of men. They are so far in a position different from all other subject classes, that their masters require something more from them than actual service. Men do not want solely the obedience of women, they want their sentiments. All men, except the most brutish, desire to have, in the woman most nearly connected with them, not a forced slave but a willing one, not a slave merely, but a favourite. They have therefore put everything in practice to enslave their minds. The masters of all other slaves rely, for maintaining obedience, on fear; either fear of themselves, or religious fears. The masters of women wanted more than simple obedience, and they turned the whole force of education to effect their purpose. All women are brought up from the very earliest years in the belief that their ideal of character is the very opposite to that of men; not self-will, and government by self-control, but submission, and yielding to the control of others. All the moralities tell them that it is the duty of women, and all the current sentimentalities that it is their nature, to live for others; to make

takes him away from home, is able to have in his own family. But it cannot be so with the wife. Above all, a female slave has (in Christian countries) an admitted right, and is considered under a moral obligation, to refuse to her master the last familiarity. Not so the wife: however brutal a tyrant she may unfortunately be chained to—though she may know that he hates her, though it may be his daily pleasure to torture her, and though she may feel it impossible not to loathe him—he can claim from her and enforce the lowest degradation of a human being, that of being made the instrument of an animal function contrary to her inclinations.

complete abnegation of themselves, and to have no life but in their affections. And by their affections are meant the only ones they are allowed to have—those to the men with whom they are connected, or to the children who constitute an additional and indefeasible tie between them and a man. When we put together three things—first, the natural attraction between opposite sexes; secondly, the wife's entire dependence on the husband, every privilege or pleasure she has being either his gift, or depending entirely on his will; and lastly, that the principal object of human pursuit, consideration, and all objects of social ambition, can in general be sought or obtained by her only through him, it would be a miracle if the object of being attractive to men had not become the polar star of feminine education and formation of character. And, this great means of influence over the minds of women having been acquired, an instinct of selfishness made men avail themselves of it to the utmost as a means of holding women in subjection, by representing to them meekness, submissiveness, and resignation of all individual will into the hands of a man, as an essential part of sexual attractiveness. Can it be doubted that any of the other yokes which mankind have succeeded in breaking, would have subsisted till now if the same means had existed, and had been as sedulously used, to bow down their minds to it? If it had been made the object of the life of every young plebeian to find personal favour in the eyes of some patrician, of every young serf with some seigneur; if domestication with him, and a share of his personal affections, had been held out as the prize which they all should look out for, the most gifted and aspiring being able to reckon on the most desirable prizes; and

if, when this prize had been obtained, they had been shut out by a wall of brass from all interests not centering in him, all feelings and desires but those which he shared or inculcated; would not serfs and seigneurs, plebeians and patricians, have been as broadly distinguished at this day as men and women are? and would not all but a thinker here and there, have believed the distinction to be a fundamental and unalterable fact in human nature?

The preceding considerations are amply sufficient to show that custom, however universal it may be, affords in this case no presumption, and ought not to create any prejudice, in favour of the arrangements which place women in social and political subjection to men. But I may go farther, and maintain that the course of history, and the tendencies of progressive human society, afford not only no presumption in favour of this system of inequality of rights, but a strong one against it; and that, so far as the whole course of human improvement up to this time, the whole stream of modern tendencies, warrants any inference on the subject, it is, that this relic of the past is discordant with the future, and must necessarily disappear. . . .

After what has been said respecting the obligation of obedience, it is almost superfluous to say anything concerning the more special point included in the general one—a woman's right to her own property; for I need not hope that this treatise can make any impression upon those who need anything to convince them that a woman's inheritance or gains ought to be as much her own after marriage as before. The rule is simple: whatever would be the husband's or wife's if they were not married, should be under their exclusive control during marriage; which need not interfere with the power to tie up property by settlement, in order to preserve it for children. Some people are sentimentally shocked at the idea of a separate interest in money matters, as inconsistent with the ideal fusion of two lives into one. For my own part, I am one of the strongest supporters of community of goods, when resulting from an entire unity of feeling in the owners, which makes all things common between them. But I have no relish for a community of goods resting on the doctrine, that what is mine is yours but what is yours is not mine; and I should prefer to decline entering into such a compact with any one, though I were myself the person to profit by it. . . .

The *power* of earning is essential to the dignity of a woman, if she has not independent property. But if marriage were an equal contract, not implying the obligation of obedience; if the connexion were no longer enforced to the oppression of those to whom it is purely a mischief, but a separation, on just terms (I do not now speak of a divorce), could be obtained by any women who was morally entitled to it; and if she would then find all honourable employments as freely open to her as to men; it would not be necessary for her protection, that during marriage she should make this particular use of her faculties. Like a man when he chooses a profession, so, when a woman marries, it may in general by understood that she makes choice of the management of a household, and the bringing up of a family, as the first call upon her exertions, during as many years of her life as may be required for the purpose; and that she renounces, not all other objects and occupations, but all which are not consistent with the requirements of this. The actual exercise, in a habitual

or systematic manner, of outdoor occupations, or such as cannot be carried on at home, would by this principle be practically interdicted to the greater number of married women. But the utmost latitude ought to exist for the adaptation of general rules to individual suitabilities; and there ought to be nothing to prevent faculties exceptionally adapted to any other pursuit, from obeying their vocation notwithstanding marriage: due provision being made for supplying otherwise any falling-short which might become inevitable, in her full performance of the ordinary functions of mistress of a family. These things, if once opinion were rightly directed on the subject, might with perfect safety be left to be regulated by opinion, without any interference of law. . . .

On the other point which is involved in the just equality of women, their admissibility to all the functions and occupations hitherto retained as the monopoly of the stronger sex, I should anticipate no difficulty in convincing any one who has gone with me on the subject of the equality of women in the family. I believe that their disabilities elsewhere are only clung to in order to maintain their subordination in domestic life; because the generality of the male sex cannot yet tolerate the idea of living with an equal. Were it not for that, I think that almost every one, in the existing state of opinion in politics and political economy, would admit the injustice of excluding half the human race from the greater number of lucrative occupations, and from almost all high social functions; ordaining from their birth either that they are not, and cannot by any possibility become, fit for employments which are legally open to the stupidest and basest of the other sex, or else that however fit they may be, those employments shall be interdicted to them, in order to be preserved for the exclusive benefit of males. In the last two centuries, when (which was seldom the case) any reason beyond the mere existence of the fact was thought to be required to justify the disabilities of women, people seldom assigned as a reason their inferior mental capacity; which, in times when there was a real trial of personal faculties (from which all women were not excluded) in the struggles of public life, no one really believed in. The reason given in those days was not women's unfitness, but the interest of society, by which was meant the interest of men: just as the *raison d'état,* meaning the convenience of the government, and the support of existing authority, was deemed a sufficient explanation and excuse for the most flagitious crimes. In the present day, power holds a smoother language, and whomsoever it oppresses, always pretends to do so for their own good: accordingly, when anything is forbidden to women, it is thought necessary to say, and desirable to believe, that they are incapable of doing it, and that they depart from their real path of success and happiness when they aspire to it. But to make this reason plausible (I do not say valid), those by whom it is urged must be prepared to carry it to a much greater length than any one ventures to do in the face of present experience. It is not sufficient to maintain that women on the average are less gifted than men on the average, with certain of the higher mental faculties, or that a smaller number of women than of men are fit for occupations and functions of the highest intellectual character. It is necessary to maintain that no women at all are fit for them, and that the most eminent women are inferior in mental faculties to the most mediocre of the

men on whom those functions at present devolve. For if the performance of the function is decided either by competition, or by any mode of choice which secures regard to the public interest, there needs to be no apprehension that any important employments will fall into the hands of women inferior to average men, or to the average of their male competitors. The only result would be that there would be fewer women than men in such employments; a result certain to happen in any case; if only from the preference always likely to be felt by the majority of women for the one vocation in which there is nobody to compete with them. Now, the most determined depreciator of women will not venture to deny, that when we add the experience of recent times to that of ages past, women, and not a few merely, but many women, have proved themselves capable of everything, perhaps without a single exception, which is done by men, and of doing it successfully and creditably. The utmost that can be said is, that there are many things which none of them have succeeded in doing as well as they have been done by some men—many in which they have not reached the very highest rank. But there are extremely few, dependent only on mental faculties, in which they have not attained the rank next to the highest. Is not this enough, and much more than enough, to make it a tyranny to them, and a detriment to society, that they should not be allowed to compete with men for the exercise of these functions? Is it not a mere truism to say, that such functions are often filled by men far less fit for them than numbers of women, and who would be beaten by women in any fair field of competition? What difference does it make that there may be men somewhere, fully employed about other things, who may be still better qualified for the things in question than these women? Does not this take place in all competitions? Is there so great a superfluity of men fit for high duties, that society can afford to reject the service of any competent person? Are we so certain of always finding a man made to our hands for any duty or function of social importance which falls vacant, that we lose nothing by putting a ban upon one-half of mankind, and refusing beforehand to make their faculties available, however distinguished they may be? And even if we could do without them, would it be consistent with justice to refuse to them their fair share of honour and distinction, or to deny to them the equal moral right of all human beings to choose their occupation (short of injury to others) according to their own preferences, at their own risk? Nor is the injustice confined to them: it is shared by those who are in a position to benefit by their services. To ordain that any kind of persons shall not be physicians, or shall not be advocates, or shall not be members of parliament, is to injure not them only, but all who employ physicians or advocates, or elect members of parliament, and who are deprived of the stimulating effect of greater competition on the exertions of the competitors, as well as restricted to a narrower range of individual choice.

It will perhaps be sufficient if I confine myself, in the details of my argument, to functions of a public nature: since, if I am successful as to those, it probably will be readily granted that women should be admissible to all other occupations to which it is at all material whether they are admitted or not. And here let me begin by marking out one function, broadly distinguished from all others, their right to which is entirely independent of any question

which can be raised concerning their faculties. I mean the suffrage, both parliamentary and municipal. The right to share in the choice of those who are to exercise a public trust, is altogether a distinct thing from that of competing for the trust itself. If no one could vote for a member of parliament who was not fit to be a candidate, the government would be a narrow oligarchy indeed. To have a voice in choosing those by whom one is to be governed, is a means of self-protection due to every one, though he were to remain for ever excluded from the function of governing: and that women are considered fit to have such a choice, may be presumed from the fact, that the law already gives it to women in the most important of all cases to themselves: for the choice of the man who is to govern a woman to the end of life, is always supposed to be voluntarily made by herself. In the case of election to public trusts, it is the business of constitutional law to surround the right of suffrage with all needful securities and limitations; but whatever securities are sufficient in the case of the male sex, no others need be required in the case of women. Under whatever conditions, and within whatever limits, men are admitted to the suffrage, there is not a shadow of justification for not admitting women under the same. The majority of the women of any class are not likely to differ in political opinion from the majority of the men of the same class, unless the question be one in which the interests of women, as such, are in some way involved; and if they are so, women require the suffrage, as their guarantee of just and equal consideration. This ought to be obvious even to those who coincide in no other of the doctrines for which I contend. Even if every woman were a wife, and if every wife ought to be a slave, all the

272 · Justice and Equality

more would these slaves stand in need of legal protection: and we know what legal protection the slaves have, where the laws are made by their masters.

With regard to the fitness of women, not only to participate in elections, but themselves to hold offices or practise professions involving important public responsibilities; I have already observed that this consideration is not essential to the practical question in dispute: since any woman, who succeeds in an open profession, proves by that very fact that she is qualified for it. And in the case of public offices, if the political system of the country is such as to exclude unfit men, it will equally exclude unfit women: while if it is not, there is no additional evil in the fact that the unfit persons whom it admits may be either women or men. As long therefore as it is acknowledged that even a few women may be fit for these duties, the laws which shut the door on those exceptions cannot be justified by any opinion which can be held respecting the capacities of women in general. But, though this last consideration is not essential, it is far from being irrelevant. An unprejudiced view of it gives additional strength to the arguments against the disabilities of women, and reinforces them by high considerations of practical utility.

Let us at first make entire abstraction of all psychological considerations tending to show, that any of the mental differences supposed to exist between women and men are but the natural effect of the differences in their education and circumstances, and indicate no radical difference, far less radical inferiority, of nature. Let us consider women only as they already are, or as they are known to have been; and the capacities which they have already practically shown. What they have

done, that at least, if nothing else, it is proved that they can do. When we consider how sedulously they are all trained away from, instead of being trained towards, any of the occupations or objects reserved for men, it is evident that I am taking a very humble ground for them, when I rest their case on what they have actually achieved. For, in this case, negative evidence is worth little, while any positive evidence is conclusive. It cannot be inferred to be impossible that a woman should be a Homer, or an Aristotle, or a Michael Angelo, or a Beethoven, because no woman has yet actually produced works comparable to theirs in any of those lines of excellence. This negative fact at most leaves the question uncertain, and open to psychological discussion. But it is quite certain that a woman can be a Queen Elizabeth, or a Deborah, or a Joan of Arc, since this is not inference, but fact. Now it is a curious consideration, that the only things which the existing law excludes women from doing, are the things which they have proved that they are able to do. There is no law to prevent a woman from having written all the plays of Shakespeare, or composed all the operas of Mozart. But Queen Elizabeth or Queen Victoria, had they not inherited the throne, could not have been intrusted with the smallest of the political duties, of which the former showed herself equal to the greatest. . . .

The concessions of the privileged to the unprivileged are so seldom brought about by any better motive than the power of the unprivileged to extort them, that any arguments against the prerogative of sex are likely to be little attended to by the generality, as long as they are able to say to themselves that women do not complain of it. That fact certainly enables men to retain the unjust privilege some time longer; but does not render it less unjust. Exactly the same thing may be said of the women in the harem of an Oriental: they do not complain of not being allowed the freedom of European women. They think our women insufferably bold and unfeminine. How rarely it is that even men complain of the general order of society; and how much rarer still would such complaint be, if they did not know of any different order existing anywhere else. Women do not complain of the general lot of women; or rather they do, for plaintive elegies on it are very common in the writings of women, and were still more so as long as the lamentations could not be suspected of having any practical object. Their complaints are like the complaints which men make of the general unsatisfactoriness of human life; they are not meant to imply blame, or to plead for any change. But though women do not complain of the power of husbands, each complains of her own husband, or of the husbands of her friends. It is the same in all other cases of servitude, at least in the commencement of the emancipatory movement. The serfs did not at first complain of the power of their lords, but only of their tyranny. The Commons began by claiming a few municipal privileges; they next asked an exemption for themselves from being taxed without their own consent; but they would at that time have thought it a great presumption to claim any share in the king's sovereign authority. The case of women is now the only case in which to rebel against established rules is still looked upon with the same eyes as was formerly a subject's claim to the right of rebelling against his king. A woman who joins in any movement which her husband disapproves, makes herself a martyr, without even being able to be an apostle, for the husband can legally put a stop to her apostleship. Women cannot be expected to devote themselves to the emancipation of women, until men in considerable number are prepared to join them in the undertaking. . . .

When we consider the positive evil caused to the disqualified half of the human race by their disqualification—first in the loss of the most inspiriting and elevating kind of personal enjoyment, and next in the weariness, disappointment, and profound dissatisfaction with life, which are so often the substitute for it; one feels that among all the lessons which men require for carrying on the struggle against the inevitable imperfections of their lot on earth, there is no lesson which they more need, than not to add to the evils which nature inflicts, by their jealous and prejudiced restrictions on one another. Their vain fears only substitute other and worse evils for those which they are idly apprehensive of: while every restraint on the freedom of conduct of any of their human fellow creatures (otherwise than by making them responsible for any evil actually caused by it), dries up *pro tanto* the principal fountain of human happiness, and leaves the species less rich, to an inappreciable degree, in all that makes life valuable to the individual human being.

30

THOMAS NAGEL
Equal Treatment and Compensatory Discrimination

It is currently easier, or widely thought to be easier, to get certain jobs or to gain admission to certain educational institutions if one is black or a woman than if one is a white man. Whether or not this is true, many people think it should be true, and many others think it should not. The question is: If a black person or a woman is admitted to a law school or medical school, or appointed to a certain academic or administrative post, in preference to a white man who is in other respects better qualified,[1] and if this is done in pursuit of a preferential policy or to fill a quota, is it unjust? Can the white man complain that he has been unjustly treated? It is important to investigate the justice of such practices, because if they are unjust, it is much more difficult to defend them on grounds of social utility. I shall argue that although preferential policies are not required by justice, they are not seriously unjust either—because the system from which they depart is already unjust for reasons having nothing to do with racial or sexual discrimination.

I

In the United States, the following steps seem to have led us to a situation in which these questions arise. First, and not very long ago, it came to be widely accepted that deliberate barriers against the admission of blacks and women to

desirable positions should be abolished. Their abolition is by no means complete, and certain educational institutions, for example, may be able to maintain limiting quotas on the admission of women for some time. But deliberate discrimination is widely condemned.

Secondly, it was recognized that even without explicit barriers there could be discrimination, either consciously or unconsciously motivated, and this gave support to self-conscious efforts at impartiality, careful consideration of candidates belonging to the class discriminated against, and attention to the proportions of blacks and women in desirable positions, as evidence that otherwise undetectable bias might be influencing the selections. (Another, related consideration is that criteria which were good predictors of performance for one group might turn out to be poor predictors of performance for another group, so that the continued employment of those criteria might introduce a concealed inequity.)

The third step came with the realization that a social system may continue to deny different races or sexes equal opportunity or equal access to de-

From Thomas Nagel, "Equal Treatment and Compensatory Discrimination," *Philosophy and Public Affairs*, vol. 2 (1972–1973), pp. 348–363. Copyright © 1973 by Princeton University Press. Reprinted by permission of Princeton University Press. This article is reprinted unabridged.

1. By saying that the white man is "in other respects better qualified" I mean that if, e.g., a black candidate with similar qualifications had been available for the position, he would have been selected in preference to the black candidate who was in fact selected; or, if the choice had been between two white male candidates of corresponding qualifications, this one would have been selected. Ditto for two white or two black women. (I realize that it may not always be easy to determine similarity of qualifications, and that in some cases similarity of credentials may give evidence of a difference in qualifications—because, e.g., one person had to overcome more severe obstacles to acquire those credentials.)

sirable positions even after the discriminatory barriers to those positions have been lifted. Socially-caused inequality in the capacity to make use of available opportunities or to compete for available positions may persist, because the society systematically provides to one group more than to another certain educational, social, or economic advantages. Such advantages improve one's competitive position in seeking access to jobs or places in professional schools. Where there has recently been widespread deliberate discrimination in many areas, it will not be surprising if the formerly excluded group experiences relative difficulty in gaining access to newly opened positions, and it is plausible to explain the difficulty at least partly in terms of disadvantages produced by past discrimination. This leads to the adoption of compensatory measures, in the form of special training programs, or financial support, or day-care centers, or apprenticeships, or tutoring. Such measures are designed to qualify those whose reduced qualifications are due to racial or sexual discrimination, either because they have been the direct victims of such discrimination, or because they are deprived as a result of membership in a group or community many of whose other members have been discriminated against. The second of these types of influence covers a great deal, and the importance of the social contribution is not always easy to establish. Nevertheless its effects typically include the loss of such goods as self-esteem, self-confidence, motivation, and ambition—all of which contribute to competitive success and none of which is easily restored by special training programs. Even if social injustice has produced such effects, it may be difficult for society to eradicate them.

This type of justification for compensatory programs raises another question. If it depends on the claim that the disadvantages being compensated for are the product of social injustice, then it becomes important how great the contribution of social injustice actually is, and to what extent the situation is due to social causes not involving injustice, or to causes that are not social, but biological. If one believes that society's responsibility for compensatory measures extends only to those disadvantages due to social injustice, one will assign political importance to the degree, if any, to which racial differences in average I.Q. are genetically influenced, or the innate contribution, if any, to the statistical differences, if any, in emotional or intellectual characteristics between men and women. Also, if one believes that among socially-produced inequalities, there is a crucial distinction for the requirement of compensation between those which are produced unjustly and those which are merely the incidental results of just social arrangements, then it will be very important to decide exactly where that line falls: whether, for example, certain intentions must be referred to in arguing that a disadvantage has been unjustly imposed. But let me put those issues aside for the moment.

The fourth stage comes when it is acknowledged that some unjustly caused disadvantages, which create difficulties of access to positions formally open to all, cannot be overcome by special programs of preparatory or remedial training. One is then faced with the alternative of either allowing the effects of social injustice to confer a disadvantage in the access to desirable positions that are filled simply on the basis of qualifications relevant to performance in those positions, or else instituting a system of compensatory discrimination in the selection process to increase access for those whose qualifications are lower at least partly as a result of unjust discrimination in other situations and at other times (and possibly against other persons). This is a difficult choice, and it would certainly be preferable to find a more direct method of rectification, than to balance inequality in one part of the social system by introducing a reverse inequality at a different point. If the society as a whole contains serious injustices with complex effects, there is probably, in any case, no way for a single institution within that society to adjust its criteria for competitive admission or employment so that the effects of injustice are nullified as far as that institution is concerned. There is consequently considerable appeal to the position that places should be filled solely by reference to the criteria relevant to performance, and if this tends to amplify or extend the effects of inequitable treatment elsewhere, the remedy must be found in a more direct attack on those differences in qualifications, rather than in the introduction of irrelevant criteria of appointment or admission which will also sacrifice efficiency, productivity, or effectiveness of the institution in its specific tasks.

At this fourth stage we therefore find a broad division of opinion. There are those who believe that nothing further can legitimately be done in the short run, once the *remediable* unjust inequalities of opportunity between individuals have been dealt with: The irremediable ones are unjust, but any further steps to counterbalance them by reverse discrimination would also be unjust, because they must employ irrelevant criteria. On the other hand, there are those who find it unacceptable in such circumstances to stay with the restricted criteria usually related to successful performance, and who believe that differential admission or hiring standards for worse-off groups are justified because they roughly, though only approximately, compensate for the inequalities of opportunity produced by past injustice.

But at this point there is some temptation to resolve the dilemma and strengthen the argument for preferential standards by proceeding to a fifth stage. One may reflect that if the criteria relevant to the prediction of performance are not inviolable it may not matter whether one violates them to compensate for disadvantages caused by injustice or disadvantages caused in other ways. The fundamental issue is what grounds to use in assigning or admitting people to desirable positions. To settle that issue, one does not have to settle the question of the degree to which racial or sexual discrepancies are socially produced, because the differentials in reward ordinarily correlated with differences in qualifications are not the result of natural justice, but simply the effect of a competitive system trying to fill positions and perform tasks efficiently. Certain abilities may be relevant to filling a job from the point of view of efficiency, but they are not relevant from the point of view of justice, because they provide no indication that one deserves the rewards that go with holding that job. The qualities, experience, and attainments that make success in a certain position likely do not in themselves merit the rewards that happen to attach to occupancy of that position in a competitive economy.

Consequently it might be concluded that if women or black people are less qualified, for *whatever* reason, in the respects that lead to success in the professions that our society rewards most highly, then it would be just to compensate for this disadvantage, within the limits permitted by efficiency, by having suitably different standards for these groups, and thus bringing their access to desirable positions more into line with that of others. Compensatory discrimination would not, on this view, have to be tailored to deal only with the effects of past injustice.

But it is clear that this is not a stable position. For if one abandons the condition that to qualify for compensation an inequity must be socially caused, then there is no reason to restrict the compensatory measures to well-defined racial or sexual groups. Compensatory selection procedures would have to be applied on an individual basis, within as well as between such groups—each person, regardless of race, sex, or qualifications, being granted equal access to the desirable positions, within limits set by efficiency. This might require randomization of law and medical school admissions, for example, from among all the candidates who were above some minimum standard enabling them to do the work. If we were to act on the principle that different abilities do not merit different rewards, it would result in much more equality than is demanded by proponents of compensatory discrimination.

There is no likelihood that such a radical course will be adopted in the United States, but the fact that it seems to follow naturally from a certain view about how to deal with racial or sexual injustice reveals something important. When we try to deal with the inequality in advantages that results from a disparity in qualifications (however produced) between races or sexes, we are up against a pervasive and fundamental feature of the system, which at every turn exacts costs and presents obstacles in response to attempts to reduce the inequalities. We must face the possibility that the primary injustice with which we have to contend lies in this feature itself, and that some of the worst aspects of what we now perceive as racial or sexual injustice are merely conspicuous manifestations of the great social injustice of differential reward.

II

If differences in the capacity to succeed in the tasks that any society rewards well are visibly correlated, for whatever reason, with other characteristics such as race or religion or social origin, then a system of liberal equality of opportunity will give the appearance of supporting racial or religious or class injustice. Where there is no such correlation, there can be the appearance of justice through equal opportunity. But in reality, there is similar injustice in both cases, and it lies in the schedule of rewards.

The liberal idea of equal treatment demands that people receive equal opportunities if they are equally qualified by talent or education to utilize those opportunities. In requiring the relativization of equal treatment to characteristics in which people are very unequal, it guarantees that the social order will reflect and probably magnify the initial distinctions produced by nature and the past. Liberalism has therefore come under increasing attack in recent years, on the ground that the familiar principle of equal treatment, with its meritocratic conception of relevant differences, seems too weak to combat the inequalities dispensed by nature and the ordinary workings of the social system.

This criticism of the view that people deserve the rewards that accrue to them as a result of their natural talents is not based on the idea that no one can be said to deserve anything.[2] For if no one deserves anything, then no inequalities are contrary to desert, and desert provides no argument for equality. Rather, I am suggesting that for many benefits and disadvantages, certain characteristics of the recipient *are* relevant to what he deserves. If people are equal in the relevant respects, that by itself constitutes a reason to distribute the benefit to them equally.[3]

The relevant features will vary with the benefit or disadvantage, and so will the weight of the resulting considerations of desert. Desert may sometimes, in fact, be a rather unimportant consideration in determining what ought to be done. But I do wish to claim, with reference to a central case, that differential abilities are not usually among the characteristics that determine whether people *deserve* economic and social benefits (though of course they determine whether people *get* such benefits). In fact, I believe that nearly all characteristics are irrelevant to what people deserve in this dimension, and that most people therefore deserve to be treated equally.[4] Perhaps voluntary differences in effort or moral differences in conduct have some bearing on economic and social desert. I do not have a precise view about what features are

relevant. I contend only that they are features in which most people do not differ enough to justify very wide differences in reward.[5] (While I realize that these claims are controversial, I shall not try to defend them here, nor to defend the legitimacy of the notion of desert itself. If these things make no sense, neither does the rest of my argument.)

A decision that people are equally or unequally deserving in some respect is not the end of the story. First of all, desert can sometimes be overridden, for example by liberty or even by efficiency. In some cases the presumption of equality is rather weak, and not much is required to depart from it. This will be so if the interest in question is minor or temporally circumscribed, and does not represent an important value in the subject's life.

Secondly, it may be that although an inequality is contrary to desert, no one can benefit from its removal: All that can be done is to worsen the position of those who benefit undeservedly from its presence. Even if one believes that desert is a very important factor in determining just distributions, one need not object to inequalities that are to no one's disadvantage. In other words, it is possible to accept something like

---

2. Rawls appears to regard this as the basis of his own view. He believes it makes sense to speak of positive desert only in the context of distributions by a just system, and not as a pre-institutional conception that can be used to measure the justice of the system. John Rawls, *A Theory of Justice* (Cambridge, Mass., 1971), pp. 310–313.

3. Essentially this view is put forward by Bernard Williams in "The Idea of Equality," in *Philosophy, Politics, and Society* (Second Series), ed. P. Laslett and W. G. Runciman (Oxford, 1964), pp. 110–131.

4. This is distinct from a case in which nothing is relevant because there *is* no desert in the matter. In that case the fact that people differed in no relevant characteristics would not create a pre-

sumption that they be treated equally. It would leave the determination of their treatment entirely to other considerations.

5. It is *not* my view that we cannot be said to deserve the *results* of anything which we do not deserve. It is true that a person does not deserve his intelligence, and I have maintained that he does not deserve the rewards that superior intelligence can provide. But neither does he deserve his bad moral character or his above-average willingness to work, yet I believe that he probably does deserve the punishments or rewards that flow from those qualities. For an illuminating discussion of these matters, see Robert Nozick, *Anarchy, State, and Utopia* (New York, Basic Books: 1974), chap. 7.

Rawls's Difference Principle from the standpoint of an egalitarian view of desert.[6] (I say it is possible. It may not be required. Some may reject the Difference Principle because they regard quality of treatment as a more stringent requirement.)

Thirdly (and most significantly for the present discussion), a determination of relative desert in the distribution of a particular advantage does not even settle the question of *desert* in every case, for there may be other advantages and disadvantages whose distribution is tied to that of the first, and the characteristics relevant to the determination of desert are not necessarily the same from one advantage to another. This bears on the case under consideration in the following way. I have said that people with different talents do not thereby deserve different economic and social rewards. They may, however, deserve different opportunities to exercise and develop those talents.[7] Whenever the distribution of two different types of benefit is connected in this way, through social or economic mechanisms or through natural human reactions, it may be impossible to avoid a distribution contrary to the conditions of desert in respect of at least one of the benefits. Therefore it is likely that a dilemma will arise in which it appears that injustice cannot be entirely avoided. It may then be necessary to decide that justice in the distribution of one advantage has priority over justice in the distribution of another that automatically goes with it.

In the case under discussion, there appears to be a conflict between justice in the distribution of educational and professional opportunities and justice in the distribution of economic and social rewards. I do not deny that there is a presumption, based on something more than efficiency, in favor of giving equal opportunities to those equally likely to succeed. But if the presumption in favor of economic equality is considerably stronger, the justification for departing from it must be stronger too. If this is so, then when "educational" justice and economic justice come into conflict, it will sometimes be necessary to sacrifice the former to the latter.

III

In thinking about racial and sexual discrimination, the view that economic justice has priority may tempt one to proceed to what I have called the fifth stage. One may be inclined to adopt admission quotas, for example, proportional to the representation of a given group in the population, because one senses the injustice of differential rewards per se. Whatever explains the small number of women or blacks in the professions, it has the result that they have less of the financial and social benefits that accrue to members of the professions, and what accounts for those differences cannot justify them. So justice requires that more women and blacks be admitted to the professions.

The trouble with this solution is that it does not locate the injustice accurately, but merely tries to correct the racially or sexually skewed economic distribution which is one of its more conspicuous symptoms. We are enabled to perceive the situation as unjust because we see it, for example, through its racial manifestations, and race is a subject by now associated in our minds with injustice. However, little is gained by merely transferring the same

6. Rawls, *op. cit.*, pp. 75–80.

7. Either because differences of ability are relevant to degree of desert in these respects or because people are equally deserving of opportunities proportional to their talents. More likely the latter.

system of differential rewards, suitably adjusted to achieve comparable proportions, to the class of blacks or the class of women. If it is unjust to reward people differentially for what certain characteristics enable them to do, it is equally unjust whether the distinction is made between a white man and a black man or between two black men, or two white women, or two black women. There is no way of attacking the unjust reward schedules (if indeed they are unjust) of a meritocratic system by attacking their racial or sexual manifestations directly.

In most societies reward is a function of demand, and many of the human characteristics most in demand result largely from *gifts* or *talents.* The greatest injustice in this society, I believe, is neither racial nor sexual but intellectual. I do not mean that it is unjust that some people are more intelligent than others. Nor do I mean that society rewards people differentially simply on the basis of their intelligence: Usually it does not. Nevertheless it provides on the average much larger rewards for tasks that require superior intelligence than for those that do not. This is simply the way things work out in a technologically advanced society with a market economy. It does not reflect a social judgment that smart people *deserve* the opportunity to make more money than dumb people. They may deserve richer educational opportunity, but they do not therefore deserve the material wealth that goes with it. Similar things could be said about society's differential reward of achievements facilitated by other talents or gifts, like beauty, athletic ability, musicality, etc. But intelligence and its development by education provide a particularly significant and pervasive example.

However, a general reform of the current schedule of rewards, even if they are unjust, is beyond the power of individual educational or business institutions, working through their admissions or appointments policies. A competitive economy is bound to reward those with certain training and abilities, and a refusal to do so will put any business enterprise in a poor competitive position. Similarly, those who succeed in medical school or law school will tend to earn more than those who do not—whatever criteria of admission the schools adopt. It is not the procedures of appointment or admission, based on criteria that predict success, that are unjust, but rather what happens as a result of success.

No doubt a completely just solution is not ready to hand. If, as I have claimed, different factors are relevant to what is deserved in the distribution of different benefits and disadvantages, and if the distribution of several distinct advantages is sometimes connected even though the relevant factors are not, then inevitably there will be injustice in some respect, and it may be practically impossible to substitute a principle of distribution which avoids it completely.

Justice may require that we try to reduce the automatic connections between material advantages, cultural opportunity, and institutional authority. But such changes can be brought about, if at all, only by large alterations in the social system, the system of taxation, and the salary structure. They will not be achieved by modifying the admissions or hiring policies of colleges and universities, or even banks, law firms, and businesses.

Compensatory measures in admissions or appointment can be defended on grounds of justice only to the extent that they compensate for specific disadvantages which have themselves been unjustly caused, by factors distinct from the general meritocratic character of the system of distribution of advantageous positions. Such contributions are difficult to verify or estimate, they probably vary among individuals in the oppressed group. Moreover, it is not obvious that where a justification for preferential treatment exists, it is strong enough to create an obligation, since it is doubtful that one element of a pluralistic society is obliged to adopt discriminatory measures to counteract injustice due to another element, or even to the society as a whole.

IV

These considerations suggest that an argument on grounds of justice for the imposition of racial or sexual quotas would be difficult to construct without the aid of premises about the source of unequal qualifications between members of different groups. The more speculative the premises, the weaker the argument. But the question with which I began was not whether compensatory discrimination is *required* by justice, but whether it is *compatible* with justice. To that question I think we can give a different answer. If the reflections about differential reward to which we have been led are correct, then compensatory discrimination need not be seriously unjust, and it may be warranted not by justice but by considerations of social utility. I say not *seriously* unjust, to acknowledge that a departure from the standards relevant to distribution of intellectual opportunities *per se* is itself a kind of injustice. But its seriousness is lessened because the factors relevant to the distribution of intellectual opportunity are irrelevant to the distribution of those material benefits that go with it. This weakens the claim of someone who argues that by virtue of those qualities that make him likely to succeed in a certain position, he deserves to be

selected for that position in preference to someone whose qualifications make it likely that he will succeed less well. He cannot claim that justice requires the allocation of positions on the basis of ability, because the result of such allocation, in the present system, is serious injustice of a different kind.

My contention, then, is that where the allocation of one benefit on relevant grounds carries with it the allocation of other, more significant benefits to which those grounds are irrelevant, the departure from those grounds need not be a serious offense against justice. This may be so for two reasons. First, the presumption of equal treatment of relevantly equal persons in respect of the first benefit may not be very strong to begin with. Second, the fairness of abiding by that presumption may be overshadowed by the unfairness of the other distribution correlated with it. Consequently, it may be acceptable to depart from the "relevant" grounds for undramatic reasons of social utility, that would not justify more flagrant and undiluted examples of unfairness. Naturally a deviation from the usual method will appear unjust to those who are accustomed to regarding ability to succeed as the correct criterion, but this appearance may be an illusion. That depends on how much injustice is involved in the usual method, and whether the reasons for departing from it are good enough, even though they do not correct the injustice.

The problem, of course, is to say what a good reason is. I do not want to produce an argument that will justify not only compensatory discrimination on social grounds, but also ordinary racial or sexual discrimination designed to preserve internal harmony in a business, for instance. Even someone who thought that the system of differential economic rewards for different abilities was unjust would presumably regard it as an *additional* justice if standard racial, religious, or sexual discrimination were a factor in the assignment of individuals to highly rewarded positions.

I can offer only a partial account of what makes systematic racial or sexual discrimination so exceptionally unjust. It has no social advantages, and it attaches a sense of reduced worth to a feature with which people are born.[8] A psychological consequence of the systematic attachment of social disadvantages to a certain inborn feature is that both the possessors of the feature and others begin to regard it as an essential and important characteristic, and one which reduces the esteem in which its possessor can be held.[9] Concomitantly, those who do not possess the characteristic gain a certain amount of free esteem by comparison, and the arrangement thus constitutes a gross sacrifice of the most basic personal interests of some for the interests of others, with those sacrificed being on the bottom. (It is because similar things can be said about the social and economic disadvantages that attach to low intelligence that I am inclined to regard that, too, as a major injustice.)

Reverse discrimination need not have these consequences, and it can have social advantages. Suppose, for example, that there is need for a great increase in the number of black doctors, because the health needs of the black community are unlikely to be met otherwise. And suppose that at the present average level of premedical qualifications among black applicants, it would require a huge expansion of total medical school enrollment to supply the desirable absolute number of black doctors without adopting differential admission standards. Such an expansion may be unacceptable either because of its cost or because it would produce a total supply of doctors, black and white, much greater than the society requires. This is a strong argument for accepting reverse discrimination, not on grounds of justice but on grounds of social utility. (In addition, there is the salutary effect on the aspirations and expectations of other blacks, from the visibility of exemplars in formerly inaccessible positions.)

The argument in the other direction, from the point of view of the qualified white applicants who are turned away, is not nearly as strong as the argument against standard racial discrimination. The self-esteem of whites as a group is not endangered by such a practice, since the situation arises only because of their general social dominance, and the aim of the practice is only to benefit blacks, and not to exclude whites. Moreover, although the interests of some are being sacrificed to further the interests of others, it is the better placed who are being sacrificed and the worst placed who are being helped.[10] It is an important feature of the case that the discriminatory measure is designed to favor a group whose social position is exceptionally depressed, with destructive consequences both for the self-

8. For a detailed and penetrating treatment of this and a number of other matters discussed here, see Owen M. Fiss, "A Theory of Fair Employment Laws," *University of Chicago Law Review* 38 (Winter 1971): 235–314.

9. This effect would not be produced by an idiosyncratic discriminatory practice limited to a few eccentrics. If some people decided they would have nothing to do with anyone left-handed, everyone else, including the left-handed, would regard it as a silly objection to an inessential feature. But if everyone shunned the left-handed, left-handedness would become a strong component of their self-image, and those discriminated against would feel they were being despised for their essence. What people regard as their essence is not independent of what they get admired and despised for.

10. This is a preferable direction of sacrifice if one accepts Rawls's egalitarian assumptions about distributive justice. Rawls, *op. cit.*, pp. 100–103.

esteem of members of the group and for the health and cohesion of the society.[11]

If, therefore, a discriminatory admissions or appointments policy is adopted to mitigate a grave social evil, and it favors a group in a particularly unfortunate social position, and if for these reasons it diverges from a meritocratic system for the assignment of positions which is not itself required by justice, then the discriminatory practice is probably not unjust.[12]

It is not without its costs, however. Not only does it inevitably produce resentment in the better qualified who are passed over because of the policy, but it also allows those in the discriminated-against group who would in fact have failed to gain a desired position in any case on the basis of their qualifications to feel that they may have lost out to someone less qualified because of the discriminatory policy. Similarly, such a practice cannot do much for the self-esteem of those who know they have benefited from it, and it may threaten the self-esteem of those in the favored group who would in fact have gained their positions even in the absence of the discriminatory policy, but who cannot be sure that they are not among its beneficiaries. This is what leads institutions to lie about their policies in this regard, or to hide them behind clouds of obscurantist rhetoric about the discriminatory character of standard admissions criteria. Such concealment is possible and even justified up to a point, but the costs cannot be entirely evaded, and discriminatory practices of this sort will be tolerable only so long as they are clearly contributing to the eradication of great social evils.

V

When racial and sexual injustice have been reduced, we shall still be left with the great injustice of the smart and the dumb, who are so differently rewarded for comparable effort. This would be an injustice even if the system of differential economic and social rewards had no systematic sexual or racial reflection. On the other hand, if the social esteem and economic advantages attaching to different occupations and educational achievements were much more uniform, there would be little cause for concern about racial, ethnic, or sexual patterns in education or work. But of course we do not at present have a method of divorcing professional status from social esteem and economic reward, at least not without a gigantic increase in total social control, on the Chinese model. Perhaps someone will discover a way in which the socially produced inequalities (especially the economic ones) between the intelligent and the unintelligent, the talented and the untalented, or even the beautiful and the ugly, can be reduced without limiting the availability of opportunities, products and services, and without resort to increased coercion or decreased liberty in the choice of work or style of life. In the absence of such a utopian solution, however, the familiar task of balancing liberty against equality will remain with us.[13]

---

11. It is therefore not, as some have feared, the first step toward an imposition of minimal or maximal quotas for all racial, religious, and ethnic subgroups of the society.

12. Adam Morton has suggested an interesting alternative, which I shall not try to develop: namely, that the practice is justified not by social utility, but because it will contribute to a more just situation in the future. The practice considered in itself may be unjust, but it is warranted by its greater contribution to justice over the long term, through eradication of a self-perpetuating pattern.

13. I have presented an earlier version of this paper to the New York Group of the Society for Philosophy and Public Affairs, the Princeton Undergraduate Philosophy Club, and the Society for Ethical and Legal Philosophy, and I thank those audiences for their suggestions.

31

PETER SINGER
All Animals Are Equal

In recent years a number of oppressed groups have campaigned vigorously for equality. The classic instance is the Black Liberation movement, which demands an end to the prejudice and discrimination that has made blacks second-class citizens. The immediate appeal of the black liberation movement and its initial, if limited, success made it a model for other oppressed groups to follow. We became familiar with liberation movements for Spanish-Americans, gay people, and a variety of other minorities. When a majority group—women—began their campaign, some thought we had come to the end of the road. Discrimination on the basis of sex, it has been said, is the last universally accepted form of discrimination, practiced without secrecy or pretense even in those liberal circles that have long prided themselves on their freedom from prejudice against racial minorities.

One should always be wary of talking of "the last remaining form of discrimination." If we have learned anything from the liberation movements, we should have learned how difficult it is to be aware of latent prejudice in our attitudes to particular groups until this prejudice is forcefully pointed out.

A liberation movement demands an expansion of our moral horizons and an extension or reinterpretation of the basic moral principle of equality. Practices that were previously regarded as natural and inevitable come to be

seen as the result of an unjustifiable prejudice. Who can say with confidence that all his or her attitudes and practices are beyond criticism? If we wish to avoid being numbered among the oppressors, we must be prepared to rethink even our most fundamental attitudes. We need to consider them from the point of view of those most disadvantaged by our attitudes, and the practices that follow from these attitudes. If we can make this unaccustomed mental switch we may discover a pattern in our attitudes and practices that consistently operate so as to benefit one group—usually the one to which we ourselves belong—at the expense of another. In this way we may come to see that there is a case for a new liberation movement. My aim is to advocate that we make this mental switch in respect of our attitudes and practices towards a very large group of beings: members of species other than our own—or, as we popularly though misleadingly call them, animals. In other words, I am urging that we extend to other species the basic principle of equality that most of us recognize should be extended to all members of our own species.

All this may sound a little farfetched, more like a parody of other liberation movements than a serious

Passages of this article appeared in a review of *Animals, Men and Morals*, edited by S. and R. Godlovitch and J. Harris (Gollancz and Taplinger, London 1972) in *The New York Review of Books*, April 5, 1973. The whole direction of my thinking on this subject I owe to talks with a number of friends in Oxford in 1970–71, especially Richard Keshen, Stanley Godlovitch, and, above all, Roslind Godlovitch.

From Peter Singer, "All Animals Are Equal," *Philosophic Exchange*, vol. 2, no. 1 (1974). Reprinted by permission of the author. This article is reprinted unabridged.

objective. In fact, in the past the idea of "The Rights of Animals" really has been used to parody the case for women's rights. When Mary Wollstonecroft, a forerunner of later feminists, published her *Vindication of the Rights of Women* in 1792, her ideas were widely regarded as absurd, and they were satirized in an anonymous publication entitled *A Vindication of the Rights of Brutes.* The author of this satire (actually Thomas Taylor, a distinguished Cambridge philosopher) tried to refute Wollstonecroft's reasonings by showing that they could be carried one stage further. If sound when applied to women, why should the arguments not be applied to dogs, cats and horses? They seemed to hold equally well for these "brutes"; yet to hold that brutes had rights was manifestly absurd; therefore the reasoning by which this conclusion had been reached must be unsound, and if unsound when applied to brutes, it must also be unsound when applied to women, since the very same arguments had been used in each case.

One way in which we might reply to this argument is by saying that the case for equality between men and women cannot validly be extended to nonhuman animals. Women have a right to vote, for instance, because they are just as capable of making rational decisions as men are; dogs, on the other hand, are incapable of understanding the significance of voting, so they cannot have the right to vote. There are many other obvious ways in which men and women resemble each other closely, while humans and other animals differ greatly. So, it might be said, men and women are similar beings, and should have equal rights, while humans and nonhumans are different and should not have equal rights.

The thought behind this reply to

Taylor's analogy is correct up to a point, but it does not go far enough. There *are* important differences between humans and other animals, and these differences must give rise to *some* differences in the rights that each have. Recognizing this obvious fact, however, is no barrier to the case for extending the basic principle of equality to nonhuman animals. The differences that exist between men and women are equally undeniable, and the supporters of Women's Liberation are aware that these differences may give rise to different rights. Many feminists hold that women have the right to an abortion on request. It does not follow that since these same people are campaigning for equality between men and women they must support the right of men to have abortions too. Since a man cannot have an abortion, it is meaningless to talk of his right to have one. Since a pig can't vote, it is meaningless to talk of its right to vote. There is no reason why either Women's Liberation or Animal Liberation should get involved in such nonsense. The extension of the basic principle of equality from one group to another does not imply that we must treat both groups in exactly the same way, or grant exactly the same rights to both groups. Whether we should do so will depend on the nature of the members of the two groups. The basic principle of equality, I shall argue, is equality of consideration; and equal consideration for different beings may lead to different treatment and different rights.

So there is a different way of replying to Taylor's attempt to parody Wollstonecroft's arguments, a way which does not deny the differences between humans and nonhumans, but goes more deeply into the question of equality, and concludes by finding nothing absurd in the idea that the basic principle of equality applies to so-called "brutes." I believe that we reach this conclusion if we examine the basis on which our opposition to discrimination on grounds of race or sex ultimately rests. We will then see that we would be on shaky ground if we were to demand equality for blacks, women, and other groups of oppressed humans, while denying equal consideration to nonhumans.

When we say that all human beings, whatever their race, creed or sex, are equal, what is it that we are asserting? Those who wish to defend a hierarchical, inegalitarian society have often pointed out that by whatever test we choose, it simply is not true that all humans are equal. Like it or not, we must face the fact that humans come in different shapes and sizes; they come with differing moral capacities, differing intellectual abilities, differing amounts of benevolent feeling and sensitivity to the needs of others, differing abilities to communicate effectively, and differing capacities to experience pleasure and pain. In short, if the demand for equality were based on the actual equality of all human beings, we would have to stop demanding equality. It would be an unjustifiable demand.

Still, one might cling to the view that the demand for equality among human beings is based on the actual equality of the different races and sexes. Although humans differ as individuals in various ways, there are no differences between the races and sexes *as such*. From the mere fact that a person is black, or a woman, we cannot infer anything else about that person. This, it may be said, is what is wrong with racism and sexism. The white racist claims that whites are superior to blacks, but this is false—although there are differences between individuals, some blacks are superior to some whites

in all of the capabilities and abilities that could conceivably be relevant. The opponent of sexism would say the same: A person's sex is no guide to his or her abilities, and this is why it is unjustifiable to discriminate on the basis of sex.

This is a possible line of objection to racial and sexual discrimination. It is not, however, the way that someone really concerned about equality would choose, because taking this line could, in some circumstances, force one to accept a most inegalitarian society. The fact that humans differ as individuals, rather than as races or sexes, is a valid reply to someone who defends a hierarchical society like, say, South Africa, in which all whites are superior in status to all blacks. The existence of individual variations that cut across the lines of race or sex, however, provides us with no defense at all against a more sophisticated opponent of equality, one who proposes that, say, the interests of all those with intelligence quotients below 100 be given less consideration than the interests of those with ratings above 100. Would a hierarchical society of this sort really be so much better than one based on race or sex? I think not. But if we tie the moral principle of equality to the factual equality of the different races or sexes, taken as a whole, our opposition to racism and sexism does not provide us with any basis for objecting to this kind of inegalitarianism.

There is a second important reason why we ought not to base our opposition to racism and sexism on any kind of factual equality, even the limited kind which asserts that variations in capacities and abilities are spread evenly between the different races and sexes: We can have no absolute guarantee that these abilities and capacities really are distributed evenly, without regard to race or sex, among human beings. So far as actual abilities are concerned, there do seem to be certain measurable differences between both races and sexes. These differences do not, of course, appear in each case, but only when averages are taken. More important still, we do not yet know how much of these differences is really due to the different genetic endowments of the various races and sexes, and how much is due to environmental differences that are the result of past and continuing discrimination. Perhaps all of the important differences will eventually prove to be environmental rather than genetic. Anyone opposed to racism and sexism will certainly hope that this will be so, for it will make the task of ending discrimination a lot easier; nevertheless it would be dangerous to rest the case against racism and sexism on the belief that all significant differences are environmental in origin. The opponent of, say, racism who takes this line will be unable to avoid conceding that if differences in ability did after all prove to have some genetic connection with race, racism would in some way be defensible.

It would be folly for the opponent of racism to stake his whole case on a dogmatic commitment to one particular outcome of a difficult scientific issue which is still a long way from being settled. While attempts to prove that differences in certain selected abilities between races and sexes are primarily genetic in origin have certainly not been conclusive, the same must be said of attempts to prove that these differences are largely the result of environment. At this stage of the investigation we cannot be certain which view is correct, however much we may hope it is the latter.

Fortunately, there is no need to pin the case for equality to one particular outcome of this scientific investigation. The appropriate response to those who claim to have found evidence of genetically-based differences in ability between the races or sexes is not to stick to the belief that the genetic explanation must be wrong, whatever evidence to the contrary may turn up: Instead we should make it quite clear that the claim to equality does not depend on intelligence, moral capacity, physical strength, or similar matters of fact. Equality is a moral ideal, not a simple assertion of fact. There is no logically compelling reason for assuming that a factual difference in ability between two people justifies any difference in the amount of consideration we give to satisfying their needs and interests. The principle of the equality of human beings is not a description of an alleged actual equality among humans: It is a prescription of how we should treat humans.

Jeremy Bentham incorporated the essential basis of moral equality into his utilitarian system of ethics in the formula: "Each to count for one and none for more than one." In other words, the interests of every being affected by an action are to be taken into account and given the same weight as the like interests of any other being. A later utilitarian, Henry Sidgwick, put the point in this way: "The good of any one individual is of no more importance, from the point of view (if I may say so) of the Universe, than the good of any other."[1] More recently, the leading figures in contemporary moral philosophy have shown a great deal of agreement in specifying as a fundamental presupposition of their moral theories some similar requirement

1. *The Methods of Ethics* (7th Ed.) p. 382.

which operates so as to give everyone's interests equal consideration—although they cannot agree on how this requirement is best formulated.[2]

It is an implication of this principle of equality that our concern for others ought not to depend on what they are like, or what abilities they possess—although precisely what this concern requires us to do may vary according to the characteristics of those affected by what we do. It is on this basis that the case against racism and the case against sexism must both ultimately rest; and it is in accordance with this principle that speciesism is also to be condemned. If possessing a higher degree of intelligence does not entitle one human to use another for his own ends, how can it entitle humans to exploit nonhumans?

Many philosophers have proposed the principle of equal consideration of interests, in some form or other, as a basic moral principle; but, as we shall see in more detail shortly, not many of them have recognized that this principle applies to members of other species as well as to our own. Bentham was one of the few who did realize this. In a forward-looking passage, written at a time when black slaves in the British dominions were still being treated much as we now treat nonhuman animals, Bentham wrote:

The day *may* come when the rest of the animal creation may acquire those rights which never could have been witholden from them but by the hand of tyranny. The French have already discovered that the blackness of the skin is no reason why a human being should be abandoned without redress to the caprice of a tormentor. It may one day come to be recognised that the number of the legs, the villosity of the skin, or the termination of the *os sacrum*, are reasons equally insufficient for abandoning a sensitive being to the same fate. What else is it that should trace the insuperable line? Is it the faculty of reason, or perhaps the faculty of discourse? But a full-grown horse or dog is

beyond comparison a more rational, as well as a more conversable animal, than an infant of a day, or a week, or even a month, old. But suppose they were otherwise, what would it avail? The question is not, Can they reason? nor Can they *talk*? but, *Can they suffer*?[3]

In this passage Bentham points to the capacity for suffering as the vital characteristic that gives a being the right to equal consideration. The capacity for suffering—or more strictly, for suffering and/or enjoyment or happiness—is not just another characteristic like the capacity for language, or for higher mathematics. Bentham is not saying that those who try to mark "the insuperable line" that determines whether the interests of a being should be considered happen to have selected the wrong characteristic. The capacity for suffering and enjoying things is a prerequisite for having interests at all, a condition that must be satisfied before we can speak of interests in any meaningful way. It would be nonsense to say that it was not in the interests of a stone to be kicked along the road by a schoolboy. A stone does not have interests because it cannot suffer. Nothing that we can do to it could possibly make any difference to its welfare. A mouse, on the other hand, does have an interest in not being tormented, because it will suffer if it is.

If a being suffers, there can be no moral justification for refusing to take that suffering into consideration. No matter what the nature of the being, the principle of equality requires that its

2. For example, R. M. Hare, *Freedom and Reason* (Oxford, 1963) and J. Rawls, *A Theory of Justice* (Harvard, 1972); for a brief account of the essential agreement on this issue between these and other positions, see R. M. Hare, "Rules of War and Moral Reasoning", *Philosophy and Public Affairs*, vol. I, no. 2 (1972).

3. *Introduction to the Principles of Morals and Legislation*, ch. XVII.

suffering be counted equally with the like suffering—in so far as rough comparisons can be made—of any other being. If a being is not capable of suffering, or of experiencing enjoyment or happiness, there is nothing to be taken into account. This is why the limit of sentience (using the term as a convenient, if not strictly accurate, shorthand for the capacity to suffer or experience enjoyment or happiness) is the only defensible boundary of concern for the interests of others. To mark this boundary by some characteristic like intelligence or rationality would be to mark it in an arbitrary way. Why not choose some other characteristic, like skin color?

The racist violates the principle of equality by giving greater weight to the interests of members of his own race, when there is a clash between their interests and the interests of those of another race. Similarly the speciesist allows the interests of his own species to override the greater interests of members of other species.[4] The pattern is the same in each case. Most human beings are speciesists. I shall now very briefly describe some of the practices that show this.

For the great majority of human beings, especially in urban, industrialized societies, the most direct form of contract with members of other species is at mealtimes: We eat them. In doing so we treat them purely as means to our ends. We regard their life and well-being as subordinate to our taste for a particular kind of dish. I say "taste" deliberately—this is purely a matter of pleasing our palate. There can be no defense of eating flesh in terms of satisfying nutritional needs, since it has been established beyond doubt that we could satisfy our need for protein and other essential nutrients far more efficiently with a diet that replaced animal flesh by soy beans, or products derived from soy beans, and other high protein vegetable products.[5]

It is not merely the act of killing that indicates what we are ready to do to other species in order to gratify our tastes. The suffering we inflict on the animals while they are alive is perhaps an even clearer indication of our speciesism than the fact that we are prepared to kill them.[6] In order to have meat on the table at a price that people can afford, our society tolerates methods of meat production that confine sentient animals in cramped, unsuitable conditions for the entire durations of their lives. Animals are treated like machines that convert fodder into flesh, and any innovation that results in a higher "conversion ratio" is liable to be adopted. As one authority on the subject has said, "cruelty is acknowledged only when profitability ceases."[7] So hens are

4. I owe the term "speciesism" to Dr. Richard Ryder.

5. In order to produce 1 lb. of protein in the form of beef or veal, we must feed 21 lbs. of protein to the animal. Other forms of livestock are slightly less inefficient, but the average ratio in the U.S. is still 1:8. It has been estimated that the amount of protein lost to humans in this way is equivalent to 90% of the annual world protein deficit. For a brief account, see Frances Moore Lappe, *Diet for a Small Planet* (Friends of The Earth/Ballantine, New York 1971) pp. 4–11.

6. Although one might think that killing a being is obviously the ultimate wrong one can do to it, I think that the infliction of suffering is a clearer indication of speciesism because it might be argued that at least part of what is wrong with killing a human is that most humans are conscious of their existence over time, and have desires and purposes that extend into the future—see, for instance, M. Tooley, "Abortion and Infanticide", *Philosophy and Public Affairs*, vol. 2, no. 1 (1972). Of course, if one took this view one would have to hold—as Tooley does—that killing a human infant or mental defective is not in itself wrong, and is less serious than killing certain higher mammals that probably do have a sense of their own existence over time.

7. Ruth Harrison, *Animal Machines* (Stuart, London, 1964). This book provides an eye-opening account of intensive farming methods for those unfamiliar with the subject.

crowded four or five to a cage with a floor area of twenty inches by eighteen inches, or around the size of a single page of the *New York Times*. The cages have wire floors, since this reduces cleaning costs, though wire is unsuitable for the hens' feet; the floors slope, since this makes the eggs roll down for easy collection, although this makes it difficult for the hens to rest comfortably. In these conditions all the birds' natural instincts are thwarted: They cannot stretch their wings fully, walk freely, dust-bathe, scratch the ground, or build a nest. Although they have never known other conditions, observers have noticed that the birds vainly try to perform these actions. Frustrated at their inability to do so, they often develop what farmers call "vices," and peck each other to death. To prevent this, the beaks of young birds are often cut off.

This kind of treatment is not limited to poultry. Pigs are now also being reared in cages inside sheds. These animals are comparable to dogs in intelligence, and need a varied, stimulating environment if they are not to suffer from stress and boredom. Anyone who kept a dog in the way in which pigs are frequently kept would be liable to prosecution, in England at least, but because our interest in exploiting pigs is greater than our interest in exploiting dogs, we object to cruelty to dogs while consuming the produce of cruelty to pigs. Of the other animals, the condition of veal calves is perhaps worst of all, since these animals are so closely confined that they cannot even turn around or get up and lie down freely. In this way they do not develop unpalatable muscle. They are also made amaemic and kept short of roughage, to keep their flesh pale, since white veal fetches a higher price; as a result they develop a craving for iron and roughage, and have been observed to gnaw wood off the sides of their stalls, and lick greedily at any rusty hinge that is within reach.

Since, as I have said, none of these practices cater to anything more than our pleasures of taste, our practice of rearing and killing other animals in order to eat them is a clear instance of the sacrifice of the most important interests of other beings in order to satisfy trivial interests of our own. To avoid speciesism we must stop this practice, and each of us has a moral obligation to cease supporting the practice. Our custom is all the support that the meat industry needs. The decision to cease giving it that support may be difficult, but it is no more difficult than it would have been for a white Southerner to go against the traditions of his society and free his slaves; if we do not change our dietary habits, how can we censure those slaveholders who would not change their own way of living?

The same form of discrimination may be observed in the widespread practice of experimenting on other species in order to see if certain substances are safe for human beings, or to test some psychological theory about the effect of severe punishment on learning, or to try out various new compounds just in case something turns up. People sometimes think that all this experimentation is for vital medical purposes, and so will reduce suffering overall. This comfortable belief is very wide of the mark. Drug companies test new shampoos and cosmetics that they are intending to put on the market by dropping them into the eyes of rabbits, held open by metal clips, in order to observe what damage results. Food additives, like artificial colorings and preservatives, are tested by what is known as the "LD$_{50}$"—a test designed to find the level of consumption at which 50% of a group of animals will die. In the process, nearly all of the animals are made very sick before some finally die, and others pull through. If the substance is relatively harmless, as it often is, huge doses have to be force-fed to the animals, until in some cases sheer volume or concentration of the substance causes death.

Much of this pointless cruelty goes on in the universities. In many areas of science, nonhuman animals are regarded as an item of laboratory equipment, to be used and expended as desired. In psychology laboratories experimenters devise endless variations and repetitions of experiments that were of little value in the first place. To quote just one example, from the experimenter's own account in a psychology journal: At the University of Pennsylvania, Perrin S. Cohen hung six dogs in hammocks with electrodes taped to their hind feet. Electric shock of varying intensity was then administered through the electrodes. If the dog learned to press its head against a panel on the left, the shock was turned off, but otherwise it remained on indefinitely. Three of the dogs, however, were required to wait periods varying from 2 to 7 seconds while being shocked before making the response that turned off the current. If they failed to wait, they received further shocks. Each dog was given from 26 to 46 "sessions" in the hammock, each session consisting of 80 "trials" or shocks, administered at intervals of one minute. The experimenter reported that the dogs, who were unable to move in the hammock, barked or bobbed their heads when the current was applied. The reported findings of the experiment were that there was a delay in the dogs' responses that increased proportionately to the time the dogs were required to endure the shock, but a gradual increase in the intensity of the shock had no systematic effect in the timing of the response. The experiment was funded by the National Institutes of Health, and the United States Public Health Service.[8]

In this example, and countless cases like it, the possible benefits to mankind are either nonexistent or fantastically remote, while the certain losses to members of other species are very real. This is, again, a clear indication of speciesism.

In the past, argument about vivesection has often missed the point, because it has been put in absolutist terms: Would the abolitionist be prepared to let thousands die if they could be saved by experimenting on a single animal? The way to reply to this purely hypothetical question is to pose another: Would the experimenter be prepared to perform his experiment on an orphaned human infant, if that were the only way to save many lives? (I say "orphan" to avoid the complication of parental feelings, although in doing so I am being overfair to the experimenter, since the nonhuman subjects of experiments are not orphans.) If the experimenter is not prepared to use an orphaned human infant, then his readiness to use nonhumans is simple discrimination, since adult apes, cats, mice and other mammals are more aware of what is happening to them, more self-directing and, so far as we can

8. *Journal of the Experimental Analysis of Behavior,* vol. 13, no. 1 (1970) Any recent volume of this journal, or of other journals in the field, like the *Journal of Comparative and Physiological Psychology,* will contain reports of equally cruel and trivial experiments. For a fuller account, see Richard Ryder, "Experiments on Animals" in *Animals, Men and Morals.*

tell, at least as sensitive to pain, as any human infant. There seems to be no relevant characteristic that human infants possess that adult mammals do not have to the same or a higher degree. (Someone might try to argue that what makes it wrong to experiment on a human infant is that the infant will, in time and if left alone, develop into more than the nonhuman, but one would then, to be consistent, have to oppose abortion, since the fetus has the same potential as the infant—indeed, even contraception and abstinence might be wrong on this ground, since the egg and sperm, considered jointly, also have the same potential. In any case, this argument still gives us no reason for selecting a nonhuman, rather than a human with severe and irreversible brain damage, as the subject for our experiments.)

The experimenter, then, shows a bias in favor of his own species whenever he carries out an experiment on a nonhuman for a purpose that he would not think justified him in using a human being at an equal or lower level of sentience, awareness, or ability to be self-directing. No one familiar with the kind of results yielded by most experiments on animals can have the slightest doubt that if this bias were eliminated the number of experiments performed would be a minute fraction of the number performed today.

Experimenting on animals, and eating their flesh, are perhaps the two major forms of speciesism in our society. By comparison, the third and last form of speciesism is so minor as to be insignificant, but it is perhaps of some special interest to those for whom this paper was written. I am referring to speciesism in contemporary philosophy.

Philosophy ought to question the basic assumptions of the age. Thinking through, critically and carefully, what most people take for granted is, I believe, the chief task of philosophy, and it is this task that makes philosophy a worthwhile activity. Regrettably, philosophy does not always live up to its historic role. Philosophers are human beings and they are subject to all the preconceptions of the society to which they belong. Sometimes they succeed in breaking free of the prevailing ideology; more often they become its most sophisticated defenders. So, in this case, philosophy as practiced in the universities today does not challenge anyone's preconceptions about our relations with other species. By their writings, those philosophers who tackle problems that touch upon the issue reveal that they make the same unquestioned assumptions as most other humans, and what they say tends to confirm the reader in his or her comfortable speciesist habits.

I could illustrate this claim by referring to the writings of philosophers in various fields—for instance, the attempts that have been made by those interested in rights to draw the boundary of the sphere of rights so that it runs parallel to the biological boundaries of the species *homo sapiens*, including infants and even mental defectives, but excluding those other beings of equal or greater capacity who are so useful to us at mealtimes and in our laboratories. I think it would be a more appropriate conclusion to this paper, however, if I concentrated on the problem with which we have been centrally concerned, the problem of equality.

It is significant, that the problem of equality, in moral and political philosophy, is invariably formulated in terms of human equality. The effect of this is that the question of the equality of other animals does not confront the philosopher, or student, as an issue in itself—and this is already an indication of the failure of philosophy to challenge accepted beliefs. Still, philosophers have found it difficult to discuss the issue of human equality without raising, in a paragraph or two, the question of the status of other animals. The reason for this, which should be apparent from what I have said already, is that if humans are to be regarded as equal to one another, we need some sense of "equal" that does not require any actual, descriptive equality of capacities, talents or other qualities. If equality is to be related to any actual characteristics of humans, these characteristics must be some lowest common denominator, pitched so low that no human lacks them—but then the philosopher comes up against the catch that any such set of characteristics which covers *all* humans will not be possessed *only* by humans. In other words, it turns out that in the only sense in which we can truly say, as an assertion of fact, that all humans are equal, at least some members of other species are also equal—equal, that is, to each other and to humans. If, on the other hand, we regard the statement "All humans are equal" in some nonfactual way, perhaps as a prescription, then, as I have already argued, it is even more difficult to exclude nonhumans from the sphere of equality.

This result is not what the egalitarian philosopher originally intended to assert. Instead of accepting the radical outcome to which their own reasonings naturally point, however, most philosophers try to reconcile their beliefs in human equality and animal inequality by arguments that can only be described as devious.

As a first example, I take William Frankena's well-known article "The Concept of Social Justice".[9] Frankena opposes the idea of basing justice on merit, because he sees that this could lead to highly inegalitarian results. Instead he proposes the principle that:

. . . all men are to be treated as equals, not because they are equal, in any respect but simply because they are human. They are human because they have emotions and desires, and are able to think, and hence are capable of enjoying a good life in a sense in which other animals are not.

But what is this capacity to enjoy the good life which all humans have, but no other animals? Other animals have emotions and desires, and appear to be capable of enjoying a good life. We may doubt that they can think—although the behavior of some apes, dolphins and even dogs suggests that some of them can—but what is the relevance of thinking? Frankena goes on to admit that by "the good life" he means "not so much the morally good life as the happy or satisfactory life", so thought would appear to be unnecessary for enjoying the good life; in fact to emphasize the need for thought would make difficulties for the egalitarian since only some people are capable of leading intellectually satisfying lives, or morally good lives. This makes it difficult to see what Frankena's principle of equality has to do with simply being *human*. Surely every sentient being is capable of leading a life that is happier or less miserable than some alternative life, and hence has a claim to be taken into account. In this respect the distinction between humans and nonhumans is not a sharp division, but rather a continuum along which we move gradually, and with overlaps between the species, from simple capacities for enjoyment

9. In R. Brandt (ed.) *Social Justice* (Prentice Hall, Englewood Cliffs, 1962); the passage quoted appears on p. 19.

and satisfaction, or pain and suffering, to more complex ones.

Faced with a situation in which they see a need for some basis for the moral gulf that is commonly thought to separate humans and animals, but can find no concrete difference that will do the job without undermining the equality of humans, philosophers tend to waffle. They resort to high-sounding phrases like "the intrinsic dignity of the human individual";[10] they talk of the "intrinsic worth of all men" as if men (humans?) had some worth that other beings did not,[11] or they say that humans, and only humans, are "ends in themselves", while "everything other than a person can only have value for a person".[12]

This idea of a distinctive human dignity and worth has a long history; it can be traced back directly to the Renaissance humanists, for instance to Pico della Mirandola's *Oration on the Dignity of Man.* Pico and other humanists based their estimate of human dignity on the idea that man possessed the central, pivotal position in the "Great Chain of Being" that led from the lowliest form of matter to God Himself; this view of the universe, in turn, goes back to both classical and Judeo-Christian doctrines. Contemporary philosophers have cast off these metaphysical and religious shackles and freely invoke the dignity of mankind without needing to justify the idea at all. Why should we not attribute "intrinsic dignity" or "intrinsic worth" to ourselves? Fellow humans are unlikely to reject the accolades we so generously bestow on them, and those to whom we deny the honor are unable to object. Indeed, when one thinks only of humans, it can be very liberal, very progressive, to talk of the dignity of all human beings. In so doing, we im-

plicitly condemn slavery, racism, and other violations of human rights. We admit that we ourselves are in some fundamental sense on a par with the poorest, most ignorant members of our own species. It is only when we think of humans as no more than a small subgroup of all the beings that inhabit our planet that we may realize that in elevating our own species we are at the same time lowering the relative status of all other species.

The truth is that the appeal to the intrinsic dignity of human beings appears to solve the egalitarian's problems only as long as it goes unchallenged. Once we ask *why* it should be that all humans—including infants, mental defectives, psychopaths, Hitler, Stalin and the rest—have some kind of dignity or worth that no elephant, pig or chimpanzee can ever achieve, we see that this question is as difficult to answer as our original request for some relevant fact that justifies the inequality of humans and other animals. In fact, these two questions are really one: Talk of intrinsic dignity or moral worth only takes the problem back one step, because any satisfactory defense of the claim that all and only humans have intrinsic dignity would need to refer to some relevant capacities or characteristics that all and only humans possess. Philosophers frequently introduce ideas of dignity, respect and worth at the point at which other reasons appear to be lacking, but this is hardly good enough. Fine phrases are the last resource of those who have run out of arguments.

10. Frankena, *op. cit.*, p. 23.

11. H. A. Bedau, "Egalitarianism and the Idea of Equality" in *Nomos IX: Equality*, ed. J. R. Pennock and J. W. Chapman, New York 1967.

12. G. Vlastos, "Justice and Equality" in Brandt, *Social Justice*, p. 48.

In case there are those who still think it may be possible to find some relevant characteristic that distinguishes all humans from all members of other species, I shall refer again, before I conclude, to the existence of some humans who quite clearly are below the level of awareness, self-consciousness, intelligence, and sentience, of many nonhumans. I am thinking of humans with severe and irreparable brain damage, and also of infant humans. To avoid the complication of the relevance of a being's potential, however, I shall henceforth concentrate on permanently retarded human beings.

Philosophers who set out to find a characteristic that will distinguish humans from other animals rarely take the course of abandoning these groups of humans by lumping them in with the other animals. It is easy to see why they do not. To take this line without rethinking our attitudes to other animals would entail that we have the right to perform painful experiments on retarded humans for trivial reasons; similarly it would follow that we had the right to rear and kill these humans for food. To most philosophers these consequences are as unacceptable as the view that we should stop treating nonhumans in this way.

Of course, when discussing the problem of equality it is possible to ignore the problem of mental defectives, or brush it aside as if somehow insignificant.[13] This is the easiest way out. What else remains? My final example of speciesism in contemporary philosophy has been selected to show what happens when a writer is prepared to face the question of human equality and animal inequality without ignoring the existence of mental defectives, and without resorting to obscurantist mumbo-jumbo. Stanley Benn's clear and honest article "Egalitarianism and Equal Consideration of Interests"[14] fits this description.

Benn, after noting the usual "evident human inequalities" argues, correctly I think, for equality of consideration as the only possible basis for egalitarianism. Yet Benn, like other writers, is thinking only of "equal consideration of human interests". Benn is quite open in his defence of this restriction of equal consideration:

. . . not to possess human shape *is* a disqualifying condition. However faithful or intelligent a dog may be, it would be a monstrous sentimentality to attribute to him interests that could be weighed in an equal balance with those of human beings . . . if, for instance, one had to decide between feeding a hungry baby or a hungry dog, anyone who chose the dog would generally be reckoned morally defective, unable to recognize a fundamental inequality of claims.

This is what distinguishes our attitude to animals from our attitude to imbeciles. It would be odd to say that we ought to respect equally the dignity or personality of the imbecile and of the rational man . . . but there is nothing odd about saying that we should respect their interests equally, that is, that we should give to the interests of each the same serious consideration as claims to considerations necessary for some standard of well-being that we can recognize and endorse.

Benn's statement of the basis of the consideration we should have for imbeciles seems to me correct, but why should there be any fundamental inequality of claims between a dog and a human imbecile? Benn sees that if equal

13. E. g. Bernard Williams, "The Idea of Equality", in *Philosophy, Politics and Society* (second series) ed. P. Laslett and W. Runciman (Blackwell, Oxford, 1962) p. 118; J. Rawls, *A Theory of Justice*, pp. 509–10.

14. *Nomos IX: Equality*; the passages quoted are on pp. 62ff.

consideration depended on rationality, no reason could be given against using imbeciles for research purposes, as we now use dogs and guinea pigs. This will not do: "But of course we do distinguish imbeciles from animals in this regard," he says. That the common distinction is justifiable is something Benn does not question; his problem is how it is to be justified. The answer he gives is this:

. . . we respect the interests of men and give them priority over dogs not *insofar* as they are rational, but because rationality is the human norm. We say it is *unfair* to exploit the deficiencies of the imbecile who falls short of the norm, just as it would be unfair and not just ordinarily dishonest, to steal from a blind man. If we do not think in this way about dogs, it is because we do not see the irrationality of the dog as a deficiency or a handicap, but as normal for the species. The characteristics, therefore, that distinguish the normal man from the normal dog make it intelligible for us to talk of other men having interests and capaciities, and therefore claims, of precisely the same kind as we make on our own behalf. But although these characteristics may provide the point of the distinction between men and other species, they are not in fact the qualifying conditions for membership, or the distinguishing criteria of the class of morally considerable persons; and this is precisely because a man does not become a member of a different species, with its own standards of normality, by reason of not possessing these characteristics.

The final sentence of this passage gives the argument away. An imbecile, Benn concedes, may have no characteristics superior to those of a dog; nevertheless this does not make the imbecile a member of "a different species" as the dog is. *Therefore* it would be "unfair" to use the imbecile for medical research as we use the dog. But why? That the imbecile is not rational is just the way things have worked out, and the same is true of the dog—neither is any more responsible for their mental level.

If it is unfair to take advantage of an isolated defect, why is it fair to take advantage of a more general limitation? I find it hard to see anything in this argument except a defence of preferring the interests of members of our own species because they are members of our own species. To those who think there might be more to it, I suggest the following mental exercise. Assume that it has been proven that there is a difference in the average, or normal, intelligence quotient for two different races, say whites and blacks. Then substitute the term "white" for every occurrence of "men" and "black" for every occurrence of "dog" in the passage quoted; and substitute "high IQ" for "rationality" and when Benn talks of "imbeciles" replace this term by "dumb whites"— that is, whites who fall well below the normal white IQ score. Finally, change "species" to "race." Now reread the passage. It has become a defense of a rigid, no-exceptions division between whites and blacks, based on IQ scores, *notwithstanding an admitted overlap* between whites and blacks in this respect. The revised passage is, of course, outrageous, and this is not only because we have made fictitious assumptions in our substitutions. The point is that in the original passage Benn was defending a rigid division in the amount of consideration due to members of different species, despite admitted cases of overlap. If the original did not, at first reading, strike us as being as outrageous as the revised version does, this is largely because although we are not racists ourselves, most of us are speciesists. Like the other authors' articles, Benn's stands as a warning of the ease with which the best minds can fall victim to a prevailing ideology.

Suggestions for Further Reading

Stanley I. Benn, "Justice," *The Encyclopedia of Philosophy*, ed. Paul Edwards (New York: Macmillan and The Free Press, 1967), vol. 4, pp. 298–302.

John Rawls, *A Theory of Justice* (Cambridge: Harvard University Press, 1971). The theory of justice as fairness is developed at great length, and with great elegance.

Joel Feinberg, *Social Philosophy* (Englewood Cliffs, N.J.: Prentice Hall, 1973), ch. 7. Unlike Rawls, Feinberg does not advance a single unified theory of justice. Rather he discusses a variety of interrelated issues, commenting independently on each one.

J. R. Lucas, "Justice," *Philosophy*, vol. 47 (1972), pp. 229–248. At the beginning of this article Lucas says: "I shall try to show why justice is, along with liberty, a peculiarly fundamental ideal, which is not merely co-ordinate with other ideals a society may value; but also that this notwithstanding, considerations of justice are not all-sufficient, and do not, and should not, always override all other political ideals."

Gregory Vlastos, "Justice and Equality," *Social Justice*, ed. Richard B. Brandt (Englewood Cliffs, N.J.: Prentice-Hall, 1962). An important treatment of these concepts, and also of the notion of human rights.

Peter Singer, *Animal Liberation* (New York: New York Review Books, 1975). A fuller treatment of the issues raised in Singer's "All Animals Are Equal."

There are several good anthologies of articles on justice and equality:

Richard B. Brandt, ed., *Social Justice* (Englewood Cliffs, N.J.: Prentice-Hall, 1962).

Frederick A. Olafson, ed., *Justice and Social Policy* (Englewood Cliffs, N.J.: Prentice-Hall, 1961).

Hugo A. Bedau, ed., *Justice and Equality* (Englewood Cliffs, N.J.: Prentice-Hall, 1971).

William T. Blackstone, ed., *The Concept of Equality* (Minneapolis: Burgess Publishing Company, 1969).

CHAPTER SIX

Human Rights

INTRODUCTION

Like many moral concepts, the concept of a *right* is both extremely important and, from a philosophical point of view, extremely puzzling. Political rhetoric is full of talk about "the rights of man," and the most important political documents, such as the United States Constitution, speak grandly of "the rights of the people." Whenever social reformers want to put their case in the strongest possible way they talk about rights: Thus, the proponents of legalized abortion did not merely say that the government ought to permit women to have abortions; they went further and claimed that women have a *right* to abortion. And on the other side, those who oppose abortion describe that procedure as a violation of the fetus's right to life.

But exactly what *is* a "right"? Do such things as rights really exist, or are they merely fictions of our imagination? Most philosophers would admit that there are such things as *legal* rights, created by the legal conventions of society. Thus, in the United States women now have a legal right to abortion up to the twenty-fourth week of pregnancy, whereas in Italy no such right exists. However, moralists frequently claim that in addition to a person's legal rights he also has certain *moral*, or *human* rights which are his regardless of whether governments recognize them. For example, it is often said that all human beings have a moral or human right to liberty, even if tyrannical governments refuse to recognize it. But this can be disputed. The great utilitarian theorist Jeremy Bentham, whose general views on ethics are presented in chapter three, firmly denied that such extralegal rights exist: Such talk, he said, is "nonsense on stilts."

The most effective way to defend the doctrine of rights is to provide a clear explanation of exactly what rights are. H. J. McCloskey takes up this problem in "Rights," the first selection in this chapter. McCloskey considers and then rejects one common way of understanding what rights are, as claims; he then offers his own analysis of rights as entitlements. McCloskey also considers the question of what sorts of beings can have rights. Human beings have rights, but do other animals? Do *plants* have rights? Why, or why not? What about fetuses? One of McCloskey's conclusions is that it is not possible for nonhuman animals—for example, dogs, horses, kangaroos, bears—to have any rights at all. (McCloskey's arguments on this point may be contrasted with Peter Singer's arguments in "All Animals Are Equal" in chapter five. Singer charges that philosophers such as McCloskey show a prejudiced attitude toward animals that is comparable to racist attitudes toward blacks.)

If there are "moral" or "human" rights shared by all people, then it is important that these rights not be violated by the legal and social arrangements of a community. Laws that infringe upon the rights of individuals are unjust for that reason. The framers of the United States Constitution thought this to be such an important point that, after enumerating many specific "rights of the people" in the first eight amendments, they added in the ninth amendment a stipulation that "the enumeration in the Constitution, of certain rights, shall not be construed to deny or disparage others retained by the people." In "Taking Rights Seriously," Ronald Dworkin discusses the implications for governments of seriously accepting the idea that individuals have rights.

The remaining three selections treat particular controversial "rights." In John Locke's famous defense, "The Right to Property," he holds that the right to property rests on the basic right of every person to his own labor and whatever he produces by it—in other words, that (with certain qualifications) we have a right to own whatever we create by our own work. In "The Right to Privacy," Hyman Gross discusses the basis of that right. And finally, Joel Feinberg takes up the question of rights of fetuses in "Is There a Right to Be Born?" Anti-abortionists often urge that fetuses do have such a right, and that abortion is immoral for this reason. Feinberg argues that they do not have a right to be born, so that abortion does not violate their "rights." But, surprisingly, he also argues that sometimes a fetus may have a right *not* to be born, so that by not allowing an abortion we are violating, at least in some instances, the fetus's rights.

32

H. J. MCCLOSKEY
Rights

In this article, I propose to consider two of three closely interrelated, questions, namely: 'What is a right?' 'Who or what may possess rights?' The third question, 'What are the grounds and nature of the rights beings actually possess?', although vitally relevant to the former two questions, raises issues too extensive in scope to be treated of in a single paper.

A. CONCEPTUAL ISSUES: RIGHTS AS ENTITLEMENTS

A moral right is commonly explained as being some sort of *claim* or *power* which ought to be recognized. D. G. Ritchie, for instance, observes that a moral right may be defined as *"the*

claim of an individual upon others recognized by society, irrespective of its recognition by the State."[1] Ryan and Boland, explaining the Catholic (Thomist) view of rights, state: "A right in the moral sense of the term may be defined as an inviolable moral *claim* to some personal good. When this claim is created as it sometimes is, by civil authority, it is a positive or legal right; when it is derived from man's rational nature it is a natural right."[2] T. H. Green, on the other hand, argues: "A right is a *power* of acting for his own ends,—for what he conceives to be his good,—secured to an individual by the community on the supposition that its exercise contributes to the good of the

From H. J. McCloskey, "Rights," *The Philosophical Quarterly*, vol. 15 (1965), pp. 115–127. Reprinted by permission of the author and the editor of *The Philosophical Quarterly*. This article is reprinted unabridged.

1. D. G. Ritchie, *Natural Rights*, London, 1894, pp. 78–9. The emphasis on the key word in this and subsequent definitions is mine.
2. J. A. Ryan and F. J. Boland, *Catholic Principles of Politics*, New York, 1940, p. 13.

community."[3] Plamenatz follows Green in explaining rights in terms of powers, but in other respects his definition differs substantially from that of Green. Plamenatz states: "A right is a *power* which a creature ought to possess because its exercise by him is itself good, or else because it is a means to what is good, and in the exercise of which all rational beings ought to protect him."[4] There are obvious grounds for rejecting such accounts of the concept of a right, whether it be a legal, moral, social, or institutional right. To consider first rights other than moral rights.

To have *a legal right* is not to have a power conferred or recognized by law, nor is it a power which ought to be recognized by law or by officials administering the law. I may have a legal right to drive a car but lack the power to do so because temporarily paralysed or because too poor to buy or rent a car. A lot of laws which confer rights are called "private power-conferring laws" but, as Cohen has argued against Hart, they are not really power-conferring laws at all.[5] The laws giving me the right to marry, divorce, or to make a will, are not conferring powers on me; yet they are clearly conferring legal rights. Similarly, criminal laws deny me legal rights but they do not interfere with my powers. Nor are legal rights powers recognized by the state, for legal rights may exist where there is no power to exercise the right. Similarly, a legal right does not amount to a claim upon others recognized by the state, although a right may provide a ground for such a claim. My legal right to marry consists primarily in the recognition of my entitlement to marry and to have my act recognized. It indirectly gives rise to claims on others not to prevent me so acting, but it does not primarily consist

in these claims. I am legally entitled under our legal system to do whatever is not forbidden by the law. Thus I have a legal right to grow roses in my garden. This legal right is not simply a claim I can make under the law that others not interfere with me when selecting plants for my garden. It is essentially an entitlement to act as I please. It may give rise to derivative entitlements, and claims on others and the state.

With *institutional rights,* for example, rights as a member of a religious organization or a social club, the possession of a right does not consist in some sort of power or claim. A right to vote in the election of the elders of the Church is an entitlement to take part in the election; and an entitlement is very different from a power, whether it be a power conferred, recognized, or which ought to be recognized. To have the right to vote is not simply or necessarily to have the power to vote, nor is it a power to act which has been conferred or recognized or which ought to be recognized. In a laxly policed election nonmembers may have the power but not the right to vote. Similarly, the right does not consist primarily in claims on others. Consider the right of the Church member to partake of Holy Communion. The right and the power are clearly distinct, and the right is related to claims only in that, besides entitling the member to partake of Holy Com-

3. T. H. Green, *Lectures on the Principles of Political Obligation,* London, 1941, p. 207.

4. J. P. Plamenatz, *Consent, Freedom and Political Obligation,* Oxford, 1938, p. 82. Plamenatz has since rejected this definition in favour of the definition, "A man (or an animal) has a right whenever other men ought not to prevent him doing what he wants or refuse some service he asks for or needs" (Ar. Soc. Suppl. Vol. XXIV (1950), p. 75.)

5. L. J. Cohen, "H. L. A. Hart, *The Concept of Law*", *Mind,* LXXI (1962), pp. 395–412, esp. pp. 396–7.

munion, it also entitles him to resist any official or member of the Church who seeks to prevent him partaking. So too with rights as a member of a social club. My right to use the club—its writing room, library, bar—is an entitlement. I may lack the power to exercise this right, and still possess it; and I may enjoy it without making claims on others—for example, if it were a small, self-service club with no staff. The right equally exists for the member who is unable to get to the club, that is, who cannot make claims on others, and for the member who admits himself to the club building and who makes no claims on others.

Rights also figure in *games*, although of course they are rights of a conceptually different kind from moral rights such as the right to liberty. However, the essence of rights in games as elsewhere consists in their being entitlements. In Australian Rules football players have the right to place-kick after a mark or free kick; and it is clearly meaningful and correct to assert that the player who doesn't know how to place-kick, and the player who never marks the ball nor receives a free kick, enjoy the right as fully as the skilful place-kick who receives many free kicks. The right consists in an entitlement, which, if denied, would provide the player with grounds for making demands and claims on others, viz., the umpire, which may or may not succeed. It is to misconstrue rights in games to construe them as the claims to which they may or may not give rise. It is a mistake comparable with that against which Hart argues, of construing rules of games as directions to scorers.[6]

If we look at *moral rights*, in particular at what we intend to claim when we claim a right, we find here too that a right is an entitlement. It may be an entitlement to do, to demand, to enjoy, to be, to have done for us. Rights may be rights to act, to exist, to enjoy, to demand. We speak of rights as being *possessed*, *exercised*, and *enjoyed*. In these respects there is an affinity between our talk about rights and our talk about capacities, powers, and the like, and a distinct contrast with talk about claims, for we *make* claims but do not possess, exercise, or enjoy them. But, since a right may exist and be possessed in the absence of the relevant power or capacity, rights are distinct from powers. I possess the rights to life, liberty and happiness; my possession of these rights means that I am entitled to live, to act freely without interference, and be unimpeded in my search for happiness.

It is often argued that rights are conceptually linked with *rules*. Benn and Peters, for instance, state: "To say that X has a right to £5 is to imply that there is a rule which, when applied to the case of X and some other person Y, imposes on Y a duty to pay X £5 if X so chooses. Without the possibility of the correlative duty resting somewhere, the attribution of the right to X would be meaningless."[7] Our foregoing consideration of legal rights suggests that this is not the case. We have legal rights in the absence of legal rules, and the way in which rules are relevant to legal rights varies. Sometimes the rule explicitly denies a right, other rules confer rights, other rules sustain rights which are rule-grounded only in the very weakened sense that 'what is not forbidden in our legal system is permitted' may be said to be itself a rule of sorts. However, it is not a rule in the same sense or senses of 'rule' as that in

6. H. L. A. Hart, *The Concept of Law*, Oxford, 1961. See, e.g., p. 40.

7. S. I. Benn and R. S. Peters, *Social Principles and the Democratic State*, London, 1959, p. 88.

which criminal and power-conferring laws are rules. With rights as members of organizations, rules figure prominently, but rights may nonetheless exist which are not grounded on rules. There may be no rule concerning private worship in the church building on weekdays, but in the absence of a rule forbidding it, and even in the absence of a general rule stating that what is not forbidden is permitted, the member may reasonably claim the right to worship privately in the church each day. He could offer good reasons, not in terms of some rule, but in terms of the purpose of the building and the character of the religious organization. The same is true of moral rights. We do not always have to point to a rule of some sort to show that we have a moral right. A claim to a right such as the right of life may be supported by a large variety of kinds of reasons. Indeed, the characteristic reasons appropriate as reasons in support of moral rights seem not to be reasons in terms of rules.

We speak of our rights as being *rights to*—as in the rights to life, liberty and happiness—not as *rights against*, as has so often mistakenly been claimed. Special rights are sometimes against specific individuals or institutions— for example, rights created by promises, contracts, etc. The wife has rights against the husband, the creditor against the debtor, but these are special, nongeneral rights which differ from the characteristic cases of general rights, where the right is simply a right to (that is an entitlement to)—for example of the man to marry the woman of his choice. It is strangely artificial to suggest that this is a right against someone or some thing. Against whom or what is it a right? My right to life is not a right against anyone. It is *my* right and by virtue of it, it is normally permissible for me to sustain my life in the face of obstacles. It does give

rise to rights against others *in the sense* that others have or may come to have duties to refrain from killing me, but it is essentially a right of mine, not an infinite list of claims, hypothetical and actual, against an infinite number of actual, potential, and as yet nonexistent human beings. Even nonmoral rights such as legal rights, rights as a member of a club, rights in games, are not typically rights against but rights to have, to do, to be, to have done for us. My legal right to drive a car, having passed a test for a licence and paid the appropriate fee, is a right to do certain things, not a right against the police, magistrates, and other officials. Similarly, the right of the tennis club member to play on the club courts is a right to play, not a right against some vague group of potential or possible obstructors. Similarly, the right of the football player to place-kick if he so chooses is a right to do just that. It is not a right against his opponent or against the umpire. And if it is a right by virtue of his having taken a mark it is especially hard to see against whom it might be said to be.

Rights are entitlements to do, have, enjoy or have done. That it is a serious error to construe general rights as rights against rather than rights to or as entitlements, is confirmed by consideration of people who live in isolation. It is meaningful to speak of the hermit on an isolated island as having rights to do or have certain things, but it would be strange to speak of him as having rights against others. His rights may give rise to rights against others, but the right— for example to live—is not primarily against others. The infliction of avoidable suffering on animals is obviously *prima facie* wrong, but the fact that a person possesses the right to life, whether he be a hermit or not, justifies him in killing animals—and in the process causing them to suffer—in order to sustain himself. His right to life is inaptly described in such a situation as a right against the animals he kills. Many, although not myself, would wish to argue that there is no right to suicide. Clearly it is not *prima facie* absurd so to argue. Yet if there is no such right, the hermit would not be entitled to take his own life, although he would have rights to do other things.

The difficulties of "rights against" talk, and of any attempt to write into the concept of a right, that it must be against someone, are evident if we consider the extreme case of the last person in the universe, who alone survives the nuclear war. Imagine that the last person is a woman capable of reproducing by artificial insemination, a large sperm bank having also survived. I suggest that talk about rights would have real application in such a situation. Suppose the woman had good reason to believe that if she reproduced, her off-spring would be monsters, defectives, imbeciles, doomed to life-long suffering. In such a case she would have to conclude that she did not possess the right to reproduce. If she had every reason to believe that her off-spring would be healthy, she would conclude that she had the right to reproduce, unless of course she regarded artificial insemination as wrong. This suggests that the actual existence of other human beings is irrelevant to whether rights may or may not be possessed. Clearly *the possible existence* of other human beings is more than adequate as a basis for talk about rights to have point. And, as I argued earlier, even this seems not to be necessary.

Other difficulties of "rights against" talk could be noted—for example the accounts it involves of what it is to lack a right, the difficulty of *possessing* rights against, where possession by us of

the right depends on the existence of others. But enough has already been said to permit us to dismiss this sort of account, which seems to be adopted, where it is adopted, to fit in with a predetermined ethical theory.

So far I have spoken of rights, whether they be legal, moral, social, institutional, or in games, as essentially entitlements of some sort; yet obviously they are different sorts of entitlements, such that we should describe them as being conceptually different from one another. The concept of a legal right is a different concept from that of a right in a game, and both are different from rights which are created by membership of a club. Similarly, although all moral rights are entitlements, there are conceptual differences between various of the rights which may be characterized as moral rights, which makes it desirable to distinguish different *concepts* of moral rights, and to speak of legal, moral, social, etc. rights as rights of different *kinds*.

It is a commonplace for political philosophers to offer *the* definition of a moral right. Some such definitions were indicated at the outset. Elsewhere, in a brief discussion of the nature and grounds of rights, I have similarly assumed that there is only one concept and only one definition of a right. In fact, if we look at the sorts of rights that are claimed as moral rights, at actual theories about rights, and at ordinary discourse, we find that there are at least four distinct concepts of moral rights, all of which are to be explained as entitlements.

(a) There is *the negative concept* of a right apparent in some of Locke's arguments for rights, particularly for the rights to life and liberty. To have a negative right to X is for it not to be wrong for us to do or have X and for other people to lack the right or have a duty

not to interfere; and here the duty is obviously not a duty against us. For example, to have a right to life of this kind, would be for it to be right (or not wrong) for us to sustain ourselves, and for others to be obliged not to take our lives or at least not to be entitled to deprive us of our lives. This concept of a right lends itself most easily to modification to permit talk about animal rights, but it will be argued later that such modification is not in order as animals cannot be possessors of rights. Negative rights are not simply rights by analogy, nor are negative rights, rights in a sense parasitic on some other concept of a right. It is logically possible that all rights be of this negative character. A community which conceived of all rights as being of this kind would obviously be said to have grasped the concept of a right, although it would not have grasped the richest and fullest concept of a right. (It is still possible to speak of such negative rights as being possessed, but the sense of 'possessed' is weaker than in the other cases.)

(b) There is also *the positive concept* of a right such that to have a right is to have a moral authority or entitlement to act in a certain way. This concept is often elucidated in terms of legitimate claims on others, but such accounts obviously will not do, for we explain and justify our claim on others in terms of having a right, that is, in terms of our having a positive moral entitlement, to act in a certain way. It is this that entitles us to demand freedom from interference. The rights for which Thomists argue on the basis of the natural law are of this kind, for example rights to seek the truth, to rear one's offspring, to preserve oneself.

(c) There is a more positive, fuller concept which we may characterize as *the welfare concept* of a right such that a right is not merely a moral entitle-

ment to do or to have, but also an entitlement to the efforts of others or to make demands on others to aid and promote our seeking after or enjoyment of some good. Thus, in terms of this welfare concept of a right, it is written into the concept that the conditions for its enjoyment be promoted. Such a concept underlies many arguments for welfare legislation, for many such arguments proceed by maintaining that respect for human rights involves removing not simply *man-made* obstacles but also *natural* hindrances and impediments to the enjoyment of some power or good. For example, many demands for conditions to promote the enjoyment of the rights to health, life, etc., proceed from such a welfare concept of a right. Indeed, if such a concept is denied significance, a great deal of controversy about rights in this century becomes meaningless.

(d) There are also *special rights* noted above as admitting of being described as rights against, and which spring from duties to particular individuals. The right of the creditor to repayment of his loan on the due date is a right or entitlement of this kind.

The above distinctions between different concepts of rights are obviously relevant to the vexed question of the relation between *rights and duties.* And, of course, the question of the relation between rights and duties raises many important issues, not the least that concerning who or what may be the possessor of rights. It is commonly argued that there is a close conceptual connexion between rights and duties. To consider in what respect this is so. (i) Where the right is of type *(a),* its existence depends in part on there being a duty on others not to interfere *or* on others lacking a right of type *(b)* to interfere. Where the right is of type *(b)* A's right creates actual and potential duties for others and for potential and hypothetical others. To explain: My right to liberty creates no duty for the Hottentot or the Eskimo, for they cannot interfere with me and do not know of my existence. If they could come to interfere, my right would constitute a ground for the duty not to interfere. Similarly with infants. My rights do not create duties for them unless and until they become full moral agents and have some relationship or connexion with me, when my right causes them to have duties not to interfere. Similarly with those as yet unborn. (ii) Rights of type *(c)* obviously give rise to duties and to potential duties. If the blind man whose sight can be restored has a right to sight (as part of the right to health) he has a right to our efforts on his behalf; and we have a duty to make the relevant effort. Such rights seem also to be possessed by those who are not full moral agents, for instances, by infants, curable lunatics, idiots, etc. If a minimal I.Q. idiot could be cured by a pill as cheap as an aspirin, it would be reasonable to claim that he has a right to the necessary treatment and that we have a duty to see that it is made available to him. (iii) Where the right is of type *(d)*, i.e. a special right against another, the right implies a duty in the person against whom it is held. The husband of the wife who has promised to obey him has a right to her obedience, and she the duty to obey. In this case the duty is primary. It springs from the wife's promise and the right is created by the promise and the duty to keep the promise. (iv) Duties and rights. To have a duty is to have a right. One has the right to do what is necessary for the fulfilment of one's duty. But to have a duty is not necessarily for another to have a right. Ross notes the case of duties to animals, and other duties could be cited.[8] For example, the duty to perfect one's talents is not a duty

against oneself, nor is it a duty to one's self. It is simply a duty and creates no rights in others. Similarly with the duty to maximize good. The last person in the universe would have the duty to maximize good and to produce other human beings if this were a means to or part of maximizing good; but there would be no one with a right resulting from the duty. The duty of the artist to produce good and not slovenly paintings does not give to others the right to demand of the artist that he produce the best paintings of which he is capable. Again, I may have a duty to the state, for example, to pay my income tax; but the sense in which the state might be said to have a right to my tax is distinct from the sense of 'right' in which we speak of moral rights as possessed by individuals. The state cannot be the possessor of the sorts of rights human beings may possess. Yet it may be the object of duties. Further, not all duties to the state or to other institutions create these rights in the institutions. It does not follow that, because the Church member has a duty to give generously to his Church, the Church has a right to his gifts.[9] In brief:

8. W. D. Ross, *The Right and The Good*, Oxford, 1930, ch. 2, appendix 1.

9. The notion of a *duty to* needs examination. We often speak of duties to when we really mean duties concerning, involving, etc., as in talk about duties to oneself. However, we do have duties which are properly described as duties to—e.g. a duty of gratitude to our benefactor, a duty to our creditor, a duty of fidelity to one's spouse, a duty of loyalty to one's country. However, it is difficult to see what the principle is that leads us to speak of such duties as "duties to." With things, and even with animals, we seem to speak of duties as involving them, rather than as being to them. If institutions such as the State and the Church may be objects of duties to, why not things and animals? Yet the duty to preserve a great painting (even if the duty of the last person in the universe) is not a duty *to* the painting. Similarly with animals. If I don't feed my cat, I can be reproached as not having done what I ought and as having no right to treat it as I did, but we should be disinclined to speak of my duty to my cat, or to

When a right is attributed, we cannot always significantly ask 'Who has the corresponding duties?' And, when a duty is postulated, we cannot always find someone who possesses a corresponding right.

B. WHO OR WHAT ARE LOGICALLY POSSIBLE POSSESSORS OF RIGHTS?

The issue as to who or what may be a possessor of rights is not simply a matter of academic, conceptual interest. Obviously, important conclusions follow from any answer. If, for instance, it is determined that gravely mentally defective human beings and monsters born of human parents are not the kinds of beings who may possess rights, this bears on how we may treat them. It does not settle such questions as to whether it is right to kill them if they are a burden or if they are enduring pointless suffering, but it does bear in an important way on such questions. Even if such beings cannot be possessors of rights it might still be wrong to kill them, but the case against killing those who endure pain is obviously easier to set out if they can be shown to be capable of possessing rights and in fact possess rights. Similarly, important conclusions follow from the question as to whether animals have rights. If they do, as Salt argued, it would seem an illegitimate invasion of animal rights to kill and eat them, if, as seems to be the case, we can sustain ourselves without killing animals.[10] If animals have rights, the case for vegetarianism is *prima facie* very strong, and is comparable with the case against cannibalism.

These issues, then, are not without importance, but they present very considerable difficulties. If we follow our unreflective moral consciousness we find ourselves drawn strongly to conclusions which seem radically inconsistent with one another; yet if we attempt to reason to a conclusion it is extremely difficult even to begin to set out an argument, let alone develop a carefully worked out, convincing argument in favour of one conclusion rather than another. And, whilst our analysis of the concept of a right takes us some way—it excludes some possibilities and some arguments—it seems on the face of it to leave open a very large number of possibilities.

Although an important and difficult problem, this is one to which few theorists have applied themselves with the attention and critical scrutiny which might be expected in such an important issue. Ross, Plamenatz and Green are typical of thinkers in this area. Ross notes difficulties in respect of idiots, infants and animals, but seems quietly to forget to deal with them, and offers his conclusions without the support of reasons. Plamenatz seems simply to legislate. He asserts that animals do have rights, and hence states that any definition of rights must be such as to admit that animals do have rights. However, no argument is offered to support the view. T. H. Green does address himself to the problem to the extent of claiming that we have rights only as members of a community, that rights involve mutual recognition, and that they can therefore only be possessed by moral persons, that is rational beings.[11] However, he offers only very general, sketchy arguments

---

justify such remarks by talk about its right to a square meal a day. Rather, we should speak of duties not to be cruel, etc.; by contrast, if parents neglected their offspring, allusions to their duties *to* their children would be made quickly and naturally.

10. H. S. Salt, *Animal Rights*, London, 1892.

11. *Ibid.*, pp. 44 and 144 (Lecture A, sn. 25, Lecture H, sn. 139).

for these contentions, and seems to fail to realize that besides excluding animals as possible possessors of rights, they exclude infants, imbeciles, and other mentally defective human beings. Ritchie perhaps comes closest to offering an argument when he notes the difficulties which arise if animals are attributed rights. If animals have rights, the cat invades the right of the mouse, the tiger of the cow, and so forth. Should we restrict the liberty of the cat and of the tiger out of respect for the rights of the mouse and the cow? And should we, out of respect for the rights of animals, allow parasites to continue to inhabit us if they do not have seriously deleterious effects on our health? Plamenatz seeks a way out of such difficulties, whilst at the same time allowing that animals have rights, by claiming that rights are *rights against rational beings*, hence the cow has no rights against the tiger but only against human beings. This obviously will not do, for the reasons noted above, namely, that rights are not primarily rights against but rights to. They may rationally be demanded only of rational beings, for the obvious reason that only rational beings are capable of complying with the demands, but this does not mean that the tiger is not invading the rights of the cow when he kills it. The absurdity of the conclusions which follow from the admission of animal rights may, as Ritchie claims, *suggest* that animals cannot be possessors of rights, but it does not *establish* that this is so.

The general tendency has been to maintain that free agents and potential free agents have rights, with idiots, and all born of human parents being treated as potentially free agents, although many are obviously not such. Those who have claimed that animals have rights have rarely explained whether they mean all animals; equally seriously, they seem not to explain why they think some or all sentient beings have rights, and why not all animate objects and even perhaps things. The unspoken premiss seems to be either that where there is a possibility of "action" of some sort there is the possibility of rights, or that where there is a possibility of pain, there is the possibility of possession of rights. But the reasons underlying the assumption are not evident. Clearly, if lower animals, especially parasitic animals such as the flea, are allowed to be capable of possessing rights, argument is needed to show why such animals, and not all animate objects, for example a beautiful oak or mountain ash, can possess rights. If it were allowed that all sentient beings and all animate objects possess some rights—for example to life—why, it might be asked, should rights be denied of inanimate things? Might not beautiful works of art, paintings of Raphael and Leonardo da Vinci also have a right to continued existence? Argument is needed here, yet argument is notably lacking. Where it is to be found, it is of the very unconvincing kind offered by Thomists, that rational beings, being subject to the natural law, have rights, since rights are grounded on the natural law; that infants, lunatics, idiots have rights and are subject to natural law since they are rational beings. Obviously, even if the theory of natural law could be established—and this I should wish to deny—infants, lunatics and idiots are not subject to it as rational agents any more than is an intelligent dog or ape. The natural law is law, and is binding on men because and in so far as it is promulgated through reason. It is not promulgated to infants, idiots and certain lunatics. And, whilst it might be argued that it is promulgated

potentially to infants, and hypothetically to idiots, potential and hypothetical promulgation are not promulgation, and to be a potential or a hypothetical possessor of rights is not to be a
possessor of potential or hypothetical
rights, nor of actual rights.

To consider what can be done
towards reaching an answer. I have
argued that rights are entitlements to
do, have, enjoy, or have done for us, and
not claims or powers. An obvious
answer to the question 'Who may possess entitlements?' is 'Free moral
agents'. They obviously may and do possess and claim entitlements of the sorts
claimed in rights to life, liberty and
health. However, it is unduly and
arbitrarily to narrow and limit the field
of possible possessors of rights to limit
it to free moral agents. Consider the
lunatic who has completely lost his grip
on the world, who is devoid of all free
choice, and who thinks (in so far as he
can be said to think) that he is a cabbage.
If he could be treated and made sane by
being given a drug costing 1/-, would it
not be meaningful to claim that he has a
right to the drug, that others ought to
exert themselves to respect his rights, to
secure his enjoyment of his rights? Here
the difficulty lies in distinguishing an
attribution of a duty and an attribution
of a right or entitlement. Clearly others
would have a duty towards the lunatic,
hence, on that account, he might in
some sort of analogous sense be said to
have a right. However, I suggest that we
should be inclined to assert that he can
have and has rights in a fuller, more
literal sense. Compare him with the
blind, rational, free agent who can
equally be cured of his blindness, but
not by his own efforts. Each would be
said to have a right to the necessary
treatment; and when we attribute the
right to the one, we seem to be using

language in the same meaningful way as
when attributing a right to the other.
We are saying that each is entitled or
has an entitlement to the efforts of
others for their own good. This suggests
that, although free agents may possess
rights, the test of who or what can be a
possessor of a right or an entitlement is
not that of freedom or rationality. A
lunatic can be a possessor of an entitle-
mentment, of kinds *(a)* and *(c)*. Further,
the lunatic does not have to be one
capable of attaining free will, that is to
be a potential or hypothetical free agent.
It is not *prima facie* absurd to claim that
an incurable lunatic is entitled to decent
treatment. His relatives can reasonably
claim that his rights be respected, and if
he is regularly being beaten up by a
sadistic attendant, they can properly
claim that his rights are being denied. So
too with infants. There seems to be no
logical paradox in asserting that the
infant is entitled to care and nurture
from his parents. This is because an
entitlement does not have to admit of
being demanded by its possessor any
more than does a legitimate claim.
Entitlements may be demanded (and
claims made) by proxies on behalf of the
holder of the entitlement. Logically we
do not have to be able to say that we are
entitled, to be entitled. The cases of the
infant and lunatic suggest this, but
obviously there are limits to those
who/which may logically be possessors
of entitlements.

Here it is useful to consider legal
rights and entitlements in respect of
animals. Legal claims may be made on
behalf of animals, for example against
trustees who embezzle money left for
the care of a cat. In such cases we should
be disinclined to speak of the courts
upholding the legal rights of the cat. Our
uneasiness, and the grounds for our uneasiness, can be brought out by the

following examples. Suppose that, as a result of deliberate legal enactment, the kangaroo came to be accorded something like the privileged position of the cow in India, the kangaroo having full rights of movement, on the roads, on private property, and so forth. I suggest that we should be reluctant to speak of the legal rights of kangaroos. This is clear from our manner of speaking of native birds and animals in sanctuaries today. We speak of our being obliged to leave them alone, not of them as having legal rights, nor of them as being legally entitled to be left alone. The law confers duties on us, not rights in the animals. This is confirmed by another possible group of cases, of legal systems in which animals which kill men are tried, and if found guilty, executed. If an animal is given an unfair trial under such a system and its legal representative demands a new trial, he could perhaps say that the animal had not received its legal rights (lawyers seem inclined to speak in this way) but it seems more accurate and less misleading simply to say that the law has not been properly observed in the original trial. Compare with a trial of a man.

Why we are reluctant to speak of the legal rights of animals, even under such legal systems, becomes clearer if we consider *things*, and why things cannot have legal rights. Things do not have legal rights in our legal system, but not because this is a peculiarity of our legal system. It is because anything which might seem to come close to a thing having legal rights is not so described. A man can leave his money to preserve a building, a park, and so forth, and appoint trustees, but we do not say of the trustees who embezzle the money that they have failed to respect the legal rights of the building or gardens they were appointed to care for.

(Similarly with legal systems where things such as cars or locomotives are given trials before being destroyed when guilty of killing men.) The reasons for this seem to be two. First, things such as parks, buildings, paintings, and so forth, do not have *interests* in the strict sense of interests, such that we could literally speak of the trustees caring for their interests. The trustees care for the thing, not for the interests of the thing. Secondly, and partly for this reason, the trustees could hardly be said to be the representatives of the thing. Here we might speak of them as custodians, and so forth.

What holds in respect of legal rights seems also to hold of moral rights. Moral rights can be possessed by beings who can claim them, and by those who can have them claimed on their behalf by others and whose interests are violated or disregarded if the rights are not respected. The concept of interests which is so important here is an obscure and elusive one. Interests are distinct from welfare, and are more inclusive in certain respects—usually what is dictated by concern for a man's welfare is in his interests. However, interests suggest much more than that which is indicated by the person's welfare. They suggest that which is or ought to be or which would be of *concern* to the person/being. It is partly for this reason—because the concept of interests has this evaluative-prescriptive overtone—that we decline to speak of the interests of animals, and speak rather of their welfare.

That the possibility of possessing rights is limited in this way is confirmed by the very fact that we speak of rights as being *possessed and enjoyed*. A right cannot not be possessed by someone; hence, only beings which can possess things can possess rights. My right to life is mine; I possess it. It is as much mine as any of my possessions—indeed more so—for I possess them by virtue of my rights. It is true that I may possess rights and not know or enjoy my possession of them. Thus, whilst rights must be possessed by a possessor, they need not be enjoyed. All we can say is that they may admit of enjoyment by their possessors.

All these considerations seem to exclude the lower animals in a decisive way, and the higher animals in a less decisive but still fairly conclusive way as possible possessors of rights. (Consider 'possess' in its literal use. Can a horse possess anything, for example its stable, its rug, in a literal sense of 'possess'?) It might, however, be argued that animals can possess special rights, for example rights arising out of relations such as the owner's "debt of gratitude" to the animal for special services. Consider the blind man and his guide dog who repeatedly saves his life. The difficulty that rights are possessed and that animals cannot possess things remains; and, in any case, the animal's special services are more naturally described as creating special duties rather than as giving rise to entitlements in the animal.

It would seem to follow from all this that monsters born of human parents whose level of existence falls far short of that of the highest animals would also seem not to be possible possessors of rights. However, two qualifications may usefully be made here. Animals, or at least the higher animals, may usefully be said to have *rights by analogy*. We have duties involving them, and these duties might be said to create rights by analogy. (The latter are not the same as rights in sense *(a)*, for a right by analogy is not an entitlement, whereas a negative right is such; and the

difference leads to important implications). With those born of human parents, even the most inferior beings, it may be *a useful lie* to attribute rights where they are not and cannot be possessed, since to deny the very inferior beings born of human parents rights, opens the way to a dangerous slide. But whether useful or not, it is a lie or a mistake to attribute rights or the possibility of rights to such beings. More difficult are the cases of the infant, lunatic, and so forth. As indicated earlier, we do attribute rights and interests to infants, lunatics, and even to incurable lunatics. Part of the reason for this is the thought that such beings, unlike the congenital idiot, etc., are possibly potential possessors of interests. Hence, until it is clear that they can never really be said to have interests, we treat them as if they do. Also relevant is the fact that even a mentally defective human being—for example an imbecile, or a lunatic with periods of sanity—may literally demand some rights and possess others and generally be attributed interests in a literal sense.

I have not considered theories to the effect that possessors of immortal souls, and only such, are logically possible possessors of rights. This is because those who argue that possessors of immortal souls possess rights—and that animals do not—usually make their claim a factual and not a logical one. They argue that this is in fact the case, and do not concern themselves with the issue as to whether it is logically possible for a being without an immortal soul to possess rights. In any case, there is a quick answer to any such contention, namely, that it is possible to deny that man has an immortal soul, without being logically impelled to deny that he may possess rights.

33

RONALD DWORKIN
Taking Rights Seriously

RONALD DWORKIN is professor of jurisprudence at Oxford, and lecturer in law at the Yale Law School. He is well known for his writings on the philosophy of law.

I

The language of rights now dominates political debate. Does our government respect the moral and political rights of its citizens? Or does the government's war policy, or its race policy, fly in the face of these rights? Do the minorities whose rights have been violated have the right to violate the law in return? Or does the silent majority itself have rights, including the right that those who break the law be punished? It is not surprising that these questions are now prominent. The concept of rights, and particularly the concept of rights against the government, has its most natural use when a political society is divided, and appeals to cooperation or a common goal are pointless.

The debate does not include the issue of whether citizens have *some* moral rights against their government. It seems accepted on all sides that they have. Conventional lawyers and politicians take it as a point of pride that our legal system recognizes, for example, individual rights of free speech, equality, and due process. They base their claim that our law deserves respect, at least in part, on that fact, for they would not claim that totalitarian systems deserve the same loyalty. Some philosophers, of course, reject the idea that citizens have rights apart from

what the law happens to give them. Bentham thought that the idea of moral rights was "nonsense on stilts." But that view has never been part of our orthodox political theory, and politicians of both parties appeal to the rights of the people to justify a great part of what they want to do. I shall not be concerned, in this essay, to defend the thesis that citizens have moral rights against their governments; I want instead to explore the implications of that thesis for those, including our present government, who profess to accept it.

It is much in dispute, of course, what *particular* rights citizens have. Does the acknowledged right to free speech, for example, include the right to participate in nuisance demonstrations? In practice the government will have the last word on what an individual's rights are, because its police will do what its officials and courts say. But that does not mean that the government's view is necessarily the correct view; anyone who thinks it does must believe that men have only such moral rights as government chooses to grant, which means that they have no moral rights at all.

All this is sometimes obscured in the United States by our constitutional system. The Constitution provides a set of individual *legal* rights in the First Amendment, and in the due process, equal protection, and similar clauses. Under present legal practice the Supreme Court has the power to declare

From Ronald Dworkin, "Taking Rights Seriously," *The New York Review of Books*, December 17, 1970. Reprinted by permission of the author. This article is reprinted unabridged.

an act of Congress or of a state legislature void if the Court finds that the act offends these provisions. This practice has led some commentators to suppose that individual moral rights are fully protected by our system, but that is hardly so, nor could it be so.

The Constitution fuses legal and moral issues, by making the validity of a law depend on the answer to complex moral problems, like the problem of whether a particular statute respects the inherent equality of all men. This fusion has important consequences for the debates about civil disobedience; I have described these elsewhere,[1] and I shall refer to them later. But it leaves open two prominent questions. It does not tell us whether the Constitution, even properly interpreted, recognizes all the moral rights our citizens have, and it does not tell us whether, as many suppose, citizens would have a duty to obey the law even if it did invade their moral rights. Both questions become crucial when some minority claims moral rights which the law denies, like the right to run its local school system, and which lawyers agree are not protected by the Constitution. The second question becomes crucial when, as now, the majority is sufficiently aroused so that constitutional amendments to eliminate rights, like the right against self-incrimination, are seriously proposed. It is also crucial in nations, like England, that have no constitution of our form.

Even if the Constitution were perfect, of course, and the majority left it alone, it would not follow that the Supreme Court could guarantee the individual rights of citizens. A Supreme Court decision is still a legal decision, and it must take into account precedent, and institutional considerations like relations between the Court and Congress, as well as morality. And no judicial decision is necessarily the right decision. Judges stand for different positions on controversial issues of law and morals, and, as the recent fights over Nixon's Supreme Court nomination showed, a President is entitled to appoint judges of his own persuasion, provided they are honest and capable.

So, though the constitutional system adds something to the protection of moral rights against the government, it falls far short of guaranteeing these rights, or even establishing what they are. It means that, on some occasions, a department other than the legislative has the last word on these issues, which can hardly satisfy someone who thinks such a department profoundly wrong.

It is of course inevitable that some department of government will have the final say on what law will be enforced. When men disagree about moral rights, there will be no way for either side to prove its case, and some decision must stand if there is not to be anarchy. But that piece of orthodox wisdom must be the beginning and not the end of a philosophy of legislation and enforcement. If we cannot insist that the government reach the right answers about the rights of its citizens, we can insist at least that it try. We can insist that it take rights seriously, follow a coherent theory of what these rights are, and act consistently with its own professions. I shall try to show what that means, and how it bears on the present political debates.

II

I shall start with the most violently argued issue. Does an American ever have the moral right to break a law? Suppose someone admits a law is valid; does he therefore have a duty to obey it?

1. "On Not Prosecuting Civil Disobedience," *New York Review of Books.* June 6, 1968.

Those who try to give an answer seem to fall into two camps. The conservatives, as I shall call them, seem to disapprove of any act of disobedience; they appear satisfied when such acts are prosecuted, and disappointed when convictions are reversed. The other group, the liberals, are much more sympathetic to at least some cases of disobedience; they sometimes disapprove of prosecutions and celebrate acquittals. If we look beyond these emotional reactions, however, and pay attention to the arguments the two parties use, we discover an astounding fact. Both groups give essentially the same answer to the question of principle that supposedly divides them.

The answer that both parties give is this. In a democracy, or at least a democracy that in principle respects individual rights, each citizen has a general moral duty to obey all the laws, even though he would like some of them changed. He owes that duty to his fellow citizens, who obey laws that they do not like, to his benefit. But this general duty cannot be an absolute duty, because even a society that is in principle just may produce unjust laws and policies, and a man has duties other than his duties to the state. A man must honor his duties to his God and to his conscience, and if these conflict with his duty to the state, then he is entitled, in the end, to do what he judges to be right. If he decides that he must break the law, however, then he must submit to the judgment and punishment that the state imposes, in recognition of the fact that his duty to his fellow citizens was overwhelmed but not extinguished by his religious or moral obligation.

Of course this common answer can be elaborated in very different ways. Some would describe the duty to the state as fundamental, and picture the dissenter as a religious or moral fanatic. Others would describe the duty to the state in grudging terms, and picture those who oppose it as moral heroes. But these are differences in tone, and the position I describe represents, I think, the view of most of those who find themselves arguing either for or against civil disobedience in particular cases. I do not claim that it is everyone's view. There must be some who put the duty to the state so high that they do not grant that it can ever be overcome. There are certainly some who would deny that a man ever has a moral duty to obey the law, at least in the United States today. But these two extreme positions are the slender tails of a bell curve, and all those who fall in between hold the orthodox position I described —that men have a duty to obey the law but have the right to follow their conscience when it conflicts with that duty.

But if that is so, then we have a paradox in the fact that men who give the same answer to a question of principle should seem to disagree so much, and to divide so fiercely, in particular cases. The paradox goes even deeper, for each party, in at least some cases, takes a position that seems flatly inconsistent with the theoretical position they both accept. This position is tested, for example, when someone evades the draft on grounds of conscience, or encourages others to commit this crime. Conservatives argue that such men must be prosecuted, even though they are sincere. Why must they be prosecuted? Because society cannot tolerate the decline in respect for the law that their act constitutes and encourages. They must be prosecuted, in short, to discourage them and others like them from doing what they have done. But there seems to be a monstrous contradiction here. If a man has a right to do what his conscience tells him he must, then how can the state be justified in discouraging him from doing it? Is it not wicked for a state to forbid and punish what it acknowledges that men have a right to do?

Moreover, it is not just conservatives who argue that those who break the law out of moral conviction should be prosecuted. The liberal is notoriously opposed to allowing southern school officials to go slow on segregation, even though he acknowledges that these school officials think they have a moral right to do what the law forbids. The liberal does not often argue, it is true, that the desegregation laws must be enforced to encourage general respect for law. He argues instead that the desegregation laws must be enforced because they are right. But his position also seems inconsistent: Can it be right to prosecute men for doing what their conscience requires, when we acknowledge their right to follow their conscience?

We are therefore left with two puzzles. How can two parties to an issue of principle, each of which thinks it is in profound disagreement with the other, embrace the same position on that issue? How can it be that each side urges solutions to particular problems which seem flatly to contradict the position of principle that both accept? One possible answer is that some or all of those who accept the common position are hypocrites, paying lip service to rights of conscience which in fact they do not grant. There is some plausibility to this charge. A sort of hypocrisy must be involved when public officials who claim to respect conscience denied Muhammad Ali the right to box in their states. If Muhammad Ali, in spite of his religious scruples, had joined the army, he would have been allowed to box even

though, on the principles these officials say they honor, he would have been a worse human being for having done so. But there are few cases that seem so straightforward as this one, and even here the officials do not seem even to recognize the contradiction between their acts and their principles. So we must search for some explanation beyond the truth that men often do not mean what they say.

The deeper explanation lies in a set of confusions that often embarrass arguments about rights. These confusions have clouded all the issues I mentioned at the outset, and have crippled attempts to develop a coherent theory of how a government that respects rights must behave.

In order to explain this, I must call attention to the fact, familiar to philosophers but often ignored in political debate, that the word "right" has different force in different contexts. In most cases, when we say that someone has a "right" to do something, we mean that it would be wrong to interfere with his doing it, or at least that some special grounds are needed for justifying any interference. I use this strong sense of "right" when I say that you have the right to spend your money gambling, if you wish, though you ought to spend it in a more worthwhile way. I mean that it would be wrong for anyone to interfere with you even though you propose to spend your money in a way that I think is wrong.

There is a clear difference between saying that someone has a right to do something in this sense, and saying that it is the "right" thing for him to do or that he does no wrong in doing it. Someone may have the right to do something that is the wrong thing for him to do, as might be the case with gambling. Conversely, something may be the right thing for him to do and yet he may have no right to do it, in the sense that it would not be wrong for someone to interfere with his trying. If our army captures an enemy soldier, we might say that the right thing for him to do is to try to escape, but it would not follow that it is wrong of us to try to stop him. We might admire him for trying to escape, and perhaps even think less of him if he did not. But there is no suggestion here that it is wrong of us to stand in his way; on the contrary, if we think our cause is just, we think it right for us to do all we can to stop him.

Ordinarily this distinction, between the issues of whether a man has a right to do something and whether it is the right thing for him to do, causes no trouble. But sometimes it does, because sometimes we say that a man has a right to do something when we mean only to deny that it is the wrong thing for him to do. Thus we say that the captured soldier has a "right" to try to escape when we mean, not that we do wrong to stop him, but that he has no duty not to make the attempt. We also use "right" this way when we speak of someone having the "right" to act on his own principles, or the "right" to follow his own conscience. We mean that he does no wrong to proceed on his honest convictions, even though we disagree with these convictions, and even though, for policy or other reasons, we must force him to act contrary to them.

Suppose a man believes that welfare payments to the poor are profoundly wrong, because they sap enterprise, and so declares his full income tax each year but declines to pay half of it. We might say that he has a right to refuse to pay, if he wishes, but that the government has a right to proceed against him for the full tax, and to fine or jail him for late payment if that is necessary to keep the collection system working efficiently.

We do not take this line in most cases; we do not say that the ordinary thief has a right to steal, if he wishes, so long as he pays the penalty. We say a man has the right to break the law, even though the state has a right to punish him, only when we think that, because of his convictions, he does no wrong in doing so.[2]

These distinctions enable us to see an ambiguity in the orthodox question: Does a man ever have a right to break the law? Does that question mean to ask whether he ever has a right to break the law in the strong sense, so that the government would do wrong to stop him, by arresting and prosecuting him? Or does it mean to ask whether he ever does the right thing to break the law, so that we should all respect him even though the government should jail him?

If we take the orthodox position to be an answer to the first—and most important—question, then the paradoxes I described arise. But if we take it as an answer to the second, they do not. Conservatives and liberals do agree that sometimes a man does not do the wrong thing to break a law, when his conscience so requires. They disagree, when they do, over the different issue of what the state's response should be. Both parties do think that sometimes the state should prosecute. But this is not inconsistent with the proposition that the man prosecuted did the right thing in breaking the law.

The paradoxes seem genuine be-

2. It is not surprising that we sometimes use the concept of having a right to say that others must not interfere with an act and sometimes to say that the act is not the wrong thing to do. Often, when someone has *no* right to do something, like attacking another man physically, it is true *both* that it is the wrong thing to do and that others are entitled to stop it, by demand, if not by force. It is therefore natural to say that someone has a right when we mean to deny *either* of these consequences, as well as when we mean to deny both.

cause the two questions are not usually distinguished, and the orthodox position is presented as a general solution to the problem of civil disobedience. But once the distinction is made, it is apparent that the position has been so widely accepted that only because, when it is applied, it is treated as an answer to the second question but not the first. The crucial distinction is obscured by the troublesome idea of a right to conscience; this idea has been at the center of most recent discussions of political obligation, but it is a red herring drawing us away from the crucial political questions. The state of a man's conscience may be decisive, or central, when the issue is whether he does something morally wrong in breaking the law; but it need not be decisive or even central when the issue is whether he has a right, in the strong sense of that term, to do so. A man does not have the right, in that sense, to do whatever his conscience demands, but he may have the right, in that sense, to do something even though his conscience does not demand it.

If that is true, then there has been almost no serious attempt to answer the questions that almost everyone means to ask. We can make a fresh start by stating these questions more clearly. Does an American ever have the right, in a strong sense, to do something which is against the law? If so, when? In order to answer these questions put in that way, we must try to become clearer about the implications of the idea, mentioned earlier, that citizens have at least some rights against their government.

I said that in the United States citizens are supposed to have certain fundamental rights against their government, certain moral rights made into legal rights by the Constitution. If this idea is significant, and worth bragging about, then these rights must be rights in the strong sense I just described. The claim that citizens have a right to free speech must imply that it would be wrong for the government to stop them from speaking, even when the government believes that what they will say will cause more harm than good. The claim cannot mean, on the prisoner-of-war analogy, only that citizens do no wrong in speaking their minds, though the government reserves the right to prevent them from doing so.

This is a crucial point, and I want to labor it. Of course a responsible government must be ready to justify anything it does, particularly when it limits the liberty of its citizens. But normally it is a sufficient justification, even for an act that limits liberty, that the act is calculated to increase what the philosophers call general utility—that it is calculated to produce more over-all benefit than harm. So, though the New York City government needs a justification for forbidding motorists to drive up Lexington Avenue, it is sufficient justification if the proper officials believe, on sound evidence, that the gain to the many will outweigh the inconvenience to the few. When individual citizens are said to have rights against the government, however, like the right of free speech, that must mean that this sort of justification is not enough. Otherwise the claim would not argue that individuals have special protection against the law when their rights are in play, and that is just the point of the claim.

Not all legal rights, or even Constitutional rights, represent moral rights against the government. I now have the legal right to drive either way on Fifty-seventh Street, but the government would do no wrong to make that street one-way, if it thought it in the general interest to do so. I have a Constitutional right to vote for a congressman every two years, but the national and state governments would do no wrong if, following the amendment procedure, they made a congressman's term four years instead of two, again on the basis of a judgment that this would be for the general good.

But those Constitutional rights that we call fundamental, like the right of free speech, are supposed to represent rights against the government in the strong sense; that is the point of the boast that our legal system respects the fundamental rights of the citizen. If citizens have a moral right of free speech, then governments would do wrong to repeal the First Amendment that guarantees it, even if they were persuaded that the majority would be better off if speech were curtailed.

I must not overstate the point. Someone who claims that citizens have a right against the government need not go so far as to say that the state is *never* justified in overriding that right. He might say, for example, that although citizens have a right to free speech, the government may override that right when necessary to protect the rights of others, or to prevent a catastrophe, or even to obtain a clear and major public benefit (though if he acknowledged this last as a possible justification, he would be treating the right in question as not among the most important or fundamental). What he cannot do is to say that the government is justified in overriding a right on the minimal grounds that would be sufficient if no such right existed. He cannot say that the government is entitled to act on no more than a judgment that its act is likely to produce, overall, a benefit to the community. That admission would make his claim of a right pointless, and would show him to be using some sense

of "right" other than the strong sense necessary to give his claim the political importance it is normally taken to have.

But then the answers to our two questions about disobedience seem plain, if unorthodox. In our society a man does sometimes have the right, in the strong sense, to disobey a law. He has that right whenever that law wrongly invades his rights against the government. If he has a moral right to free speech, that is, then he has a moral right to break any law that the government, by virtue of his right, had no right to adopt. The right to disobey the law is not a separate right, having something to do with conscience, additional to other rights against the government. It is simply a feature of these rights against the government, and it cannot be denied in principle without denying that any such rights exist.

These answers seem obvious once we take rights against the government in the strong sense I described. If I have a right to speak my mind on political issues, then the government does wrong to make it illegal for me to do so, even if it thinks this is in the general interest. If, nevertheless, the government does make my act illegal, then it does a further wrong to enforce that law against me. My right against the government means that it is wrong for the government to stop me from speaking; the government cannot make it right to stop me just by taking the first step.

This does not, of course, tell us exactly what rights men do have against the government. It does not tell us whether the right of free speech includes the right of demonstration. But it does mean that passing a law cannot affect such rights as men do have, and that is of crucial importance, because it dictates the attitude that an individual is entitled to take toward his personal decision when civil disobedience is in question. Both conservatives and liberals suppose that in a society which is generally decent everyone has a duty to obey the law, whatever it is. That is the source of the "general duty" clause in the orthodox position, and though liberals believe that his duty can sometimes be "overridden," even they suppose, as the orthodox position maintains, so that the duty of obedience remains in some submerged form, so that a man does well to accept punishment in recognition of that duty. But this general duty is almost incoherent in a society that recognizes rights. If a man believes he has a right to demonstrate, then he must believe that it would be wrong for the government to stop him, with or without benefit of a law. If he is entitled to believe that, then it is silly to speak of a duty to obey the law as such, or of a duty to accept the punishment that the state has no right to give.

Conservatives will object to the short work I have made of their point. They will argue that even if the government was wrong to adopt some law, like a law limiting speech, there are independent reasons why the government is justified in enforcing the law once adopted. When the law forbids demonstration, then, so they argue, some principle more important than the individual's right to speak is brought into play; namely, the principle of respect for law. If a law, even a bad law, is left unenforced, then respect for law is weakened, and society as a whole suffers. So an individual loses his moral right to speak when speech is made criminal, and the government must, for the common good and for the general benefit, enforce the law against him.

But this argument, though popular, is plausible only if we forget what it means to say that an individual has a right against the state. It is far from plain that civil disobedience lowers respect for law, but even if we suppose that it does, this fact is irrelevant. The prospect of utilitarian gains cannot justify preventing a man from doing what he has a right to do, and the supposed gains in respect for law are simply utilitarian gains. There would be no point in the boast that we respect individual rights unless that involved some sacrifice, and the sacrifice in question must be that we give up whatever marginal benefits our country would receive from overriding these rights when they prove inconvenient. So the general benefit cannot be a good ground for abridging rights, even when the benefit in question is a heightened respect for law.

But perhaps I do wrong to assume that the argument about respect for law is only an appeal to general utility. I said that a state may be justified in overriding or limiting rights on other grounds, and we must ask, before rejecting the conservative position, whether any of these apply. The most important—and least well understood —of these other grounds invokes the notion of *competing rights* that would be jeopardized if the right in question were not limited. Citizens have personal rights to the state's protection as well as personal rights to be free from the state's interference, and it may be necessary for the government to choose between these two sorts of rights. The law of defamation, for example, limits the personal right of any man to say what he thinks, because it requires him to have good grounds for what he says. But this law is justified, even for those who think that it does invade a personal right, by the fact that it protects the right of others not to have their reputations ruined by a careless statement.

The individual rights that our society acknowledges often conflict in this way, and when they do it is the job of government to discriminate. If the government makes the right choice, and protects the more important at the cost of the less, then it has not weakened or cheapened the notion of a right; on the contrary, it would have done so had it failed to protect the more important of the two. So we must acknowledge that the government has a reason for limiting rights if it plausibly believes that a competing right is more important.

May the conservative seize on this fact? He might argue that I did wrong to characterize his argument as one that appeals to the general benefit, because it appeals instead to competing rights; namely, the moral right of the majority to have its laws enforced or the right of society to maintain the degree of order and security it wishes. These are the rights, he would say, that must be weighed against the individual's right to do what the wrongful law prohibits.

But this argument is confused, because it depends on yet another ambiguity in the language of rights. It is true that we speak of the "right" of society to do what it wants, but this cannot be a "competing right" of the sort that might justify the invasion of a right against the government. The existence of rights against the government would be jeopardized if the government were able to defeat such a right by appealing to the right of a democratic majority to work its will. A right against the government must be a right to do something even when the majority thinks it would be wrong to do it, and even when the majority would be worse off for having it done. If we now say that society has a right to do whatever is in the general benefit, or the right to preserve whatever sort of environ-ment the majority wishes to live in—and we mean that these are the sort of rights that provide justification for over-ruling any rights against the government that may conflict—then we have anni-hilated the latter rights.

In order to save them, we must recognize as competing rights only the rights of other members of the society as individuals. We must distinguish the "rights" of the majority as such, which cannot count as justification for over-ruling individual rights, and the per-sonal rights of members of a majority, which might well count. The test we must use is this. Someone has a com-peting right to protection, which must be weighed against an individual right to act, if that person would be entitled to demand that protection from his gov-ernment on his own title, as an individ-ual, without regard to whether a ma-jority of his fellow citizens joined in the demand.

It cannot be true, on this test, that anyone has a right to have all the laws of the nation enforced. He has a right to have enforced only those criminal laws that he would have a right to have enacted if they were not already law. The laws against personal assault may well fall into that class. If the physically vulnerable members of the community —those who need police protection against personal violence—were only a small minority, it would still seem plausible to say that they were enti-tled to that protection. But the laws that provide a certain level of quiet in public places, or that authorize and fi-nance a foreign war, cannot be thought to rest on individual rights. The timid lady on the streets of Chicago is not entitled to just the degree of quiet that now obtains, nor is she entitled to have boys drafted to fight in wars she ap-proves. There are laws—perhaps desirable laws—that provide these advantages for her, but the justification for these laws, if they can be justified at all, is the common desire of a large majority, not her personal right. If, therefore, these laws do abridge someone else's moral right to protest, or his right to personal security, she cannot urge a competing right to justify the abridgment. She has no personal right to have such laws passed, and she has no competing right to have them enforced either.

So the conservative cannot advance his argument much on the ground of competing rights, but he may want to use another ground. A government, he may argue, may be justified in abridging the personal rights of its citizens in an emergency, or when a very great loss may be prevented, or perhaps when some major benefit may clearly be secured. If the nation is at war, a policy of censorship may be justified even though it invades the right to say what one thinks on matters of political controversy. But the emergency must be genuine. There must be what Oliver Wendell Holmes described as a clear and present danger, and the danger must be one of magnitude.

Can the conservative argue that when any law is passed, even a wrongful law, this sort of justification is available for enforcing it? His argument might be something of this sort. If the government once acknowledges that it may be wrong—that the legislature might have adopted, the executive approved, and the courts left standing a law that in fact abridges important rights—then this admission will lead not simply to a marginal decline in respect for law, but to a crisis of order. Citizens may decide to obey only those laws they personally approve, and that is anarchy. So the government must insist that whatever a

citizen's rights may be before a law is passed and upheld by the courts, his rights thereafter are determined by that law.

But this argument ignores the primitive distinction between what may happen and what will happen. If we allow speculation to support the justification of emergency or decisive benefit, then, again, we have annihilated rights. We must, as Learned Hand said, discount the gravity of the evil threatened by the likelihood of reaching that evil. I know of no genuine evidence to the effect that tolerating some civil disobedience, out of respect for the moral position of its authors, will increase such disobedience, let alone crime in general. The case that it will must be based on vague assumptions about the contagion of ordinary crimes, assumptions that are themselves unproved, and that are in any event largely irrelevant. It seems at least as plausible to argue that tolerance will increase respect for officials and for the bulk of the laws they promulgate, or at least retard the rate of growing disrespect.

If the issue were simply the question whether the community would be marginally better off under strict law enforcement, then the government would have to decide on the evidence we have, and it might not be unreasonable to decide, on balance, that it would. But since rights are at stake, the issue is the very different one of whether tolerance would destroy the community or threaten it with great harm, and it seems to me simply mindless to suppose that the evidence makes that probable or even conceivable.

The argument from emergency is confused in another way as well. It assumes that the government must take the position either that a man never has the right to break the law, or that he always does. I said that any society that claims to recognize rights at all must abandon the notion of a general duty to obey the law that holds in all cases. This is important, because it shows that there are no shortcuts to meeting a citizen's claim of right. If a citizen argues that he has a moral right not to serve in the army, or to protest in a way he finds effective, then an official who wants to answer him, and not simply bludgeon him into obedience, must respond to the particular points he makes, and cannot point to the draft law or a Supreme Court decision as having even special, let alone decisive, weight. Sometimes an official who considers the citizen's moral arguments in good faith will be persuaded that the citizen's claim is plausible, or even right. It does not follow, however, that he will always be persuaded or that he always should be.

I must emphasize that all these propositions concern the strong sense of right, and they therefore leave open important questions about the right to do so. If a man believes he has the right to break the law, he must then ask whether he does the right thing to exercise that right. He must remember that reasonable men can differ about whether he has a right against the government, and therefore a right to break the law, that he thinks he has; and therefore that reasonable men can oppose him in good faith. He must take into account the various consequences his acts will have, whether they involve violence, and such other considerations as the context makes relevant. He must not go beyond the rights he can in good faith claim to acts that violate the rights of others. On the other hand, if some official, like a prosecutor, believes that the citizen does *not* have the right to break the law, then *he* must ask whether he does the right thing to

enforce it. In the article I mentioned earlier, I argued that certain features of our legal system, and in particular the fusion of legal and moral issues in our Constitution, mean that citizens often do the right thing in exercising what they take to be moral rights to break the law, and that prosecutors often do the right thing in failing to prosecute them for it. I will not repeat those arguments here; instead I want to ask whether the requirement that government take its citizens' rights seriously has anything to do with the crucial question of what these rights are.

III

The argument so far has been hypothetical: If a man has a particular moral right against the government, that right survives contrary legislation or adjudication. But this does not tell us what rights he has, and it is notorious that reasonable men disagree about that. There is wide agreement on certain clearcut cases. Almost everyone who believes in rights at all would admit, for example, that a man has a moral right to speak his mind in a nonprovocative way on matters of political concern, and that this is an important right, that the state must go to great pains to protect. But there is great controversy as to the limits of such paradigm rights, and the so-called "anti-riot" law involved in the Chicago Seven trial is a case in point.

The defendants were accused of conspiring to cross state lines with the intention of causing a riot. This charge is vague—perhaps unconstitutionally vague—but the law apparently defines as criminal emotional speeches which argue that violence is justified in order to secure political equality. Does the right of free speech protect this sort of speech? That, of course, is a legal issue, because it invokes the free-speech clause of the First Amendment of the Constitution. But it is also a moral issue, because, as I said, we must treat the First Amendment as an attempt to protect a moral right. It is part of the job of governing to "define" moral rights through statutes and judicial decisions; that is, to declare officially the extent that moral rights will be taken to have in law. Congress faced this task in voting on the anti-riot bill, and the Supreme Court will face it if the Chicago Seven case goes that far. How should the different departments of government go about defining moral rights?

They should begin with a sense that whatever they decide might be wrong. History and their descendants may judge that they acted unjustly when they thought they were right. If they take their duty seriously, they must try to limit their mistakes, and they must therefore try to discover where the dangers of mistake lie.

They might choose one of two very different models for this purpose. The first model recommends striking a balance between the rights of the individual and the demands of society at large. If the government *infringes* a moral right (for example, by defining the right of free speech more narrowly than justice requires), then it has done the individual a wrong. On the other hand, if the government *inflates* a right (by defining it more broadly than justice requires), then it cheats society of some general benefit, like safe streets, that it is perfectly entitled to have. So a mistake on one side is as serious as a mistake on the other. The course of government is to steer to the middle, to balance the general good and personal rights, giving to each its due.

When the government, or any branch, defines a right, it must bear in mind, according to the first model, the social cost of different proposals and make the necessary adjustments. It must not grant the same freedom to noisy demonstrations as it grants to calm political discussion, for example, because the former causes much more trouble than the latter. Once it decides how much of a right to recognize, it must enforce its decision to the full. That means permitting an individual to act within his rights, as the government has defined them, but not beyond, so that if anyone breaks the law, even on grounds of conscience, he must be punished. No doubt any government will make mistakes, and will regret decisions once taken. That is inevitable. But this middle policy will ensure that errors on one side will balance out errors on the other over the long run.

The first model, described in this way, has great plausibility, and most laymen and lawyers, I think, would respond to it warmly. The metaphor of balancing the public interest against personal claims is established in our political and judicial rhetoric, and this metaphor gives the model both familiarity and appeal. Nevertheless, the first model is a false one, certainly in the case of rights generally regarded as important, and the metaphor is the heart of its error.

The institution of rights against the government is not a gift of God, or an ancient ritual, or a national sport. It is a complex and troublesome practice that makes the government's job of securing the general benefit more difficult and more expensive, and it would be a frivolous and wrongful practice unless it served some point. Anyone who professes to take rights seriously, and who praises our government for respecting them, must have some sense of what that point is. He must accept, at the minimum, one or both of two important ideas. The first is the vague but powerful idea of human dignity. This idea, associated with Kant, but defended by philosophers of different schools, supposes that there are ways of treating a man that are inconsistent with recognizing him as a full member of the human community, and holds that such treatment is profoundly unjust. The second is the more familiar idea of political equality. This supposes that the weaker members of a political community are entitled to the same concern and respect of their government as the more powerful members have secured for themselves, so that if some men have freedom of decision, whatever the effect on the general good, then all men must have the same freedom. I do not want to defend or elaborate these ideas here, but only to insist that anyone who claims that citizens have rights must accept ideas very close to these.[3] It makes sense to say that a man has a fundamental right against the government, in the strong sense, like free speech, if that right is necessary to protect his dignity, or his standing as equally entitled to concern and respect, or some other personal value of like consequence. It does not make sense otherwise.

So if rights make sense at all, then the invasion of a right must be a very serious matter. It means treating a man as less than a man, or as less worthy of concern than other men. The institution of rights rests on the conviction that this is a grave injustice, and that it is worth paying the incremental cost in social policy or efficiency that is necessary to prevent it. But then it must be wrong to say that inflating rights is as serious as invading them. If the government errs on the side of the individual, then it simply pays a little more in social efficiency than it has to pay; it pays a little more, that is, of the same

coin that it has already decided must be spent. But if it errs against the individual, it inflicts an insult upon him that, on its own reckoning, it is worth a great deal of that coin to avoid.

So the first model is indefensible. It rests, in fact, on a mistake I discussed earlier; namely, the confusion of society's rights with the rights of members of society. "Balancing" is appropriate when the government must choose between competing claims of right; between the southerner's claim to freedom of association, for example, and the black man's claim to an equal education. Then the government can do nothing but estimate the merits of the competing claims, and act on its estimate. The first model assumes that the "right" of the majority is a competing right that must be balanced in this way; but that, as I argued before, is a confusion that threatens to destroy the concept of individual rights. It is worth noticing that the community rejects the first model in that area where the stakes for the individual are highest, the criminal process. We say that it is better that a great many guilty men go free than that one innocent man be punished, and that homily rests on the choice of the second model for government.

The second model treats abridging a right as much more serious than

3. He need not consider these ideas to be axiomatic. He may, that is, have reasons for insisting that dignity or equality are important values, and these reasons may be utilitarian. He may believe, for example, that the general good will be advanced, *in the long run*, only if we treat indignity or inequality as very great injustices, and never allow our *opinions* about the general good to justify them. I do not know of any good arguments for or against this sort of "institutional" utilitarianism, but it is consistent with my point, because it argues that we must treat violations of dignity and equality as special moral crimes, beyond the reach of ordinary utilitarian justification.

inflating one, and its recommendations follow from that judgment. It stipulates that once a right is recognized in clear-cut cases, then the government should act to cut off that right only when some compelling reason is presented, some reason that is consistent with the suppositions on which the original right must be based. It cannot be an argument for curtailing a right, once granted, simply that society would pay a further price in extending it. There must be something special about that further cost, or there must be some other feature of the case, that makes it sensible to say that although great social cost is warranted to protect the original right, this particular cost is not necessary. Otherwise, the government's failure to extend the right will show that its recognition of the right in the original case is a sham, a promise that it intends to keep only until that becomes inconvenient.

How can we show that a particular cost is not worth paying without taking back the initial recognition of a right? I can think of only three sorts of grounds that can consistently be used to limit the definition of a particular right. First, the government might show that the values protected by the original right are not really at stake in the marginal case, or are at stake only in some attenuated form. Second, it might show that if the right is defined to include the marginal case, then some competing right, in the strong sense I described earlier, would be abridged. Third, it might show that if the right were so defined, then the cost to society would not be simply incremental but would be of a degree far beyond the cost paid to grant the original right, a degree great enough to justify whatever assault on dignity or equality might be involved.

It is fairly easy to apply these grounds to one problem the Supreme Court has recently faced, and must face soon again. The draft law provides an exemption for conscientious objectors, but this exemption, as interpreted by the draft boards, has been limited to those who object to *all* wars on *religious* grounds. If we suppose that the exemption is justified on the ground that an individual has a moral right not to kill in violation of his own principles, then the question is raised whether it is proper to exclude those whose morality is not based on religion, or whose morality is sufficiently complex to distinguish among wars. The Court has held that the draft boards are wrong to exclude the former, and it will soon be asked to decide whether it is wrong to exclude the latter as well.

None of the three grounds I listed can justify either of these exclusions. The invasion of personality in forcing men to kill when they believe killing immoral is just as great when these beliefs are based on secular grounds, or take account of the fact that wars differ in morally relevant ways, and there is no pertinent difference in competing rights or in national emergency. There are differences among the cases, of course, but they are insufficient to justify the distinction. A government that is secular on principle cannot prefer a religious to a nonreligious morality as such. There are utilitarian arguments in favor of limiting the exemption to religious or universal grounds—an exemption so limited may be less expensive to administer, and may allow easier discrimination between sincere and insincere applicants. But these utilitarian reasons are irrelevant, because they cannot count as grounds for limiting a right.

What about the anti-riot law as applied in the Chicago trial? Does that law represent an improper limitation of the right to free speech, supposedly protected by the First Amendment? If we were to apply the first model for government to this issue, the argument for the anti-riot law would look strong. But if we set aside talk of balancing as inappropriate, and turn to the proper grounds for limiting a right, then the argument becomes a great deal weaker. The original right of free speech must suppose that it is an assault on human personality to stop a man from expressing what he honestly believes, particularly on issues affecting how he is governed. Surely the assault is greater, and not less, when he is stopped from expressing those principles of political morality that he holds most passionately, in the fact of what he takes to be outrageous violations of these principles. It may be said that the anti-riot law leaves him free to express these principles in a nonprovocative way. But that misses the point of the connection between expression and dignity. A man cannot express himself freely when he cannot match his rhetoric to his outrage, or when he must trim his sails to protect values he counts as nothing next to those he is trying to vindicate. It is true that some political dissenters speak in ways that shock the majority, but it is arrogant for the majority to suppose that the orthodox methods of expression are the proper ways to speak, for this is a denial of equal concern and respect. If the point of the right is to protect the dignity of dissenters, then we must make judgments about appropriate speech with the personality of the dissenters in mind, not the personality of the "silent" majority for whom the anti-riot law is no restraint at all.

So the argument that the personal values protected by the original right are less at stake in this marginal case fails. We must consider whether competing rights, or some grave threat to society, nevertheless justify the anti-riot law. We can consider these two grounds together, because the only plausible competing rights are rights to be free from violence, and violence is the only plausible threat to society that the context provides.

I have no right to burn your house, or stone you or your car, or swing a bicycle chain against your skull, even if I find these natural means of expression. But the defendants in the Chicago trial were not accused of direct violence; the argument runs that the acts of speech they planned made it likely that others would do acts of violence, either in support of or out of hostility to what they said. Does this provide a justification?

The question would be different if we could say with any confidence how much and what sort of violence the anti-riot law might be expected to prevent. Will it save two lives a year, or two hundred, or two thousand? Two thousand dollars' worth of property, or two hundred thousand, or two million? No one can say, not simply because prediction is next to impossible, but because we have no firm understanding of the process whereby demonstration disintegrates into riot, and in particular of the part played by inflammatory speech, as distinct from poverty, police brutality, blood lust, and all the rest of human and economic failure. The government must try, of course, to reduce the violent waste of lives and property, but it must recognize that any attempt to locate and remove a cause of riot, short of a reorganization of society, must be an exercise in speculation, trial and error. It must make its decisions under conditions of high uncertainty, and the institution of rights, taken seriously limits its freedom to experiment under such conditions.

It forces the government to bear in

mind that preventing a man from speaking or demonstrating offers him a certain and profound insult, in return for a speculative benefit that may in any event be achieved in other if more expensive ways. When lawyers say that rights may be limited to protect other rights, or to prevent catastrophe, they have in mind cases in which cause and effect are relatively clear, like the familiar example of a man falsely crying "Fire" in a crowded theater. But the Chicago story shows how obscure the causal connections can become. Were the speeches of Hoffman or Rubin necessary conditions of the riot? Or had thousands of people come to Chicago for the purpose of rioting anyway, as the government also argues? Were they in any case sufficient conditions? Or could the police have contained the violence if they had not been so busy contributing to it, as the staff of the President's Commission on Violence said they were? These are not easy questions, but if rights mean anything, then the government cannot simply assume answers that justify its conduct. If a man has a right to speak, if the reasons that support that right extend to provocative political speech, and if the effects of such speech on violence are unclear, then the government is not entitled to make its first attack on that problem by denying that right. It may be that abridging the right to speak is the least expensive course, or the least damaging to police morale, or the most popular politically. But these are utilitarian arguments in favor of starting one place rather than another, and such arguments are ruled out by the concept of rights.

This point may be obscured by the popular belief that political activists look forward to violence and "ask for trouble" in what they say. They can hardly complain, in the general view, if they are taken to be the authors of the violence they expect, and treated accordingly. But this repeats the confusion I tried to explain earlier, between having a right and doing the right thing. The speaker's motives may be relevant in deciding whether he does the right thing in speaking passionately about issues that may inflame or enrage his audience. But if he has a right to speak, because the danger in allowing him to speak is speculative, his motives cannot count, as independent evidence, in the argument that justifies stopping him.

But what of the individual rights of those who will be destroyed by a riot, of the passerby who will be killed by a sniper's bullet, or the shopkeeper who will be ruined by looting? Putting the issue this way, in terms of competing rights, suggests a principle that would undercut the effect of uncertainty. Shall we say that some rights to protection are so important that the government is justified in doing all it can to maintain them? Shall we therefore say that the government may abridge the rights of others to act when their acts might simply increase the risk, by however slight or speculative a margin, that some person's rights to life or property will be violated?

Some such principle is relied on by those who oppose the Supreme Court's liberal rulings on police procedure. These rulings increase the chance that a guilty man will go free, and therefore marginally increase the risk that any particular member of the community will be murdered or raped or robbed. Some critics believe that the Court's decisions must therefore be wrong.

But no society that purports to recognize a variety of rights, on the ground that a man's dignity or equality may be invaded in a variety of ways, can accept such a principle. If forcing a man to testify against himself, or forbidding him to speak, does the damage that the rights against self-incrimination and the right of free speech assume, then it would be contemptuous for the state to tell a man that he must suffer this damage against the possibility that other men's risk of loss may be marginally reduced. If rights make sense, then the degrees of their importance cannot be so different that some count not at all when others are mentioned. Of course the government may discriminate and may stop a man from exercising his right to speak when there is a clear and substantial risk that his speech will do great damage to the person or property of others, and no other means of preventing this are at hand, as in the case of a man falsely shouting "Fire" in a theater. But we must reject the suggested principle that the government can ignore rights to speak when life and property are in question. So long as the impact of speech on these other rights remains speculative and marginal, it must look elsewhere for levers to pull.

IV

I said, at the beginning of this essay, that I wanted to show what a government must do that professes to recognize individual rights. It must dispense with the claim that citizens never have a right to break its law, and it must not define citizens' rights so that these are cut off for supposed reasons of the general good. The present government's policy toward civil disobedience, and its companion against vocal protest, its enforcement of the anti-riot law, may therefore be thought to count against its sincerity.

One might well ask, however, whether it is wise to take rights all that seriously after all. America's genius, at least in her own legend, lies in not taking any abstract doctrine to its logical extreme. It may be time to ignore abstractions, and concentrate instead on giving the majority of our citizens a new sense of their government's concern for their welfare, and of their title to rule.

That, in any event, is what the Vice-President seems to believe. In a policy statement on the issue of weirdoes and social misfits, he said that the liberals' concern for individual rights was a headwind blowing in the face of the ship of state. That is a poor metaphor, but the philosophical point it expresses is very well taken. He recognizes, as many liberals do not, that the majority cannot travel as fast or as far as it would like if it recognizes the rights of individuals to do what, in the majority's terms, is the wrong thing to do.

The Vice-President supposes that rights are divisive, and that national unity and a new respect for law may be developed by taking them more skeptically. But he is wrong. Our country will continue to be divided by its social and foreign policy, and if the economy grows weaker the divisions will become more bitter. If we want our laws and our legal institutions to provide the ground rules within which these issues will be contested, then these ground rules must not be the conqueror's law that the dominant class imposes on the weaker, as Marx supposed the law of a capitalist society must be. The bulk of the law—that part which defines and implements social, economic and foreign policy—cannot be neutral. It must state, in its greatest part, the majority's view of the common good. The institution of rights is therefore crucial, because it represents the majority's promise to the minorities that their dignity and equality will be respected. When the divisions among the groups are most violent, then this gesture, if law is to work, must be most sincere.

The institution requires an act of faith on the part of the minorities, because the scope of their rights will be controversial whenever they are important, and because the officers of the majority will act on their own notions of what these rights really are. Of course these officials will disagree with many of the claims that a minority makes. That makes it all the more important that they take their decisions gravely. They must show that they understand what rights are, and they must not cheat on the full implications of the doctrine. The government will not re-establish respect for law without giving the law some claim to respect. It cannot do that if it neglects the one feature that distinguishes law from ordered brutality, and makes that claim plausible. If the government does not take rights seriously, then it does not take law seriously either.

34

JOHN LOCKE
The Right to Property

JOHN LOCKE (1632–1704) was one of the most important British empirical philosophers. His major work was the *Essay Concerning Human Understanding* (1690).

Whether we consider natural reason, which tells us that men, being once born, have a right to their preservation, and consequently to meat and drink and such other things as nature affords for their subsistence; or revelation, which gives us an account of those grants God made of the world to Adam, and to Noah and his sons; it is very clear that God, as King David says (Psalm cxv. 16), "has given the earth to the children of men," given it to mankind in common. But this being supposed, it seems to some a very great difficulty how any one should ever come to have a property in anything. I will not content myself to answer that if it be difficult to make out property upon a supposition that God gave the world to Adam and his posterity in common, it is impossible that any man but one universal monarch should have any property upon a supposition that God gave the world to Adam and his heirs in succession, exclusive of all the rest of his posterity. But I shall endeavor to show how men might come to have a property in several parts of that which God gave to mankind in common, and that without any express compact of all the commoners.

God, who has given the world to men in common, has also given them reason to make use of it to the best advantage of life and convenience. The

From John Locke, *Second Treatise of Government* (1690), chapter 5.

earth and all that is therein is given to men for the support and comfort of their being. And though all the fruits it naturally produces and beasts it feeds belong to mankind in common, as they are produced by the spontaneous hand of nature; and nobody has originally a private dominion exclusive of the rest of mankind in any of them, as they are thus in their natural state; yet, being given for the use of men, there must of necessity be a means to appropriate them some way or other before they can be of any use or at all beneficial to any particular man. The fruit or venison which nourishes the wild Indian, who knows no enclosure and is still a tenant in common, must be his, and so his, that is, a part of him, that another can no longer have any right to it before it can do him any good for the support of his life.

Though the earth and all inferior creatures be common to all men, yet every man has a property in his own person; this nobody has any right to but himself. The labor of his body and the work of his hands, we may say, are properly his. Whatsoever then he removes out of the state that nature has provided and left it in, he has mixed his labor with, and joined to it something that is his own, and thereby makes it his property. It being by him removed from the common state nature has placed it in, it has by this labor something annexed to it that excludes the common right of other men. For this labor being the unquestionable property of the laborer, no man but he can have a right to what that is once joined to, at least where there is enough and as good left in common for others.

He that is nourished by the acorns he picked up under an oak, or the apples he gathered from the trees in the wood, has certainly appropriated them to himself. Nobody can deny but the nourishment is his. I ask, then, When did they begin to be his? When he digested or when he ate or when he boiled or when he brought them home? Or when he picked them up? And it is plain, if the first gathering made them not his, nothing else could. That labor put a distinction between them and common; that added something to them more than nature, the common mother of all, had done; and so they became his private right. And will anyone say he had no right to those acorns or apples he thus appropriated because he had not the consent of all mankind to make them his? Was it a robbery thus to assume to himself what belonged to all in common? If such a consent as that was necessary, man had starved, notwithstanding the plenty God had given him. We see in commons, which remain so by compact, that it is the taking any part of what is common and removing it out of the state nature leaves it in which begins the property, without which the common is of no use. And the taking of this or that part does not depend on the express consent of all the commoners. Thus the grass my horse has bit, the turfs my servant has cut, and the ore I have digged in any place where I have a right to them in common with others, become my property without the assignation or consent of anybody. The labor that was mine, removing them out of that common state they were in, has fixed my property in them.

By making an explicit consent of every commoner necessary to any one's appropriating to himself any part of what is given in common, children or servants could not cut the meat which their father or master had provided for them in common without assigning to every one his peculiar part. Though the water running in the fountain be every one's, yet who can doubt but that in the pitcher is his only who drew it out? His labor has taken it out of the hands of nature where it was common and belonged equally to all her children, and has thereby appropriated it to himself.

Thus this law of reason makes the deer that Indian's who has killed it; it is allowed to be his goods who has bestowed his labor upon it, though before it was the common right of every one. And amongst those who are counted the civilized part of mankind who have made and multiplied positive laws to determine property, this original law of nature, for the beginning of property in what was before common, still takes place; and by virtue thereof what fish any one catches in the ocean, that great and still remaining common of mankind, or what ambergris any one takes up here, is, by the labor that removes it out of that common state nature left it in, made his property who takes that pains about it. And even amongst us, the hare that anyone is hunting is thought his who pursues her during the chase; for, being a beast that is still looked upon as common and no man's private possession, whoever has employed so much labor about any of that kind as to find and pursue her has thereby removed her from the state of nature wherein she was common, and has begun a property.

It will perhaps be objected to this that "if gathering the acorns, or other fruits of the earth, etc., makes a right to them, then any one may engross as much as he will." To which I answer: not so. The same law of nature that does by this means give us property does also bound that property, too. "God has given us all things richly" (I Tim. vi. 17), is the voice of reason confirmed by inspiration. But how far has he given it us? To enjoy. As much as any one can make use of to any advantage of life before it spoils, so much he may by his labor fix a property in; whatever is beyond this is more than his share and belongs to others. Nothing was made by God for man to spoil or destroy. And thus considering the plenty of natural provisions there was a long time in the world, and the few spenders, and to how small a part of that provision the industry of one man could extend itself and engross it to the prejudice of others, especially keeping within the bounds set by reason of what might serve for his use, there could be then little room for quarrels or contentions about property so established.

But the chief matter of property being now not the fruits of the earth and the beasts that subsist on it, but the earth itself, as that which takes in and carries with it all the rest, I think it is plain that property in that, too, is acquired as the former. As much land as a man tills, plants, improves, cultivates, and can use the product of, so much is his property. He by his labor does, as it were, enclose it from the common. Nor will it invalidate his right to say everybody else has an equal title to it, and therefore he cannot appropriate, he cannot enclose, without the consent of all his fellow commoners—all mankind. God, when he gave the world in common to all mankind, commanded man also to labor, and the penury of his condition required it of him. God and his reason commanded him to subdue the earth, that is, improve it for the benefit of life, and therein lay out something upon it that was his own, his labor. He that in obedience to this command of God subdued, tilled, and sowed any part of it, thereby annexed to it something that was his property, which another had no title to, nor could without injury take from him.

Nor was this appropriation of any parcel of land by improving it any prejudice to any other man, since there was still enough and as good left, and more than the yet unprovided could use. So that, in effect, there was never the less left for others because of his enclosure for himself; for he that leaves as much as another can make use of does as good as take nothing at all. Nobody could think himself injured by the drinking of another man, though he took a good draught, who had a whole river of the same water left him to quench his thirst; and the case of land and water, where there is enough for both, is perfectly the same.

God gave the world to men in common; but since he gave it them for their benefit and the greatest conveniences of life they were capable to draw from it, it cannot be supposed he meant it should always remain common and uncultivated. He gave it to the use of the industrious and rational—and labor was to be his title to it—not to the fancy or covetousness of the quarrelsome and contentious. He that had as good left for his improvement as was already taken up needed not complain, ought not to meddle with what was already improved by another's labor; if he did, it is plain he desired the benefit of another's pains which he had no right to, and not the ground which God had given him in common with others to labor on, and whereof there was as good left as that already possessed, and more than he knew what to do with, or his industry could reach to.

It is true, in land that is common in England or any other country where there are plenty of people under government who have money and commerce, no one can enclose or appropriate any part without the consent of all his fellow commoners; because this is left common by compact, that is, by the law of the land, which is not to be violated. And though it be common in respect of some men, it is not so to all mankind, but is the joint property of this country or this parish. Besides, the remainder after such enclosure would not be as good to the rest of the commoners as the whole was when they could all make use of the whole; whereas in the beginning and first peopling of the great common of the world it was quite otherwise. The law man was under was rather for appropriating. God commanded, and his wants forced, him to labor. That was his property which could not be taken from him wherever he had it fixed. And hence subduing or cultivating the earth and having dominion, we see, are joined together. The one gave title to the other. So that God, by commanding to subdue, gave authority so far to appropriate; and the condition of human life which requires labor and material to work on necessarily introduces private possessions.

The measure of property nature was well set by the extent of men's labor and the conveniences of life. No man's labor could subdue or appropriate all, nor could his enjoyment consume more than a small part, so that it was impossible for any man, this way, to entrench upon the right of another, or acquire to himself a property to the prejudice of his neighbor, who would still have room for as good and as large a possession—after the other had taken out his—as before it was appropriated. This measure did confine every man's possession to a very moderate proportion, and such as he might appropriate to himself without injury to anybody, in the first ages of the world, when men were more in danger to be lost by wandering from their company in the then vast wilderness of the earth than to be straitened for want of room to plant in. And the same measure may be allowed still without prejudice to any-body, as full as the world seems; for supposing a man or family in the state they were at first peopling of the world by the children of Adam or Noah, let him plant in some inland, vacant places of America; we shall find that the possessions he could make himself, upon the measures we have given, would not be very large, nor, even to this day, prejudice the rest of mankind, or give them reason to complain or think themselves injured by this man's encroachment, though the race of men have now spread themselves to all the corners of the world and do infinitely exceed the small number which was at the beginning. Nay, the extent of ground is of so little value without labor that I have heard it affirmed that in Spain itself a man may be permitted to plough, sow, and reap, without being disturbed, upon land he has no other title to but only his making use of it. But, on the contrary, the inhabitants think them-selves beholden to him who by his industry on neglected and consequently waste land has increased the stock of corn which they wanted. But be this as it will, which I lay no stress on, this I dare boldly affirm—that the same rule of property, viz., that every man should have as much as he could make use of, would hold still in the world without straitening anybody, since there is land enough in the world to suffice double the inhabitants, had not the invention of money and the tacit agreement of men to put a value on it introduced—by consent—larger possessions and a right to them; which, how it has done, I shall by-and-by show more at large.

This is certain, that in the begin-ning, before the desire of having more than man needed had altered the in-trinsic value of things which depends only on their usefulness to the life of man, or had agreed that a little piece of yellow metal which would keep with-out wasting or decay should be worth a great piece of flesh or a whole heap of corn, though men had a right to appro-priate, by their labor, each one to him-self as much of the things of nature as he could use, yet this could not be much, nor to the prejudice of others, where the same plenty was still left to those who would use the same industry. To which let me add that he who appropriates land to himself by his labor does not lessen but increase the common stock of mankind; for the provisions serving to the support of human life produced by one acre of enclosed and cultivated land are—to speak much within com-pass—ten times more than those which are yielded by an acre of land of an equal richness lying waste in common. And therefore he that encloses land, and has a greater plenty of the conveniences of life from ten acres than he could have from a hundred left to nature, may truly be said to give ninety acres to mankind; for his labor now supplies him with provisions out of ten acres which were by the product of a hun-dred lying in common. I have here rated the improved land very low in mak-ing its product but as ten to one, when it is much nearer a hundred to one; for I ask whether in the wild woods and un-cultivated waste of America, left to na-ture, without any improvement, tillage, or husbandry, a thousand acres yield the needy and wretched inhabitants as many conveniences of life as ten acres of equally fertile land do in Devonshire, where they are well cultivated.

Before the appropriation of land, he who gathered as much of the wild fruit, killed, caught, or tamed as many of the beasts as he could; he that so employed his pains about any of the spontaneous products of nature as any way to alter them from the state which nature put them in, by placing any of his labor on them, did thereby acquire a propriety in them; but, if they perished in his possession without their due use, if the fruits rotted or the venison putrified before he could spend it, he offended against the common law of nature and was liable to be punished; he invaded his neighbor's share, for he had no right further than his use called for any of them and they might serve to afford him conveniences of life.

The same measures governed the possession of land, too: whatsoever he tilled and reaped, laid up and made use of before it spoiled, that was his peculiar right; whatsoever he enclosed and could feed and make use of, the cattle and product was also his. But if either the grass of his enclosure rotted on the ground, or the fruit of his planting perished without gathering and laying up, this part of the earth, notwithstanding his enclosure, was still to be looked on as waste and might be the possession of any other. Thus, at the beginning, Cain might take as much ground as he could till and make it his own land, and yet leave enough to Abel's sheep to feed on; a few acres would serve for both their possessions. But as families increased and industry enlarged their stocks, their possessions enlarged with the need of them; but yet it was commonly without any fixed property in the ground they made use of till they incorporated, settled themselves together, and built cities; and then, by consent, they came in time to set out the bounds of their distinct territories, and agree on limits between them and their neighbors, and by laws within themselves settled the properties of those of the same society; for we see that in that part of the world which was first inhabited, and therefore like to be best peopled, even as low down as Abraham's time they wandered with their flocks and their herds, which was their substance, freely up and down; and this Abraham did in a country where he was a stranger. Whence it is plain that at least a great part of the land lay in common, that the inhabitants valued it not, nor claimed property in any more than they made use of. But when there was not room enough in the same place for their herds to feed together, they, by consent, as Abraham and Lot did (Gen. xiii. 5), separated and enlarged their pasture where it best liked them. And for the same reason Esau went from his father and his brother and planted in Mount Seir (Gen. xxxvi. 6).

And thus, without supposing any private dominion and property in Adam over all the world exclusive of all other men, which can in no way be proven, nor any one's property be made out from it; but supposing the world given, as it was, to the children of men in common, we see how labor could make men distinct titles to several parcels of it for their private uses, wherein there could be no doubt of right, no room for quarrel.

Nor is it so strange, as perhaps before consideration it may appear, that the property of labor should be able to overbalance the community of land; for it is labor indeed that put the difference of value on everything; and let anyone consider what the difference is between an acre of land planted with tobacco or sugar, sown with wheat or barley, and an acre of the same land lying in common without any husbandry upon it, and he will find that the improvement of labor makes the far greater part of the value. I think it will be but a very modest computation to say that, of the products of the earth useful to the life of man, nine-tenths are the effects of labor; nay, if we will rightly estimate things as they come to our use and cast up the several expenses about them, what in them is purely owing to nature, and what to labor, we shall find that in most of them ninety-nine hundredths are wholly to be put on the account of labor.

There cannot be a clearer demonstration of anything than several nations of the Americans are of this, who are rich in land and poor in all the comforts of life; whom nature having furnished as liberally as any other people with the materials of plenty, that is, a fruitful soil, apt to produce in abundance what might serve for food, raiment, and delight, yet for want of improving it by labor have not one-hundredth part of the conveniences we enjoy. And a king of a large and fruitful territory there feeds, lodges, and is clad worse than a day-laborer in England.

To make this a little clear, let us but trace some of the ordinary provisions of life through their several progresses before they come to our use and see how much of their value they receive from human industry. Bread, wine, and cloth are things of daily use and great plenty; yet, notwithstanding, acorns, water, and leaves, or skins must be our bread, drink, and clothing, did not labor furnish us with these more useful commodities; for whatever bread is more worth than acorns, wine than water, and cloth or silk than leaves, skins, or moss, that is wholly owing to labor and industry: the one of these being the food and raiment which unassisted nature furnishes us with; the other, provisions which our industry and pains prepare for us, which how much they exceed the other in value when anyone has computed, he will then see how much labor makes the far greatest part of the value of things we enjoy in this world. And the ground which produces the materials is scarce to be reckoned in as any, or at most but a very small, part of it; so little that even amongst us land that is left wholly to nature, that has no improvement of pasturage, tillage, or planting, is called, as indeed it is, 'waste'; and we shall find the benefit of it amount to little more than nothing.

This shows how much numbers of men are to be preferred to largeness of dominions; and that the increase of lands and the right employing of them is the great art of government; and that prince who shall be so wise and godlike as by established laws of liberty to secure protection and encouragement to the honest industry of mankind, against the oppression of power and narrowness of party, will quickly be too hard for his neighbors; but this by the bye.

To return to the argument in hand.

An acre of land that bears here twenty bushels of wheat, and another in America which with the same husbandry would do the like, are, without doubt, of the same natural intrinsic value; but yet the benefit mankind receives from the one in a year is worth £5, and from the other possibly not worth a penny if all the profit an Indian received from it were to be valued and sold here; at least, I may truly say, not one-thousandth. It is labor, then, which puts the greatest part of the value upon land, without which it would scarcely be worth anything; it is to that we owe the greatest part of all its useful products; for all that the straw, bran, bread of that acre of wheat is more worth than the product of an acre of as good land which lies waste is all the effect of labor. For it is not barely the ploughman's pains, the reaper's and thresher's toil, and the baker's sweat [that] is to be counted into the bread we eat; the labor of those who broke the oxen, who digged and wrought the iron and stones, who felled and framed the timber employed about the plough, mill, oven, or any other utensils, which are a vast number requisite to this corn, from its being seed to be sown to its being made bread, must all be charged on the account of labor, and received as an effect of that; nature and the earth furnished only the almost worthless materials as in themselves. It would be a strange "catalogue of things that industry provided and made use of, about every loaf of bread" before it came to our use, if we could trace them; iron, wood, leather, bark, timber, stone, bricks, coals, lime, cloth, dyeing drugs, pitch, tar, masts, ropes, and all the materials made use of in the ship that brought any of the commodities used by any of the workmen to any part of the work; all which it would be almost impossible, at least too long, to reckon up.

From all which it is evident that, though the things of nature are given in common, yet man, by being master of himself and proprietor of his own person and the actions or labor of it, had still in himself the great foundation of property; and that which made up the greater part of what he applied to the support or comfort of his being, when invention and arts had improved the conveniences of life, was perfectly his own and did not belong in common to others.

Thus labor, in the beginning, gave a right of property wherever anyone was pleased to employ it upon what was common, which remained a long while the far greater part and is yet more than mankind makes use of. Men, at first, for the most part contented themselves with what unassisted nature offered to their necessities; and though afterwards, in some parts of the world—where the increase of people and stock, with the use of money, had made land

scarce and so of some value—the several communities settled the bounds of their distinct territories and, by laws within themselves, regulated the properties of the private men of their society, and so, by compact and agreement, settled the property which labor and industry began. And the leagues that have been made between several states and kingdoms either expressly or tacitly disowning all claim and right to the land in the others' possession have, by common consent, given up their pretenses to their natural common right which originally they had to those countries, and so have, by positive agreement, settled a property amongst themselves in distinct parts and parcels of the earth; yet there are still great tracts of ground to be found which—the inhabitants thereof not having joined with the rest of mankind in the consent of the use of their common money—lie waste, and are more than the people who dwell on it do or can make use of, and so still lie in common; though this can scarce happen amongst that part of mankind that have consented to the use of money.

The greatest part of things really useful to the life of man, and such as the necessity of subsisting made the first commoners of the world look after, as it does the Americans now, are generally things of short duration, such as, if they are not consumed by use, will decay and perish of themselves; gold, silver, and diamonds are things that fancy or agreement has put the value on, more than real use and the necessary support of life. Now of those good things which nature has provided in common, every one had a right, as has been said, to as much as he could use, and property in all that he could effect with his labor; all that his industry could extend to, to alter from the state nature had put it in, was his. He that gathered a hundred bushels of acorns or apples had thereby a property in them; they were his goods as soon as gathered. He was only to look that he used them before they spoiled, else he took more than his share and robbed others. And indeed it was a foolish thing, as well as dishonest, to hoard up more than he could make use of. If he gave away a part to anybody else so that it perished not uselessly in his possession, these he also made use of. And if he also bartered away plums that would have rotted in a week for nuts that would last good for his eating a whole year, he did no injury; he wasted not the common stock, destroyed no part of the portion of the goods that belonged to others, so long as nothing perished uselessly in his hands. Again, if he would give his nuts for a piece of metal, pleased with its color, or exchange his sheep for shells, or wool for a sparkling pebble or a diamond, and keep those by him all his life, he invaded not the right of others; he might heap as much of these durable things as he pleased; the exceeding of the bounds of his just property not lying in the largeness of his possession, but the perishing of anything uselessly in it.

And thus came in the use of money—some lasting thing that men might keep without spoiling, and that by mutual consent men would take in exchange for the truly useful but perishable supports of life.

And as different degrees of industry were apt to give men possessions in different proportions, so this invention of money gave them the opportunity to continue and enlarge them; for supposing an island, separate from all possible commerce with the rest of the world, wherein there were but a hundred families, but there were sheep, horses, and cows, with other useful animals, wholesome fruits, and land

enough for corn for a hundred thousand times as many, but nothing in the island, either because of its commonness or perishableness, fit to supply the place of money; what reason could anyone have there to enlarge his possessions beyond the use of his family and a plentiful supply to its consumption, either in what their own industry produced or they could barter for like perishable, useful commodities with others? Where there is not something both lasting and scarce, and so valuable to be hoarded up, there men will not be apt to enlarge their possessions of land were it ever so rich, ever so free for them to take. For, I ask, what would a man value ten thousand or a hundred thousand acres of excellent land, ready cultivated and well stocked, too, with cattle, in the middle of the inland parts of America where he had no hopes of commerce with other parts of the world to draw money to him by the sale of the product? It would not be worth the enclosing, and we should see him give up again to the wild common of nature whatever was more than would supply the conveniences of life to be had there for him and his family.

Thus in the beginning all the world was America, and more so than that is now; for no such thing as money was anywhere known. Find out something that has the use and value of money amongst his neighbors, you shall see the same man will begin presently to enlarge his possessions.

But since gold and silver, being little useful to the life of man in proportion to food, raiment, and carriage, has its value only from the consent of men, whereof labor yet makes, in great part, the measure, it is plain that men have agreed to a disproportionate and unequal possession of the earth, they having, by a tacit and voluntary consent, found out a way how a man may fairly possess more land than he himself can use the product of, by receiving in exchange for the overplus gold and silver which may be hoarded up without injury to any one, these metals not spoiling or decaying in the hands of the possessor. This partage of things in an inequality of private possessions men have made practicable out of the bounds of society and without compact, only by putting a value on gold and silver, and tacitly agreeing in the use of money; for, in governments, the laws regulate the right of property, and the possession of land is determined by positive constitutions.

And thus, I think, it is very easy to conceive how labor could at first begin a title of property in the common things of nature, and how the spending it upon our uses bounded it. So that there could then be no reason of quarreling about title, nor any doubt about the largeness of possession it gave. Right and convenience went together; for as a man had a right to all he could employ his labor upon, so he had no temptation to labor for more than he could make use of. This left no room for controversy about the title, nor for encroachment on the right of others; what portion a man carved to himself was easily seen, and it was useless, as well as dishonest, to carve himself too much or take more than he needed.

35

HYMAN GROSS
The Right to Privacy

HYMAN GROSS is a New York attorney and former law professor at New York University who has written on a variety of legal issues.

Why is privacy desirable? When is its loss objectionable and when is it not? How much privacy is a person entitled to? These questions challenge at the threshold our concern about protection of privacy. Usually they are pursued by seeking agreement on the boundary between morbid and healthy reticence, and by attempting to determine when unwanted intrusion or notoriety is

From Hyman Gross, "Privacy and Autonomy," *Privacy:* Nomos XIII, J. Roland Pennock and John W. Chapman, eds. Reprinted by permission of the Publishers, Lieber-Atherton, Inc. Copyright © 1971 by Atherton Press, Inc. All rights reserved. This article is reprinted unabridged.

justified by something more important than privacy. Seldom is privacy considered as the condition under which there is *control* over acquaintance with one's personal affairs by the one enjoying it, and I wish here to show how consideration of privacy in this neglected aspect is helpful in answering the basic questions. First I shall attempt to make clear this part of the idea of privacy, next suggest why privacy in this aspect merits protection, then argue that some important dilemmas are less vexing when we do get clear about these things, and finally offer a cautionary remark regarding the relation of privacy and autonomy.

I

What in general is it that makes certain conduct offensive to privacy? To distinguish obnoxious from innocent interference with privacy we must first see clearly what constitutes loss of privacy at all, and then determine why loss of privacy when it does occur is sometimes objectionable and sometimes not.

Loss of privacy occurs when the limits one has set on acquaintance with his personal affairs are not respected. Almost always we mean not respected by *others*, though in unusual cases we might speak of a person not respecting his own privacy—he is such a passionate gossip, say, that he gossips even about himself and later regrets it. Limits on acquaintance may be maintained by the physical insulation of a home, office, or other private place within which things that are to be private may be confined. Or such bounds may exist by virtue of exclusionary social conventions, for example, those governing a private conversation in a public place; or through restricting conventions which impose an obligation to observe such limits, as when disclosure is made in confidence. Limits operate in two ways. There are restrictions on what is known, and restrictions on who may know it. Thus, a curriculum vitae furnished to or for a prospective employer is not normally an invitation to undertake a detective investigation using the items provided as clues. Nor is there normally license to communicate to others the information submitted. In both instances there would be disregard of limitations implied by considerations of privacy, unless the existence of such limitations is unreasonable under the circumstances (the prospective employer

is the CIA, or the information is furnished to an employment agency). But there is no loss of privacy when such limits as do exist are respected, no matter how ample the disclosure or how extensive its circulation. If I submit a detailed account of my life while my friend presents only the barest réumé of his, I am not giving up more of privacy than he. And if I give the information to a hundred employers, I lose no more in privacy than my friend who confides to only ten, provided those informed by each of us are equally restricted. More people know more about me, so my *risk* of losing privacy is greater and the threatened loss more serious. Because I am a less private person than my friend, I am more willing to run that risk. But until there is loss of control over what is known, and by whom, my privacy is uncompromised—though much indeed may be lost in secrecy, mystery, obscurity, and anonymity.

Privacy is lost in either of two ways. It may be given up, or it may be taken away. Abandonment of privacy (though sometimes undesired) is an inoffensive loss, while deprivation by others is an offensive loss.

If one makes a public disclosure of personal matters or exposes himself under circumstances that do not contain elements of restriction on further communication, there is loss of control for which the person whose privacy is lost is himself responsible. Such abandonment may result from indifference, carelessness, or a positive desire to have others become acquainted. There are, however, instances in which privacy is abandoned though this was not intended. Consider indiscretions committed while drunk which are rued when sober. If the audience is not under some obligation (perhaps the duty of a confidant) to keep dark what was revealed, there has been a loss of privacy for which the one who suffers it is responsible. But to constitute an abandonment, the loss of privacy must result from voluntary conduct by the one losing it, and the loss must be an expectable result of such conduct. If these two conditions are not met, the person who suffers the loss cannot be said to be responsible for it. Accordingly, a forced revelation, such as an involuntary confession, is not an abandonment of privacy, because the person making it has not given up control but has had it taken from him.

Regarding the requirement of expectability, we may see its significance by contrasting the case of a person whose conversation is overheard in Grand Central Station with the plight of someone made the victim of eavesdropping in his living room. In a public place loss of control is expectable by virtue of the circumstances of communication: Part of what we mean when we say a place is public is that there is not present the physical limitation upon which such control depends. But a place may be called private only when there is such limitation, so communication in it is expectably limited and the eavesdropping an offensive violation for which the victim is not himself responsible. And consider the intermediate case of eavesdropping on a conversation in a public place—a distant parabolic microphone focused on a street-corner conversation, or a bugging device planted in an airplane seat. The offensive character of such practices derives again from their disregard of expectable limitations, in this instance the force of an exclusionary social convention which applies to all except those whose immediate presence enables them to overhear.

So far there has been consideration of what constitutes loss of privacy, and

when it is objectionable. But to assess claims for protection of privacy we must be clear also about *why* in general loss of privacy is objectionable. This becomes especially important when privacy and other things we value are in competition, one needing to be sacrificed to promote the other. It becomes important then to understand what good reasons there are for valuing privacy, and this is our next item of business.

II

There are two sorts of things we keep private, and with respect to each privacy is desirable for somewhat different reasons. Concern for privacy is sometimes concern about what of us can become known, and to whom. This includes acquaintance with all those things which make up the person as he may become known—identity, appearance, traits of personality and character, talents, weaknesses, tastes, desires, habits, interests—in short, things which tell us who a person is and what he's like. The other kind of private matter is about our lives—what we've done, intend to do, are doing now, how we feel, what we have, what we need— and concern about privacy here is to restrict acquaintance with these matters. Together these two classes of personal matters comprise all those things which can be private. Certain items of information do indeed have aspects which fit them for either category. For example, a person's belief is something which pertains to him when viewed as characteristic of him, but pertains to the events of his life when viewed as something he has acquired, acts on, and endeavors to have others adopt.

Why is privacy of the person important? This calls mainly for consideration of what is necessary to maintain an integrated personality in a social setting. Although we are largely unaware of what influences us at the time, we are constantly concerned to control how we appear to others, and act to implement this concern in ways extremely subtle and multifarious. Models of image and behavior are noticed, imitated, adopted, so that nuances in speech, gesture, facial expression, *politesse,* and much more become a person as known on an occasion. The deep motive is to influence the reactions of others, and this is at the heart of human social accommodation. Constraints to imitation and disguise can become a pathological problem of serious proportions when concern with appearances interferes with normal functioning, but normal behavior allows, indeed requires, that we perform critically in presenting and withholding in order to effect certain appearances. If these editorial efforts are not to be wasted, we must have a large measure of control over what of us is seen and heard, when, where, and by whom. For this reason we see as offensive the candid camera which records casual behavior with the intention of later showing it as entertainment to a general audience. The victim is not at the time aware of who will see him and so does not have the opportunity to exercise appropriate critical restraint in what he says and does. Although subsequent approval for the showing eliminates grounds for objection to the publication as an offense to privacy, there remains the lingering objection to the prior disregard of limits of acquaintance which are normal to the situation and so presumably relied on by the victim at the time. The nature of the offense is further illuminated by considering its aggravation when the victim has been deliberately introduced unawares into the situation for the purpose of filming his behavior, or its still greater offensiveness if the setting is a place normally providing privacy and

assumed to be private by the victim. What we have here are increasingly serious usurpations of a person's prerogative to determine how he shall appear, to whom, and on what occasion.

The same general objection applies regarding loss of privacy where there is information about our personal affairs which is obtained, accumulated, and transmitted by means beyond our control. It is, however, unlike privacy of personality in its untoward consequences. A data bank of personal information is considered objectionable, but not because it creates appearances over which we have no control. We are willing to concede that acquaintance with our reputation is in general not something we are privileged to control, and that we are not privileged to decide just what our reputation shall be. If the reputation is correct we cannot object because we do not appear as we would wish. What then are the grounds of objection to a data bank, an objection which indeed persists even if its information is correct and the inferences based on the information are sound? A good reason for objecting is that a data bank is an offense to self-determination. We are subject to being acted on by others because of conclusions about us which we do not know and whose effect we have no opportunity to counteract. There is a loss of control over reputation which is unacceptable because we no longer have the ability to try to change what is believed about us. We feel entitled to know what others believe, and why, so that we may try to change misleading impressions and on occasion show why a decision about us ought not to be based on reputation even if the reputation is justified. If our account in the data bank were made known to us and opportunity given to change its effect, we should drop most (though not all) of our objection to it. We might still fear the danger of abuse by public forces concerned more with the demands of administrative convenience than justice, but because we could make deposits and demand a statement reflecting them we would at least no longer be in the position of having what is known and surmised about us lie beyond our control.

Two aspects of privacy have been considered separately, though situations in which privacy is violated sometimes involve both. Ordinary surveillance by shadowing, peeping, and bugging commonly consists of observation of personal behavior as well as accumulation of information. Each is objectionable for its own reasons, though in acting against the offensive practice we protect privacy in both aspects. Furthermore, privacy of personality and of personal affairs have some common ground in meriting protection, and this has to do with a person's role as a responsible moral agent.

In general we do not criticize a person for untoward occurrences which are a result of his conduct if (through no fault of his own) he lacked the ability to do otherwise. Such a person is similarly ineligible for applause for admirable things which would not have taken place but for his conduct. In both instances we claim that he is not responsible for what happened, and so should not be blamed or praised. The principle holds true regarding loss of privacy. If a person cannot control how he is made to appear (nor could he have prevented his loss of control), he is not responsible for how he appears or is thought of, and therefore cannot be criticized as displeasing or disreputable (nor extolled as the opposite). He can, of course, be condemned for conduct which is the basis of the belief about

him, but that is a different matter from criticism directed solely to the fact that such a belief exists. Personal gossip (even when believed) is not treated by others as something for which the subject need answer, because its existence defies his control. Responsible appraisal of anyone whose image or reputation is a matter of concern requires that certain private items illicitly in the public domain be ignored in the assessment. A political figure may, with impunity, be known as someone who smokes, drinks, flirts, and tells dirty jokes, so long (but only so long) as this is not the public image *he* presents. The contrasting fortunes of two recent political leaders remind us that not being responsible for what is believed by others can be most important. If such a man is thought in his private life to engage in discreet though illicit liaisons he is not held accountable for rumors without more. However, once he has allowed himself to be publicly exposed in a situation which is in the slightest compromising, he must answer for mere appearances. And on this same point, we might consider why a woman is never held responsible for the way she appears in the privacy of her toilette.

To appreciate the importance of this sort of disclaimer of responsibility we need only imagine a community in which it is not recognized. Each person would be accountable for himself however he might be known, and regardless of any precautionary seclusion which was undertaken in the interest of shame, good taste, or from other motives of self-regard. In such a world modesty is sacrificed to the embarrassment of unwanted acclaim, and self-criticism is replaced by the condemnation of others. It is part of the vision of Orwell's *1984*, in which observation is so thorough that it forecloses the possibility of a private sector of life under a person's exclusionary control, and so makes him answerable for everything observed without limits of time or place. Because of this we feel such a condition of life far more objectionable than a community which makes the same oppressive social demands of loyalty and conformity but with the opportunity to be free of concern about appearances in private. In a community without privacy, furthermore, there can be no editorial privilege exercised in making oneself known to others. Consider, for example, the plight in which Montaigne would find himself. He observed that "No quality embraces us purely and universally. If it did not seem crazy to talk to oneself, there is not a day when I would not be heard growling at myself: 'Confounded fool!' And yet I do not intend that to be my definition." Respect for privacy is required to safeguard our changes of mood and mind, and to promote growth of the person through self-discovery and criticism. We want to run the risk of making fools of ourselves and be free to call ourselves fools, yet not be fools in the settled opinion of the world, convicted out of our own mouths.

III

Privacy is desirable, but rights to enjoy it are not absolute. In deciding what compromises must be made some deep quandaries recur, and three of them at least seem more manageable in light of what has been said so far.

In the first place, insistence on privacy is often taken as implied admission that there is cause for shame. The assumption is that the only reason for keeping something from others is that one is ashamed of it (although it is conceded that sometimes there is in fact no cause for shame even though the per-

son seeking privacy thinks there is). Those who seek information and wish to disregard interests in privacy often play on this notion by claiming that the decent and the innocent have no cause for shame and so no need for privacy; "Only those who have done or wish to do something shameful demand privacy." But it is unsound to assume that a claim for privacy implies such an admission. Pride, or at least wholesome self-regard, is the motive in many situations. The famous Warren and Brandeis article on privacy which appeared in the *Harvard Law Review* in 1890 was impelled in some measure, we are told, by Samuel Warren's chagrin. His daughter's wedding, a very social Boston affair, had been made available to the curious at every newsstand by the local press. Surely he was not ashamed of the wedding even though outraged by the publicity. Or consider Miss Roberson, the lovely lady whose picture was placed on a poster advertising the product of Franklin Mills with the eulogistic slogan "Flour of the family," thereby precipitating a lawsuit whose consequences included the first statutory protection of privacy in the United States. What was exploited was the lady's face, undoubtedly a source of pride.

Both these encroachments on privacy illustrate the same point. Things which people like about themselves are taken by them to belong to them in a particularly exclusive way, and so control over disclosure or publication is especially important to them. The things about himself which a person is most proud of he values most, and thus are things over which he is most interested to exercise control. It is true that shame is not infrequently the motive for privacy, for often we do seek to maintain conditions necessary to avoid criticism and punishment. But since it is not the only motive, the quest for privacy does not entail tacit confessions. Confusion arises here in part because an assault on privacy always does involve humiliation of the victim. But this is because he has been deprived of control over something personal which is given over to the control of others. In short, unwilling loss of privacy always results in the victim being shamed, not because of what others learn, but because they and not he may then determine who else shall know it and what use shall be made of it.

Defining the privilege to make public what is otherwise private is another source of persistent difficulty. There is a basic social interest in making available information about people, in exploring the personal aspects of human affairs, in stimulating and satisying curiosity about others. The countervailing interest is in allowing people who have not offered themselves for public scrutiny to remain out of sight and out of mind. In much of the United States the law has strained with the problem of drawing a line of protection which accords respect to both interests. The result, broadly stated, has been recognition of a privilege to compromise privacy for news and other material whose primary purpose is to impart information, but to deny such privileged status to literary and other art, to entertainment, and generally to any approppriation for commercial purposes. Development of the law in New York after Miss Roberson's unsuccessful attempt to restrain public display of her picture serves as a good example. A statute was enacted prohibiting unauthorized use of the name, portrait, or picture of any living person for purposes of trade or advertising, and the legislation has been interpreted by the courts along the general lines indicated. But it is still open to speculation why a

writer's portrayal of a real person as a character in a novel could qualify as violative, while the same account in a biographical or historical work would not. It has not been held that history represents a more important social interest than art and so is more deserving of a privileged position in making known personal matters, or, more generally, that edification is more important than entertainment. Nor is the question ever raised, as one might expect, whether an item of news is sufficiently newsworthy to enjoy a privilege in derogation of privacy. Further, it was not held that the implied statutory criterion of intended economic benefit from the use of a personality would warrant the fundamental distinctions. Indeed, the test of economic benefit would qualify both television's public affairs programs and its dramatic shows as within the statute, and the reportage of *Life* magazine would be as restricted as the films of De Mille or De Sica. But in each instance the former is in general free of the legal prohibition while the latter is not. What, then, is the basis of distinction? Though not articulated, a sound criterion does exist.

Unauthorized *use* of another person—whether for entertainment, artistic creation, or economic gain—is offensive. So long as we remain in charge of how we are used, we have no cause for complaint. In those cases in which a legal wrong is recognized, there has been use by others in disregard of this authority, but in those cases in which a privilege is found, there is not *use* of personality or personal affairs at all, at least not use in the sense of one person assuming control over another, which is the gist of the offense to autonomy. We do indeed suffer a loss of autonomy whenever the power to place us in free circulation is exercised by others, but we consider such loss offensive only when another person assumes the control of which we are deprived, when we are used and not merely exposed. Failure to make clear this criterion of offensiveness has misled those who wish to define the protectable area and they conceive the problem as one of striking an optimal balance between two valuable interests, when in fact it is a matter of deciding whether the acts complained of are offensive under a quite definite standard of offensiveness. The difficult cases here have not presented a dilemma of selecting the happy medium, but rather the slippery job of determining whether the defendant had used the plaintiff or whether he had merely caused things about him to become known, albeit to the defendant's profit. The difference is between managing another person as a means to one's own ends, which is offensive, and acting merely as a vehicle of presentation (though not gratuitously) to satisfy established social needs, which is not offensive. Cases dealing with an unauthorized biography that was heavily anecdotal and of questionable accuracy, or with an entertaining article that told the true story of a former child prodigy who became an obscure eccentric, are perplexing ones because they present elements of both offensive and inoffensive publication, and a decision turns on which is predominant.

There remains another balance-striking quandary to be dismantled. It is often said that privacy as an interest must be balanced against security. Each, we think, must sacrifice something of privacy to promote the security of all, though we are willing to risk some insecurity to preserve a measure of privacy. Pressure to reduce restrictions on wiretapping and searches by police seeks to push the balance toward greater security. But the picture we are given is

seriously misleading. In the first place we must notice the doubtful assumption on which the argument rests. It may be stated this way: The greater the ability to watch what is going on, or obtain evidence of what has gone on, the greater the ability to prevent crime. It is a notion congenial to those who believe that more efficient law enforcement contributes significantly to a reduction in crime. We must, however, determine if such a proposition is in fact sound, and we must see what crimes are suppressible, even in principle, before any sacrifice of privacy can be justified. There is, at least *in limine*, much to be said for the conflicting proposition that once a generally efficient system of law enforcement exists an increase in its efficiency does not result in a corresponding reduction in crime, but only in an increase in punishments. Apart from that point, there is an objection relating more directly to what has been said here about privacy. Security and privacy are both desirable, but measures to promote each are on different moral footing. Men ought to be secure, we say, because only in that condition can they live a good life. Privacy, however, like peace and prosperity, is itself part of what we mean by a good life, a part having to do with self-respect and self-determination. Therefore, the appropriate attitudes when we are asked to sacrifice privacy for security are first a critical one which urges alternatives that minimize or do not at all require the sacrifice, and ultimately regret for loss of a cherished resource if the sacrifice proves necessary.

IV

In speaking of privacy and autonomy there is some danger that privacy may be conceived as autonomy. Such confusion has been signaled in legal literature by early and repeated use of the phrase "right to be let alone" as a synonym for "right of privacy." The United States Supreme Court succumbed completely in 1965 in its opinion in *Griswold v. Connecticut*, and the ensuing intellecual disorder warrants comment.

In that case legislative prohibition of the use of contraceptives was said to be a violation of a constitutional right of privacy, at least when it affected married people. The court's opinion relied heavily on an elaborate *jeu de mots*, in which different senses of the word "privacy" were punned upon, and the legal concept generally mismanaged in ways too various to recount here. In the *Griswold* situation there had been an attempt by government to regulate personal affairs, not get acquainted with them, and so there was an issue regarding autonomy and not privacy. The opinion was not illuminating on the question of what are proper bounds for the exercise of legislative power,

which was the crucial matter before the court. It is precisely the issue of what rights to autonomous determination of his affairs are enjoyed by a citizen. The *Griswold* opinion not only failed to take up that question in a forthright manner, but promoted confusion about privacy in the law by unsettling the intellectual focus on it which had been developed in torts and constitutional law. If the confusion in the court's argument was inadvertent, one may sympathize with the deep conceptual difficulties which produced it, and if it was deliberately contrived, admire its ingenuity. Whatever its origin, its effect is to muddle the separate issues, which must be analyzed and argued along radically different lines when protection is sought either for privacy or for autonomy. Hopefully, further developments will make clear that while an offense to privacy is an offense to autonomy, not every curtailment of autonomy is a compromise of privacy.

36

JOEL FEINBERG
Is There a Right to Be Born?

If a person is told that voluntary sterilization is wicked and therefore forbidden, he or she might cogently reply that what a person does with his own body is his own business, or a matter entirely between him and his physician, so that no one else has a right to interfere. Similarly, if a couple is told that the use of "mechanical" contraceptives is wicked

Published here for the first time.

and not to be permitted, they might reply with equal cogency that the decision whether or not to use contraceptives ought to be theirs alone, since no other parties have their interests directly involved. More exactly, the decision should ultimately be the woman's alone, since her will should reign sovereign on the question of what is to be done in or to her body.

Appeal to the right to determine the

use of one's own body is also commonly made these days in support of the mother's right to abortion. But here the issue is much more complicated. Deciding whether or not to have a fetus removed from the womb does not at first sight seem quite the same sort of thing as deciding whether or not to have one's nose straightened, or one's gall bladder removed. Nor is a fetus a *part* of a woman's body in the same sense as that in which her vermiform appendix is a part of her body. Opponents of legalized abortion point out that a fetus is not a constituent organ of the mother but an independent entity temporarily growing inside the mother, and to the question whose interests other than the mother's are involved in the decision whether to abort, these parties answer triumphantly that the fetus too has an interest in what is done to it. In fact, the fetus is said itself to have rights that command respect, one of which is the right to be born, violation of which is said to be as clearly murder as the deliberate killing of an innocent human being outside of the womb.

Now, from the fact that a fetus is not a "part," or a constitutive organ, of its mother's body it does not yet follow that it is a being possessed of claims against others to be treated in certain ways. Surely this minimal and negative characterization of the fetus (as a "nonorgan") leaves the question of its status as a right-holder entirely open. And yet this is the crucial question in the controversy over the legalization of abortion. If the fetus does have a right to be born, then we owe it *to it* not to prevent its birth; and a legal duty of noninterference might be imposed upon us *for the fetus's sake.* On the other hand, if the fetus has no right to be born, we owe no more to it than we do to a gall bladder or a wart or a contraceptive coil,

and the mother's bodily sovereignty applies as much to this internal nonorgan as it does to her own genuine bodily parts.

I

Gall bladders and contraceptive coils, of course, are not the kinds of beings of which it even makes sense to say that they could have rights of their own. To ascribe rights to such things as bodily organs, rocks, stones, artifacts, machines, natural processes, and other "mere things" is to commit a kind of "category mistake" analogous to talk of home runs learning to tap dance or virtues having weight. It is absurd to say that *rocks* can have rights, for example, not because rocks are morally inferior things unworthy of rights (that statement makes no sense either), but because rocks belong to a category of entities of whom rights cannot meaningfully be predicated. That is not to say that there are no circumstances in which we ought to treat rocks carefully, but only that the rocks themselves cannot claim good treatment from us. Our first question about fetuses, then, should not be the normative one, "Do they have rights?," but rather the conceptual one, "Are they even the kinds of beings that *can* have rights?" Fetuses appear to fall somewhere between the clear cases of normal human beings, whose categorical suitability for right-ownership would be admitted even by extreme misanthropes who deny that anyone in fact has rights, and mere rocks, at the other extreme, to which the attribution of rights is conceptually impossible. Fetuses, then, are among a variety of bewildering borderline cases for the application of rights, which raise separate riddles of precisely the same form: Is it meaningful or conceptually possible to ascribe rights to individual animals? to whole species of animals? to plants? to idiots and madmen? to our dead ancestors? to generations yet unborn? Until we know how to settle these puzzling cases, we cannot claim fully to grasp the concept of a right or to know the shape of its logical boundaries.

In another paper[1] I have tried to answer all of these questions with one stroke by formulating a criterion for distinguishing the kinds of beings who can have rights from the kinds that cannot. I argued there that only beings who have interests are conceptually suitable subjects for the attribution of rights. I came to that conclusion for two main reasons. First, interests are necessary for a being to be *represented* by proxies. Various kinds of incompetents, infants, insane and senile persons, even some of the higher animals, can be represented by guardians, or trustees, not in the sense in which a mere stand-in or mouthpiece represents the *will* of his principal, for these incompetents may have no will to be represented, but rather in the sense in which an attorney, for example, is delegated authority to represent his client's *interests* or to be his agent. Second, interests are essential to a creature's being the sort of thing that can have a *good of its own*, for to act for a creature's good simply *is* to act in its interest. It may seem at first sight as though even plants and "mere things," which most assuredly do not have interests of their own, might yet have a good or welfare that we can promote or retard. Certain kinds of fertilizer are "good for" lawns (as we say) and certain kinds of gasoline or oil are "good for" automobiles. But clearly all we can mean by these useful idioms is that the fertilizer or the gasoline and oil promotes *our* interest in the lawn or the automobile. Particularly in the case of the mere thing, where the absence of an interest of its own is certain, it is clear that the object, though it can *be* good or bad in a great variety or respects, can *have* no good of its own. "An automobile needs gasoline and oil to function, but it is no tragedy for *it* if it runs out—an empty tank does not hinder or retard *its* interests."[2]

This account, I think, explains why those who debate the question of animal rights often find it crucial to determine whether animals are the directly intended beneficiaries of protective legislation. To concede that animals can *be* beneficiaries (as the deniers of the possibility of animal rights were reluctant to do) is to acknowledge that they are the sorts of beings who can have interests and therefore a good of their own which can be represented by proxies and protected by guardians. Possession of interests by no means automatically confers any particular right or even any rights at all upon a being. What it does is show that the being in question is the kind of being to whom moral or legal rights can be ascribed without conceptual absurdity. To have a right, after all, is to have a claim, and to have a claim is to be in a legitimate position to make certain demands against others. A mute creature can make claims only by means of a vicarious representative speaking for it, but *if* it has no interests of its own

1. Joel Feinberg "The Rights of Animals and Future Generations," *Philosophy and Environmental Crisis*, ed. by William Blackstone (Athens, Georgia: University of Georgia Press, 1974).

2. *Ibid.* Cf. Aristotle's discussion of why we cannot be friends with inanimate objects, *Nicomachean Ethics*, Book VIII, Chap. 2: "We cannot wish for the good of such objects." And in a note: "It would be absurd, for example, for a man to wish his wine well. If he has any wish in the matter, it is that the wine may keep, so that he can taste the joys of possession." J. A. K. Thomson translation, Penguin Books (1953), p. 230.

it cannot be represented in this way, having *no "behalf" that another can speak in.* Moreover, if a creature has no interests of its own, it has no welfare or good of its own, and cannot be helped or hindered, benefited or aided, in which case, it has *no "sake" that one could act for.* In that event there could be no coherent reason for regarding any conduct of others as its due, and thus the concept of a right would simply not apply to it.

Applying the interest principle to the hard cases, I concluded that the higher animals *are* among the sorts of beings who *can* have rights, even though the rights they actually have are minimal, perhaps a general right not to be treated cruelly and rather rare specific rights derived from agreements between human beings. I denied that vegetables can have rights on the grounds that however interests are ultimately to be analyzed, they must be compounded somehow out of wants and purposes, both of which in turn presuppose something like expectation, belief, and cognitive awareness, which are presumably missing in vegetables (even in "human vegetables"). I hesitantly conceded, however, that dead persons can have rights against us, namely rights to the fulfillment of promises made to them when they were alive, and rights not to be falsely defamed to those who once knew and loved them. This admittedly paradoxical conclusion is supported by the idea that certain of a dead person's interests can be thought to survive their owner's death and constitute claims against us that persist beyond the life of the claimant. This in turn requires us to think of interests as fulfilled only by the coming into existence of that which is desired, and not simply as "satisfaction of desire" in the sense of contentment in

the mind of the desirer when he believes that his desire has been fulfilled. It is too late, after all, for a dead man to experience contentment.

II

If the interest principle is to permit us to ascribe rights to fetuses and generations yet unborn, it can only be on the grounds that interests can exert a claim upon us even before their possessors actually come into being, just the reverse of the situation respecting dead men where interests are respected even after their possessors have ceased to be. The rights our law confers on the unborn child, both proprietary and personal, are for the most part placeholders or reservations for the rights he shall inherit when he becomes a full-fledged interested being. The law protects a potential interest in these cases before it has even grown into actuality, as a garden fence protects newly seeded flower beds long before blooming flowers have emerged from them. The unborn child's present right to property, for example, is a legal protection offered now to his future interest, contingent upon his birth, and instantly voidable if he dies before birth. As Coke put it: "The law in many cases hath consideration of him in respect of the apparent expectation of his birth";[3] but this is quite another thing than recognizing a right actually to be born. *Assuming* that the child will be born, the law seems to say, various interests that he will come to have after birth must be protected from damage that they can incur even before birth.

"There is nothing in law," says Salmond, "to prevent a man from owning property before he is born. His

3. William Salmond, *Jurisprudence*, Twelfth Edition, ed. by P. J. Fitzgerald (London: Sweet & Maxwell, 1966), p. 303.

ownership is contingent, for he may never be born at all; but it is nonetheless a real and present ownership. A man may settle property on his wife and the children to be born of her. Or he may die intestate and his unborn child will inherit his estate."[4] To say of an unborn fetus that he has a right of ownership *now* is to say that funds have been left in trust for him on the expectation of his arrival. His right to use the funds is contingent upon his birth as a living human being. As Salmond puts it, "The legal personality attributed to him by way of anticipation falls away *ab initio* if he never takes his place among the living . . . A posthumous child, for example, may inherit; but if he dies in the womb, or is stillborn, his inheritance fails to take effect, and *no one can claim through him*, though it would be otherwise if he lived for an hour after his birth."[5] Even though it deviates from a certain technical legal usage, let us call the legal rights a fetus has in anticipation of his future postnatal interests, *contingent rights*, rights reserved for him on the expectation of his birth.

In recent years American jurisdictions have conferred another set of contingent rights upon fetuses—conditional (again) upon their eventually being born alive. I refer to rights to be free of bodily injury that will handicap them after they are born. With this contingent fetal right goes a corresponding postnatal right *ex delicto*, or right of action in tort, to sue for damages in compensation for injuries inflicted before he was born, a right which he can exercise through a proxy-attorney and in his own name any time *after* he is born. Thus, a child born with malformed limbs because a motorist negligently ran over his mother while he was in her womb is entitled to recover damages after he is born from the negligent motorist. If he dies *in utero*, however, no one can sue in his name, for his death. His prenatal legal rights that can be violated by another's negligence apparently do not include a right to be born alive, but only the conditional right *if* born alive, to be free of physical injury. (It is interesting to note parenthetically that the conduct that causes injury to the fetus for which it can recover after it is born may have occurred before it was even *conceived*. A pharmaceutical manufacturer who carelessly prepares medicine six months before an infant's conception will be answerable to a child fifteen months later, if the medicine taken by the mother damaged the embryo, and the fetus nevertheless survived until birth. Or consider the case where a blood transfusion to a mother gives her syphilis. One year later she conceives, and her child is subsequently born syphilitic. In an actual German case of a few years ago, the infant was able to recover damages from the hospital for its negligence in administering the blood transfusion to his mother almost two years before *he* was even born.)

Let me reiterate that these rights to sue, and the rights to be free of bodily injury that they presuppose, do *not* imply *unconditional* recognition of prenatal rights. The fetus's rights are recognized in Lord Coke's words "on condition only that it be born alive." If it dies *in utero* or is stillborn, then no person will exist to claim that he himself has been damaged; nor will anyone be able to represent the claimant, or derive any kind of rights by transmission from the fetus. There are certain older decisions that no longer have the force of precedent that awarded com-

4. *Loc. cit.*
5. *Ibid.*, p. 304.

pensation to the fetus's estate for wrongful injuries suffered *in utero* resulting in stillbirth. Those decisions seemed to imply a noncontingent right of the fetus to be born alive, but they have now fallen out of our law.

There are numerous other places, however, where our law does seem to imply an unconditional legal right to be born, and very few commentators seem to have found that idea conceptually absurd. Of decisions that might be construed as recognizing the fetus's right while still a fetus to be born alive, two interesting ones can be mentioned here. The first is from the law governing treatment of condemned criminals: "A pregnant woman condemned to death is respited as of right, until she has been delivered of her child."[6] (The "as of right" mentioned in the quoted sentence must surely refer to a right of the fetus, not the mother, since the mother is denied the right to let her child die with her; that is, she is not given a discretionary right herself to decide the child's fate.)

The other interesting example of apparent judicial recognition of the right to be born comes from an article given the following headline by the *New York Times*: "Unborn Child's Right Upheld Over Religion." A hospital patient in her eighth month of pregnancy refused to take a blood transfusion even though warned by her physician that "she might die at any minute and take the life of her child as well." The ground of her refusal was that blood transfusions are repugnant to the principles of her (Jehovah's Witnesses) religion. The Supreme Court of New Jersey expressed uncertainty over the constitutional question of whether a nonpregnant adult might refuse, on religious grounds, a blood transfusion pronounced necessary to her own survival, but nevertheless ordered the patient in the present case to receive the transfusion, on the grounds that "the unborn child is entitled to the law's protection."[7]

It is important to reemphasize here that the questions of whether fetuses *do* or *ought to have* rights are substantive questions of laws and morals, open to argument and decision. The prior question of whether features are the kinds of beings that *can have* rights, however, is a conceptual, not a moral, question, amenable only to what is called "logical analysis," and irrelevant to moral judgment. The correct answer to the conceptual question, I believe, is that unborn children *are* among the sorts of beings of whom posession of rights can meaningfully be predicated, even though they are (temporarily) incapable of having interests, because their future interests can be protected now, and it does make sense to protect a potential interest even before it has grown into actuality. The interest-principle, however, makes perplexing, at best, talk of a noncontingent fetal right to be born; for fetuses, lacking actual wants and goals, have no actual interests in being born, and it is difficult to think of any other reason for ascribing any rights to them other than on the assumption that they will in fact be born.

I now turn to the difficult normative question of whether there are any noncontingent fetal rights.

III

To begin with, it does seem *morally* (though not "conceptually") *absurd* to

6. *Ibid.*, p. 303.

7. *New York Times*, June 17, 1966, p. 1. The New Jersey Supreme Court denied the right of a nonpregnant adult to refuse a blood transfusion necessary to her survival in the later case, *John F. Kennedy Memorial Hospital v. Heston* (1971).

claim that there is a general across-the-board right possessed by *all* human fetuses, simply as such, to be born. There may well be rights held by all human beings as such, for example, the rights not to be exploited, or degraded, or treated in cruel or inhuman ways. These of course are the claims we call "human rights," since one automatically acquires them simply by being born a human being. Most theorists formulate the basic human rights in such a way that they cannot, logically, conflict with one another, so that their claim upon others can be treated as absolute and unconditional. We have a human right, for example, not to be subjected to physical torture, which we think cannot be justly infringed in any circumstances. Whatever the tenability of this claim, it surely seems more plausible than a parallel claim on behalf of all fetuses that they enjoy a human or "fetal-human" right to be born that can *never* be justly infringed (or more narrowly redefined) even for the sake of those already alive. The latter claim would entail that fundamental interests of living persons are automatically to be forfeited whenever they conflict with a claim to be born made on behalf of an entity which is nothing more than a cluster of splitting cells still incapable of consciousness or desire, a judgment which seems utterly perverse.

The fetus, of course, has *future interests*, "contingent upon its being born" which can be protected in advance for it, on the expectation that it *will* be born. But it does not have an actual interest now that it be born later, because it is not yet capable of having *any* actual interests. That fact might tempt us to the view that a fetus *never* has a right to be born, that whatever rights it does have now are those "con-tingent rights" whose full statement has the form: "Assuming that the fetus *will* be born, we owe it to him now not to damage, or preclude the satisfaction of the interests he *will* have after his birth." This normative view tempts me very strongly. It does not, however, follow from the analytic view presented above. My position there was *not* that for every right there is a particular interest corresponding to it. That view is patently false, for at any given time I have rights to do many things that are *contrary* to my interests, and I may have interests that do not qualify or even deserve legal protection. My analytic conclusion, on the contrary, was only that it is a (conceptually) necessary condition for the possession of any rights at all that the possessor be the kind of being who is, was, or will be capable of having interests. I did not claim further that there need be a neat one-to-one correspondence between specific interests and specific rights. Therefore, without further premises, the fact that a given fetus at a given time does not have a specific actual interest in being born does not entail that he has no right, at that time, to be born. So the question is still open.

But now I wonder what *reasons* can be given in support of the normative judgment that a fetus has at least a general *claim* to be born even though that claim may be overridden in certain circumstances by stronger claims or rights. I should think that the fact that a being has an interest in X would be a very good reason, speaking generally, in support of the claim that he has a right to X, even though it is admittedly not, all by itself, a decisive reason; and similarly the fact that a being has no interest in X would at least put something of a heavier burden on the shoulders of the person who claims that

that being has a right to X. For all I know there are reasons of still other kinds that have relevance to right-claims and particularly to prenatal right-claims, so I cannot be dogmatic. Some reasons clearly do not apply to fetuses. For example, it cannot be claimed that anyone has made a *promise* to a given fetus to bestow the so-called "gift of life" upon it. I should think that it is impossible to make a promise to a fetus. So the fact that a fetus has no actual interest in being born at any time before it is in fact born seems to me to be a very good reason (though not perhaps a conclusive one) for denying that it has an unconditional right to be born, even though it may be said to have contingent rights conditional upon its subsequent birth and the actualization of its future interests. I have some hesitation in endorsing this view, however, mainly because of the apparent examples, cited earlier, of legal acknowledgment of a right to be born.

One of these examples, that of the convicted pregnant murderess, raises some interesting questions. I find myself tempted in this case to the currently popular view that it should be the mother's exclusive right to decide whether or not her baby should be born, especially when there is no known father to be considered. To be sure, it fills me with horror to think of a conspicuously pregnant woman being hanged, unborn child and all; but that may be mainly because of the reprobative symbolism of the hanging ritual. Where the example is less complicated by guilt, the maternal prerogative principle is easier to apply. Imagine an impoverished, husbandless, pregnant lady dying of consumption in her hovel, amidst a brood of other illegitimate or else deserted children. It would seem utterly inhumane in this case to deny her the right to abort her child or otherwise prevent its birth, say, by dying with it still unborn. Indeed, if we did grant the right to decide the question of birth to the convicted murderess or the deserted consumptive, we might well expect them to exercise it, at least insofar as they are exclusively concerned with the welfare of the potential child they carry, by choosing abortion, unless, *mirabile dictu,* there is reason to think that the child would receive the parental love, family life, and economic necessities that would be its "birth right." Only in the latter case would a choice made on the ground of the infant's future welfare be a choice of birth rather than death.[8]

But now a new and startling possibility suggests itself. The conscientious mother will be determined to do her child justice, to make the right decision for *its* sake, to give it its due, and this seems to be another way of saying: *to honor its rights.* Whatever the circumstances may be, since the fetus has no actual interest, at the time, in being born, there is still no reason that I am sure of for ascribing to it a right to be born, though the existence of such a reason, as we have seen, is not logically precluded. But if the circumstances are very unhappy ones (for example prenatal damage, poverty, malnutrition, no father) there may very well be future interests of the child whose eventual fulfillment has already been blocked, so that if the child is allowed to be born, his rights to the protection of those interests will have *already* been violated, and that fact seems to me to be a very good reason for *not* permitting it to be born. Moreover,

8. Note a new interpretation of the idea of a birth-right suggested by this point: If you can't have that to which you have a birth-right then you are wronged if you are brought to birth.

it seems a reason for saying that non-birth is something we now owe it, that it is something that can now be claimed on its behalf as its due. Thus, even before we have been able to come to a strong conclusion about whether there is ever a right to be born, we seem to have stumbled onto an argument for the startling conclusion that there can be a *right not to be born,*

Here is a brief recapitulation of that argument:

1. The absence of an actual interest of a fetus in being born leaves open the question of whether there can ever be a right to be born.

2. The clearest cases of rights that a fetus does have, therefore, are rights to the present protection of future interests, *on the assumption* that it will be born. To say he's got such a right to *x* is to say that *x* must be held for his arrival.

3. Thus, if the conditions for the eventual fulfillment of his future interests are destroyed before he is born, the child can claim, after he has been born, that his *rights* (his present rights) have been violated.

4. But if, before the child has been born, we know that the conditions for the fulfillment of his most basic interests have already been destroyed, and we permit him nevertheless to be born, we become a party to the violation of his rights.

5. In such circumstances, therefore, a proxy for the fetus might plausibly claim on its behalf, a *right not to be born.* That right is based on his future rather than his present interests (he has no actual present interests); but of course it is not contingent on his birth because he has it before birth, from the very moment that satisfaction of his

most basic future interests is rendered impossible.

I am suggesting then that the only noncontingent rights fetuses ever have is the right not to be born (when all chance of fulfillment of birth-rights is already destroyed).

IV

Could a child then sue for damages on the ground that he was improperly allowed to be born? Surprisingly, this has already been done. And not only have infants sued defendants for "wrongful birth," so-called, they have in at least two cases sued defendants for wrongfully permitting them to be *conceived* in the first place! (Wrongful conception is what is implied by "wrongful birth" wherever abortion is illegal.) In *Williams v. State*[9] an infant girl sued the State of New York for damages resulting from the state's negligent operation of a mental hospital. It seems that the infant's mother, a mentally deficient patient in the state institution, was sexually assaulted by an attendant, as a result of which the plaintiff was born out of wedlock to an incompetent mother. The suit, which charged the state with negligence in failing to protect the mother from the rape, met with success in the trial court, but was overturned on appeal. It was part of the plaintiff's pleading at the trial court that she had been "deprived of property rights; deprived of a normal childhood and home life; deprived of proper parental care, support and rearing; caused to bear the stigma of ille-

9. *Williams v. State of New York*, 46 Misc. 2d 824, 260 N. Y. S. 2d 953 (Ct. Claims, 1965); *reversed*, 25 A. D. 2d 906, 269 N. Y. S. 2d 786 (App. Div. 1966); *reversal affirmed*, 18 N. Y. 2d 481, 233 N. E. 2d 343 (1966). I am grateful to Herbert Spiegelberg for calling this case to my attention.

gitimacy and has otherwise been greatly injured all to her damage in the sum of $100,000." From the philosophical point of view this bill of injuries would have been more interesting still had it included inherited mental retardation, genetically transmitted from the mother, and perhaps also an inherited tendency (say) to some chronically painful and incurable condition. In that (fictitious) case, the attorney for the plaintiff might have been in a stronger position to counter the argument that:

What does disturb us is the nature of the new action and the related suits which would be encouraged. Encouragement would extend to all others born into the world under conditions they might regard as adverse. One might seek damages for being born of a certain color, another because of race; one for being born with a hereditary disease, another for inheriting unfortunate family characteristics; one for being born into a large and destitute family, another because a parent has an unsavory reputation . . .[10]

To this objection, from the opinion in *Zepeda v. Zepeda* cited by judge in the *Williams* case, the reply should be that not all interests of the newborn child should or can qualify for prenatal legal protection, but only those very basic ones whose satisfaction is indispensable to a decent life. The state cannot insure all or even many of its citizens against bad luck in the lottery of life. As the eventual Appeals Court opinion put it: "Being born under one set of circumstances rather than another or to one pair of parents rather than another is not a suable wrong that is cognizable in court." On the other hand, to be dealt feeble-mindedness or syphilis, or advanced heroin addition, or guaranteed malnutrition, or economic deprivation so far below a reasonable minimum as to be inescapably degrading and sordid, is not merely to have "bad luck." It is to be dealt a card from a stacked deck in a transaction that is not a "game" so much as a swindle.

The only reservations of the trial judge in allowing the case to be tried were that there was at the time no clear precedent for that kind of suit and that there was something approaching paradox in the idea that a tort can "be inflicted upon a being simultaneously with its conception."[11] He took neither of these misgivings seriously, but the second one proved to be the plaintiff's undoing at the appellate level. The Court of Appeals in its majority opinion held that the infant had no right to recover, "rejecting the idea that there could be an obligation of the State to a person not yet conceived." If my sketch of an argument above is correct, however, the court was too hasty. The obligation of the State, in my view, was not owed to some shadowy creature waiting in its metaphysical limbo to be born. Rather it was an obligation to its patient to protect her from assault, and as a consequence of its breach of duty to her, the rights of another human being, her daughter, which like most prenatal rights, are contingent upon later birth, were violated. Or perhaps the duty of the state can be characterized more felicitously still as a duty of care owed to anybody likely to be affected by its conduct, on analogy with the duty of a producer of canned baby food toward *all* eventual consumers of its product including some children yet unborn or even unconceived.

10. From the opinion in a somewhat similar case, *Zepeda v. Zepeda*, 41 Ill. App. 2d 240, 190 N. E. 2d 849 (1963); *certiorari denied*, 379 U. S. 945, 85 S. Ct. 444, 13 L. Ed. 2d 545 (Dec. 1964); quoted by Judge Sidney Squire in *State v. Williams*, 260 N. Y. S. 2d 953.

11. We have seen that it can be inflicted before conception or after conception and before birth.

In a separate concurring opinion, Judge Kenneth Keating found another ground for ruling against the infant:

Damages are awarded in tort cases on the basis of a comparison between the position the plaintiff would have been in, had the defendant not committed the acts causing injury, and the position in which the plaintiff presently finds herself. The damages sought by the plaintiff in the case at bar involve a determination as to whether nonexistence or nonlife is preferable to life as an illegitimate with all the hardship attendant thereon. It is impossible to make that choice.[12]

Now, it is perhaps true as a matter of law, that assessments of damages in tort cases (or at any rate, in all *other* kinds of tort cases) rest upon a hypothetical comparison of the plaintiff's condition after his injury with what his condition would have been had the defendant not affected it by his intentional or negligent wrong-doing; and of course that kind of compaison cannot be made when the alleged injury occurs at the very moment of conception, for it would have us consider the "condition" the plaintiff would have been in had he never been conceived, which is a contradiction in terms. In this kind of case, then, assessments of damages would have to be made in some other way; but even if assessments were made on *admittedly arbitrary* grounds, they might better serve justice than if no damages are awarded at all. In any case, the question of damages aside, the grounds for charging that a wrongdoer has violated another's right not to be born do not include reference to a strange never-never land from which phantom beings are dragged struggling and kicking into their mothers' wombs and thence into existence as persons in the real world. Talk of a "right not to be born" is a compendious way of referring to the plausible moral requirement that

no child be brought into the world unless certain very minimal conditions of well-being are assured, and certain basic "future interests" are protected in advance, at least in the sense that the *possibility* of his fulfilling those interests be kept open. When a child is brought into existence even though those requirements have not been observed, *he has been wronged* thereby; and that is not to say that any metaphysical interpretation, or any sense at all, can be given to the statement that he would have been better off had he never been born.

Now it might be asked why there should be such a striking asymmetry between a plausibly defensible right not to be born and its implausibly maintained counterpart, the alleged right of fetuses to be born. Just as we hurt a potential person when we *allow* him to be born in a condition such that he will have no chance to fulfill his most basic future interests, don't we also hurt a potential person when we *deny* him a chance to be born into a life quite sure to give him love and wealth and fulfillment? To be sure, there is no person around to complain that he himself was wronged or to sue for damages in the latter case, for the prospective plaintiff in that case is not in existence. But that doesn't prove that the fetus or potential person was not wronged in not being permitted to become an actual person. Perhaps, a proxy might have been permitted to seek an injunction on behalf of the unborn fetus with the promising future, so that there would be some parallel legal consequences in ascribing to it a right to be born, after all. There are other practical differences between the two cases, however. One is that the right not to be born is to be conferred

12. Judge Kenneth Keating in *Williams v. State*, 223 N. E. 2d 344.

only in those rare circumstances in which the fetus has no chance whatever of a decent life and we can know this with near certainty in advance. There could be no corresponding necessity or certainty in the case of the fetus with the especially promising future. Moreover, in the case where the right in question is violated, the fetus with no chance becomes a human being who gets badly hurt, but the fetus with the glittering future never learns what he is missing and never "knows what hits him." The main asymmetry between the two cases, however, derives from the differing moral statuses of harm and mere nonbenefit. It is generally much more plausible to make claim against others not to be harmed than to make the claim to be positively benefitted, contractual considerations aside. A claim not to be sunk into poverty is, in its very nature, easier to support than a claim to be kept in one's riches. The right not to be born is typical of a large and familiar class of rights *not to* be forced into a situation in which one's important interests are certain to be damaged. A general right *to be* born based on an exceptionally promising future would be an instance of a quite different sort of thing: a right to be permitted into a situation in which there is a good chance, as far as anyone can tell, that one's interests, basic and otherwise, will be advanced. In any case, when the right of a fetus not to be born is violated, there is an assignable living person who has been harmed. When a fetus with a promising future is aborted, neither he nor any other existing being is hurt by it (unless hurt is confused with nonbenefit.)

V

My doubts about the existence of a right to be born transfer neatly to the question of a similar right to come into existence ascribed to future generations. The rights that future generations certainly have against us are contingent rights: The interests they are sure to have when they come into being (assuming of course that they *will* come into being) cry out for protection from invasions that can take place *now*. Yet there are no actual interests, presently existent, that future generations, presently nonexistent, have *now*. Hence, there is no actual interest that they have in simply coming into being; and I am at a loss to think of any *other* reason for claiming that they have a right to come into existence (though there may well be such a reason). Suppose then that all human beings at a given time voluntarily form a compact never again to produce children, thus leading within a few decades to the end of our species. We can imagine, say, that the whole world is converted to a strange ascetic religion which absolutely requires sexual abstinence for everyone. Would this arrangement violate the rights of *anyone?* No one can complain on behalf of presently nonexistent future generations that their future interests which give them a contingent right of protection have been violated, since they will never come into existence to be wronged. My inclination then is to conclude that the suicide of our species would be deplorable, lamentable, and a deeply moving tragedy, but that it would violate no one's *rights*. Indeed, if, contrary to fact, all human beings could ever agree to such a thing, that very agreement would be a symptom of our species' biological unsuitability for survival anyway.[13]

13. This paragraph is taken from my article "The Rights of Animals and Future Generations," *op. cit.*

Suggestions for Further Reading

Stanley I. Benn, "Rights," *The Encyclopedia of Philosophy*, ed. Paul Edwards (New York: Macmillan and The Free Press, 1967), vol. 7, pp. 195–199.

Joel Feinberg, "Duties, Rights, and Claims," *American Philosophical Quarterly*, vol. 3 (1966), pp. 137–144. [Reprinted in E. Kent (ed.), *Law and Philosophy* (New York: Appleton-Century-Crofts, 1970).] Feinberg discusses the nature of rights and the relation between rights, duties, and claims.

Joel Feinberg, *Social Philosophy* (Englewood Cliffs, N.J.: Prentice-Hall, 1973), chs. 4–6. This is especially good on legal rights.

H. L. A. Hart, "Are There Any Natural Rights?" *The Philosophical Review*, vol. 64 (1955), pp. 175–191. In this classic article Hart argues that "if there are any moral rights at all, it follows that there is at least one natural right, the equal right of all men to be free."

Richard Wasserstrom, "Rights, Human Rights, and Racial Discrimination," *The Journal of Philosophy*, vol. 61 (1964), pp. 628–641. Wasserstrom discusses the nature of human rights and then what happens when rights are denied, as in the case of racial discrimination.

A. I. Melden, ed., *Human Rights* (Belmont, Cal.: Wadsworth, 1970). This is a good collection of essays on human rights. It includes the papers by Hart and Wasserstrom cited above.

CHAPTER SEVEN

Morality and the Law

INTRODUCTION

We now take up two questions concerning the relationship between morality and the law. First, do we have a moral obligation to obey the law, and if so, how extensive is this obligation? And second, is it right for a society to have laws the only purpose of which is to force people to behave "morally"?

Almost everyone would agree that citizens do have an obligation to obey the laws of their community. However, it is not clear exactly *why* we should obey the law. Why should we be obligated to act in a certain way, simply because a group of legislators in some distant city decide we must act in that way?

The classical argument for the obligation to obey the law was formulated by the great seventeenth-century political theorist Thomas Hobbes. Hobbes argued that without a system of laws binding on everyone life would be intolerable. In order to secure the advantages that we take for granted in civilized societies, we must be able to assume that people will obey certain rules: principally, rules requiring them to keep their agreements with us, and rules requiring us not to harm one another. Moreover, when we have disputes with other people, or complaints against them, we need to have some way of settling the dispute or seeking redress other than getting a gun and fighting it out. The law serves both these purposes: It secures compliance with the rules necessary for social living, and it provides a referee (the courts) for peacefully adjudicating disputes between individuals or groups of individuals. As Hobbes puts it, without the law to provide these services,

there is no place for industry; because the fruit thereof is uncertain: and consequently no culture of the earth; no navigation, nor use of the commodities that may be imported by sea; no commodious building; no instruments of moving, and removing, such things as require much force; no knowledge of the face of the earth; no account of time; no arts; no letters; no society; and which is worst of all, continual fear, and danger of violent death; and the life of man, solitary, poor, nasty, brutish, and short.

Hobbes's argument is presented in "The Nature of Legal Obligation." Then in "Legal Obligation and the Duty of Fair Play," John Rawls argues that, at least in societies such as the United States, we have a duty to obey the law which is derived from the more fundamental duty of fair play.

Very few people, however, would say that we should *always* obey the law; there are at least some circumstances in which disobedience to law is justified. To take a simple case: The law may require a motorist to signal before turning, yet in an emergency a driver may have to make a sudden turn, without signalling, in order to avoid an accident. Again, some regimes may be so blatantly immoral that citizens are released from virtually all duties of allegiance: Nazi Germany is an obvious example.

More troublesome cases arise when some particular law or government policy requires an individual to act against his conscience, although the system of laws is not objectionable as a whole. Laws enforcing racial segregation and laws requiring individuals to participate in a war they consider immoral are recent examples. Should a person continue to obey the law in such circumstances, or should he follow his own conscience? In "The Morality of Civil Disobedience," Charles Frankel explains and defends the traditional liberal theory of civil disobedience, which allows that in some circumstances a person may follow his conscience and disobey the law, provided that certain carefully stated conditions are satisfied. Henry David Thoreau takes a more radical view in "There Is No Obligation to Obey the Law." Thoreau did not agree that governments and laws are necessary; he argued that we would be better off without them, and that no one ever has a duty to violate his own conscience merely because some legal "authority" tells him that he must.

There are also philosophical problems about the moral *content* of the law. Whenever a sizeable majority of people within a community regard a form of behavior as seriously immoral, there is a tendency to write that judgment into law and formally prohibit behavior of that type. For example, in most jurisdictions in the United States there are laws prohibiting homosexual behavior and the production and distribution of pornographic literature. These laws were enacted at least in part because most people have felt that homosexuality and pornography are immoral. It may be argued, however, that there should be no such laws, because, even if the practices in question are "immoral," they do no harm to anyone except the people who voluntarily decide to engage in them. Or, to put the same point in different words, the law should not forbid a citizen from doing anything that would not harm others. This was essentially the view of John Stuart Mill in his essay *On Liberty*, parts of which are reprinted in "The Limits to the Authority of the State Over the Individual":

The object of this Essay is to assert one very simple principle, as entitled to govern absolutely the dealings of society with the individual . . . That principle is, that the sole end for which mankind are warranted, individually or collectively, in interfering with the liberty of action of any of their number, is self-protection. That the only purpose for which power can be rightfully exercised over any member of a civilized community, against his will, is to prevent harm to others. His own good, either physical or moral, is not a sufficient warrant.

Of course Mill's principle would not rule out all laws prohibiting immorality. Murder and rape are immoral, and it is quite all right to have laws against them because those offenses involve harming others. On the other hand, if one person writes a pornographic book, and another buys and reads it, it would not seem that they are harming anyone but themselves—if, indeed, they are even doing that.

Mill's principle has become one of the cornerstones of modern liberal theory. The principle has been vigorously debated since its first presentation, but it has been especially on the minds of philosophers during the past twenty years. In 1954 a committee was established in England, under the chairmanship of John Wolfenden, to consider changes in the laws concerning prostitution and homosexuality. Three years later the committee issued its now famous Report, recommending that there be no laws prohibiting either of those practices, and arguing for this on grounds very much like Mill's. The Wolfenden Committee Report touched off a controversy that still continues. Lord Patrick Devlin, formerly a judge of the Queen's Bench, has been the leading critic of the Report. He has argued, against the Committee and against Mill, that society does have a right to use the law to force compliance with its moral code. Some of Devlin's leading arguments are presented in "Mill on Liberty in Morals." There have been many replies to Devlin, and one of the most thoughtful, "Homosexuality, Pornography, and the Law" by Ronald Dworkin, concludes this chapter.

37

THOMAS HOBBES
The Nature of Legal Obligation

THOMAS HOBBES (1588–1679), the great English materialist and political philosopher, published his most important work, the *Leviathan*, when he was 63 years old.

OF THE NATURAL CONDITION OF MANKIND AS CONCERNING THEIR FELICITY, AND MISERY

Nature hath made men so equal, in the faculties of the body, and mind; as that though there be found one man sometimes manifestly stronger in body, or of quicker mind than another; yet when all is reckoned together, the difference between man, and man, is not so considerable, as that one man can thereupon claim to himself any benefit, to which another may not pretend, as well as he. For as to the strength of body, the weakest has strength enough to kill the strongest, either by secret machination, or by confederacy with others, that are in the same danger with himself.

And as to the faculties of the mind, setting aside the arts grounded upon words, and especially that skill of pro-

Excerpted from Thomas Hobbes, *Leviathan* (1651), chs. 13, 14, 17.

ceeding upon general, and infallible rules, called science; which very few have, and but in few things; as being not a native faculty, born with us; nor attained, as prudence, while we look after somewhat else, I find yet a greater equality amongst men, than that of strength. For prudence, is but experience; which equal time, equally bestows on all men, in those things they equally apply themselves unto. That which may perhaps make such equality incredible, is but a vain conceit of one's own wisdom, which almost all men think they have in a greater degree, than the vulgar; that is, than all men but themselves, and a few others, whom by fame, or for concurring with themselves, they approve. For such is the nature of men, that howsoever they may acknowledge many others to be more witty, or more eloquent, or more learned; yet they will hardly believe there be many so wise as themselves; for they see their own wit at hand, and other men's at a distance. But this proveth rather that men are in that point equal, than unequal. For there is not ordinarily a greater sign of the equal distribution of anything, than that every man is contented with his share.

From this equality of ability, ariseth equality of hope in the attaining of our ends. And therefore if any two men desire the same thing, which nevertheless they cannot both enjoy, they become enemies; and in the way to their end, which is principally their own conservation, and sometimes their delectation only, endeavour to destroy, or subdue one another. And from hence it comes to pass that where an invader hath no more to fear, than another man's single power; if one plant, sow, build, or possess a convenient seat, others may probably be expected to come prepared with forces united, to dispossess, and deprive him, not only of the fruit of his labour, but also of his life, or liberty. And the invader again is in the like danger of another.

And from this diffidence of one another, there is no way for any man to secure himself, so reasonable, as anticipation; that is, by force, or wiles, to master the persons of all men he can, so long, till he see no other power great enough to endanger him: and this is no more than his own conservation requireth, and is generally allowed. Also because there be some, that taking pleasure in contemplating their own power in the acts of conquest, which they pursue farther than their security requires; if others, that otherwise would be glad to be at ease within modest bounds, should not by invasion increase their power, they would not be able, long time, by standing only on their defence, to subsist. And by consequence, such augmentation of dominion over men being necessary to a man's conservation, it ought to be allowed him.

Again, men have no pleasure, but on the contrary a great deal of grief, in keeping company, where there is no power able to over-awe them all. For every man looketh that his companion should value him, at the same rate he sets upon himself: and upon all signs of contempt, or undervaluing, naturally endeavours, as far as he dares, (which amongst them that have no common power to keep them in quiet, is far enough to make them destroy each other), to extort a greater value from his contemners, by damage; and from others, by the example.

So that in the nature of man, we find three principal causes of quarrel. First, competition; secondly, diffidence; thirdly, glory.

The first, maketh men invade for gain; the second, for safety; and the third, for reputation. The first use violence, to make themselves masters of other men's persons, wives, children, and cattle; the second to defend them; the third, for trifles, as a word, a smile, a different opinion, and any other sign of undervalue, either direct in their persons, or by reflection in their kindred, their friends, their nation, their profession, or their name.

Hereby it is manifest, that during the time men live without a common power to keep them all in awe, they are in that condition which is called war; and such a war, as is of every man, against every man. For WAR, consisteth not in battle only, or the act of fighting; but in a tract of time, wherein the will to contend by battle is sufficiently known: and therefore the notion of *time*, is to be considered in the nature of war; as it is in the nature of weather. For as the nature of foul weather, lieth not in a shower or two of rain; but in an inclination thereto of many days together: so the nature of war, consisteth not in actual fighting; but in the known disposition thereto, during all the time there is no assurance to the contrary. All other time is PEACE.

Whatsoever therefore is consequent to a time of war, where every man is enemy to every man; the same is consequent to the time, wherein men live without other security, than what their own strength, and their own invention shall furnish them withal. In such condition, there is no place for industry; because the fruit thereof is uncertain: and consequently no culture of the earth; no navigation, nor use of the commodities that may be imported by sea; no commodious building; no instruments of moving, and removing, such things as require much force; no knowledge of the face of the earth; no account of time; no arts; no letters; no society; and which is worst of all, continual fear, and danger of violent death; and the life of man, solitary, poor, nasty, brutish, and short.

It may seem strange to some man, that has not well weighed these things; that nature should thus dissociate, and render men apt to invade, and destroy one another: and he may therefore, not trusting to this inference, made from the passions, desire perhaps to have the same confirmed by experience. Let him therefore consider with himself, when taking a journey, he arms himself, and seeks to go well accompanied; when going to sleep, he locks his doors; when even in his house he locks his chests; and this when he knows there be laws, and public officers, armed, to revenge all injuries shall be done him; what opinion he has of his fellow-subjects, when he rides armed; of his fellow citizens, when he locks his doors; and of his children, and servants, when he locks his chests. Does he not there as much accuse mankind by his actions, as I do by my words? But neither of us accuse man's nature in it. The desires, and other passions of man, are in themselves no sin. No more are the actions, that proceed from those passions, till they know a law that forbids them: which till laws be made they cannot know: nor can any law be made, till they have agreed upon the person that shall make it.

It may peradventure be thought, there was never such a time, nor condition of war as this; and I believe it was never generally so, over all the world: but there are many places, where they live so now. For the savage people in many places of America, except the government of small families, the concord whereof dependeth on natural lust, have no government at all; and live at this day in that brutish manner, as I said before. Howsoever, it may be perceived what manner of life there would be, where there were no common power to fear, by the manner of life, which men that have formerly lived under a peaceful government use to degenerate into, in a civil war.

But though there had never been any time, wherein particular men were in a condition of war one against another; yet in all times, kings, and persons of sovereign authority, because of their independency, are in continual jealousies, and in the state and posture of gladiators; having their weapons pointing, and their eyes fixed on one another; that is, their forts, garrisons, and guns upon the frontiers of their kingdoms; and continual spies upon their neighbours; which is a posture of war. But because they uphold thereby, the industry of their subjects; there does not follow from it, that misery, which accompanies the liberty of particular men.

To this war of every man, against every man, this also is consequent; that nothing can be unjust. The notions of right and wrong justice and injustice have there no place. Where there is no common power, there is no law: where no law, no injustice. Force, and fraud, are in war the two cardinal virtues. Justice, and injustice are none of the faculties neither of the body, nor mind. If they were, they might be in a man that were alone in the world, as well as his senses, and passions. They are qualities, that relate to men in society, not in solitude. It is consequent also to the same condition, that there be no propriety, no dominion, no *mine* and *thine* distinct; but only that to be every man's, that he can get; and for so long, as he can keep it. And thus much of the ill condition, which man by mere nature is actually placed in; though with a possibility to come out of it, consisting partly in the passions, partly in his reason.

The passions that incline men to peace, are fear of death; desire of such things as are necessary to commodious living; and a hope by their industry to obtain them. And reason suggesteth convenient articles of peace, upon which men may be drawn to agreement. These articles, are they, which otherwise are called the Laws of Nature: whereof I shall speak more particularly, in the two following chapters.

OF THE FIRST AND SECOND NATURAL LAWS, AND OF CONTRACTS

The right of nature, which writers commonly call *jus naturale,* is liberty each man hath, to use his own power, as he will himself, for the preservation of his own nature; that is to say, of his own life; and consequently, of doing any thing, which in his own judgment, and reason, he shall conceive to be the aptest means thereunto.

By *liberty,* is understood, according to the proper signification of the word, the absence of external impediments: which impediments, may oft take away part of a man's power to do what he would; but cannot hinder him from using the power left him, according as his judgment, and reason shall dictate to him.

A *law of nature, lex naturalis,* is a precept or general rule, found out by reason, by which a man is forbidden to do that, which is destructive of his life, or taketh away the means of preserving the same; and to omit that, by which he thinketh it may be best preserved. For though they that speak of this subject, use to confound *jus,* and *lex, right* and *law:* yet they ought to be distinguished; because *right,* consisteth in liberty to do, or to forbare; whereas *law,* determineth, and bindeth to one of them: so that law, and right, differ as much, as obligation, and liberty; which in one and the same matter are inconsistent.

And because the condition of man, as hath been declared in the precedent chapter, is a condition of war of every one against every one: in which case every one is governed by his own reason; and there is nothing he can make use of, that may not be a help unto him, in preserving his life against his enemies; it followeth, that in such a condition, every man has a right to every thing; even to one another's body. And therefore, as long as this natural right of every man to every thing endureth, there can be no security to any man, how strong or wise soever he be, of living out the time, which nature ordinarily alloweth men to live, and consequently it is a precept, or general rule of reason, *that every man, ought to endeavour peace, as far as he has hope of obtaining it; and when he cannot obtain it, that he may seek, and use, all helps, and advantages of war.* The first branch of which rule, containeth the first, and fundamental law of nature; which is, *to seek peace, and follow it.*

The second, the sum of the right of nature; which is, *by all means we can, to defend ourselves.*

From this fundamental law of nature, by which men are commanded to endeavour peace, is derived this second law; *that a man be willing, when others are so too, as far-forth, as for peace, and defence of himself he shall think it necessary, to lay down this right to all things; and be contented with so much liberty against other men, as he would allow other men against himself.* For as long as every man holdeth this right, of doing any thing he liketh; so long are all men in the condition of war. But if other men will not lay down their right, as well as he; then there is no reason for any one, to divest himself of his: for that were to expose himself to prey, which no man is bound to, rather than to dispose himself to peace. This is that law of the Gospel; *whatsoever you require that others should do to you, that do ye to them.* And that law of all men, *quod tibi fieri non vis, alteri ne feceris.*

To *lay down* a man's *right* to any thing, is to *divest* himself of the *liberty,* of hindering another of the benefit of his own right to the same. For he that renounceth, or passeth away his right, giveth not to any other man a right which he had not before; because there is nothing to which every man had not right by nature: but only standeth out of his way, that he may enjoy his own original right, without hindrance from him; not without hindrance from another. So that the effect which redoundeth to one man, by another man's defect of right, is but so much diminution of impediments to the use of his own right original.

Right is laid aside, either by simply renouncing it; or by transferring it to another. By *simply renouncing;* when

he cares not to whom the benefit thereof redoundeth. By *transferring;* when he intendeth the benefit thereof to some certain person, or persons. And when a man hath in either manner abandoned, or granted away his right; then he is said to be *obliged,* or *bound,* not to hinder those, to whom such right is granted, or abandoned, from the benefit of it: and that he *ought,* and it is his *duty,* not to make void that voluntary act of his own: and that such hindrance is *injustice,* and *injury,* as being *sine jure;* the right being before renounced, or transferred. So that *injury,* or *injustice,* in the controversies of the world, is somewhat like to that, which in the disputations of scholars is called *absurdity.* For as it is there called an absurdity, to contradict what one maintained in the beginning: so in the world, it is called injustice, and injury, voluntarily to undo that, which from the beginning he had voluntarily done. The way by which a man either simply renounceth, or transferreth his right, is a declaration, or signification, by some voluntary and sufficient sign, or signs, that he doth so renounce, or transfer; or hath so renounced, or transferred the same, to him that accepteth it. And these signs are either words only, or actions only; or, as it happeneth most often, both words, and actions. And the same are the *bonds,* by which men are bound, and obliged: bonds, that have their strength, not from their own nature, for nothing is more easily broken than a man's word, but from fear of some evil consequence upon that rupture.

Whensoever a man transferreth his right, or renounceth it; it is either in consideration of some right reciprocally transferred to himself; or for some other good he hopeth for thereby. For it is a voluntary act: and of the voluntary acts of every man the object is some *good to himself*. And therefore there be some rights, which no man can be understood by any words, or other signs to have abandoned, or transferred. As first a man cannot lay down the right of resisting them, that assault him by force, to take away his life; because he cannot be understood to aim thereby, at any good to himself. The same may be said of wounds, and chains, and imprisonment; both because there is no benefit consequent to such patience; as there is to the patience of suffering another to be wounded, or imprisoned: as also because a man cannot tell, when he seeth men proceed against him by violence, whether they intend his death or not. And lastly the motive, and end for which this renouncing, and transferring of right is introduced, is nothing else but the security of a man's person, in his life, and in the means of so preserving life, as not to be weary of it. And therefore if a man by words, or other signs, seem to despoil himself of the end, for which those signs were intended; he is not to be understood as if he meant it, or that it was his will; but that he was ignorant of how such words and actions were to be interpreted.

The mutual transferring of right, is that which men call *contract*.

. . .

And though this may seem too subtle a deduction of the laws of nature, to be taken notice of by all men; whereof the most part are too busy in getting food, and the rest too negligent to understand; yet to leave all men inexcusable, they have been contracted into one easy sum, intelligible even to the meanest capacity; and that is, *Do not that to another, which thou wouldest not have done to thyself*; which sheweth him, that he has no

more to do in learning the laws of nature, but, when weighing the actions of other men with his own, they seem too heavy, to put them into the other part of the balance, and his own into their place, that his passions, and self-love, may add nothing to the weight; and then there is none of these laws of nature that will not appear unto him very reasonable.

The laws of nature oblige *in foro interno*; that is to say, they bind to a desire they should take place: but *in foro externo*; that is, to the putting them in act, not always. For he that should be modest, and tractable, and perform all he promises, in such time, and place, where no man else should do so, should but make himself a prey to others, and procure his own certain ruin, contrary to the ground of all laws of nature, which tend to nature's preservation. And again, he that having sufficient security, that others shall observe the same laws towards him, observes them not himself, seeketh not peace but war; and consequently the destruction of his nature by violence.

And whatsoever laws bind *in foro interno*, may be broken, not only by a fact contrary to the law, but also by a fact according to it, in case a man think it contrary. For though his action in this case, be according to the law; yet his purpose was against the law; which, where the obligation is *in foro interno*, is a breach.

The laws of nature are immutable and eternal; for injustice, ingratitude, arrogance, pride, iniquity, acception of persons, and the rest, can never be made lawful. For it can never be that war shall preserve life, and peace destroy it.

The same laws, because they oblige only to a desire, and endeavour, I mean an unfeigned and constant endeavour, are easy to be observed. For in that they require nothing but endeavour, he that endeavoureth their performance, fulfilleth them; and he that fulfilleth the law, is just.

And the science of them, is the true and only moral philosophy. For moral philosophy is nothing else but the science of what is *good*, and *evil*, in the conversation, and society of mankind. *Good*, and *evil*, are names that signify our appetites, and aversions; which in different tempers, customs, and doctrines of men, are different: and divers men, differ not only in their judgment, on the senses of what is pleasant, and unpleasant to the taste, smell, hearing, touch, and sight; but also of what is comfortable, or disagreeable to reason, in the actions of common life. Nay, the same man in divers times, differs from himself; and one time praiseth, that is, calleth good, what another time he dispraiseth, and calleth evil: from whence arise disputes, controversies, and at last war. And therefore so long as a man is in the condition of mere nature, which is a condition of war, as private appetite is the measure of good, and evil: and consequently all men agree on this, that peace is good, and therefore also the way, or means of peace, which, as I have shewed before, are *justice, gratitude, modesty, equity, mercy*, and the rest of the laws of nature, are good; that is to say; *moral virtues*; and their contrary *vices*, evil.

OF THE CAUSES, GENERATION, AND DEFINITION OF A COMMONWEALTH

The final cause, end, or design of men, who naturally love liberty, and dominion over others, in the introduction of that restraint upon themselves, in which we see them live in commonwealths, is the foresight of their own preservation, and of a more contented life thereby; that is to say, of getting themselves out from that miserable condition of war, which is necessarily consequent to the natural passions of men, when there is no visible power to keep them in awe, and tie them by fear of punishment to the performance of their covenants, and observation of those laws of nature set down in the fourteenth and fifteenth chapters.

For the laws of nature, as *justice, equity, modesty, mercy*, and, in sum, *doing to others, as we would be done to*, of themselves, without the terror of some power, to cause them to be observed, are contrary to our natural passions, that carry us to partiality, pride, revenge, and the like. And covenants, without the swords, are but words, and of no strength to secure a man at all. Therefore notwithstanding the laws of nature, which every one hath then kept, when he has the will to keep them, when he can do it safely, if there be no power erected, or not great enough for our security; every man will, and may lawfully rely on his own strength and art, for caution against all other men. And in all places, where men have lived by small families, to rob and spoil one another, has been a trade, and so far from being reputed against the law of nature, that the greater spoils they gained, the greater was their honour; and men observed no other laws therein, but the laws of honour; that is, to abstain from cruelty, leaving to men their lives, and instruments of husbandry. And as small families did then; so now do cities and kingdoms which are but greater families, for their own security, enlarge their dominions, upon all pretences of danger, and fear of invasion, or assistance that may be given to invaders, and endeavour as much as they can, to subdue, or weaken their neighbours, by open force, and secret arts, for want of other caution, justly; and are remembered for it in after ages with honour.

Nor is it the joining together of a small number of men, that gives them this security; because in small numbers, small additions on the one side or the other, make the advantage of strength so great, as is sufficient to carry the victory; and therefore gives encouragement to an invasion. The multitude sufficient to confide in for our security, is not determined by any certain number, but by comparison with the enemy we fear; and is then sufficient, when the odds of the enemy is not of so visible and conspicuous moment, to determine the event of war, as to move him to attempt.

And be there never so great a multitude; yet if their actions be directed according to their particular judgments, and particular appetites, they can expect thereby no defence, nor protection, neither against a common enemy, nor against the injuries of one another. For being distracted in opinions concerning the best use and application of their strength, they do not help but hinder one another; and reduce their strength by mutual opposition to nothing: whereby they are easily, not only subdued by a very few that agree together; but also when there is no common enemy, they make war upon each other, for their particular interests. For if we could suppose a great multitude of men to consent in the observation of justice, and other laws of nature, without a common power to keep them all in awe; we might as well suppose all mankind to do the same; and then there neither would be, nor need to be any civil government, or commonwealth at all; because there would be peace without subjection.

Nor is it enough for the security,

which men desire should last all the time of their life, that they be governed, and directed by one judgment, for a limited time; as in one battle, or one war. For though they obtain a victory by their unanimous endeavour against a foreign enemy; yet afterwards when either they have no common enemy, or he that by one part is held for an enemy, is by another part held for a friend, they must needs by the difference of their interests dissolve, and fall again into a war amongst themselves.

It is true, that certain living creatures, as bees, and ants, live sociably one with another, which are therefore by Aristotle numbered amongst political creatures; and yet have no other direction, than their particular judgments and appetites; nor speech, whereby one of them can signify to another, what he thinks expedient for the common benefit: and therefore some man may perhaps desire to know, why mankind cannot do the same. To which I answer.

First, that men are continually in competition for honour and dignity, which these creatures are not; and consequently amongst men there ariseth on that ground, envy and hatred, and finally war; but amongst these not so.

Secondly, that amongst these creatures, the common good differeth not from the private; and being by nature inclined to their private, they procure thereby the common benefit. But man, whose joy consisteth in comparing himself with other man, can relish nothing but what is eminent.

Thirdly, that these creatures, having not, as man, the use of reason, do not see, nor think they see any fault, in the administration of their common business; whereas amongst men, there are very many, that think themselves wiser, and abler to govern the public, better than the rest; and these strive to reform and innovate, one this way, another that way; and thereby bring it into distraction and civil war.

Fourthly, that these creatures, though they have some use of voice, in making known to one another their desires, and other affections; yet they want that art of words, by which some men can represent to others, that which is good, in the likeness of evil; and evil, in the likeness of good; and augment, or diminish the apparent greatness of good and evil; discontenting men, and troubling their peace at their pleasure.

Fifthly, irrational creatures cannot distinguish between *injury*, and *damage*; and therefore as long as they be at ease, they are not offended with their fellows: whereas man is then most troublesome, when he is most at ease: for then it is that he loves to shew his wisdom, and control the actions of them that govern the commonwealth.

Lastly, the agreement of these creatures is natural; that of men, is by covenant only, which is artificial: and therefore it is no wonder if there be somewhat else required, besides covenant, to make their agreement constant and lasting; which is a common power, to keep them in awe, and to direct their actions to the common benefit.

The only way to erect such a common power, as may be able to defend them from the invasion of foreigners, and the injuries of one another, and thereby to secure them in such sort, as that by their own industry, and by the fruits of the earth, they may nourish themselves and live contentedly; is, to confer all their power and strength upon one man, or upon one assembly of men, that may reduce all their wills, by plurality of voices, unto one will: which is as much as to say, to appoint one man, or assembly of men, to bear their person;

and every one to own, and acknowledge himself to be author of whatsoever he that so beareth their person, shall act, or cause to be acted, in those things which concern the common peace and safety; and therein to submit their wills, every one to his will, and their judgments, to his judgment. This is more than consent, or concord; it is a real unity of them all, in one and the same person, made by covenant of every man with every man, in such manner, as if every man should say to every man, *I authorize and give up my right of governing myself, to this man, or to this assembly of men, on this condition, that thou give up thy right to him, and authorize all his actions in like manner.* This done, the multitude so united in one person, is called a *commonwealth*, in Latin *civitas*. This is the generation of the great *leviathan*, or rather, to speak more reverently, of that *mortal god*, to which we owe under the *immortal God*, our peace and defence. For by this authority, given him by every particular man in the commonwealth, he hath the use of so much power and strength conferred on him, that by terror thereof, he is enabled to perform the wills of them all, to peace at home, and mutual aid against their enemies abroad. And in him consisteth the essence of the commonwealth; which, to define it, is *one person, of whose acts a great multitude, by mutual covenants one with another, have made themselves every one the author, to the end he may use the strength and means of them all, as he shall think expedient, for their peace and common defence.*

And he that carrieth this person, is called *sovereign*, and said to have *sovereign power*; and every one besides, his *subject*.

The attaining to this sovereign power, is by two ways. One, by natural force; as when a man maketh his children, to submit themselves, and their children to his government, as being able to destroy them if they refuse; or by war subdueth his enemies to his will, giving them their lives on that condition. The other, is when men agree amongst themselves, to submit to some man, or assembly of men, voluntarily, on confidence to be protected by him against all others. This latter, may be called a political commonwealth, or commonwealth by *institution*; and the former, a commonwealth by *acquisition*.

38

JOHN RAWLS
Legal Obligation and the Duty of Fair Play

The subject of law and morality suggests many different questions. In particular, it may consider the historical and sociological question as to the way and manner in which moral ideas influence and are influenced by the legal system; or it may involve the question whether moral concepts and principles enter into an adequate definition of law. Again, the topic of law and morality suggests the problem of the legal enforcement of morality and whether the fact that certain conduct is immoral by accepted precepts is sufficient to justify making that conduct a legal offense. Finally, there is the large subject of the study of the rational principles of moral criticism of legal institutions and the moral grounds of our acquiescence in them. I shall be concerned solely with a fragment of this last question: with the grounds for our moral obligation to obey the law, that is, to carry out our legal duties and to fulfill our legal obligations. My thesis is that the moral obligation to obey the law is a special case of the prima facie duty of fair play.

I shall assume, as requiring no argument, that there is, at least in a society such as ours, a moral obligation to obey the law, although it may, of course, be overridden in certain cases by other more stringent obligations. I shall assume also that this obligation must rest on some general moral principle; that is, it must depend on some principle of justice or upon some principle of social utility or the common good, and the like. Now, it may appear to be a truism, and let us suppose it is, that a moral obligation rests on some moral principle. But I mean to exclude the possibility that the obligation to obey the law is based on a special principle of its own. After all, it is not, without further argument, absurd that there is a moral principle such that when we find ourselves subject to an existing system of rules satisfying the definition of a legal system, we have an obligation to obey the law; and such a principle might be final, and not in need of explanation, in the way in which the principles of justice or of promising and the like are final. I do not know of anyone who has said that there is a special principle of legal obligation in this sense. Given a rough agreement, say, on the possible principles as being those of justice, of social utility, and the like, the question has been on which of one or several is the obligation to obey the law founded, and which, if any, has a special importance. I want to give a special place to the principle defining the duty of fair play.

In speaking of one's obligation to obey the law, I am using the term "obligation" in its more limited sense, in which, together with the notion of a duty and of a responsibility, it has a connection with institutional rules. Duties and responsibilities are assigned to certain positions and offices, and obligations are normally the consequence of voluntary acts of persons, and while perhaps most of our obligations are assumed by ourselves, through the making of promises and the accepting of benefits, and so forth, others may put us under obligation to them (as when on some occasion they help us, for example, as children). I should not claim that the moral grounds for our obeying the law is derived from the duty of fair play except insofar as one is referring to an obligation in this sense. It would be incorrect to say that our duty not to commit any of the legal offenses, specifying crimes of violence, is based on the duty of fair play, at least entirely. These crimes involve wrongs as such, and with such offenses, as with the vices of cruelty and greed, our doing them is wrong independently of there being a legal system the benefits of which we have voluntarily accepted.

I shall assume several special features about the nature of the legal order in regard to which a moral obligation arises. In addition to the generally strategic place of its system of rules, as defining and relating the fundamental institutions of society that regulate the pursuit of substantive interests, and to the monopoly of coercive powers, I shall suppose that the legal system in question satisfies the concept of the *rule of law* (or what one may think of as justice as regularity). By this I mean that its rules are public, that similar cases are treated similarly, that there are no bills of attainder, and the like. These are all features of a legal system insofar as it embodies without deviation the notion of a public system of rules addressed to rational beings for the organization of their conduct in the pursuit of their substantive interests. This concept imposes, by itself, no limits on the *content* of legal rules, but only on their regular administration. Finally, I shall assume that the legal order is that of a constitutional democracy: that is, I shall suppose that there is a constitution establishing a position of equal citizenship and securing freedom of the person, freedom of thought and liberty of conscience, and such political equality as in suffrage and the right to participate in the political process. Thus I am confining discussion to a legal system of a special kind, but there is no harm in this.

The moral grounds of legal obligation may be brought out by considering what at first seem to be two anomalous facts: first, that sometimes we have an obligation to obey what we think, and think correctly, is an unjust law; and second, that sometimes we have an obligation to obey a law even in a situation where more good (thought of as a sum of social advantages) would seem to result from not doing so. If the moral obligation to obey the law is founded on the principle of fair play, how can one become bound to obey an unjust law, and what is there about the principle that explains the grounds for forgoing the greater good?

It is, of course, a familiar situation in a constitutional democracy that a person finds himself morally obligated to obey an unjust law. This will be the case whenever a member of the minority, on some legislative proposal, opposes the majority view for reasons of justice. Perhaps the standard case is where the majority, or a coalition sufficient to constitute a majority, takes advantage of its strength and votes in its own interests. But this feature is not essential. A person belonging to the minority may be advantaged by the majority proposal and still oppose it as unjust, yet when it is enacted he will normally be bound by it.

Some have thought that there is ostensibly a paradox of a special kind when a citizen, who votes in accordance with his moral principles (conception of justice), accepts the majority decision when he is in the minority. Let us suppose the vote is between two bills, *A* and *B* each establishing an income tax procedure, rates of progression, or the like, which are contrary to one another. Suppose further that one thinks of the constitutional procedure for enacting legislation as a sort of machine that yields a result when the votes are fed into it—the result being that a certain bill is enacted. The question arises as to how a citizen can accept the machine's choice, which (assuming that *B* gets a majority of the votes) involves thinking that *B* ought to be enacted when, let us suppose, he is of the declared opinion that *A* ought to be enacted. For some the paradox seems to be that in a constitutional democracy a citizen is often put in a situation of believing that both *A* and *B* should be enacted when *A* and *B* are contraries: that *A* should be enacted because *A* is the best policy, and that *B* should be enacted because *B* has a majority—and moreover, and this is essential, that this conflict is different from the usual sort of conflict between prima facie duties.

There are a number of things that may be said about this supposed paradox, and there are several ways in which it may be resolved, each of which brings out an aspect of the situation. But I think the simplest thing to say is to deny straightway that there is anything different in this situation than in any other situation where there is a conflict of prima facie principles. The essential of the matter seems to be as follows: (1) Should *A* or *B* be enacted and implemented, that is, administered? Since it is supposed that everyone accepts the outcome of the vote, within limits, it is appropriate to put the enactment and implementation together. (2) Is *A* or *B* the best policy? It is assumed that everyone votes according to his political opinion as to which is the best policy and that the decision as to how to vote is not based on personal interest. There is no special conflict in this situation: The citizen who knows that he will find himself in the minority believes that, taking into account only the relative merits of *A* and *B* as prospective statutes, and leaving aside how the vote will go, *A* should be enacted and implemented. Moreover, on his own principles he should vote for what he thinks is the best policy, and leave aside how the vote will go. On the other hand, given that a majority will vote for *B*, *B* should be enacted and implemented, and he may know that a majority will vote for *B*. These judgments are relative to different principles (different arguments). The first is based on the person's conception of the best social policy; the second is based on the principles on which he accepts the constitution. The real decision, then, is as follows: A person has to decide, in each case where he is in the minority, whether the nature of the statute is such that, given that it will get, or has got, a majority vote, he should oppose its being implemented, engage in civil disobedience, or take equivalent action. In this situation he simply has to balance his obligation to oppose an unjust statute against his obligation to abide by a just constitution. This is, of course, a difficult situation, but not one introducing any deep logical paradox. Normally, it is hoped that the obligation to the constitution is clearly the decisive one.

Although it is obvious, it may be worthwhile mentioning, since a relevant feature of voting will be brought out, that the result of a vote is that a rule of law is enacted, and although given the fact of its enactment, everyone agrees that it should be implemented, no one is required to believe that the statute enacted represents the best policy. It is consistent to say that another statute would have been better. The vote does not result in a statement to be believed: namely, that B is superior, on its merits, to A. To get this interpretation one would have to suppose that the principles of the constitution specify a device which gathers information as to what citizens think should be done and that the device is so constructed that it always produces from this information the morally correct opinion as to which is the best policy. If in accepting a constitution it was so interpreted, there would, indeed, be a serious paradox: for a citizen would be torn between believing, on his own principles, that A is the best policy, and believing at the same time that B is the best policy as established by the constitutional device, the principles of the design of which he accepts. This conflict could be made a normal one only if one supposed that a person who made his own judgment on the merits was always prepared to revise it given the opinion constructed by the machine. But it is not possible to determine the best policy in this way, nor is it possible for a person to give such an undertaking. What this misinterpretation of the constitutional procedure shows, I think, is that there is an important difference between voting and spending. The constitutional procedure is not, in an essential respect, the same as the market: Given the usual assumptions of perfect competition of price theory, the actions of private persons spending according to their interests will result in the best situation, as judged by the criterion of Pareto. But in a perfectly just constitutional procedure, people voting their political opinions on the merits of policies may or may not reflect the best policy. What this misinterpretation brings out, then, is that when citizens vote for policies on their merits, the constitutional procedure cannot be viewed as acting as the market does, even under ideal conditions. A constitutional procedure does not reconcile differences of opinion into an opinion to be taken as true—this can only be done by argument and reasoning—but rather it decides whose opinion is to determine legislative policy.

Now to turn to the main problem, that of understanding how a person can properly find himself in a position where, by his own principles, he must grant that, given a majority vote, B should be enacted and implemented even though B is unjust. There is, then, the question as to how it can be morally justifiable to acknowledge a constitutional procedure for making legislative enactments when it is certain (for all practical purposes) that laws will be passed that by one's own principles are unjust. It would be impossible for a person to undertake to change his mind whenever he found himself in the minority; it is not impossible, but entirely reasonable, for him to undertake to abide by the enactments made, whatever they are, provided that they are within certain limits. But what more exactly are the conditions of this undertaking?

First of all, it means, as previously suggested, that the constitutional procedure is misinterpreted as a procedure for making legal rules. It is a process of social decision that does not produce a statement to be believed (that *B* is the best policy) but a rule to be followed. Such a procedure, say involving some form of majority rule, is necessary because it is certain that there will be disagreement on what is the best policy. This will be true even if we assume, as I shall, that everyone has a similar sense of justice and everyone is able to agree on a certain constitutional procedure as just. There will be disagreement because they will not approach issues with the same stock of information, they will regard different moral features of situations as carrying different weights, and so on. The acceptance of a constitutional procedure is, then, a necessary political device to decide between conflicting legislative proposals. If one thinks of the constitution as a fundamental part of the scheme of social cooperation, then one can say that if the constitution is just, and if one has accepted the benefits of its working and intends to continue doing so, and if the rule enacted is within certain limits, then one has an obligation, based on the principle of fair play, to obey it when it comes one's turn. In accepting the benefits of a just constitution one becomes bound to it, and in particular one becomes bound to one of its fundamental rules: Given a majority vote in behalf of a statute, it is to be enacted and properly implemented.

The principle of fair play may be defined as follows. Suppose there is a mutually beneficial and just scheme of social cooperation, and that the advantages it yields can only be obtained if everyone, or nearly everyone, cooperates. Suppose further that cooperation requires a certain sacrifice from each person, or at least involves a certain restriction of his liberty. Suppose finally that the benefits produced by cooperation are, up to a certain point, free: that is, the scheme of cooperation is unstable in the sense that if any one person knows that all (or nearly all) of the others will continue to do their part, he will still be able to share a gain from the scheme even if he does not do his part. Under these conditions a person who has accepted the benefits of the scheme is bound by a duty of fair play to do his part and not to take advantage of the free benefit by not cooperating. The reason one must abstain from this attempt is that the existence of the benefit is the result of everyone's effort, and prior to some understanding as to how it is to be shared, if it can be shared at all, it belongs in fairness to no one. (I return to this question below.)

Now I want to hold that the obligation to obey the law, as enacted by a constitutional procedure, even when the law seems unjust to us, is a case of the duty of fair play as defined. It is, moreover, an obligation in the more limited sense in that it depends upon our having accepted and our intention to continue accepting the benefits of a just scheme of cooperation that the constitution defines. In this sense it depends on our own voluntary acts. Again, it is an obligation owed to our fellow citizens generally: that is, to those who cooperate with us in the working of the constitution. It is not an obligation owed to public officials, although there may be such obligations. That it is an obligation owed by citizens to one another is shown by the fact that they are entitled to be indignant with one another for failure to comply. Further, an essential condition of the obligation is the justice of the constitution and the general system of law being roughly in accordance with it. Thus the obligation to obey (or not to resist) an unjust law depends strongly on there being a just constitution. Unless one obeys the law enacted under it, the proper equilibrium, or balance, between competing claims defined by the constitution will not be maintained. Finally, while it is true enough to say that the enactment by a majority binds the minority, so that one may be bound by the acts of others, there is no question of their binding them in conscience to certain beliefs as to what is the best policy, and it is a necessary condition of the acts of others binding us that the constitution is just, that we have accepted its benefits, and so forth.

Now a few remarks about the principles of a just constitution. Here I shall have to presuppose a number of things about the principles of justice. In particular, I shall assume that there are two principles of justice that properly apply to the fundamental structure of institutions of the social system and, thus, to the constitution. The first of these principles requires that everyone have an equal right to the most extensive liberty compatible with a like liberty for all; the second is that inequalities are arbitrary unless it is reasonable to expect that they will work out for everyone's advantage and provided that the positions and offices to which they attach or from which they may be gained are open to all. I shall assume that these are the principles that can be derived by imposing the constraints of morality upon rational and mutually self-interested persons when they make conflicting claims

on the basic form of their common institutions: that is, when questions of justice arise.

The principle relevant at this point is the first principle, that of equal liberty. I think it may be argued with some plausibility that it requires, where it is possible, the various equal liberties in a constitutional democracy. And once these liberties are established and constitutional procedures exist, one can view legislation as rules enacted that must be ostensibly compatible with both principles. Each citizen must decide as best he can whether a piece of legislation, say the income tax, violates either principle; and this judgment depends on a wide body of social facts. Even in a society of impartial and rational persons, one cannot expect agreement on these matters.

Now recall that the question is this: How is it possible that a person, in accordance with his own conception of justice, should find himself bound by the acts of another to obey an unjust law (not simply a law contrary to his interests)? Put another way: Why, when I am free and still without my chains, should I accept certain a priori conditions to which any social contract must conform, a priori conditions that rule out all constitutional procedures that would decide in accordance with my judgment of justice against everyone else? To explain this (Little has remarked),[1] we require two hypotheses: that among the very limited number of procedures that would stand any chance

1. The metaphor of being free and without one's chains is taken from I. M. D. Little's review of K. Arrow's book *Social Choice and Individual Values*, (New York, 1951) which appeared in *Journal of Political Economy*, LX (1952). See p. 431. My argument follows his in all essential respects, the only addition being that I have introduced the concept of justice in accounting for what is, in effect, Arrow's nondictatorship condition.

of being established, none would make my decision decisive in this way; and that all such procedures would determine social conditions that I judge to be better than anarchy. Granting the second hypothesis, I want to elaborate on this in the following way: The first step in the explanation is to derive the principles of justice that are to apply to the basic form of the social system and, in particular, to the constitution. Once we have these principles, we see that no just constitutional procedure would make my judgment as to the best policy decisive (would make me a dictator in Arrow's sense).[2] It is not simply that, among the limited number of procedures actually possible as things are, no procedure would give me this authority. The point is that even if such were possible, given some extraordinary social circumstances, it would not be just. (Of course it is not possible for everyone to have this authority). Once we see this, we see how it is possible that within the framework of a just constitutional procedure to which we are obligated, it may nevertheless happen that we are bound to obey what seems to us to be and is an unjust law. Moreover, the possibility is present even though everyone has the same sense of justice (that is, accepts the same principles of justice) and everyone regards the constitutional procedure itself as just. Even the most efficient constitution cannot prevent the enactment of unjust laws if, from the complexity of the social situation and like conditions, the majority decides to enact them. A just constitutional procedure cannot foreclose all injustice; this depends on those who carry out the procedure. A constitutional procedure is not like a market reconciling interests to an optimum result.

So far I have been discussing the first mentioned anomaly of legal obligation, namely, that though it is founded on justice, we may be required to obey an unjust law. I should now like to include the second anomaly: that we may have an obligation to obey the law even though more good (thought of as a sum of advantages) may be gained by not doing so. The thesis I wish to argue is that not only is our obligation to obey the law a special case of the principle of fair play, and so dependent upon the justice of the institutions to which we are obligated, but also the principles of justice are absolute with respect to the principle of utility (as the principle to maximize the net sum of advantages). By this I mean two things. First, unjust institutions cannot be justified by an appeal to the principle of utility. A greater balance of net advantages shared by some cannot justify the injustice suffered by others; and where unjust institutions are tolerable it is because a certain degree of injustice sometimes cannot be avoided, that social necessity requires it, that there would be greater injustice otherwise, and so on. Second, our obligation to obey the law, which is a special case of the principle of fair play, cannot be overridden by an appeal to utility, though it may be overridden by another duty of justice. These are sweeping propositions and most likely false, but I should like to examine them briefly.

I do not know how to establish these propositions. They are not established by the sort of argument used above to show that the two principles, previously mentioned, are the two principles of justice, that is, when the subject is the basic structure of the social system. What such an argument might show is that, if certain natural condi-

2. See Arrow, *opus cit. supra.*

tions are taken as specifying the concept of justice, then the two principles of justice are the principles logically associated with the concept when the subject is the basic structure of the social system. The argument might prove, if it is correct, that the principles of justice are incompatible with the principle of utility. The argument might establish that our intuitive notions of justice must sometimes conflict with the principle of utility. But it leaves unsettled what the more general notion of right requires when this conflict occurs. To prove that the concept of justice should have an absolute weight with respect to that of utility would require a deeper argument based on an analysis of the concept of right, at least insofar as it relates to the concepts of justice and utility. I have no idea whether such an analysis is possible. What I propose to do instead is to try out the thought that the concept of justice does have an absolute weight, and to see whether this suggestion, in view of our considered moral opinions, lead to conclusions that we cannot accept. It would seem as if to attribute to justice an absolute weight is to interpret the concept of right as requiring that a special place be given to persons capable of a sense of justice and to the principle of their working together, from an initial position of equality, the form of their common institutions. To the extent that this idea is attractive, the concept of justice will tend to have an absolute weight with respect to utility.

Now to consider the two anomalous cases. First: In the situation where the obligation requires obedience to an unjust law, it seems true to say that the obligation depends on the principle of fair play and, thus, on justice. Suppose it is a matter of a person being required to pay an income tax of a kind that he thinks is unjust, not simply by reference to his interests. He would not want to try to justify the tax on the ground that the net gain to certain groups in society is such as to outweigh the injustice. The natural argument to make is to his obligation to a just constitution.

But in considering a particular issue, a citizen has to make two decisions: how he will vote (and I assume that he votes for what he thinks is the best policy, morally speaking), and, in case he should be in the minority, whether his obligation to support, or not obstruct, the implementation of the law enacted is not overridden by a stronger obligation that may lead to a number of courses including civil disobedience. Now in the sort of case imagined, suppose there is a real question as to whether the tax law should be obeyed. Suppose, for example, that it is framed in such a way that it seems deliberately calculated to undermine unjustly the position of certain social or religious groups. Whether the law should be obeyed or not depends, if one wants to emphasize the notion of justice, on such matters as (1) the justice of the constitution and the real opportunity it allows for reversal; (2) the depth of the injustice of the law enacted; (3) whether the enactment is actually a matter of calculated intent by the majority and warns of further such acts; and (4) whether the political sociology of the situation is such as to allow of hope that the law may be repealed. Certainly, if a social or religious group reasonably (not irrationally) and correctly supposes that a permanent majority, or majority coalition, has deliberately set out to undercut its basis and that there is no chance of successful constitutional resistance, then the obligation to obey that particular law (and perhaps other laws more generally) ceases. In such a case a minority may no longer be obligated by the duty of fair play. There may be other reasons, of course, at least for a time, for obeying the law. One might say that disobedience will not improve the justice of their situation or of their descendants' situation; or that it will result in injury and harm to innocent persons (that is, members not belonging to the unjust majority). In this way, one might appeal to the balance of justice, if the principle of not causing injury to the innocent is a question of justice; but, in any case, the appeal is not made to the greater net balance of advantages (irrespective of the moral position of those receiving them). The thesis I want to suggest then, is that in considering whether we are obligated to obey an unjust law, one is led into no absurdity if one simply throws out the principle of utility altogether, except insofar as it is included in the general principle requiring one to establish the most efficient just institutions.

Second: Now the other sort of anomaly arises when the law is just and we have a duty of fair play to follow it, but a greater net balance of advantages could be gained from not doing so. Again, the income tax will serve to illustrate this familiar point: The social consequences of any one person (perhaps even many people) not paying his tax are unnoticeable, and let us suppose zero in value, but there is a noticeable private gain for the person himself, or for another to whom he chooses to give it (the institution of the income tax is subject to the first kind of instability). The duty of fair play binds us to pay our tax, nevertheless, since we have accepted, and intend to continue doing so, the benefits of the fiscal system to which the income tax belongs. Why is this reasonable and not a blind following of a rule, when a greater net sum of advantages is pos-

sible?—because the system of cooperation consistently followed by everyone else itself produces the advantages generally enjoyed and in the case of a practice such as the income tax there is no reason to given exemptions to anyone so that they might enjoy the possible benefit. (An analogous case is the moral obligation to vote and so to work the constitutional procedure from which one has benefited. This obligation cannot be overridden by the fact that our vote never makes a difference in the outcome of an election; it may be overridden, however, by a number of other considerations, such as a person being disenchanted with all parties, being excusably uninformed, and the like.)

There are cases, on the other hand, where a certain number of exemptions can be arranged for in a just or fair way; and if so, the practice, including the exemptions, is more efficient, and when possible it should be adopted (waiving problems of transition) in accordance with the principle of establishing the most efficient just practice. For example, in the familiar instance of the regulation to conserve water in a drought, it might be ascertained that there would be no harm in a certain extra use of water over and above the use for drinking. In this case some rotation scheme can be adopted that allots exemptions in a fair way, such as houses on opposite sides of the street being given exemptions on alternate days. The details are not significant here. The main idea is simply that if the greater sum of advantages can effectively and fairly be distributed amongst those whose cooperation makes these advantages possible, then this should be done. It would indeed be irrational to prefer a lesser to a more efficient just scheme of cooperation; but this fact is not to be confused with justifying an unjust scheme by its greater efficiency or excusing ourselves from a duty of fair play, the equilibrium between conflicting claims, as defined by possible benefit, as in the case of the income tax, or in the case of voting, or if there is no way to do so that does not involve such problems as excessive costs, then the benefit should be foregone. One may disagree with this view, but it is not irrational, not a matter of rule worship: It is, rather, an appeal to the duty of fair play, which requires one to abstain from an advantage that cannot be distributed fairly to those whose efforts have made it possible. That those who make the efforts and undergo the restrictions of their liberty should share in the benefits produced is a consequence of the assumption of an initial position of equality, and it falls under the second principle. But the question of distributive justice is too involved to go into here. Moreover, it is unlikely that there is any substantial social benefit for the distribution of which some fair arrangement cannot be made.

To summarize, I have suggested that the following propositions may be true:

First, that our moral obligation to obey the law is a special case of the duty of fair play. This means that the legal order is construed as a system of social cooperation to which we become bound because: first, the scheme is just (that is, it satisfies the two principles of justice), and no just scheme can ensure against our ever being in the minority in a vote; and second, we have accepted, and intend to continue to accept, its benefits. If we failed to obey the law, to act on our duty of fair play, the equilibrium between conflicting claims, as defined by the concept of justice, would be upset. The duty of fair play is not, of course, intended to account for its being wrong for us to commit crimes of violence, but it is intended to account, in part, for the obligation to pay our income tax, to vote, and so on.

Second, I then suggested that the concept of justice has an absolute weight with respect to the principle of utility (not necessarily with respect to other moral concepts). By that I meant that the union of the two concepts of justice and utility must take the form of the principle of establishing the most efficient just institution. This means that an unjust institution or law cannot be justified by an appeal to a greater net sum of advantages, and that the duty of fair play cannot be analogously overridden. An unjust institution or law or the overriding of the duty of fair play can be justified only by a greater balance of justice. I know of no way to prove this proposition. It is not proved by the analytic argument to show that the principles of justice are indeed the principles of justice. But I think it may be shown that the principle to establish the most efficient just institutions does not lead to conclusions counter to our intuitive judgments and that it is not in any way irrational. It is, moreover, something of a theoretical simplification, in that one does not have to balance justice against utility. But this simplification is no doubt not a real one, since it is as difficult to ascertain the balance of justice as anything else.

39

CHARLES FRANKEL
The Morality of Civil Disobedience

CHARLES FRANKEL is professor of philosophy at Columbia University and the author of several books, including *The Case for Modern Man* (1956), *The Democratic Prospect* (1962), and *The Love of Anxiety* (1965). He is a former Assistant Secretary of State for Educational and Cultural Affairs. This article was written during the early 1960s, when the American civil rights movement was at its peak.

For some time past an old and troublesome philosophical issue has been at the center of public events, and it is likely to remain there for some time to come. This is the question of the morality of civil disobedience. A teachers' union threatens a strike even though a state law prohibits strikes by public employees; advocates of civil rights employ mass demonstrations of disobedience to the law to advance their cause; the governor of a Southern state deliberately obstructs the enforcement of federal laws, and declares himself thoroughly within his rights in doing so. An observer can approve the motives that lead to some of these actions and disapprove others. All, nevertheless, raise the same fundamental question: Does the individual have the right—or perhaps the duty—to disobey the law when his mind, his conscience, or his religious faith tells him that the law is unjust?

The question is as old as Socrates. It has regularly propelled men into radical examination of the premises of personal morality and civic obligation and, indeed, of government itself. And it is an interesting question not only for its philosophical implications but because it has always been a painfully practical question as well, and never more so than today.

Our period in history is frequently described as "materialistic" and "conformist," an age in which governments have enormous powers to crush the bodies and anesthetize the minds of their subjects, and in which the great masses of men and women—presumably in contrast with men and women of other times—prefer to play it safe rather than raise questions of basic moral principle. It is to the point to note, however, that massive resistance to law, justified in the name of higher moral principles like "freedom," "equality," and "national independence," has been a conspicuous feature of our period, and one of its most effective techniques of social action. Millions of ordinary people with no pretensions to being either heroes or saints have employed it in India, in South Africa, in the resistance movements against the Nazis, and in the struggle for equality for Negroes in the United States.

Moreover, such massive resistance to law is by no means confined only to supremely glorious or dangerous causes; nor is it used only by revolutionaries, underdogs, or outsiders. During Prohibition, a large number of respectable, conservative Americans dutifully broke the law in defense of what they regarded as an inalienable human right. In this

From Charles Frankel, "The Morality of Civil Disobedience," *The New York Times Magazine,* January 12, 1964. © 1964 by the New York Times Company. Reprinted by permission. This article is reprinted unabridged.

case, doing one's duty happened also to be agreeable and even fashionable, but this does not change the fact that many right-thinking citizens, who today condemn pacifists or integrationists for using illegal methods to advance their cause, have themselves used such methods happily and unashamedly.

When is it justified, then, for the citizen to act as his own legislator and to decide that he will or will not obey a given law?

An answer that covers all the issues this question raises cannot be given here, nor can a set of principles be proposed that will allow anyone to make automatic and infallible judgments concerning the legitimacy or illegitimacy of specific acts of civil disobedience. Such judgments require detailed knowledge of the facts of specific cases, and such knowledge is often unavailable to the outsider. Nevertheless, it is possible to indicate some of the principal issues that are raised by civil disobedience, some of the more common mistakes that are made in thinking about these issues, and, at least in outline, the approach that one man would take toward such issues.

We can begin, it seems to me, by rejecting one extreme position. This is the view that disobedience to the law can never be justified in any circumstances. To take this position is to say one of two things: either every law that exists is a just law, or a greater wrong is always done by breaking the law. The first statement is plainly false. The second is highly doubtful. If it is true, then the signers of the Declaration of Independence, and those Germans who refused to carry out Hitler's orders, committed acts of injustice.

It is possible, however, to take a much more moderate and plausible version of this position, and many quite reasonable people do. Such people concede that disobedience to the law can sometimes be legitimate and necessary under a despotic regime. They argue, however, that civil disobedience can never be justified in a democratic society, because such a society provides its members with legal instruments for the redress of their grievances.

This is one of the standard arguments that is made, often quite sincerely, against the activities of people like supporters of the Congress of Racial Equality, who set about changing laws they find objectionable by dramatically breaking them. Such groups are often condemned for risking disorder and for spreading disrespect for the law when, so it is maintained, they could accomplish their goals a great deal more fairly and patriotically by staying within the law, and confining themselves to the courts and to methods of peaceful persuasion.

Now it is perfectly true, I believe, that there is a stronger case for obedience to the law, including bad law, in a democracy than in a dictatorship. The people who must abide by the law have presumably been consulted, and they have legal channels through which to express their protests and to work for reform. One way to define democracy is to say that it is a system whose aim is to provide alternatives to civil disobedience. Nevertheless, when applied to the kind of situation faced, say, by CORE, these generalizations, it seems to me, become cruelly abstract.

The basic fallacy in the proposition that, in a democracy, civil disobedience can never be justified, is that it confuses the *ideals* or *aims* of democracy with the inevitably less than perfect accomplishments of democracy at any given moment. In accordance with democratic ideals, the laws of a democracy may give rights and powers to individuals which, in theory, enable them to work legally for the elimination of injustices. In actual fact, however, these rights and powers may be empty. The police may be hostile, the courts biased, the elections rigged—and the legal remedies available to the individual may be unavailing against these evils.

Worse still, the majority may have demonstrated, in a series of free and honest elections, that it is unwavering in its support of what the minority regards as an unspeakable evil. This is obviously the case today in many parts of the South, where the white majority is either opposed to desegregation or not so impatient to get on with it as is the Negro minority. Are we prepared to say that majorities never err? If not, there is no absolutely conclusive reason why we must invariably give the results of an election greater weight than considerations of elementary justice.

It is true, of course, that one swallow does not make a summer, and that the test of legal democratic processes is not this or that particular success or failure, but rather the general direction in which these processes move over the long run. Still, the position that violation of the law is never justifiable so long as there are legal alternatives overstates this important truth. It fails to face at least three important exceptions to it.

In the first place, dramatic disobedience to the law by a minority may be the only effective way of catching the attention or winning the support of the majority. Most classic cases of civil disobedience, from the early Christians to Gandhi and his supporters, exemplify this truth. Civil disobedience, like almost no other technique, can shame a majority and make it ask itself just how far it is willing to go, just how seriously it really is committed to defending the status quo.

Second, there is the simple but painful factor of time. If a man is holding you down on a bed of nails, it is all very well for a bystander to say that you live in a great country in which there are legal remedies for your condition, and that you ought, therefore, to be patient and wait for these remedies to take effect. But your willingness to listen to this counsel will depend, quite properly, on the nature of the injury you are suffering.

Third, it is baseless prejudice to assume that observance of the law is *always* conducive to strengthening a democratic system while disobedience to the law can never have a salutary effect. A majority's complacent acquiescence in bad laws can undermine the faith of a minority in the power of democratic methods to rectify manifest evils; yet a vigorous democracy depends on the existence of minorities holding just such a faith. Disobedience to bad laws can sometimes jolt democratic processes into motion. Which strengthens one's hope for democracy more—the behavior of the Negroes in Birmingham who broke municipal ordinances when they staged their protest marches, or the behavior of the police, using dogs and fire hoses to assert their legal authority?

Another factor should also be taken into account. In our federal system, there are often legitimate doubts concerning the legal validity, under our Constitution, of various state or local ordinances. Disobedience to these laws is in many cases simply a practical, though painful, way of testing their legality. But even where no thought of such a test is involved, there is often present a moral issue which no one can easily dodge—least of all the man whose personal dignity and self-respect are caught up in the issue. A citizen caught in a conflict between local laws and what he thinks will be upheld as the superior federal law can sometimes afford to wait until the courts have determined the issue for him. But often he cannot afford to wait, or must take a stand in order to force a decision. This is the situation of many Negro citizens in Southern states as they confront the conflict between local and federal laws.

Yet there is another side to the story. It would be a mistake to conclude from what has been said that civil disobedience is justified, provided only that it is disobedience in the name of higher principles. Strong moral conviction is not all that is required to turn breaking the law into service to society.

Civil disobedience is not simply like other acts in which men stand up courageously for their principles. It involves violation of the law. And the law can make no provision for its violation except to hold the offender liable to punishment. This is why President Kennedy was in such a delicate position at the time of the Negro demonstrations in Birmingham. He gave many signs that, as an individual, he was in sympathy with the goals of the demonstrators. As a political leader, he probably realized that these goals could not be attained without dramatic actions that crossed the line into illegality. But as Chief Executive he could not give permission or approval to such actions.

We may admire a man like Martin Luther King, who is prepared to defy the authorities in the name of a principle, and we may think that he is entirely in the right; just the same, his right to break the law cannot be officially recognized. No society, whether free or tyrannical, can give its citizens the right to break its laws: To ask it to do so is to ask it to proclaim, as a matter of law,

that its laws are not laws. If anybody ever has a right to break the law, this cannot be a legal right under the law. It has to be a moral right against the law. And this moral right is not an unlimited right to disobey any law which one regards as unjust. It is a right that is hedged about, it seems to me, with important restrictions.

First of all, the exercise of this right is subject to standards of just and fair behavior. I may be correct, for example, in thinking that an ordinance against jaywalking is an unnecessary infringement of my rights. This does not make it reasonable, however, for me to organize a giant sit-down strike in the streets which holds up traffic for a week. Conformity to the concept of justice requires that there be some proportion between the importance of the end one desires to attain and the power of the means one employs to attain it.

When applied to civil disobedience, this principle constitutes a very large restriction. Civil disobedience is an effort to change the law by making it impossible to enforce the law, or by making the price of such enforcement extremely high. It is a case, as it were, of holding the legal system to ransom. It can arouse extreme passions on one side or the other, excite and provoke the unbalanced, and make disrespect for the law a commonplace and popular attitude.

Moreover, although violence may be no part of the intention of those who practice civil disobedience, the risks of violence are present, and are part of what must be taken into account when a program of civil disobedience is being contemplated. In short, civil disobedience is a grave enterprise. It may sometimes be justified, but the provocation for it has to be equally grave. Basic principles have to be at issue. The evils being combated have to be serious evils that are liable to endure unless they are fought. And there should be reasonable grounds to believe that legal methods of fighting them are likely to be insufficient by themselves.

Nor is this the only limitation on the individual's moral right to disobey the law. The most important limitation is that his cause must be a just one. It was right for General de Gaulle to disobey Marshal Pétain; it was wrong for the commanders of the French Army in Algeria, twenty years later, to disobey General de Gaulle. Similarly, if it is absolutely necessary, and if the consequences have been properly weighed, then it is right to break the law in order to eliminate inequalities based on race. But it can never be necessary, and no weighing of consequences can ever make it right, to break the law in the name of Nazi principles. In sum, the goals of those who disobey the law have to lie at the very heart of what we regard as morality before we can say that they have a moral right to do what they are doing.

But who is to make these difficult decisions? Who is to say that one man's moral principles are right and another man's wrong? We come here to the special function that civil disobedience serves in a society. The man who breaks the law on the ground that the law is immoral asks the rest of us, in effect, to trust him, or to trust those he trusts, in preference to the established conventions and authorities of our society. He has taken a large and visible chance, and implicitly asked us to join him in taking that chance, on the probity of his personal moral judgment. In doing so, he has put it to us whether we are willing to take a similar chance on the probity of our own judgment.

Thomas Hobbes, who knew the trouble that rebels and dissenters convinced of their rectitude could cause, once remarked that a man may be convinced that God has commanded him to act as he has, but that God, after all, does not command other men to believe that this is so. The man who chooses to disobey the law on grounds of principle may be a saint, but he may also be a madman. He may be a courageous and lonely individualist, but he may also merely be taking orders and following his own crowd. Whatever he may be, however, his existence tends to make us painfully aware that we too are implicitly making choices, and must bear responsibility for the ones we make.

This, indeed, may be the most important function of those who practice civil disobedience. They remind us that the man who obeys the law has as much of an obligation to look into the morality of his acts and the rationality of his society as does the man who breaks the law. The occurrence of civil disobedience can never be a happy phenomenon; when it is justified, something is seriously wrong with the society in which it takes place. But the man who puts his conscience above the law, though he may be right or he may be wrong, does take personal moral responsibility for the social arrangements under which he lives. And so he dramatizes the fascinating and fearful possibility that those who obey the law might do the same. They might obey the law and support what exists, not out of habit or fear, but because they have freely chosen to do so, and are prepared to live with their consciences after having made that choice.

40

HENRY DAVID THOREAU
There Is No Obligation to Obey the Law

HENRY DAVID THOREAU (1817–1862), American transcendentalist philosopher, first delivered his essay on civil disobedience, from which this article is excerpted, as a lecture explaining his refusal to pay state taxes in protest over the Mexican war, Southern slavery, the treatment of Indians, and other injustices. His collected works fill twenty volumes.

I heartily accept the motto—"That government is best which governs least"; and I should like to see it acted up to more rapidly and systematically. Carried out, it finally amounts to this, which also I believe—"That government is best which governs not at all"; and when men are prepared for it, that will be the kind of government which they will have. Government is at best but an expedient; but most governments are usually, and all governments are sometimes, inexpedient. The objections which have been brought against a standing army, and they are many and weighty, and deserve to prevail, may also at last be brought against a standing government. The standing army is only an arm of the standing government. The standing government itself, which is only the mode which the people have chosen to execute their will, is equally liable to be abused and perverted before the people can act through it. Witness the present Mexican war, the work of comparatively a few individuals using the standing government as their tool; for, in the outset, the people would not have consented to this measure.

This American government—what is it but a tradition, though a recent one, endeavoring to transmit itself unimpaired to posterity, but each instant losing some of its integrity? It has not the vitality and force of a single living man; for a single man can bend it to his will. It is a sort of wooden gun to the people themselves. But it is not the less necessary for this; for the people must have some complicated machinery or other, and hear its din, to satisfy that idea of government which they have. Governments show thus how successfully men can be imposed on, even impose on themselves, for their own advantage. It is excellent, we must all allow. Yet this government never of itself furthered any enterprise, but by the alacrity with which it got out of its way. *It* does not keep the country free. *It* does not settle the West. *It* does not educate. The character inherent in the American people has done all that has been accomplished; and it would have done somewhat more, if the government had not sometimes got in its way. For government is an expedient by which men would fain succeed in letting one another alone; and, as has been said, when it is most expedient, the governed are most let alone by it. Trade and commerce, if they were not made of India-rubber, would never manage to bounce over the obstacles which legislators are continually putting in their way; and, if one were to judge these men wholly by the effects of their actions and not partly by their intentions, they would deserve to be classed and pun-

Excerpted from Henry David Thoreau, *Civil Disobedience* (1849).

ished with those mischievous persons who put obstructions on the railroads.

But, to speak practically and as a citizen, unlike those who call themselves no-government men, I ask for, not at once no government, but *at once* a better government. Let every man make known what kind of government would command his respect, and that will be one step toward obtaining it.

After all, the practical reason why, when the power is once in the hands of the people, a majority are permitted, and for a long period continue, to rule, is not because they are most likely to be in the right, nor because this seems fairest to the minority, but because they are physically the strongest. But a government in which the majority rule in all cases cannot be based on justice, even as far as men understand it. Can there not be a government in which majorities do not virtually decide right and wrong, but conscience?—in which majorities decide only those questions to which the rule of expediency is applicable? Must the citizen ever for a moment, or in the least degree, resign his conscience to the legislator? Why has every man a conscience, then? I think that we should be men first, and subjects afterward. It is not desirable to cultivate a respect for the law, so much as for the right. The only obligation which I have a right to assume, is to do at any time what I think right. It is truly enough said, that a corporation has no conscience; but a corporation of conscientious men is a corporation *with* a conscience. Law never made men a whit more just; and, by means of their respect for it, even the well-disposed are daily made the agents of injustice. A common and natural result of an undue respect for law is, that you may see a file of soldiers, colonel, captain, corporal, privates, powder-monkeys, and all, marching in admirable order over hill and dale, to the wars, against their wills, ay, against their common sense and consciences, which makes it very steep marching indeed, and produces a palpitation of the heart. They have no doubt that it is a damnable business in which they are concerned; they are all peaceably inclined. Now, what are they? Men at all? or small movable forts and magazines, at the service of some unscrupulous man in power? Visit the Navy-Yard, and behold a marine, such a man as an American government can make, or such as it can make a man with its black arts—a mere shadow and reminiscence of humanity, a man laid out alive and standing, and already, as one may say, buried under arms with funeral accompaniments, though it may be—

"Not a drum was heard, not a funeral note,
 As his corpse to the rampart we hurried;
Not a soldier discharged his farewell shot
 O'er the grave where our hero we buried."

The mass of men serve the state thus, not as men mainly, but as machines, with their bodies. They are the standing army, and the militia, jailers, constables, posse comitatus, &c. In most cases there is no free exercise whatever of the judgment or of the moral sense; but they put themselves on a level with wood and earth and stones; and wooden men can perhaps be manufactured that will serve the purpose as well. Such command no more respect than men of straw or a lump of dirt. They have the same sort of worth only as horses and dogs. Yet such as these even are commonly esteemed good citizens. Others—as most legislators, politicians, lawyers, ministers, and officeholders—serve the state chiefly with their heads; and, as they rarely make any moral distinctions, they are as likely to serve the Devil, without *intending* it, as God. A very few, as heroes, patriots, martyrs, reformers in the great sense, and *men,* serve the state with the consciences also, and so necessarily resist it for the most part; and they are commonly treated as enemies by it. A wise man will only be useful as a man, and will not submit to be "clay," and "stop a hole to keep the wind away," but leave that office to his dust at least:

> *"I am too high-born to be propertied,*
> *To be a secondary at control,*
> *Or useful serving-man and instrument*
> *To any sovereign state throughout the*
> *world."*

He who gives himself entirely to his fellow-men appears to them useless and selfish; but he who gives himself partially to them is pronounced a benefactor and philanthropist.

How does it become a man to behave toward this American government to-day? I answer, that he cannot without disgrace be associated with it. I cannot for an instant recognize the political organization as *my* government which is the *slave's government also.*

All men recognize the right of revolution; that is the right to refuse allegiance to, and to resist, the government, when its tyranny or its inefficiency are great and unendurable. But almost all say that such is not the case now. But such was the case, they think, in the Revolution of '75. If one were to tell me that this was a bad government because it taxed certain foreign commodities brought to its ports, it is most probable that I should not make an ado about it, for I can do without them. All machines have their friction; and possibly this does enough good to counterbalance the evil. At any rate, it is a great evil to make a stir about it. But when the friction

comes to have its machine, and oppression and robbery are organized, I say, let us not have such a machine any longer. In other words, when a sixth of the population of a nation which has undertaken to be the refuge of liberty are slaves, and a whole country is unjustly overrun and conquered by a foreign army, and subjected to military law, I think that it is not too soon for honest men to rebel and revolutionize. What makes this duty the more urgent is the fact, that the country so overrun is not our own, but ours is the invading army. . . .

All voting is a sort of gaming, like checkers or backgammon, with a slight moral tinge to it, a playing with right and wrong, with moral questions; and betting naturally accompanies it. The character of the voters is not staked. I cast my vote, perchance, as I think right; but I am not vitally concerned that that right should prevail. I am willing to leave it to the majority. Its obligation, therefore, never exceeds that of expediency. Even voting *for the right* is *doing* nothing for it. It is only expressing to men feebly your desire that it should prevail. A wise man will not leave the right to the mercy of chance, not wish it to prevail through the power of the majority. There is but little virtue in the action of masses of men. When the majority shall at length vote for the abolition of slavery, it will be because they are indifferent to slavery, or because there is but little slavery left to be abolished by their vote. *They* will then be the only slaves. Only *his* vote can hasten the abolition of slavery who asserts his own freedom by his vote. . . .

It is not a man's duty, as a matter of course, to devote himself to the eradication of any, even the most enormous wrong; he may still properly have other concerns to engage him; but it is his duty, at least, to wash his hands of it, and, if he gives it no thought longer, not to give it practically his support. If I devote myself to other pursuits and contemplations, I must first see, at least, that I do not pursue them sitting upon another man's shoulders. I must get off him first, that he may pursue his contemplations too. See what gross inconsistency is tolerated. I have heard some of my townsmen say, "I should like to have them order me out to help put down an insurrection of the slaves, or to march to Mexico—see if I would go"; and yet these very men have each, directly by their allegiance, and so indirectly, at least, by their money, furnished a substitute. The soldier is applauded who refuses to serve in an unjust war by those who do not refuse to sustain the unjust government which makes the war; is applauded by those whose own act and authority he disregards and sets at naught; as if the State were penitent to that degree that it hired one to scourge it while it sinned, but not to that degree that it left off sinning for a moment. Thus, under the name of Order and Civil Government, we are all made at last to pay homage to and support our own meanness. After the first blush of sin comes its indifference; and from immoral it becomes, as it were, *un*moral, and not quite unnecessary to that life which we have made.

The broadest and most prevalent error requires the most disinterested virtue to sustain it. The slight reproach to which the virtue of patriotism is commonly liable, the noble are most likely to incur. Those who, while they disapprove of the character and measures of a government, yield to it their allegiance and support, are undoubtedly its most conscientious supporters, and so frequently the most serious obstacles to reform. Some are petitioning the State to dissolve the Union, to disregard the requisitions of the President. Why do they not dissolve it themselves—the union between themselves and the State—and refuse to pay their quota into its treasury? Do not they stand in the same relation to the State, that the State does to the Union? And have not the same reasons prevented the State from resisting the Union, which have prevented them from resisting the State?

How can a man be satisfied to entertain an opinion merely, and enjoy *it*? Is there any enjoyment in it, if his opinion is that he is aggrieved? If you are cheated out of a single dollar by your neighbor, you do not rest satisfied with knowing that you are cheated, or with saying that you are cheated, or even with petitioning him to pay you your due; but you take effectual steps at once to obtain the full amount, and see that you are never cheated again. Action from principle, the perception and the performance of right, changes things and relations; it is essentially revolutionary, and does not consist wholly with anything which was. It not only divides states and churches, it divides families; ay, it divides the *individual*, separating the diabolical in him from the divine.

Unjust laws exist: shall we be content to obey them, or shall we endeavor to amend them, and obey them until we have succeeded, or shall we transgress them at once? Men generally, under such a government as this, think that they ought to wait until they have persuaded the majority to alter them. They think that, if they should resist, the remedy would be worse than the evil. But it is the fault of the government itself that the remedy *is* worse than the evil. *It* makes it worse. Why is it not more apt to anticipate and provide for reform? Why does it not cherish its wise minority? Why does it cry and resist before it is hurt? Why does it not encourage its citizens to be on the alert to point out its faults, and *do* better than it would have them? Why does it always crucify Christ, and excommunicate Copernicus and Luther, and pronounce Washington and Franklin rebels?

One would think, that a deliberate and practical denial of its authority was the only offence never contemplated by government; else, why has it not assigned its definite, its suitable and proportionate penalty? If a man who has no property refuses but once to earn nine shillings for the State, he is put in prison for a period unlimited by any law that I know, and determined only by the discretion of those who placed him there; but if he should steal ninety times nine shillings from the State, he is soon permitted to go at large again.

If the injustice is part of the necessary friction of the machine of government, let it go, let it go: perchance it will wear smooth—certainly the machine will wear out. If the injustice has a spring, or a pulley, or a rope, or a crank, exclusively for itself, then perhaps you may consider whether the remedy will not be worse than the evil; but if it is of such a nature that it requires you to be the agent of injustice to another, then, I say, break the law. Let your life be a counter friction to stop the machine. What I have to do is to see, at any rate, that I do not lend myself to the wrong which I condemn.

As for adopting the ways which the State has provided for remedying the evil, I know not of such ways. They take too much time, and a man's life will be gone. I have other affairs to attend to. I came into this world, not chiefly to make this a good place to live in, but to live in it, be it good or bad. A man has not everything to do, but something; and because he cannot do *everything*, it is not necessary that he should do *something* wrong. It is not my business to be petitioning the Governor or the Legislature any more than it is theirs to petition me; and, if they should not hear my petition, what should I do then? But in this case the state has provided no way: its very Constitution is the evil. This may seem to be harsh and stubborn and unconciliatory; but it is to treat with the utmost kindness and consideration the only spirit that can appreciate or deserves it. So is all change for the better, like birth and death, which convulse the body. . . .

41

JOHN STUART MILL
The Limits to the Authority of the State over the Individual

What, then, is the rightful limit to the sovereignty of the individual over himself? Where does the authority of society begin? How much of human life should be assigned to individuality, and how much to society?

Each will receive its proper share, if

Excerpted from John Stuart Mill, *On Liberty* (1859), ch. 4.

each has that which more particularly concerns it. To individuality should belong the part of life in which it is chiefly the individual that is interested; to society, the part which chiefly interests society.

Though society is not founded on a contract, and though no good purpose is answered by inventing a contract in order to deduce social obligations from it, every one who receives the protection of society owes a return for the benefit, and the fact of living in society renders it indispensable that each should be found to observe a certain line of conduct towards the rest. This conduct consists, first, in not injuring the interests of one another; or rather certain interests, which, either by express legal provision or by tacit understanding, ought to be considered as rights; and secondly, in each person's bearing his share (to be fixed on some equitable principle) of the labours and sacrifices incurred for defending the society or its members from injury and molestation. These conditions society is justified in enforcing, at all costs to those who endeavour to withhold fulfillment. Nor is this all that society may do. The acts of an individual may be hurtful to others, or wanting in due consideration for their welfare, without going the length of violating any of their constituted rights. The offender may then be justly punished by opinion, though not by law. As soon as any part of a person's conduct affects prejudicially the interests of others, society has jurisdiction over it, and the question whether the general welfare will or will not be promoted by interfering with it, becomes open to discussion. But there is no room for entertaining any such question when a person's conduct affects the interests of no persons besides himself, or needs not affect them unless they like (all the per-

sons concerned being of full age, and the ordinary amount of understanding). In all such cases there should be perfect freedom, legal and social, to do the action and stand the consequences.

It would be a great misunderstanding of this doctrine, to suppose that it is one of selfish indifference, which pretends that human beings have no business with each other's conduct in life, and that they should not concern themselves about the well-doing or well-being of one another, unless their own interest is involved. Instead of any diminution, there is need of a great increase of disinterested exertion to promote the good of others. But disinterested benevolence can find other instruments to persuade people to their good, than whips and scourges, either of the literal or the metaphorical sort. I am the last person to undervalue the self-regarding virtues; they are only second in importance, if even second, to the social. It is equally the business of education to cultivate both. But even education works by conviction and persuasion as well as by compulsion, and it is by the former only that, when the period of education is past, the self-regarding virtues should be inculcated. Human beings owe to each other help to distinguish the better from the worse, and encouragement to choose the former and avoid the latter. They should be for ever stimulating each other to increased exercise of their higher faculties, and increased direction of their feelings and aims towards wise instead of foolish, elevating instead of degrading, objects and contemplations. But neither one person, nor any number of persons, is warranted in saying to another human creature of ripe years, that he shall not do with his life for his own benefit what he chooses to do with it. He is the person most interested in his own well-being; the interest which any other person, except in cases of strong personal attachment, can have in it, is trifling, compared with that which he himself has; the interest which society has in him individually (except as to his conduct to others) is fractional, and altogether indirect: while, with respect to his own feelings and circumstances, the most ordinary man or woman has means of knowledge immeasurably surpassing those that can be possessed by any one else. The interference of society to overrule his judgment and purposes in what only regards himself, must be grounded on general presumptions: which may be altogether wrong, and even if right, are as likely as not to be misapplied to individual cases, by persons no better acquainted with the circumstances of such cases than those are who look at them merely from without. In this department, therefore, of human affairs, individuality has its proper field of action. In the conduct of human beings towards one another, it is necessary that general rules should for the most part be observed, in order that people may know what they have to expect; but in each person's own concerns, his individual spontaneity is entitled to free exercise. Considerations to aid his judgment, exhortations to strengthen his will, may be offered to him, even obtruded on him, by others; but he himself is the final judge. All errors which he is likely to commit against advice and warning, are far outweighed by the evil of allowing others to constrain him to what they deem his good.

The distinction here pointed out between the part of a person's life which conerns only himself, and that which concerns others, many persons will refuse to admit. How (it may be asked) can any part of the conduct of a member of society be a matter of indifference to the other members? No person is an entirely isolated being; it is impossible for a person to do anything seriously or permanently hurtful to himself, without mischief reaching at least to his near connexions, and often far beyond them. If he injures his property, he does harm to those who directly or indirectly derived support from it, and usually diminishes, by a greater or less amount, the general resources of the community. If he deteriorates his bodily or mental faculties, he not only brings evil upon all who depended on him for any portion of their happiness, but disqualifies himself for rendering the services which he owes to his fellow creatures generally; perhaps becomes a burthen on their affection or benevolence; and if such conduct were very frequent, hardly any offence that is committed would detract more from the general sum of good. Finally, if by his vices or follies a person does no direct harm to others, he is nevertheless (it may be said) injurious by his example; and ought be be compelled to control himself, for the sake of those whom the sight or knowledge of his conduct might corrupt or mislead.

And even (it will be added) if the consequences of misconduct could be confined to the vicious or thoughtless individual, ought society to abandon to their own guidance those who are manifestly unfit for it? If protection against themselves is confessedly due to children and persons under age, is not society equally bound to afford it to persons of mature years who are equally incapable of self-government? If gambling, or drunkenness, or incontinence, or idleness, or uncleanliness, are as injurious to happiness, and as great a hindrance to improvement, as many or most of the acts prohibited by law, why (it may be asked) should not law, so far as is consistent with practicability and social convenience, endeavour to repress these also? And as a supplement to the unavoidable imperfections of law, ought not opinion at least to organize a powerful police against these vices, and visit rigidly with social penalties those who are known to practise them? There is no question here (it may be said) about restricting individuality, or impeding the trial of new and original experiments in living. The only things it is sought to prevent are things which have been tried and condemned from the beginning of the world until now; things which experience has shown not to be useful or suitable to any person's individuality. There must be some length of time and amount of experience, after which a moral or prudential truth may be regarded as established: and it is merely desired to prevent generation after generation from falling over the same precipice which has been fatal to their predecessors.

I fully admit that the mischief which a person does to himself, may seriously affect, both through their sympathies and their interests, those nearly connected with him, and in a minor degree, society at large. When, by conduct of this sort, a person is led to violate a distinct and assignable obligation to any other person or persons, the case is taken out of the self-regarding class and becomes amenable to moral disapprobation in the proper sense of the term. If, for example, a man, through intemperance or extravagance, becomes unable to pay his debts, or, having undertaken the moral responsibility of a family, becomes from the same cause incapable of supporting or educating them, he is deservedly reprobated, and might be justly punished; but it is for the breach of duty to his family or creditors, not for the extravagance. If the resources which ought to have been

devoted to them, had been diverted from them for the most prudent investment, the moral culpability would have been the same. George Barnwell murdered his uncle to get money for his mistress, but if he had done it to set himself up in business, he would equally have been hanged. Again, in the frequent case of a man who causes grief to his family by addiction to bad habits, he deserves reproach for his unkindness or ingratitude; but so he may for cultivating habits not in themselves vicious, if they are painful to those with whom he passes his life, or who from personal ties are dependent on him for their comfort. Whoever fails in the consideration generally due to the interests and feelings of others, not being compelled by some more imperative duty, or justified by allowable self-preference, is a subject of moral disapprobation for that failure, but not for the cause of it, nor for the errors, merely personal to himself which may have remotely led to it. In like manner, when a person disables himself, by conduct purely self-regarding, from the performance of some definite duty incumbent on him to the public, he is guilty of a social offence. No person ought to be punished simply for being drunk; but a soldier or a policeman should be punished for being drunk on duty. Whenever, in short, there is a definite damage, or a definite risk of damage, either to an individual or to the public, the case is taken out of the province of liberty, and placed in that of morality or law.

But with regard to the merely contingent, or, as it may be called, constructive injury which a person causes to society, by conduct which neither violates any specific duty to the public, nor occasions perceptible hurt to any assignable individual except himself;

the inconvenience is one which society can afford to bear, for the sake of the greater good of human freedom. If grown persons are to be punished for not taking proper care of themselves, I would rather it were for their own sake, than under pretence of preventing them from impairing their capacity of rendering to society benefits which society does not pretend it has a right to exact. But I cannot consent to argue the point as if society had no means of bringing its weaker members up to its ordinary standard of rational conduct, except waiting till they do something irrational, and then punishing them, legally or morally, for it. Society has had absolute power over them during all the early portion of their existence: it has had the whole period of childhood and nonage in which to try whether it could make them capable of rational conduct in life. The existing generation is master both of the training and the entire circumstances of the generation to come; it cannot indeed make them perfectly wise and good, because it is itself so lamentably deficient in goodness and wisdom; and its best efforts are not always, in individual cases, its most successful ones; but it is perfectly well able to make the rising generation, as a whole, as good as, and a little better than, itself. If society lets any considerable number of its members grow up mere children, incapable of being acted on by rational consideration of distant motives, society has itself to blame for the consequences. Armed not only with all the powers of education, but with the ascendancy which the authority of a received opinion always exercises over the minds who are least fitted to judge for themselves; and aided by the *natural* penalties which cannot be prevented from falling on those who incur the distaste or the contempt of those who

know them; let not society pretend that it needs, besides all this, the power to issue commands and enforce obedience in the personal concerns of individuals, in which, on all principles of justice and policy, the decision ought to rest with those who are to abide the consequences. Nor is there anything which tends more to discredit and frustrate the better means of influencing conduct, than a resort to the worse. If there be among those whom it is attempted to coerce into prudence of temperance, any of the material of which vigorous and independent characters are made, they will infallibly rebel against the yoke. No such person will ever feel that others have a right to control him in his concerns, such as they have to prevent him from injuring them in theirs; and it easily comes to be considered a mark of spirit and courage to fly in the face of such usurped authority, and do with ostentation the exact opposite of what it enjoins; as in the fashion of grossness which succeeded, in the time of Charles II, to the fanatical moral intolerance of the Puritans. With respect to what is said of the necessity of protecting from the bad example set to others by the vicious or the self-indulgent; it is true that bad example may have a pernicious effect, especially the example of doing wrong to others with impunity to the wrong-doer. But we are now speaking of conduct which, while it does no wrong to others, is supposed to do great harm to the agent himself; and I do not see how those who believe this, can think otherwise than that the example, on the whole, must be more salutary than hurtful, since, if it displays the misconduct, it displays also the painful or degrading consequences which, if the conduct is justly censured, must be supposed to be in all or most cases attendant on it.

But the strongest of all the arguments against the interference of the public with purely personal conduct, is that when it does interfere, the odds are that it interferes wrongly, and in the wrong place. On questions of social morality, of duty to others, the opinion of the public, that is, of an overruling majority, though often wrong, is likely to be still oftener right; because on such questions they are only required to judge of their own interests; of the manner in which some mode of conduct, if allowed to be practised, would affect themselves. But the opinion of a similar majority, imposed as a law on the minority, on questions of self-regarding conduct, is quite as likely to be wrong as right; for in these cases public opinion means, at the best, some people's opinion of what is good or bad for other people; while very often it does not even mean that; the public, with the most perfect indifference, passing over the pleasure or convenience of those whose conduct they censure, and considering only their own preference. There are many who consider as an injury to themselves any conduct which they have a distaste for, and resent it as an outrage to their feelings; as a religious bigot, when charged with disregarding the religious feelings of others, has been known to retort that they disregard his feelings, by persisting in their abominable worship or creed. But there is no parity between the feeling of a person for his own opinion, and the feeling of another who is offended at his holding it; no more than between the desire of a thief to take a purse, and the desire of the right owner to keep it. And a person's taste is as much his own peculiar concern as his opinion or his purse. It is easy for any one to imagine an ideal public, which leaves the freedom and choice of individuals in all un-certain matters undisturbed, and only requires them to abstain from modes of conduct which universal experience has condemned. But where has there been seen a public which set any such limit to its censorship? or when does the public trouble itself about universal experience? In its interferences with personal conduct it is seldom thinking of anything but the enormity of acting or feeling differently from itself; and this standard of judgment, thinly disguised, is held up to mankind as the dictate of religion and philosophy, by nine-tenths of all moralists and speculative writers. These teach that things are right because they are right; because we feel them to be so. They tell us to search in our own minds and hearts for laws of conduct binding on ourselves and on all others. What can the poor public do but apply these instructions, and make their own personal feelings of good and evil, if they are tolerably unanimous in them, obligatory on all the world?

The evil here pointed out is not one which exists only in theory; and it may perhaps be expected that I should specify the instances in which the public of this age and country improperly invests its own preferences with the character of moral laws. I am not writing an essay on the aberrations of existing moral feeling. That is too weighty a subject to be discussed parenthetically, and by way of illustration. Yet examples are necessary, to show that the principle I maintain is of serious and practical moment, and that I am not endeavouring to erect a barrier against imaginary evils. And it is not difficult to show, by abundant instances, that to extend the bounds of what may be called moral police, until it encroaches on the most unquestionably legitimate liberty of the individual, is one of the most universal of all human propensities.

As a first instance, consider the antipathies which men cherish on no better grounds than that persons whose religious opinions are different from theirs, do not practise their religious observances, especially their religious abstinences. To cite a rather trivial example, nothing in the creed or practice of Christians does more to envenom the hatred of Mahomedans against them, than the fact of their eating pork. There are few acts which Christians and Europeans regard with more unaffected disgust, than Mussulmans regard this particular mode of satisfying hunger. It is, in the first place, an offence against their religion; but this circumstance by no means explains either the degree or the kind of their repugnance; for wine also is forbidden by their religion, and to partake of it is by all Mussulmans accounted wrong, but not disgusting. Their aversion to the flesh of the 'unclean beast' is, on the contrary, of that peculiar character, resembling an instinctive antipathy, which the idea of uncleanness, when once it thoroughly sinks into the feelings, seems always to excite even in those whose personal habits are anything but scrupulously clean, and of which the sentiment of religious impurity, so intense in the Hindoos, is a remarkable example. Suppose now that in a people, of whom the majority were Mussulmans, that majority should insist upon not permitting pork to be eaten within the limits of the county. This would be nothing new in Mahomedan countries.[1] Would it be a legitimate exercise of the moral authority of public opinion? and if not, why not? The practice is really revolting to such a public. They also sincerely think that it is forbidden and abhorred by the Deity. Neither could the prohibition be censured as religious persecution. It might be religious in its origin, but it would not be

persecution for religion, since nobody's religion makes it a duty to eat pork. The only tenable ground of condemnation would be, that with the personal tastes and self-regarding concerns of individuals the public has no business to interfere. . . .

Under the name of preventing intemperance, the people of one English colony, and of nearly half the United States, have been interdicted by law from making any use whatever of fermented drinks, except for medical purposes: for prohibition of their sale is in fact, as it is intended to be, prohibition of their use. And though the impracticability of executing the law has caused its repeal in several of the States which had adopted it, including the one from which it derives its name, an attempt has notwithstanding been commenced, and is prosecuted with considerable zeal by many of the professed philanthropists, to agitate for a similar law in this country. The association, or 'Alliance' as it terms itself, which has been formed for this purpose, has acquired some notoriety through the publicity given to a correspondence between its Secretary and one of the very few English public men who hold that a politician's opinions ought to be founded on principles. Lord Stanley's share in this corre-

1. The case of the Bombay Parsees is a curious instance in point. When this industrious and enterprising tribe, the descendants of the Persian fire-worshippers, flying from their native country before the Caliphs, arrived in Western India, they were admitted to toleration by the Hindoo sovereigns, on condition of not eating beef. When those regions afterwards fell under the dominion of Mahomedan conquerors, the Parsees obtained from them a continuance of indulgence, on condition of refraining from pork. What was at first obedience to authority became a second nature, and the Parsees to this day abstain both from beef and pork. Though not required by their religion, the double abstinence has had time to grow into a custom of their tribe: and custom, in the East, is a religion.

spondence is calculated to strengthen the hopes already built on him, by those who know how rare such qualities as are manifested in some of his public appearances, unhappily are among those who figure in political life. The organ of the Alliance, who would 'deeply deplore the recognition of any principle which could be wrested to justify bigotry and persecution,' undertakes to point out the 'broad and impassable barrier' which divides such principles from those of the association. 'All matters relating to thought, opinion, conscience, appear to me,' he says, 'to be without the sphere of legislation; all pertaining to social act, habit, relation, subject only to a discretionary power vested in the State itself, and not in the individual, to be within it.' No mention is made of a third class, different from either of these, viz. acts and habits which are not social, but individual; although it is to this class, surely, that the act of drinking fermented liquors belongs. Selling fermented liquors, however, is trading, and trading is a social act. But the infringement complained of is not on the liberty of the seller, but on that of the buyer and consumer; since the State might just as well forbid him to drink wine, as purposely make it impossible for him to obtain it. The Secretary, however, says, 'I claim, as a citizen, a right to legislate whenever my social rights are invaded by the social act of another.' And now for the definition of these 'social rights.' 'If anything invades my social rights, certainly the traffic in

strong drink does. It destroys my primary right of security, by constantly creating and stimulating social disorder. It invades my right of equality, by deriving a profit from the creation of a misery, I am taxed to support. It impedes my right to free moral and intellectual development, by surrounding my path with dangers, and by weakening and demoralizing society, from which I have a right to claim mutual aid and intercourse.' A theory of 'social rights,' the like of which probably never before found its way into distinct language—being nothing short of this—that it is the absolute social right of every individual, that every other individual shall act in every respect exactly as he ought; that whosoever fails thereof in the smallest particular, violates my social right, and entitles me to demand from the legislature the removal of the grievance. So monstrous a principle is far more dangerous than any single interference with liberty; there is no violation of liberty which it would not justify; it acknowledges no right to any freedom whatever, except perhaps to that of holding opinions in secret without ever disclosing them: for the moment an opinion which I consider noxious, passes any one's lips, it invades all the 'social rights' attributed to me by the Alliance. The doctrine ascribes to all mankind a vested interest in each other's moral, intellectual, and even physical perfection to be denied by each claimant according to his own standard. . . .

42

LORD PATRICK DEVLIN
Mill on Liberty in Morals

LORD PATRICK DEVLIN, a leading English jurist, was a judge of the Queen's Bench from 1948 to 1960. His essays on law and morality are collected in his book *The Enforcement of Morals* (1965).

John Stuart Mill thought to resolve the struggle between liberty and authority that is inherent in every society. We who belong to the societies of the United States or of the British Commonwealth or of other like-minded peoples say that we belong to a free society. By this I think we mean no more than that we strike a balace in favour of individual freedom. The law is the boundary that marks the limit of authority and it is not drawn in a straight line. As it traverses the field of human activities it inclines from side to side, in some allowing much more freedom than in others. At each point we try to strike the right balance. What I mean by striking it in favour of freedom is that the question to be asked in each case is: 'How much authority is necessary?' and not: 'How much liberty is to be conceded?' That the question should be put in that form, that authority should be a grant and liberty not a privilege, is, I think, the true mark of a free society.

Is it possible to drive a straight line across the field running from one end to the other, marking out for all time the private domain on one side and the public on the other? If it is, the value to the individual in the minority would be immense. As things are, in the constant struggle between liberty and authority the individual is at a disadvantage. Each time the Government, backed by the power of the majority, brings forward some new piece of legislation designed to benefit the majority and involving some further invasions of the private domain, the minority can only appeal to an undefined concept of liberty. Lack of definition suits the stronger party. What is wanted, if it can be got, is a comprehensive principle, clear and precise, by which any proposed law can be tested.

This sort of thing—the idea of formulating a law above ordinary law and by which ordinary law may be tested, is attempted on a grand scale in the Constitution of the United States. The scale was not grand enough for Mill. The Constitution was built to be permanent: Mill's doctrine was designed as perdurable. The Articles of the Constitution were made difficult to alter, but Mill dealt in immutabilities. No society, he said,[1] in which the liberties which he prescribed were not on the whole respected was free, whatever might be its form of government; and none was completely free in which they did not exist absolutely and unqualified. Again, where the Constitution protects only specific freedoms, such as the freedom to exercise religion, freedom of speech and of the press, and so forth, Mill induced from the specific freedoms he enumerated a definition wide enough

The Ernst Freund Lecture delivered at the University of Chicago on 15 October 64 and printed in the *University of Chicago Law Review*, vol. 32, No. 2.

1. Mill, *On Liberty*, p. 75.

From *The Enforcement of Morals* by Lord Devlin, published by Oxford University Press. Reprinted by permission of the publisher. Abridged.

to cover all freedom. He regarded the Constitution as inadequate. The fact that in his day 'nearly half the United States have been interdicted by law from making any use whatever of fermented drinks, except for medical purposes' was placed first in his list of 'gross usurpations upon the liberty of private life'.[2] What Mill declared was a fundamental doctrine, to be kept as in a tabernacle in the hearts of men, to which all law, including the law that makes and amends constitutions, should be subject.

Mill therefore set out to define once and for all 'the nature and limits of the power which can be legitimately exercised by society over the individual'.[3] He did this by asserting 'one very simple principle, as entitled to cover absolutely the dealings of society with the individual in the way of compulsion and control. . . . That principle is, that the sole end for which mankind are warranted, individually or collectively, in interfering with the liberty of action of any of their number, is self-protection. That the only purpose for which power can be rightfully exercised over any member of a civilised community, against his will, is to prevent harm to others. His own good, either physical or moral, is not a sufficient warrant. He cannot rightfully be compelled to do or forbear because it will be better for him to do so, because it will make him happier, because in the opinion of others, to do so would be wise, or even right.'[4]

The core of this principle is that a man must be allowed to pursue his own good in his own way. Its opposite has come to be identified as paternalism. But an identifying mark is not a line. To secure the citadel of freedom Mill flung a line beyond which the law must not trespass. The law was not to interfere with a man unless what he did caused harm to others. What Mill included in 'harm to others' was chiefly physical harm to other individuals.

. . .

The incident in England which has recently revived interest in Mill's doctrine is the publication of the Wolfenden Report in 1957. The Report based its proposals for the reform of criminal law on homosexuality upon the principle of the realm of private morality which is not the law's business. This use of the principle is, as Professor Hart observed,[5] 'strikingly similar' to Mill's doctrine. Professor Hart immediately conferred upon it his full approval with all the authority which that carries and in 1963 devoted a series of comprehensive and penetrating lectures to expounding it. The idea that in a free society a man's morals should be his own affair is superficially at least an attractive one. We have built a society in which a man's religion is his own affair: Can we not go a step further and build one in which his morals are his own affair too? The law knows nothing of any religion. Is there any need for it to know anything of morals?

Let me for a moment stop talking about society as an abstract conception and talk instead about a hundred men and women. Ninety are virtuous and ten are vicious. Are the virtuous to be compelled to associate with the vicious? The natural answer is—certainly not. For even granted that the vicious do no physical harm to others against their will, association with them may cause the vice to be spread. Moreover, the object of the association being to share the

2. ibid. p. 144.

3. ibid. p. 65.

4. ibid. p. 72.

5. Hart, *Law, Liberty and Morality*, p. 14.

burdens and benefits of life among the community as a whole, it is likely that the vicious will be more benefited than burdened; men who are constantly drunk, drugged or debauched are not likely to be useful members of the community.

What then are the ninety to do about it? If all that was involved was the membership of a social club, the situation would be simple. The vicious ten would be expelled and no one would think the expulsion harsh. But a society in which a man has his whole social life is something more than a club. Men can no longer be driven into the desert; outlawry and banishment are things of the past. Even when in use they were as punishments so severe that mercy enjoined, at least at first, a lesser penalty. Is it therefore permissible for the ninety to deprive the ten of their liberty for the purpose at best of reformation and at worst of restraint? Or must they in the name of freedom leave the ten at large, relying on the strength of their own virtue to resist contamination and in time to convert the vicious?

. . .

Granted then that the law can play some part in the war against vice, ought it to be excluded for the reason that private vice cannot do any harm to society? I think that it is capable of doing both physical harm and spiritual harm. Tangible and intangible may be better words; body and soul a better simile.

Let me consider first the tangible harm. It is obvious that an individual may by unrestricted indulgence in vice so weaken himself that he ceases to be a useful member of society. It is obvious also that if a sufficient number of individuals so weaken themselves, society will thereby be weakened. That is what I mean by tangible harm to society. If the proportion grows sufficiently large, society will succumb either to its own disease or to external pressure. A nation of debauchees would not in 1940 have responded satisfactorily to Winston Churchill's call to blood and toil and sweat and tears. I doubt if any of this would be denied. The answer that is made to it is that the danger, if private immorality were tolerated, of vice spreading to such an extent as to affect society as a whole is negligible and in a free society ought to be ignored.

There is here a distinction to be made. As I have said, the question is not whether at any given time the spread of a particular vice has reached such proportions as to constitute a danger, but whether all vice that can be committed in private is of its nature harmless to society. It is therefore proper to distinguish between natural and unnatural vice; and it is usually an example, such as homosexuality, selected from unnatural vice that is taken to illustrate the absurdity of supposing that private immorality could ever develop into a menace to society. Of course, looking at the thing in the crudest way, a completely homosexual society would, unless continuously reinforced from outside, soon cease to exist because it would not breed. But, as has been pointed out, the same might be said of a completely celibate society, yet no one regards celibacy as injurious to society. The natural demand for heterosexual intercourse, it is argued, will always be strong enough to ensure that homosexuality is kept to a harmless minority.

This is, within limits, a formidable argument and I shall return to consider the curious results which flow from it. It does not however apply to natural vice where the pressure is the other way. There may be those who argue that men and women are inherently virtuous so that the vicious few, even if allowed free rein, will always be in a harmless and unattractive minority. This seems to me like arguing that the vast majority of men and women in society are inherently loyal so that it would be quite safe to ignore the treacherous few. No doubt traitors, as also vice-mongers, are often in it only for money and no one would applaud that. But there are noble as well as ignoble traitors; and—it might well be argued on the lines of Mill—it is worth putting up with the almost negligible harm that is caused by treachery as it is ordinarily practised so as to make sure that we do not stifle some new political conception, which although now regarded with abhorrence by all right-minded people, may in the end, because we are all fallible, turn out to be a great improvement. The danger that some traitors or spies may deliver up to the enemy some vital secrets is, it can be urged, an imaginary one existing only in story books. In real life the damage they do, at any rate in peacetime, is hardly likely to do more than dent the structure of a strong society.

But this is not the way in which treachery is considered. We do not estimate the achievements of treason over the last century and ask what they have amounted to. So with incitement to mutiny; we do not ask how much can safely be permitted without seriously endangering the discipline of the armed forces. So with sedition; we do not argue that the loyalty of the robust majority and its belief in the merits of our polity is all that is necessary for the safety of the realm. When we are constitution-making—whether what is being formulated is a clause in writing or a principle supported by tacit consent—it is the nature of the subject-matter that is the determinant. Whether society should have the power to restrain any activity de-pends on the nature of the activity. Whether it should exercise the power at any given time in its history depends on the situation at that time and requires a balance to be struck between the foreseeable danger to society and the foreseeable damage to the freedom and happiness of the individual.

This distinction, which one might with some exaggeration call a distinction between eternity and time, is the answer to a modified and more attractive way of putting the argument I have just been considering. Granted that society cannot allow private vice to rampage, ought not its power of interference be confined to the excess? It is, it can be urged, only the excess that is dangerous. It is indeed with this in mind that anti-vice laws are generally framed, that is, to contain rather than to eliminate the vice. It is considered impracticable to use the law to eliminate fornication or even prostitution; the criminal law against soliciting, procuring, living on immoral earnings, and running brothels is designed to keep the vice within limits. But there is no Plimsoll line which can define the safety level.

In the same way, while a few people getting drunk in private cause no problem at all, widespread drunkenness, whether in private or public, would create a social problem. The line between drunkenness that creates a social problem of sufficient magnitude to justify the intervention of the law and that which does not, cannot be drawn on the distinction between private indulgence and public sobriety. It is a practical one, based on an estimate of what can safely be tolerated whether in public or in private, and shifting from time to time as circumstances change. The licensing laws coupled with high taxation may be all that is needed. But if more be needed there is no doctrinal answer even to complete prohibition. It cannot be said that so much is the law's business but more is not.

I move now to consideration of intangible harm to society and begin by noting a significant distinction. When considering tangible damage to society we are concerned chiefly with immoral activity. Moral belief is relevant only in so far as the lack of it contributes to immoral activity. A vicious minority diminishes the physical strength of society even if all its members believe themselves to be sinning. But if they all believed that, they would not diminish the common belief in right and wrong which is the intangible property of society. When considering intangible injury to society it is moral belief that matters; immoral activity is relevant only in so far as it promotes disbelief.

It is generally accepted that some shared morality, that is, some common agreement about what is right and what is wrong, is an essential element in the constitution of any society.[6] Without it there would be no cohesion. But polygamy can be as cohesive as monogamy and I am prepared to believe that a society based on free love and a community of children could be just as strong (though according to our ideas it could not be as good) as one based on the family. What is important is not the quality of the creed but the strength of the belief in it. The enemy of society is not error but indifference.

On this reasoning there is nothing inherently objectionable about the change of an old morality for a new one. Why then is the law used to guard existing moral beliefs? It is because an old morality cannot be changed for a new morality as an old coat for a new one. The old belief must be driven out by disbelief. Polygamy could not be established in England or in the United States unless there was first created a disbelief in the value of monogamy. If change is in progress there will for a long period be no common belief in the value of either institution. Disbelief in the virtue of chastity is not confined to those who from the purest motives would like to help spinsters to lead a fuller life; and through the breach in the walls made by the new moralist there will come pouring a horde which he would loathe and despise. Whether the new belief is better or worse than the old, it is the interregnum of disbelief that is perilous. During the interregnum, society will be attacked by forces which those, who in the course of their rational discussions have generated the disbelief, will have no power to control and which will be as hostile to the new belief as to the old.

But no one, it will be said, wants to subvert a whole morality. All that is sought is freedom to make peripheral changes or, if not quite peripheral, changes that will leave the bulk of morality intact; nothing will be done that will seriously diminish the cohesive force of a common morality. That brings us back to the old difficulty: How much can be allowed and how can it be measured? If it is proper and indeed necessary for the law to guard some part of public morality, how shall we determine what part to leave unguarded? There is in this respect a special difficulty due to the nature of moral belief. It is not for most men based on a number of separate rational judgements arrived at after weighing the arguments for and against chastity, for and against honesty, for and against homosexuality, and so on. Most men take their morality as a whole and in fact derive it, though this is irrelevant, from some religious doctrine. To destroy the belief in one

6. See Hart, p. 51.

part of it will probably result in weakening the belief in the whole. Professor Hart says that to argue in this way is to treat morality as if it 'forms a single seamless web'[7] which he finds unconvincing. Seamlessness presses the simile rather hard but, apart from that, I should say that for most people morality is a web of beliefs rather than a number of unconnected ones. This may or may not be the most rational way of arriving at a moral code. But when considering the degree of injury to a public morality, what has to be considered is how the morality is in fact made up and not how in the opinion of rational philosophers it ought to be made up.

But then if the law is required to guard the whole of public morality, is that not, as Professor Hart puts it graphically, using 'legal punishment to freeze into immobility the morality dominant at a particular time in a society's existence'?[8] I do not see why it should have that effect. At the worst it leaves morality as mobile as the law; and though it may not be easy to change the law, it is far easier than to change a moral belief of a community. In fact, for practical reasons the law never attempts to cover the whole of public morality and the area left uncovered is naturally that which is most susceptible to change. But assume that it did cover the whole of public morality, its effect would be not to freeze but to regulate the process of liquefaction and to help distinguish the changes which are motivated by a genuine search after moral improvement from those which are relaxation into vice. It is in this way that the law acts as a winnower, if I may return to the metaphor of the wheat and the chaff. Admittedly it is an unscientific way. There is no phased programme, no planners to say that if free love is let in in the 60's, the homo-

sexualist must wait until the 70's. But relaxation, if it seems to be going too far, sets off a movement for tightening up what is left. The law is brought in to do the tightening as well as to hold off the evil-doers who flourish whenever moral principle is uncertain. A detached observer, who favoured neither the old nor the new morality, would see this as a natural, albeit a rough and ready, method of regulation.

In any society in which the members have a deeply-rooted desire for individual freedom—and where there is not that desire, it is useless to devise methods for securing it—there is also a natural respect for opinions that are sincerely held. When such opinions accumulate enough weight, the law must either yield or it is broken. In a democratic society, especially one like ours in which laymen play a conspicuous part in the enforcement of the law, there will be a strong tendency for it to yield—not to abandon all defences so as to let in the horde, but to give ground to those who are prepared to fight for something that they prize. To fight may be to suffer. A willingness to suffer is the most convincing proof of sincerity. Without the law there would be no proof. The law is the anvil on which the hammer strikes.

Much of what I have just said is more appropriate to a society in which freedom is still young than to ours. In England today there is no question of the law being used to suppress any activity which is not generally thought to be immoral. The climate of a free society is naturally clement to individuality of any sort and uncongenial to compulsion, so that the criminal law will withdraw its support, if it has ever

7. Hart, p. 51.
8. ibid. p. 72.

given it, from a moral belief which is seriously challenged.

It may be that in the case of homosexuality this is too sweeping a statement. I do not think that there is anyone who asserts vocally that homosexuality is a good way of life but there may be those who believe it to be so. This brings me back to the point where I left that subject when distinguishing between natural and unnatural vice. That distinction does not affect the intangible harm that immorality does to society but it is relevant, I suggested, to assessing the likelihood of tangible injury. If the intangible harm is ignored, there is a strong case for arguing that homosexuality between adults should be excluded altogether from the ambit of the law on the ground that as a practice it is incapable of causing appreciable injury to society. I cannot say more than that there is a strong case, for many would argue that homosexuality if tolerated would spread to significant proportions. If one ignores that argument as well, the result would be that the charter of freedom should not encompass the whole of morality but only so much of it as is concerned with unnatural vice—freedom of morality in matters unnatural.

Is this the sort of result that is really worth striving for on a high theoretical plane? Any law reformer who raises this sort of issue must be the sort of man who likes to bang his head against a brick wall in the hope that he will be able to get through on his own terms and so avoid a little argument at the gate. It will not improve his chances of getting through the gate if he tells the janitor that there ought not to be a wall there at all. So it is much easier to obtain the repeal of a law by persuading the law-maker that on balance it is doing more harm than good than by denouncing him as a meddler who ought to be minding his own business. . . .

43

RONALD DWORKIN
Homosexuality, Pornography, and the Law

No doubt most Americans and Englishmen think that homosexuality, prostitution, and the publication of pornography are immoral. What part should this fact play in the decision whether to make them criminal? This is a tangled question, full of issues with roots in philosophical and sociological controversy. It is a question lawyers must face, however, and two recent and controversial events—publication of the Wolfenden Report in England,[1] followed by a public debate on prostitution and homosexuality, and a trio of obscenity

From Ronald Dworkin, "Lord Devlin and the Enforcement of Morals." Reprinted by permission of The Yale Law Journal Company and Fred B. Rothman & Company from *The Yale Law Journal*, vol. 75, pp. 986–87, 988–1005. This article is slightly abridged. Footnotes are numbered as in the original.

1. Report of the Committee on Homosexual Offenses and Prostitution, CMD. No. 247 (1957).

decisions in the United States Supreme Court[2]—press it upon us.

Several positions are available, each with its own set of difficulties. Shall we say that public condemnation is sufficient, in and of itself, to justify making an act a crime? This seems inconsistent with our traditions of individual liberty, and our knowledge that the morals of even the largest mob cannot come warranted for truth. If public condemnation is not sufficient, what more is needed? Must there be some demonstration of present harm to particular persons directly affected by the practice in question? Or is it sufficient to show some effect on social customs and institutions which alters the social environment, and thus affects all members of society indirectly? If the latter, must it also be demonstrated that these social changes threaten long-term harm of some standard sort, like an increase in crime or a decrease in productivity? Or would it be enough to show that the vast bulk of the present community would deplore the change? If so, does the requirement of harm add much to the bare requirement of public condemnation?

In 1958 Lord Devlin delivered the second Maccabaean Lecture to the British Academy. He called his lecture "The Enforcement of Morals," and devoted it to these issues of principle.[3] His conclusions he summarized in these remarks about the practice of homosexuality: "We should ask ourselves in the first instance whether, looking at it calmly and dispassionately, we regard it as a vice so abominable that its mere presence is an offense. If that is the genuine feeling of the society in which we live, I do not see how society can be denied the right to eradicate it."[4] . . .

There are two chief arguments. The first is set out in structured form in the Maccabaean Lecture. It argues from society's right to protect its own existence. The second, a quite different and much more important argument, develops in disjointed form through various essays. It argues from the majority's right to follow its own moral convictions in defending its social environment from change it opposes. I shall consider these two arguments in turn, but the second at greater length.

THE FIRST ARGUMENT: SOCIETY'S RIGHT TO PROTECT ITSELF

The first argument—and the argument which has received by far the major part of the critics' attention—is this:[9]

(1) In a modern society there are a variety of moral principles which some men adopt for their own guidance and do not attempt to impose upon others. There are also moral standards which the majority places beyond toleration and imposes upon those who dissent. For us, the dictates of a particular religion are an example of the former class, and the practice of monogamy an example of the latter. A society cannot survive unless some standards are of the second class, because some moral conformity is essential to its life. Every society has a right to preserve its own existence, and therefore the right to insist on some such conformity.

2. Memoirs v. Massachusetts (Fanny Hill), 383 U.S. 413 (1966), Ginzburg v. United States, 383 U.S. 463 (1966), Mishkin v. New York, 383 U.S. 502 (1966).

3. Devlin, The Enforcement of Morals (Oxford University Press 1959). Reprinted in Devlin, The Enforcement of Morals (Oxford University Press 1965). [The latter is hereinafter cited as Devlin.]

4. Devlin 17. This position was carefully stated as hypothetical. Apparently Lord Devlin does not now think that the condition is met, because he has publically urged modification of the laws on homosexuality since the book's publication.

9. It is developed chiefly in Devlin 7–25.

(2) If society has such a right, then it has the right to use the institutions and sanctions of its criminal law to enforce the right—"[S]ociety may use the law to preserve morality in the same way it uses it to safeguard anything else if it is essential to its existence."[10] Just as society may use its law to prevent treason, it may use it to prevent a corruption of that conformity which ties it together.

(3) But society's right to punish immorality by law should not necessarily be exercised against every sort and on every occasion of immorality—we must recognize the impact and the importance of some restraining principles. There are several of these, but the most important is that there "must be toleration of the maximum individual freedom that is consistent with the integrity of society."[11] These restraining principles, taken together, require that we exercise caution in concluding that a practice is considered profoundly immoral. The law should stay its hand if it detects any uneasiness or halfheartedness or latent toleration in society's condemnation of the practice. But none of these restraining principles apply, and hence society is free to enforce its rights, when public feeling is high, enduring and relentless, when, in Lord Devlin's phrase, it rises to "intolerance, indignation and disgust."[12] Hence the summary conclusion about homosexuality: If it is genuinely regarded as an abominable vice, society's right to eradicate it cannot be denied.

We must guard against a possible, indeed tempting, misconception of this argument. It does not depend upon any assumption that when the vast bulk of a community thinks a practice is immoral they are likely right. What Lord Devlin thinks is at stake, when our public morality is challenged, is the very survival of society, and he believes that society is entitled to preserve itself

without vouching for the morality that holds it together.

Is this argument sound? Professor H. L. A. Hart, responding to its appearance at the heart of the Maccabaean lecture,[13] thought that it rested upon a confused conception of what a society is. If one holds anything like a conventional notion of a society, he said, it is absurd to suggest that every practice the society views as profoundly immoral and disgusting threatens its survival. This is as silly as arguing that society's existence is threatened by the death of one of its members or the birth of another, and Lord Devlin, he reminds us, offers nothing by way of evidence to support any such claim. But if one adopts an artificial definition of a society, such that a society consists of that particular complex of moral ideas and attitudes which its members happen to hold at a particular moment in time, it is intolerable that each such moral status quo should have the right to preserve its precarious existence by force. So, Professor Hart argued, Lord Devlin's argument fails whether a conventional or an artificial sense of "society" is taken.

Lord Devlin replies to Professor Hart in a new and lengthy footnote. After summarizing Hart's criticism he comments, "I do not assert that *any* deviation from a society's shared morality threatens its existence any more than I assert that *any* subversive activity threatens its existence. I assert that they are both activities which are capable in their nature of threatening the existence of society so that neither can be put beyond the law."[14] This reply

10. *Id.* at 11.

11. *Id.* at 16.

12. *Id.* at 17.

13. H. L. A. Hart, *Law, Liberty and Morality* 51 (1963).

14. Devlin 13.

exposes a serious flaw in the architecture of the argument.

It tells us that we must understand the second step of the argument—the crucial claim that society has a right to enforce its public morality by law—as limited to a denial of the proposition that society never has such a right. Lord Devlin apparently understood the Wolfenden Report's statement of a "realm of private morality . . . not the law's business" to assert a fixed jurisdictional barrier placing private sexual practices forever beyond the law's scrutiny. His arguments, the new footnote tells us, are designed to show merely that no such constitutional barrier should be raised, because it is possible that the challenge to established morality might be so profound that the very existence of a conformity in morals, and hence of the society itself, would be threatened.[15]

We might well remain unconvinced, even of this limited point. We might believe that the danger which any unpopular practice can present to the existence of society is so small that it would be wise policy, a prudent protection of individual liberty from transient hysteria, to raise just this sort of constitutional barrier and forbid periodic reassessments of the risk.

But if we were persuaded to forego this constitutional barrier we would expect the third step in the argument to answer the inevitable next question: Granted that a challenge to deep-seated and genuine public morality may conceivably threaten society's existence, and so must be placed above the threshold of the law's concern, how shall we know when the danger is sufficiently clear and present to justify not merely scrutiny but action? What more is needed beyond the fact of passionate public disapproval to show that we are in the presence of an actual threat?

The rhetoric of the third step makes it seem responsive to this question—there is much talk of "freedom" and "toleration" and even "balancing." But the argument is not responsive, for freedom, toleration and balancing turn out to be appropriate only when the public outrage diagnosed at the second step is shown to be overstated, when the fever, that is, turns out to be feigned. When the fever is confirmed, when the intolerance, indignation and disgust are genuine, the principle that calls for "the maximum individual freedom consis-

---

15. This reading had great support in the text even without the new footnote:

"I think, therefore, that it is not possible to set theoretical limits to the power of the State to legislate against immorality. It is not possible to settle in advance exceptions to the general rule or to define inflexibly areas of morality into which the law is in no circumstances to be allowed to enter."

Devlin 12–13.

The arguments presented bear out this construction. They are of the *reductio ad absurdum* variety, exploiting the possibility that what is immoral can in theory become subversive of society.

"But suppose a quarter or a half of the population got drunk every night, what sort of society would it be? You cannot set a theoretical limit to the number of people who can get drunk before society is entitled to legislate against drunkenness. The same may be said of gambling."

Id. at 14.

Each example argues that no jurisdictional limit may be drawn, not that every drunk or every act of gambling threatens society. There is no suggestion that society is entitled actually to make drunkenness or gambling crimes if the practice in fact falls below the level of danger. Indeed Lord Devlin quotes the Royal Commission on Betting, Lotteries, and Gaming to support his example on gambling:

"If we were convinced that whatever the degree of gambling this effect [on the character of the gambler as a member of society] must be harmful we should be inclined to think that it was the duty of the state to restrict gambling to the greatest extent practicable."

(Cmd. No. 8190 at para. 150 (1951), quoted in Devlin 14.

The implication is that society may scrutinize and be ready to regulate, but should not actually do so until the threat of harm in fact exists.

tent with the integrity of society" no longer applies. But this means that nothing more than passionate public disapproval is necessary after all.

In short, the argument involves an intellectual sleight of hand. At the second step, public outrage is presented as a threshold criterion, merely placing the practice in a category which the law is not forbidden to regulate. But offstage, somewhere in the transition to the third step, this threshold criterion becomes itself a dispositive affirmative reason for action, so that when it is clearly met the law may proceed without more. The power of this manoeuvre is proved by the passage on homosexuality. Lord Devlin concludes that if our society hates homosexuality enough it is justified in outlawing it, and forcing human beings to choose between the miseries of frustration and persecution, because of the danger the practice presents to society's existence. He manages this conclusion without offering evidence that homosexuality presents any danger at all to society's existence, beyond the naked claim that all "deviations from a society's shared morality . . . are capable in their nature of threatening the existence of society" and so "cannot be put beyond the law."[16]

THE SECOND ARGUMENT: SOCIETY'S RIGHT TO FOLLOW ITS OWN LIGHTS

We are therefore justified in setting aside the first argument and turning to the second. My reconstruction includes making a great deal explicit which I believe implicit, and so involves some risk of distortion, but I take the second argument to be this:[17]

(1) If those who have homosexual desires freely indulged them, our social environment would change. What the changes would be cannot be calculated with any precision, but it is plausible to suppose, for example, that the position of the family, as the assumed and natural institution around which the educational, economic and recreational arrangements of men center, would be undermined, and the further ramifications of that would be great. We are too sophisticated to suppose that the effects of an increase in homosexuality would be confined to those who participate in the practice alone, just as we are too sophisticated to suppose that prices and wages affect only those who negotiate them. The environment in which we and our children must live is determined, among other things, by patterns and relationships formed privately by others than ourselves.

(2) This in itself does not give society the right to prohibit homosexual practices. We cannot conserve every custom we like by jailing those who do not want to preserve it. But it means that our legislators must inevitably decide some moral issues. They must decide whether the institutions which seem threatened are sufficiently valuable to protect at the cost of human freedom. And they must decide whether the practices which threaten that institution are immoral, for if they are then the freedom of an individual to pursue them counts for less. We do not need so strong a justification, in terms of the social importance of the institutions being protected, if we are confident that no one has a moral right to do what we want to prohibit. We need less of a case, that is, to abridge someone's freedom to lie, cheat or drive recklessly, than his freedom to choose his own

16. Devlin 13 n.l.

17. Most of the argument appears in Devlin chapters V, VI and VII. See also an article published after the book: *Law and Morality*, 1 Manitoba L.S.J. 243 (1964/65).

jobs or to price his own goods. This does not claim that immorality is sufficient to make conduct criminal; it argues, rather, that on occasion it is necessary.

(3) But how shall a legislator decide whether homosexual acts are immoral? Science can give no answer, and a legislator can no longer properly turn to organized religion. If it happens, however, that the vast bulk of the community is agreed upon an answer, even though a small minority of educated men may dissent, the legislator has a duty to act on the consensus. He has such a duty for two closely connected reasons: (a) In the last analysis the decision must rest on some article of moral faith, and in a democracy this sort of issue, above all others, must be settled in accordance with democratic principles. (b) It is, after all, the community which acts when the threats and sanctions of the criminal law are brought to bear. The community must take the moral responsibility, and it must therefore act on its own lights—that is, on the moral faith of its members.

This, as I understand it, is Lord Devlin's second argument. It is complex, and almost every component invites analysis and challenge. Some readers will dissent from its central assumption, that a change in social institutions is the sort of harm a society is entitled to protect itself against. Others who do not take this strong position (perhaps because they approve of laws which are designed to protect economic institutions) will nevertheless feel that society is not entitled to act, however immoral the practice, unless the threatened harm to an institution is demonstrable and imminent rather than speculative. Still others will challenge the thesis that the morality or immorality of an act ought even to count in determining whether to make it criminal (though they would

no doubt admit that it does count under present practice), and others still will argue that even in a democracy legislators have the duty to decide moral questions for themselves, and must not refer such issues to the community at large. I do not propose to argue now for or against any of these positions. I want instead to consider whether Lord Devlin's conclusions are valid on his own terms, on the assumption, that is, that society does have a right to protect its central and valued social institutions against conduct which the vast bulk of its members disapproves on moral principle.

I shall argue that his conclusions are not valid, even on these terms, because he misunderstands what it is to disapprove on moral principle. I might say a cautionary word about the argument I shall present. It will consist in part of reminders that certain types of moral language (terms like "prejudice" and "moral position," for example) have standard uses in moral argument. My purpose is not to settle issues of political morality by the fiat of a dictionary, but to exhibit what I believe to be mistakes in Lord Devlin's moral sociology. I shall try to show that our conventional moral practices are more complex and more structured than he takes them to be, and that he consequently misunderstands what it means to say that the criminal law should be drawn from public morality. This is a popular and appealing thesis, and it lies near the core not only of Lord Devlin's, but of many other, theories about law and morals. It is crucial that its implications be understood.

THE CONCEPT OF A MORAL POSITION

We might start with the fact that terms like "moral position" and "moral conviction" function in our conventional morality as terms of justification and criticism, as well as of description. It is true that we sometimes speak of a group's "morals," or "morality," or "moral beliefs," or "moral positions" or "moral convictions," in what might be called an anthropological sense, meaning to refer to whatever attitudes the group displays about the propriety of human conduct, qualities or goals. We say, in this sense, that the morality of Nazi Germany was based on prejudice, or was irrational. But we also use some of these terms, particularly "moral position" and "moral conviction," in a discriminatory sense, to contrast the positions they describe with prejudices, rationalizations, matters of personal aversion or taste, arbitrary stands, and the like. One use—perhaps the most characteristic use—of this discriminatory sense is to offer a limited but important sort of justification for an act, when the moral issues surrounding that act are unclear or in dispute.

Suppose I tell you that I propose to vote against a man running for a public office of trust because I know him to be a homosexual and because I believe that homosexuality is profoundly immoral. If you disagree that homosexuality is immoral, you may accuse me of being about to cast my vote unfairly, acting on prejudice or out of a personal repugnance which is irrelevant to the moral issue. I might then try to convert you to my position on homosexuality, but if I fail in this I shall still want to convince you of what you and I will both take to be a separate point—that my vote was based upon *a* moral position, in the discriminatory sense, even though one which differs from yours. I shall want to persuade you of this, because if I do I am entitled to expect that you will alter your opinion of me and of what I am about to do. Your judgment of my character will be different—you might still think me eccentric (or puritanical or unsophisticated) but these are types of character and not faults of character. Your judgment of my act will also be different, in this respect. You will admit that so long as I hold my moral position, I have a moral right to vote against the homosexual, because I have a right (indeed a duty) to vote my own convictions. You would not admit such a right (or duty) if you were still persuaded that I was acting out of a prejudice or a personal taste.

I am entitled to expect that your opinion will change in these ways, because these distinctions are a part of the conventional morality you and I share, and which forms the background for our discussion. They enforce the difference between positions we must respect, although we think them wrong, and positions we need not respect because they offend some ground rule of moral reasoning. A great deal of debate about moral issues (in real life, although not in philosophy texts) consists of arguments that some position falls on one or the other side of this crucial line.

It is this feature of conventional morality that animates Lord Devlin's argument that society has the right to follow its own lights. We must therefore examine that discriminatory concept of a moral position more closely, and we can do so by pursuing our imaginary conversation. What must I do to convince you that my position is a moral position?

(a) I must produce some reasons for it. This is not to say that I have to articulate a moral principle I am following or a general moral theory to which I subscribe. Very few people can do either, and the ability to hold a moral position is not limited to those who can.

My reason need not be a principle or theory at all. It must only point out some aspect or feature of homosexuality which moves me to regard it as immoral: the fact that the Bible forbids it, for example, or that one who practices homosexuality becomes unfit for marriage and parenthood. Of course, any such reason would presuppose my acceptance of some general principle or theory, but I need not be able to state what it is, or realize that I am relying upon it.

Not every reason I might give will do, however. Some will be excluded by general criteria stipulating sorts of reasons which do not count. We might take note of four of the most important such criteria:

(i) If I tell you that homosexuals are morally inferior because they do not have heterosexual desires, and so are not "real men," you would reject that reason as showing one type of prejudice. Prejudices, in general, are postures of judgment that take into account considerations our conventions exclude. In a structured context, like a trial or a contest, the ground rules exclude all but certain considerations, and a prejudice is a basis of judgment which violates these rules. Our conventions stipulate some ground rules of moral judgment which obtain even apart from such special contexts, the most important of which is that a man must not be held morally inferior on the basis of some physical, racial or other characteristic he cannot help having. Thus a man whose moral judgments about Jews, or Negroes, or Southerners, or women, or effeminate men are based on his belief that any member of these classes automatically deserves less respect, without regard to anything he himself has done, is said to be prejudiced against that group.

(ii) If I base my view about homosexuals on a personal emotional reaction ("they make me sick") you would reject that reason as well. We distinguish moral positions from emotional reactions, not because moral positions are supposed to be unemotional or dispassionate—quite the reverse is true—but because the moral position is supposed to justify the emotional reaction, and not vice versa. If a man is unable to produce such reasons, we do not deny the fact of his emotional involvement, which may have important social or political consequences, but we do not take this involvement as demonstrating his moral conviction. Indeed, it is just this sort of position—a severe emotional reaction to a practice or a situation for which one cannot account—that we tend to describe, in lay terms, as a phobia or an obsession.

(iii) If I base my position on a proposition of fact ("homosexual acts are physically debilitating") which is not only false, but is so implausible that it challenges the minimal standards of evidence and argument I generally accept and impose upon others, then you would regard my belief, even though sincere, as a form of rationalization, and disqualify my reason on that ground. (Rationalization is a complex concept, and also includes, as we shall see, the production of reasons which suggest general theories I do not accept.)

(iv) If I can argue for my own position only by citing the beliefs of others ("everyone knows homosexuality is a sin") you will conclude that I am parroting and not relying on a moral conviction of my own. With the possible (though complex) exception of a deity, there is no moral authority to which I can appeal and so automatically make my position a moral one. I must have my own reasons, though of course I may have been taught these reasons by others.

No doubt many readers will disagree with these thumbnail sketches of prejudice, mere emotional reaction, rationalization and parroting. Some may have their own theories of what these are. I want to emphasize now only that these are distinct concepts, whatever the details of the differences might be, and that they have a role in deciding whether to treat another's position as a moral conviction. They are not merely epithets to be pasted on positions we strongly dislike.

(b) Suppose I do produce a reason which is not disqualified on one of these (or on similar) grounds. That reason will presuppose some general moral principle or theory, even though I may not be able to state that principle or theory, and do not have it in mind when I speak. If I offer, as my reason, the fact that the Bible forbids homosexual acts, or that homosexual acts make it less likely that the actor will marry and raise children, I suggest that I accept the theory my reason presupposes, and you will not be satisfied that my position is a moral one if you believe that I do not. It may be a question of my sincerity—do I in fact believe that the injunctions of the Bible are morally binding as such, or that all men have a duty to procreate? Sincerity is not, however, the only issue, for consistency is also in point. I may believe that I accept one of these general positions, and be wrong, because my other beliefs, and my own conduct on other occasions, may be inconsistent with it. I may reject certain Biblical injunctions, or I may hold that men have a right to remain bachelors if they please or use contraceptives all their lives.

Of course, my general moral positions may have qualifications and exceptions. The difference between an exception and an inconsistency is that the former can be supported by reasons which presuppose other moral positions I can properly claim to hold. Suppose I condemn all homosexuals on Biblical authority, but not all fornicators. What reasons can I offer for the distinction? If I can produce none which supports it, I cannot claim to accept the general position about Biblical authority. If I do produce a reason which seems to support the distinction, the same sorts of question may be asked about that reason as were asked about my original reply. What general position does the reason for my exception presuppose? Can I sincerely claim to accept that further general position? Suppose my reason, for example, is that fornication is now very common and has been sanctioned by custom. Do I really believe that what is immoral becomes moral when it becomes popular? If not, and if I can produce no other reason for the distinction, I cannot claim to accept the general position that what the Bible condemns is immoral. Of course, I may be persuaded, when this is pointed out, to change my views on fornication. But you would be alert to the question of whether this is a genuine change of heart, or only a performance for the sake of the argument.

In principle there is no limit to these ramifications of my original claim, though of course, no actual argument is likely to pursue very many of them.

(c) But do I really have to have a reason to make my position a matter of moral conviction? Most men think that acts which cause unnecessary suffering, or break a serious promise with no excuse, are immoral, and yet they could give no reason for these beliefs. They feel that no reason is necessary, because they take it as axiomatic or self-evident that these are immoral acts. It seems contrary to common sense to deny that a position held in this way can be a moral position.

Yet there is an important difference between believing that one's position is self-evident and just not having a reason for one's position. The former presupposes a positive belief that no further reason is necessary, that the immorality of the act in question does not depend upon its social effects, or its effects on the character of the actor, or its proscription by a deity, or anything else, but follows from the nature of the act itself. The claim that a particular position is axiomatic, in other words, does supply a reason of a special sort, namely that the act is immoral in and of itself, and this special reason, like the others we considered, may be inconsistent with more general theories I hold.

The moral arguments we make presuppose not only moral principles, but also more abstract positions about moral reasoning. In particular, they presuppose positions about what kinds of acts can be immoral in and of themselves. When I criticize your moral opinions, or attempt to justify my own disregard of traditional moral rules I think are silly, I will proceed by denying that the act in question has any of the several features that can make an act immoral—that it involves no breach of an undertaking or duty, for example, harms no one including the actor, is not proscribed by any organized religion, and is not illegal. I proceed in this way because I assume that the ultimate grounds of immorality are limited to some such small set of very general standards. I may assert this assumption directly or it may emerge from the pattern of my argument. In either event, I will enforce it by calling positions which can claim no support from any of these ultimate standards *arbitrary*, as I

should certainly do if you said that photography was immoral, for instance, or swimming. Even if I cannot articulate this underlying assumption, I shall still apply it, and since the ultimate criteria I recognize are among the most abstract of my moral standards, they will not vary much from those my neighbors recognize and apply. Although many who despise homosexuals are unable to say why, few would claim affirmatively that one needs no reason, for this would make their position, on their own standards, an arbitrary one.

(d) This anatomy of our argument could be continued, but it is already long enough to justify some conclusions. If the issue between us is whether my views on homosexuality amount to a moral position, and hence whether I am entitled to vote against a homosexual on that ground, I cannot settle the issue by reporting my feelings. You will want to consider the reasons I can produce to support my belief, and whether my other views and behavior are consistent with the theories these reasons presuppose. You will have, of course, to apply your own understanding, which may differ in detail from mine, of what a prejudice or a rationalization is, for example, and of when one view is inconsistent with another. You and I may end in disagreement over whether my position is a moral one, partly because of such differences in understanding, and partly because one is less likely to recognize these illegitimate grounds in himself than in others.

We must avoid the skeptical fallacy of passing from these facts to the conclusion that there is no such thing as a prejudice or a rationalization or an inconsistency, or that these terms mean merely that the one who uses them strongly dislikes the positions he describes this way. That would be like arguing that because different people have different understandings of what jealousy is, and can in good faith disagree about whether one of them is jealous, there is no such thing as jealousy, and one who says another is jealous merely means he dislikes him very much.

LORD DEVLIN'S MORALITY

We may now return to Lord Devlin's second argument. He argues that when legislators must decide a moral issue (as by his hypothesis they must when a practice threatens a valued social arrangement), they must follow any consensus of moral position which the community at large has reached, because this is required by the democratic principle, and because a community is entitled to follow its own lights. The argument would have some plausibility if Lord Devlin meant, in speaking of the moral consensus of the community, those positions which are moral positions in the discriminatory sense we have been exploring.

But he means nothing of the sort. His definition of a moral position shows he is using it in what I called the anthropological sense. The ordinary man whose opinions we must enforce, he says, ". . . is not expected to reason about anything and his judgment may be largely a matter of feeling."[18] "If the reasonable man believes," he adds, "that a practice is immoral and believes also—no matter whether the belief is right or wrong, so be it that it is honest and dispassionate—that no right-minded member of his society could think otherwise, then for the purpose of the law it is immoral."[19] Elsewhere he quotes with approval Dean Rostow's attribution to him of the view that ". . . the common morality of a society at any time is a blend of custom and

conviction, of reason and feeling, of experience and prejudice."[20] His sense of what a moral conviction is emerges most clearly of all from the famous remark about homosexuals. If the ordinary man regards homosexuality "as a vice so abominable that its mere presence is an offence,"[21] this demonstrates for him that the ordinary man's feelings about homosexuals are a matter of moral conviction.[22]

His conclusions fail because they depend upon using "moral position" in this anthropological sense. Even if it is true that most men think homosexuality an abominable vice and cannot tolerate its presence, it remains possible that this common opinion is a compound of prejudice (resting on the assumption that homosexuals are morally inferior creatures because they are effeminate), rationalization (based on assumptions of fact so unsupported that they challenge the community's own standards of rationality), and personal aversion (representing no conviction

18. Devlin 15.

19. *Id.* at 22–23.

20. Rostow, *The Enforcement of Morals*, 1960 Camb. L.J. 174, 197; reprinted in E. V. Rostow, *The Sovereign Prerogative* 45, 78 (1962). Quoted in Devlin 95.

21. *Id.* at 17.

22. In the preface (*Id.* at viii) Lord Devlin acknowledges that the language of the original lecture might have placed "too much emphasis on feeling and too little on reason," and he states that the legislator is entitled to disregard "irrational" beliefs. He gives as an example of the latter the belief that homosexuality causes earthquakes, and asserts that the exclusion of irrationality "is usually an easy and comparatively unimportant process." I think it fair to conclude that this is all Lord Devlin would allow him to exclude. If I am wrong, and Lord Devlin would ask him to exclude prejudices, personal aversions, arbitrary stands and the rest as well, he should have said so, and attempted to work some of these distinctions out. If he had, his conclusions would have been different and would no doubt have met with a different reaction.

but merely blind hate rising from un-acknowledged self-suspicion). It remains possible that the ordinary man could produce no reason for his view, but would simply parrot his neighbor who in turn parrots him, or that he would produce a reason which presupposes a general moral position he could not sincerely or consistently claim to hold. If so, the principles of democracy we follow do not call for the enforcement of the consensus, for the belief that prejudices, personal aversions and rationalizations do not justify restricting another's freedom itself occupies a critical and fundamental position in our popular morality. Nor would the bulk of the community then be entitled to follow its own lights, for the community does not extend that privilege to one who acts on the basis of prejudice, rationalization, or personal aversion. Indeed, the distinction between these and moral convictions, in the discriminatory sense, exists largely to mark off the former as the sort of positions one is not entitled to pursue.

A conscientious legislator who is told a moral consensus exists must test the credentials of that consensus. He cannot, of course, examine the beliefs or behavior of individual citizens; he cannot hold hearings on the Clapham omnibus. That is not the point.

The claim that a moral consensus exists is not itself based on a poll. It is based on an appeal to the legislator's sense of how his community reacts to some disfavored practice. But this same sense includes an awareness of the grounds on which that reaction is generally supported. If there has been a public debate involving the editorial columns, speeches of his colleagues, the testimony of interested groups, and his own correspondence, these will sharpen his awareness of what arguments and positions are in the field. He must sift

these arguments and positions trying to determine which are prejudices or rationalizations, which presuppose general principles or theories vast parts of the population could not be supposed to accept, and so on. It may be that when he has finished this process of reflection he will find that the claim of a moral consensus has not been made out. In the case of homosexuality, I expect, it would not be, and that is what makes Lord Devlin's undiscriminating hypothetical so serious a misstatement. What is shocking and wrong is not his idea that the community's morality counts, but his idea of what counts as the community's morality.

Of course the legislator must apply these tests for himself. If he shares the popular views he is less likely to find them wanting, though if he is self-critical the exercise may convert him. His answer, in any event, will depend upon his own understanding of what our shared morality requires. That is inevitable, for whatever criteria we urge him to apply, he can apply them only as he understands them.

A legislator who proceeds in this way, who refuses to take popular indignation, intolerance and disgust as the moral conviction of his community, is not guilty of moral elitism. He is not simply setting his own educated views against those of a vast public which rejects them. He is doing his best to enforce a distinct, and fundamentally important, part of his community's morality, a consensus more essential to society's existence in the form we know it than the opinion Lord Devlin bids him follow.

No legislator can afford to ignore the public's outrage. It is a fact he must reckon with. It will set the boundaries of what is politically feasible, and it will determine his strategies of persuasion and enforcement within these boundaries. But we must not confuse strategy with justice, nor facts of political life with principles of political morality. Lord Devlin understands these distinctions, but his arguments will appeal most, I am afraid, to those who do not.

POSTSCRIPT ON PORNOGRAPHY

I have been discussing homosexuality because that is Lord Devlin's example. I should like to say a word about pornography, if only because it is, for the time being, more in the American legal headlines than homosexuality. This current attention is due to the Supreme Court's decisions and opinions in three recent cases: *Ginzburg, Mishkin* and *Fanny Hill*.[23] In two of these, convictions (and jail sentences) for the distribution of pornography, were upheld, and in the third, while the Court reversed a state ban on an allegedly obscene novel, three justices dissented.

Two of the cases involved review of state procedures for constitutionality, and the third the interpretation and application of a federal statute. The Court therefore had to pass on the constitutional question of how far a state or the nation may legally restrict the publication of erotic literature, and on questions of statutory construction. But each decision nevertheless raises issues of political principle of the sort we have been considering.

A majority of the Court adheres to the constitutional test laid down some years ago in *Roth*.[24] As that test now stands, a book is obscene, and as such not protected by the first amendment, if: "(a) the dominant theme of the material taken as a whole appeals to a prurient interest in sex; (b) the material is patently offensive because it affronts contemporary community standards relating to the description or representation of sexual matters; and (c) the material is utterly without redeeming social value."[25] We might put the question of political principle this way: What gives the federal government, or any state, the moral right to prohibit the publication of books which are obscene under the *Roth* test?

Justice Brennan's opinion in *Mishkin* floated one answer: Erotic literature, he said, incites some readers to crime. If this is true, if in a significant number of such cases the same readers would not have been incited to the same crime by other stimuli, and if the problem cannot effectively be handled in other ways, this might give society a warrant to ban these books. But these are at least speculative hypotheses, and in any event they are not pertinent to a case like *Ginzburg*, in which the Court based its decision not on the obscene character of the publications themselves, but on the fact that they were presented to the public as salacious rather than enlightening. Can any other justification be given for the prohibition of obscene books?

An argument like Lord Devlin's second argument can be constructed, and many of those who feel society is entitled to ban pornography are in fact moved by some such argument. It might take this form:

(1) If we permit obscene books freely to be sold, to be delivered as it were with the morning milk, the whole tone of the community will eventually change. That which is now thought filthy and vulgar in speech and dress, and in public behavior, will become acceptable. A public which could enjoy pornography legally would soon settle for nothing very much tamer, and all

---

23. *Supra* note 2.

24. Roth v. United States, 354 U.S. 476 (1957).

25. Memoirs v. Massachusetts (Fanny Hill), 383 U.S. 413, 418 (1966).

forms of popular culture would inevitably move closer to the salacious. We have seen these forces at work already —the same relaxations in our legal attitudes which enabled books like *Tropic of Cancer* to be published have already had an effect on what we find in movies and magazines, on beaches and on the city streets. Perhaps we must pay that price for what many critics plausibly consider works of art, but we need not pay what would be a far greater price for trash—mass-manufactured for profit only.

(2) It is not a sufficient answer to say that social practices will not change unless the majority willingly participates in the change. Social corruption works through media and forces quite beyond the control of the mass of the people, indeed quite beyond the control of any conscious design at all. Of course, pornography attracts while it repels, and at some point in the deterioration of community standards the majority will not object to further deterioration, but that is a mark of the corruption's success, not proof that there has been no corruption. It is precisely that possibility which makes it imperative that we enforce our standards while we still have them. This is an example—it is not the only one—of our wishing the law to protect us from ourselves.

(3) Banning pornography abridges the freedom of authors, publishers and would-be readers. But if what they want to do is immoral, we are entitled to protect ourselves at that cost. Thus we are presented with a moral issue: Does one have a moral right to publish or to read "hard-core" pornography which can claim no value or virtue beyond its erotic effect? This moral issue should not be solved by fiat, nor by self-appointed ethical tutors, but by submission to the public. The public at present believes that hard-core pornography is immoral, that those who produce it are panderers, and that the protection of the community's sexual and related mores is sufficiently important to justify restricting their freedom.

But surely it is crucial to this argument, whatever else one might think of it, that the consensus described in the last sentence be a consensus of moral conviction. If it should turn out that the ordinary man's dislike of pornographers is a matter of taste, or an arbitrary stand, the argument would fail because these are not satisfactory reasons for abridging freedom.

It will strike many readers as paradoxical even to raise the question whether the average man's views on pornography are moral convictions. For most people the heart of morality is a sexual code, and if the ordinary man's views on fornication, adultery, sadism, exhibitionism and the other staples of pornography are not moral positions, it is hard to imagine any beliefs he is likely to have that are. But writing and reading about those adventures is not the same as performing in them, and one may be able to give reasons for condemning the practices (that they cause pain, or are sacrilegious, or insulting, or cause public annoyance) which do not extend to producing or savoring fantasies about them.

Those who claim a consensus of moral convictions on pornography must provide evidence that this exists. They must provide moral reasons or arguments which the average member of society might sincerely and consistently advance in the manner we have been describing. Perhaps this can be done, but it is no substitute simply to report that the ordinary man—within or without the jury box—turns his thumb down on the whole business.

Suggestions for Further Reading

Hugo A. Bedau, ed., *Civil Disobedience* (New York: Pegasus Books, 1969).

Jeffrie G. Murphy, ed., *Civil Disobedience and Violence* (Belmont, Cal.: Wadsworth, 1971). Two good anthologies of articles on civil disobedience.

Peter Singer, *Democracy and Disobedience* (Oxford: Clarendon Press, 1973). A study of the special reasons for obeying the law in a democracy. Singer also considers the question of whether countries such as the United States and England actually are democracies, in the sense necessary for us to have special obligations to obey their laws. He concludes that they are not.

Ronald Dworkin, "On Not Prosecuting Civil Disobedience," *The New York Review of Books*, June 6, 1968. [Reprinted in *Trials of the Resistance* (New York: New York Review Books, 1970).] Dworkin points out that prosecutors and judges have wide discretionary powers in proceeding against lawbreakers—they must decide whether or not to prosecute, whether to bring more or less serious charges, whether to impose light or heavy sentences, and so forth. He argues that when a person breaks the law for reasons of conscience, prosecutors and judges should opt for leniency.

Robert Paul Wolff, *In Defense of Anarchism* (New York: Harper Torchbooks, 1970). Wolff argues that there can be no such thing as a legitimate government—that is, a government with the authority to force us to obey its laws—because the very idea of political authority conflicts with the moral autonomy of the individual.

Lord Patrick Devlin, *The Enforcement of Morals* (Oxford: Oxford University Press, 1965). In this collection of essays Lord Devlin argues, against Mill, that a society does have the right to use the power of the law to enforce its moral code.

H. L. A. Hart, *Law, Liberty, and Morality* (Stanford, Cal.: Stanford University Press, 1963). A defense of a position similar to Mill's. Hart specifically attempts to refute Devlin's arguments.

Richard Wasserstrom, ed., *Morality and the Law* (Belmont, Cal.: Wadsworth, 1971). A collection of essays on the question of whether the law should be used to enforce moral rules.

Norman Care and Thomas Trelogan, eds., *Issues in Law and Morality* (Cleveland: Case Western Reserve University Press, 1973). Essays by various writers on the topics indicated in the title.